Foreword

"MILITARY CRYPTANALYTICS, PART II," was originally published in October, 1959, as a classified text by the U.S. Government. Recently declassified and expanded with computer programs written by Wayne G. Barker, we are proud to add this book to our Cryptographic Series. The book is probably the most comprehensive and one of the best books ever written concerning the intermediate phase of military cryptanalytics.

— AEGEAN PARK PRESS

MILITARY CRYPTANALYTICS
PART II — VOLUME 1

by
Lambros D. Callimahos
and
William F. Friedman

ISBN: 0-89412-075-1

AEGEAN PARK PRESS
P.O. Box 2837
Laguna Hills, California 92654
(714) 586-8811

Manufactured in the United States of America

A likely impossibility is always preferable to an unconvincing possibility.
                                                                    —Aristotle.

Preface

This text represents a manifold expansion and revision, both in scope and content, of the earlier work entitled "Military Cryptanalysis, Part II" by William F. Friedman. This extensive expansion and revision was necessitated by the considerable advancement made in the art since the publication of the previous text.

I am indebted to my colleague Dr. Robert H. Shaw for reviewing the manuscript of this volume and making numerous valuable comments and suggestions.

                                                                    —*L. D. C.*

TABLE OF CONTENTS

Military Cryptanalytics, Part II

Periodic Polyalphabetic Substitution Systems

INTRODUCTORY REMARKS

1. **General.**—*a.* This text constitutes the second in the series of six basic texts on the science of cryptanalytics as applied to military communications in general, without regard to the particular Service involved (i.e., army, navy, or air force traffic). The first two texts together cover most of the necessary fundamentals of cryptanalytics; the last four will deal with specialized aspects of the science.

b. It is assumed that the reader has studied *Military Cryptanalytics, Part I,* and is familiar with the cryptologic concepts, principles, and techniques of solution of the various cryptosystems treated in that text; this background is a necessary prerequisite to the understanding of the principles expounded in the present text.

c. It is taken for granted that the student has acquired a foundation of generalized cryptologic terminology from the study of the first text and its accompanying glossary. The new terms which appear in this text are usually defined upon their first occurrence; these terms, as well as others which are necessary for cross-reference, are included in the glossary to this volume (Appendix 1).

d. As has been already indicated, each text has its accompanying course of problems in cryptanalysis, so that the student may have the opportunity of applying the principles learned to practical examples, and in so doing develop skill in the analysis of the types of cryptosystems treated in this text. The problems which pertain to this text constitute Appendix 9.

e. As was the case in the preceding text, this present volume assumes that the reader has had but a minimum of mathematical background, not beyond elementary algebra; the authors have endeavored to enhance this background gradually and progressively, to enable the student to be better versed in the mathematical techniques and applications in the art of cryptanalysis. As before, footnotes are used to give additional general information about the subject being treated, or to amplify mathematical principles in details which may be beyond the average reader; therefore certain footnotes may be passed over by the student.

2. **The essential difference between monoalphabetic and polyalphabetic substitution.**—*a.* In the substitution methods thus far discussed the basic feature is monoalphabeticity. From the cryptanalytic standpoint, neither the nature of the cipher symbols nor their method of production is an essential feature, although these may be differentiating characteristics from the cryptographic standpoint. It is true that in the cases of monoalphabetic substitution with

1

variants and in syllabary squares and code charts, there is a departure, more or less considerable, from strict monoalphabeticity. In some of the cases of variant systems, indeed, there may be available two or more wholly independent sets of equivalents, which, moreover, may even be arranged in the form of completely separate alphabets. Thus, while a loose terminology might permit one to designate such systems as polyalphabetic, it is better to reserve this nomenclature for those cases wherein polyalphabeticity is the essence of the method, specifically introduced with the purpose of imparting a *positional* variation in the substitutive equivalents for plaintext letters, in accordance with some rule directly or indirectly connected with the absolute *positions* the plaintext letters occupy in the message. This point calls for amplification.

b. In monoalphabetic substitution with variants the object of having different or multiple equivalents is to suppress, so far as possible by simple methods, the characteristic frequencies of the individual letters occurring in plain text. As has been noted, it is by means of these characteristic frequencies that the cipher equivalents can usually be identified. In these systems the varying equivalents for plaintext letters are subject to the free choice and caprice of the enciphering clerk; if he is careful and conscientious in the work, he will really make use of all the different equivalents afforded by the system; but if he is slipshod and hurried in his work, he will use the same equivalents repeatedly rather than take pains and time to refer to the charts, tables, or diagrams to find the variants. Moreover, and this is a crucial point, even if the individual enciphering clerks are extremely careful, when many of them employ the same system it is entirely impossible to insurè a complete diversity in the encipherments [1] produced by two or more clerks working at different message centers. The result is inevitably to produce plenty of repetitions and *near-repetitions* or isologous sequences in the texts emanating from several stations, and when texts such as these are all available for study they are open to solution by a comparison of their similarities and differences.

c. In true polyalphabetic systems, on the other hand, there is established a rather definite procedure which automatically determines the shifts or changes in equivalents or in the manner in which they are introduced, so that these changes are beyond the momentary whim or choice of the enciphering clerk. When the method of shifting or changing the equivalents is scientifically sound and sufficiently complex, the research necessary to establish the values of the cipher characters is much more prolonged and difficult than is the case even in complicated monoalphabetic substitution with variants, as will later be seen. These are the objects of true polyalphabetic substitution systems. The number of such systems is quite large, and it will be possible to describe in detail the cryptanalysis of only a few of the more common or typical examples of methods encountered in practical military communications.

d. The three methods, (1) single-equivalent monoalphabetic substitution, (2) monoalphabetic substitution with variants, and (3) true polyalphabetic substitution, show the following relationships as regards the equivalency between plaintext and ciphertext units:

A. In method (1), there is a set of symbols, usually 26; a plaintext letter is always represented by one and only one of these symbols; conversely, a symbol always represents the same plaintext letter. The equivalence between the plaintext and the cipher letters is constant in both encipherment and decipherment.

B. In method (2), there is a set of *n* symbols, where *n* may be any number greater than 26 and often is a multiple of that number; a plaintext letter may be represented by 1, 2, 3, . . .

---

[1] It must be noticed, however, that a complete diversity of enciphering is sometimes not necessarily an optimum desideratum from the standpoint of cryptosecurity; a complete diversity of encipherments, in the case of isologs, would lay bare all the elements of a variant system. See in this connection the example given in subpar. 62*b* in *Military Cryptanalytics, Part I*.

different symbols; conversely, a symbol always represents the same plaintext letter, the same as is the case in method (1). The equivalence between the plaintext and the cipher letters is variable in encipherment but constant in decipherment.[2]

C. In method (3), there is, as in the first method, a set of [usually] 26 symbols; a plaintext letter may be represented by 1, 2, 3, . . . 26 different symbols; conversely, a symbol may represent 1, 2, 3, . . . 26 different plaintext letters, depending upon the system and the specific key. The equivalence between the plaintext and the cipher letters is variable in both encipherment and decipherment.

3. Example of polyalphabetic substitution.—*a.* A simple example may be used to illustrate what is meant by true polyalphabetic substitution. Suppose that two correspondents agree upon a numerical key, for example, 74030274, each digit of which means that the plaintext letter to which the digit applies as a key number is to be replaced by the letter that stands a corresponding number of places to the right of it in the normal alphabet. For example, if R_p is to be enciphered by key number 7, it is to be replaced by Y_c. The numerical key is written over the letters of the plain text, letter for letter, and is repeated until the whole text is covered.[3] Let the message be REINFORCEMENTS BEING RUSHED. The encipherment of this message is shown in Fig. 1, below. For convenience in counting forward (to the right) to find cipher equivalents, a normal alphabet is given at the top of the figure. To decipher such a crypto-

Normal alphabet:	ABCDEFGHIJKLMNOPQRSTUVWXYZ
Key:	74030 27474 03027 47403 02747
Plain text:	REINF ORCEM ENTSB EINGR USHED
Cipher text:	YIIQF QYGLQ EQTUI IPRGU UUOIK

FIGURE 1

gram, the clerk writes the numerical key over the cipher letters and then counts backward (i.e., to the left) in the normal alphabet as many places as indicated by the key number standing over each letter.

---

[2] As has been pointed out in the previous text, there is a monoalphabetic method in which the inverse result obtains, the correspondence being constant in encipherment but variable in decipherment; this is a method not found in the usual books on cryptography but in an essay on that subject by Edgar Allan Poe, entitled, in some editions of his works, "A few words on secret writing" and, in other editions, "Cryptography." The method is to draw up an enciphering alphabet such as the following (using Poe's example):

Plain: A B C D E F G H I J K L M N O P Q R S T U V W X Y Z
Cipher: S U A V I T E R I N M O D O F O R T I T E R I N R E

In such an alphabet, because of repetitions in the cipher component, the plaintext equivalents are subject to a considerable degree of variability, as will be seen in the deciphering alphabet:

Cipher:	A	B	C	D	E	F	G	H	I	J	K	L	M	N	O	P	Q	R	S	T	U	V	W	X	Y	Z
Plain:	C		M	G	O			E			K	J	L			H	A	F	B	D						
			U					I			X	N				Q	R									
			Z					S				P				V	T									
								W				Y														

This type of variability gives rise to ambiguities in decipherment. A cipher group such as TIE_c would yield such plaintext sequences as REG, FIG, TEU, REU, etc., which could be read only by *context*. No system of such a character would be practical for serious usage. For a further discussion of this type of cipher alphabet see Friedman, William F., "Edgar Allan Poe, Cryptographer," *Signal Corps Bulletins* Nos. 97 (July–Sept.) and 98 (Oct.–Dec.), 1937.

[3] This system is known in cryptologic literature as the *Gronsfeld cipher.*

3

b. Instead of writing the key over and over again in order to cover the plain text completely, the text may be written in sets of letters corresponding in length to the length of the key. Thus the text may be written underneath a single appearance of the key in successive short horizontal lines, leaving space between the lines for the insertion of cipher equivalents, as shown in Fig. 2. Instead of enciphering the letters by individual, repeated countings, two strips bearing normal alphabets may be juxtaposed in the proper relative positions to encipher

```
7 4 0 3 0 2 7 4
R E I N F O R C
E M E N T S B E
I N G R U S H E
D
```

FIGURE 2

a whole column of letters at one setting of the strips. Thus for the first column, with the key number 7, the strips are juxtaposed so that the first letter in the column, *viz.*, R_p (which is to be represented by the seventh letter to the right of it, and is therefore to be enciphered by Y_c of the lower strip) is directly above Y_c, as follows:

Plain: ABCDEFGHIJKLMNOPQRSTUVWXYZ
Cipher: ABCDEFGHIJKLMNOPQRSTUVWXYZABCDEFGHIJKLMNOPQRSTUVWXYZ

The equivalents for the rest of the letters of the first column may now be written under their respective plaintext letters, reference being made to the enciphering alphabet to see what the cipher letters should be: $E_p=L_c$; $I_p=P_c$; and $D_p=K_c$. For the second column, the two strips are juxtaposed as follows:

Plain: ABCDEFGHIJKLMNOPQRSTUVWXYZ
Cipher: ABCDEFGHIJKLMNOPQRSTUVWXYZABCDEFGHIJKLMNOPQRSTUVWXYZ

The cipher equivalents for the second column are: $E_p=I_c$; $M_p=Q_c$; and $N_p=R_c$. The process is continued in this manner until all the columns have been enciphered as shown in the diagram below:

```
7 4 0 3 0 2 7 4
R E I N F O R C
Y I I Q F Q Y G

E M E N T S B E
L Q E Q T U I I

I N G R U S H E
P R G U U U O I

D
K
```

The cipher text is then transcribed in five-letter groups for transmission, *viz.*, YIIQF QYGLQ EQTUI IPRGU UUOIK. This systematized procedure has the merit of being faster, less laborious, and less liable to error than the method shown in subpar. 3*a*.

4. **Primary classification of polyalphabetic systems.**—*a*. A primary classification of polyalphabetic systems into two rather distinct types may be made: (1) periodic systems and (2)

aperiodic systems. When the enciphering process involves a cryptographic treatment which is repetitive in character, and which results in the production of *cyclic phenomena* in the cryptographic text, the system is termed *periodic*. When the enciphering process is not of the type described in the foregoing general terms, the system is termed *aperiodic*. The substitution in both cases involves the use of two or more cipher alphabets.

b. The cyclic phenomena inherent in a periodic system may be exhibited externally, in which case they are said to be *patent*, or they may not be exhibited externally, and must be uncovered by a preliminary step in the analysis, in which case they are said to be *latent*. The periodicity may be quite definite in nature, and therefore determinable with mathematical exactitude allowing for no variability, in which case the periodicity is said to be *fixed*. In other instances the periodicity is more or less flexible in character and even though it may be determinable mathematically, allowance must be made for a degree of variability subject to limits controlled by the specific system under investigation. The periodicity is in this case said to be *flexible*, or *variable within limits*.

5. Primary classification of periodic systems.—Periodic polyalphabetic substitution systems may primarily be classified into two kinds:

a. Those in which only a few of a whole set of cipher alphabets are used in enciphering individual messages, these alphabets being employed repeatedly in a fixed sequence throughout each message. Because it is usual to employ a secret word, phrase, or number as a key to determine the number, identity, and sequence with which the cipher alphabets are employed, and this key is used over and over again in encipherment, this method is often called the *repeating-key system*, or the *repeating-alphabet system*. In this text the designation "repeating-key system" will be used.[4]

b. Those in which all the cipher alphabets comprising the complete set for the system are employed one after the other successively in the encipherment of a message, and when the last alphabet of the series has been used, the encipherer begins over again with the first alphabet. This is commonly referred to as a *progressive alphabet system*.

6. Sequence of study of polyalphabetic systems.—*a*. In the studies to be followed in connection with polyalphabetic systems, the order in which the work will proceed conforms very closely to the classifications made in pars. 4 and 5. Periodic polyalphabetic substitution ciphers will come first, because they are, as a rule, simpler and because a thorough understanding of the principles of their analysis is prerequisite to a comprehension of how aperiodic systems are solved. But in the final analysis the solution of examples of both types rests upon the conversion or reduction of polyalphabeticity into monoalphabeticity. If this is possible, solution can always be achieved, granted there are sufficient data in the final monoalphabetic distributions to permit solution by recourse to the ordinary principles of frequency.

b. First in the order of study of periodic systems will come the analysis of repeating-key systems. Some of the more simple varieties will be discussed in detail, with examples. Subsequently, ciphers of progressive alphabet systems will be discussed. There will then follow a treatment of polyalphabetic bipartite systems, monome-dinome systems with cyclic additives, and periodic digraphic systems.

---

[4] French terminology calls this the "double-key method," but there is no logic in such nomenclature.

THEORY OF REPEATING-KEY SYSTEMS

7. Classification of cipher alphabets upon the basis of their derivation.—*a.* The substitution processes in polyalphabetic methods involve the use of a plurality of cipher alphabets. The latter may be derived by various schemes, the exact nature of which determines the principal characteristics of the cipher alphabets and plays a very important role in the preparation and solution of polyalphabetic cryptograms. For these reasons it is advisable, before proceeding to a discussion of the principles and methods of analysis, to point out these various types of cipher alphabets, show how they are produced, and how the method of their production or derivation may be made to yield important clues and short cuts in analysis.

b. A primary classification of cipher alphabets for polyalphabetic substitution may be made into the two following types:

(1) Independent or unrelated cipher alphabets.

(2) Derived or interrelated cipher alphabets.

c. Independent cipher alphabets may be disposed of in a very few words. They are merely separate and distinct alphabets showing no relationship to one another in any way. They may be compiled by the various methods discussed in par. 39 of *Military Cryptanalytics, Part I.* The solution of cryptograms written by means of such alphabets is rendered more difficult by reason of the absence of any relationship between the equivalents of one cipher alphabet and those of any of the other alphabets of the same cryptogram. On the other hand, from the point of view of practicability in their production and their handling in encrypting and decrypting, they present some difficulties which make them less popular with cryptographers than interrelated cipher alphabets.

d. Derived or interrelated alphabets, as their name indicates, are most commonly produced by the *interaction* of two primary components, which when juxtaposed at the various points of coincidence can be made to yield *secondary alphabets.*

8. Primary components and secondary alphabets.—Two basic, slidable sequences or components of *n* characters each will yield *n* secondary alphabets. The components may be classified according to various schemes. For cryptanalytic purposes the following classification will be found useful:

Case I. The primary components are both normal sequences.

a. The sequences proceed in the same direction. (The secondary alphabets are direct standard alphabets.) (Pars. 20–22.)

b. The sequences proceed in opposite directions. (The secondary alphabets are reversed standard alphabets; they are also reciprocal cipher alphabets.) (Subpars. 20*i*, 21*c*.)

Case II. The primary components are not both normal sequences.

a. The plain component is normal, the cipher component is a mixed sequence. (The secondary alphabets are mixed alphabets.) (Pars. 26–35.)

b. The plain component is a mixed sequence, the cipher component is normal. (The secondary alphabets are mixed alphabets.) (Par. 36.)

c. Both components are mixed sequences.

    1. Components are identical mixed sequences

        (a) Sequences proceed in the same direction. (The secondary alphabets are mixed alphabets.) (Par. 41.)

        (b) Sequences proceed in opposite directions. (The secondary alphabets are reciprocal mixed alphabets.) (Par. 55.)

    2. Components are different mixed sequences. (The secondary alphabets are mixed alphabets.) (Par. 56.)

9. The use of key words to indicate number, identity, and sequence of cipher alphabets employed.—*a*. If reference is made to the two settings of alphabet strips in subpar. 3*b*, it will be noted that in the first setting, $A_p = H_c$, and in the second setting, $A_p = E_c$. If the eight settings of the strips are studied it will be found that the letters which A_p represents successively are H, E, A, D, A, C, H, and E, giving the word HEADACHE. These settings, when first presented in the foregoing description, correspond merely to the numerical key 74030274, but this numerical key is also expressible in terms of letters, which when put together properly spell a word. This is only another way of showing that key words may be employed in this type of substitution as in those previously described. Key words of various lengths and composition may be used, consisting of single words, long phrases or sentences. In general, the longer the key the greater is the degree of cryptographic security.

b. The number of elements in the key—that is, that number of letters or figures composing it—determines the number of alphabets to be employed. The identity of each element of the key, the specific letter or figure it happens to be, determines specifically which of a set of cipher alphabets pertaining to the whole system will be used. And the specific sequence or relative order of the elements of the key determines specifically the sequence with which the cipher alphabets are employed within the encipherment. The total number of cipher alphabets pertaining to or composing the system may be limited or unlimited. When they are produced as a result of the sliding of two basic or primary alphabets against each other, the number is limited to 26 in the English alphabet.

c. A brief notation for indicating or designating a specific key letter is to suffix the subscript "k" to it, just as the subscripts "p" and "c" are suffixed to letters to indicate letters of the plain text or cipher text, respectively. When the key letter occurs in an equation, it can be enclosed within parentheses to avoid ambiguity. Thus $B_p(D_k) = E_c$ means that the plaintext letter B when enciphered by the key letter D (in a certain alphabet system) yields the cipher letter E.

10. Cipher disks.—*a*. In subpar. 3*b*, it was noted that the separate alphabets employed in the encipherment are produced by the use of only two strips of paper bearing the normal alphabet. Such strips are often referred to as *sliding alphabets*, because they can be shifted or slid against each other in any one of 26 points of contact or coincidence. Exactly the same results, so far as cipher equivalents are concerned, can be obtained by the use of other devices. First, there are the so-called cipher wheels or cipher disks in which an alphabet is written on the periphery of a *rotating disk*, the circumference of which is divided into 26 equal segments, and this disk is made to revolve concentrically upon a similar but slightly larger *fixed disk*. Fig. 3 shows the now obsolete U.S. Army Cipher Disk, which is of this simple type. Here the alphabetic sequences are printed on glossy celluloid, are permanent, and admit of no variation. The use of unglazed celluloid upon which blank segments appear would permit writing letters and erasing them as often as desirable. Thus, quick and easy change of alphabets would be possible.

b. The cipher alphabets produced by the cipher disk shown in the figure are merely reversed standard alphabets, the same as are produced by the use of sliding strips of paper, and by the use of certain tables which are discussed below. The method of employing the disk needs no discussion. It may serve in monoalphabetic or polyalphabetic substitution with a key word or key number.

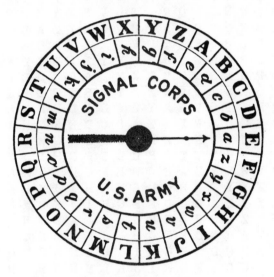

FIGURE 3

11. **Square tables.**—*a*. Tables known in the literature of cryptography under various names, such as "Vigenère Square," "Vigenère Table," "Square Table," "Pythagorean Table," etc., are often employed in polyalphabetic substitution. All the results produced by their use can be duplicated by the employment of sliding alphabets or revolving disks. The modern form of the Vigenère Square is shown in Fig. 4. Such a square may be used in various ways, differing from one another in minor details. The most common method is to consider the top line of the table as containing the plaintext letters, the first column at the left as containing the key letters. Then each successive horizontal line contains the cipher equivalents for the plaintext sequence ABC...Z enciphered by the key letter which stands at its left in the first column. Thus, the cipher alphabet corresponding to key letter D is the sequence of letters in the fourth horizontal line under the plaintext line, where $A_p = D_c$, $B_p = E_c$, etc. It will be easy to remember, in using such a table, that the equivalent of a given plaintext letter, T_p, for example, enciphered by a given key letter, O_k, lies at the intersection of the vertical column headed by T, and the horizontal row begun by O. In this case $T_p(O_k) = H_c$. The same result will be found on referring to sliding, direct standard alphabets.

9

Plain text

```
        A B C D E F G H I J K L M N O P Q R S T U V W X Y Z
     A | A B C D E F G H I J K L M N O P Q R S T U V W X Y Z
     B | B C D E F G H I J K L M N O P Q R S T U V W X Y Z A
     C | C D E F G H I J K L M N O P Q R S T U V W X Y Z A B
     D | D E F G H I J K L M N O P Q R S T U V W X Y Z A B C
     E | E F G H I J K L M N O P Q R S T U V W X Y Z A B C D
     F | F G H I J K L M N O P Q R S T U V W X Y Z A B C D E
     G | G H I J K L M N O P Q R S T U V W X Y Z A B C D E F
     H | H I J K L M N O P Q R S T U V W X Y Z A B C D E F G
     I | I J K L M N O P Q R S T U V W X Y Z A B C D E F G H
     J | J K L M N O P Q R S T U V W X Y Z A B C D E F G H I
     K | K L M N O P Q R S T U V W X Y Z A B C D E F G H I J
     L | L M N O P Q R S T U V W X Y Z A B C D E F G H I J K
 M   M | M N O P Q R S T U V W X Z Y A B C D E F G H I J K L
     N | N O P Q R S T U V W X Y Z A B C D E F G H I J K L M
     O | O P Q R S T U V W X Y Z A B C D E F G H I J K L M N
     P | P Q R S T U V W X Y Z A B C D E F G H I J K L M N O
     Q | Q R S T U V W X Y Z A B C D E F G H I J K L M N O P
     R | R S T U V W X Y Z A B C D E F G H I J K L M N O P Q
     S | S T U V W X Y Z A B C D E F G H I J K L M N O P Q R
     T | T U V W X Y Z A B C D E F G H I J K L M N O P Q R S
     U | U V W X Y Z A B C D E F G H I J K L M N O P Q R S T
     V | V W X Y Z A B C D E F G H I J K L M N O P Q R S T U
     W | W X Y Z A B C D E F G H I J K L M N O P Q R S T U V
     X | X Y Z A B C D E F G H I J K L M N O P Q R S T U V W
     Y | Y Z A B C D E F G H I J K L M N O P Q R S T U V W X
     Z | Z A B C D E F G H I J K L M N O P Q R S T U V W X Y
```

Key (left)   Cipher (right)

FIGURE 4

b. Minor modifications of the Vigenère Square are encountered. If the top line is made a reversed normal sequence, leaving the interior of the table unchanged, or if the successive horizontal rows are made to contain the reversed normal sequence, leaving the top row (plain text) unchanged, then the results given by using the table are the same as those given by using the cipher disk shown in Fig. 3. Again, the same general results can be obtained by using a set of alphabets in tabular form known under the names of Porta's Table and Napoleon's Table, which is shown in Fig. 5. In this table the alphabets are all reciprocal, for example, $G_p(W_k)=R_c$, $R_p(W_k)=G_c$. Reciprocal alphabets when arranged in this form are sometimes called *complementary alphabets*. Note that in each alphabet either of two letters may serve as key letter indifferently: $G_p(W_k)$ or $G_p(X_k)=R_c$.

c. Another modification of the basic table, and one that employs numbers instead of letters as cipher equivalents is shown in Fig. 6. Since many more than 26 different equivalents are available (100 pairs of digits from 00 to 99), it is possible to insert many plaintext elements in the top line of the table in addition to the 26 letters. For example, one could have the 10 digits;

	A B C D E F G H I J K L M
AB	N O P Q R S T U V W X Y Z
CD	A B C D E F G H I J K L M
	O P Q R S T U V W X Y Z N
EF	A B C D E F G H I J K L M
	P Q R S T U V W X Y Z N O
GH	A B C D E F G H I J K L M
	Q R S T U V W X Y Z N O P
IJ	A B C D E F G H I J K L M
	R S T U V W X Y Z N O P Q
KL	A B C D E F G H I J K L M
	S T U V W X Y Z N O P Q R
MN	A B C D E F G H I J K L M
	T U V W X Y Z N O P Q R S
OP	A B C D E F G H I J K L M
	U V W X Y Z N O P Q R S T
QR	A B C D E F G H I J K L M
	V W X Y Z N O P Q R S T U
ST	A B C D E F G H I J K L M
	W X Y Z N O P Q R S T U V
UV	A B C D E F G H I J K L M
	X Y Z N O P Q R S T U V W
WX	A B C D E F G H I J K L M
	Y Z N O P Q R S T U V W X
YZ	A B C D E F G H I J K L M
	Z N O P Q R S T U V W X Y

FIGURE 5

a few common double-letter combinations, such as DD, LL, RR, and SS; a few of the most frequently used digraphs, such as TH, ER, IN; or even such common syllables as ENT, ING, and ION. The table shown in Fig. 6 was used by the Italian army in World War I, and was known as the "Cifrario militare tascabile" (Pocket military cipher).

12. **Square tables employing mixed alphabets.**—*a.* In the tables thus far shown the alphabets have been direct or reversed standard sequences, but just as mixed sequences may be written upon sliding strips and revolving disks, so can mixed alphabets appear in tabular form. The table shown in Fig. 7, based upon the keyword-mixed sequence derived from the word LEAVENWORTH, is an example that is equivalent to the use of a strip bearing that keyword sequence sliding against another strip bearing the normal alphabet. The usual method of using such a table is the same as that in the preceding cases. The only difference is that the key letters must now be sought in a mixed sequence, whereas in the preceding tables they were located in direct or reversed standard sequences. Example, using Fig. 7: $C_p(S_k)=X_c$.

b. Fig. 8 illustrates a case in which a mixed alphabet is sliding against itself. The usual method of employing such a table is exactly the same as that explained before. The only differ-

11

Figure 6

*	a	b	c	d	e	f	g	h	i	j	k	l	m	n	o	p	q	r	s	t	u	v	w	x	y	z	0	1	2	3	4	5	6	7	8	9
a	10	11	12	13	14	15	16	17	18	19	20	21	22	23	24	25	26	27	28	29	30	31	32	33	34	35	36	37	38	39	40	41	42	43	44	45
b	11	12	13	14	15	16	17	18	19	20	21	22	23	24	25	26	27	28	29	30	31	32	33	34	35	36	37	38	39	40	41	42	43	44	45	10
c	12	13	14	15	16	17	18	19	20	21	22	23	24	25	26	27	28	29	30	31	32	33	34	35	36	37	38	39	40	41	42	43	44	45	10	11
d	13	14	15	16	17	18	19	20	21	22	23	24	25	26	27	28	29	30	31	32	33	34	35	36	37	38	39	40	41	42	43	44	45	10	11	12
e	14	15	16	17	18	19	20	21	22	23	24	25	26	27	28	29	30	31	32	33	34	35	36	37	38	39	40	41	42	43	44	45	10	11	12	13
f	15	16	17	18	19	20	21	22	23	24	25	26	27	28	29	30	31	32	33	34	35	36	37	38	39	40	41	42	43	44	45	10	11	12	13	14
g	16	17	18	19	20	21	22	23	24	25	26	27	28	29	30	31	32	33	34	35	36	37	38	39	40	41	42	43	44	45	10	11	12	13	14	15
h	17	18	19	20	21	22	23	24	25	26	27	28	29	30	31	32	33	34	35	36	37	38	39	40	41	42	43	44	45	10	11	12	13	14	15	16
i	18	19	20	21	22	23	24	25	26	27	28	29	30	31	32	33	34	35	36	37	38	39	40	41	42	43	44	45	10	11	12	13	14	15	16	17
j	19	20	21	22	23	24	25	26	27	28	29	30	31	32	33	34	35	36	37	38	39	40	41	42	43	44	45	10	11	12	13	14	15	16	17	18
k	20	21	22	23	24	25	26	27	28	29	30	31	32	33	34	35	36	37	38	39	40	41	42	43	44	45	10	11	12	13	14	15	16	17	18	19
l	21	22	23	24	25	26	27	28	29	30	31	32	33	34	35	36	37	38	39	40	41	42	43	44	45	10	11	12	13	14	15	16	17	18	19	20
m	22	23	24	25	26	27	28	29	30	31	32	33	34	35	36	37	38	39	40	41	42	43	44	45	10	11	12	13	14	15	16	17	18	19	20	21
n	23	24	25	26	27	28	29	30	31	32	33	34	35	36	37	38	39	40	41	42	43	44	45	10	11	12	13	14	15	16	17	18	19	20	21	22
o	24	25	26	27	28	29	30	31	32	33	34	35	36	37	38	39	40	41	42	43	44	45	10	11	12	13	14	15	16	17	18	19	20	21	22	23
p	25	26	27	28	29	30	31	32	33	34	35	36	37	38	39	40	41	42	43	44	45	10	11	12	13	14	15	16	17	18	19	20	21	22	23	24
q	26	27	28	29	30	31	32	33	34	35	36	37	38	39	40	41	42	43	44	45	10	11	12	13	14	15	16	17	18	19	20	21	22	23	24	25
r	27	28	29	30	31	32	33	34	35	36	37	38	39	40	41	42	43	44	45	10	11	12	13	14	15	16	17	18	19	20	21	22	23	24	25	26
s	28	29	30	31	32	33	34	35	36	37	38	39	40	41	42	43	44	45	10	11	12	13	14	15	16	17	18	19	20	21	22	23	24	25	26	27
t	29	30	31	32	33	34	35	36	37	38	39	40	41	42	43	44	45	10	11	12	13	14	15	16	17	18	19	20	21	22	23	24	25	26	27	28
u	30	31	32	33	34	35	36	37	38	39	40	41	42	43	44	45	10	11	12	13	14	15	16	17	18	19	20	21	22	23	24	25	26	27	28	29
v	31	32	33	34	35	36	37	38	39	40	41	42	43	44	45	10	11	12	13	14	15	16	17	18	19	20	21	22	23	24	25	26	27	28	29	30
w	32	33	34	35	36	37	38	39	40	41	42	43	44	45	10	11	12	13	14	15	16	17	18	19	20	21	22	23	24	25	26	27	28	29	30	31
x	33	34	35	36	37	38	39	40	41	42	43	44	45	10	11	12	13	14	15	16	17	18	19	20	21	22	23	24	25	26	27	28	29	30	31	32
y	34	35	36	37	38	39	40	41	42	43	44	45	10	11	12	13	14	15	16	17	18	19	20	21	22	23	24	25	26	27	28	29	30	31	32	33
z	35	36	37	38	39	40	41	42	43	44	45	10	11	12	13	14	15	16	17	18	19	20	21	22	23	24	25	26	27	28	29	30	31	32	33	34

FIGURE 6

12

A B C D E F G H I J K L M N O P Q R S T U V W X Y Z

```
L E A V N W O R T H B C D F G I J K M P Q S U X Y Z
E A V N W O R T H B C D F G I J K M P Q S U X Y Z L
A V N W O R T H B C D F G I J K M P Q S U X Y Z L E
V N W O R T H B C D F G I J K M P Q S U X Y Z L E A
N W O R T H B C D F G I J K M P Q S U X Y Z L E A V
W O R T H B C D F G I J K M P Q S U X Y Z L E A V N
O R T H B C D F G I J K M P Q S U X Y Z L E A V N W
R T H B C D F G I J K M P Q S U X Y Z L E A V N W O
T H B C D F G I J K M P Q S U X Y Z L E A V N W O R
H B C D F G I J K M P Q S U X Y Z L E A V N W O R T
B C D F G I J K M P Q S U X Y Z L E A V N W O R T H
C D F G I J K M P Q S U X Y Z L E A V N W O R T H B
D F G I J K M P Q S U X Y Z L E A V N W O R T H B C
F G I J K M P W S U X Y Z L E A V N W O R T H B C D
G I J K M P Q S U X Y Z L E A V N W O R T H B C D F
I J K M P Q S U X Y Z L E A V N W O R T H B C D F G
J K M P Q S U X Y Z L E A V N W O R T H B C D F G I
K M P Q S U X Y Z L E A V N W O R T H B C D F G I J
M P Q S U X Y Z L E A V N W O R T H B C D F G I J K
P Q S U X Y Z L E A V N W O R T H B C D F G I J K M
Q S U X Y Z L E A V N W O R T H B C D F G I J K M P
S U X Y Z L E A V N W O R T H B C D F G I J K M P Q
U X Y Z L E A V N W O R T H B C D F G I J K M P Q S
X Y Z L E A V N W O R T H B C D F G I J K M P Q S U
Y Z L E A V N W O R T H B C D F G I J K M P Q S U X
Z L E A V N W O R T H B C D F G I J K M P Q S U X Y
```

FIGURE 7

ence is that both the plaintext letters and the key letters must be looked for in mixed sequences. Example, using Fig. 8: $U_p(R_k) = V_c$.

c. In employing sliding alphabets it is usual to set the key letter as located in the cipher component opposite the letter A as located in the plain component, or the key letter as located in the cipher component may be set opposite the initial letter of the plain component. In all examples preceding that in Fig. 8, the key letter has been A. In Fig. 8, since the plain component is also a mixed sequence and its initial letter is Q, the sliding alphabets are set against each other so that the given key letter in the cipher component is opposite Q in the plain component. Thus, to duplicate the results given by the use of Fig. 8 in finding the value of $U_p(R_k)$, it is necessary to set the sliding strips in the following relative positions:

```
Plain:                          QUESTIONABLYCDFGHJKMPRVWXZ
Cipher: QUESTIONABLYCDFGHJKMPRVWXZQUESTIONABLYCDFGHJKMPRVWXZ
```

Here it is seen that $U_p(R_k) = V_c$, which is identical with the result obtained from the use of the table. There are other ways of using the table, however, each having a correspondingly modified

```
Q U E S T I O N A B L Y C D F G H J K M P R V W X Z
U E S T I O N A B L Y C D F G H J K M P R V W X Z Q
E S T I O N A B L Y C D F G H J K M P R V W X Z Q U
S T I O N A B L Y C D F G H J K M P R V W X Z Q U E
T I O N A B L Y C D F G H J K M P R V W X Z Q U E S
I O N A B L Y C D F G H J K M P R V W X Z Q U E S T
O N A B L Y C D F G H J K M P R V W X Z Q U E S T I
N A B L Y C D F G H J K M P R V W X Z Q U E S T I O
A B L Y C D F G H J K M P R V W X Z Q U E S T I O N
B L Y C D F G H J K M P R V W X Z Q U E S T I O N A
L Y C D F G H J K M P R V W X Z Q U E S T I O N A B
Y C D F G H J K M P R V W X Z Q U E S T I O N A B L
C D F G H J K M P R V W X Z Q U E S T I O N A B L Y
D F G H J K M P R V W X Z Q U E S T I O N A B L Y C
F G H J K M P R V W X Z Q U E S T I O N A B L Y C D
G H J K M P R V W X Z Q U E S T I O N A B L Y C D F
H J K M P R V W X Z Q U E S T I O N A B L Y C D F G
J K M P R V W X Z Q U E S T I O N A B L Y C D F G H
K M P R V W X Z Q U E S T I O N A B L Y C D F G H J
M P R V W X Z Q U E S T I O N A B L Y C D F G H J K
P R V W X Z Q U E S T I O N A B L Y C D F G H J K M
R V W X Z Q U E S T I O N A B L Y C D F G H J K M P
V W X Z Q U E S T I O N A B L Y C D F G H J K M P R
W X Z Q U E S T I O N A B L Y C D F G H J K M P R V
X Z Q U E S T I O N A B L Y C D F G H J K M P R V W
Z Q U E S T I O N A B L Y C D F G H J K M P R V W X
```

FIGURE 8

method of employing sliding strips in order to obtain identical results; these methods will be discussed in the next paragraph.

d. In addition to cryptographic schemes in which there are cipher squares composed of slides of a basic sequence to produce the various alphabets, it is of course possible to have *n* unrelated, random-mixed alphabets (here *n* can be *any* number) used cyclically to encipher the letters of a message. Such a scheme cannot be reduced to two components, and therefore would require the alphabets written out in a matrix or in tabular form. For instance, a system might incorporate 1,000 different mixed alphabets, numbered from 1–1,000; then alphabet 1 might be used to encipher the first letter of each message, alphabet 2 the second letters, etc. There are also cryptographic schemes in which certain alphabets of a set are selected for enciphering a given message, the selection being governed by an indicator, by the date, or other convention.

13. Further remarks on primary components.—*a.* In preceding paragraphs it has been shown that the equivalents obtainable from the use of square tables may be duplicated by the use of revolving cipher disks or of sliding primary components. It was also stated that there are various ways of employing such tables, disks, and sliding components. Cryptographically the results may be quite diverse from different methods of using such paraphernalia, since the specific equivalents obtained from one method may be altogether different from those obtained from

14

another method. But from the cryptanalytic point of view the diversity referred to is of little significance; only in one or two cases does the specific method of employing these cryptographic instrumentalities have an important bearing upon the procedure in cryptanalysis. However, it is advisable that the student learn something about these different methods before proceeding with further work.

b. There are, not *two*, but *four* letters involved in every case of finding equivalents by means of sliding primary components; furthermore, the determination of an equivalent for a given plaintext letter is representable by *two* equations involving *four* elements, usually letters. Three of these letters are by this time well-known to and understood by the student, *viz.*, θ_k, θ_p, and θ_c. The fourth element or letter has been passed over without much comment, but cryptographically it is just as important a factor as the other three. Its function may best be indicated by noting what happens when two primary components are juxtaposed, for the purpose of finding equivalents. Suppose these components are the following sequences:

(1) A B C D E F G H I J K L M N O P Q R S T U V W X Y Z
(2) F B P Y R C Q Z I G S E H T D J U M K V A L W N O X

Now suppose one is merely asked to find the equivalent of P_p when the key letter is K. Without further specification, the cipher equivalent cannot be stated; for it is necessary to know not only which K will be used as the key letter, the one in the component labeled (1) or the one in the component labeled (2), but also what letter the K_k will be set against, in order to juxtapose the two components. Most of the time, in the preceding text, these two factors have been tacitly assumed to be fixed and well understood: the K_k is sought in the mixed, or cipher component, and this K is set against A in the normal, or plain component. Thus:

$$\begin{array}{cc} \text{Index} & \text{Plain} \\ \downarrow & \downarrow \end{array}$$

(1) Plain: ABCDEFGHIJKLMNOPQRSTUVWXYZ
(2) Cipher: FBPYRCQZIGSEHTDJUMKVALWNOXFBPYRCQZIGSEHTDJUMKVALWNOX

$$\begin{array}{cc} \uparrow & \uparrow \\ \text{Key} & \text{Cipher} \end{array}$$

With this setting, $P_p = Z_c$.

c. The letter A in this case may be termed the *index letter*, symbolized A_i. The index letter constitutes the fourth element involved in the two equations applicable to the finding of equivalents by sliding components. The four elements are therefore these:

(1) The key letter, θ_k
(2) The index letter, θ_i
(3) The plaintext letter, θ_p
(4) The cipher letter, θ_c

The index letter is commonly the initial letter of the component; but this, too, is only a convention. It might be *any letter* of the sequence constituting the component, as agreed upon by the correspondents. *However, in the subsequent discussion it will be assumed that the index letter is the initial letter of the component in which it is located, unless otherwise stated.*

d. In the foregoing case the enciphering equations are as follows:

$$\text{(I)} \quad K_k = A_i; \ P_p = Z_c$$

But there is nothing about the use of sliding components which excludes other methods of finding equivalents than that shown above. For instance, despite the labeling of the two components as shown above, there is nothing to prevent one from seeking the plaintext letter

15

in the component labeled (2), that is, the cipher component, and taking as its cipher equivalent the letter opposite it in the other component labeled (1).   Thus:

$$\text{Index} \quad\quad \text{Cipher}$$
$$\downarrow \quad\quad\quad \downarrow$$

(1)　　　　　　　ABCDEFGHIJKLMNOPQRSTUVWXYZ

(2) FBPYRCQZIGSEHTDJUMKVALWNOXFBPYRCQZIGSEHTDJUMKVALWNOX

$$\uparrow \quad\quad\quad \uparrow$$
$$\text{Key} \quad\quad \text{Plain}$$

Thus:

(II) $K_k = A_1$; $P_p = K_c$

e. Since equations (I) and (II) yield different resultants, even with the same index, key, and plaintext letters, it is obvious that an accurate formula to cover a specific pair of enciphering equations must include data showing in what component each of the four letters comprising the equations is located.   Thus, equations (I) and (II) should read:

(I) K_k in component (2) = A_1 in component (1); P_p in component (1) = Z_c in component (2).

(II) K_k in component (2) = A_1 in component (1); P_p in component (2) = K_c in component (1).

For the sake of brevity, the following notations will be used:

(1) $K_{k/2} = A_{1/1}$; $P_{p/1} = Z_{c/2}$
(2) $K_{k/2} = A_{1/1}$; $P_{p/2} = K_{c/1}$

f. Employing two sliding components and the four letters entering into an enciphering equation, there are, in all, twelve different resultants possible for the same set of components and the same set of four basic elements.   These twelve differences in resultants arise from a set of twelve different enciphering conditions,[1] as set forth below (the notation adopted in subpar. *e* is used):

(1) $\theta_{k/2} = \theta_{1/1}$; $\theta_{p/1} = \theta_{c/2}$
(2) $\theta_{k/2} = \theta_{1/1}$; $\theta_{p/2} = \theta_{c/1}$
(3) $\theta_{k/1} = \theta_{1/2}$; $\theta_{p/1} = \theta_{c/2}$
(4) $\theta_{k/1} = \theta_{1/2}$; $\theta_{p/2} = \theta_{c/1}$
(5) $\theta_{k/2} = \theta_{p/1}$; $\theta_{1/1} = \theta_{c/2}$
(6) $\theta_{k/2} = \theta_{c/1}$; $\theta_{1/1} = \theta_{p/2}$

(7) $\theta_{k/2} = \theta_{p/1}$; $\theta_{1/2} = \theta_{c/1}$
(8) $\theta_{k/2} = \theta_{c/1}$; $\theta_{1/2} = \theta_{p/1}$
(9) $\theta_{k/1} = \theta_{p/2}$; $\theta_{1/1} = \theta_{c/2}$
(10) $\theta_{k/1} = \theta_{c/2}$; $\theta_{1/1} = \theta_{p/2}$
(11) $\theta_{k/1} = \theta_{p/2}$; $\theta_{1/2} = \theta_{c/1}$
(12) $\theta_{k/1} = \theta_{c/2}$; $\theta_{1/2} = \theta_{p/1}$

g. The twelve resultants obtainable from juxtaposing sliding components as indicated under the preceding subparagraph may also be obtained either from *one* square table, in which case *twelve* different methods of finding equivalents must be applied, or from *twelve* different square tables, in which case *one* standard method of finding equivalents will serve all purposes.

h. If but one table such as that shown below in Fig. 9 is employed, the various methods of finding equivalents are difficult to keep in mind.

---

[1] Equations (1) and (2) are the most widely used, and are referred to in cryptographic literature as the Vigenère type of encipherment; (5) and (6) are the equations of the Beaufort type; and (9) and (10) are the Delastelle type.

```
A B C D E F G H I J K L M N O P Q R S T U V W X Y Z
┌─────────────────────────────────────────────────┐
│ F B P Y R C Q Z I G S E H T D J U M K V A L W N O X │
│ B P Y R C Q Z I G S E H T D J U M K V A L W N O X F │
│ P Y R C Q Z I G S E H T D J U M K V A L W N O X F B │
│ Y R C Q Z I G S E H T D J U M K V A L W N O X F B P │
│ R C Q Z I G S E H T D J U M K V A L W N O X F B P Y │
│ C Q Z I G S E H T D J U M K V A L W N O X F B P Y R │
│ Q Z I G S E H T D J U M K V A L W N O X F B P Y R C │
│ Z I G S E H T D J U M K V A L W N O X F B P Y R C Q │
│ I G S E H T D J U M K V A L W N O X F B P Y R C Q Z │
│ G S E H T D J U M K V A L W N O X F B P Y R C Q Z I │
│ S E H T D J U M K V A L W N O X F B P Y R C Q Z I G │
│ E H T D J U M K V A L W N O X F B P Y R C Q Z I G S │
│ H T D J U M K V A L W N O X F B P Y R C Q Z I G S E │
│ T D J U M K V A L W N O X F B P Y R C Q Z I G S E H │
│ D J U M K V A L W N O X F B P Y R C Q Z I G S E H T │
│ J U M K V A L W N O X F B P Y R C Q Z I G S E H T D │
│ U M K V A L W N O X F B P Y R C Q Z I G S E H T D J │
│ M K V A L W N O X F B P Y R C Q Z I G S E H T D J U │
│ K V A L W N O X F B P Y R C Q Z I G S E H T D J U M │
│ V A L W N O X F B P Y R C Q Z I G S E H T D J U M K │
│ A L W N O X F B P Y R C Q Z I G S E H T D J U M K V │
│ L W N O X F B P Y R C Q Z I G S E H T D J U M K V A │
│ W N O X F B P Y R C Q Z I G S E H T D J U M K V A L │
│ N O X F B P Y R C Q Z I G S E H T D J U M K V A L W │
│ O X F B P Y R C Q Z I G S E H T D J U M K V A L W N │
│ X F B P Y R C Q Z I G S E H T D J U M K V A L W N O │
└─────────────────────────────────────────────────┘
```

FIGURE 9

For example:

(1) For enciphering equations $\theta_{k/2}=\theta_{1/1}$; $\theta_{p/1}=\theta_{c/2}$:
Locate θ_p in top sequence; locate θ_k in first column; θ_c is the letter within the square at intersection of the two lines thus determined.   Thus:

$$K_{k/2}=A_{1/1}; P_{p/1}=Z_{c/2}$$

(2) For enciphering equations $\theta_{k/2}=\theta_{1/1}$; $\theta_{p/2}=\theta_{c/1}$:
Locate θ_k in first column; follow line to right to θ_p; proceed up this column, and θ_c is letter at top.   Thus:

$$K_{k/2}=A_{1/1}; P_{p/2}=K_{c/1}$$

(3) For enciphering equations $\theta_{k/1}=\theta_{1/2}$; $\theta_{p/1}=\theta_{c/2}$:
Locate θ_k in top sequence and proceed down column to θ_1; locate θ_p in top sequence; θ_c is letter at other corner of rectangle thus formed.   Thus:

$$K_{k/1}=A_{1/2}; P_{p/1}=X_{c/2}$$

17

Only three different methods have been shown and the student no doubt already has encountered difficulty in keeping them segregated in his mind. It would obviously be very confusing to try to remember all twelve methods, but fortunately this is not necessary. If one standard or fixed method of finding equivalents is followed with several different tables, this difficulty disappears. Suppose that the following method is adopted: Arrange the square so that the plaintext letter may be sought in a separate sequence, arranged alphabetically, above the square and so that the key letter may be sought in a separate sequence, also arranged alphabetically, to the left of the square; look for the plaintext letter in the top row; locate the key letter in the 1st column to the left; find the letter standing within the square at the intersection of the vertical and horizontal lines thus determined. Then *twelve* squares, equivalent to the twelve different conditions listed in subpar. *f*, can readily be constructed.[2] However, to avoid confusing the student with a multiplicity of unnecessary details which have no direct bearing upon basic principles, one and only one standard method of finding equivalents by means of sliding components will be selected from among the twelve available, as set forth in the preceding subparagraphs. Unless otherwise stated, this method will be the one denoted by the first of the formulas listed in subpar. *f*, *viz.*:

$$\theta_{k/2} = \theta_{1/1}\,;\; \theta_{p/1} = \theta_{c/2}$$

Calling the plain component "1" and the cipher component "2", this will mean that the key letter on the cipher component will be set opposite the index, which will be the first letter of the plain component; the plaintext letter to be enciphered will then be sought on the plain component and its equivalent will be the letter opposite it on the cipher component.

---

[2] Cf. subpar. 100*a*.

THEORY OF SOLUTION OF REPEATING-KEY SYSTEMS

14. The three steps in the analysis of repeating-key systems.—*a.* The method of enciphering according to the principle of the repeating key has been illustrated in subpar. 3*b.* The analysis of a cryptogram produced by a periodic polyalphabetic system, regardless of the kind of cipher alphabets employed, or their method of production, resolves itself into three distinct and successive steps:

(1) Determination of the length of the repeating key, which is the same as the determination of the number of alphabets involved in the cryptogram.

(2) Allocation or distribution of the letters of the cipher text into the respective cipher alphabets to which they belong. This is the step which reduces the polyalphabetic text to monoalphabetic terms.

(3) Analysis of the individual monoalphabetic distributions to determine plaintext values of the cipher letters in each distribution or alphabet.

b. The foregoing steps will be treated in the order in which mentioned. The first step may be described briefly as that of *determining the period.* The second step may be described briefly as that of *reduction to monoalphabetic terms.* The third step may be designated as *identification of ciphertext values.*

15. First step: finding the length of the period.—*a.* The determination of the period, that is, the length of the key or the number of cipher alphabets involved in a cryptogram enciphered by the repeating-key method is, as a rule, a relatively simple matter. The cryptogram itself usually manifests externally certain phenomena which are the direct result of the use of a repeating key. The principles involved are, however, so fundamental in cryptanalytics that their elucidation warrants a somewhat detailed treatment. This will be done in connection with a short example of encipherment, shown in Fig. 10.

b. Regardless of what system is used, identical plaintext letters enciphered by the same cipher alphabet [1] must yield identical cipher letters. Referring to Fig. 10, such a condition is brought about every time that identical plaintext letters happen to be enciphered with the same key letter (i.e., every time identical plaintext letters fall into the same column in the encipherment).[2] Now since the number of columns or positions with respect to the key is very limited (except in the case of very long key words), and since the repetition of letters is an inevitable condition in plain text, it follows that there will be in a message of fair length many

---

[1] It is to be understood, of course, that cipher alphabets with single equivalents are meant in this case.

[2] The frequency with which this condition may be *expected* to occur can be definitely calculated.

Message

THE ARTILLERY BATTALION MARCHING IN THE REAR OF THE ADVANCE GUARD
KEEPS ITS COMBAT TRAIN WITH IT INSOFAR AS PRACTICABLE.

(Repeating key: BLUE, using direct standard alphabets)

Cipher Alphabets

```
Plain: A B C D E F G H I J K L M N O P Q R S T U V W X Y Z
  (1): B C D E F G H I J K L M N O P Q R S T U V W X Y Z A
  (2): L M N O P Q R S T U V W X Y Z A B C D E F G H I J K
  (3): U V W X Y Z A B C D E F G H I J K L M N O P Q R S T
  (4): E F G H I J K L M N O P Q R S T U V W X Y Z A B C D
```

```
B L U E   B L U E   B L U E   B L U E   B L U E   B L U E   B L U E
T H E A   R T I L   L E R Y   B A T T   A L I O   N M A R   C H I N
U S Y E   S E C P   M P L C   C L N X   B W C S   O X U V   D S C R

G I N T   H E R E   A R O F   T H E A   D V A N   C E G U   A R D K
H T H X   I P L I   B C I J   U S Y E   E G U R   D P A Y   B C X O

E E P S   I T S C   O M B A   T T R A   I N W I   T H I T   I N S O
F P J W   J E M G   P X V E   U E L E   J Y Q M   U S C X   J Y M S

F A R A   S P R A   C T I C   A B L E
G L L E   T A L E   D E C G   B M F I
```

Cryptogram

```
U S Y E S   E C P M P   L C C L N   X B W C S   O X U V D   S C R H T
H X I P L   I B C I J   U S Y E E   G U R D P   A Y B C X   O F P J W
J E M G P   X V E U E   L E J Y Q   M U S C X   J Y M S G   L L E T A
L E D E C   G B M F I
```

FIGURE 10

cases where identical plaintext letters *must* fall into the same column. They will thus be enciphered by the same cipher alphabet, resulting, therefore, in the production of many identical letters in the cipher text and these will represent identical letters in the plain text. When identical plaintext polygraphs fall into identical columns the result is the formation of identical ciphertext polygraphs, that is, repetitions of groups of 2, 3, 4, . . . letters are exhibited in the cryptogram. Repetitions of this type will hereafter be called *causal repetitions*, because they are produced by a definite, traceable cause, *viz.*, the encipherment of identical letters by the same cipher alphabets.

c. It will also happen, however, that *different* plaintext letters falling in *different* columns will, by mere accident, produce identical cipher letters. Note, for example, in Fig. 10 that in the columns under the key letter B, R_p becomes S_c, and that in the columns under the key letter L, H_p also becomes S_c. The production of an identical ciphertext letter in these two cases (that is, a repetition where the plaintext letters are different and enciphered by different alphabets) is merely fortuitous. It is, in everyday language, "a mere coincidence," or "an accident." For this reason repetitions of this type will hereafter be called *accidental repetitions*.

20

d. A consideration of the phenomenon pointed out in subpar. *c* makes it obvious that in polyalphabetic ciphers it is important that the cryptanalyst be able to tell whether the repetitions he finds in a specific case are causal or accidental in their origin, that is, whether they represent actual encipherments of identical plaintext letters by identical keying elements, or mere coincidences brought about purely fortuitously.

e. Now accidental repetitions will, of course, happen fairly frequently with individual letters, but less frequently with digraphs, because in this case the same kind of an "accident" must take place twice in succession. Intuitively one feels that the chances that such a purely fortuitous coincidence will happen two times in succession must be much less than that it will happen every once in a while in the case of single letters. Similarly, intuition makes one feel that the chances of such accidents happening in the case of three or more consecutive letters are still less than in the case of digraphs, decreasing very rapidly as the repetition increases in length.

f. The phenomena of cryptographic repetition may, fortunately, be dealt with statistically, thus taking the matter outside the realm of intuition and putting it on a firm, objective basis. Moreover, often the statistical analysis will tell the cryptanalyst when he has arranged or rearranged his text properly, that is, when he is approaching or has reached monoalphabeticity in his efforts to reduce polyalphabetic text to its simplest terms. By means of the binomial distribution,[3] it is possible to compute tables of the expected number of digraphs, trigraphs, and other polygraphs occurring exactly 0, 1, 2, 3, . . . *x* times in a sample of random text of a given size; then the repetitive phenomena in a cryptogram under study may be compared with the phenomena expected by pure chance (i.e., in samples of random text of the same size as the cryptogram) as a means of evaluating whether or not the observed repetitions and their number are significant. If the observed repetitive phenomena are no more than would normally be expected by chance, then these phenomena cannot be used as a basis for cryptanalytic attack; if, however, these repetitions are highly unlikely to have occurred by chance, then they are open to interpretation and exploitation. Tables derived from the binomial distribution are given in subpar. *g*, below.[4]

g. Fig. 11*a* is a table of the expected number of digraphs appearing exactly 2, 3, 4, . . . 10 times in samples of *random* text of sizes 100 to 1,000 letters, by hundreds. Fig. 11*b* is a table of the expected number of trigraphs appearing exactly 2, 3, and 4 times *by chance* in these sample sizes; and Figs. 11*c* and *d* contain the data for tetragraphs and pentagraphs, respectively. As an illustration of the use of these tables, from Fig. 11*a* we observe that in a sample of 300 letters of random text we may expect about 43 (rounded off to the nearest integer) digraphs to occur twice, 6 digraphs to occur three times, and about 1 digraph to occur four times. The meaning of the decimal fractions in that row under E(4), E(5), and E(6) may be interpreted as follows: the entry 0.683 under E(4) means that in 100 samples of 300 random letters each, about

---

[3] This distribution, as well as the Poisson exponential distribution (which is an approximation to the binomial), will be treated in *Military Cryptanalytics, Part III*.

[4] The tables illustrated here have been computed using the formula for the number of comparisons as $\frac{(N-t+1)(N-t)}{2}$, where N is the number of letters in the sample size and *t* is the length of the polygraph. Strictly speaking, the formula $\frac{(N-2t+2)(N-2t+1)}{2}$ should be used, to discount overlapping repetitions such as the repeated tetragraph in the sequence ABCABCA; however, in most statistical computations, especially where analytical machine techniques are employed, the scoring is almost invariably predicated upon the first formula. The two formulas are practically equivalent, except for small values of N when the second formula is the more precise one for the number of comparisons.

Number of letters	Expected number of digraphs occurring exactly x times								
	E(2)	E(3)	E(4)	E(5)	E(6)	E(7)	E(8)	E(9)	E(10)
100	6.21	0.298	0.011						
200	21.8	2.12	0.154	0.009					
300	42.5	6.23	0.683	0.060	0.004				
400	65.3	12.8	1.87	0.220	0.022	0.002			
500	88.1	21.6	3.97	0.582	0.071	0.008			
600	110	32.3	7.11	1.25	0.184	0.023	0.003		
700	129	44.3	11.4	2.35	0.403	0.059	0.008	0.001	
800	145	57.1	16.8	3.96	0.777	0.130	0.019	0.003	
900	158	70.1	23.2	6.16	1.36	0.257	0.043	0.006	0.001
1000	169	83.0	30.6	9.03	2.21	0.466	0.085	0.014	0.002

FIGURE 11a

Number of letters	Exp. number of trigraphs		
	E(2)	E(3)	E(4)
100	0.269	0.001	
200	1.10	0.004	
300	2.48	0.014	
400	4.40	0.033	
500	6.85	0.064	
600	9.81	0.111	0.001
700	13.3	0.175	0.002
800	17.3	0.261	0.003
900	21.8	0.371	0.005
1000	26.8	0.505	0.008

FIGURE 11b

Number of letters	Tetragraphs	
	E(2)	E(3)
100	0.010	
200	0.043	
300	0.096	
400	0.171	
500	0.270	
600	0.389	
700	0.530	
800	0.693	
900	0.877	
1000	1.08	0.001

FIGURE 11c

Number of letters	Pentagraphs
	E(2)
100	
200	0.002
300	0.004
400	0.007
500	0.011
600	0.015
700	0.021
800	0.027
900	0.034
1000	0.042

FIGURE 11d

68 of them will have a digraph occurring 4 times within the sample; the entry 0.060 under E(5) means that in 100 samples of 300 random letters each, 6 of them will have a digraph occurring 5 times; and the entry 0.004 under E(6) means that in 1,000 samples of 300 random letters, 4 of them may be expected to have a digraph occurring 6 times. From Fig. 11b, we note that a sample of 300 random letters may be expected to contain 2 or 3 trigraphs occurring twice; and in 1,000 of such samples, 14 may be expected to contain a trigraph occurring three times. From Fig. 11c, we note that in 1,000 samples of 300 random letters, 96 of them may be expected to contain a repeated tetragraph, while the chance of a tetragraph occurring three times in these 1,000 samples is so small as to be practically nonexistent; note that, under E(3) of the last row of this Figure, if we had 1,000 samples of 1,000 letters each, only 1 of them may be expected to contain a threefold occurrence of a tetragraph. From Fig. 11d, we see that if we had 1,000 samples of 300 random letters, only 4 of them may be expected to contain a pentagraphic repetition (i.e., a pentagraph occurring twice), and that in these 1,000 samples there is, in unmathematical but nevertheless precise language, not a ghost of a chance that a pentagraph will occur three times.

22

h. The foregoing tables may also be used to determine the *cumulative* values of digraphs and polygraphs expected to appear *x or more* times in samples of random text. Using Fig. 11*a* as an example, in a 300-letter sample of random text, if the entries under E(2) to E(6) are added together, the sum (49.477) indicates that about 49 digraphs may be expected to occur at least twice (i.e., two or more times); if the values E(3) to E(6) are added together, the sum (6.977) shows that 7 digraphs may be expected to occur three or more times; if the entries under E(4) to E(6) are added together, the sum (0.747) shows that in *100* such samples of random text, about 75 of them will contain a digraph occurring at least four times; and if the entries under E(5) and E(6) are added, their sum (0.065) shows that in *1,000* 300-letter samples of random text, 65 of these may be expected to contain a digraph occurring five or more times.

i. As an illustration of the application of the foregoing discussion, it is indicated that if a cryptanalyst were to have at hand only the cryptogram of Fig. 10, with the repetitions underlined as below, a statistical study of the number and length of the repetitions within the message would tell him that while some of the digraphic repetitions may be accidental, the chances that they all are accidental are small. In the case of the tetragraphic repetition he would realize that the chances of its being accidental are very small indeed.

```
U S Y E S   E C P M P   L C C L N   X B W C S   O X U V D   S C R H T
H X I P L   I B C I J   U S Y E E   G U R D P   A Y B C X   O F P J W
J E M G P   X V E U E   L E J Y Q   M U S C X   J Y M S G   L L E T A
L E D E C   G B M F I
```

j. A consideration of the facts therefore leads to but one conclusion, *viz.*, that the repetitions exhibited by the cryptogram under investigation are *not accidental* but are *causal* in their origin; and the cause is in this case not difficult to find: repetitions in the plain text were actually enciphered by identical alphabets. In order for this to occur, it was necessary that the tetragraph USYE, for example, fall *both* times in *exactly* the same relative position with respect to the key. Note, for example, that USYE in Fig. 10 represents in both cases the plaintext polygraph THEA. The first time it occurred it fell in positions 1–2–3–4 with respect to the key; the second time it occurred it happened to fall in the very same relative positions, although it might just as well have happened to fall in any of the other three possible relative positions with respect to the key, *viz.*, 2–3–4–1, 3–4–1–2, or 4–1–2–3.

k. Lest the student be misled, however, a few more words are necessary on this subject. In the preceding subparagraph the word "happened" was used; this word correctly expresses the idea in mind, because the insertion or deletion of a single plaintext letter between the two occurrences would have thrown the second occurrence one letter forward or backward, respectively, and thus caused the polygraph to be enciphered by a sequence of alphabets such as can no longer produce the cipher polygraph USYE from the plaintext polygraph THEA. On the other hand, the insertion or deletion of this one letter might bring the letters of some other polygraph into similar columns so that some other repetition would be exhibited in case the USYE repetition had thus been suppressed.

l. The encipherment of identical letters by identical cipher alphabets is therefore the *cause* of the production of repetitions in the cipher text in the case of repeating-key ciphers. What principles can be derived from this fact, and how can they be employed in the solution of cryptograms of this type?

m. If a count is made of the number of letters from and including the first USYE to, but not including, the second occurrence of USYE, a total of 40 letters is found to intervene between the two occurrences. This number, 40, must, of course, be an exact multiple of the length of the key.[5] Having the plain text before one, it is easily seen that it is the 10th multiple; that is, the 4-letter key has repeated itself 10 times between the first and the second occurrence of USYE. It follows, therefore, that if the length of the key were not known, the number 40 could safely be taken to be an exact multiple of the length of the key; in other words, one of the *factors* of the number 40 would be equal to the length of the key. The word "safely" is used in the preceding sentence to mean that the interval 40 applies to a repetition of 4 letters and it has been shown that the chances are small that this repetition is accidental. The factors of 40 are 2, 4, 5, 8, 10, and 20. So far as this single repetition of USYE is concerned, if the length of the key were not known, all that could be said about the latter would be that it is equal to one of these factors. The repetition by itself gives no further indications. How can the exact factor be selected from among a list of several possible factors?

n. Let the intervals between all the repetitions in the cryptogram be listed. They are as follows:

Repetition	Interval	Factors
1st USYE to 2d USYE	40	2, 4, 5, 8, 10, 20
1st BC to 2d BC	16	2, 4, 8
1st CX to 2d CX	25	5
1st EC to 2d EC	88	2, 4, 11, 22, 44
1st LE to 2d LE	16	2, 4, 8
2d LE to 3d LE	4	2
1st LE to 3d LE	20	2, 4, 5, 10
1st JY to 2d JY	8	2, 4
1st PL to 2d PL	24	2, 3, 4, 6, 8, 10, 12
1st SC to 2d SC	52	2, 4, 13, 26
(1st SY to 2d SY, already included in USYE.)		
(1st US to 2d US, already included in USYE.)		
2d US to 3d US	36	2, 3, 4, 6, 9, 18
1st US to 3d US	76	2, 4, 19, 38
(1st YE to 2d YE, already included in USYE.)		

o. Are all these repetitions *causal* repetitions? Since, from Fig. 11c, we find that the expected number of tetragraphs appearing twice (i.e., a tetragraphic repetition) in 100 letters of random text is 0.01, this decimal fraction means that in 100 such cases only 1 may be expected to contain a repeated tetragraph; thus it is a 99-to-1 chance of the USYE repetition occurring accidentally. From Fig. 11a, the expected number of digraphs occurring 3 times is 0.298; so the chances against the threefold occurrence of the two digraphs LE and US are quite high. We expect only 6.5 digraphs to occur *at least* 2 times in 100 letters of random text, but in our sample we have *10* digraphs appearing two or more times. The chances are very great, therefore, that the majority of these repetitions are causal, so that it is not astonishing that the intervals between all the various repetitions, except in one case, contain the factors 2 and 4.

p. This means that if the cipher is written out in either 2 columns or 4 columns, all these repetitions (except the CX repetition) would fall into the same columns. From this it follows that the length of the key is either 2 or 4, the latter, on practical grounds, being more probable

---

[5] Barring, that is, cases such as those mentioned in subpar. 16b and in footnote 8 on p. 26.

than the former. Doubts concerning the matter of choosing between a 2-letter and a 4-letter key will be dissolved when the cipher text is distributed into its component uniliteral frequency distributions.

q. The repeated digraph CX in the foregoing message is an accidental repetition, as will be apparent by referring to Fig. 10. Had the message been longer there would have been more such accidental repetitions, but, on the other hand, there would be a proportionately greater number of causal repetitions.

r. Sometimes it happens that the cryptanalyst quickly notes a repetition of a polygraph of four or more letters, the interval between the first and second occurrences of which has only two factors, of which one is a relatively small number, the other a relatively high prime number.[6] He may therefore assume at once that the length of the key is equal to the smaller factor without searching for additional recurrences upon which to corroborate his assumption. Suppose, for example, that in a relatively short cryptogram the interval between the first and second occurrences of a polygraph of five letters happens to be a number such as 203, the factors of which are 7 and 29. Evidently the number of alphabets may at once be assumed to be 7, unless one is dealing with messages exchanged among correspondents known to use long keys. In the latter case one could assume the number of alphabets to be 29—or even 203.

s. The foregoing method of determining the period in a polyalphabetic cipher is commonly referred to in the literature as "factoring the intervals between repetitions"; or more often it is simply called "factoring." Because the latter is an apt term and is brief, it will be employed hereafter in this text to designate the process.

t. As an aid in the determination of possible periods in cases under study, there is given in Appendix 2, "Basic formulas and useful tables," a table of the factors of all numbers from 1 to 400, inclusive (cf. pp. 345–348).

16. General remarks on factoring.—*a.* The statement made in par. 4 with respect to the cyclic phenomena said to be exhibited in cryptograms of the periodic type now becomes clear. The use of a short repeating key produces a periodicity of repetitions collectively termed "cyclic phenomena," an analysis of which leads to a determination of the length of the period or cycle, and this gives the length of the key.[7] Save for a rare exception mentioned below, only in the case of relatively short cryptograms enciphered by a relatively long key does factoring fail to lead to the correct determination of the number of cipher alphabets in a repeating-key cipher; and of course, the fact that a cryptogram contains repetitions whose factors show constancy is in itself an indication and test of its periodic nature. It also follows that if the cryptogram is not a repeating-key cipher, then factoring will show no definite results, and conversely the fact that it does not yield definite results at once indicates that the cryptogram is not a periodic, repeating-key cipher.

b. There are two main cases in which factoring leads to no definite results. One is in the case of monoalphabetic substitution ciphers. Here recurrences are very plentiful as a rule, and the intervals separating these recurrences may be factored, *but the factors will show no constancy*; there will be several factors common to many or most of the recurrences. This in itself is an indication of a monoalphabetic (monographic) substitution cipher, if the very fact of the presence of many recurrences fails to impress itself upon the inexperienced cryptanalyst.

---

[6] A prime number is defined as one which has no integral divisors except itself and 1.

[7] The principle of factoring was first expounded by the German cryptologist, Major F. W. Kasiski, in his book *Die Geheimschriften und die Dechiffrirkunst*, Berlin 1863. Prior to that time, repeating-key ciphers of the Vigenère and similar types were regarded as absolutely secure against cryptanalysis—indeed, the Vigenère cipher was often alluded to in the literature as "le chiffre indéchiffrable."

The other case in which the process of factoring is nonsignificant involves certain types of nonperiodic, polyalphabetic ciphers. In certain of these ciphers, recurrences of digraphs, trigraphs, and even longer polygraphs may be plentiful in a long message, but the intervals between such recurrences bear no definite multiple relation to the length of the key, such as in the case of the true periodic, repeating-key cipher, in which the alphabets change with successive letters and repeat themselves over and over again.[8]

c. Factoring is not the only method of determining the length of the period of a periodic, polyalphabetic substitution cipher, although it is by far the most common and easily applied. At this point it will merely be stated that when the message under study is relatively short in comparison with the length of the key, so that there are only a few cycles of cipher text and no long repetitions affording a basis for factoring, there are several other methods available; these will be explained subsequently. It is desirable at this juncture merely to indicate that methods other than factoring do exist and are used in practical work.

d. Fundamentally, the factoring process is merely a more-or-less simple mathematical method of studying the phenomena of periodicity in cryptograms. It will usually enable the cryptanalyst to ascertain definitely whether or not a given cryptogram is periodic in nature, and if so, the length of the period, *stated in terms of the cryptographic unit involved*. By the latter statement is meant that the factoring process may be applied not only in analyzing the periodicity manifested by cryptograms in which the plaintext units subjected to cryptographic treatment are monographic in nature (i.e., are single letters) but also in studying the periodicity exhibited by those occasional cryptograms wherein the plaintext units are digraphic, trigraphic, or n-graphic in character. The student should bear this point in mind when he comes to the study of substitution systems of the latter sort.

17. Second step: distributing the cipher text into the component monoalphabets.—a. After the number of cipher alphabets involved in the cryptogram has been ascertained, the next step is to rewrite the message in groups corresponding to the length of the key, or in columnar fashion, whichever is more convenient, and this automatically divides up the text so that the letters belonging to the same cipher alphabet occupy similar positions in the groups, or, if the columnar method is used, fall in the same column. The letters are thus distributed into the respective cipher alphabets to which they belong. This reduces the polyalphabetic text to monoalphabetic terms.

b. Separate uniliteral frequency distributions for the thus isolated individual alphabets are now compiled. For example, in the case of the cipher in subpar. 15i, having determined that four alphabets are involved, and having rewritten the message in four columns, one makes a frequency distribution of the letters in the first column, another of the letters in the second column, and so on for the four columns. *Each of the resulting distributions is therefore a monoalphabetic frequency distribution.* If these distributions do not give the characteristic irregular crest-and-trough appearance of monoalphabetic frequency distributions, including the expected number of blanks (Λ), and if the observed values of phi (ϕ_o) of these distributions are not sufficiently close to the expected value of ϕ_p (or do not yield I.C.'s in the close vicinity of the expected value), then the analysis which led to the hypothesis as regards the number of alphabets in-

---

[8] One further case which might be mentioned is that of periodic ciphers in which the key word or phrase contains repeated polygraphic segments, such as in NATIONAL ORGANIZATION. A five-letter word enciphered in alphabets 2–6 will have the same ciphertext equivalents as the same word enciphered in alphabets 16–20, thus giving rise to a *causal* repetition, but the interval between the occurrences will not reflect the length of the true period. Such repetitions are referred to as being the result of the *subcycles* in the total key; these phenomena are encountered in the study of certain machine cipher systems.

volved is fallacious. In fact, the ϕ or I.C. of these individual distributions may be considered to be an index of the correctness of the factoring process; for theoretically, and practically, the individual distributions constructed upon the *correct* hypothesis will tend to conform more closely to the expected ϕ or I.C. of a monoalphabetic frequency distribution than will the distributions constructed upon an incorrect hypothesis. These considerations will be discussed in the next paragraph.

18. Statistical proof of the monoalphabeticity of the distributions.—*a*. The student is already familiar with the monographic ϕ test for determining the relative monoalphabeticity of a distribution; this test was discussed in detail in par. 27 of *Military Cryptanalytics, Part I*. The formulas for monographic ϕ_p and ϕ_r were stated as ϕ_p (for English) $=.0667N(N-1)$, and $\phi_r=.0385N(N-1)$, where N is the total number of elements in the distribution. The ϕ_o was calculated by the formula $\phi_o=\Sigma f(f-1)$, where f is the frequency of each element of the distribution. The index of coincidence (I.C.) was defined as the ratio of ϕ_o to ϕ_r; the monographic I.C. of English plain text was given as 1.73, as compared with the I.C. of 1.00 for random text.[9]

b. The ϕ test may be applied to the distributions of periodic polyalphabetic ciphers to confirm the monoalphabeticity of the distributions (made on an hypothesis of *n* alphabets) and thereby confirm the length of the period; this test is particularly applicable in difficult cases, as for instance where there are insufficient polygraphic repetitions in a short text, or where the factoring resolves itself into two or more periods. If the correct period is assumed, then the ϕ test applied to each of the alphabets should approximate fairly closely and consistently the value for ϕ_p; and, conversely, if an incorrect period is assumed, the ϕ_o should approximate the value of ϕ_r more closely than it does ϕ_p. It is to be remarked that small deviations from the expected values are usual, and indeed is the normal situation, but that large deviations are rare. The degree of deviation that may be expected may be determined by statistical means, under the concept of the *standard deviation of* ϕ.

c. For reference purposes, there is included in Appendix 2 (on p. 344) a table of the expected values of ϕ_p and ϕ_r for sample sizes (N) from 11 to 100, inclusive. Since the I.C. is an expression of monoalphabeticity in terms of a *ratio*, the evaluation of distributions will be expressed in terms of the I.C. in the future, unless the ϕ values are more convenient in specific cases.

d. The uniliteral distributions for the cipher text of the four alphabets of the cryptogram in Fig. 10 are made, and are shown below together with the ϕ and I.C. values for these distributions:

$\phi=36$

A B C D E F G H I J K L M N O P Q R S T U V W X Y Z (I.C.$=1.56$)

Alphabet 1

$\phi=44$

A B C D E F G H I J K L M N O P Q R S T U V W X Y Z (I.C.$=1.91$)

Alphabet 2

$\phi=46$

A B C D E F G H I J K L M N O P Q R S T U V W X Y Z (I.C.$=1.99$)

Alphabet 3

$\phi=44$

A B C D E F G H I J K L M N O P Q R S T U V W X Y Z (I.C.$=1.91$)

Alphabet 4

---

[9] A more convenient formula for the monographic I.C. of 26-character text is $\dfrac{26\Sigma f(f-1)}{N(N-1)}$, which is equivalent to $\dfrac{\phi_o}{\phi_r}$.

It can be seen that these distributions are clearly monoalphabetic, since the ϕ values are in the vicinity of ϕ_p (which, for this size sample, is 40) rather than close to ϕ_r (in this case, 23). It is pointed out that any other assumed periods, *which are not a multiple of 4*, will not yield monoalphabetic distributions. But if in this case a period of 8 were assumed, these 8 distributions would be monoalphabetic; however it would be noticed that the distributions for alphabets 1 and 5 would be quite similar, and likewise alphabets 2 and 6, 3 and 7, and 4 and 8— therefore these 8 distributions could then be combined into the four distributions of the correct hypothesis.[10]

e. A further application of the ϕ test should be considered at this time, that is, the cases where the length of the period is large as compared with the size of the sample of cipher text.[11] Although a single ϕ test for small values of N would rarely give a reliable result, it is nevertheless possible to apply this test for small values of N, provided it is possible to obtain the average for a number of such tests. Thus it is usually possible to determine the period of a polyalphabetic cipher, where the number of alphabets is large and the number of letters per distribution is small, even though there are no long repetitions.

(1) Let us consider the following cryptogram which is known to be enciphered by periodic polyalphabetic substitution, where the number of alphabets is between 40 and 50:

```
HSKUS   PMFHD   UJJIX   MSPTP   OIPCI   WKZVU
YPPNE   USAIG   BOOGA   OPGPR   HBOUC   SHPVG
HQXZS   ACKRK   VBGHM   VSFRY   TTKHK   VWZXV
LIJHW   ARLKF   IJSLT   MHKAH   QTUVT   XSMEC
FCSKT   GOOYB   XZVLI   JRYAC   DWEJM   SCAFP
IEAXO   KAQDW   EXPYP   QHDNO   JIXNZ   JGNUD
OARFU   ERJOY   BDOKE   IKDUV   TDVEV   LETDO
AFROU   NYNBD   VQOBE   GGSHQ   HXOPU   ZCOCU
KKZLT   PHKRT   CCOAS   BZUGB   UBBUN   OVTPO
VMIZD   EPQFV   KZ
```

If we assume a period of 50, the cryptogram would be written out on this width, as illustrated below; the ϕ_o value for each column is obtained and is included in the diagram:

```
         5    10   15   20   25   30   35   40   45   50
HSKUSPMFHDUJJIXMSPTPOIPCIWKZVUYPPNEUSAIGBOOGAOPGPR
HBOUCSHPVGHQXZSACKRKVBGHMVSFRYTTKHKVWZXVLIJHWARLKF
IJSLTMHKAHQTUVTXSMECFCSKTGOOYBXZVLIJRYACDWEJMSCAFP
IEAXOKAQDWEXPYPQHDNOJIXNZJGNUDOARFUERJOYBDOKEIKDUV
TDVEVLETDOAFROUNYNBDVQOBEGGSHQHXOPUZCOCUKKZLTPHKRT
CCOASBZUGBUBBUNOVTPOVMIZDEPQFVKZ
40222020202000002002620000220000200202000020200000000
```

We note that there are 32 columns wherein N=6, and 18 columns wherein N=5; we also note that the ϕ values range between 0 and 6. In the diagram below, keeping the data from the two categories of N separate, the column labelled "ϕ" is the observed value of ϕ; the column labelled "x" is the number of times the particular value of ϕ occurred; and the column labelled "ϕx" is the product of the preceding two columns (given as a means of arriving at the *average value of* ϕ).

---

[10] Cf. the discussion on the χ (chi) test in par. 37.

[11] The discussion which follows and the example illustrated are based on certain parts of the pioneer work of Dr. Solomon Kullback in his treatise, *Statistical Methods in Cryptanalysis*.

N=6		
ϕ	x	ϕx
0	18	0
2	12	24
4	1	4
6	1	6
	32	34

N=5		
ϕ	x	ϕx
0	14	0
2	4	8
4	0	0
6	0	0
	18	8

The average value of ϕ (symbolized by $\bar{\phi}$, which is read as "phi bar"), where N=6, is $\frac{34}{32}$, or 1.06; the $\bar{\phi}$, where N=5, is $\frac{8}{18}$, or 0.44; in other words, *the average value of ϕ is derived by adding up all the ϕ values for a given column length, and then dividing by the number of columns of that length.* The values of $\bar{\phi}$ are compared with ϕ_p and ϕ_r below, and, since $\bar{\phi}$ more closely approximates ϕ_r than it does ϕ_p, the conclusion is reached that the period of the cryptogram is not 50.[12]

	N=6	N=5
$\bar{\phi}$	1.06	0.44
ϕ_p	2.00	1.33
ϕ_r	1.15	0.77

(2) Since we have discarded 50 as a possible period, we write the cryptogram on a width of 49 and examine its statistics; if this width fails, then we write the cryptogram on widths of 48, 47, . . . etc. The results of assumptions of widths from 49 down to 44 are shown in the diagram below:

	49 alphabets		48 alphabets		47 alphabets N=6
	N=6	N=5	N=6	N=5	
$\bar{\phi}$	1.57	0.67	1.33	0.33	0.85
ϕ_p	2.00	1.33	2.00	1.33	2.00
ϕ_r	1.15	0.77	1.15	0.77	1.15

	46 alphabets		45 alphabets		44 alphabets	
	N=7	N=6	N=7	N=6	N=7	N=6
$\bar{\phi}$	1.00	1.15	1.50	0.69	1.22	1.23
ϕ_p	2.80	2.00	2.80	2.00	2.80	2.00
ϕ_r	1.66	1.15	1.66	1.15	1.66	1.15

[12] Kullback, *ibid.*, p. 42, carries the analysis further by considering the sigmages of the deviations, and expresses these in terms of probability statements (assuming for convenience that this sigmage is Normally distributed). He shows that, for N=6, only 15% of monoalphabetic text would yield a value of $\bar{\phi}$ as small as or smaller than 1.13, whereas 52% of random text would yield a value of ϕ as large as or larger than 1.13; for N=5, only 35% of monoalphabetic text would yield a value of $\bar{\phi}$ as small as or smaller than 0.56, whereas 75% of random text would yield a value of $\bar{\phi}$ as large as or larger than that observed. This is more compactly illustrated in the diagram below:

	N=6	N=5
$\bar{\phi}$, N letters of monoalphabetic text	$P(\bar{\phi}\leq1.13)=.15$	$P(\bar{\phi}\leq0.56)=.35$
$\bar{\phi}$, N letters of random text	$P(\bar{\phi}\geq1.13)=.52$	$(P(\bar{\phi}\geq0.56)=.75$

These assumed periods are discarded one by one because $\bar{\phi}$ did not come up to plaintext expectations.

(3) Now testing for a period of 43 we write out the cryptogram on this width and take the ϕ_o of the columns, as is illustrated below:

```
        5         10        15        20        25        30        35        40  43
        HSKUSPMFHDUJJIXMSPTPOIPCIWKZVUYPPNEUSAIGBOO
        GAOPGPRHBOUCSHPVGHQXZSACKRKVBGHMVSFRYTTKHKV
        WZXVLIJHWARLKFIJSLTMHKAHQTUVTXSMECFCSKTGOOY
        BXZVLIJRYACDWEJMSCAFPIEAXOKAQDWEXPYPQHDNOJI
        XNZJGNUDOARFUERJOYBDOKEIKDUVTDVEVLETDOAFROU
        NYNBDVQOBEGGSHQHXOPUZCOCUKKZLTPHKRTCCOASBZU
        GBUBBUNOVTPOVMIZDEPQFVKZ
2 0 2 4 4 4 2 4 2 6 4 0 2 4 2 4 6 0 4 0 4 4 4 6 2 0 14 8 2 2 0 4 2 0 4 2 2 2 4 2 4 6 2
```

The data from this hypothesis are tabulated in the following diagram:

N=7				N=6		
ϕ	x	ϕx		ϕ	x	ϕx
0	4	0		0	3	0
2	6	12		2	9	18
4	11	44		4	4	16
6	3	18		6	1	6
	24	74		8	1	8
				14	1	14
					19	62

$$\bar{\phi}=\frac{74}{24}=3.08 \qquad\qquad \bar{\phi}=\frac{62}{19}=3.26$$

The comparison of the $\bar{\phi}$ values with the values for ϕ_p and ϕ_r is illustrated in the following diagram:

	N=7	N=6
$\bar{\phi}$	3.08	3.26
ϕ_p	2.80	2.00
ϕ_r	1.66	1.15

There seems to be no doubt that the period of the cryptogram is 43.

(4) In this example, it is noted that ϕ counts were made of the columns of the write-outs of the cryptogram on the various widths; in this case, ϕ's are more convenient to use than their translation in terms of the decimal values of I.C.'s. If, however, we had much *longer* columns, the I.C. values might give a quicker portrayal of the relative goodness of the columns. Note

that we could have used I.C.'s in expressing the *final* result of each assumption of a period, as follows:

50 alphabets		49 alphabets		48 alphabets		47 alphabets
N=6	N=5	N=6	N=5	N=6	N=5	N=6
I.C. 0.92	0.57	1.36	0.87	1.15	0.43	0.74

46 alphabets		45 alphabets		44 alphabets		43 alphabets	
N=7	N=6	N=7	N=6	N=7	N=6	N=7	N=6
I.C. 0.62	1.00	0.93	0.60	0.76	1.07	1.91	2.83

It will be observed that the data may be evaluated much more rapidly in the case of I.C.'s, since we need to keep only one invariant index (1.73) in mind in comparing our results with the expected value of the I.C. for English plain text.[13]

19. **Third step: solving the monoalphabetic distributions.**—The difficulty experienced in analyzing the individual or isolated frequency distributions depends mostly upon the type of cipher alphabets used. It is apparent that mixed alphabets may be used just as easily as standard alphabets, and, of course, the cipher letters themselves give no indication as to which is the case. However, just as it was found that in the case of monoalphabetic substitution ciphers a uniliteral frequency distribution gives clear indications as to whether the cipher alphabet is a

---

[13] In the calculations of this problem, Kullback treated the statistics for the long and short columns separately; this was done primarily to make easier the determination of the sigmages of the deviations. However, it is possible to derive a *single* statistic (either ϕ or I.C.) for each hypothesis of a period, eliminating the necessity of looking at two sets of data for each assumption.

For instance, in the hypothesis of 50 alphabets, the total number of comparisons is $32\left(\frac{6\times5}{2}\right)+18\left(\frac{5\times4}{2}\right)=660$,

thus the ϕ values (which, by definition, are *twice* the expected number of coincidences) are the following:

$$\phi_p=2(660)(.0667)=88$$
$$\phi_r=2(660)(.0385)=51$$

The observed ϕ is the sum of the ϕ values for the long and short columns, so that $\phi_o=36+10=46$. The I.C. is thus $\frac{46}{51}=0.90$.

In the hypothesis of 43 alphabets, the number of comparisons is $24\left(\frac{7\times6}{2}\right)+19\left(\frac{6\times5}{2}\right)=789$; thus

$$\phi_p=\frac{2(789)}{15}=105$$

$$\phi_r=\frac{2(789)}{26}=61$$

$$\phi_o=74+62=136$$

The I.C. of $\frac{136}{61}=2.23$ points to this hypothesis as the correct period. (Note that .0667 is approximately equal to $\frac{1}{15}$, so that computation is facilitated by using $\frac{1}{15}$ and $\frac{1}{26}$ instead of .0667 and .0385 for the plaintext and random constants, respectively.)

Having established the period as 43, solution of this example is predicated on the trial that standard alphabets are involved; this procedure will be taken up in par. 21 in the next chapter.

standard or a mixed alphabet, by the relative positions and extensions of the crests and troughs in the distribution, so it is found that in the case of repeating-key ciphers, uniliteral frequency distributions for the isolated or individual alphabets will also give clear indications as to whether these alphabets are standard alphabets or mixed alphabets. Only two or three such frequency distributions are necessary for this determination;[14] if they appear to be standard alphabets, similar distributions can be made for the rest of the alphabets; but if they appear to be mixed alphabets, then it is best to compile triliteral frequency distributions for all the alphabets. The analysis of the values of the cipher letters in each distribution proceeds along the same lines as in the case of monoalphabetic ciphers. The analysis is more difficult only because of the reduced size of the distributions, but if the message is very long, then each frequency distribution will contain enough elements to permit a speedy solution.

---

[14] In certain mixed-alphabet periodic ciphers, it is possible that a distribution for one alphabet might reflect the phenomena expected for a standard alphabet; for instance, if the plain- and cipher components are identically mixed sequences running in the same direction, and if for one alphabet $A_p = A_c$, then the distribution for that alphabet will be the normal uniliteral distribution. It is for this reason that we must make distributions for *at least two* alphabets to determine whether or not a polyalphabetic cipher is composed of standard alphabets.

Chapter IV

REPEATING-KEY SYSTEMS WITH STANDARD CIPHER ALPHABETS

20. **Solution by fitting the distributions to the normal.**—*a*. In the light of the foregoing principles, let the following cryptogram be studied:

Message

```
          5           10          15          20          25
A  A U K H Y   J A M K I   Z Y M W M   J M I G X   N F M L X
B  E T I M I   Z H B H R   A Y M Z M   I L V M E   J K U T G
C  D P V X K   Q U K H Q   L H V R M   J A Z N G   G Z V X E
D  N L U F M   P Z J N V   C H U A S   H K Q G K   I P L W P
E  A J Z X I   G U M T V   D P T E J   E C M Y S   Q Y B A V
F  A L A H Y   P O I X W   P V N Y E   E Y X E E   U D P X R
G  B V Z V I   Z I I V O   S P T E G   K U B B R   Q L L X P
H  W F Q G K   N L L L E   P T I K W   D J Z X I   G O I O I
J  Z L A M V   K F M W F   N P L Z I   O V V F M   Z K T X G
K  N L M D F   A A E X I   J L U F M   P Z J N V   C A I G I
L  U A W P R   N V I W E   J K Z A S   Z L A F M   H S
```

All repetitions of trigraphs and longer polygraphs are underlined; these repetitions are tabulated in the diagram below, together with their locations, intervals, and factors.

Repetition	Location	Interval	Factors
LUFMPZJNVC	D2, K12	160	2, 4, 5, 8, 10, 16, 20, 32, 40, 80
JZXIG	E2, H17	90	2, 3, 5, 6, 9, 10, 15, 18, 30, 45
EJK	B20, L10	215	5, 43
PTE	E12, G12	50	2, 5, 10, 25
QGK	D18, H3	85	5, 17
UKH	A2, C7	55	5, 11
ZLA	J1, L16	65	5, 13

b. The factor 5 appears in all cases; it is practically certain that the number of alphabets is five, and the I.C.'s should confirm this hypothesis. Since the text already appears in groups of five letters, it is unnecessary to rewrite the message. The next step is to make a uniliteral frequency distribution for Alphabet 1 to see if it can be determined whether or not standard alphabets are involved. It is as follows:

Alphabet 1

$$A \; B \; C \; D \; E \; F \; G \; H \; I \; J \; K \; L \; M \; N \; O \; P \; Q \; R \; S \; T \; U \; V \; W \; X \; Y \; Z \qquad I.C.=1.44$$

c. Although the indications for fitting the distribution to the normal are not very clear cut, yet if one takes into consideration the small amount of data, the assumption of a direct standard alphabet with $W_c = A_p$ is worth further test. Accordingly a similar distribution is made for Alphabet 2.

Alphabet 2

$$A \; B \; C \; D \; E \; F \; G \; H \; I \; J \; K \; L \; M \; N \; O \; P \; Q \; R \; S \; T \; U \; V \; W \; X \; Y \; Z \qquad I.C.=1.47$$

d. There is every indication of a direct standard alphabet, with $H_c = A_p$. Let similar distributions be made for the last three alphabets. They are as follows:

Alphabet 3

$$A \; B \; C \; D \; E \; F \; G \; H \; I \; J \; K \; L \; M \; N \; O \; P \; Q \; R \; S \; T \; U \; V \; W \; X \; Y \; Z \qquad I.C.=1.71$$

Alphabet 4

$$A \; B \; C \; D \; E \; F \; G \; H \; I \; J \; K \; L \; M \; N \; O \; P \; Q \; R \; S \; T \; U \; V \; W \; X \; Y \; Z \qquad I.C.=1.36$$

Alphabet 5

$$A \; B \; C \; D \; E \; F \; G \; H \; I \; J \; K \; L \; M \; N \; O \; P \; Q \; R \; S \; T \; U \; V \; W \; X \; Y \; Z \qquad I.C.=1.91$$

e. After but little experiment it is found that the distributions can best be made to fit the normal when the following values are assumed:

Alphabet 1 . . . . $A_p = W_c$
Alphabet 2 . . . . $A_p = H_c$
Alphabet 3 . . . . $A_p = I_c$
Alphabet 4 . . . . $A_p = T_c$
Alphabet 5 . . . . $A_p = E_c$

f. Note the key word given by the successive equivalents of A_p: WHITE. And also note what may appear to be too low values of three of the I.C.'s above.[1] Nevertheless, the real proof of the cryptanalytic pudding is, of course, the unmistakable and indisputable plaintext flavor of the values of the solved alphabets on the cryptogram. The five complete cipher alphabets are shown in matrix form in Fig. 12, below:

Plain text

```
  A B C D E F G H I J K L M N O P Q R S T U V W X Y Z
1 W X Y Z A B C D E F G H I J K L M N O P Q R S T U V
2 H I J K L M N O P Q R S T U V W X Y Z A B C D E F G
3 I J K L M N O P Q R S T U V W X Y Z A B C D E F G H
4 T U V W X Y Z A B C D E F G H I J K L M N O P Q R S
5 E F G H I J K L M N O P Q R S T U V W X Y Z A B C D
```

FIGURE 12

g. Applying these values to the first few groups of our message, the following is found:

```
        1 2 3 4 5   1 2 3 4 5   1 2 3 4 5   1 2 3 4 5   1 2 3 4 5
Cipher: A U K H Y   J A M K I   Z Y M W M   J M I G X   N F M L X . . .
Plain:  E N C O U   N T E R E   D R E D I   N F A N T   R Y E S T . . .
```

---

[1] As has been remarked in subpar. 18*b*, small deviations from the expected values are usual and in fact may be anticipated, whereas large deviations are rare. In the case of the I.C.'s at hand, the value for the third alphabet (1.71) almost coincides with the expected 1.73; but the values for the 1st, 2d, and 4th alphabets *seem* too low, while the value for the 5th (1.91) is "on the high side," i.e., a *positive* deviation instead of a *negative* deviation. For the benefit of the mathematical reader, these deviations from the expected plain can be proven to be in the nature of only about 1σ *for samples of these sizes* (55 and 54 tallies), so that the deviations observed are not really significant after all. For the statistically curious, the formulas for the standard deviation of ϕ and I.C. for English plain text are given below (where N is the sample size):

$$\sigma(\phi) = \sqrt{(.0048)N^3 + (.1101)N^2 - (.1149)N}$$

$$\sigma(\text{I.C.}) = \frac{26}{(N-1)\sqrt{N}} \sqrt{(.0048)N^2 + (.1101)N - .1149}$$

Derivation of these formulas will be left for the extensive treatment of cryptomathematics in *Military Cryptanalytics, Part III*. It might be noted that cryptanalysts are usually much more deeply concerned with the deviation of an observed ϕ or I.C. from *random* rather than from an estimated or expected *plain*. This is of course especially true in situations wherein the value of the ϕ_p is unknown (such as would be in the case of a 10 x 10 bipartite matrix of unknown composition, or in the case of a polyalphabetic encipherment of an unknown code); in such situations only the deviations from random *could* be measured. The formulas for the standard deviation of ϕ and I.C. for 26-letter random text are as follows:

$$\sigma(\phi) = .2720 \sqrt{N(N-1)}$$

$$\sigma(\text{I.C.}) = \frac{7.0711}{\sqrt{N(N-1)}}$$

Since sigmage is defined as the difference between the observed and the expected number, divided by the standard deviation, it may be shown that the I.C. of Alphabet 1 in the example is $\frac{1.44 - 1.00}{.13} = 3.38\sigma$ over random; for this type of distribution (which follows the χ^2 distribution), this amounts to less than 1 chance in 300 of being produced at random.

35

h. Intelligible text at once results, and the solution can now be completed very quickly. The complete message is as follows:

ENCOUNTERED RED INFANTRY ESTIMATED AT ONE REGIMENT AND MACHINE GUN COMPANY IN TRUCKS NEAR EMMITTSBURG. AM HOLDING MIDDLE CREEK NEAR HILL 543 SOUTHWEST OF FAIRPLAY. WHEN FORCED BACK WILL CONTINUE DELAYING REDS AT MARSH CREEK. HAVE DESTROYED BRIDGES ON MIDDLE CREEK BETWEEN EMMITTSBURG—TANEYTOWN ROAD AND RHODES MILL.

i. In the foregoing example (which is typical of the system erroneously attributed, in cryptographic literature, to the French cryptographer Blaise de Vigenère, although to do him justice, he made no claim of having "invented" it), direct standard alphabets were used, but it is obvious that reversed standard alphabets may be used and the solution accomplished in the same manner. In fact, the cipher disk used by the United States Army for a number of years yields exactly this type of cipher, which is also known in the literature as the Beaufort Cipher, and by other names. In fitting the isolated frequency distributions to the normal, the direction of reading the crests and troughs is merely reversed.[2]

21. Solution by completing the plain-component sequence.—*a.* There is another method of solving this type of cipher which is worth explaining because the underlying principles will be found useful in many cases. It is a modification of the method of solution by completing the plain-component sequence, already explained in *Military Cryptanalytics, Part I.*

b. After all, the individual alphabets of a cipher such as the one just solved are merely direct standard alphabets. It has been seen that monoalphabetic ciphers in which standard cipher alphabets are used may be solved almost mechanically by completing the plain-component sequence. The plain text reappears on only one generatrix and this generatrix is the same for the whole message. It is easy to pick this generatrix out of all the other generatrices because it is the only one which yields intelligible text. Is it not apparent that if the same process is applied to the cipher letters of the *individual alphabets* of the cipher just solved, the plaintext equivalents of these letters must all reappear on one and the same generatrix? But how will the generatrix which actually contains the plaintext letters be distinguishable from the other generatrices, since these plaintext letters are not consecutive letters in the plain text but only letters separated from one another by a constant interval? The answer is simple. The plaintext generatrix should be distinguishable from the others *because it will show more and a better assortment of high-frequency letters, and can thus be selected by the eye from the whole set of generatrices.* If this is done with all the alphabets in the cryptogram, it will merely be necessary to assemble the letters of the thus selected generatrices in proper order, and the result should be consecutive letters forming intelligible text.

c. An example will serve to make the process clear. Let the same message be used as before. Factoring showed that it involves five alphabets. Let the first ten cipher letters *in each alphabet*

---

[2] If standard alphabets are employed wherein a letter (usually J) is omitted, this omission must be taken into consideration in fitting the distributions to the normal, or in applying the method of completing the plain-component sequence treated in par. 21.

be set down in a horizontal line and, under the assumption that direct standard alphabets are involved, let the normal alphabet sequences be completed.[3] Thus:

Gen.	Alphabet 1	Alphabet 2	Alphabet 3	Alphabet 4	Alphabet 5
1	AJZJNEZAIJ	UAYMFTHYLK	KMMIMIBMVU	HKWGLMHZMT	YIMXXIRMEG
2	BKAKOFABJK	VBZNGUIZML	LNNJNJCNWV	ILXHMNIANU	ZJNYYJSNFH
3	CLBLPGBCKL	WCAOHVJANM	MOOKOKDOXW	JMYINOJBOV	AKOZZKTOGI
4	DMCMQHCDLM	XDBPIWKBON	NPPLPLEPYX	KNZJOPKCPW	BLPAALUPHJ
5	ENDNRIDEMN	YECQJXLCPO	OQQMQMFQZY	LOAKPQLDQX	CMQBBMVQIK
6	FOEOSJEFNO	ZFDRKYMDQP	PRRNRNGRAZ	MPBLQRMERY	DNRCCNWRJL
7	GPFPTKFGOP	AGESLZNERQ	QSSOSOHSBA	NQCMRSNFSZ	EOSDDOXSKM
8	HQGQULGHPQ	BHFTMAOFSR	RTTPTPITCB	ORDNSTOGTA	FPTEEPYTLN
9	IRHRVMHIQR	CIGUNBPGTS	SUUQUQJUDC	PSEOTUPHUB	GQUFFQZUMO
10	JSISWNIJRS	DJHVOCQHUT	TVVRVRKVED	QTFPUVQIVC	HRVGGRAVNP
11	KTJTXOJKST	EKIWPDRIVU	UWWSWSLWFE	RUGQVWRJWD	ISWHHSBWOQ
12	LUKUYPKLTU	FLJXQESJWV	VXXTXTMXGF	SVHRWXSKXE	JTXIITCXPR
13	MVLVZQLMUV	GMKYRFTKXW	WYYUYUNYHG	TWISXYTLYF	KUYJJUDYQS
14	NWMWARMNVW	HNLZSGULYX	XZZVZVOZIH	UXJTYZUMZG	LVZKKVEZRT
15	OXNXBSNOWX	IOMATHVMZY	YAAWAWPAJI	VYKUZAVNAH	MWALLWFASU
16	PYOYCTOPXY	JPNBUIWNAZ	ZBBXBXQBKJ	WZLVABWOBI	NXBMMXGBTV
17	QZPZDUPQYZ	KQOCVJXOBA	ACCYCYRCLK	XAMWBCXPCJ	OYCNNYHCUW
18	RAQAEVQRZA	LRPDWKYPCB	BDDZDZSDML	YBNXCDYQDK	PZDOOZIDVX
19	SBRBFWRSAB	MSQEXLZQDC	CEEAEATENM	ZCOYDEZREL	QAEPPAJEWY
20	TCSCGXSTBC	NTRFYMARED	DFFBFBUFON	ADPZEFASFM	RBFQQBKFXZ
21	UDTDHYTUCD	OUSGZNBSFE	EGGCGCVGPO	BEQAFGBTGN	SCGRRCLGYA
22	VEUEIZUVDE	PVTHAOCTGF	FHHDHDWHQP	CFRBGHCUHO	TDHSSDMHZB
23	WFVFJAVWEF	QWUIBPDUHG	GIIEIEXIRQ	DGSCHIDVIP	UEITTENIAC
24	XGWGKBWXFG	RXVJCQEVIH	HJJFJFYJSR	EHTDIJEWJQ	VFJUUFOJBD
25	YHXHLCXYGH	SYWKDRFWJI	IKKGKGZKTS	FIUEJKFXKR	WGKVVGPKCE
26	ZIYIMDYZHI	TZXLESGXKJ	JLLHLHALUT	GJVFKLGYLS	XHLWWHQLDF

FIGURE 13

d. If the high-frequency generatrices underlined in Fig. 13 are selected and their letters are juxtaposed *in columns*, the consecutive letters of intelligible plain text immediately present themselves. Thus:

Selected generatrices
{
For Alphabet 1, generatrix 5___E N D N R I D E M N
For Alphabet 2, generatrix 20__N T R F Y M A R E D
For Alphabet 3, generatrix 19__C E E A E A T E N M
For Alphabet 4, generatrix 8___O R D N S T O G T A
For Alphabet 5, generatrix 23__U E I T T E N I A C
}

---

[3] If reversed standard alphabets are assumed, it would first be necessary to convert the cipher letters of each isolated alphabet into their normal, plain-component equivalents, and then to proceed as in the case of direct standard alphabets.

```
                                    1 2 3 4 5
                                   ⎡E N C O U
                                   │N T E R E
                                   │D R E D I
                                   │N F A N T
Columnar juxtaposition of letters  │R Y E S T
from selected generatrices         ⎨I M A T E
                                   │D A T O N
                                   │E R E G I
                                   │M E N T A
                                   ⎣N D M A C
```

Plain text: ENCOUNTERED RED INFANTRY ESTIMATED AT ONE REGIMENT AND MAC . . .

e. Solution by this method can thus be achieved without the compilation of any frequency tables and is very quick. The inexperienced cryptanalyst may have difficulty at first in selecting the generatrices which contain the most and the best assortment of high-frequency letters, but with increased practice one can attain a high degree of proficiency. It is only a matter of experiment, trial, and error to select and assemble the proper generatrices so as to produce intelligible text. The selection of the correct generatrix in each alphabet may be narrowed down to a considerably restricted choice from a comparatively few generatrices, using a short-cut procedure which has much merit and is easy to apply, as will now be demonstrated.

f. Let the generatrices be completed as in Fig. 13, and then let us encircle all the letters J, K, Q, X, and Z in each of the ten columns belonging to Alphabet 1. Now let us cross out all generatrices containing *two or more* of these low-frequency letters, under the premise that it is unlikely that the correct generatrix will contain more than one of these low-frequency letters.[4] This procedure is extended to the generatrices pertaining to Alphabets 2–5 (cf. Fig. 14). It will be observed that with this procedure there have been eliminated 13, 15, 11, 16, and 16 generatrices from Alphabets 1–5, respectively, thus considerably simplifying the inspection of the remaining generatrices.

g. The selection of the correct generatrix from those remaining may now be facilitated by the use of a rough weighting or "scoring" procedure, in which the eight highest-frequency letters (ETNROAIS) are assigned a weight of 1 and the remaining letters a weight of 0.[5] The sum of

[4] This premise can be substantiated statistically. By means of the binomial theorem, it may be shown that for 10-letter generatrices an average of 60% (i.e., 16 generatrices out of 26) of incorrect generatrices will be eliminated, while the chance of rejecting the correct case is only 0.8%. If the generatrices contained 15 letters, an average of 82% (i.e., 21 out of 26) of incorrect generatrices may be expected to be eliminated, with a risk of 1.8% as the chance of rejecting the correct case. Thus, to avoid excessive risk, the threshold of only 2 letters of the JKQXZ group should be raised when the generatrices contain more than 12–15 letters.

[5] In considering the highest-frequency English plaintext letters in descending frequency order, there is a sharp drop after the S; therefore this seems the obvious place to divide the letters into two classes or categories. There are also other more cogent mathematical reasons to substantiate the fact that this 8–18 split is the best possible division of the English plaintext letters into two classes for weighting purposes. The scoring system discussed is tantamount to using *three* weights, 1, 0, and $-\infty$; the elimination of generatrices on the basis of two or more occurrences of one of the low frequency letters (JKQXZ) is equivalent to assigning a weight of $-\infty$ to the eliminated generatrices.

The set of alphabet strips prepared for use in connection with the courses in Military Cryptanalytics has been designed with this weighting system in mind. The letters ETNROAIS are printed in red, the rest of the letters in black, with the letters JKQXZ in minuscule type. Thus, in using these strips, one searches for the most "redness" in the generatrices, discounting those generatrices in which two or more of the minuscule letters are present.

38

the weights for each generatrix is then recorded at the side of the generatrix; the correct generatrix may be expected to have the highest or near-highest score in that particular alphabet. The result of the generatrix elimination and the summing of the weights is shown in Fig. 14, below:

Gen.	Alphabet 1	Alphabet 2	Alphabet 3	Alphabet 4	Alphabet 5
1	~~AJZJNEZAIJ~~	2 UAYMFTHYLK	2 KMMIMIBMVU	~~HKWGLMHZMT~~	~~YIMXXIRMEG~~
2	~~BKAKOFABJK~~	~~VBZNGUIZML~~	~~LNNJNJCNWV~~	5 ILXHMNIANU	~~ZJNYYJSNFH~~
3	0 CLBLPGBCKL	4 WCAOHVJANM	~~MOOKOKDOXW~~	~~JMYINOJBOV~~	~~AKOZZKTOGI~~
4	0 DMCMQHCDLM	~~XDBPIWKBON~~	2 NPPLPLEPYX	~~KNZJOPKGPW~~	2 BLPAALUPHJ
5	7 ENDNRIDEMN	~~YEOQJXLCPO~~	~~OQQMQMFQZY~~	~~LOAKPQLDQX~~	~~CMQBBMVQIK~~
6	7 FOEOSJEFNO	~~ZFDRKYMDQP~~	7 PRRNRNGRAZ	3 MPBLQRMERY	4 DNRCCNWRJL
7	2 GPFPTKFGOP	~~AGESLZNERQ~~	7 QSSOSOHSBA	~~NQCMRSNFSZ~~	~~EOSDDOXSKM~~
8	~~HQGQULGHPQ~~	5 BHFTMAOFSR	6 RTTPTPITCB	8 ORDNSTOGTA	5 FPTEEPYTLN
9	5 IRHRVMHIQR	4 CIGUNBPGTS	~~SUUQUQJUDC~~	4 PSEOTUPHUB	~~GQUFFQZUMO~~
10	~~JSISWNIJRS~~	~~DJHVOCQHUT~~	4 TVVRVRKVED	~~QTFPUVQIVG~~	4 HRVGGRAVNP
11	~~KTJTXOJKST~~	4 EKIWPDRIVU	3 UWWSWSLWFE	~~RUGQVWRJWD~~	4 ISWHHSBWOQ
12	~~LUKUYPKLTU~~	~~FLJXQESJWV~~	~~VXXTXTMXGF~~	~~SVHRWXSKXE~~	~~JTXIITCXPR~~
13	~~MVLVZQLMUV~~	~~GMKYRFTKXW~~	1 WYYUYUNYHG	3 TWISXYTLYF	~~KUYJJUDYQS~~
14	4 NWMWARMNVW	~~HNLZSGULYX~~	~~XZZVZVOZIH~~	~~UXJTYZUMZG~~	~~LVZKKVEZRT~~
15	~~OXNXBSNOWX~~	4 IOMATHVMZY	5 YAAWAWPAJI	~~VYKUZAVNAH~~	3 MWALLWFASU
16	3 PYOYCTOPXY	~~JPNBUIWNAZ~~	~~ZBBXBXQBKJ~~	3 WZLVABWOBI	~~NXBMMXGBTV~~
17	~~QZPZDUPQYZ~~	~~KQOCVJXOBA~~	2 ACCYCYRCLK	~~XAMWBGXPGJ~~	3 OYCNNYHCUW
18	~~RAQAEVQRZA~~	1 LRPDWKYPCB	~~DDDZDZSDML~~	~~YBNXCDYQDK~~	~~PZDOOZIDVX~~
19	5 SBRBFWRSAB	~~MSQEXLZQDC~~	8 CEEAEATENM	~~ZCOYDEZREL~~	~~QAEPPAJEWY~~
20	4 TCSCGXSTBC	6 NTRFYMARED	2 DFFBFBUFON	4 ADPZEFASFM	~~RBFQQBKFXZ~~
21	2 UDTDHYTUCD	5 OUSGZNBSFE	2 EGGCGCVGPO	4 BEQAFGBTGN	4 SCGRRCLGYA
22	4 VEUEIZUVDE	4 PVTHAOCTGF	0 FHHDHDWHQP	2 CFRBGHCUHO	3 TDHSSDMHZB
23	2 WFVFJAVWEF	1 QWUIBPDUHG	~~GIIEIEXIRQ~~	3 DGSCHIDVIP	8 UEITTENIAC
24	~~XGWGKBWXFG~~	~~RXVJCQEVIH~~	~~HJJFJFYJSR~~	~~EHTDIJEWJQ~~	~~VFJUUFOJBD~~
25	~~YHXHLCXYGH~~	~~SYWKDRFWJI~~	~~IKKGKGZKTS~~	~~FIUEJKFXKR~~	~~WGKVVGPKCE~~
26	~~ZIYIMDYZIH~~	~~TZXLESGXKJ~~	2 JLLHLHALUT	~~GJVFKLGYLS~~	~~XHLWWHQLDF~~

FIGURE 14

Note that in this example the correct generatrix in each alphabet is the one with the highest score.[6] This weighting system, crude as it may appear, suffices in cases where the generatrices contain at least 8–10 letters. When the number of letters per generatrix is small, there exist more refined statistical methods for the selection of the correct generatrices; these methods will be treated in par. 34 in the next chapter.

---

[6] Theoretically, the generatrix with the greatest value should be the correct generatrix. In actual practice, of course, the generatrix with the greatest value may not be the correct one, but the correct one will certainly be among the three or four generatrices or so with the largest values. In any case, the test of "correctness" is whether, when juxtaposed, a set of two or three generatrices selected will yield "good" digraphs or trigraphs, i.e., high-frequency digraphs or trigraphs such as occur in normal plain text.

h. It has been seen how the key word may be discovered in this type of cryptogram.[7] Usually the key is made up of those letters in the successive alphabets whose equivalents are A_p, but other conventions are of course possible. Sometimes a key number is used, such as 8–4–7–1–2, which means merely that A_p is represented by the eighth letter from A (in the normal alphabet) in the first cipher alphabet, by the fourth letter from A in the second cipher alphabet, and so on, as in the classic Gronsfeld cipher. However, the method of solution as illustrated above, being independent of the nature of the key, is the same as before.

22. Solution by the probable-word method.—*a.* The common use of plaintext words as key words in cryptograms such as the foregoing makes possible a method of solution that is simple and can be used where the more detailed method of analysis using frequency distributions or by completing the plain-component sequence is of no avail. In the case of a very short message which may show no recurrences and give no indications as to the number of alphabets involved, this modified method will be found most useful.

b. Briefly, the method consists in assuming the presence of a probable word or crib in the message, and referring to the alphabets to find the key letters applicable when this hypothetical word is assumed to be present in various positions in the cipher text. If the assumed word happens to be correct, and is placed in the correct position in the message, the key letters produced by referring to the alphabets will yield the key word. In the following message it is assumed that reversed standard alphabets are known to be used by the enemy.

PGSGG DNRUH VMBGR YOUUC WMSGL VTQDO

c. Collateral information leads to the assumption of the presence of the word REGIMENT. One may assume that this word begins the message. Using sliding normal components, one reversed, the other direct, the key letters are ascertained by noting what the successive equivalents of A_p are. Thus:

```
Cipher:      P G S G G D N R
Plain text:  R E G I M E N T
"Key":       G K Y O S H A K
```

The key does not spell any intelligible word. One therefore shifts the assumed word one letter forward and another trial is made.

```
Cipher:      G S G G D N R U
Plain text   R E G I M E N T
"Key":       X W M O P R E N
```

This also yields no intelligible key word. One continues to shift the assumed word forward one space at a time until the following point is reached:

```
Cipher:      U H V M B G R Y
Plain text:  R E G I M E N T
"Key":       L L B U N K E R
```

The key now becomes evident. It is a cyclic permutation of BUNKER HILL. It should be clear that since the key word or key phrase repeats itself during the encipherment of such a message, the plaintext word upon whose assumed presence in the message this test is being based may begin to be enciphered at any point in the key, and continue over into the next repetition of the

---

[7] Cf. subpar. 20*e.*

key if the probable word is longer than the key. When this is the case it is merely necessary to shift the latter part of the sequence of key letters to the first part, as in the case noted: LLBUNKER is permuted cyclically into BUNKER..LL, and thus BUNKER HILL.

d. The examples in subpar. *c*, above, merely illustrate the *theory* of "placing" a probable word and recovering the key word. In actual practice, the application of the probable-word method proceeds along slightly different lines of a short-cut manner, as will be described below, using the same message and probable word as stated in the preceding subparagraph.

(1) The cipher text is written in a horizontal line on cross-section paper, and the first five letters or so of the probable word are written columnarwise to the left of the cipher text and one space below it. Assuming first that direct standard alphabets have been used, the successive letters of the cipher are *deciphered* as R_p, writing the respective *key letters* (as derived under A_p or the assumed index letter) [8] on the first line just below the cipher text; this assumes that R_p exists at one of the N–7 possible positions (for the word REGIMENT). Then the presence of the letter E_p is assumed in the text (beginning with the second letter of the message), and the successive key letters from these decipherments are inscribed in the second line for N–6 positions. On the third line the process is repeated, assuming that G_p is present in N–5 possible positions beginning with the third letter of the cryptogram, writing the key letters from the respective decipherments under each θ_c.

(2) Now if the trigraph REG_p exists in the message, then the juxtaposition of REG_p at its correct location in the cipher text will yield on a diagonal a plaintext trigraph which is a part of the repeating key, *if the key is a plaintext word or phrase.* So by examining the possible plaintext trigraphs and extending them to 1, 2, 3, or more places if necessary, all but one will be eliminated by inconsistencies (i.e., implausible plaintext polygraphs), as only one polygraph will keep on yielding valid plain text. If the first trials with direct standard alphabets are not successful, then reversed standard alphabets are tried. It is important to keep in mind that plaintext trigraphs are not necessarily only those which are contained within words; observe the LLB trigraph in Fig. 15*b*, below, which occurs between words at a cyclical repetition of the key phrase BUNKER HILL.

(3) In the following three figures, Fig. 15*a* is the attempted solution under the premise that the alphabets employed are direct standard; Fig. 15*b* is the successful trial with reversed standard alphabets; [9] and Fig. 15*c* is the complete decipherment of the message after the key word has been recovered.

---

[8] See also in this connection subpar. 39*d*.

[9] It is interesting to point out a further short cut to this already short-cut method. In Fig. 15*a*, we derive the first row of key letters (representing R_p) under the cipher; i.e., YPBBP.... For the second row, we derive C_k under G_c as the first equivalent of E_p; this equivalent is of course under the P_k derived in the first row. We now take an alphabet composed of two direct standard sequences, and juxtapose them so that P in the upper component is over C in the lower component. The rest of the letters in the E_p row (*viz.*, the second row) may now be read directly by referring to the direct standard alphabet; i.e., if P_k in component (1) is equivalent to C_k in component (2), then $B_k(1)=O_k(2)$, $M_k(1)=Z_k(2)$, etc. In Fig. 15*b* the same procedure is followed, *still using the direct standard alphabet* for finding the equivalents of the key letters in the second and third rows; the reason that direct standard alphabets may still be used is that there has been in effect a conversion into plain-component equivalents. The method just described is much faster and less laborious in finding the equivalents for the second and third rows, once the initial key letter of each row has been determined.

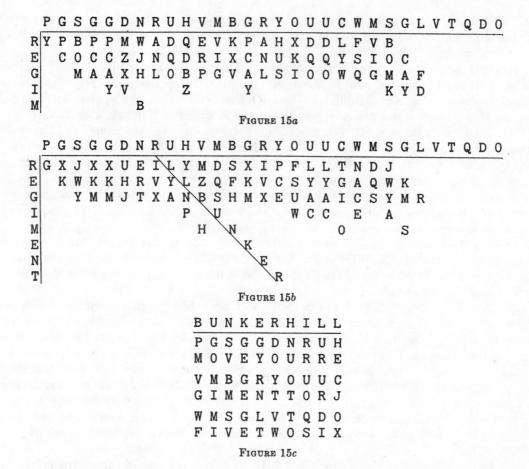

```
  P G S G G D N R U H V M B G R Y O U U C W M S G L V T Q D O
R Y P B P P M W A D Q E V K P A H X D D L F V B
E C O C C Z J N Q D R I X C N U K Q Q Y S I O C
G   M A A X H L O B P G V A L S I O O W Q G M A F
I     Y V     Z     Y           K Y D
M   B
```

FIGURE 15a

```
  P G S G G D N R U H V M B G R Y O U U C W M S G L V T Q D O
R G X J X X U E I L Y M D S X I P F L L T N D J
E K W K K H R V Y L Z Q F K V C S Y Y G A Q W K
G   Y M M J T X A N B S H M X E U A A I C S Y M R
I           P   U       W C C   E       A
M           H   N           O       S
E               K
N               E
T               R
```

FIGURE 15b

```
B U N K E R H I L L
P G S G G D N R U H
M O V E Y O U R R E

V M B G R Y O U U C
G I M E N T T O R J

W M S G L V T Q D O
F I V E T W O S I X
```

FIGURE 15c

e. Another method for testing cribs where the components are known is illustrated in Fig. 16, below. This method involves the completion of all the generatrices from the cipher text, and searching for the key by means of a stencil pre-cut to the probable word being tested.

(1) In this example, using the same message and crib as in the preceding subparagraph, the top row of the diagram is the cipher message; the identical row just beneath the cipher consists of the key letters (on the hypothesis of reversed standard alphabets) if the ciphertext letters represent encipherments of A_p; the next row (QHTHH...) consists of the key letters if the ciphertext letters represent encipherments of B_p; and so forth. A stencil or mask is made on cross-section paper of the same size cells as the cross-section paper used to complete the generatrices, with appropriate cells cut out in successive columns to represent the letters of the crib (located by means of the reference alphabet to the left of the diagram). This stencil can now be slid along the horizontal axis through successive positions of the diagram; when the correct placement of the crib is reached, the letters of the key (in this case, LLBUNKER) will manifest themselves in the apertures.

(2) If we are to test the crib on the basis of direct standard alphabets (instead of reversed standard as above), the completion diagram of Fig. 16 may still be used; the only change necessary is that the plaintext reference alphabet at the left must be changed to the AZYXW...DCB sequence, to reflect the difference in deriving the key letters in the diagram.

Cipher text

```
            P G S G G D N R U H V M B G R Y O U U C W M S G L V T Q D O
            ─────────────────────────────────────────────────────────
        A   P G S G G D N R U H V M B G R Y O U U C W M S G L V T Q D O
        B   Q H T H H E O S V I W N C H S Z P V V D X N T H M W U R E P
        C   R I U I I F P T W J X O D I T A Q W W E Y O U I N X V S F Q
        D   S J V J J G Q U X K Y P E J U B R X X F Z P V J O Y W T G R
        E   T K W K K H R V Y L Z Q F K V C S Y Y G A Q W K P Z X U H S
        F   U L X L L I S W Z M A R G L W D T Z Z H B R X L Q A Y V I T
        G   V M Y M M J T X A N B S H M X E U A A I C S Y M R B Z W J U
        H   W N Z N N K U Y B O C T I N Y F V B B J D T Z N S C A X K V
Plain   I   X O A O O L V Z C P D U J O Z G W C C K E U A O T D B Y L W
text    J   Y P B P P M W A D Q E V K P A H X D D L F V B P U E C Z M X
        K   Z Q C Q Q N X B E R F W L Q B I Y E E M G W C Q V F D A N Y
        L   A R D R R O Y C F S G X M R C J Z F F N H X D R W G E B O Z
        M   B S E S S P Z D G T H Y N S D K A G G O I Y E S X H F C P A
        N   C T F T T Q A E H U I Z O T E L B H H P J Z F T Y I G D Q B
        O   D U G U U R B F I V J A P U F M C I I Q K A G U Z J H E R C
        P   E V H V V S C G J W K B Q V G N D J J R L B H V A K I F S D
        Q   F W I W W T D H K X L C R W H O E K K S M C I W B L J G T E
        R   G X J X X U E I L Y M D S X I P F L L T N D J X C M K H U F
        S   H Y K Y Y V F J M Z N E T Y J Q G M M U O E K Y D N L I V G
        T   I Z L Z Z W G K N A O F U Z K R H N N V P F L Z E O M J W H
        U   J A M A A X H L O B P G V A L S I O O W Q G M A F P N K X I
        V   K B N B B Y I M P C Q H W B M T J P P X R H N B G Q O L Y J
        W   L C O C C Z J N Q D R I X C N U K Q Q Y S I O C H R P M Z K
        X   M D P D D A K O R E S J Y D O V L R R Z T J P D I S Q N A L
        Y   N E Q E E B L P S F T K Z E P W M S S A U K Q E J T R O B M
        Z   O F R F F C M Q T G U L A F Q X N T T B V L R F K U S P C N
```

FIGURE 16

(3) This particular method is very valuable if there are many cribs to be tested; this method also has related applications in other fields of cryptanalysis.

f. Two further important ramifications of the probable-word method should be pointed out at this time; these apply to cases wherein the crib is considerably shorter than the repeating key, and to cases where the repeating key is composed of a sequence of random letters.

(1) Suppose that in the previous example we were testing the crib $YOUR_p$; at the 5th position of the cipher text we would have recovered the key fragment $ERHI_k$ which appears likely as a part of a key word in English. We would then take this key fragment and *slide it along all the remaining positions of the cipher text*; at position 15 we would obtain the fragment $NTTO_p$ as possible plain text, and at position 25 we would obtain the fragment $TWOS_p$. Factoring the intervals between the fragments which yielded plain text, we would conclude that the period of the message is 10. The $NTTO_p$ sequence might be preceded by an E_p, which might be expanded into $MENTTO_p$, which would yield the fragments $(MO?)VEYOUR_p$ at position 3 and $(FI?)VETWOS_p$ at position 23. This procedure would be continued until the message is completely solved.

(2) In the foregoing case, $ERHI_k$ was recognized as a possible key fragment because it looked like a plausible sequence of a plaintext key word. If the key had not been a plaintext

43

word, but instead had been, let us say, the arbitrary letters CBNOMRGOWB, then the fragment MRGO$_k$ of this sequence would not have been recognized as part of the key when the crib YOUR$_p$ was tried at the 5th position. The procedure followed in cases where the key is composed of random letters is to assume the crib at position 1, derive the "key," and slide this "key" along the rest of the message to see whether possible plain text results; then the crib is tried at positions 2, 3, 4 . . . in turn, until its placement at the correct position yields decipherments in other parts of the message which are recognized as valid plain text. This technique, although laborious when done by hand, is a basis for solution when analytical machine methods are employed.

g. It has been seen in the probable-word method described in this paragraph that the length of the key is of no particular interest or consequence in the steps taken in effecting the solution. The determination of the length and elements of the key come after the solution rather than before it. In the case illustrated the length of the period is seen to be 10, corresponding to the length of the key (BUNKER HILL).

h. The foregoing method is one of the other methods of determining the length of the key (besides factoring), referred to in subpar. 16*c.* As will be shown subsequently, the method can also be used as a last resort when known mixed alphabets are employed. This method of solution by searching for a word is contingent upon the following circumstances:

(1) That the word whose presence is assumed actually occurs in the message, is properly spelled, and correctly enciphered.

(2) That the sliding components (or equivalent cipher disks or squares) employed in the search for the assumed word are actually the ones which were employed in the encipherment, or are such as to give identical results as the ones which were actually used.

(3) That the pair of enciphering equations used in the test is actually the pair which was employed in the encipherment; or if a cipher square is used in the test, the method of finding equivalents gives results that correspond with those actually obtained in the encipherment.

i. The foregoing appears to be quite an array of contingencies and the student may think that on this account the method will often fail. But examining these contingencies one by one, it will be seen that successful application of the method may not be at all rare—after the solution of some messages has disclosed what sort of paraphernalia and methods of employing them are favored by the enemy. From the foregoing remark it is to be inferred that the probable-word method has its greatest usefulness not in an initial solution of a system, but only after successful study of enemy communications by more difficult processes of analysis has told its story to the alert cryptanalyst. Although it is commonly attributed to Bazeries, the French cryptanalyst of 1900, the probable-word method is very old in cryptanalysis and goes back several centuries. Its usefulness in practical work may best be indicated by quoting from a competent observer: [10]

"There is another [method] which is to this first method what the geometric method is to analysis in certain sciences, and, according to the whims of individuals, certain cryptanalysts prefer one to the other. Certain others, incapable of getting the answer with one of the methods in the solution of a difficult problem, conquer it by means of the other, with a disconcerting masterly stroke. This other method is that of the probable word. We may have more or less definite opinions concerning the subject of the cryptogram. We may know something about its date, and the correspondents, who may have been indiscreet in the subject they have treated. On this basis, the hypothesis is made that a certain word probably appears in the text. . . . In certain classes of documents, military or diplomatic telegrams, banking and mining affairs, etc.,

---

[10] Givierge, M., *Cours de Cryptographie*, Paris, 1925, p. 30.

it is not impossible to make very important assumptions about the presence of certain words in the text. After a cryptanalyst has worked for a long time with the writings of certain correspondents, he gets used to their expressions. He gets a whole load of words to try out; then the changes of key, and sometimes of system, no longer throw into his way the difficulties of an absolutely new study, which might require the analytical method."

To which I am prompted to add the amusing definition of cryptanalysis attributed to a British wag: "All cryptanalysis is divided into two parts: trance-titution and supposition."

23. The Porta system.—*a.* The solution of the Porta system, described in subpar. 11*b*, may properly be treated at this point along with repeating-key systems with standard alphabets, since the enciphering matrix is a known matrix with normal components. The Porta matrix illustrated in Fig. 5 on p. 11 may be visualized as follows:

Plain text

```
          A B C D E F G H I J K L M N O P Q R S T U V W X Y Z
     A,B │N O P Q R S T U V W X Y Z│A B C D E F G H I J K L M│
     C,D │O P Q R S T U V W X Y Z N│M A B C D E F G H I J K L│
     E,F │P Q R S T U V W X Y Z N O│L M A B C D E F G H I J K│
     G,H │Q R S T U V W X Y Z N O P│K L M A B C D E F G H I J│
  s  I,J │R S T U V W X Y Z N O P Q│J K L M A B C D E F G H I│
  r  K,L │S T U V W X Y Z N O P Q R│I J K L M A B C D E F G H│
  e  M,N │T U V W X Y Z N O P Q R S│H I J K L M A B C D E F G│
  t  O,P │U V W X Y Z N O P Q R S T│G H I J K L M A B C D E F│
  t  Q,R │V W X Y Z N O P Q R S T U│F G H I J K L M A B C D E│
  e  S,T │W X Y Z N O P Q R S T U V│E F G H I J K L M A B C D│
  l  U,V │X Y Z N O P Q R S T U V W│D E F G H I J K L M A B C│
  y  W,X │Y Z N O P Q R S T U V W X│C D E F G H I J K L M A B│
  e  Y,Z │Z N O P Q R S T U V W X Y│B C D E F G H I J K L M A│
  K
```

b. If the message in par. 20 were enciphered by means of the Porta table, the key word still being WHITE, the distributions for the five alphabets would appear as follows:

1. A B C D E F G H I J K L M │ N O P Q R S T U V W X Y Z

2. A B C D E F G H I J K L M │ N O P Q R S T U V W X Y Z

3. A B C D E F G H I J K L M │ N O P Q R S T U V W X Y Z

4. A B C D E F G H I J K L M │ N O P Q R S T U V W X Y Z

5. A B C D E F G H I J K L M │ N O P Q R S T U V W X Y Z

45

Now if a vertical dividing line is drawn between the M and the N of the distributions, each *half* of the distribution may be used to fit half of the normal frequency distribution (following the Porta rule of encipherment, i.e., each half of the alphabet going to the opposite half). Thus in Alphabet 1 the sequence $CDEFGHIJ_c$ may easily be identified as $NOPQRSTU_p$; this would fix the key letters as WX, and therefore the $A \ldots M_p$ sequence should begin at Y_c. This latter fit may not be ideal, but it is nevertheless plausible. In Alphabets 2, 3, and 5 the RST_p sequence may be spotted at BCD_c, ABC_c, and CDE_c, respectively, whereas in Alphabet 4 the trial of E_p as N_c gives a reasonably good matching of that half of the distribution. These assumptions in the first halves of the distributions will of course determine the placements of the letters in the second halves, since, for example in Alphabet 4, if $N_c=E_p$, then $E_c=N_p$; therefore the original assumptions for the first halves will be confirmed or rejected by the goodness of fit of the distributions for the second halves. The keys for these five alphabets are derived as (W,X), (G,H), (I,J), (S,T), and (E,F); from these letters, the repeating key WHITE is obvious.[11]

c. In completing the plain-component sequence in the case of Porta encipherment, the cipher letters of each alphabet are first converted to their [Porta] plain-component equivalents, and then the plain-component sequence is completed from these letters, with a minor modification. This modification consists in completing the converted cipher letters A–M in a downward direction, while the letters N–Z are completed in the opposite (i.e., *upward*) direction. As an example of this process, let us assume that the message in subpar. 20*h* has been enciphered by five alphabets in the Porta system; the first forty letters of this encipherment are:

```
PKTFF  CDVIT  OBVZX  CVREE  GIVJE  TPRKT
OQCFL  PBVPX . . .
```

The conversion process and plain-component completion of the first three alphabets are shown in the diagram below (employing the procedure of generatrix elimination and weighting as described in subpars. 21*f* and *g*):

	Alphabet 1			Alphabet 2			Alphabet 3
	P C O C G T O P			K D B V I P Q B			T V V R V R C V
1	C P B P T G B C			~~X Q O I V C D O~~		6	G I I E I E P I
3	D O C O S H C D		3	W P N J U D E N			~~H J J F J F O J~~
6	E N D N R I D E			~~V O Z K T E F Z~~			~~I K K G K G N K~~
	~~F Z E Z Q J E F~~		2	U N Y L S F G Y			~~J L L H L H Z L~~
O	G Y F Y P K F G			~~T Z X M R G H X~~		2	K M M I M I Y M
	~~H X G X O L G H~~		3	S Y W A Q H I W			~~L A A J A J X A~~
3	I W H W N M H I			~~R X V B P I J V~~			~~M B B K B K W B~~
	~~J V I V Z A I J~~			~~Q W U C O J K U~~		1	A C C L C L V C
	~~K U J U Y B J K~~		3	P V T D N K L T		0	B D D M D M U D
	~~L T K T X C K L~~		3	O U S E Z L M S		7	C E E A E A T E
2	M S L S W D L M		5	N T R F Y M A R		1	D F F B F B S F
5	A R M R V E M A			~~Z S Q G X A B Q~~		2	E G G C G C R G
	~~B Q A Q U F A B~~		1	Y R P H W B C P		0	F H H D H D Q H

The generatrices with the highest scores are the correct ones.

d. Just as the Vigenère table (consisting of direct standard alphabets) has its complementary table of reversed standard alphabets, a variant of the Porta table might be constructed

---

[11] In some cases the lower half of the Porta alphabets shifts to the *right*, instead of to the left as in the normal form; this possibility must be taken into account in the recovery of the key word.

wherein the lower halves of the sequences run in the opposite direction to the upper half, as is illustrated below:

A,B
A	B	C	D	E	F	G	H	I	J	K	L	M
Z	Y	X	W	V	U	T	S	R	Q	P	O	N

C,D
A	B	C	D	E	F	G	H	I	J	K	L	M
Y	X	W	V	U	T	S	R	Q	P	O	N	Z

.
.
.

Y,Z
A	B	C	D	E	F	G	H	I	J	K	L	M
N	Z	Y	X	W	V	U	T	S	R	Q	P	O

In this case, the method of fitting the distributions to the normal and the method of completing the plain-component sequence must of course be modified to take care of the new situation. Other variations of the Porta idea are possible; these will be treated in subsequent chapters.

e. In applying the probable-word method in Porta, the cryptographic peculiarities of the system greatly facilitate the testing and placing of cribs. As an illustration, let us suppose we have at hand the 40-letter fragment in subpar. 23c (the period being unknown), and let us place under each cipher letter a notation of its class (using "1" to designate a cipher letter from the group A–M in the normal sequence and "2" to designate a letter from the group N–Z. The cipher text and notations will look as follows:

```
P K T F F   C D V I T   O B V Z X   C V R E E   G I V J E   T P R K T
2 1 2 1 1   1 1 2 1 2   2 1 2 2 2   1 2 2 1 1   1 1 2 1 1   2 2 2 1 2

O Q C F L   P B V P X...
2 2 1 1 1   2 1 2 2 2
```

Let us suppose that the probable word is INFANTRY; the letters of this word have the class notation of 12112222, but in encipherment the classes would be reversed, *viz.*, 21221111. We now look for the pattern 21221111 in the cipher text, and we find it beginning at the 15th position. The derived key $\begin{pmatrix} E & W & G & I & S & E & W & G \\ F & X & H & J & T & F & X & H \end{pmatrix}$ can easily be recognized as a cyclical repetition of the key word WHITE.

24. The Gronsfeld system.—The Gronsfeld system (described in par. 3) is identical with a Vigenère system with direct standard alphabets (where only the first 10 alphabets are used), except that a numerical key is involved, the digits of the key indicating how much displacement the plaintext letters should have along the normal sequence; thus only the first ten rows of the Vigenère table are used. The Gronsfeld system is solved just like any Vigenère system, except (when the system is known to be a Gronsfeld) for a minor modification in the use of the probable-word method. The severe limitation of the cipher equivalents possible for a given plaintext letter greatly restricts the placement of trial cribs. For example, in trying the crib YOUR$_p$ in a message, the diagram below (analogous to Fig. 15a) shows, in the first row beneath the cipher,

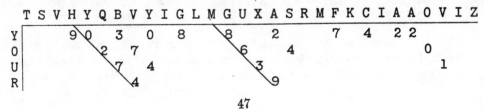

the keys resulting from the only possible Gronsfeld decipherments of Y_p; the row just beneath that gives the keys for O_p (*where* Y_p *has been a possibility for the preceding cipher letter*); etc. In the example, there are only two places where $YOUR_p$ is a possibility: at the 5th and 14th positions, with the corresponding keys being 0274 and 8639, respectively. If 0274 is slid through the remainder of the cipher text, the appearance of the plaintext fragments MENT (at position 13) and FIVE (at position 21) shows that this key fragment is correct, and that the period is 8. If the solution proved difficult, the plain-component sequences could be completed for the remaining cipher text as shown below, as an aid in recovering the rest of the text. It must be pointed

```
     0 2 7 4           0 2 7 4           0 2 7 4             0 2
  T S V H Y Q B V Y I G L M G U X A S R M F K C I A A O V I Z
  S R U G Y O U R X H F K M E N T Z R Q L F I V E Z Z N U I X
  R Q T F     W G E J     Y Q P K     Y Y M T
  Q P S E     V F D I     X P O J     X X L S
  P O R D     U E C H     W O N I     W W K R
  O N Q C     T D B G     V N M H     V V J Q
  N M P B     S C A F     U M L G     U U I P
  M L O A     R B Z E     T L K F     T T H O
  L K N Z     Q A Y D     S K J E     S S G N
  K J M Y     P Z X C     R J I D     R R F M
```

out that, although reading a Gronsfeld cipher of a lengthy period on ten generatrices alone is quite possible, it may be rather difficult to do so in actual practice unless something concerning the contents or nature of the message plain text is known.

25. Polyalphabetic numerical systems.—*a.* Periodic number ciphers may be encountered in which the plain component is the normal sequence and the cipher component is what may be regarded as a standard [numerical] sequence. For instance, if the cipher component consisted of the dinomes 01–26 in normal order, this component is in effect an A–Z sequence and analysis would proceed along the lines of any direct standard alphabet cipher. In Fig. 6 we have a numerical Vigenère square consisting of a 36-element "normal" plain component and a cipher component consisting of the dinomes 10–45 in ascending order; this system involves nothing new in techniques of solution, except that in fitting the cipher distributions to the normal (after factoring), allowance has to be made for the beginning and ending points of the A–Z sequence in the 36 elements of the cipher distributions.

b. If periodic numerical ciphers are encountered in which the cipher components are slides of the 00, 01 . . . 98, 99 sequence in normal order, the occurrence in certain alphabets of dinomes within a comparatively narrow range will be an aid to factoring. For example, if the matrix in the illustration below were used for encipherment, the occurrence of the "low dinomes"

	A	B	C	D	E	F	G	H		V	W	X	Y	Z
1	03	04	05	06	07	08	09	10	....	24	25	26	27	28
2	41	42	43	44	45	46	47	48	....	62	63	64	65	66
3	28	29	30	31	32	33	34	35	....	49	50	51	52	53
4	70	71	72	73	74	75	76	77	....	91	92	93	94	95
5	32	33	34	35	36	37	38	39	....	53	54	55	56	57

(resulting from encipherments by Alphabet 1) spaced along the cipher text at an interval of 5, and the "high dinomes" (resulting from encipherments by Alphabet 4) likewise spaced along the cipher text at that same interval, would quickly identify the length of the period.

CHAPTER V

REPEATING-KEY SYSTEMS WITH MIXED CIPHER ALPHABETS, I; DIRECT SYMMETRY OF POSITION

26. Reason for the use of mixed alphabets.—*a.* It has been seen in the examples considered thus far that the use of several alphabets in the same message does not greatly complicate the analysis of such a cryptogram. There are three reasons why this is so. Firstly, only relatively few alphabets were employed; secondly, these alphabets were employed in a periodic or repeating manner, giving rise to cyclic phenomena in the cryptogram by means of which the number of alphabets could be determined; and, thirdly, the cipher alphabets were *known* alphabets, by which is meant merely that the sequences of letters in both components of the cipher alphabets were known sequences.

b. In the case of monoalphabetic ciphers it was found that the use of a mixed alphabet delayed the solution to a considerable degree, and it will now be seen that the use of mixed alphabets in polyalphabetic ciphers renders the analysis much more difficult than the use of standard alphabets, but that the solution is still fairly easy to achieve.

27. Interrelated mixed alphabets.—*a.* It was stated in par. 7 that the method of producing the mixed alphabets in a polyalphabetic cipher often affords clues which are of great assistance in the analysis of the cipher alphabets. This is so, of course, primarily when the cipher alphabets are interrelated secondary alphabets produced by sliding components or their equivalents. Reference is now made to the classification set forth in par. 8, in connection with the types of alphabets which may be employed in polyalphabetic substitution. It will be seen that thus far only Cases I*a* and *b* have been treated. Case II*a* will now be discussed.

b. Here one of the components, the plain component, is the normal sequence, while the cipher component is a mixed sequence, the various juxtapositions of the two components yielding mixed alphabets. The mixed component may be a systematically-mixed or a random-mixed sequence. If the 26 successive displacements of the mixed component are recorded in separate lines, a symmetrical cipher square such as that shown in Fig. 17 results therefrom. It is identical in form with the square table shown in Fig. 9.

Plain

A B C D E F G H I J K L M N O P Q R S T U V W X Y Z

Cipher

```
L E A V N W O R T H B C D F G I J K M P Q S U X Y Z
E A V N W O R T H B C D F G I J K M P Q S U X Y Z L
A V N W O R T H B C D F G I J K M P Q S U X Y Z L E
V N W O R T H B C D F G I J K M P Q S U X Y Z L E A
N W O R T H B C D F G I J K M P Q S U X Y Z L E A V
W O R T H B C D F G I J K M P Q S U X Y Z L E A V N
O R T H B C D F G I J K M P Q S U X Y Z L E A V N W
R T H B C D F G I J K M P Q S U X Y Z L E A V N W O
T H B C D F G I J K M P Q S U X Y Z L E A V N W O R
H B C D F G I J K M P Q S U X Y Z L E A V N W O R T
B C D F G I J K M P Q S U X Y Z L E A V N W O R T H
C D F G I J K M P Q S U X Y Z L E A V N W O R T H B
D F G I J K M P Q S U X Y Z L E A V N W O R T H B C
F G I J K M P Q S U X Y Z L E A V N W O R T H B C D
G I J K M P Q S U X Y Z L E A V N W O R T H B C D F
I J K M P Q S U X Y Z L E A V N W O R T H B C D F G
J K M P Q S U X Y Z L E A V N W O R T H B C D F G I
K M P Q S U X Y Z L E A V N W O R T H B C D F G I J
M P Q S U X Y Z L E A V N W O R T H B C D F G I J K
P Q S U X Y Z L E A V N W O R T H B C D F G I J K M
Q S U X Y Z L E A V N W O R T H B C D F G I J K M P
S U X Y Z L E A V N W O R T H B C D F G I J K M P Q
U X Y Z L E A V N W O R T H B C D F G I J K M P Q S
X Y Z L E A V N W O R T H B C D F G I J K M P Q S U
Y Z L E A V N W O R T H B C D F G I J K M P Q S U X
Z L E A V N W O R T H B C D F G I J K M P Q S U X Y
```

FIGURE 17

c. Such a cipher square may be used in exactly the same manner as the Vigenère square. With the key word BLUE and with the normal enciphering equations ($\theta_{k/2}=\theta_{1/1}$; $\theta_{p/1}=\theta_{c/2}$), the appropriate lines of the square could be arranged in the form of the matrix below:

```
P:   A B C D E F G H I J K L M N O P Q R S T U V W X Y Z
C₁:  B C D F G I J K M P Q S U X Y Z L E A V N W O R T H
C₂:  L E A V N W O R T H B C D F G I J K M P Q S U X Y Z
C₃:  U X Y Z L E A V N W O R T H B C D F G I J K M P Q S
C₄:  E A V N W O R T H B C D F G I J K M P Q S U X Y Z L
```

FIGURE 18a

50

These lines would, of course, yield the following cipher alphabets:

```
(1) Plain:  A B C D E F G H I J K L M N O P Q R S T U V W X Y Z
    Cipher: B C D F G I J K M P Q S U X Y Z L E A V N W O R T H

(2) Plain:  A B C D E F G H I J K L M N O P Q R S T U V W X Y Z
    Cipher: L E A V N W O R T H B C D F G I J K M P Q S U X Y Z

(3) Plain:  A B C D E F G H I J K L M N O P Q R S T U V W X Y Z
    Cipher: U X Y Z L E A V N W O R T H B C D F G I J K M P Q S

(4) Plain:  A B C D E F G H I J K L M N O P Q R S T U V W X Y Z
    Cipher: E A V N W O R T H B C D F G I J K M P Q S U X Y Z L
```

FIGURE 18b

28. Principles of direct symmetry of position.—*a.* It was stated directly above that Fig. 17 is a symmetrical cipher square, by which is meant that the letters in its successive horizontal lines show a *symmetry of position* with respect to one another. They constitute, in reality, one and only one sequence or series of letters, the sequences being merely displaced successively 1, 2, 3, . . . 25 intervals. The symmetry exhibited is obvious and is said to be visible, or *direct*. This fact can be used to good advantage, as will presently be demonstrated.

b. Consider, for example, the pair of letters G_c and V_c in cipher alphabet (1) of Fig. 18b. The letter V_c is the 15th letter to the right of G_c. In cipher alphabet (2), V_c is also the 15th letter to the right of G_c, as is the case in each of the four cipher alphabets in Fig. 18b, since the *relative* positions they occupy are the same in each horizontal line in Fig. 18a, that is, in each of the successive recordings of the cipher component as the latter is slid to the right against the plain or normal component. If, therefore, the relative positions occupied by two letters, θ_1 and θ_2, in such a cipher alphabet, C_1, are known, and if the position of θ_1 in another cipher alphabet, C_2, belonging to the same series is known, then θ_2 may at once be placed into its correct position in C_2. Suppose, for example, that as the result of an analysis based upon considerations of frequency, the following values in four cipher alphabets have been tentatively determined:

```
    Plain:  A B C D E F G H I J K L M N O P Q R S T U V W X Y Z
(1) Cipher:        G                     Y         V

    Plain:  A B C D E F G H I J K L M N O P Q R S T U V W X Y Z
(2) Cipher:      N                   G           P

    Plain:  A B C D E F G H I J K L M N O P Q R S T U V W X Y Z
(3) Cipher:        L                   B           I

    Plain:  A B C D E F G H I J K L M N O P Q R S T U V W X Y Z
(4) Cipher:      W                       I           Q
```

FIGURE 19a

c. The cipher components of these four secondary alphabets may, for convenience, be assembled into a cellular structure, hereinafter called a *sequence reconstruction matrix,* as shown in Fig. 19b. Regarding the top line of the reconstruction matrix in Fig. 19b as being common to all four secondary cipher alphabets listed in Fig. 19a, the successive lines of the reconstruction matrix may now be termed cipher alphabets, and may be referred to by the numbers at the left.

51

```
Plain:    A B C D E F G H I J K L M N O P Q R S T U V W X Y Z
Cipher 1:         G                   Y         V
Cipher 2:         N                   G         P
Cipher 3:         L                   B         I
Cipher 4:         W                   I         Q
```

FIGURE 19b

d. The letter G is common to Alphabets 1 and 2. In Alphabet 2 it is noted that N occupies the 10th position to the left of G, and the letter P occupies the 5th position to the right of G. One may therefore place these letters, N and P, in their proper positions in Alphabet 1, the letter N being placed 10 letters before G, and the letter P, 5 letters after G. Thus:

```
Plain:    A B C D E F G H I J K L M N O P Q R S T U V W X Y Z
Cipher 1:         G         P         Y         V N
```

Thus, the values of two new letters in Alphabet 1, *viz.*, $P_c = J_p$, and $N_c = U_p$ have been automatically determined; these values were obtained without any analysis based upon the frequency of P_c and N_c. Likewise, in Alphabet 2, the letters Y and V may be inserted in these positions:

```
Plain:    A B C D E F G H I J K L M N O P Q R S T U V W X Y Z
Cipher 2:       V N                   G         P         Y
```

This gives the new values $V_c = D_p$ and $Y_c = Y_p$ in Alphabet 2. Alphabets 3 and 4 have a common letter I, which permits of the placement of Q and W in Alphabet 3, and of B and L in Alphabet 4.

e. The new values thus found are of course immediately inserted throughout the cryptogram, thus leading to the assumption of further values in the cipher text. This process, *viz.*, *the reconstruction of the primary components*, by the application of the principles of direct symmetry of position to the cells of the reconstruction matrix, thus facilitates and hastens solution.

f. It must be clearly understood that before the principles of direct symmetry of position can be applied in cases such as the foregoing, *it is necessary that one of the components* (in this case, the plain component) *be a known sequence.* Whether it is the normal sequence or not is immaterial, so long as the sequence is *known.* Obviously, if the sequence is unknown, symmetry, even if present, cannot be detected by the cryptanalyst because he has no base upon which to try out his assumptions for symmetry. In other words, direct symmetry of position is manifested in the illustrated example because the plain component is a *known sequence,* and not because it is the normal alphabet. The significance of this point will become apparent later on in connection with the problem to be discussed in par. 36.

29. Initial steps in the solution of a typical example.—*a.* In the light of the foregoing principles let us study a typical message.

	5	10	15	20	25	30
A	Q W B R I	V W Y C A	I S P J L	R B Z E Y	Q W Y E U	L W M G W
B	I C J C I	M T Z E I	M I B K N	Q W B R I	V W Y I G	B W N B Q
C	Q C G Q H	I W J K A	G E G X N	I D M R U	V E Z Y G	Q I G V N
D	C T G Y O	B P D B L	V C G X G	B K Z Z G	I V X C U	N T Z A O
E	B W F E Q	Q L F C O	M T Y Z T	C C B Y Q	O P D K A	G D G I G
F	V P W M R	Q I I E W	I C G X G	B L G Q Q	V B G R S	M Y J J Y
G	Q V F W Y	R W N F L	G X N F W	M C J K X	I D D R U	O P J Q Q
H	Z R H C N	V W D Y Q	R D G D G	B X D B N	P X F P U	Y X N F G
J	M P J E L	S A N C D	S E Z Z G	I B E Y U	K D H C A	M B J J F
K	K I L C J	M F D Z T	C T J R D	M I Y Z Q	A C J R R	S B G Z N
L	Q Y A H Q	V E D C Q	L X N C L	L V V C S	Q W B I I	I V J R N
M	W N B R I	V P J E L	T A G D N	I R G Q P	A T Y E W	C B Y Z T
N	E V G Q U	V P Y H L	L R Z N Q	X I N B A	I K W J Q	R D Z F Y
P	K W F Z L	G W F J Q	Q W J Y Q	I B W R X		

b. The principal repetitions of three or more letters have been underlined in the message and the factors (up to 26 only) of the intervals between them are as follows:

QWBRIVWY	45	3, 5, 9, 15
CGXGB	60	2, 3, 4, 5, 6, 10, 12, 15, 20
PJEL	95	5, 19
ZZGI	145	5
BRIV	330	2, 3, 5, 6, 10, 11, 13, 22
BRIV	285	3, 5, 15, 19
KAG	75	3, 5, 15, 25
QRD	165	3, 5, 15
QWB	45	3, 5, 9, 15
QWB	275	5, 11, 25
WIC	130	2, 5, 10, 13, 26
XNF	45	3, 5, 9, 15
YZT	225	3, 5, 15, 25
ZTC	145	5

53

The factor 5 is common to all of these repetitions, and there seems to be every indication that five alphabets are involved. Since the message already appears in groups of five letters, it is unnecessary in this case to rewrite it in groups corresponding to the length of the key. The uniliteral frequency distribution for Alphabet 1 is as follows:

```
 ≡  卌  ‖‖   _  ‖‖    卌    ‖‖‖‖  卌  _  ‖  _  卌  ‖‖‖  _   卌   _  _  _  _
 A  B  C  D  E  F  G  H  I  J  K  L  M  N  O  P  Q  R  S  T  U  V  W  X  Y  Z
```

c. Attempts to fit this distribution to the normal on the basis of a direct or reversed standard alphabet do not give positive results, and it is assumed that mixed alphabets are involved. Individual triliteral frequency distributions are then compiled and are shown below. These tables are similar to those made for single mixed-alphabet ciphers, and are made in the same way except that instead of taking the letters one after the other, the letters which belong to the separate alphabets now must be assembled in separate tables. For example, in Alphabet 1, the trigraph QAC means that A occurs in Alphabet 1; Q, its prefix, occurs in Alphabet 5, and C, its suffix, occurs in Alphabet 2. All confusion may be avoided by placing numbers indicating the alphabets in which they belong above the letters, thus: Q[5]A[1]C[2]

Alphabet 1

A	B	C	D	E	F	G	H	I	J	K	L	M	N	O	P	Q	R	S	T	U	V	W	X	Y	Z
QC	GW	NT		TV		AE	AS	UD	UW	IT	UT	QP	NX	-W	LB	LA	LA		IW	NN	QI		UX		QR
PT	OP	TC				AD	WC	FI	QX	II		UP		YW	YW	DE			IW						
	GK	TT				LX	HW	FW	LV	OT				NW	QD	RB			UE						
	OW	WB				LW	ND		LR	SY				QC	QD				LC						
	GL						GV			WC				GI					GP						
	GX						WC			GP				QL					QB						
							XD			AB				RI					NW						
							GB			JF				YV					QE						
							IV			DI				NY					IP						
							NR							SW					UP						
							AK							QW											
							QB																		

Alphabet 2

A	B	C	D	E	F	G	H	I	J	K	L	M	N	O	P	Q	R	S	T	U	V	W	X	Y	Z
SN	RZ	IJ	IM	GG	MD			MB		IW	QF			WB	BD		ZH	IP	MZ		IX	QB	GN	MJ	
TG	VG	QG	GG	VZ				QG		BZ	BG				OD		IG		CG		QF	VY	BD	QA	
IE	VG	ID	SZ					QI							VW		LZ		NZ		LV	QY	PF		
MJ	CB	RG	VD					KL							OJ				MY		IJ	LM	YN		
SG	IG	KH						MY							MJ				CJ		EG	QB	LN		
CY	MJ	RZ						XN							VJ				AY		VY				
IW		AJ													VY						BN				
																					IJ				
																					BF				
																					RN				
																					VD				
																					QB				
																					KF				
																					GF				
																					QJ				

54

Alphabet 3

A	B	C	D	E	F	G	H	I	J	K	L	M	N	O	P	Q	R	S	T	U	V	W	X	Y	Z
YH	WR		PB	BY	WE	CQ	RC	IE	CC		IC	WG	WB		SJ						VC	PM	VC	WC	BE
IK	PK		LC			EX	DC		WK		DR	WF										KJ		WE	TE
WR	DR		VW			IV			YJ			XF										BR		WI	EY
CY	WY		XP			TY			CK			XF												TZ	KZ
WI	XB		WZ			CX			PQ			AC												IZ	TA
NR	FZ		WJ			DI			PE			XC												TE	EZ
	EC					CX			BJ			IB												BZ	RN
						LQ			TR															PH	DY
						BR			CR																
						DD			VR																
						BZ			PE																
						AD			WY																
						RQ																			
						VQ																			

Alphabet 4

A	B	C	D	E	F	G	H	I	J	K	L	M	N	O	P	Q	R	S	T	U	V	W	X	Y	Z
ZO	NQ	YA	GG	ZY	NL	MW	AQ	YG	PL	BN	WR	ZQ		FU		GH	BI				GN	FY	GN	ZG	ZG
DL	JI	GN	YU	NW			YL	GG	JY	JA						GQ	BI						GG	GO	YT
DN	XU		ZI	NG				BI	JF	DA						JQ	MU						GG	BQ	ZG
NA	FO		FQ					WQ	JX							GP	GS						DQ	DT	
HN			IW					FQ								GU	DU						EU	YQ	
ND			JL													JD							ZF	GN	
HA			JL													JR							JQ	YT	
LJ			YW													JN							FL		
DQ																BI									
NL																WX									
VS																									

Alphabet 5

A	B	C	D	E	F	G	H	I	J	K	L	M	N	O	P	Q	R	S	T	U	V	W	X	Y	Z
CI			CS			JK	IB	QI	RV	CM	JR		KQ	YB	QA	BQ	MQ	RM	ZC	EL		GI	KI	EQ	
KG			RM			YK	YQ		CM		BV		XI	AB		EQ	RS	CQ	ZC	RV		EI	R–	JQ	
KG						XB	EM				FG		VC	CM		YO	ZE		CN			FM		WR	
CM						ZI	RV				ES		CV			QV				RO		EC			
BI						IV	II				CL		BP			QZ				PY					
						XB	RV				ET		ZQ			YR				QV					
						DB	HL						RW			ZA				YK					
						FM	ZG						DI			HV									
						ZI										CL									
																NX									
																JR									
																JQ									
																YI									

Condensed table of repetitions

1 2 3 4 5 1 2 3	1 2 3	4 5 1	1 2	3 4
Q W B R I V W Y–2	Q W B–3	K A G–2	Q W–5	B R–3
		Z T C–2	V P–3	G Q–4
2 3 4 5 1	**2 3 4**		V W–3	G X–3
C G X G B–2	X N F–2	**5 1 2**		J R–3
		Q R D–2	**2 3**	N F–3
2 3 4 5	**3 4 5**	W I C–2	C G–3	Y Z–3
P J E L–2	Y Z T–2		C J–3	
			P J–3	
3 4 5 1			W B–3	**4 5**
B R I V–3			W F–3	R I–3
Z Z G I–2			W Y–3	Y Q–3
			X N–3	Z T–3
			5 1	
			G B–4	
			I V–3	
			Q Q–3	

d. One now proceeds to analyze each alphabet distribution, in an endeavor to establish identifications of cipher equivalents. First, of course, attempts should be made to separate the vowels from the consonants in each alphabet, using the same test as in the case of a single mixed-alphabet cipher. There seems no doubt that $\overset{2}{W_c}$ and $\overset{5}{Q_c}$ are equivalents of E_p. In the other alphabets the equivalents of E_p are not so clear-cut, but for the moment, let us assume that E_p is the highest θ_c in the particular alphabet, *viz.*, $\overset{1}{I_c}$, $\overset{3}{G_c}$, and $\overset{4}{C_c}$.

e. The letters of greatest frequency in Alphabet 1 are I, M, Q, V, B, G, L, R, S, and C. I_c has already tentatively been assumed to be E_p. If $\overset{2}{W_c}$ and $\overset{5}{Q_c} = E_p$, then one should be able to distinguish the vowels from the consonants among the letters I, M, Q, V, B, G, L, R, S, and C of Alphabet 1 by examining the prefixes of $\overset{2}{W_c}$, and the suffixes of $\overset{5}{Q_c}$. The prefixes and suffixes of these letters, as shown by the triliteral frequency distributions, are these:

Prefixes of $\overset{2}{\overset{2}{W_c}}$ $(=E_p)$ Suffixes of $\overset{5}{\overset{5}{Q_c}}$ $(=E_p)$

Q G K V R B I L   I Q R X L V A Z O

f. Consider now the letter $\overset{1}{M_c}$; it does not occur either as a prefix of $\overset{2}{W_c}$, or as a suffix of $\overset{5}{Q_c}$. Hence it is most probably a vowel, and on account of its high frequency it may be assumed to be $\overset{1}{O_p}$. On the other hand, note that Q_c occurs five times as a prefix of $\overset{1}{W_c}$ and three times as a suffix of $\overset{5}{Q_c}$. It is therefore a consonant, most probably R_p, for it would give the digraph $\overset{5\ 1}{ER_p}(=QQ_c)$ as occurring three times and $\overset{1\ 2}{RE_p}(=QW_c)$ as occurring five times.

g. The letter V_c occurs three times as a prefix of $\overset{2}{W_c}$ and twice as a suffix of $\overset{5}{Q_c}$. It is therefore a consonant; on account of its frequency, let it be assumed to be $\overset{1}{T_p}$. The letter B_c occurs

56

twice as a prefix of $\overset{2}{W}_c$ but not as a suffix of $\overset{5}{Q}_c$. Its frequency is only medium, and it is probably a consonant. In fact, the twice repeated digraph $\overset{1\,2}{BW}_c$ is once a part of the trigraph $\overset{5\,1\,2}{GBW}$, and $\overset{5}{G}_c$, the letter of second highest frequency in Alphabet 5, looks excellent for T_p. Might not the trigraph $\overset{5\,1\,2}{GBW}$ be THE_p? It will be well to keep this possibility in mind.

h. The letter $\overset{1}{G}_c$ occurs only once as a prefix of $\overset{2}{W}_c$ and does not occur as a suffix of $\overset{5}{Q}_c$. It may be a vowel, but one cannot be sure. The letter $\overset{1}{L}_c$ occurs once as a prefix of $\overset{2}{W}_c$ and once as a suffix of $\overset{5}{Q}_c$. It may be considered to be a consonant. $\overset{1}{R}_c$ occurs once as a prefix of $\overset{2}{W}_c$, and twice as a suffix of $\overset{5}{Q}_c$, and is certainly a consonant. Neither the letter $\overset{1}{S}_c$ nor the letter $\overset{1}{C}_c$ occurs as a prefix of $\overset{2}{W}_c$ or as a suffix of $\overset{5}{Q}_c$; both would seem to be vowels, but a study of the prefixes and suffixes of these letters lends more weight to the assumption that $\overset{1}{C}_c$ is a vowel than that $\overset{1}{S}_c$ is a vowel. For all the prefixes of C, *viz.*, $\overset{5}{N}$, $\overset{5}{T}$, and $\overset{5}{W}$, are in subsequent analysis of Alphabet 5 classified as consonants, as are likewise its suffixes, *viz.*, T, C, and B in Alphabet 2. On the other hand, only one prefix, $\overset{5}{L}_c$, and one suffix, $\overset{2}{B}_c$, of $\overset{1}{S}_c$ are later classified as consonants. Since vowels are more often associated with consonants than with other vowels, it would seem that $\overset{1}{C}_c$ is more likely to be a vowel than $\overset{1}{S}_c$. At any rate $\overset{1}{C}_c$ is assumed to be a vowel, for the present, leaving $\overset{1}{S}_c$ unclassified.

i. Going through the same steps with the remaining alphabets, we obtain the following results:

Alphabet	Vowels	Consonants
1	I, M, C.	Q, V, B, L, R, G?
2	W, P, I.	B, C, D, T.
3	G, Z.	J, N, D, Y, F.
4	C, E?, R?, B?.	Y, Z, J, Q.
5	Q, U.	G, N, A, I, W, L, T.

30. Application of principles of direct symmetry of position.—a. The next step is to try to determine a few values in each alphabet. In Alphabet 1, from the foregoing analysis, the following data are on hand:

Plain: A B C D E F G H I J K L M N O P Q R S T U V W X Y Z
Cipher: C?   I   C?   M   Q   V

Let the values of E_p already assumed in the remaining alphabets, be set down in a reconstruction matrix, as follows:

Plain: A B C D E F G H I J K L M N O P Q R S T U V W X Y Z

	A B C D E F G H I J K L M N O P Q R S T U V W X Y Z
1	C? I C? M Q V
2	W
Cipher: 3	G
4	C
5	Q

57

b. It is seen that by good fortune the letter Q is common to Alphabets 1 and 5, and the letter C is common to Alphabets 1 and 4. If it is assumed that one is dealing with a case in which a mixed component is sliding against the normal component, one can apply the principles of direct symmetry of position to these alphabets, as outlined in par. 28. For example, one may insert the following values in Alphabet 5:

```
Plain:    A B C D E F G H I J K L M N O P Q R S T U V W X Y Z
         ┌─────────────────────────────────────────────────────┐
Cipher: 1│C?          I       C?            M     Q   V         │
        5│   M    Q   V              C?         I       C?      │
         └─────────────────────────────────────────────────────┘
```

c. The process at once gives three definite values: $M_c=B_p$, $V_c=G_p$, $I_c=R_p$. Let these deduced values be substantiated by referring to the frequency distribution. Since B and G are normally low or medium frequency letters in plain text, one should find that M_c and V_c, their hypothetical equivalents in Alphabet 5, should have low frequencies. As a matter of fact, they do not appear in this alphabet, which thus far corroborates the assumption. On the other hand, since $\overset{5}{I_c}=R_p$, if the values derived from symmetry of position are correct, $\overset{5}{I_c}$ should be of high frequency and reference to the distribution shows that I_c is of high frequency. The position of C is doubtful; it belongs either under N_p or V_p. If the former is correct, then the frequency of $\overset{5}{C_c}$ should be high, for it would equal N_p; if the latter is correct, then its frequency should be low, for it would equal V_p. As a matter of fact, $\overset{5}{C_c}$ does not occur, and it must be concluded that it belongs under V_p. This in turn settles the value of $\overset{1}{C_c}$, for it must now be placed definitely under I_p and removed from beneath A_p.

d. The definite placement of C now permits the insertion of new values in Alphabet 4, and one now has the following:

```
Plain:    A B C D E F G H I J K L M N O P Q R S T U V W X Y Z
         ┌─────────────────────────────────────────────────────┐
        1│          I       C            M     Q   V            │
        2│          W                                           │
Cipher: 3│          G                                           │
        4│I         C           M       Q   V                   │
        5│   M    Q V                          I       C        │
         └─────────────────────────────────────────────────────┘
```

58

31. Subsequent steps in solution.—*a.* It is high time that the thus far deduced values, as recorded in the reconstruction matrix, be inserted in the cipher text, for by this time it must seem that the analysis has certainly gone too far upon unproved hypotheses. The following results are obtained:

```
              5         10        15        20        25        30
A  QWBRI VWYCA ISPJL RBZEY QWYEU LWMGW→
   RE    RTE E E                 RE         E
B  ICJCI MTZEI MIBKN QWBRI VWYIG BWNBQ
   E     ERO      RO       RE    RTE A  E     E
C  QCGQH IWJKA GEGXN IDMRU VEZYG QIGVN
   R EN  EE        E         E       T      R EP
D  CTGYO BPDBL VCGXG BKZZG IVXCU NTZAO
   IE          T   E       E     E
E  BWFEQ QLFCO MTYZT CCBYQ OPDKA GDGIG
   E     ERE O     I     E              E A
F  VPWMR QIIEW ICGXG BLGQQ VBGRS MYJJY
   T K   R     E   E     E NET    E     O
G  QVFWY RWNFL GXNFW MCJKX IDDRU OPJQQ
   R           E         O       E         NE
H  ZRHCN VWDYQ RDGDG BXDBN PXFPU YXNFG
     E     TE   E     E
J  MPJEL SANCD SEZZG IBEYU KDHCA MBJJF
   O         E       E            E   O
K  KILCJ MFDZT CTJRD MIYZQ ACJRR SBGZN
     E    O  I       O       E            E
L  QYAHQ VEDCQ LXNCL LVVCS QWBII IVJRN
   R      ET  EE      E       E  RE ARE
M  WNBRI VPJEL TAGDN IRGQP ATYEW CBYZT
     RT    E          E  EN          I
N  EVGQU VPYHL LRZNQ XINBA IKWJQ RDZYF
   EN    T             E         E  E
P  KWFZL GWFJQ QWJYQ IBWRX
   E       E    ERE    E E
```

b. The combinations given are excellent throughout and no inconsistencies appear. Note the trigraph QWB, which is repeated in the following polygraphs (underlined in the foregoing text):

```
          1 2 3 4 5 1          5 1 2 3 4 5 1
          Q W B R I V . . .  S Q W B I I I
          R E   R T . . .    R E   A R E
```

c. The letter B_c is common to both polygraphs, and a little imagination will lead to the assumption of the value $B_c = P_p$, yielding the following:

```
1 2 3 4 5 1        5 1 2 3 4 5 1
Q W B R I V . . .  S Q W B I I I
R E P O R T . . .  P R E P A R E
```

d. Note also (at E29) the polygraph $\overset{4\,5\,1\,2\,3\,4}{I\ G\ V\ P\ W\ M}$, which looks like the word ATTACK.

```
A   T     K
```

The frequency distributions are consulted to see whether the frequencies given for $\overset{5}{G_c}$ and $\overset{2}{P_c}$ are high enough for T_p and A_p, respectively, and also whether the frequency of $\overset{3}{W_c}$ is good enough for C_p; it is noted that they are excellent. Moreover, the digraph $\overset{5\,1}{GB_c}$, which occurs four times, looks like TH_p, thus making $\overset{1}{B_c}=H_p$. Does the insertion of these four new values in our diagram of alphabets bring forth any inconsistencies? The insertion of the value $\overset{2}{P_c}=A_p$ and $\overset{1}{B_c}=H_p$ gives no indications either way, since neither letter has yet been located in any of the other alphabets. The insertion of the value $\overset{5}{G_c}=T_p$ gives a value common to Alphabets 3 and 5, for the value $\overset{3}{G_c}=E_p$ was assumed long ago. Unfortunately an inconsistency is found here. The letter $\overset{1}{I}$ has been placed two letters to the left of G in the mixed component, and has given good results in Alphabets 1 and 5; if the value $\overset{3}{W_c}=C_p$ (obtained above from the assumption of the word ATTACK) is correct, then W, and not I, should be the second letter to the left of G. Which shall be retained? There has been so far nothing to establish the value of $\overset{3}{G_c}=E_p$; this value was assumed from frequency considerations solely. Perhaps it is wrong. It certainly behaves like a vowel, and one may see what happens when one changes its value to O_p. The following placements in the reconstruction matrix result from the analysis, when only two or three new values have been added as a result of the clues afforded by the deductions:

Plain:	A	B	C	D	E	F	G	H	I	J	K	L	M	N	O	P	Q	R	S	T	U	V	W	X	Y	Z
1			S			I		G	B	C					M		P	Q	R	V	W					
2	P	Q	R	V	W								S			I		G	B	C					M	
Cipher: **3**	R	V	W								S			I		G	B	C					M		P	Q
4	I		G	B	C					M		P	Q	R	V	W								S		
5		M		P	Q	R	V	W								S			I		G	B	C			

e. Many new values are produced, and these are inserted throughout the message, yielding the following:

```
          5           10          15          20          25          30
A | Q W B R I   V W Y C A   I S P J L   R B Z E Y   Q W Y E U   L W M G W →
  | R E P O R   T E   E     E   M Y     S R         R E         E W C H
B | I C J C I   M T Z E I   M I B K N   Q W B R I   V W Y I G   B W N B Q  ←
  | E S   E R   O           R O O P     R E P O R   T E   A T   H E   D E
C | Q C G Q H   I W J K A   G E G X N   I D M R U   V E Z Y G   Q I G V N
  | R S O N     E E         G   O       E   W O     T           T R O O P
D | C T G Y O   B P D B L   V C G X G   B K Z Z G   I V X C U   N T Z A O
  | I   O       H A D       T S O   T   H       T   E D   E
E | B W F E Q   Q L F C O   M T Y Z T   C C B Y Q   O P D K A   G D G I G
  | H E   E     R   E       O         I S P   E     A           G   O A T
F | V P W M R   Q I I E W   I C G X G   B L G Q Q   V B G R S   M Y J J Y
  | T A C K F   R O M       H E S O   T H   O N E   T R O O P   O
G | Q V F W Y   R W N F L   G X N F W   M C J K X   I D D R U   O P J Q Q
  | R D   Q     S E         G           H O S       E   O       A   N E
H | Z R H C N   V W D Y Q   R D G D G   B X D B N   P X F P U   Y X N F G
  |   C E       T E         S O   T     H   D       Q   M           T
J | M P J E L   S A N C D   S E Z Z G   I B E Y U   K D H C A   M B J J F
  | O A         C   E C     T E R                   E           O R
K | K I L C J   M F D Z T   C T J R D   M I Y Z Q   A C J R R   S B G Z N
  |   O E       O       I     O         O O     E     S   O F   C R O
L | Q Y A H Q   V E D C Q   L X N C L   L V V C S   Q W B I I   I V J R N
  | R           E T   E E           E     D B E P   R E P A R   E D   O
M | W N B R I   V P J E L   T A G D N   I R G Q P   A T Y E W   C B Y Z T
  | U   P O R   T A         O           E C O N D         H I   R
N | E V G Q U   V P Y H L   L R Z N Q   X I N B A   I K W J Q   R D Z Y F
  |   D O N     T A         C     E     O   D       E       S
P | K W F Z L   G W F J Q   Q W J Y Q   I B W R X
  |   E         G E         E R E       E E   R O
```

32. Completing the solution.—*a.* Completion of solution is now a very easy matter. The mixed component is finally found to be the following sequence, based upon the word EXHAUSTING:

E X H A U S T I N G B C D F J K L M O P Q R V W Y Z

The completely reconstructed enciphering matrix is shown in Fig. 19.

Plain: A B C D E F G H I J K L M N O P Q R S T U V W X Y Z

Cipher:
```
1  A U S T I N G B C D F J K L M O P Q R V W Y Z E X H
2  P Q R V W Y Z E X H A U S T I N G B C D F J K L M O
3  R V W Y Z E X H A U S T I N G B C D F J K L M O P Q
4  I N G B C D F J K L M O P Q R V W Y Z E X H A U S T
5  L M O P Q R V W Y Z E X H A U S T I N G B C D F J K
```

FIGURE 19

b. Note that the successive equivalents of A_p spell the word APRIL, which is the specific key for the message. The plaintext message is as follows:

REPORTED ENEMY HAS RETIRED TO NEWCHESTER. ONE TROOP IS REPORTED AT HENDERSON MEETING HOUSE. TWO OTHER TROOPS IN ORCHARD AT SOUTHWEST EDGE OF NEWCHESTER. SECOND SQ IS PREPARING TO ATTACK FROM THE SOUTH. ONE TROOP OF THIRD SQ IS ENGAGING HOSTILE TROOP AT NEWCHESTER. REST OF THIRD SQ IS MOVING TO ATTACK NEWCHESTER FROM THE NORTH. MOVE YOUR SQ INTO WOODS EAST OF CROSSR[OADS] FIVE THREE NINE AND BE PREPARED TO SUPPORT ATTACK OF SECOND AND THIRD SQ. DO NOT ADVANCE BEYOND NEWCHESTER. MESSAGES HERE.

                                                         TREER, COL.

c. The preceding case is a good example of the value of the principles of direct symmetry of position when applied properly to a cryptogram enciphered by the sliding of a mixed component against the normal. The cryptanalyst starts off with only a very limited number of assumptions and builds up many new values as a result of the placement of the few original values in the reconstruction matrix.

33. Solution of subsequent messages enciphered by the same cipher component.—*a.* Let us suppose that the correspondents are using the same basic or primary components but with different key words for other messages. Can the knowledge of the sequence of letters in the reconstructed mixed primary component be used to solve the subsequent messages? It has been shown that in the case of a monoalphabetic cipher in which a mixed alphabet was used, the process of completing the plain-component sequence could be applied to solve subsequent messages in which the same components were used, even though the cipher component was set at a different key letter. A modification of the procedure used in that case can be used in this case, where a plurality of cipher alphabets based upon sliding primary components is used.

b. Let us suppose that the following message passing between the same two correspondents as in the preceding message has been intercepted:

SFDZR YRRKX MIWLL AQRLU RQFRT IJQKF XUWBS MDJZK MICQC UDPTV
TYRNH TRORV BQLTI QBNPR RTUHD PTIVE RMGQN LRATQ PLUKR KGRZF
JCMGP IHSMR GQRFX BCABA OEMTL PCXJM RGQSZ VB

c. The presence in this sized sample of a tetragraphic repetition whose interval is 21 letters suggests a key word of three or seven letters; the repeated trigraph at an interval of 28 makes seven the more probable hypothesis. There are very few other repetitions; this is to be expected in short messages with a key of such length.

62

d. Let the message be written in groups of seven letters, in columnar fashion, as shown in Fig. 20*a.* The letters in each column belong to a single alphabet. Let the first ten letters in each column be converted into their plain-component equivalents by setting the reconstructed cipher component against the normal plain component at any arbitrarily selected point, such as in the following alphabet:

Plain: A B C D E F G H I J K L M N O P Q R S T U V W X Y Z
Cipher: E X H A U S T I N G B C D F J K L M O P Q R V W Y Z

The columns of equivalents are now as shown in Fig. 20*b.*

```
1 2 3 4 5 6 7          1 2 3 4 5 6 7
S F D Z R Y R          F N M Z V Y V
R K X M I W L          V P B R H X Q
L A Q R L U R          Q D U V Q E V
Q F R T I J Q          U N V G H O U
K F X U W B S          P N B E X K F
M D J Z K M I          R M O Z P R H
C Q C U D P T          L U L E M T G
V T Y R N H T          W G Y V I C G
R O R V B Q L          V S V W K U Q
T I Q B N P R          G H U K I T V
R T U H D P T            FIGURE 20b
I V E R M G Q
N L R A T Q P
L U K R K G R
Z F J C M G P
I H S M R G Q
R F X B C A B
A O E M T L P
C X J M R G Q
S Z V B
   FIGURE 20a
```

e. It has been shown that in the case of a monoalphabetic cipher involving a mixed cipher component it was merely necessary to complete the normal alphabetic sequence beneath the plain-component equivalents and all the plain text reappeared on one generatrix. It was also found that in the case of a polyalphabetic cipher involving standard alphabets, the plaintext equivalents of each alphabet reappeared on the same generatrix, and it was necessary only to combine the proper generatrices in order to produce the plain text of the message. In the case at hand both processes are combined: the normal alphabetical sequence is continued beneath the letters of each column and then the generatrices are combined to produce the plain text. The generatrix diagrams for the first five alphabets (i.e., columns) are shown in Fig. 21, below. Only the first ten letters in each generatrix are used in the diagrams, since the application of the generatrix elimination and rough scoring procedures discussed in pars. 21*f* and *g* will yield a solution.

f. A trial of the generatrices with the highest scores in the first three alphabets yields the trigraphs shown in Fig. 22*a.* The generatrices of the subsequent columns are examined to

Gen.	Alphabet 1	Alphabet 2	Alphabet 3	Alphabet 4	Alphabet 5
	SRLQKMCVRT	FKAFFDQTOI	DXQRXJCYRQ	ZMRTUZURVB	RILIWKDNBN
1	1 FVQUPRLWVG	4 NPDNNMUGSH	1 MBUVBOLYVU	~~ZRVGEZEVWK~~	~~VHQHXPMIKI~~
2	~~GWRVQSMXWH~~	7 OQEOONVHTI	1 NCVWCPMZWV	3 ASWHFAFWXL	~~WIRIYQNJLJ~~
3	~~HXSWRTNYXI~~	3 PRFPPOWIUJ	~~ODWXDQNAXW~~	~~BTXIGBGXYM~~	~~XJSJZROKMK~~
4	~~IYTXSUOZYJ~~	~~QSGQQPXJVK~~	~~PEXYEROBYX~~	~~CUYJHCHYZN~~	~~YKTKASPLNL~~
5	~~JZUYTVPAZK~~	~~RTHRRQYKWL~~	~~QFYZFSPCZY~~	~~DVZKIDIZAO~~	~~ZLULBTQMOM~~
6	~~KAVZUWQBAL~~	~~SUISSRZLXM~~	~~RGZAGTQDAZ~~	~~EWALJEJABP~~	3 AMVMCURNPN
7	2 LBWAVXRCBM	6 TVJTTSAMYN	5 SHABHUREBA	~~FXBMKFKBCQ~~	5 BNWNDVSOQO
8	2 MCXBWYSDCN	~~UWKUUTBNZO~~	4 TIBCIVSFCB	2 GYCNLGLCDR	5 COXOEWTPRP
9	~~NDYCXZTEDO~~	2 VXLVVUCOAP	~~UJCDJWTGDC~~	3 HZDOMHMDES	~~DPYPFXUQSQ~~
10	4 OEZDYAUFEP	0 WYMWWVDPBQ	~~VKDEKXUHED~~	8 IAEPNINEFT	~~EQZQGYVRTR~~
11	~~PFAEZBVGFQ~~	~~XZNXXWEQCR~~	3 WLEFLYVIFE	~~JBFQOJOFGU~~	5 FRARHZWSUS
12	2 QGBFACWHGR	4 YAOYYXFRDS	~~XMFGMZWJGF~~	~~KCGRPKPGHV~~	6 GSBSIAXTVT
13	3 RHCGBDXIHS	~~ZBPZZYGSET~~	~~YNGHINAXKHG~~	~~LDHSQLQHIW~~	2 HTCTJBYUWU
14	5 SIDHCEYJIT	~~ACQAAZHTFU~~	4 ZOHIOBYLIH	~~MEITRMRIJX~~	~~IUDUKGZVXV~~
15	~~TJEIDFZKJU~~	3 BDRBBAIUGV	~~APIJPCZMJI~~	~~NFJUSNSJKY~~	2 JVEVLDAWYW
16	~~UKFJEGALKV~~	2 CESCCBJVHW	~~BQJKQDANKJ~~	~~OGKVTOTKLZ~~	~~KWFWMEBXZX~~
17	0 VLGKFHBMLW	~~DFTDDCKWIX~~	~~CRKLREBOLK~~	1 PHLWUPULMA	~~LXGXNFCYAY~~
18	2 WMHLGICNMX	~~EGUEEDLXJY~~	2 DSLMSFCPML	~~QIMXVQVMNB~~	~~MYHYOGDZBZ~~
19	~~XNIMHJDONY~~	~~FHVFFEMYKZ~~	5 ETMNTGDQNM	5 RJNYWRWNOC	~~NZIZPHEACA~~
20	~~YOJNIKEPOZ~~	3 GIWGGFNZLA	6 FUNOUHERON	~~SKOZXSXOPD~~	~~OAJAQIFBDB~~
21	~~ZPKOJLFQPA~~	~~HJXHHGOAMB~~	4 GVOPVIFSPO	4 TLPAYTYPQE	~~PBKBRJGCEC~~
22	~~AQLPKMGRQB~~	4 IKYIIHPBNC	~~HWPQWJGTQP~~	~~UMQBZUZQRF~~	~~QCLCSKHDFD~~
23	4 BRMQLNHSRC	~~JLZJJIQCOD~~	~~IXQRXKHURQ~~	6 VNRCAVARSG	5 RDMDTLIEGE
24	7 CSNRMOITSD	~~KMAKKJRDPE~~	5 JYRSYLIVSR	4 WOSDBWBSTH	4 SENEUMJFHF
25	6 DTOSNPJUTE	~~LNBLLKSEQF~~	~~KZSTZMJWTS~~	~~XPTECXCTUI~~	4 TFOFVNKGIG
26	~~EUPTOQKVUF~~	3 MOCMMLTFRG	~~LATUANKXUT~~	~~YQUFDYDUVJ~~	1 UGPGWOLHJH

FIGURE 21

select those which may be added to those already selected in order to build up the plain text. The results are shown in Fig. 22b. Note that, in this case, the correct generatrix for Alphabet 5 is not the one with the highest score (6), but one of the four generatrices with a score of 5. The generatrix process is a very valuable aid in the solution of messages after the primary components have been recovered as a result of the longer and more detailed analysis of the

```
1 2 3
C O F
S Q U
N E N
R O O
M O U
O N H
I V E
T H R
S T O
D I N
```

FIGURE 22a

```
1 2 3 4 5 6 7
C O F I R S T
S Q U A D R O
N E N E M Y T
R O O P D I S
M O U N T E D
O N H I L L F
I V E N I N E
T H R E E W E
S T O F G O O
D I N T E N T
```

FIGURE 22b

64

frequency distributions of the first message intercepted. Very often a short message can be solved in no other way than the one shown, if the primary components are completely known.

g. It may be of interest to find the key word for the message. Assuming that enciphering method number 1 (see subpar. 13*f*) is known to be employed, all that is necessary is to set the mixed component of the cipher alphabet underneath the plain component so as to produce the cipher letter indicated as the equivalent of any given plaintext letter in each of the alphabets. For example, in the first alphabet it is noted that $C_p = S_c$. Adjust the two components under each other so as to bring S of the cipher component beneath C of the plain component, thus:

```
Plain:   ABCDEFGHIJKLMNOPQRSTUVWXYZ
Cipher:  EXHAUSTINGBCDFJKLMOPQRVWYZEXHAUSTINGBCDFJKLMOPQRVWYZ
```

It is noted that $A_p = A_c$. Hence, the first letter of the key word to the message is A. The 2d, 3d, 4th, . . . 7th key letters are found in exactly the same manner, and the following is obtained:

```
When  C O F I R S T  equals
      S F D Z R Y R, then A_p successively equals
      A Z I M U T H
```

34. Statistical methods for the determination of correct generatrices.—*a.* The student has seen the advantages of the simple two-category weighting procedure, as demonstrated in subpars. 21*f* and *g*, over the method of ocular inspection. These advantages are that, first of all, the two-category weighting system is very easy to apply mentally, and, secondly, almost *any* scoring system will be more accurate (and *measurable*) than will a mere appraisal by eye which is subjective or intuitive in nature. This second point is especially true when the number of letters in the generatrices is small, that is, around 10 letters or so.

b. Instead of the system of two-category weights, it is possible to use the summation of the *relative frequencies* of plaintext letters to evaluate generatrices. For convenience in assigning whole numbers as the frequencies, the following scale (summing to 100) has been used:

```
7  1  3  4  13  3  2  3  7  0  0  4  2  8  8  3  0  8  6  9  3  2  2  0  2  0
A  B  C  D  E   F  G  H  I  J  K  L  M  N  O  P  Q  R  S  T  U  V  W  X  Y  Z
```

This system is only a trifle more sensitive than the two-category system, but the convenience of only two categories for mental arithmetic is lost. Besides, the two-category system actually involves *ratios* of the frequencies of the two classes of letters and in effect gives a *multiplication* of the weights of a generatrix, whereas the summation of the plaintext frequencies involves an *addition* of these frequencies which is not a precise statistical measure of the relative goodness of a generatrix. The summation of the relative frequencies of letters takes into account only the probability of occurrence of each letter in the generatrix, *considered separately*; that is, the occurrence of an E has a value of 13, regardless of whatever other letters are present in the same generatrix, and this value is *added* to the frequencies of the other letters.

c. If instead of the summation of the arithmetical frequencies, *logarithms* of the frequencies are used and these logarithms are added together, then a more nearly true picture of the generatrix is obtained. The reason underlying this fact is that the summation of logarithmic weights is equivalent to *multiplying* the probabilities of occurrence of all the letters in the generatrix taken together, thus giving an accurate evaluation of the generatrix *as a whole*. This method is especially valuable when generatrices contain as few as 5 or 6 letters. As an aid to the solution of problems wherein the plain component is a standard alphabet, a set of strips has been printed containing the normal sequence and the respective logarithmic weights over each letter. (If the plain component is any other sequence, strips would have to be prepared manually with that particular sequence inscribed.) The logarithmic weights on these strips are as follows:

```
8 4 7 7 9 6 5 7 8 1 2 7 6 8 8 6 2 8 8 9 6 5 5 3 6 0
A B C D E F G H I J K L M N O P Q R S T U V W X Y Z
```

The numbers on these strips are one-digit logarithms (to the base 133) of the relative frequencies of English plaintext letters as found in Table 3, Appendix 2, *Military Cryptanalytics, Part I*. For the interested student, the derivation of these one-digit logarithms will be discussed in the next two subparagraphs.

d. Let the following table be examined. Column (a) represents the uniliteral frequencies on a basis of 1000 letters; column (b) represents the logarithms (to the base 10) of these frequencies; column (c) contains the figures of the preceding column with the addition of .009 to each logarithm; column (d) is a conversion of the basic frequencies in column (a) to two-digit logarithms (base 133); and column (e) is a one-digit logarithmic weight based on the logarithms of the preceding column.

e. The addition of .009 to the common logarithms is for the purpose of transforming the letter of the lowest frequency (Z_p) to the value of .000 for convenience; this addition (which is

	(a)	(b)	(c)	(d)	(e)
A	73.7	1.868	1.877	.87	8
B	9.7	0.987	0.996	.41	4
C	30.7	1.487	1.496	.70	7
D	42.4	1.628	1.637	.76	7
E	130.0	2.113·	2.122	.99	9
F	28.3	1.452	1.461	.68	6
G	16.4	1.214	1.223	.57	5
H	33.9	1.530	1.539	.72	7
I	73.5	1.866	1.875	.87	8
J	1.64	0.214	0.223	.12	1
K	2.96	0.471	0.480	.22	2
L	36.4	1.560	1.569	.73	7
M	24.7	1.392	1.401	.65	6
N	79.5	1.900	1.909	.89	8
O	75.3	1.875	1.884	.88	8
P	26.7	1.427	1.436	.67	6
Q	3.50	0.544	0.553	.26	2
R	75.8	1.880	1.889	.88	8
S	61.2	1.787	1.796	.84	8
T	91.9	1.963	1.972	.92	9
U	26.0	1.415	1.424	.66	6
V	15.3	1.184	1.193	.56	5
W	15.6	1.192	1.201	.56	5
X	4.62	0.664	0.673	.31	3
Y	19.3	1.285	1.294	.61	6
Z	.98	0.991–10	0.000	.00	0

equivalent to an arithmetic multiplication) does not change the ratios between the basic frequencies. Now the highest frequency (E_p) is arbitrarily given the value .99 and all the other logarithms are then scaled proportionally down to Z_p which is 0: this is equivalent to expressing the frequencies in logarithms with a base other than 10, which in this case is 133. The new base (C) used to convert each of the uniliteral frequencies to the logarithmic range 0 to 0.99 is derived as follows, when 130 is the highest frequency (E_p):

$$\text{Let } 130 = C^{0.99}$$

$$\text{Log}_{10}\ 130 = \text{Log}_{10}\ C^{0.99}$$

$$\text{Log}_{10}\ 130 = (0.99)(\text{Log}_{10}\ C)$$

$$C = \text{Antilog}\ \frac{\text{Log}_{10}\ 130}{0.99} = \text{Antilog}\ \frac{2.122}{0.99}$$

$$C = 133$$

The formula for the computation of the logarithm to the new base (C) of any actual frequency (Y) of a series is:

$$\text{Log}_C Y = \frac{\text{Log}_{10} Y}{\text{Log}_{10} C}$$

It is more convenient to use reciprocals in the conversion of a whole series of logarithmic values, as in this instance. The formula is:

$$(\text{Log}_{10} Y)(\text{Log}_{10} C)^{-1} = \text{Log}_C Y$$

After these two-digit logarithms are derived, they are converted into one-digit logarithms by multiplying them by 10, dropping the single decimal.[1]

f. As an example of the sensitivity of these logarithmic weights, let us consider the generatrices of Alphabet 5 in Fig. 21. In this example, Generatrix No. 12 (an *incorrect* generatrix) had a two-category score of 6, and Generatrix Nos. 7, 8, 11, and 23 had scores of 5. If logarithmic weights had been used, these generatrices would have had the following scores:[2]

```
Gen. 12: G  S  B  S  I  A  X  T  V  T
         5  8  4  8  8  8  3  9  5  9 = 67
Gen.  7: B  N  W  N  D  V  S  O  Q  O
         4  8  5  8  7  5  8  8  2  8 = 63
Gen.  8: C  O  X  O  E  W  T  P  R  P
         7  8  3  8  9  5  9  6  8  6 = 69
Gen. 11: F  R  A  R  H  Z  W  S  U  S
         6  8  8  8  7  0  5  8  6  8 = 64
Gen. 23: R  D  M  D  T  L  I  E  G  E
         8  7  6  7  9  7  8  9  5  9 = 75
```

---

[1] Logarithms multiplied by 10 are called *decibans;* logarithms multiplied by 100 are called *centibans.* Logarithmic weights are usually expressed in decibans or centibans for convenience in treatment as integral values.

[2] It is interesting to determine the numerical expectation of the sum of the logarithmic weights for correct generatrices, as well as the expectation for incorrect ones—in other words, a sort of logarithmic ϕ test. The expected value for the correct (i.e., plaintext) generatrices is calculated by multiplying the logarithmic weights by the probabilities of each letter, summing the results; this sum is then multiplied by the number of letters in the generatrix to give the expected value of the sum of the logarithmic weights for the generatrix. The random expectation is the sum of the logarithmic weights in the scale (151) divided by 26, multiplied by the number of letters in the generatrix. Thus the plaintext expectation is 7.6N and the random expectation is 5.8N, where N is the number of letters in the generatrix.

The results clearly point to Generatrix No. 23 as the correct generatrix. Even if these generatrices had contained only six letters instead of 10, the logarithmic weights would have pointed to the correct generatrix.

g. In order to illustrate the degree of refinement between logarithmic weights and the arithmetical frequency weights mentioned in subpar. 34*b*, let us consider the following case. Below are the best generatrices from the first three alphabets of a seven-alphabet polyalphabetic cipher; the number at the left of the generatrices is the sum of the arithmetical weights, while the number to the right is the sum of the logarithmic weights.

Alphabet 1		Alphabet 2		Alphabet 3	
40 O I A G N N 45		40 Z O T W E N 39		32 H N H Z T N 39	
37 S M E K R R 41		35 O D I L T C 46		31 C I C U O I 44	
36 T N F L S S 46		32 D S X A I R 42		31 M S M E Y S 43	
34 B V N T A A 42				31 O U O G A U 41	
33 U O G M T T 43				29 S Y S K E Y 39	

It will be seen that, although the generatrix OIAGNN in Alphabet 1 has the highest arithmetic sum, nevertheless the most *probably* correct generatrix as shown by the logarithmic weights is TNFLSS. In Alphabet 2, the generatrix ODILTC has the highest probability of being the correct one; and in the third alphabet the logarithmic sum points to CICUOI as the most likely generatrix.[3] These generatrices when juxtaposed yield the following plaintext fragments, attesting to the validity of the selection:

```
T O C . . . .
N D I . . . .
F I C . . . .
L L U . . . .
S T O . . . .
S C I . . . .
```

h. In difficult cases wherein generatrices contain very few letters, one more statistical resource is available to the cryptanalyst. Suppose that in a certain short cryptogram the number of letters in each alphabet is only four, and that in this particular case the generatrix RTIS is selected from the generatrices for Alphabet 1. In Alphabet 2, the generatrices EINP, IMRT, and PTYA (logarithmic weights of 31, 31, and 29, respectively) appear to be the most likely candidates for the correct generatrix. The generatrix RTIS is juxtaposed against the three generatrices of the second alphabet, and now we record the logarithmic weights [4] of the digraphs thus formed, as follows:

RE	96	RI	75	RP	59
TI	82	TM	45	TT	67
IN	92	IR	73	IY	0
SP	55	ST	88	SA	71
	325		281		197

---

[3] In Alphabet 1, the difference between the logarithmic scores of OIAGNN (45) and TNFLSS (46) shows that the latter generatrix is $133^{0.1}=1.6$ times better than the first generatrix; in Alphabet 2, the difference (7) between the logarithmic scores of ZOTWEN and ODILTC shows that the latter is $133^{0.7}=31$ times better than the first generatrix; and in Alphabet 3, the difference (5) between the logarithmic scores of HNHZTN and CICUOI shows that the latter is $133^{0.5}=11$ times better than the first generatrix.

[4] These weights are taken from Table 15, Appendix 2, *Military Cryptanalytics, Part I*. The table gives two-digit logarithms to the base 224 of the digraphic frequencies of plain text; for convenience, these logarithms are treated here as centibans by dropping the decimal point. This logarithmic method is much more precise than a method wherein only the digraphic frequencies are used to obtain a score.

The logarithmic score of 325 points to the generatrix EINP as the most probable for Alphabet 2.[5] Thus the selection of the correct generatrices has been reduced to a purely statistical basis which is of great assistance in effecting a quick solution. Moreover, an understanding of the principles involved will be of considerable value in subsequent work.

35. Solution by the probable-word method.—*a*. Occasionally one may encounter a cryptogram which is so short that it contains no recurrences even of digraphs, and thus gives no indications of the number of alphabets involved. If the sliding mixed components are known, one may apply the methods illustrated in par. 22, assuming the presence of a probable word, checking it against the text and the sliding components to establish a key, if the correspondents are using key words.

b. For example, suppose that the presence of the word ENEMY is assumed in the message in subpar. 33*b* above. One proceeds to check it against an unknown key word, sliding the already reconstructed mixed component against the normal and starting with the first letter of the cryptogram, in this manner:

> When   ENEMY   equals
> SFDZR, then A_p successively equals
> XENFW

The sequence XENFW spells no intelligible word. Therefore, the location of the assumed word ENEMY is shifted one letter forward in the cipher text, and the test is made again, just as was explained in subpar. 22*d*. When the group AQRLU is tried, the key letters ZIMUT are obtained, which, taken as a part of a word, suggest the word AZIMUTH. The method must yield solution when the correct assumptions are made.

c. The placement of probable words in polyalphabetic ciphers may be facilitated by considering (1) the *frequency patterns* of the letters composing cribs, and (2) the *partial idiomorphisms* which may be produced in the periodic encipherment of certain cribs.

(1) For instance, in the first case, the plaintext frequency pattern of the word CAVALRY has a distinctive relative high- (H), medium- (M), and low-frequency (L) pattern of MHLHMHL; if the individual monoalphabetic frequencies of a periodic cipher are written over the cipher letters of a cryptogram, possible placements for the word CAVALRY might be seen. It is important to note that, although the frequencies of high- and medium-frequency plaintext letters might be distorted in a polyalphabetic cryptogram, it is not expected that *low-frequency* letters will be changed appreciably; therefore these low-frequency letters are a more accurate guide to crib-placing than are the other letters. It goes without saying that polygraphic repetitions may be used as a basis on which to assume probable words, depending on the length of the polygraphs; these repetitions, together with the frequency pattern of the cipher letters composing the repetitions, form one of the most valuable means of plaintext entries in a cryptogram.

(2) The aspect of partial idiomorphism is based on the fact that, if there is a pair of repeated letters at a distance of N in a plaintext word, this idiomorphism will show through in the cipher when there has been a polyalphabetic encipherment of a period of length N (or a factor of N). For example, if the word DIVISION is enciphered by a polyalphabetic substitution of four alphabets, the first and third I_p must of necessity be represented by the same ciphertext equivalent. Thus if in a four-alphabet system an A...A pattern is found in the cipher text, reference may be made to compilations of words containing like letters repeated

---

[5] The generatrix EINP is better than IMRT by a factor of $224^{(3.25-2.81)} = 224^{0.44} = 11$; likewise, the generatrix EINP is better than PTYA by a factor of $224^{(3.25-1.97)} = 224^{1.28} = 1019$. (For an additional example of digraphic weighting, see also subpar. 81*f*(3).)

at various intervals,[6] and under the listing of "A(3)A" will be found DIVISION, among other words, which may be used as possible assumptions.

36. Solution when the plain component is a mixed sequence, the cipher component, the normal.—*a*. This falls under Case II*b* outlined in par. 8.   It is not the usual method of employing a single mixed component, but may be encountered occasionally in cipher devices.

b. The preliminary steps, as regards factoring to determine the length of the period, are the same as usual.   The message is then transcribed into its periods.   Frequency distributions are then made, as usual, and these are attacked by the principles of frequency and recurrence. An attempt is made to apply the principles of direct symmetry of position as demonstrated thus far, but this attempt will be futile, for the reason that the plain component is in this case an *unknown* mixed sequence.   Any attempt to find symmetry in the secondary alphabets based upon the normal sequence for the plain component can therefore disclose no symmetry because the symmetry which exists is based upon a wholly different sequence.

c. However, if the usual principles of direct symmetry of position are of no avail in this case, there are certain other principles of symmetry which may be employed to great advantage. To explain them an actual example will be used.   Let it be assumed that it is known to the cryptanalyst that the enemy is using the general system under discussion, *viz.*, a mixed sequence, variable from day to day, is used as the plain component; the normal sequence is used as the cipher component; and a repeating key, variable from message to message, is used in the ordinary manner.   The following message has been intercepted:

```
           5          10          15          20          25          30
A.  Q E O V K   L R M L Z   J V G T G   N D L V K   E V N T Y   E R M U E
B.  V R Z M O   Y A A M P   D K E I J   S F M Y O   Y H M M E   G Q A M B
C.  U Q A X R   H U F B U   K Q Y M U   N E L V T   K Q I L E   K Z B U E
D.  U L I B K   N D A X B   X U D G L   L A D V K   P O A Y O   D K K Y K
E.  L A D H Y   B V N F V   U E E M E   F F M T E   G V W B Y   T V D Z L
F.  S P B H B   X V A Z C   U D Y U E   L K M M A   E U D D K   N C F S H
G.  H S A H Y   T M G U J   H Q X P P   D K O U E   X U Q V B   F V W B X
H.  N X A L B   T C D L M   I V A A A   N S Z I L   O V W V P   Y A G Z L
J.  S H M M E   G Q D H O   Y H I V P   N C R R E   X K D Q Z   G K N C G
K.  N Q G U Y   J I W Y Y   T M A H W   X R L B L   O A D L G   N Q G U Y
L.  J U U G B   J H R V X   E R F L E   G W G U O   X E D T P   D K E I Z
M.  V X N W A   F A A N E   M K G H B   S S N L O   K J C B Z   T G G L O
N.  P K M B X   H G E R Y   T M W L Z   N Q C Y Y   T M W I P   D K A T E
P.  F L N U J   N D T V X   J R Z T L   O P A H C   D F Z Y Y   D E Y C L
Q.  G P G T Y   T E C X B   H Q E B R   K V W M U   N I N G J   I Q D L P
R.  J K A T E   G U W B R   H U Q W M   V R Q B W   Y R F B F   K M W M B
S.  T M U L Z   L A A H Y   J G D V K   L K R R E   X K N A O   N D S B X
T.  X C G Z A   H D G T L   V K M B W   I S A U E   F D N W P   N L Z I J
U.  S R Q Z L   A V N H L   G V W V K   F I G H P   G E C Z U   K Q A P
```

[6] In this connection, see Appendix 3.

d. A study of the repetitions and of the factors of their intervals discloses that five alphabets are involved. Uniliteral frequency distributions are made and are shown in Fig. 23*a*:

Alphabet 1

Alphabet 2

Alphabet 3

Alphabet 4

Alphabet 5

FIGURE 23*a*

e. Since the cipher component in this case is the normal alphabet, *it follows that the five frequency distributions are based upon a sequence which is known, and therefore, the five frequency distributions should manifest a direct symmetry of distribution of crests and troughs.* By virtue of this symmetry and by shifting the five distributions relative to one another to proper superimpositions, the several distributions may be combined into a single uniliteral distribution.

Note how this shifting has been done in the case of the five illustrative distributions:

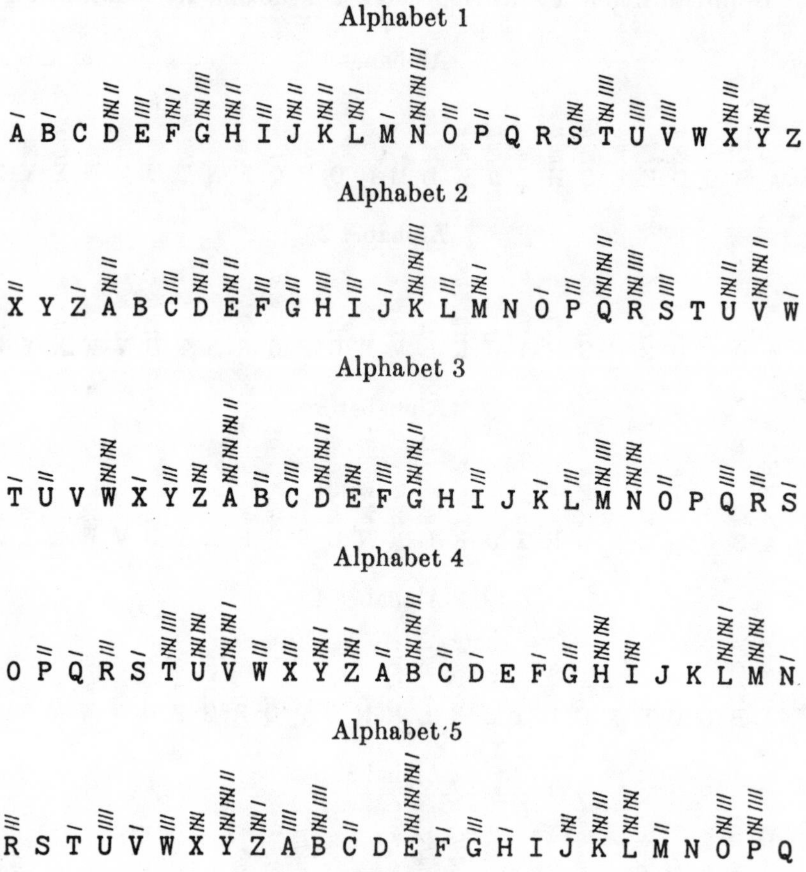

Alphabet 1

A B C D E F G H I J K L M N O P Q R S T U V W X Y Z

Alphabet 2

X Y Z A B C D E F G H I J K L M N O P Q R S T U V W

Alphabet 3

T U V W X Y Z A B C D E F G H I J K L M N O P Q R S

Alphabet 4

O P Q R S T U V W X Y Z A B C D E F G H I J K L M N

Alphabet 5

R S T U V W X Y Z A B C D E F G H I J K L M N O P Q

FIGURE 23b

f. The superimposition of the respective distributions enables one to convert the cipher letters of the five alphabets into one alphabet. Suppose it is decided to convert Alphabets 2, 3, 4, and 5 into terms of Alphabet 1. It is merely necessary to substitute for the respective letters in the four alphabets those which stand above them in Alphabet 1. For example, in Fig. 23b, X_c in Alphabet 2 is directly under A_c in Alphabet 1; hence, if the superimposition is correct then $X_c = A_c$. Therefore, in the cryptogram it is merely necessary to replace every X_c in the second position by A_c. Again T_c in Alphabet 3 = A_c in Alphabet 1; therefore in the cryptogram one replaces every T_c in the third position by A_c. The entire process, hereinafter designated as *reduction to monoalphabetic terms*, gives the following converted cipher text:

```
             5           10          15          20          25          30
A.  Q H V H T   L U T X I   J Y N F P   N G S H T   E Y U F H   E U T G N
B.  V U G Y X   Y D H Y Y   D N L U S   S I T K X   Y K T Y N   G T H Y K
C.  U T H J A   H X M N D   K T F Y D   N H S H C   K T P X N   K C I G N
D.  U O P N T   N G H J K   X X K S U   L D K H T   P R H K X   D N R K T
E.  L D K T H   B Y U R E   U H L Y N   F I T F N   G Y D N H   T Y K L U
F.  S S I T K   X Y H L L   U G F G N   L N T Y J   E X K P T   N F M E Q
G.  H V H T H   T P N G S   H T E B Y   D N V G N   X X X H K   F Y D N G
H.  N A H X K   T F K X V   I Y H M J   N V G U U   O Y D H Y   Y D N L U
J.  S K T Y N   G T K T X   Y K P H Y   N F Y D N   X N K C I   G N U O P
K.  N T N G H   J L D K H   T P H T F   X U S N U   O D K X P   N T N G H
L.  J X B S K   J K Y H G   E U M X N   G Z N G X   X H K F Y   D N L U I
M.  V A U I J   F D H Z N   M N N T K   S V U X X   K M J N I   T J N X X
N.  P N T N G   H J L D H   T P D X I   N T J K H   T P D U Y   D N H F N
P.  F O U G S   N G A H G   J U G F U   O S H T L   D I G K H   D H F O U
Q.  G S N F H   T H J J K   H T L N A   K Y D Y D   N L U S S   I T K X Y
R.  J N H F N   G X D N A   H X X I V   V U X N F   Y U M N O   K P D Y K
S.  T P B X I   L D H T H   J J K H T   L N Y D N   X N U M X   N G Z N G
T.  X F N L J   H G N F U   V N T N F   I V H G N   F G U I Y   N O G U S
U.  S U X L U   A Y U T U   G Y D H T   F L N T Y   G H J L D   K T H B
```

g. The uniliteral frequency distribution for this converted text follows. Note that the frequency of each letter is the sum of the five frequencies in the corresponding columns of Fig. 23*b*.

A	B	C	D	E	F	G	H	I	J	K	L	M	N	O	P	Q	R	S	T	U	V	W	X	Y	Z
7	5	3	31	7	25	36	54	17	21	38	22	8	69	9	15	2	3	19	48	38	12		38	39	3

FIGURE 24

The problem having been reduced to monoalphabetic terms, solution is readily attained by the application of simple principles; [7] the beginning of the message is found to read as follows:

JAPAN CONSULTED GERMANY TODAY ON REPORTS THAT THE COMMUNIST...

h. The reconstruction of the plain component is now a very simple matter. It is found to be as follows:

H Y D R A U L I C B E F G J K M N O P Q S T V W X Z

Note also, in Fig. 23*b*, the key word for the message, HEAVY, the letters being in the columns headed by the letter H.

i. The solution of subsequent messages with different keys can now be reached directly, by a simple modification of the principles explained in par. 33. This modification consists in using for the completion sequence the *mixed plain component* (now known) instead of the normal alphabet, after the cipher letters have been converted into their plain-component equivalents. Let the student confirm this by experiment.

j. The probable-word method of solution discussed under par. 22 is also applicable here, in case of very short cryptograms. This method presupposes, of course, possession of the mixed component and the procedure is essentially the same as that in par. 22. In the example discussed in the present paragraph, the letter A on the plain component was successively set against the key letters HEAVY; but this is not the only possible procedure.

k. The student should go over carefully the principle of "reduction to monoalphabetic terms" explained in subpar. *f* above until he thoroughly understands it. Later on he will encounter cases in which this principle is of very great assistance in the cryptanalysis of more complex problems.

l. The principle illustrated in subpar. *e*, above, that is, shifting two or more monoalphabetic frequency distributions relatively so as to bring them into proper alignment for amalgamation into a single monoalphabetic distribution, is called *matching*. It is a very important cryptanalytic principle. Note that its practical application consists in sliding one monoalphabetic distribution against the other so as to obtain the best coincidence between the *entire sequence* of crests and troughs of the other distribution. When the best point of coincidence has been found, the two sequences may be amalgamated and *theoretically* the single resultant distribution will also be monoalphabetic in character. The successful application of the principle of matching depends upon several factors. First, the cryptographic situation must be such that matching is a correct cryptanalytic step. For example, the distributions in Fig. 23*a* are properly subject to matching because the cipher component in the basic sequences concerned in this problem is the normal sequence, while the plain component is a mixed sequence. But it would be futile to try to match the distributions in subpar. 29*c*, for in that case the cipher component is a mixed sequence, the plain component is the normal sequence. Hence, no

---

[7] An interesting technique is possible at this point to recover the key word for the plain component from the composite uniliteral frequency distribution of the cipher text at one fell swoop, if the plain component is a keyword-mixed sequence. Note the distribution in Fig. 24. If this represents the "profile" of a keyword-mixed sequence, then it appears that the key word begins at D_c, with the letters Z_c, A_c, B_c, C_c, being the equivalents of four of the five plaintext letters VWXYZ. Q_c and R_c are obviously J_p and K_p, respectively; and $W_c = Q_p$. The sequence $STUV_c$ represents either $LNOP_p$ or $MNOP_p$; XY_c must be two of the letters RST_p. If $N_c = E_p$, then $OP_c = FG_p$; M_c is probably B_p, thus delineating the key word of 9 letters beginning at D_c. From this analysis it can be conjectured that the key word contains the letters A, C, D, H, I, U, one from the group LM, one from the group RST, and probably Y (for a more likely percentage of vowels). From this point on, anagramming of the key word presents no problem.

amount of shifting or matching can bring the distributions of subpar. 29c into proper superimposition for correct amalgamation.   (If the occurrences in the various distributions in subpar. 29c had been distributed according to the sequence of letters in the mixed component, then matching would be possible; but in order to be able to distribute these occurrences according to the mixed component, the latter has to be *known*—and that is just what is unknown until the problem has been solved.)   A second factor involved in successful matching is the number of elements in the two distributions forming the subject of the test.   If both of them have very few tallies, there is hardly sufficient information to permit matching by eye with any degree of assurance that the work is not in vain.   If one of them has many tallies, the other only a few, the chances for success are better than before, because the positions of the *blanks* in the two distributions can be used as a guide for their proper superimposition.   Fortunately, there exist certain mathematical and statistical procedures which can be brought to bear upon the matter of cryptanalytic matching.   One of these, involving the χ (chi) test, will be discussed in par. 37.

m. The normal conditions existing that permit the exploitation of direct symmetry of position in polyalphabetic ciphers are those cases already treated wherein the plain component is a known sequence.   In such examples the sequence of the plain component is inscribed along the top of the sequence reconstruction matrix, and direct symmetry will manifest itself among the cipher components within the matrix.   When the inverse conditions are present, i.e., those cases wherein the cipher component is a known sequence and the plain component unknown, the usual method of solution is, of course, the matching of distributions and the conversion of the cryptogram to monoalphabetic terms.   However, when the number of elements in the distribution is very small, this method is inapplicable, and the only feasible solution involves the assumption of probable words.   If the usual type of matrix is made (with an A to Z sequence outside for the plain component), only *indirect symmetry of position* [8] will be manifested.   But if an inverse matrix is made having the known *cipher* component on the outside, then *direct* symmetry will be evident among the various plain-component alphabets.   We will now consider an example to illustrate this technique.

(1) Let it be assumed that the enemy has been using for his low-echelon cryptosystems a small cipher disk in which the cipher component is a standard alphabet, the plain component a mixed sequence which is changed daily.   The following is the beginning of an intercepted message, the remaining portion having been lost through operational difficulties:

```
K O L N T   E Q Z D F   I X K T K   X K Y M B   J J G B R   H R T A F
R W W V C   F M K B Y   Q B D T . . .
```

This message having originated from a headquarters that has frequently been guilty of stereotypic phraseology, it is suspected that the plain text begins with the opening phrase "REFERENCE YOUR MESSAGE NUMBER . . ."   Superimposing the assumed plain text against the cipher text,

```
          5          10          15          20          25
     K O L N T E Q Z D F I X K T K X K Y M B J J G B R H
     R E F E R E N C E Y O U R M E S S A G E N U M B E R,
```

[8] Indirect symmetry of position will be taken up in the next chapter.

it is observed that R_p is enciphered as K_c at the first and thirteenth positions, thereby tentatively establishing the period-length as 12:

```
K O L N T E Q Z D F I X
R E F E R E N C E Y O U

K T K X K Y M B J J G B
R M E S S A G E N U M B

R H R T A F R W W V C F
E R

M K B Y Q B D T . . .
```

The student will observe that all other periods from 2 to 14 are ruled out because of coincidences in the plain text which are not substantiated by like coincidences in the cipher for the assumed period-length. For example, the blocks for the periods 9, 10, and 11 yield the following:

```
       (9)                  (10)                    (11)
R E F E R E N C E     R E F E R E N C E Y     R E F E R E N C E Y O
Y O U R M E S S A     O U R M E S S A G E     U R M E S S A G E N U
G E N U M B E R       N U M B E R             M B E R
```

(2) An inverse matrix is made, and the *plaintext* values from the plain-cipher relationships above are inscribed within the matrix, as follows:

	A	B	C	D	E	F	G	H	I	J	K	L	M	N	O	P	Q	R	S	T	U	V	W	X	Y	Z
1	.	.	.	.	.	.	.	.	R	.	.	.	.	.	E	.	.	.	.	.	.	.	.	.	.	.
2	.	.	.	.	.	.	R	.	.	.	.	E	.	.	M	.	.	.	.	.	.	.	.	.	.	.
3	.	.	.	.	.	.	.	E	F	.	.	.	.	.	.	.	.	.	.	.	.	.	.	.	.	.
4	.	.	.	.	.	.	.	.	.	E	.	.	.	.	.	.	.	.	.	S	.	.	.	.	.	.
5	.	.	.	.	.	.	.	.	S	.	.	.	.	.	.	.	R	.	.	.	.	.	A	.	.	.
6	.	.	.	E	.	.	.	.	.	.	.	.	.	.	.	.	.	.	.	.	.	.	.	A	.	.
7	.	.	.	.	.	.	.	.	G	.	.	N	.	.	.	.	.	.	.	.	.	.	.	.	.	.
8	.	E	.	.	.	.	.	.	.	.	.	.	.	.	.	.	.	.	.	.	.	.	.	.	.	C
9	.	.	E	.	.	.	.	N	.	.	.	.	.	.	.	.	.	.	.	.	.	.	.	.	.	.
10	.	.	.	Y	.	.	.	U	.	.	.	.	.	.	.	.	.	.	.	.	.	.	.	.	.	.
11	.	.	.	.	M	O	.	.	.	.	.	.	.	.	.	.	.	.	.	.	.	.	.	.	.	.
12	.	B	.	.	.	.	.	.	.	.	.	.	.	.	.	.	.	.	.	.	.	.	.	U	.	.

Plain: (rows 1–12)
Cipher: A B C D E F G H I J K L M N O P Q R S T U V W X Y Z

76

After application of the principles of direct symmetry of position, the matrix will now look like this:

Plain:

```
 1 | . S . . . . . . . R A . . . C . E F G . . M N O .
 2 | . . . . . . . R A . . . C . E F G . . M N O . . S .
 3 | . . . R A . . . C . E F G . . M N O . . S . . . . .
 4 | . . . . . . R A . . . C . E F G . . M N O . . S . .
 5 | E F G . . M N O . . S . . . . . . . . R A . . . C .
 6 | . . C . E F G . . M N O . . S . . . . . . . . R A .
 7 | . . . R A . . . C . E F G . . M N O . . S . . . . .
 8 | . E F G . . M N O . . S . . . . . . . R A . . . C
 9 | . C . E F G . . M N O . . S . . . . . . . R A . .
10 | . . . . . Y . . U . . . B . . . . . . . . . . . . .
11 | . E F G . . M N O . . S . . . . . . . . R A . . . C
12 | . B . . . . . . . . . . . . . . . . . . Y . . U . .
```

Cipher: A B C D E F G H I J K L M N O P Q R S T U V W X Y Z

When these new derived values are substituted in the cryptogram,

```
K O L N T E Q Z D F I X
R E F E R E N C E Y O U

K T K X K Y M B J J G B
R M E S S A G E N U M B

R H R T A F R W W V C F
E R O N E F O   R   F

M K B Y Q B D T
              R
```

the U_p of the segment ONE FOUR in the third line permits the amalgamation of the two partial sequences into one, *viz.*:

```
R A U . . C B E F G . . M N O . . S . . . . . Y .
```

(3) With but little further experimentation, we can synthesize the entire plain text and find the plain component to be based on HYDRAULIC. The complete message fragment is now as follows:

```
K O L N T E Q Z D F I X
R E F E R E N C E Y O U

K T K X K Y M B J J G B
R M E S S A G E N U M B

R H R T A F R W W V C F
E R O N E F O U R O F J

M K B Y Q B D T
U L Y T H I R D
```

77

There is no evidence of a key word for the repeating key in the inverse matrix; but if the matrix is rewritten in the usual enciphering form, the key word HEADQUARTERS will be apparent under H_p. Thus:

Plain: H Y D R A U L I C B E F G J K M N O P Q S T V W X Z

Cipher:

1	H	I	J	K	L	M	N	O	P	Q	R	S	T	U	V	W	X	Y	Z	A	B	C	D	E	F	G
2	E	F	G	H	I	J	K	L	M	N	O	P	Q	R	S	T	U	V	W	X	Y	Z	A	B	C	D
3	A	B	C	D	E	F	G	H	I	J	K	L	M	N	O	P	Q	R	S	T	U	V	W	X	Y	Z
4	D	E	F	G	H	I	J	K	L	M	N	O	P	Q	R	S	T	U	V	W	X	Y	Z	A	B	C
5	Q	R	S	T	U	V	W	X	Y	Z	A	B	C	D	E	F	G	H	I	J	K	L	M	N	O	P
6	U	V	W	X	Y	Z	A	B	C	D	E	F	G	H	I	J	K	L	M	N	O	P	Q	R	S	T
7	A	B	C	D	E	F	G	H	I	J	K	L	M	N	O	P	Q	R	S	T	U	V	W	X	Y	Z
8	R	S	T	U	V	W	X	Y	Z	A	B	C	D	E	F	G	H	I	J	K	L	M	N	O	P	Q
9	T	U	V	W	X	Y	Z	A	B	C	D	E	F	G	H	I	J	K	L	M	N	O	P	Q	R	S
10	E	F	G	H	I	J	K	L	M	N	O	P	Q	R	S	T	U	V	W	X	Y	Z	A	B	C	D
11	R	S	T	U	V	W	X	Y	Z	A	B	C	D	E	F	G	H	I	J	K	L	M	N	O	P	Q
12	S	T	U	V	W	X	Y	Z	A	B	C	D	E	F	G	H	I	J	K	L	M	N	O	P	Q	R

37. The χ (chi) test for evaluating the relative matching of distributions.—*a.* The student by now is well familiar with the ϕ test which is used to determine the monoalphabeticity of a single distribution. If two messages were enciphered monoalphabetically by the same cipher alphabet, it follows not only that their corresponding distributions would be monoalphabetic, but also that these distributions would be strikingly similar in respect to their corresponding peaks and troughs. Likewise, if in a polyalphabetic cipher there are repeated letters in the key, then the distributions appertaining to the repeated letters will show identical spatial relationships of the positions of the peaks and troughs. Furthermore, in situations wherein the cipher component is a standard alphabet (or any other *known* sequence), these spatial relationships are relative and require only the correct juxtaposition of the distributions to make the relationships absolute. When the number of tallies in the distributions is large, matching by eye is a simple matter; however if the number of tallies is small, ocular matching becomes difficult and recourse must be had to statistical means for evaluating the relative matching of distributions.

b. One of the simplest means for determining the relative matching or nonmatching attributes of distributions is the χ (*chi*) *test*, sometimes called the "cross-products sum test." With this test, which is related to the ϕ test,[9] the "observed value of χ" (symbolized by χ_o) is compared with the "expected value of χ for matching distributions" (symbolized by χ_m) and the "expected value of χ for nonmatching distributions" (symbolized by χ_r). The formulas used for the expected values of χ for matching and nonmatching distributions, respectively, are

$$\chi_m = .0667(N_1 N_2) \text{ and } \chi_r = .0385(N_1 N_2),$$

where $(N_1 N_2)$ represents the product of the total number of tallies in each distribution. The observed value of χ is calculated by multiplying the frequency of each element in the first distribution by its homologous counterpart in the second distribution, and totalling the result; i.e., the frequency of A_c in the first distribution is multiplied by the frequency of A_o in the second distribution, etc., and then the sum of these cross products is obtained. Mathematically, this is expressed by the formula $\chi_o = \Sigma f_i f_i'$.

---

[9] The ϕ and χ tests were first described by Dr. Solomon Kullback in *Statistical Methods in Cryptanalysis.*

78

c. The use of the χ test is best illustrated by an example. Suppose the following two distributions are to be matched:

No. 1: A B C D E F G H I J K L M N O P Q R S T U V W X Y Z

No. 2: A B C D E F G H I J K L M N O P Q R S T U V W X Y Z

Now let the frequencies be juxtaposed, for convenience in finding the cross products, thus:

f_1------ 1 4 0 3 0 1 0 0 1 0 0 1 0 0 1 0 0 3 2 2 1 0 1 3 0 2 $N_1 = 26$
       A B C D E F G H I J K L M N O P Q R S T U V W X Y Z
f_2------ 0 2 0 0 0 3 0 0 1 0 1 0 0 1 1 0 0 3 1 1 0 0 0 0 1 2 $N_2 = 17$
$f_1 f_2$---- 0 8 0 0 0 3 0 0 1 0 0 0 0 0 1 0 0 9 2 2 0 0 0 0 0 4 $\Sigma f_1 f_2 = 30 = \chi_o$

$$\chi_m = .0667(26 \times 17) = 29.5; \quad \chi_r = .0385(26 \times 17) = 17$$

The fact that the observed value of χ, 30, agrees very closely with the expected value for matching distributions, 29.5, means that the two distributions very probably belong together or are properly matched. Note the qualifying phrase "very probably." It implies that there is uncertainty about this business of matching distributions by statistical methods; the arithmetic serves only as a measuring device, so to speak, which can be employed to measure the degree of similarity that exists. There are other statistical tests for matching, in addition to the χ test.[10] Moreover, it is possible to go further with the χ test and find a measure of reliance that may be placed upon the value obtained; but these points will be left for discussion in the next text.

d. One more point will, however, here be added in connection with the χ test. Suppose the very same two distributions in the preceding subparagraph are again juxtaposed, with f_2 shifted one interval to the left of the position shown above, and let us take the cross-products sum. Thus:

f_1------ 1 4 0 3 0 1 0 0 1 0 0 1 0 0 1 0 0 3 2 2 1 0 1 3 0 2 $N = 26$
       A B C D E F G H I J K L M N O P Q R S T U V W X Y Z
f_2------ 2 0 0 0 3 0 0 1 0 1 0 0 1 1 0 0 3 1 1 0 0 0 0 1 2 0 $N = 17$
       B C D E F G H I J K L M N O P Q R S T U V W X Y Z A
$f_1 f_2$---- 2 0 0 0 0 0 0 0 0 0 0 0 0 0 0 0 0 3 2 0 0 0 0 0 3 0 0 $\Sigma f_1 f_2 = 10 = \chi_o$

Since the observed value of χ, 10, more closely approximates the expected value of χ for nonmatching distributions, 17, it may be concluded that if the two distributions pertain to the same primary components they are not properly superimposed. In other words, the χ test may also be applied in cases where two or more frequency distributions must be shifted relatively in order to find their correct superimposition. The theory underlying this application of the χ test is, of course, the same as before: two monoalphabetic distributions when properly combined will yield a single distribution which should still be monoalphabetic in character. In applying the χ test in such cases it may be necessary to shift two 26-element distributions to various superimpositions, make the χ test for each superimposition, and take as correct that one which yields the best value for the test. The nature of the problem will, of course, determine whether the frequency distributions which are to be matched should be compared (1) by direct

---

[10] The most important of these is the chi-square test, based on the χ^2 distribution.

superimposition, that is, setting the A to Z tallies of one distribution directly opposite the corresponding tallies of the other distribution, as in subpar. *c*; or (2) by shifted superimposition, that is, keeping the A to Z tallies of the first distribution fixed and sliding the whole sequence of tallies of the second distribution to various superimpositions against the first.

e. A very common method of expressing the relative matching quality of a pair of distributions involves the ratio of the observed χ to the expected value for χ_r. This ratio of $\frac{\chi_o}{\chi_r}$ is called the "cross I.C." (abbr. ξ I.C.). The cross I.C. is usually the preferred expression, rather than the χ value, since the ratio gives a quick measure (when compared with the expected ξ I.C.'s of 1.73 and 1.00 for matching and nonmatching distributions, respectively) of the relative goodness of a particular matching. For instance, in the example given in subpar. *c*, the ξ I.C. of the two distributions is $\frac{30}{17} = 1.76$; in the example in subpar. *d*, the ξ I.C. is $\frac{10}{17} = 0.59$.

The ordinary monographic I.C., i.e., $\frac{\phi_o}{\phi_r}$, is often referred to as the δ I.C. (read "delta I.C."), in order to distinguish between this and other I.C.'s such as the cross I.C.

38. Modified Porta systems.—*a*. Variations of the Porta system are possible, wherein either the A–M sequence is left undisturbed and the N–Z portion is mixed, or the A–M portion is mixed and the N–Z sequence is the normal; these situations are exemplified in Figs. 25*a* and *b*, below:

	A	B	C	D	E	F	G	H	I	J	K	L	M
AB	S	P	U	R	T	N	O	Q	V	W	X	Y	Z
CD	P	U	R	T	N	O	Q	V	W	X	Y	Z	S
EF	U	R	T	N	O	Q	V	W	X	Y	Z	S	P
GH	R	T	N	O	Q	V	W	X	Y	Z	S	P	U
IJ	T	N	O	Q	V	W	X	Y	Z	S	P	U	R
KL	N	O	Q	V	W	X	Y	Z	S	P	U	R	T
MN	O	Q	V	W	X	Y	Z	S	P	U	R	T	N
OP	Q	V	W	X	Y	Z	S	P	U	R	T	N	O
QR	V	W	X	Y	Z	S	P	U	R	T	N	O	Q
ST	W	X	Y	Z	S	P	U	R	T	N	O	Q	V
UV	X	Y	Z	S	P	U	R	T	N	O	Q	V	W
WX	Y	Z	S	P	U	R	T	N	O	Q	V	W	X
YZ	Z	S	P	U	R	T	N	O	Q	V	W	X	Y

FIGURE 25*a*

	F	L	A	M	E	B	C	D	G	H	I	J	K
AB	N	O	P	Q	R	S	T	U	V	W	X	Y	Z
CD	O	P	Q	R	S	T	U	V	W	X	Y	Z	N
EF	P	Q	R	S	T	U	V	W	X	Y	Z	N	O
GH	Q	R	S	T	U	V	W	X	Y	Z	N	O	P
IJ	R	S	T	U	V	W	X	Y	Z	N	O	P	Q
KL	S	T	U	V	W	X	Y	Z	N	O	P	Q	R
MN	T	U	V	W	X	Y	Z	N	O	P	Q	R	S
OP	U	V	W	X	Y	Z	N	O	P	Q	R	S	T
QR	V	W	X	Y	Z	N	O	P	Q	R	S	T	U
ST	W	X	Y	Z	N	O	P	Q	R	S	T	U	V
UV	X	Y	Z	N	O	P	Q	R	S	T	U	V	W
WX	Y	Z	N	O	P	Q	R	S	T	U	V	W	X
YZ	Z	N	O	P	Q	R	S	T	U	V	W	X	Y

FIGURE 25*b*

In such situations, after factoring, approximately 50% of the cipher text may be reduced to monoalphabetic terms, while in the other 50% there will be manifested direct symmetry of position; this is best illustrated by an example.

80

b. Let the following cryptogram and its accompanying distributions be studied:

```
W P A V V    Q E X G J    K R A S G    R D B S N    S I D I Z    H P C T Q
C D L G F    T H Y G K    E I D D J    R M Q A J    K U O T V    Z W R F F
H N O O Z    E T D J K    S M N G K    E H A C X    I N D F R    J E A G P
H P K A F    I J L G H    H G Q U L    J I R V F    E X C U Z    F V R F Z
E M Y Y O    Y J C E R    J F Q B U    K H D O I    W E X V X    V N K A R
K I K C K    I N P O Z    K G W T Y    W D X E B    K P F S O    G X B V L
J G Q A L    Q L Q A G    G G L G F    S J V U L    J D B D H    Y H Y G K
E H D B X    K E Y T F    K U L Q L    I J W D V    F T K P Z    T I W A Z
J H B G D    K F A Q Z    W S E C V    H H Q D F    X B R V I    Y J M D R
S G P T V    M N C O U    S G Q S J    K I Q N L    G G V G H    H U Y I Z
```

(1) A B C D E F G H I J K L M N O P Q R S T U V W X Y Z

(2) A B C D E F G H I J K L M N O P Q R S T U V W X Y Z

(3) A B C D E F G H I J K L M N O P Q R S T U V W X Y Z

(4) A B C D E F G H I J K L M N O P Q R S T U V W X Y Z

(5) A B C D E F G H I J K L M N O P Q R S T U V W X Y Z

It is noted that the A–M halves of the cipher distributions may be matched by sliding them at appropriate intervals; this is proof that a Porta matrix of the type shown in Fig. 25a has been used in the encipherment. The correct matching is obvious:

(1) A B C D E F G H I J K L M

(2) M A B C D E F G H I J K L

(3) G H I J K L M A B C D E F

(4) J K L M A B C D E F G H I

(5) B C D E F G H I J K L M A

81

c. The cipher letters A–M of the cryptogram may now be reduced to monoalphabetic terms, using Alphabet 1 as a base, as shown below:

```
            5          10         15         20         25         30
A   WPAVV  QEXGJ  KRASG  RDBSN  SIDIZ  HPCTQ
     H      F KIK  H F    EI      JKM    H J
B   CDLGF  THYGK  EIDDJ  RMQAJ  KUOTV  ZWRFF
    CEFKE    I KJ  EJKHI   A EI  K          JE
C   HNOOZ  ETDJK  SMNGK  EHACX  INDFR  JEAGP
    H       E KAJ   A     KJEIH  G  I   KJFHK
D   HPKAF  IJLGH  HGQUL  JIRVF  EXCUZ  FVRFZ
    H  EEE   IKF  KGH H     K  JJ     E  E  J    F    J
E   EMYYO  YJCER  JFQBU  KHDOI  WEXVX  VNKAR
    EA        KJI  JG  F    KIK   H    F          EE
F   KIKCK  INPOZ  KGWTY  WDXEB  KPFSO  GXBVL
    KJEGJ  I       KH    E  IAK  M   G  I K
G   JGQAL  QLQAG  GGLGF  SJVUL  JDBDH  YHYGK
    JH  EK    M  EF GHFKE    K    KJEIH  G   I KJ
H   EHDBX  KEYTF  KULQL  IJWDV  FTKPZ  TIWAZ
    EIKF   KF      EK    F KIK  H   F  E        J E
J   JHBGD  KFAQZ  WSECV  HHQDF  XBRVI  YJMDR
    JIIKC  KGH       LG    HI   HE    C     H     KGH
K   SGPTV  MNCOU  SGQSJ  KIQNL  GGVGH  HUYIZ
    H       M  J    H       IKJ   K GH   KGH   M
```

The conversion process makes patent several new polygraphic repetitions which were previously latent in the cipher text. The threefold occurrence of the sequence F.KIK.H.F. at A6, E14, and H13 can be established as probably comprising a 10-letter repetition. The X_c at A8 and E23 shows that θ_c^2 and θ_c^{10} of the repetition are identical plaintext letters, thus establishing the partial idiomorphic pattern as ABCDC...AB which may be identified in a pattern list as belonging to the plaintext word PHOTOGRAPH. At D3, the EEE_o is most probably SSS_p, with the preceding P_c most likely an E_p. With these entries, reconstruction of the matrix and recovery of the rest of the plain text is an easy matter.

39. Additional remarks.—*a.* It might be well to bring in at this point several observations in connection with the solution of the systems discussed thus far in this text. These observations are treated as brief notes below.

b. When factoring does not indicate a period uniquely, write out the cipher text on the fewest number of widths that will accommodate the possible periods. For instance if factoring indicates a maximum of 12 alphabets, then writing the cipher text on the widths of 12, 10, and 8 will facilitate examination and taking of distributions on the basis of 2, 3, 4, 5, 6, 8, 10, and 12 alphabets. If only two periods are possible and one is a multiple of the other, write out the text on the longer period; in other cases where there are only two possible periods, select the least common multiple for the first trial.

c. When the cryptanalyst is confronted by a polyalphabetic cipher of a fairly lengthy period, and the problem involves the matching of comparatively small distributions, the χ test should be used to match the distributions, beginning with a pair of distributions having the best "profiles," and after all the distributions have been matched, the cipher text is converted to monoalphabetic terms. Even if some of the distributions are mismatched, it will usually be possible to solve the resulting monoalphabet; systematic garbles every nth position will point to the distributions incorrectly matched. However, if the repeating key is a plaintext key, a search for plaintext fragments in one of the columns of the matched distributions might make possible a quick recovery of the repeating key and thereby bypass difficulties in matching some of the "less good" distributions.

d. If the repeating key of a polyalphabetic cipher is not found under the first letter of the plain component, and it is known or assumed that the normal equation $\theta_{k/2} = \theta_{1/1}$, $\theta_{p/1} = \theta_{c/2}$ is used, then completing the plain-component sequence, if known, on the "key" under any θ_p will disclose the key word if one was used.

e. During the course of reconstruction of the mixed component, the student should be on the alert to take advantage of any evidence of systematic construction or derivation. If the fragmentary component does not display the characteristics of a keyword-mixed sequence, it should be examined for manifestations of other types of systematic mixing (see par. 51 of *Military Cryptanalytics, Part I*); it is often possible to determine the method of mixing, recover the key word involved, and reconstruct the entire component from a fragmentary sequence of 15 letters or less, and thus materially speed up solution of the problem.

f. If in a polyalphabetic cryptogram there are two or more sets of long polygraphic repetitions of equal length, consider the possibility that these two sets might be different encipherments of the same plain text, and look for corroborating evidence. For example, if Set "A" was partially recovered as .EA...A.TE.S$_p$ and Set "B" was recovered as .EA....R.ER.$_p$, these values may be amalgamated into .EA...ARTERS$_p$ and further expanded into HEADQUARTERS.

g. The student should keep his mind open to possible variations of a basic idea, even if a particular variation might seem at first blush to contradict a general principle. For instance, although in Porta encipherment it is not expected that a letter may be enciphered by itself, nevertheless in the matrix illustrated below such a contingency is possible.

```
        A B C D E F G H I K L M *
    AB | N O P Q R S T U V W X Y Z
    CD | O P Q R S T U V W X Y Z N
    EF | P Q R S T U V W X Y Z N O
    GH | Q R S T U V W X Y Z N O P
    IJ | R S T U V W X Y Z N O P Q
    KL | S T U V W X Y Z N O P Q R
    MN | T U V W X Y Z N O P Q R S
    OP | U V W X Y Z N O P Q R S T
    QR | V W X Y Z N O P Q R S T U
    ST | W X Y Z N O P Q R S T U V
    UV | X Y Z N O P Q R S T U V W
    WX | Y Z N O P Q R S T U V W X
    YZ | Z N O P Q R S T U V W X Y
```

The A–M component has been shortened by combining I and J, so by convention a letter appearing in the asterisked column may be represented by itself; e.g., with the key word FACE, PLATOON would be enciphered as AXOEOBN.

h. Polyalphabetic numerical systems with "standard" alphabets have been discussed in par. 25. When, however, the cipher component consists of a mixed numerical sequence, then direct symmetry of position will of course be manifested, and this fact can be exploited in the solution of a cryptogram. If, however, the cipher component is a "normal" numerical sequence (say, a sequence of the dinomes 01–26 or the dinomes 10–45 in numerical order) and the plain component is an unknown mixed sequence, then the methods discussed in par. 36 are applicable.

i. Mixed numerical sequences are often derived in some manner from key words. A typical method involves repeating a short key word enough times to obtain a 26-letter sequence, from which a numerical key is derived by the usual process,[11] as in the following example:

```
          5              10             15             20             25 26
 H  Y  D  R  A  U  L  I  C  H  Y  D  R  A  U  L  I  C  H  Y  D  R  A  U  L  I
 9 24  6 18  1 21 15 12  4 10 25  7 19  2 22 16 13  5 11 26  8 20  3 23 17 14
```

When the cipher component is a systematically mixed numerical sequence based on a key word, phenomena are usually disclosed which will make possible the analysis of its construction. For example, let us assume that our recovered sequence is as follows:

1 21 15 12 4 10 25 7 19 2 22 16 13 5 11 26 8 20 3 23 17 14 9 24 6 18

We note a repetition of a pattern after an interval of 9, so we begin writing the sequence as shown in Fig. 26a, below. After the dinome 14, the pattern seems to stop; but we notice that

```
                                        9 24  6 18  |  9 24  6 18  1 21 15 12  4
 1 21 15 12  4 10 25  7 19  | 1 21 15 12  4 10 25  7 19  | 10 25  7 19  2 22 16 13  5
 2 22 16 13  5 11 26  8 20  | 2 22 16 13  5 11 26  8 20  | 11 26  8 20  3 23 17 14
 3 23 17 14                 | 3 23 17 14
        FIGURE 26a                    FIGURE 26b                    FIGURE 26c
```

we can place the four remaining numbers at the top of our diagram, as shown in Fig. 26b. Then by permuting the diagram cyclically, we arrive at that shown in Fig. 26c. If we now examine the order of the numbers in the top row of Fig. 26c, we will have the sequence 4 9 3 7 1 8 6 5 2, which is the numerical key derived from the literal key used to mix the component. From this numerical key we can now derive the original literal key; the method of derivation is treated in par. 6 of Appendix 5.

---
[11] Cf. par. 38 of *Military Cryptanalytics, Part I.*

CHAPTER VI

REPEATING-KEY SYSTEMS WITH MIXED CIPHER ALPHABETS, II; INDIRECT SYMMETRY OF POSITION

40. Further cases to be considered.—*a.* Thus far Cases II*a* and *b* of the mixed-alphabet cases mentioned in par. 8 have been treated. There remains Case II*c* which has been further subdivided as follows:

Case II*c*. Both components are mixed sequences.

1. Components are identical mixed sequences.

(a) Sequences proceed in the same direction. (The secondary alphabets are mixed alphabets.)

(b) Sequences proceed in opposite directions. (The secondary alphabets are reciprocal mixed alphabets.)

2. Components are different mixed sequences. (The secondary alphabets are mixed alphabets.)

b. The first of the foregoing subcases, i.e., Case II*c*1(a), will now be examined. Case II*c*1(b) will be taken up in subpar. 44*n*, and Case II*c*2 will be treated in subpar. 44*o*.

41. Identical primary mixed components proceeding in the same direction.—*a.* It is often the case that the mixed components are derived from an easily remembered word or phrase, so that they can be reproduced at any time from memory. Thus, for example, given the key word QUESTIONABLY, the following mixed sequence is derived:

QUESTIONABLYCDFGHJKMPRVWXZ

b. By using this sequence as both plain and cipher component, that is, by sliding this sequence against itself, a series of 25 secondary mixed alphabets may be produced; in the one remaining alphabet, *viz.*, where $Q_p=Q_c$, all letters will be self-enciphered. In enciphering a message, sliding strips may be employed with a key word to designate the particular and successive positions in which the strips are to be set, the same as was the case in previous examples of the use of sliding components. The method of designating the positions, however, requires a word or two of comment at this point. In the examples thus far shown, the key letter, as located on the cipher component, was always set opposite A, as located on the plain component; possibly an erroneous impression has been created that this is invariably the rule. This is decidedly not true, as has already been explained in par. 13*c*. If it has seemed to be the case that θ_1 always equals A_p, it is only because the text has dealt thus far principally with cases in

85

which the plain component is the normal sequence and its initial letter, which usually constitutes the index for juxtaposing cipher components, is A. It must be emphasized, however, that various conventions may be adopted in this respect; but the most common of them is to employ the initial letter of the plain component as the index letter. That is, the index letter, θ_1, will be the initial letter of the mixed sequence, in this case, Q. Furthermore, to prevent the possibility of ambiguity it will be stated again that the pair of enciphering equations employed in the ensuing discussion will be the first of the 12 set forth under par. 13f, viz., $\theta_{k/2}=\theta_{1/1}$; $\theta_{p/1}=\theta_{c/2}$. In this case the subscript "1" means the plain component, the subscript "2", the cipher component, so that the enciphering equation is the following: $\theta_{k/c}=\theta_{1/p}$; $\theta_{p/p}=\theta_{c/c}$.

c. By setting the two sliding components against each other in the two positions shown below, the cipher alphabets labeled (1) and (2) given by two key letters, A and B, are seen to be different.

Key letter=A

Plain component:

QUESTIONABLYCDFGHJKMPRVWXZ

Cipher component: QUESTIONABLYCDFGHJKMPRVWXZQUESTIONABLYCDFGHJKMPRVWXZ

Secondary alphabet (1):

```
Plain:  A B C D E F G H I J K L M N O P Q R S T U V W X Y Z
Cipher: H J P R L V W X D Z Q K U G F E A S Y C B T I O M N
```

Key letter=B

Plain component:

QUESTIONABLYCDFGHJKMPRVWXZ

Cipher component: QUESTIONABLYCDFGHJKMPRVWXZQUESTIONABLYCDFGHJKMPRVWXZ

Secondary alphabet (2):

```
Plain:  A B C D E F G H I J K L M N O P Q R S T U V W X Y Z
Cipher: J K R V Y W X Z F Q U M E H G S B T C D L I O N P A
```

d. Very frequently a square table is employed by the correspondents, instead of sliding strips, but the results are the same. The cipher square based upon the word QUESTIONABLY is shown in Fig. 27. It will be noted that it does nothing more than set forth the successive positions of the two primary sliding components; the top line of the square is the plain component, the successive horizontal lines below it, the cipher component in its various juxtapositions. The usual method of employing such a square (i.e., corresponding to the enciphering equations $\theta_{k/c}=\theta_{1/p}$; $\theta_{p/p}=\theta_{c/c}$) is to take as the cipher equivalent of a plaintext letter that letter which lies at the intersection of the vertical column headed by the plaintext letter and the horizontal row begun by the key letter. For example, the cipher equivalent of E_p with key letter T is the letter O_c; or $E_p (T_k)=O_c$. The method given in subpar. b for determining the cipher equivalents by means of the two sliding strips yields the same results as does the cipher square.

42. Enciphering and deciphering by means of identical primary mixed components.—There is nothing of special interest to be noted in connection with the use either of identical mixed components or of an equivalent square table such as that shown in Fig. 27, in enciphering or deciphering a message. The basic principles are the same as in the case of the sliding of one

```
 1  2  3  4  5  6  7  8  9 10 11 12 13 14 15 16 17 18 19 20 21 22 23 24 25 26
 Q  U  E  S  T  I  O  N  A  B  L  Y  C  D  F  G  H  J  K  M  P  R  V  W  X  Z
 U  E  S  T  I  O  N  A  B  L  Y  C  D  F  G  H  J  K  M  P  R  V  W  X  Z  Q
 E  S  T  I  O  N  A  B  L  Y  C  D  F  G  H  J  K  M  P  R  V  W  X  Z  Q  U
 S  T  I  O  N  A  B  L  Y  C  D  F  G  H  J  K  M  P  R  V  W  X  Z  Q  U  E
 T  I  O  N  A  B  L  Y  C  D  F  G  H  J  K  M  P  R  V  W  X  Z  Q  U  E  S
 I  O  N  A  B  L  Y  C  D  F  G  H  J  K  M  P  R  V  W  X  Z  Q  U  E  S  T
 O  N  A  B  L  Y  C  D  F  G  H  J  K  M  P  R  V  W  X  Z  Q  U  E  S  T  I
 N  A  B  L  Y  C  D  F  G  H  J  K  M  P  R  V  W  X  Z  Q  U  E  S  T  I  O
 A  B  L  Y  C  D  F  G  H  J  K  M  P  R  V  W  X  Z  Q  U  E  S  T  I  O  N
 B  L  Y  C  D  F  G  H  J  K  M  P  R  V  W  X  Z  Q  U  E  S  T  I  O  N  A
 L  Y  C  D  F  G  H  J  K  M  P  R  V  W  X  Z  Q  U  E  S  T  I  O  N  A  B
 Y  C  D  F  G  H  J  K  M  P  R  V  W  X  Z  Q  U  E  S  T  I  O  N  A  B  L
 C  D  F  G  H  J  K  M  P  R  V  W  X  Z  Q  U  E  S  T  I  O  N  A  B  L  Y
 D  F  G  H  J  K  M  P  R  V  W  X  Z  Q  U  E  S  T  I  O  N  A  B  L  Y  C
 F  G  H  J  K  M  P  R  V  W  X  Z  Q  U  E  S  T  I  O  N  A  B  L  Y  C  D
 G  H  J  K  M  P  R  V  W  X  Z  Q  U  E  S  T  I  O  N  A  B  L  Y  C  D  F
 H  J  K  M  P  R  V  W  X  Z  Q  U  E  S  T  I  O  N  A  B  L  Y  C  D  F  G
 J  K  M  P  R  V  W  X  Z  Q  U  E  S  T  I  O  N  A  B  L  Y  C  D  F  G  H
 K  M  P  R  V  W  X  Z  Q  U  E  S  T  I  O  N  A  B  L  Y  C  D  F  G  H  J
 M  P  R  V  W  X  Z  Q  U  E  S  T  I  O  N  A  B  L  Y  C  D  F  G  H  J  K
 P  R  V  W  X  Z  Q  U  E  S  T  I  O  N  A  B  L  Y  C  D  F  G  H  J  K  M
 R  V  W  X  Z  Q  U  E  S  T  I  O  N  A  B  L  Y  C  D  F  G  H  J  K  M  P
 V  W  X  Z  Q  U  E  S  T  I  O  N  A  B  L  Y  C  D  F  G  H  J  K  M  P  R
 W  X  Z  Q  U  E  S  T  I  O  N  A  B  L  Y  C  D  F  G  H  J  K  M  P  R  V
 X  Z  Q  U  E  S  T  I  O  N  A  B  L  Y  C  D  F  G  H  J  K  M  P  R  V  W
 Z  Q  U  E  S  T  I  O  N  A  B  L  Y  C  D  F  G  H  J  K  M  P  R  V  W  X
```

FIGURE 27

mixed component against the normal, the displacements of the two components being controlled by changeable key words of varying lengths. The components may be changed at will and so on. All this has been discussed adequately enough in Chapter II.

43. Principles of solution.—*a.* Basically the principles of solution in the case of a cryptogram enciphered by two identical mixed sliding components are the same as in the preceding case. Primary recourse is had to the principles of frequency and repetition of single letters, digraphs, trigraphs, and longer polygraphs. Once an entering wedge has been forced into the problem, the subsequent steps may consist merely in continuing along the same lines as before, building up the solution bit by bit.

b. Doubtless the question has already arisen in the student's mind as to whether any principles of symmetry of position can be used to assist in the solution and in the reconstruction of the cipher alphabets in cases of this kind. This phase of the subject will be taken up in the succeeding paragraphs and will be treated in a detailed manner, because the theory and principles involved are of very wide application in cryptanalytics.

44. Theory of indirect symmetry of position in secondary alphabets.—*a.* Note the two secondary alphabets (1) and (2) given in subpar. 41c. Superficially they show no resemblance or symmetry despite the fact that they were produced from the same primary components. Nevertheless, when the matter is studied with care, a symmetry of position is discoverable.

87

Because it is a hidden or latent phenomenon, it may be termed *latent symmetry of position*. However, the phenomenon has a long-standing designation in cryptologic literature as *indirect symmetry of position* and this terminology has grown into usage, so that a change now is perhaps inadvisable. Indirect symmetry of position is a very interesting and exceedingly useful phenomenon in cryptanalytics.

b. Consider the following secondary alphabet (the one labeled (2) in subpar. 41*c*):

(2) $\begin{cases}$ Plain: A B C D E F G H I J K L M N O P Q R S T U V W X Y Z \
Cipher: J K R V Y W X Z F Q U M E H G S B T C D L I O N P A $\end{cases}$

c. Assuming it to be known that this is a secondary alphabet produced by two identical mixed primary components, it is desired to reconstruct the latter. Construct a chain of alternating plaintext and ciphertext equivalents, beginning at any point and continuing until the chain has been completed. Thus, for example, beginning with $A_p = J_c$, $J_p = Q_c$, $Q_p = B_c$, . . ., and dropping out the letters common to successive pairs, there results the sequence A J Q B . . . By completing the chain the following sequence of letters is established:

$$\text{A J Q B K U L M E Y P S C R T D V I F W O G X N H Z}$$

d. This sequence consists of 26 letters. *When slid against itself it will produce exactly the same secondary alphabets as do the primary components based upon the word* QUESTIONABLY. To demonstrate that this is the case, compare the secondary alphabets given by the two settings of the externally different components shown below:

Plain component: QUESTIONABLYCDFGHJKMPRVWXZ
Cipher component: QUESTIONABLYCDFGHJKMPRVWXZQUESTIONABLYCDFGHJKMPRVWXZ

Secondary alphabet (1):

Plain: A B C D E F G H I J K L M N O P Q R S T U V W X Y Z
Cipher: J K R V Y W X Z F Q U M E H G S B T C D L I O N P A

Plain component: AJQBKULMEYPSCRTDVIFWOGXNHZ
Cipher component: AJQBKULMEYPSCRTDVIFWOGXNHZAJQBKULMEYPSCRTDVIFWOGXNHZ

Secondary alphabet (2):

Plain: A B C D E F G H I J K L M N O P Q R S T U V W X Y Z
Cipher: J K R V Y W X Z F Q U M E H G S B T C D L I O N P A

e. Since the sequence A J Q B K... gives exactly the same equivalents in the secondary alphabets as does the sequence Q U E S T ... X Z, the former sequence is cryptographically equivalent to the latter sequence. For this reason the A J Q B K... sequence is termed an *equivalent primary component*.[1] If the real or original primary component is a keyword-mixed sequence, it is hidden or *latent* within the equivalent primary sequence; but it can be made *patent* by decimation of the equivalent primary component. The procedure is as fol-

---

[1] Such an equivalent component is merely a sequence which has been or can be derived from the original sequence or basic primary component by applying a *decimation* process to the latter; conversely, the original or basic component can be derived from an equivalent component by applying the same sort of process to the equivalent component. By decimation is meant the selection of elements from a sequence according to some fixed interval. For example, the sequence A E I M . . . is derived, by decimation, from the normal alphabet by selecting every fourth letter.

lows: Find three letters in the equivalent primary component such as are likely to have formed an unbroken sequence in the original primary component, and see if the interval between the first and second is the same as that between the second and third. Such a case is presented by the letters W, X, and Z in the equivalent primary component above. Note the sequence ...W O G X N H Z...; the distance or interval between the letters W, X, and Z is three letters. Continuing the chain by adding letters three intervals removed, the latent original primary component is made patent. Thus:

```
 1  2  3  4  5  6  7  8  9 10 11 12 13 14 15 16 17 18 19 20 21 22 23 24 25 26
 W  X  Z  Q  U  E  S  T  I  O  N  A  B  L  Y  C  D  F  G  H  J  K  M  P  R  V
```

f. It is possible to perform the steps given in *c* and *e* in a combined single operation when the original primary component is a keyword-mixed sequence. Starting with any pair of letters (in the cipher component of the secondary alphabet) likely to be sequent in the keyword-mixed sequence, such as JK$_c$ in the secondary alphabet labeled (2), the following chain of digraphs may be set up. Thus, J and K in the plain component stand over Q and U, respectively, in the cipher component; Q and U in the plain component stand over B and L, respectively, in the cipher component, and so on. Connecting the pairs in a series, the following results are obtained:

JK → QU → BL → KM → UE → LY → MP → ES → YC → PR → ST → CD → RV →
TI → DF → VW → IO → FG → WX → ON → GH → XZ → NA → HJ → ZQ → AB → JK...

These may now be united by means of their common letters:

JK → KM → MP → PR → RV → etc. = J K M P R V W X Z Q U E S T I O N A B L Y C D F G H

The original primary component is thus completely reconstructed.

g. Not all of the 26 secondary alphabets of the series yielded by two sliding primary components may be used to develop a complete equivalent primary component. Only 12 of these secondary alphabets will yield complete equivalent primary components when the method of reconstruction shown in subpar. *c* above is followed. For example, the following secondary alphabet, which is also derived from the primary components based upon the word QUESTIONABLY, will not yield a complete chain of 26 plaintext-ciphertext equivalents:

Plain: A B C D E F G H I J K L M N O P Q R S T U V W X Y Z
Cipher: C D H J O K M P B R V F W Y L X T Z N A I Q U E G S

Equivalent primary components:

```
 1  2  3  4  5  6  7  8  9 10 11 12 13 │ 1  2  3
 A  C  H  P  X  E  O  L  F  K  V  Q  T │ A  C  H...  (The A C H sequence begins again.)
```

h. It is seen that only 13 letters of the chain have been established before the sequence begins to repeat itself. Exactly one-half of the chain has been established. The other half may be established by beginning with a letter not in the first half. Thus:

```
 1  2  3  4  5  6  7  8  9 10 11 12 13 │ 1  2  3
 B  D  J  R  Z  S  N  Y  G  M  W  U  I │ B  D  J...  (The B D J sequence begins again.)
```

i. There are several methods for combining two 13-letter chains. The simplest method, applicable when the primary component is a keyword-mixed sequence, will now be described. If we assume two letters to be sequent in the original keyword-mixed sequence, such as for example J and K, and if these letters *are not in the same 13-letter chain*, we would then write the two 13-letter chains over one another, with the J of the one chain superimposed over the K in the other chain. Thus, using for an example the chains A C H P X E O L F K V Q T and B D J R Z S N Y G M W U I established in subpars. *g* and *h* above, we would have the following:

```
B D J R Z S N Y G M W U I
L F K V Q T A C H P X E O
```

The vertical digraphs thus formed look as if the primary component were a keyword-mixed sequence. Now noting the vertical digraph $\frac{W}{X}$, we may assume that Y will follow it in the mixed component; the Y is not in the same 13-letter chain that contains the X, so this looks promising. The chain containing the Y is now written beneath the diagram, properly juxtaposed so that Y is under the X, thus:

```
B D J R Z S N Y G M W U I
L F K V Q T A C H P X E O
W U I B D J R Z S N Y G M
```

The resulting vertical trigraphs are not satisfactory as portions of a keyword-mixed sequence, so it appears that Y must be in the key word and not in the remaining semi-alphabetical portion of the sequence. If we now assume that WX is followed by Z (which is not in the same chain as X) in the sequence, we have the following:

```
B D J R Z S N Y G M W U I
L F K V Q T A C H P X E O
Y G M W U I B D J R Z S N
```

The "good" trigraphs produced (DFG, JKM, etc.) attest to the correctness of the trial. We now have in effect a series of three-letter chains, which may be interconnected by the common letters in the first and third rows, thus: WXZ, ZQU, UES, ..; this quickly yields the QUESTIONABLY ... XZ sequence. Note that these three-letter chains will always be at a constant interval apart; in this case, the interval was +7.

j. The reason why a complete chain of 26 letters cannot be constructed from the secondary alphabet given under subpar. *g* is that it represents a case in which two primary components of 26 letters were slid an *even* number of intervals apart. (This will be explained in further detail in subpar. *p* below.) There are 12 such cases in all, none of which will admit of the construction of a complete chain of 26 letters. In addition, there is one *odd* slide case wherein the secondary alphabet cannot be made to yield a complete chain of 26 letters for an equivalent primary component. This is the case when the displacement is at an interval of 13. Note the secondary alphabet based upon the primary components below (which are the same as those shown in subpar. *d*):

Primary Components

```
Q U E S T I O N A B L Y C D F G H J K M P R V W X Z
D F G H J K M P R V W X Z Q U E S T I O N A B L Y C
```

Secondary Alphabet

```
Plain:  A B C D E F G H I J K L M N O P Q R S T U V W X Y Z
Cipher: R V Z Q G U E S K T I W O P M N D A H J F B L Y X C
```

k. If an attempt is made to construct a chain of letters from this secondary alphabet alone, no progress can be made because the alphabet is completely reciprocal, and all chains are of length 2. However, the cryptanalyst can still proceed; the attack will follow along the lines shown below in subpars. *l* and *m.*

l. If the original primary component is a keyword-mixed sequence, the cryptanalyst may reconstruct it by attempting to dovetail the 13 reciprocal pairs (AR, BV, CZ, DQ, EG, FU, HS, IK, JT, LW, MO, NP, and XY) into one sequence. The members of these pairs are all 13 intervals apart. Thus:

```
  0  1  2  3  4  5  6  7  8  9 10 11 12 13
A  .  .  .  .  .  .  .  .  .  .  .  .  .  R
B  .  .  .  .  .  .  .  .  .  .  .  .  .  V
C  .  .  .  .  .  .  .  .  .  .  .  .  .  Z
D  .  .  .  .  .  .  .  .  .  .  .  .  .  Q
E  .  .  .  .  .  .  .  .  .  .  .  .  .  G
F  .  .  .  .  .  .  .  .  .  .  .  .  .  U
H  .  .  .  .  .  .  .  .  .  .  .  .  .  S
I  .  .  .  .  .  .  .  .  .  .  .  .  .  K
J  .  .  .  .  .  .  .  .  .  .  .  .  .  T
L  .  .  .  .  .  .  .  .  .  .  .  .  .  W
M  .  .  .  .  .  .  .  .  .  .  .  .  .  O
N  .  .  .  .  .  .  .  .  .  .  .  .  .  P
X  .  .  .  .  .  .  .  .  .  .  .  .  .  Y
```

Write out the series of 26 numbers from 0 to 25 and insert as many pairs into position as possible, being guided by considerations of probable partial sequences in the keyword-mixed sequence. Thus:

```
0 1 2 3 4 5 6 7 8 9 10 11 12 13 14 15 16
A B C D . . . . . . .  .  .  R  V  Z  Q
```

It begins to look as though the key word commences with the letter **Q**, in which case it should be followed by U. This means that the next pair to be inserted is FU. Thus:

```
0 1 2 3 4 5 6 7 8 9 10 11 12 13 14 15 16 17
A B C D F . . . . . .  .  .  R  V  Z  Q  U
```

The sequence A B C D F means that E is in the key. Perhaps the sequence is A B C D F G H. Upon trial, using the pairs EG and HS, the following placements are obtained:

```
0 1 2 3 4 5 6 7 8 9 10 11 12 13 14 15 16 17 18 19
A B C D F G H . . . .  .  .  R  V  Z  Q  U  E  S
```

This suggests the word **QUEST** or **QUESTION**. The pair JT is added:

```
0 1 2 3 4 5 6 7 8 9 10 11 12 13 14 15 16 17 18 19 20
A B C D F G H J . . .  .  .  R  V  Z  Q  U  E  S  T
```

The sequence G H J suggests G H J K, which places an I after T. Enough of the process has been shown to make the steps clear.

m. Another method of circumventing the difficulties introduced by the 14th secondary alphabet (displacement interval, 13) is to use it in conjunction with another secondary alphabet which is produced by an even-interval displacement.   For example, suppose the following two secondary alphabets are available.[2]

	1	2	3	4	5	6	7	8	9	10	11	12	13	14	15	16	17	18	19	20	21	22	23	24	25	26
Ø.........	A	B	C	D	E	F	G	H	I	J	K	L	M	N	O	P	Q	R	S	T	U	V	W	X	Y	Z
1.........	R	V	Z	Q	G	U	E	S	K	T	I	W	O	P	M	N	D	A	H	J	F	B	L	Y	X	C
2.........	X	Z	E	S	K	T	I	O	R	N	A	Q	B	W	V	L	H	Y	M	P	J	C	D	F	U	G

The first of these secondaries is the 13-interval secondary; the second is one of the even-interval secondaries, from which only half-chain sequences can be constructed.   But if the construction be based upon the two sequences, 1 and 2 in the foregoing diagram, the following is obtained:

R X U T N L D H M V Z E I A Y F J P W Q S O B C G K

This is a complete equivalent primary component.   The original keyword-mixed component can be recovered from it by decimation at an interval of +9.

R V W X Z Q U E S T I O N A B L Y C D F G H J K M P

n. (1) When the primary components are identical mixed sequences proceeding in *opposite* directions, all the secondary alphabets will be reciprocal alphabets.   One can reconstruct the primary component by the procedure of subpar. *m* above.   Note the following three reciprocal secondary alphabets:

	1	2	3	4	5	6	7	8	9	10	11	12	13	14	15	16	17	18	19	20	21	22	23	24	25	26
Ø.........	A	B	C	D	E	F	G	H	I	J	K	L	M	N	O	P	Q	R	S	T	U	V	W	X	Y	Z
1.........	P	M	H	G	Q	F	D	C	W	Y	L	K	B	R	V	A	E	N	Z	X	U	O	I	T	J	S
2.........	W	V	M	K	S	J	H	G	Q	F	D	R	C	X	Z	Y	I	L	E	U	T	B	A	N	P	O
3.........	T	S	Q	Z	L	X	W	V	N	R	P	E	M	I	O	K	C	J	B	A	Y	H	G	F	U	D

(2) Using lines 1 and 2, the following chain can be constructed (equivalent primary component):

P W Q S O B C G K R X U T N L D H M V Z E I A Y F J

Or, using lines 2 and 3:

W T Y K Z O D P U A G V S L J X I C M Q N F R E B H

The original keyword-mixed primary component (based on the word QUESTIONABLY) can be recovered from either of the two foregoing equivalent primary components.   But if lines 1 and 3 are used, only half-chains can be constructed:

P T F X A K E C V O H Q L and M S D W N J U Y R I G Z B

_____

[2] The method of writing down the secondary alphabets shown in the diagram below will hereafter be followed in all cases when alphabet reconstruction matrices are necessary.   The top line will be understood to be the plain component; it is common to all the secondary alphabets, and is set off from the cipher components by the heavy black line.   This top line of letters will be designated by the digit Ø, and will be referred to as "the zero line" in the diagram.   The successive lines of letters, which occupy the space below the zero line and which contain the various cipher components of the several secondary alphabets, will be numbered serially.   These numbers may then be used as reference numbers for designating the horizontal lines in the diagram.   The numbers standing above the letters may be used as reference numbers for the vertical columns in the diagram.   Hence, any letter in the reconstruction matrix may be designated by coordinates, giving the row coordinate first.   Thus, A (2–11) means the letter A standing in row 2, column 11.

This is because 1 and 3 are both odd-interval secondary alphabets, whereas 2 is an even-interval secondary. It may be added that odd-interval secondaries are characterized by having two cases in which a plaintext letter is enciphered by itself; that is, θ_p is identical with θ_c. This phrase "identical with" will be represented by the symbol $\equiv$; the phrase "not identical with" will be represented by the symbol $\not\equiv$. (Note that in secondary alphabet number 1 above, $F_p \equiv F_c$ and $U_p \equiv U_c$; in secondary alphabet number 3 above, $M_p \equiv M_c$ and $O_p \equiv O_c$). This characteristic will enable the cryptananalyst to select at once the proper two secondaries to work with in case several are available; one should show two cases where $\theta_p \equiv \theta_c$; the other should show none.

o. (1) When the primary components are different mixed sequences, their reconstruction from secondary cipher alphabets follows along the same lines as set forth above, under *b* to *j*, inclusive, with the exception that the selection of letters for building up the chain of equivalents for the primary cipher component is restricted to those below the zero line in the reconstruction matrix. Having reconstructed the primary cipher component, we can readily reconstruct the plain component. This will become clear if the student will study the following example:

```
Ø........  A B C D E F G H I J K L M N O P Q R S T U V W X Y Z
1........  T V A B U L I Q X Y C W S N D P F E Z G R H J K M O
2........  Z J S T V I Q R M O N K X E A G B W P L H Y C D F U
```

(2) Using only lines 1 and 2, the following chain is constructed:

T Z P G L I Q R H Y O U V J C N E W K D A S X M F B

This is an equivalent primary cipher component. By finding the value of the successive letters of this chain in terms of the plain component of secondary alphabet number 1 (the zero line), the following is obtained:

A S P T F G H U V J Z E B W K N R L X O C M I Y Q D
T Z P G L I Q R H Y O U V J C N E W K D A S X M F B

The sequence A S P T . . . is an equivalent primary plain component. The original key-word-mixed components may be recovered from each of the equivalent primary components. That for the primary plain component is based upon the key PUBLISHERS MAGAZINE; that for the primary cipher component is based upon the key QUESTIONABLY.

(3) Another method of accomplishing the process indicated above can be illustrated graphically by the following two chains, based upon the two secondary alphabets set forth in subpar. *o* (1):

```
          1 2 3 4 5 6 7 8 9 10 11 12 13 14 15 16 17 18 19 20 21 22 23 24 25 26
Ø.....  A B C D E F G H I J  K  L  M  N  O  P  Q  R  S  T  U  V  W  X  Y  Z
1.....  T V A B U L I Q X Y  C  W  S  N  D  P  F  E  Z  G  R  H  J  K  M  O
2.....  Z J S T V I Q R M O  N  K  X  E  A  G  B  W  P  L  H  Y  C  D  F  U
```

```
        Col. 1.          Col. 2.
A (Ø–1)  → T (1–1);   → T (2–4)  → D (Ø–4);  →
D (Ø–4)  → B (1–4);   → B (2–17) → Q (Ø–17); →
Q (Ø–17) → F (1–17);  → F (2–25) → Y (Ø–25); →
Y (Ø–25) → M (1–25);  → M (2–9)  → I (Ø–9);  →
I (Ø–9)  → X (1–9);   → X (2–13) → M (Ø–13); →
M (Ø–13) → S (1–13);  → S (2–3)  → C (Ø–3);  →
    etc.            etc.
```

(4) By joining the letters in Column 1, we can obtain the following chain: ADQYIM, etc. If this be examined, it will be found to be an equivalent primary of the sequence based upon PUBLISHERS MAGAZINE. By joining the letters in Column 2, we can obtain the following chain: TBFMXS. This is an equivalent primary of the sequence based upon QUESTIONABLY.

p. A final word concerning the reconstruction of primary components in general may be added. It has been seen that in the case of a 26-element component sliding against itself (both components proceeding in the same direction), it is only the secondary alphabets resulting from odd-interval displacements of the primary components which permit reconstructing a single 26-letter chain of equivalents. This is true except for the 13th interval displacement, which, in spite of its being an odd number, still acts like an even-number displacement in that no complete chain of equivalents can be established from the secondary alphabet. This exception gives the clue to the basic reason for this phenomenon: it is that the number 26 has two factors, 2 and 13. With the exception of displacement-interval 1, *any displacement interval which has a factor in common with the number of letters in the primary sequence will yield a secondary alphabet from which no complete chain of 26 equivalents can be derived for the construction of a complete equivalent primary component.* This general rule is applicable only to components which progress in the same direction; if they progress in opposite directions, all the secondary alphabets are reciprocal alphabets and they behave exactly like the reciprocal secondaries resulting from the 13-interval displacement of two 26-letter identical components progressing in the same direction.

q. The foregoing remarks give rise to the following observations based upon the general rule pointed out above. Whether or not a complete equivalent primary component is derivable by decimation from an original primary component (and if not, the lengths and numbers of chains of letters, or incomplete components, that can be constructed in attempts to derive such equivalent components) will depend upon the number of letters in the original primary component and the specific decimation interval selected. For example, in a 26-letter original primary component, decimation interval 5 will yield a complete equivalent primary component of 26 letters, whereas decimation intervals 4 or 8 will yield 2 chains of 13 letters each. In a 24-letter component, decimation interval 5 will also yield a complete equivalent primary component (of 24 letters), but decimation interval 4 will yield 6 chains of 4 letters each, and decimation interval 8 will yield 3 chains of 8 letters each. It also follows that in the case of an original primary component in which the total number of characters is a prime number, *all* decimation intervals will yield complete equivalent primary components. The following table has been drawn up in the light of these observations, for original primary sequences from 16 to 32 elements. (All prime-number sequences have been omitted.) In this table, the column at the extreme left gives the various decimation intervals, omitting in each case the first interval, which merely gives the original primary sequence, and the last interval, which merely gives the original sequence reversed. The top line of the table gives the various lengths of original primary sequences from 32 down to 16. (The student should bear in mind that sequences containing characters in addition to the letters of the alphabet may be encountered; he can add to this table when he is interested in sequences of more than 32 characters.) The numbers within the table then show, for each combination of decimation interval and length of original sequence, the lengths of the chains of characters that can be constructed. (The student may note the symmetry in each column.) The bottom line shows the total number of complete equivalent primary components which can be derived for each different length of original component.

Decimation interval	Number of characters in original primary component											
	32	30	28	27	26	25	24	22	21	20	18	16
2	16	15	14	27	13	25	12	11	21	10	9	8
3	32	10	28	9	26	25	8	22	7	20	6	16
4	8	15	7	27	13	25	6	11	21	5	9	4
5	32	6	28	27	26	5	24	22	21	4	18	16
6	16	5	14	9	13	25	4	11	7	10	3	8
7	32	30	4	27	26	25	24	22	3	20	18	16
8	4	15	7	27	13	25	3	11	21	5	9	2
9	32	10	28	3	26	25	8	22	7	20	2	16
10	16	3	14	27	13	5	12	11	21	2	9	8
11	32	30	28	27	26	25	24	2	21	20	18	16
12	8	5	7	9	13	25	2	11	7	5	3	4
13	32	30	28	27	2	25	24	22	21	20	18	16
14	16	15	2	27	13	25	12	11	3	10	9	8
15	32	2	28	9	26	5	8	22	7	4	6	
16	2	15	7	27	13	25	3	11	21	5	9	
17	32	30	28	27	26	25	24	22	21	20		
18	16	5	14	3	13	25	4	11	7	10		
19	32	30	28	27	26	25	24	22	21			
20	8	3	7	27	13	5	6	1l				
21	32	10	4	9	26	25	8					
22	16	15	14	27	13	25	12					
23	32	30	28	27	26	25						
24	4	5	7	9	13							
25	32	6	28	27								
26	16	15	14									
27	32	10										
28	8	15										
29	32											
30	16											
Total number of complete sequences	14	6	10	16	10	18	6	8	10	6	4	6

45. Reconstruction of primary components by employing principles of indirect symmetry of position.—*a.* Let us now consider the application of indirect symmetry in a typical example. In a certain periodic polyalphabetic cryptogram under study which factored to five alphabets, the following assumptions based on repetitions in the cipher text have been made:

```
1 2 3 4 5 1 2 3     3 4 5 1 2 3 4 5     1 2 3 4 5 1 2 3 4     5 1 2 3 4 5
ZFOOWATF            XSMAQUHX            YINOBRKXF           IPZZPO
DIVISION            REGIMENT            ARTILLERY           ATTACK
```

These values are inserted in a sequence reconstruction matrix, as illustrated below:

Ø	A	B	C	D	E	F	G	H	I	J	K	L	M	N	O	P	Q	R	S	T	U	V	W	X	Y	Z
1	Y		Z					A			R										P						
2					K			F					Q		T				I		Z						
3	Z				U									F				X		N		O					
4			P	S			O					H													F		
5	I					M				O	B									W	X						

FIGURE 28

It is clear from the intervals (X...O), (S...O), and (M...O) in rows 3, 4, and 5 that the plain component is not the normal sequence. If an inverse matrix were constructed, it would disclose that neither is the cipher component the normal sequence, if this possibility had not already been ruled out by the absence of matching qualities of the distributions for the five alphabets. It is also evident that this is not a case of identical mixed sequences proceeding in opposite directions, since reciprocity between the plain and cipher is contradicted (e.g., in Alphabet 1, $A_p = Y_c$, but $A_c = I_p$). At the moment, we do not know whether the plain component is identical with the cipher component, or whether it is a different mixed sequence; in the absence of evidence to the contrary,[3] we will assume the former hypothesis.

b. In order to derive additional values for possible insertion in the cryptogram, around which values further assumptions may be made and thus speed up the process of solution, we may study certain relationships among the letters in the matrix. For convenience, we may refer to these relationships as "proportions," arising from the process of "proportioning."[4] Proportioning should be done in a systematic manner, if it is to be efficient; this is especially true in the initial stages of solution, when it is important not to overlook a possible derived value. The following procedure is suggested to insure thoroughness of method.

(1) Each vertical pairing in the matrix is transferred to the horizontal, and a four-element proportion is utilized to complete another proportion which has three elements in common

---

[3] An hypothesis of identical components proceeding in the same direction would be ruled out by a situation in which, for example, in one of the alphabets $A_p = A_c$, and in the same alphabet $B_p \neq B_c$; or this hypothesis would be ruled out if in one alphabet there were evidences of only *partial* reciprocity (such as $A_p = L_c$, $A_c = L_p$, $N_p = R_c$, but $N_c \neq R_p$).

[4] As an example of cryptologic proportions, let us rearrange the first five rows of the matrix shown in Fig. 27, with an arbitrary permutation applied to the rows and columns such as in the following diagram:

```
    9 24  6 18  1 21 15 12  4 10 25  7 19  2 22 16 13  5 11 26  8 20  3 23 17 14
3   Y  Q  A  P  S  W  J  F  O  C  U  B  R  T  X  K  G  N  D  E  L  V  I  Z  M  H
5   L  Z  N  M  E  V  H  D  I  Y  Q  A  P  S  W  J  F  O  C  U  B  R  T  X  K  G
2   A  W  I  J  Q  P  F  Y  S  B  X  O  K  U  R  G  C  T  L  Z  N  M  E  V  H  D
1   C  U  B  R  T  X  K  G  N  D  E  L  V  I  Z  M  H  A  F  S  Y  W  O  Q  P  J
4   B  X  O  K  U  R  G  C  T  L  Z  N  M  E  V  H  D  I  Y  Q  A  P  S  W  J  F
```

We note in this diagram the rectangular relationship of the vertical pair YL (3–9, 5–9) to the vertical pair BA (3–7, 5–7). If we now consider the vertical pair YL (5–10, 4–10), we find the identical relationship to BA (5–8, 4–8); furthermore, we also find that YL (3–9, 3–8) = BA (4–9, 4–8), YL (5–10, 5–9) = BA (2–10, 2–9), YL (1–8, 3–8) = BA (1–6, 3–6), YL (1–8, 1–7) = BA (3–8, 3–7), and YL (4–11, 2–11) = BA (4–9, 2–9). What this shows us is that if we start with an observed particular proportion of four elements as the YL = BA in this instance, we can automatically fill in the missing value of a similar proportion having three elements in common with the first proportion. *The relationships present in the original Vigenère square have not been changed by the rearrangement of the rows and columns of that square.*

with the first proportion. Referring to Fig. 28, we shall start with the vertical pairing AY (Ø–1, 1–1) and transfer whatever data is available to the horizontal pairing AY (Ø–1, Ø–25). The vertical pairing AY includes proportionally, between rows Ø and 1, the pairs DZ, IA, LR, and TP; or, expressed differently, A:Y=D:Z=I:A=L:R=T:P. The horizontal pairing AY (Ø–1, Ø–25) includes no other proportional pairs—*however*, there are present the latent proportions A:Y=Y:θ, A:Y=Z:θ, A:Y=θ:F, and A:Y=I:θ. Now as we have already established the four-element proportion A:Y=I:A from the vertical pairing, then we know that the θ in the last horizontal proportion A:Y=I:θ must be the letter A; therefore we place A in the matrix at position 5–25.

(2) This process of transferring values is then attempted for the vertical pairing AZ (Ø–1, 3–1), and then for AK, but with negative results. When the vertical pairing AI is considered, the proportion A:I=Y:A turns up once again, but this yields no additional information since this proportion has already been established when we placed the A at 5–25. The subsequent vertical pairings CP, DZ, EK, EU, ES, and GM yield nothing further until IA is reached, wherein IA (Ø–9, 1–9)=AY (Ø–1, 1–1). But it is noted that the homologous proportion IA (Ø–9, Ø–1)=AY (1–9, 1–1) has its elements in exactly the same locations as IA (Ø–9, Ø–1)=AY (Ø–1, 1–1), so no transference of data from one alphabet to another is possible. In other words, the data within a proportion of four elements in one particular "rectangular" reading may be transferred to a *different* rectangular reading having three of the elements in common. The need, of course, for seeking a *four*-element proportion first is that proportions in cryptanalytics must be defined by four elements (for a given set of enciphering components), because unlike ordinary arithmetic wherein the missing member of 2:4=3:x *must* be a 6, the cryptanalytic proportion A:B=C:θ could be satisfied by *any* letter, depending upon the components involved. What we were actually saying by the proportion A:Y=I:A is that in a *certain* pair of components (the case under study) we have established an empirical cryptanalytic proportion, and that this relationship will be true in *all* cases involving these same four elements.

(3) The vertical pairing IA nevertheless yields a good proportion, namely IA (Ø–9, 1–9)= DZ (Ø–4, 1–4), which permits the insertion of the letter D in position 3–9 after the homologous rectangular reading IA (Ø–9, Ø–1)=DZ (3–9, 3–1). Then the vertical pairing IF will yield the value T at the position 4–6 from the proportion I:F=O:T. This process is continued until the last vertical pairings at the extreme right of the matrix have been treated.

c. The matrix will now appear as in Fig. 29, below, after we have systematically proportioned once straight across the matrix from left to right:

Ø	A	B	C	D	E	F	G	H	I	J	K	L	M	N	O	P	Q	R	S	T	U	V	W	X	Y	Z
1	Y	L		Z	I			A		F	R	G		K			O	P			S	T				
2				K				F		P	E	Q		T			I	X	Z			H		D			
3	Z			U			T	D					F				X	N			O						
4	K		P		S	T			O					H											F		
5	I			U		K	M		E		O	B			S	T		L	W	X					A	D	

FIGURE 29

It should be emphasized that this has been a very detailed treatment of the problem in order to demonstrate the principles of proportioning. In actual practice, of course, the derivation of additional values would be a basis upon which to make further plaintext assumptions, probably rendering unnecessary the rigorous systematization of the process of proportioning across the width of the matrix, as just described.

d. From the matrix in Fig. 29, the following partial chains, fragments of equivalent primary components, are derived:

```
Ø-1  E I A Y   B L R   D Z   W S O K F   M G   X T P
Ø-2  L E K P   R I F   M Q   O T Z   S X D   V H
Ø-3  A Z   E U   H T N F   I D   R X   V O
Ø-4  A K   C P   E S   Y F T   I O   N H
Ø-5  Y A I E   Z D U   F K O S W   G M   R L B   T X
1-2  A F P Z   I K T D   R E   O X
```

It is observed that the chains Ø-3 and 1-2 bear a 1:3 relationship, i.e., one is an expansion at an interval of 3 of the other (cf. AZ and ID in line Ø-3, and AFPZ and IKTD in line 1-2).   Let then the chains in 1-2 be considered as a relative +1 decimation of the primary sequence, and inscribe AFPZ in the first four positions of a line of 26 cells on cross-section paper, thus:

```
1  2  3  4  5  6  7  8  9  10 11 12 13 14 15 16 17 18 19 20 21 22 23 24 25 26
A  F  P  Z
```

Now since the chains in line Ø-3 are a 1:3 contraction of the chains in line 1-2, then in order to equate line Ø-3 with line 1-2 we must expand the former at an interval of 3.   That is, the interval between the letters AZ must be 3 instead of 1.   This expansion, of course, also applies to the remaining chains in line Ø-3.   Thus HTNF must be expanded into H..T..N..F; and since we already have an F in our basic AFPZ sequence, these letters are then interpolated as follows:

```
1  2  3  4  5  6  7  8  9  10 11 12 13 14 15 16 17 18 19 20 21 22 23 24 25 26
A  F  P  Z                                H        T        N
```

e. With these new values, the sequence IKTD from the assumed +1 decimation in line 1-2 may be added, because of the presence of T in both sequences,

```
1  2  3  4  5  6  7  8  9  10 11 12 13 14 15 16 17 18 19 20 21 22 23 24 25 26
A  F  P  Z                                H  I  K  T  D     N
```

and the remaining fragments in the various chains may be amalgamated to permit the completion of the sequence as follows:

```
1  2  3  4  5  6  7  8  9  10 11 12 13 14 15 16 17 18 19 20 21 22 23 24 25 26
A  F  P  Z  L  J  S  Y  C  M  V  R  E  O  X  U  G  Q  H  I  K  T  D  B  N  W
```

This complete equivalent primary component, reconstructed from a series of smaller chains derived from a number of other equivalent primary components, may now be decimated to produce the original primary component which is a keyword-mixed sequence.

f. It must be noted that proportioning does not yield any *new* basic data, but merely gives a *restatement* of data already latent or inherent in the matrix; what the process does is to make all the relationships patent and this restatement facilitates the derivation of chains.   Furthermore, in the sets of partial chains given in subpar. *d*, the first five chains (Ø-1 to Ø-5) give all the latent relationships present in the matrix.   However, the addition of one more set of chains (line 1-2) brings out the existing relationships in a much clearer light than would have otherwise been possible, and this materially speeds up solution.

g. Another example may be presented to demonstrate further the principles of indirect symmetry. In a polyalphabetic cryptogram which factored to six alphabets, the following message beginning is assumed, based on collateral information:

```
123456 123456 123456 123456 123456 1
EKIIBK KGOZVZ DIWBBH LFCRKZ WKODBB Q...
ONEFIV EFIVEM MHOWIT ZERAMM UNITIO N
```

The values from this crib are put into a sequence reconstruction matrix, as follows:

```
Ø A B C D E F G H I J K L M N O P Q R S T U V W X Y Z
1 |      K           D Q E           W           L
2 |    F G   I         K
3 |    I       O           W     C
4 |R   I                       D   Z B
5 |    V     B       K
6 |                Z B           H   K
```

Noting an apparent +1 decimation of a keyword-mixed primary component between lines Ø–2, E:F = F:G = H:I, we may begin to reconstruct the original primary component by inspection directly without deriving additional values by proportions:[5]

```
          1 2 3 4 5 6 7 8 9 10 11 12 13 14 15 16 17 18 19 20 21 22 23 24 25 26
(Ø–2)  E:F = F:G = HI    E F G H I
(Ø–3)  E:I = I:O = OW    E F G H I . . . O . . . W
(Ø–4)  F:I = W:B         E F G H I . . . O . . . W . . B
(3–5)  I:V = O:B         E F G H I . . . O . . V W . . B
(Ø–1)  O:E = U:W         E F G H I . . . O . . V W . . B . . . . U
```

Continuing in this vein, we quickly recover the original primary component; let the student finish the solution as an exercise.

46. Theory of a graphical method of indirect symmetry.[6]—*a.* It has been shown that the interval between letters of a sequence obtained from a secondary alphabet is a constant function of the interval separating the letters in the original primary component. Consider the following sequence:

$$\text{Q U E S T I O N A B L Y C D F G H J K M P R V W X Z}$$

Assume that this component is slid against itself and that the following groups of partial sequences are obtained from three secondary alphabets:

> Group 1—S T I; U E; N A
> Group 2—I N; E T; O A
> Group 3—T N; Q S O

FIGURE 30

---

[5] It must be pointed out that there is no proof at this stage that the **HI** ties in with **EFG**; the **HI** *might* be in the key word, but intuitively it is felt that there is a greater probability that it is a part of the remaining alphabetical sequence after the occurrence of the key word.

[6] The basic theory underlying this modified method of applying the principles was first set forth in a brief paper in November 1941 by 1st Lt. Paul E. Neff, Sig. C. His original notes, slightly modified, comprise pars. 46 and 52, and subpars. 53*a* to *d*, inclusive.

Referring to the primary component, it will be seen that the letters of the partial sequences obtained from group 1 coincide in their interval (i.e., a +1 decimation) with that in the primary component; the letters of the partial sequences obtained from group 2 represent a decimation interval of two in the primary component; and those obtained from group 3, a decimation interval of three.

b. In the foregoing case, decimation was accomplished by taking intervals to the right along a horizontal component. Referring to the square based on **QUESTIONABLY** given in Fig. 27 on p. 87, let a portion of that square or matrix be considered, as shown in Fig. 31 below:

```
Column No.   1  2  3  4  5  6  7  8      1  2  3  4  5  6  7  8

             Q  U  E  S  T  I  O  N      Q  U  E  S  T  I  O  N
             U  E  S  T  I  O  N  A      U  E  S  T  I  O  N  A
             E  S  T  I  O  N  A  B      E  S  T  I  O  N  A  B
             S  T  I  O  N  A  B  L      S  T  I  O  N  A  B  L

                      (a)                         (b)


Column No.   1  2  3  4  5  6  7  8      1  2  3  4  5  6  7  8

             Q  U  E  S  T  I  O  N      Q  U  E  S  T  I  O  N
             U  E  S  T  I  O  N  A      U  E  S  T  I  O  N  A
             E  S  T  I  O  N  A  B      E  S  T  I  O  N  A  B
             S  T  I  O  N  A  B  L      S  T  I  O  N  A  B  L
             T  I  O  N  A  B  L  Y      T  I  O  N  A  B  L  Y

                      (c)                         (d)
```

FIGURE 31

c. Again referring to Fig. 30, we note that the partial sequences STI, UE, and NA can be obtained from Fig. 31a by reading down columns 4, 2, and 8, respectively. This can be represented graphically by the symbol ↓1, which means that all partial sequences obtained from Fig. 31a by proceeding downward in any column would be in the same group (i.e., secondary alphabet) and have the same decimation interval.

d. The partial sequences IN, ET, and OA can be represented graphically by 1⌐, or simply

↘1, which indicates that all partial sequences obtained by taking letters one space down and one space to the right, or one space down a diagonal to the right would represent the same decimation interval.

e. The partial sequences TN and QSO can be represented by the symbol 1⌐; but they can also be represented by 2⌐ and, if the entire matrix of Fig. 27 is considered, by other possible routes.

f. The decimation interval of a secondary sequence derived from a primary is the sum of the horizontal and vertical components of the route selected. Since the partial sequence TN can be

100

represented by $1\underset{2}{\llcorner\!\!\to}$, the decimation interval of this sequence is equal to the vertical decimation interval of the basic square plus twice the horizontal decimation interval in that square. Any other route selected for the same sequence would give an equivalent of this.

g. It is seen, therefore, that the decimation interval of a component can be represented graphically in various ways other than along the horizontal, by use of diagrams such as in Fig. 31, in which the successive juxtaposed components have the same relative displacement. In this case the successive horizontal lines had a one-letter displacement to the left.

h. Not being limited to one dimension, reconstruction of the primary component or an equivalent should be possible in one combined matrix by reversing the foregoing process and graphically integrating partial sequences from different secondary alphabets into a single diagram. Suppose the partial sequences in Fig. 30 are given and it is desired to reconstruct the primary component.

```
Group _____   1        2       3
                    S T I    I N     T N
Partial sequences   U E      E T     Q S O
                    N A      O A
                    ‾‾‾→     ↓1     ↘1
                     1
```

FIGURE 32

i. (1) Using cross-section paper one can arbitrarily select the STI sequence in group 1 and write this sequence horizontally, making the graphical notation ___→ below group 1.

(2) Proceeding to group 2, we note that the partial sequence IN contains one letter in common with the sequence STI already entered, but since NA forms a sequence in group 1 and OA forms a sequence in group 2, it is clear that two different decimations are involved and therefore it would be incorrect to integrate the STI and the IN into STIN. However, the letter N can arbitrarily be placed in any position *other* than along the horizontal line on which STI has been placed. It will be placed directly below the letter I and the group will be denoted graphically by ↓1, giving:

```
S T I
. . N
```

FIGURE 33a

(3) The skeleton of the matrix or diagram is now fixed in two dimensions, and no further letters can be *arbitrarily* placed within it. However, additional sequences from groups 1 and 2 can be added, provided a common letter is available in the diagram; sequences from other groups can be added, provided one pair is already entered in the diagram which would fix the proper graphical decimation.

(4) Moving to group 3, there is the partial sequence TN and it is noted that this pair of letters is present in the diagram. The symbol ↘1 can therefore be placed under group 3.

(5) In group 3 the partial sequence QSO appears and the letter S is in the diagram. It therefore follows that the letters Q and O can be placed thus:

```
(1)  Q . . .
(2)  . S T I
(3)  . . O N
```

FIGURE 33b

101

(6) Similarly the letter E of the partial sequence ET in group 2 goes directly above the T:

```
(1)  Q . E .
(2)  . S T I
(3)  . . O N
```

FIGURE 33c

(7) The letter U of the sequence UE in group 1 goes before the E:

```
(1)  Q U E .
(2)  . S T I
(3)  . . O N
```

FIGURE 33d

(8) Likewise the letter A of NA in group 1 follows N:

```
(1)  Q U E . .
(2)  . S T I .
(3)  . . O N A
```

FIGURE 33e

(9) The sequence OA in group 2 remains to be entered. Since both these letters are already in the diagram, the letter A can be placed under the existing O or the letter O can be placed above the existing A. Either alternative would be correct. Selecting the latter alternative yields the following:

```
(1)  Q U E . .
(2)  . S T I O
(3)  . . O N A
```

FIGURE 33f

j. All the original information has now been entered in the diagram seen in Fig. 33f and the letter O appears twice therein. This letter O may be termed the "tie-in" letter since it indicates the horizontal interval between the juxtaposed reconstructed sequences of the basic matrix. The absence of a tie-in letter in the diagram would indicate that insufficient data are present for the reconstruction of a complete sequence.

k. (1) By sliding the last row of Fig. 33f two intervals to the right we can superimpose the two O's, giving:

```
(1)  Q U E . . . .
(2)  . S T I O . .
(3)  . . . . O N A
```

FIGURE 33g

(2) Since each horizontal sequence must be shifted two intervals to the right of its initial position in relation to the line above, row (1) must be moved two intervals to the left of its original position. Thus:

```
(1)  Q U E . . . . .
(2)  . . . S T I O . .
(3)  . . . . . . O N A
```

FIGURE 33h

102

(3) Since the three rows involve the same decimation, and since the O of ONA coincides with the O of STIO, the ONA sequence may be raised up one row and united with the STIO sequence. If this is legitimate then the new row (2) may likewise be raised up one row. This yields the united sequence QUESTIONA.... This last step may be more clearly understood by studying the following partially reconstructed matrix:

```
(1)  Q U E S T I O N . .
(2)  E S T I O N A B . .
(3)  T I O N A B L Y . .
(4)  O N A B L Y C D . .
```

FIGURE 33i

l. The application of this graphical method of indirect symmetry to a specific example will be illustrated in par. 52, in the next chapter.

47. Further remarks.—*a.* A study of the principles and techniques discussed in this chapter should impress the student with the importance and value of indirect symmetry of position as a tool in cryptanalytics. Admittedly, indirect symmetry is a difficult subject to treat in writing, as it lends itself much better to blackboard demonstration in a classroom to insure thorough understanding of the principles. In any case, it is only by practice on a multitude of different examples and cases that these principles can be firmly implanted in the mind of the student— and even then the practice must be a continuous process, as it is only too easy to lose adroitness and facility in the application of these principles.

b. It is recommended that the student prepare as training aids five strips bearing the following sequences, double length:

(1) A normal A–Z sequence.
(2) A keyword-mixed sequence based on QUESTIONABLY.
(3) A keyword-mixed sequence based on QUESTIONABLY.
(4) A QUESTIONABLY keyword-mixed sequence, running in reverse.
(5) A keyword-mixed sequence based on HYDRAULIC.

With these strips the phenomena arising in all cases of direct and indirect symmetry may be duplicated, and the strips will be found useful in further experimentation and study. For example, strips (1) and (2) may be used to produce the phenomena of direct symmetry; (2) and (3) may be employed to produce the manifestations inherent in indirect symmetry extending to the Ø (plaintext) alphabet; (3) and (4) will bring out the peculiarities inherent in cases of indirect symmetry within the matrix only, but with the added feature of reciprocity between the plain and cipher components; and (4) and (5) will duplicate the idiosyncracies of indirect symmetry within the matrix only.

c. There are two principal methods of the application of indirect symmetry, and both are useful. In most cases it is usually easier to employ the graphical method, but occasionally there is encountered a problem which is easier to solve by the linear method.[7] But both methods should be practiced constantly, in order to maintain facility in the application of these principles.

d. Thus far there has been treated the recovery of primary components based on keyword-mixed sequences only. What would happen if the primary component were, say, a transposi-

---

[7] As an example, it should be noted that the chains in subpar. 45*d* permit easier treatment by the linear method than by the graphical method; the student should confirm this by experiment.

tion-mixed sequence? In the previous text [8] it has been shown how to recover the key word in various types of sequences, including transposition-mixed sequences. If, however, a transposition-mixed sequence were decimated, as it would be in the case of an equivalent primary component, a slight modification of procedure is necessary.

(1) Let us consider the following sequence:

A J V C O D F S H B P I N Z L M X R G T U K W Y E Q

This can easily be reduced to its original transposition rectangle:

4 9 3 7 1 8 6 5 2
H Y D R A U L I C
B E F G J K M N O
P Q S T V W X Z

However, if the basic sequence were decimated at an interval of three,

A C F B N M G K E J O S P Z X T W Q V D H I L R U Y,

the usual procedures of uncovering the transposition do not apply. The sequence must be decimated at the intervals of $+3$, $+5$, $+7$, $+9$, and $+11$; these resultant sequences are then examined in turn in an attempt to remove the transposition, reading these sequences both forwards and backwards. When the $+9$ decimation is considered, it will yield the original transposition.

(2) In unusual circumstances wherein all the secondary alphabets consist of even decimations, thus giving rise exclusively to 13-letter chains, there is an approach which may be used. For instance, let us suppose that we have the two chains (AEPTOQDCHYNMK) and (BZWXLIJRVUSGF). We will assume that the letters VWXYZ are at the end of the transposition matrix, and we will complete the sequences on these letters from the foregoing chains, thus:

V W X Y Z
U X L N W
S L I M X
G I J K L
F J R A I
B R V E J
Z V U P R
W U S T V
X S G O U
L G F Q S
I F B D G
J B Z C F
R Z W H B

---

[8] *Military Cryptanalytics, Part I,* par. 51.

The sequence GIJKL on the fourth line certainly looks like part of the transposition matrix *two* rows above the VWXYZ row. The diagram may now be expanded to the left and right, as is shown below:

```
S T U V W X Y Z
G O S U X L N W
F Q G S L I M X
B D F G I J K L M N O P Q
        F J R A I K M Q T D
        B R V E J A K D O C
        Z V U P R E A C Q H
        W U S T V P E H D Y
        X S G O U T P Y C N
        L G F Q S O T N H M
        I F B D G Q O M Y K
        J B Z C F D Q K N A
        R Z W H B C D A M E
                H C E K P
                Y H P A T
                N Y T E O
```

The key word PREACH (or PREACHER) is manifested, and, with a little experimentation, the original transposition matrix is recovered as follows:

```
5 6 3 1 2 4
P R E A C H
B D F G I J
K L M N O Q
S T U V W X
Y Z
```

This example admittedly is a simple case because of the brevity and particular composition of the key word; longer key words quickly complicate the problem of recovery, but the general lines just indicated will apply. Each case must be treated as a special case; the cryptanalyst has to be on the alert to capitalize on any peculiarities or phenomena manifested.

e. In treating a periodic cipher, the first step is, of course, to determine the number of alphabets involved by factoring the intervals between the various polygraphic repetitions. The cryptogram is then written out in proper period-lengths, and distributions for each alphabet are made; if necessary (that is, where the number of tallies per distribution is small), I.C.'s of the distributions are calculated, for further proof of the correctness of the factoring. These distributions are now carefully examined for (1) a possible fitting of all the distributions to the normal frequency distribution or its reverse, which would show that standard alphabets are involved; (2) a possible matching of all the distributions in respect to each other, which would show that the cipher component is the normal sequence; (3) a possible direct matching, "head on," of two or more distributions, which would show that the repeating key has repeated letters in the homologous positions; and (4) a possible fitting of only one or so of the distributions to the normal, "head on." If case (4) is present, then it is indicative that the cryptogram involves indirect symmetry extending to the ∅ (i.e., plaintext) row of the reconstruction matrix, since this manifestation is brought about by the interaction of a mixed sequence against itself, running in the same direction, with the juxtaposition $A_p = A_c$, so that every letter in that particular alphabet would be enciphered by itself.[9]

f. After the distributions have been examined, assumptions of high frequency letters or of probable words are inserted in the sequence reconstruction matrix, which in turn is examined for evidences or contradictions of direct symmetry or of indirect symmetry either within or without the matrix. (If reciprocity in more than one alphabet is observed, then it may be assumed that the cryptogram involves a mixed sequence running against itself in reverse.[10]) Whenever an assumption of a plaintext value for a cipher letter is made, the student should be sure to *finish* four things before making any further assumptions: (1) the plaintext value should be entered *below* all occurrences of the cipher letters; (2) the value should be entered in the reconstruction matrix; (3) examination should be made if any inconsistencies are produced either in the plain text or in the matrix; and (4) an attempt should be made to derive new values by direct symmetry or by proportioning within the matrix. Adherence to this systematization of method will save much time, contribute to the proper cryptanalytic education of the student, and will prove of considerable importance in the solution of difficult problems.

g. As a final remark on indirect symmetry, it must be noted that Porta matrices, as well as Vigenère-type matrices, might be encountered in which indirect symmetry will be manifested; this situation will obtain when both "families" of the Porta matrix are mixed sequences. It also follows that indirect symmetry will be present in schemes wherein the cipher component is a mixed numerical sequence and the plain component is also a mixed sequence.

---

[9] A fitting of only one or so of the distributions to the normal, at an interval of 13, is an earmark of a normal Porta system with the particular key involved being (A,B); a fitting of only one or so of the distributions to the reversed normal, "head on," is a characteristic of a complementary Porta system (cf. subpar. 23*d*), with the key involved being (A,B). The trial matching at various slides of the sets of letters A–M or N–Z should also not be overlooked as Porta characteristics (cf. subpars. 23*b* and 38*b*).

[10] Reciprocity in only one alphabet could be caused by a sequence shifted 13 positions against itself, in the case of 26-letter components.

Chapter VII

APPLICATION OF PRINCIPLES OF INDIRECT SYMMETRY OF POSITION

48. Applying the principles to a specific example.—*a.* The preceding chapter, with the many details covered, now forms a sufficient base for proceeding with an exposition of how the principles of indirect symmetry of position can be applied very early in the solution of a poly-alphabetic substitution cipher in which sliding primary components were employed to produce the secondary cipher alphabets for the enciphering of the cryptogram.

b. The case described below will serve not only to explain the method of applying these principles but will at the same time show how their application greatly facilitates the solution of a single, rather difficult, polyalphabetic substitution cipher. It is realized, of course, that the cryptogram could be solved by the usual methods of frequency and long, patient experimentation. However, the method to be described was actually applied and very materially reduced the amount of time and labor that would otherwise have been required for solution.

49. The cryptogram employed in the exposition.—*a.* The problem that will be used in this exposition involves an actual cryptogram submitted for solution in connection with a cipher device having two concentric disks upon which the same random-mixed alphabet appears, both alphabets progressing in the same direction. This was obtained from a study of the descriptive circular accompanying the cryptogram. By the usual process of factoring, it was determined that the cryptogram involved 10 alphabets. The message as arranged according to its period is shown in Fig. 34, in which all repetitions of two or more letters are indicated.

b. The triliteral frequency distributions are given in Fig. 35. It will be seen that on account of the brevity of the message, considering the number of alphabets involved, the frequency distributions do not yield many clues. By a very careful study of the repetitions, tentative individual determinations of values of cipher letters, as illustrated in Figs. 36, 37, 38, and 39, were made. These are given in sequence and in detail in order to show that there is nothing artificial or arbitrary in the preliminary stages of analysis here set forth.

107

									10										20										30

```
         10                    20                    30
A  W F U P C F O C J Y   G B Z D P F B O U O   G R F T Z M Q M A V
B  K Z U G D Y F T R W   G J X N L W Y O U X   I K W E P Q Z O K Z
C  P R X D W L Z I C W   G K Q H O L O D V M   G O X S N Z H A S E
D  B B J I P Q F J H D   Q C B Z E X Q T X Z   J C Q R Q F V M L H
E  S R Q E W M L N A E   G S X E R O Z J S E   G V Q W E J M K G H
F  R C V O P N B L C W   L Q Z A A A M D C H   B Z Z C K Q O I K F →
G ←C F B S C V X C H Q   Z T Z S D M X W C M   R K U H E Q E D G X
H  F K V H P J J K J Y   Y Q D P C J X L L L   G H X E R O Q P S E →
J ←G K B W T L F D U Z   O C D H W M Z T U Z   K L B P C J O T X E
K  H S P O P N M D L M   G C K W D V B L S E   G S U G D P O T H X
L  B K D Z F M T G Q J   L F U Y D T Z V H Q   Z G W N K X J T R N →
M ←Y T X C D P M V L W   B G B W O Q R G N   H H V L A Q Q V A V
N  J Q W O O T T N V Q   B K X D S O Z R S N   Y U X O P P Y O X Z
P  H O Z O W M X C G Q   J J U G D W Q R V M   U K W P E F X E N F →
Q ←C C U G D W P E U H   Y B W E W V M D Y J   R Z X
```

FIGURE 34

108

I

A	B	C	D	E	F	G	H	I	J	K	L	M	N	O	P	Q	R	S	T	U	V	W	X	Y	Z
	EB	FF			XK	YB	ES	XK	ZC	VZ	WQ			ZC	ZR	DC	HC	HR		MK		-F		YQ	QT
	HZ	FC				OR	NH		VQ	ZL	JF						MK							NT	QG
	XK					WJ	ZO		QJ								JZ							NU	
	WG					WK																		HB	
	QK					MO																			
						ES																			
						EV																			
						LH																			
						EK																			
						MC																			
						ES																			

II

A	B	C	D	E	F	G	H	I	J	K	L	M	N	O	P	Q	R	S	T	U	V	W	X	Y	Z
	GZ	QB			WU	ZW	GX		GX	IW	KB			GX		LZ	ZF	GX	GZ	YX	GQ				KU
	BJ	JQ			CB	BB	HV		JU	GQ				HZ		YD	PX	HP	YX						BZ
	YW	RV			LU					RU						JW	SQ	GU							RX
		OD								FV															
		GK								GB															
		CU								BD															
										BX															
										UW															

III

A	B	C	D	E	F	G	H	I	J	K	L	M	N	O	P	Q	R	S	T	U	V	W	X	Y	Z
	CZ		QP		RT				BI	CW				SO		KH				FP	CO	KE	JN		BD
	FS		CH													CR				ZG	KH	GN	RD		QA
	KW		KZ													RE				KH	HL	QO	OS		ZC
	LP															VW				SG		KP	SE		TS
	GW																			FY		BE	HE		00
																				JG		TC			
																				CG		KD			
																						UO			
																						Z-			

IV

A	B	C	D	E	F	G	H	I	J	K	L	M	N	O	P	Q	R	S	T	U	V	W	X	Y	Z
ZA		ZK	ZP	WP		UD	QO	JP			VA		XL	VP	UC		QQ	XN	FZ			QE		UD	BE
		XD	XW	QW		UD	UE				WK	PP	DC			BC					BT			DF
		XS	XR			UD	VP						WO	BC			ZD					KD			
		XR				UD	DW						XP	WE								BW			
		WW											ZW												

V

A	B	C	D	E	F	G	H	I	J	K	L	M	N	O	P	Q	R	S	T	U	V	W	X	Y	Z
AA		PF	GY	ZX	ZM					CQ	NW		SZ	HL	DF	RF	EO	DO	WL			DL			TM
LQ		SV	SM	WJ						NX				OT	EQ		EO					EM			
		PJ	WV	HQ											IQ							HM			
		.PJ	GP	PF											ON							WO			
			YT												HJ							OM			
			GP												ON							EV			
			GW												OP										
			GW																						

Figure 35

Triliteral Frequency Distributions

VI

A	B	C	D	E	F	G	H	I	J	K	L	M	N	O	P	Q	R	S	T	U	V	W	X	Y	Z
AM					CO				EM		WZ	ZQ	PB	RZ	DO	PZ			DZ		CX	LY	EQ	DF	NH
					PB				PJ		OO	WL	PM	RQ	DM	PF			OT		DB	DQ	KJ		
					QV				CX		TF	DX		WQ	PY	KO					WM	DP			
					EX				CO			WZ		SZ		EE									
												FT				AQ									
												WX													

VII

A	B	C	D	E	F	G	H	I	J	K	L	M	N	O	P	Q	R	S	T	U	V	W	X	Y	Z
	FO			QD	YT		ZA		JK		MN	JK	FC	WE	MM		MG		FM		VC	WO			QO
	NL			QJ					XT			AD	LD	XT			TN				MW	PO			LI
	VL			LD								ND	QI	OP							JL				OJ
												PV	JT	OR							MC				MT
												VD	PT	QV							FE				TV
														WR											OR

VIII

A	B	C	D	E	F	G	H	I	J	K	L	M	N	O	P	Q	R	S	T	U	V	W	X	Y	Z
HS	OJ	OV	XN			TQ	ZC	FH	MG	BC	QA	LA	BU	QS		QG		FR		ZH	XC				
	XH	MC	PU				OK	ZS	JJ	XL	VL	TV	YU			ZS		QX		ML					
	XG	EG								BS			ZK			QV		ZU		QA					
	FU												YX					OX							
	ML																	OH							
	MY																	JR							

IX

A	B	C	D	E	F	G	H	I	J	K	L	M	N	O	P	Q	R	S	T	U	V	W	X	Y	Z
MV		IW				KH	JD		CY	OZ	MH		EF			GJ	TW	AE		OO	DM		TZ	DJ	
NE		LW				DX	CQ		KY	IF	LL						TN	JE		OX	NQ		TE		
VV		DH				RN	TX				DM							PE		DZ	RM		OZ		
		WM				CQ	VQ				VW							LE		TZ					
																		RN		EH					

X

A	B	C	D	E	F	G	H	I	J	K	L	M	N	O	P	Q	R	S	T	U	V	W	X	Y	Z
				HQ	SB	KC		LS	QL		LG	VG	RY	UG		HZ				AK		RG	UI	JG	KP
				AG	NC			GR	YR			CR	GH			HZ				AJ		CG	GF	JY	XJ
				SG				CB			LG		SY			VB						CL	HB		UO
				SG				UY			VU					GJ						LB			UK
				XH																					XH
				SG																					

FIGURE 35—Continued.

[1] $G_c=E_p$; [2] $K_c=E_p$; [3] $X_c=E_p$; and [5] $D_c=E_p$, from frequency considerations.

[3 4 5] $UGD=THE_p$; [4 5 6] $PCJ=THE_p$; and [9 10 1] $SEG=THE_p$, from study of repetitions.

```
                       10                    20                  30
A   W F U P C F O C J Y   G B Z D P F B O U O   G R F T Z M Q M A V
        T T H       E                   E                       E

B   K Z U G D Y F T R W   G J X N L W Y O U X   I K W E P Q Z O K Z
        T H E     E                 E               E

C   P R X D W L Z I C W   G K Q H O L O D V M   G O X S N Z H A S E
        E           E E               E   E                   T H

D   B B J I P Q F J H D   Q C B Z E X Q T X Z   J C Q R Q F V M L H
            E                     E

E   S R Q E W M L N A E   G S X E R O Z J S E   G V Q W E J M K G H
            H       E           E       T H         E

F   R C V O P N B L C W   L Q Z A A A M D C H   B Z Z C K Q O I K F→

G  ←C F B S C V X C H Q   Z T Z S D M X W C M   R K U H E Q E D G X
                H                 E                 E T

H   F K V H P J J K J Y   Y Q D P C J X L L L   G H X E R O Q P S E→
        E       E             T H E                 E   E       T H

J  ←G K B W T L F D U Z   O C D H W M Z T U Z   K L B P C J O T X E
        E E       E               E     E             T H E       H

K   H S P O P N M D L M   G C K W D V B L S E   G S U G D P O T H X
                    E         E             T H E     T H E

L  ←B K D Z F M T G Q J   L F U Y D T Z V H Q   Z G W N K X J T R N→
        E                     T   E           E

M  ←Y T X C D P M V L W   B G B W W O Q R G N   H H V L A Q Q V A V
            E E                 E     E                         E

N   J Q W O O T T N V Q   B K X D S O Z R S N   Y U X O P P Y O X Z
                              E E   T               E       E   E

P   H O Z O W M X C G Q   J J U G D W Q R V M   U K W P E F X E N F→
                              T H E                 E T

Q  ←C C U G D W P E U H   Y B W E W V M D Y J   R Z X
        T H E         E           E
```

FIGURE 36

Refer to position K–22 in Fig. 36; S_c^2 assumed to be N_p.

Refer to position E–9 in Fig. 36; A_c^9 assumed to be W_p.

Then at position A–29, $\overset{9\ 10\ 1\ 2\ 3\ 4\ 5}{A\ V\ K\ Z\ U\ G\ D}$ is assumed to be WITH THE.

```
                    10                      20                    30
A │ W F U P C F O C J Y  G B Z D P F B O U O  G R F T Z M Q M A V
      T T H            E                    E                W I

B │ K Z U G D Y F T R W  G J X N L W Y O U X  I K W E P Q Z O K Z
    T H T H E          E           E            E

C │ P R X D W L Z I C W  G K Q H O L O D V M  G O X S N Z H A S E
        E            E E                E      E              T H

D │ B B J I P Q F J H D  Q C B Z E X Q T X Z  J C Q R Q F V M L H

E │ S R Q E W M L N A E  G S X E R O Z J S E  G V Q W E J M K G H
        W H E N E        W H E N E      T H E              E

F │ R C V O P N B L C W  L Q Z A A A M D C H  B Z Z C K Q O I K F→
                                      H

G │←C F B S C V X C H Q  Z T Z S D M X W C M  R K U H E Q E D G X
              H                E              E T

H │ F K V H P J J K J Y  Y Q D P C J X L L L  G H X E R O Q P S E→
      E            E            T H E            E E          T H

J │←G K B W T L F D U Z  O C D H W M Z T U Z  K L B P C J O T X E
    E E            E E              T        T H E            H

K │ H S P O P N M D L M  G C K W D V B L S E  G S U G D P O T H X
      N            E          E    T H E N T H E

L │ B K D Z F M T G Q J  L F U Y D T Z V H Q  Z G W N K X J T R N→
    E                      T   E

M │←Y T X C D P M V L W  B G B W W O Q R G N  H H V L A Q Q V A V
              E E            E E              W I

N │ J Q W O O T T N V Q  B K X D S O Z R S N  Y U X O P P Y O X Z
                        E E            T

P │ H O Z O W M X C G Q  J J U G D W Q R V M  U K W P E F X E N F→
                            T H E              E   T

Q │←C C U G D W P E U H  Y B W E W V M D Y J  R Z X
        T H E            H E                  H E
```

FIGURE 37

Additional Values From Assumptions (II)

Refer to position A–1, Fig. 37;
W F U P C F O C J Y; assume to be BUT THOUGH.
(positions 1 2 3 4 5 6 7 8 9 10)
– – T T H – – – – –

Refer to positions E–13 and H–23, Fig. 37; X E R O is assumed to be EACH.
(positions 3 4 5 6)
E – – –

```
                    10                    20                    30
A │ W F U P C F O C J Y    G B Z D P F B O U O    G R F T Z M Q M A V
  │   B U T T H O U G H        E           O          E           W I

B │ K Z U G D Y F T R W    G J X N L W Y O U X    I K W E P Q Z O K Z
  │   T H T H E            E         E                K W   A

C │ P R X D W L Z I C W    G K Q H O L O D V M    G O X S N Z H A S E
  │     E                  E E           U        E   E           T H

D │ B B J I P Q F J H D    Q C B Z E X Q T X Z    J C Q R Q F V M L H
  │                                      O

E │ S R Q E W M L N A E    G S X E R O Z J S E    G V Q W E J M K G H
  │       A                W H E N E A C H   T H   E           E

F │ R C V O P N B L C W    L Q Z A A A M D C H    B Z Z C K Q O I K F→
  │                                    H              U

G │←C F B S C V X C H Q    Z T Z S D M X W C M    R K U H E Q E D G X
  │   U     H     G                E                  E T

H │ F K V H P J J K J Y    Y Q D P C J X L L L    G H X E R O Q P S E→
  │           E       E    H       T H E          E   E A C H     T H

J │←G K B W T L F D U Z    O C D H W M Z T U Z    K L B P C J O T X E
  │  E E                           T           T        T H E U     H

K │ H S P O P N M D L M    G C K W D V B L S E    G S U G D P O T H X
  │   N                    E           E   T H    E N T H E   U

L │ B K D Z F M T G Q J    L F U Y D T Z V H Q    Z G W N K X J T R N→
  │   E                      U T   E     E

M │←Y T X C D P M V L W    B G B W W O Q R G N    H H V L A Q Q V A V
  │       E   E              E   H                              W I

N │ J Q W O O T T N V Q    B K X D S O Z R S N    Y U X O P P Y O X Z
  │                        E E   E     H     T        H         T

P │ H O Z O W M X C G Q    J J U G D W Q R V M    U K W P E F X E N F→
  │           G            T H E                  E   T       O

Q │←C C U G D W P E U H    Y B W E W V M D Y J    R Z X
  │   T H E                    A                  H E
```

Figure 38

113

4 5 6

OPN—assume ING from repetition and frequency.

9 10 1

HQZ—assume ING from repetition and frequency.

```
                10                        20                       30
A  W F U P C F O C J Y   G B Z D P F B O U O   G R F T Z M Q M A V
   B U T T H O U G H         E         N O         E             W I

B  K Z U G D Y F T R W   G J X N L W Y O U X   I K W E P Q Z O K Z
   T H T H E                 E       E             E   A N

C  P R X D W L Z I C W   G K Q H O L O D V M   G O X S N Z H A S E
       E             E E                 U       E     E         T H

D  B B J I P Q F J H D   Q C B Z E X Q T X Z   J C Q R Q F V M L H
             N     I                 T X           O

E  S R Q E W M L N A E   G S X E R O Z J S E   G V Q W E J M K G H
       A         W H     E N E A C H     T H   E         E

F  R C V O P N B L C W   L Q Z A A A M D C H   B Z Z C K Q O I K F →
       I N G                     H                         U

G ←C F B S C V X C H Q   Z T Z S D M X W C M   R K U H E Q E D G X
   U       H   G I N G   G         E               E T

H  F K V H P J J K J Y   Y Q D P C J X L L L   G H X E R O Q P S E →
   E       N E     H         T H E             E   E A C H     T H

J ←G K B W T L F D U Z   O C D H W M Z T U Z   K L B P C J O T X E
   E E                       W M     U Z         T     T H E U     H

K  H S P O P N M D L M   G C K W D V B L S E   G S U G D P O T H X
   N     I N G           E           E     T H   E N T H E   U   I

L  B K D Z F M T G Q J   L F U Y D T Z V H Q   Z G W N K X J T R N →
   E                       U T     E     I N   G

M ←Y T X C D P M V L W   B G B W W O Q R G N   H H V L A Q Q V A V
       E   E                 H       H                         W I

N  J Q W O O T T N V Q   B K X D S O Z R S N   Y U X O P P Y O X Z
         I         N     E E       H     T           I N

P  H O Z O W M X C G Q   J J U G D W Q R V M   U K W P E F X E N F →
         I   G   N           T H E             E T       O

Q ←C C U G D W P E U H   Y B W E W V M D Y J   R Z X
     T H E                   A                 H E
```

FIGURE 39

c. From the initial and subsequent tentative identifications shown in Figs. 36, 37, 38, and 39, the values obtained were arranged in the form of the secondary alphabets in a reconstruction matrix, shown in Fig. 40.

	1	2	3	4	5	6	7	8	9	10	11	12	13	14	15	16	17	18	19	20	21	22	23	24	25	26
ø	A	B	C	D	E	F	G	H	I	J	K	L	M	N	O	P	Q	R	S	T	U	V	W	X	Y	Z
1			W				G		Z											K						
2							K		Z					S							F					
3							X														U					
4	E							G		O											P					
5		R		D				C					P													
6					J		N	O							F											
7																				O						
8								C																		
9								J	H										S					A		
10								E	V					Q												

FIGURE 40

50. Application of principles.—*a.* Throughout this paragraph, reference will be made to Fig. 40, above. Hereafter, in order to avoid all ambiguity and for ease in reference, the position of a letter in Fig. 40 will be indicated as stated in footnote 2, p. 92. Thus, $N(6-7)$ refers to the letter N in row 6 and in column 7 of Fig. 40.

b. (1) Let us consider the following pairs of letters:

$$E(\text{ø}-5) \qquad J(6-5)$$
$$G(\text{ø}-7) \qquad N(6-7)$$
$$\left.\begin{array}{ll} H(\text{ø}-8) & O(6-8) \\ O(\text{ø}-15) & F(6-15) \end{array}\right\} \text{HO, OF = HOF}$$

(We are able to use the row marked "ø" in Fig. 40 since this is a case of a mixed sequence sliding against *itself*.)

(2) The immediate results of this set of values will now be given. Having HOF as a sequence, with EJ as belonging to the same displacement interval, suppose HOF and EJ are placed into juxtaposition as portions of sliding components. Thus:

Plain: . . . H O F . . .
Cipher: . . . E J . . . .

When $H_p = E_c$, then $O_p = J_c$.

(3) Refer now to alphabet 10, Fig. 40, where it is seen that $H_p = E_c$. *The derived value, $O_p = J_c$, can be inserted immediately in the same alphabet* and substituted in the cryptogram.

(4) The student may possibly get a clearer idea of the principles involved if he will regard the matter as though he were dealing with arithmetical proportion. For instance, given any three terms in the proportion $2:8 = 4:16$, the 4th term can easily be found. Furthermore, given the pair of values on the left-hand side of the equation, one may find numerous pairs of values which may be inserted in the right-hand side, or vice versa. For instance, $2:8 = 4:16$ is the same as $2:8 = 5:20$, or $9:36 = 4:16$, and so on. An illustration of each of these principles will now be given, reference being made to Fig. 40. As an example of the first principle, note that $E(\text{ø}-5)$:

$H(\emptyset-8)=J(6-5):O(6-8)$. Now find $E(10-8):H(\emptyset-8) = ?(10-15):O(\emptyset-15)$. It is clear that J may be inserted as the 3d term in this proportion, thus giving the important new value $O_p=J_c$,[10] which is exactly what was obtained directly above, by means of the partial sliding components. As an example of the second principle, note the following pairs:

$$E(\emptyset-5) \qquad H(\emptyset-8)$$
$$K(2-5) \qquad Z(2-8)$$
$$D(5-5) \qquad C(5-8)$$
$$J(6-5) \qquad O(6-8)$$

These additional pairs are also noted:

$$K(1-20) \qquad Z(1-7)$$
$$T(\emptyset-20) \qquad G(\emptyset-7)$$

Therefore, $E:H = K:Z = D:C = J:O = T:G$, and T may be inserted in position (4-5).

  c. (1) Again, GN belongs to the same set of displacement-interval values as do EJ and HOF. Hence, by superimposition:

$$\text{Plain: . . . H O F . . .}$$
$$\text{Cipher: . . . G N . . . .}$$

  (2) Referring to alphabet 4, when $H_p=G_c$, then $O_p=N_c$. Therefore, the letter N can be inserted in position (4-15) in Fig. 40, and the value $N_c=O_p$[6] can be substituted in the cryptogram.

  (3) Furthermore, note the corroboration found from this particular superimposition:

$$H(\emptyset-8) \qquad G(\emptyset-7)$$
$$O(6-8) \qquad N(6-7)$$

This checks up the value in alphabet 6, $G_p=N_c$.

  d. (1) Again superimpose HOF and GN:

$$\text{. . . H O F . . .}$$
$$\text{. . . G N . . .}$$

  (2) Note this corroboration:

$$O(6-8) \qquad G(4-8)$$
$$F(6-15) \qquad N(4-15)$$

which has just been inserted in Fig. 40, as stated above.

  e. (1) Again using HOF and EJ, but in different superimposition:

$$\text{. . . H O F . .}$$
$$\text{. . E J . . . .}$$

  (2) Refer now to H(9-9), J(9-8). Directly under these letters is found V(10-9), E(10-8). Therefore, the V can be added immediately before HOF, making the sequence VHOF.

  f. (1) Now take VHOF and juxtapose it with EJ, thus:

$$\text{. . . V H O F . . .}$$
$$\text{. . . E J . . .}$$

(2) Refer now to Fig. 40, and find the following:

$$V(10-9) \quad E(10-8)$$
$$H(9-9) \quad J(9-8)$$
$$0(4-9) \quad G(4-8)$$
$$I(\emptyset-9) \quad H(\emptyset-8)$$

(3) From the value OG it follows that G can be set next to J in EJ. Thus:

```
. . . V H O F . . .
. . . E J G . . .
```

(4) But GN already is known to belong to the same set of displacement-interval values as EJ. Therefore, it is now possible to combine EJ, JG, and GN into one sequence, EJGN, yielding:

```
. . . V H O F . . .
. . . E J G N . . .
```

g. (1) Refer now to Fig. 40.

$$V(\emptyset-22) \quad E(\emptyset-5)$$
$$?(1-22) \quad G(1-5)$$
$$?(2-22) \quad K(2-5)$$
$$?(3-22) \quad X(3-5)$$
$$?(5-22) \quad D(5-5)$$
$$?(6-22) \quad J(6-5)$$

(2) The only values which can be inserted are:

$$0(1-22) \quad G(1-5)$$
$$H(6-22) \quad J(6-5)$$

(3) This means that $V_p=0_c$ in alphabet 1 and that $V_p=H_c$ in alphabet 6. There is one 0_c in the frequency distribution for Alphabet 1, and no H_c in that for Alphabet 6. The frequency distribution is, therefore, corroborative insofar as these values are concerned.

h. (1) Further, taking EJGN and VHOF, superimpose them thus:

```
. . . E J G N . . .
. . . V H O F . . .
```

(2) Refer now to Fig. 40.

$$E(\emptyset-5) \quad H(\emptyset-8)$$
$$G(1-5) \quad ?(1-8)$$

(3) From the diagram of superimposition the value G(1-5) F(1-8) can be inserted, which gives $H_p=F_c$ in alphabet 1.

i. (1) Again, VHOF and EJGN are juxtaposed:

```
. . . V H O F . . .
. . . E J G N . . .
```

(2) Refer to Fig. 40 and find the following:

$$H(\emptyset-8) \quad G(4-8)$$
$$A(\emptyset-1) \quad E(4-1)$$

117

This means that it is possible to add A, thus:

```
. . . A V H O F . . .
. . . E J G N . . .
```

(3) In the set there are also:

```
E(∅–5)    G(1–5)
G(∅–7)    Z(1–7)
```

Then in the superimposition

```
. . . E J G N . . .
. . . E J G N . . .
```

it is possible to add Z under G, making the sequence EJGNZ.

(4) Then taking

```
. . . A V H O F . . .
. . . E J G N Z . . .
```

and referring to Fig. 40:

```
H(∅–8)    N(∅–14)
O(6–8)    ?(6–14)
```

It will be seen that O=Z from superimposition, and hence in alphabet 6 $N_p = Z_c$, an important new value, but occurring only once in the cryptogram. Has an error been made? The work so far seems too corroborative in interlocking details to think so.

j. (1) The possibilities of the superimposition and sliding of the AVHOF and the EJGNZ sequences have by no means been exhausted as yet, but a little different trail this time may be advisable.

```
E(∅–5)    T(∅–20)
G(1–5)    K(1–20)
X(3–5)    U(3–20)
```

(2) Then:

```
. . . E J G N Z . . .
. . . T . K . . .
```

(3) Now refer to the following:

```
E(∅–5)     K(2–5)
N(∅–14)    S(2–14)
```

whereupon the value S can be inserted:

```
. . . E J G N Z . . . .
. . . T . K . . S . . .
```

k. (1) Consider all the values based upon the displacement interval corresponding to JG:

```
J(6–5)    G(1–5)    │ J(9–8)    G(4–8)
N(6–7)    Z(1–7)    │ H(9–9)    O(4–9)
                    │ S(9–20)   P(4–20)   │ S(2–14)    P(5–14)
                    │                     │ Z(2–8)     C(5–8)
                    │                     │ K(2–5)     D(5–5)
```

(2) Since J and G are sequent in the EJGNZ sequence, it can be said that all the letters of the foregoing pairs are also sequent. Hence ZC, SP, and KD are available as new data. These give EJGNZC and T.KD.SP.

(3) Now consider:

$$T(\emptyset{-}20) \quad P(4{-}20)$$
$$A(\emptyset{-}1) \quad E(4{-}1)$$
$$H(\emptyset{-}8) \quad G(4{-}8)$$
$$I(\emptyset{-}9) \quad O(4{-}9)$$

Now in the T.KD.SP sequence the interval between T and P is T . . . . . . P. Hence, the interval between A and E is 6 also. It follows therefore that the sequences AVHOF and EJGNZC should be united, thus:

```
      1 2 3 4 5 6
. . . A V H O F . E J G N Z C . . .
```

(4) Corroboration is found in the interval between H and G, which is also 6. The letter I can be placed into position, from the relation I($\emptyset{-}9$) O(4$-$9), thus:

```
      1 2 3 4 5 6
. . . I . . A V H O F . E J G N Z C . . .
```

l. (1) From Fig. 40:

$$H(\emptyset{-}8) \quad Z(2{-}8)$$
$$E(\emptyset{-}5) \quad K(2{-}5)$$
$$N(\emptyset{-}14) \quad S(2{-}14)$$
$$U(\emptyset{-}21) \quad F(2{-}21)$$

(2) Since in the I..AVHOF.EJGNZC sequence the letters H and Z are separated by 8 intervals one can write:

```
          1 2 3 4 5 6 7 8
. . . H . . . . . . . Z . . .
. . . E . . . . . . . K . . .
. . . N . . . . . . . S . . .
. . . U . . . . . . . F . . .
```

(3) Hence one can make the sequence

```
                1 2 3 4 5 6 7 8
. . . I . . A V H O F . E J G N Z C . . K . . .
Then . . . I . . A V H O F . E J G N Z C T . K D . S P . . .
and . . U I . . A V H O F . E J G N Z C T . K D . S P . . .
         1 2 3 4 5 6 7 8                 1 2 3 4 5 6 7 8
```

m. (1) Subsequent derivations can be indicated very briefly as follows:

$$E(\emptyset{-}5) \quad C(\emptyset{-}3)$$
$$D(5{-}5) \quad R(5{-}3)$$

```
       1 2 3 4 5 6 7 8 9 10 11 12 13 14 15 16 17 18 19 20 21 22 23 24 25 26
From U I . . A V H O F . E J G N Z C T . K D . S P . . .
one can write         . . . E . . . . C . . .
                              1 2 3 4 5
```

and

```
                                      . . . D . . . . R .
                                            1 2 3 4 5
```

making the sequence

```
   1 2 3 4 5 6 7 8 9 10 11 12 13 14 15 16 17 18 19 20 21 22 23 24 25 26
   U I . . A V H O F . E J G N Z C T . K D . S P . R .
```

119

(2) Another derivation:

$$U(3\text{–}20) \quad T(\emptyset\text{–}20)$$
$$X(3\text{–}5) \quad E(\emptyset\text{–}5)$$

<pre>
        1 2 3 4 5 6 7 8 9 10 11 12 13 14 15 16 17 18 19 20 21 22 23 24 25 26
From   U I . . A V H O F . E J G N Z C T . K D . S P . R .
one can write U . . . . T . . .
and   . . . . E . . . . X . . . . .
</pre>

making the sequence

<pre>
        1 2 3 4 5 6 7 8 9 10 11 12 13 14 15 16 17 18 19 20 21 22 23 24 25 26
        U I . . A V H O F . E J G N Z C T . K D X S P . R .
</pre>

(3) Another derivation:

$$E(\emptyset\text{–}5) \quad G(1\text{–}5)$$
$$B(\emptyset\text{–}2) \quad W(1\text{–}2)$$

<pre>
From   . . . E J G . . .
one can write . . . E . G . . .
and then   . . . B . W . . .
</pre>

There is only one place where B.W can fit, *viz.*, at the end:

<pre>
        1 2 3 4 5 6 7 8 9 10 11 12 13 14 15 16 17 18 19 20 21 22 23 24 25 26
        U I . . A V H O F . E J G N Z C T . K D X S P B R W
</pre>

n. Only four letters remain to be placed into the sequence, *viz.*, L, M, Q, and Y. Their positions are easily found by application of the primary component to the message. The complete sequence is as follows:

<pre>
        1 2 3 4 5 6 7 8 9 10 11 12 13 14 15 16 17 18 19 20 21 22 23 24 25 26
        U I M Y A V H O F L E J G N Z C T Q K D X S P B R W
</pre>

With the primary component fully reconstructed, the decipherment of the rest of the text can be accomplished with speed and precision.   The complete plain text is shown in the figure below:

```
                    10                  20                  30
A │ W F U P C F O C J Y   G B Z D P F B O U O   G R F T Z M Q M A V
  │ B U T T H O U G H W   E C A N N O T A S Y   E T R E V I E W W I

B │ K Z U G D Y F T R W   G J X N L W Y O U X   I K W E P Q Z O K Z
  │ T H T H E M I N D S   E Y E O U R P A S T   W E C A N T O A N E

C │ P R X D W L Z I C W   G K Q H O L O D V M   G O X S N Z H A S E
  │ X T E N T F O R E S   E E O U R F U T U R   E W E C A N W I T H

D │ B B J I P Q F J H D   Q C B Z E X Q T X Z   J C Q R Q F V M L H
  │ S C I E N T I F I C   C O N F I D E N C E   L O O K F O R W A R

E │ S R Q E W M L N A E   G S X E R O Z J S E   G V Q W E J M K G H
  │ D T O A T I M E W H   E N E A C H O F T H   E B O D I E S C O M

F │ R C V O P N B L C W   L Q Z A A A M D C H   B Z Z C K Q O I K F →
  │ P O S I N G T H E S   O L A R S Y S T E M   S H A L L T U R N A

G │ ← C F B S C V X C H Q   Z T Z S D M X W C M   R K U H E Q E D G X
  │ N U N C H A N G I N   G F A C E I N P E R   P E T U I T Y T O T

H │ F K V H P J J K J Y   Y Q D P C J X L L L   G H X E R O Q P S E →
  │ H E S U N E A C H W   I L L T H E N H A V   E R E A C H E D T H

J │ ← G K B W T L F D U Z   O C D H W M Z T U Z   K L B P C J O T X E
  │ E E N D O F I T S E   V O L U T I O N S E   T I N T H E U N C H

K │ H S P O P N M D L M   G C K W D V B L S E   G S U G D P O T H X
  │ A N G I N G S T A R   E O F D E A T H T H   E N T H E S U N I T

L │ B K D Z F M T G Q J   L F U Y D T Z V H Q   Z G W N K X J T R N →
  │ S E L F W I L L G O   O U T B E C O M I N   G A C O L D A N D L

M │ ← Y T X C D P M V L W   B G B W W O Q R G N   H H V L A Q Q V A V
  │ I F E L E S S M A S   S A N D T H E S O L   A R S Y S T E M W I

N │ J Q W O O T T N V Q   B K X D S O Z R S N   Y U X O P P Y O X Z
  │ L L C I R C L E U N   S E E N G H O S T L   I K E I N S P A C E

P │ H O Z O W M X C G Q   J J U G D W Q R V M   U K W P E F X E N F →
  │ A W A I T I N G O N   L Y T H E R E S U R   R E C T I O N O F A

Q │ C C U G D W P E U H   Y B W E W V M D Y J   R Z X
  │ N O T H E R C O S M   I C C A T A S T R O   P H E
```

FIGURE 41

121

o. The primary component appears to be a random-mixed sequence; no key word for the repeating key is to be found, at least none reappears on experimentation with various hypotheses as to enciphering equations. Nevertheless, the random construction of the primary component did not complicate or retard the solution.

p. Some analysts may prefer to work exclusively with the reconstruction matrix, rather than with sliding strips. One method is as good as the other and personal preferences will dictate which will be used by the individual student. If the reconstruction matrix is used, the original letters should be inserted in red pencil, so as to differentiate them from derived letters.

51. General remarks on the foregoing solution.—*a*. The sequence of steps described in the preceding paragraphs corresponds quite closely with that actually followed in solving the problem. It is also to be pointed out that this method can be used as a control in the early stages of analysis because it will allow the cryptanalyst to check assumptions for values. For example, the very first value derived in applying the principles of indirect symmetry to the problem herein described was $H_c = A_p$ in alphabet 1. As a matter of fact the author had been inclined toward this value, from a study of the frequency and combinations which H_c showed; when the indirect-symmetry method actually substantiated his tentative hypothesis he immediately proceeded to substitute the value given. If he had assigned a different value to H_c, or if he had assumed a letter other than H_c for A_p in that alphabet, the conclusion would immediately follow that either the assumed value for H_c was erroneous, or that one of the values which led to the derivation of $H_c = A_p$ by indirect symmetry was wrong. Thus, these principles aid not only in the systematic and nearly automatic derivation of new values (with only occasional, or incidental references to the actual frequencies of letters), but they also assist very materially in serving as corroborative checks upon the validity of the assumptions already made.

b. Furthermore, while the author has set forth, in the reconstruction matrix in Fig. 40, a set of 30 values apparently obtained before he began to reconstruct the primary component, this was done for purposes of clarity and brevity in exposition of the principles herein described. As a matter of fact, what he did was to watch very carefully, when inserting values in the reconstruction matrix to find the very first chance to employ the principles of indirect symmetry; and just as soon as a value could be derived, he substituted the value in the cryptographic text. This is good procedure for two reasons. Not only will it disclose impossible combinations but also it gives opportunity for making further assumptions for values by the addition of the derived values to those previously assumed. Thus, the processes of reconstructing the primary component and finding additional data for the reconstruction proceed simultaneously in an ever-widening circle.

c. It is worth noting that the careful analysis of only 30 cipher equivalents in the reconstruction matrix shown in Fig. 40 results in the derivation of the entire table of secondary alphabets, 676 values in all. And while the elucidation of the method seems long and tedious, in its actual application the results are speedy, accurate, and gratifying.

d. (1) The problem here used as an illustrative case is by no means one that most favorably presents the application and the value of the method, for it has been applied in other cases with much speedier success. For example, suppose that in a cryptogram of 6 alphabets the equivalents of only THE_p in all 6 alphabets are fairly certain. As in the previous case, it is supposed

122

that the secondary alphabets are obtained by sliding a mixed alphabet against itself. Suppose the partial secondary alphabets to be as follows:

```
  Ø A B C D E F G H I J K L M N O P Q R S T U V W X Y Z
1         B     Q                             E
2         C     L                             X
3         I     V                             C
4         N     P                             B
5         X     O                             P
6         T     Z                             V
```

FIGURE 42

(2) Consider the following chain of derivatives arranged diagrammatically:

```
    H(Ø-8)    O(5-8)
    T(Ø-20)   P(5-20)
    E(Ø-5)    X(5-5)    E(1-20)   X(2-20)
              Q(1-8)    L(2-8)
              B(1-5)    C(2-5)───▶B(4-20)   C(3-20)
                                  N(4-5)    I(3-5)
                                  P(4-8)    V(3-8)───▶

──▶P(5-20)   V(6-20)
    O(5-8)    Z(6-8)
    X(5-5)    T(6-5)───▶X(2-20)   T(Ø-20)
              L(2-8)    H(Ø-8)
              C(2-5)    E(Ø-5)───▶C(3-20)   E(1-20)
                                  V(3-8)    Q(1-8)
                                  I(3-5)    B(1-5)
```

FIGURE 43

(3) These pairs manifestly all belong to the same displacement interval, and therefore unions can be made immediately. The complete list is as follows:

EX, QL, NI, LH, HO, BC, OZ, CE, TP, PV, XT, VQ, IB.

(4) Joining pairs by their common letters, the following sequence is obtained:

. . . N I B C E X T P V Q L H O Z . . .

e. With this as a nucleus the cryptogram can be solved speedily and accurately. When it is realized that the cryptanalyst can assume THE's rather readily in some cases, the value of this principle becomes apparent. When it is further realized that if a cryptogram has sufficient text to enable the THE's to be found easily, it is usually also not at all difficult to make correct assumptions of values for two or three other high-frequency letters; it is then clear that the principles of indirect symmetry of position may often be used with gratifyingly quick success to reconstruct the complete primary component.

f. When the probable-word method is combined with the principles of indirect symmetry the solution of a difficult case is often accomplished with astonishing ease and rapidity.

52. Use of the graphical method in the foregoing example.—a. As an illustration of the application of the graphical method of indirect symmetry, we shall use as an example the crypto-

gram given in par. 49. It is desired to reconstruct the original primary component, or an equivalent, from the values entered in the reconstruction matrix shown in Fig. 40 on p. 115. Since a mixed sequence is sliding against itself, all the partial sequences (pairs or greater) which can be established by studying the reconstruction matrix are listed as shown in Fig. 44a, below. The single pairs in $\emptyset$–7 and $\emptyset$–8 are crossed out since they offer no data for reconstruction. This yields the following groups of partial sequences:

$\emptyset$– 1	2	3	4	5	6	7	8	9	10
BW	EK	EX	AE	ED	EJ	~~UO~~	~~GC~~	IHJ	HE
EGZ	HZ	TU	HG	HCR	GN			TS	IV
TK	NS		IO	NP	HOF			WA	NQ
	UF		TP						

FIGURE 44a

b. (1) The sequences HOF and EJ in group 6 and HE in group 10 are noted. The HOF will be placed horizontally and the notation ⟶ is made under group 6. The letter E of the pair

HE of group 10 will be placed under the H, and the notation ↓1 added under group 10. Thus:

$\emptyset$– 1	2	3	4	5	6	7	8	9	10
BW	EK	EX	AE	ED	EJ	~~UO~~	~~GU~~	IHJ	HE
EGZ	HZ	TU	HG	HCR	GN			TS	IV
TK	NS		IO	NP	HOF			WA	NQ
	UF		TP						

⟶ (under group 4), ↓1 (under group 10)

FIGURE 44b

Since the sequence EJ belongs to the same displacement interval as HOF, the letter J can be inserted after the letter E, giving:

```
H O F
E J .
```

FIGURE 45a

No more pairs can be added immediately from groups 6 or 10. Those pairs already entered are crossed out in their respective groups and an inspection is made for additional data in another group.

(2) The sequence IHJ is noted in group 9. The letters H and J are already entered in the diagram. One can therefore place the letter I, and the notation ↘1 is placed under group 9. The addition of the letter I now permits the insertion of the letter V of the sequence IV in group 10, giving:

```
I . . .
V H O F
. E J .
```

FIGURE 45b

(3) In group 4 there is the sequence IO which is obtainable in the diagram by the route 1⌐₂ .

This notation is made beneath group 4; the letter A of the sequence AE and the letter G of the

124

sequence HG can now also be entered.   The addition of the letter **A** permits the placement of the letter **W** of the pair **WA** of group 9; likewise the addition of the letter **G** permits the insertion of the letter **N** of the sequence **GN** of group 6; finally, the placement of the letter **N** permits the placement of the **Q** of group 9.   One now has:

```
W . I . . . .
. A V H O F .
. . . E J G N
. . . . . . Q
```

FIGURE 45c

(4) Referring to group 1, we note the sequence EGZ, of which EG appears in the diagram at The letter Z can therefore be placed and the letter B of the sequence BW can be inserted two intervals to the left of the letter W, giving:

```
B . W . I . . . .
. . . A V H O F . .
. . . . . E J G N Z
. . . . . . . Q .
```

FIGURE 45d

(5) Noting the sequence HZ of group 2 as being graphically represented in the diagram by, we place the letters K, S, and U of the sequence EK, NS and UF.   Thus:

```
B . W U I . . . . . .
. . . A V H O F . . . .
. . . . . E J G N Z . . .
. . . . . . . . Q K . . S
```

FIGURE 45e

(6) The letter **T** of the sequence **TK** of group 1 can now be placed, which permits the addition of the letter **P** of the sequence **TP** of group 4.   A study of the diagram shows the pair **TU** of group 3 at interval 3, which allows the placing of the letter **X** of the pair **EX** of the same group.

One then has:

```
. X . . . . . . . . .
B . W U I . . . . . . .
. . . A V H O F . . . .
. . . . . E J G N Z . . .
. . . . . . . T Q K . . S
. . . . . . . . P . . .
```

FIGURE 45f

125

(7) The diagram now shows the pair NP of group 5 at 2⌐→ , the letter D of the sequence ED
                                                          1
and the letters C and R of HCR can therefore be inserted.   Thus:

```
. X . . . . .   . . .   .
B . W U I . . .   . . .   .
. . . A V H O F .   . . . .
. . . . . E J G N Z . . .
. . . . . C T Q K . . S
. . . . . . D . . P . . .
. . . . . . . R . . . .
```

FIGURE 45g

(8) Pair TS of group 9 remains.   It has already been noted that the notation ↘1 has
been applied to group 9.   Hence the letter S can also be placed one interval to the right and
below the T, as shown in Fig. 45h, in which all the available data are now entered.

```
(1) . X . . . . .   . . .   .
(2) B . W U I . . .   . . .   .
(3) . . . A V H O F .   . . . .
(4) . . . . . E J G N Z . . .
(5) . . . . . C T Q K . . S
(6) . . . . . . D . S P . . .
(7) . . . . . . . R . . . .
```

FIGURE 45h

c. (1) The letter S appears in rows (5) and (6) at a displacement interval of four.   This
letter then serves as the "tie-in" letter.   Marking off 26 squares on cross-section paper the D.SP
of row (6) is written, and row (5) is moved four intervals to the left, at which position the letter
S is properly superimposed as follows:

```
        1 2 3 4 5 6 7 8 9 10 11 12 13 14 15 16 17 18 19 20 21 22 23 24 25 26
Row (5) C T Q K . . S .
Row (6) . . . . D . S P
```

(2) Likewise row (4) is moved four intervals to the left of its original relative position to
row (5) and dropped into position.   Row (3) is moved the same distance in relation to row (4),
etc.   These steps may be illustrated as follows:

```
        1 2 3 4 5 6 7 8 9 10 11 12 13 14 15 16 17 18 19 20 21 22 23 24 25 26
Row (4) . . . . E J G N Z C T Q K D . S P . . . . . . . . .
Row (3) H O F . E J G N Z C T Q K D . S P . . . . . . . A V
Row (2) H O F . E J G N Z C T Q K D . S P B . W U T . . A V
```

(3) The placing of the letter X of row (1) and the letter R of row (7) gives the final sequence:

```
        1 2 3 4 5 6 7 8 9 10 11 12 13 14 15 16 17 18 19 20 21 22 23 24 25 26
        H O F . E J G N Z C T Q K D X S P B R W U I . . A V
```

(4) It will be noted that the foregoing component is identical with that obtained in subpar.
50m(3).

53. Additional remarks on the graphical method.—*a.* In the example given above only one tie-in letter was available and it was located in adjacent rows. Although only one is necessary, in most cases several tie-in letters are present after all pairs of letters have been entered in the diagram; then the superimposed sequences can be easily connected by their common letters. If the tie-in letter had appeared in adjacent columns instead of adjacent rows as in the foregoing example, the columns would have been shifted vertically and the sequence taken from the diagram in that manner.

b. When only a few pairs of letters forming partial sequences are available, frequently only one tie-in letter may be encountered. If it does not occur in adjacent rows or columns the component can still be written with additional considerations. For example, adjacent diagonals might be used. However, the student will experience no difficulty after the application of this method to a few problems.

c. Since all the data are entered in one diagram, the graphical method of reconstruction quickly discloses erroneous assumptions and enables one to ascertain in a short time whether sufficient data are present for the reconstruction of the component. Even if this is not the case, the diagram automatically offers new values which may be substituted in the cryptogram. One may then assume additional values which can be entered in the diagram or which will serve to corroborate sequences already entered.

d. The placing of the first two sequences of different displacement intervals in the diagram determines the type of sequences that will be established. If the original sequence entered horizontally in the diagram is an odd decimation (other than 13) of the primary component, a 26-letter sequence can be obtained horizontally. If this original sequence is initially tied in vertically with another sequence of an odd decimation interval, a 26-letter sequence can also be obtained vertically from the diagram.

e. (1) In certain instances, however, it will happen that the available partial sequences have all resulted from even decimations of the basic sequence and that no tie-in letters are present to permit the integration of all the data into a single diagram. In such cases the reconstruction of the basic sequence may take place by taking data from two or more different diagrams, and then, using the relative positions of the letters with respect to each other in these diagrams, the basic sequence may be established. This method can best be demonstrated by means of an example, and the following one is based upon the QUEST... sequence of subpar. 46*a.* Suppose the reconstruction diagram from the derivation of a few plaintext-ciphertext relationships yields the following partial sequences:

Group	1	2	3
	Q H O	Q X V	Q T A
	F T	O T	X E
	C E	P K	F K
Sequences	J N	F C	U I B
	W D S	U Z W	Z S
		N I	Y G M
		G D	

FIGURE 46

(2) The partial sequences in the three groups can be combined to form two diagrams. This may be accomplished by considering the sequences of group 1 as parts of a horizontal component and those of group 2 as parts of a vertical component of a cipher square based upon

127

the original or an equivalent primary sequence. When all the letters of these two groups have been entered into the two resultant diagrams in Figs. 47a and b, it will be observed that the positions occupied in these two diagrams by the letters of group 3 represent the interval $1 \rfloor_{2}$. Thus:

```
Q H O . .          Y U J N . .
X F T P .          . Z G I . .
V C E K A          . W D S M B
    (a)                (b)
```

FIGURE 47

(3) It will be noted that there are 12 letters in each of the two diagrams and that all the letters appearing in the original partial sequences have been included in these two groups. It appears, first, that two 13-letter sequences are involved and second, that the partial sequences in all three groups represent even decimations of the basic component. The problem now remains to reconstruct the original or an equivalent primary cipher square to which these diagrams belong, or to find the original or an equivalent primary component of which the partial sequences in groups 1, 2, and 3 are derivatives.

(4) Since the two diagrams are linked by the partial sequences of group 3 (because the interval $1 \rfloor_{2}$ is common to both of them), it follows that any two letters in one of the diagrams

will be separated from each other in the basic sequence by the same interval as any two letters occupying the same relative positions in the other diagram. Another way of saying the same thing is, that while the intervals between V and C, C and E, E and K, and K and A, in the basic component (or an equivalent thereof) are unknown, whatever they may be they are identical and the same as that between W and D, D and S, S and M, M and B (from WDSMB), or between Y and U, U and J, J and N (from YUJN), and so on. Likewise, Q and K (interval $2 \rfloor_{3}$) are sep-

arated by the same interval as Y and S, or U and M, and so on.

(5) Making the easiest assumption first, suppose the basic sequence is a keyword-mixed sequence, and that the letter Z is the final letter thereof. If it is preceded by Y, then, because of the relative positions occupied by Y and Z in Fig. 47b, the following would also be sequent in the basic sequence: QF, HT, OP, XC, FE, TK, PA; UG, JI, ZD, GS, and IM. Since the majority of these are hardly likely to occur in a keyword-mixed sequence, the assumption that Y precedes Z is discarded. Suppose X precedes Z (implying that Y is in the key word). But X and Z are not in the same diagram, so no test can be made. Suppose the sequence is W . Z. Then the following sequences would be valid:

```
W . Z . U          V . X . Q
D . G . J          C . F . H
S . I . N          E . T . O
                   K . P
```

These look very likely. In fact, noting the D . G . J and the C . F . H sequences it seems logical to integrate or dovetail them thus: CDFGHJ. This then suggests that W . Z . U and V . X . Q may be integrated into VWXZQU; S . I . N and E . T . O may be integrated into ESTION. From this point on the matter of extending the partial sequences into the basic one is simple and rather obvious.

128

f. (1) Suppose, however, that the basic sequence is not a keyword-mixed sequence, so that clues of the nature of those employed in the preceding subparagraph are no longer available. Then what?

(2) Referring back to subpar. 53*e*(2), it has already been noted that the two diagrams, each containing 12 letters, represent half-sequences (of 13 letters) derived from an even decimation of the original component. (The decimation must be the same in both cases because the interval 1⌐→ is common to them.) Suppose an attempt is made to integrate the QHO, XFTP, and VCEKA sequences of Fig. 47*a* into a 13-letter cycle or half sequence. The three partial sequences in this diagram may be united into a 13-letter cycle in a number of ways but the correct integration will be that which will satisfy all the conditions set up by the partial sequences in groups 1, 2, and 3. After a bit of experimentation it is found that the only one which will satisfy all conditions is this:

```
1  2  3  4  5  6  7  8  9  10 11 12 13
Q  H  O  V  C  E  K  A  X  F  T  P  .
```

Note, for example, that the conditions represented by QXV in group 2 are satisfied in that the intervals between these letters are the same in the 13-letter cycle; the same is true as regards the intervals between O and T, P and K, and so on. Likewise, the conjugate sequence from Fig. 47*b* is established as

```
1  2  3  4  5  6  7  8  9  10 11 12 13
Y  U  J  N  W  D  S  M  B  Z  G  I  .
```

Thus there have been established the two half-sequences involved. The problem now remains to integrate them into a single sequence which is either the primary one or an equivalent primary component.

(3) Each of these sequences may, of course, be expanded to form a 26-element sequence, the elements of which will satisfy the interval relationships among the letters in each 13-letter sequence. Thus:

```
     1  2  3  4  5  6  7  8  9  10 11 12 13 14 15 16 17 18 19 20 21 22 23 24 25 26
(1)  Q  .  O  .  C  .  K  .  X  .  T  .  .  H  .  V  .  E  .  A  .  F  .  P  .
(2)  Y  .  J  .  W  .  S  .  B  .  G  .  .  U  .  N  .  D  .  M  .  Z  .  I  .
```

FIGURE 48

There remains the problem of integrating these two sequences into a single sequence.

(4) Suppose a start is made thus:

```
1  2  3  4  5  6  7  8  9  10 11 12 13 14 15 16 17 18 19 20 21 22 23 24 25 26
Q  Y  O  J  C  W  K  S  X  B  T  G  .  .  H  U  V  N  E  D  A  M  F  Z  P  I
```

FIGURE 49

All the interval relationships of groups 1, 2, and 3 of Fig. 46 are satisfied by this sequence. If the sequence is written on a pair of sliding strips, any even-interval displacement of one of the strips will produce plaintext-ciphertext relationships fully satisfied by the requirements of the sequences in Fig. 46 or Fig. 47. Thus:

```
(1)  Q Y O J C W K S X B T G . . H U V N E D A M F Z P I
     H U V N E D A M F Z P I Q Y O J C W K S X B T G . .

(2)  Q Y O J C W K S X B T G . . H U V N E D A M F Z P I
     X B T G . . H U V N E D A M F Z P I Q Y O J C W K S

(3)  Q Y O J C W K S X B T G . . H U V N E D A M F Z P I
     T G . . H U V N E D A M F Z P I Q Y O J C W K S X B
```

FIGURE 50

The foregoing three juxtapositions will satisfy all the requirements of the sequences indicated in groups 1, 2, and 3 of Fig. 46, as well as those indicated in Figs. 47a and b. *Without further restrictions or additional data, therefore, it is impossible to tell whether the reconstructed single sequence is correct or not.* In fact, there are 13 possible integrations of the two expanded 13-letter sequences which will yield equivalent results, since there are 13 positions in which the dovetailing of the second sequence may be commenced with respect to the first sequence. Only one of these, however, will be correct in that it will yield a single sequence which, when slid against itself at all juxtapositions (both odd and even displacements) will invariably yield the full quota of plaintext-ciphertext relationships that the original basic or an equivalent primary component yields when slid against itself. (An incorrect integration will often yield a series of equivalents of which only a few are wrong.)

(5) The correct integration will, however, be disclosed quickly enough when the cryptanalyst refers to the cipher text and one or two additional values are derived. Thus, suppose an additional word is deciphered and it yields a pair of values in a new secondary alphabet, for example, $A_p = D_c$ and $U_p = O_c$. The single sequence reconstructed as shown in Fig. 49 will not yield this pair of values, as seen in the following juxtaposition of the sliding strips:

```
Q Y O J C W K S X B T G . . H U V N E D A M F Z P I
I Q Y O J C W K S X B T G . . H U V N E D A M F Z P
```

FIGURE 51

Here $A_p = D_c$ but $U_p = H_c$, not O_c. However, if the dovetailing is commenced with the letter S of Fig. 48 and the resultant 26-letter sequence is juxtaposed against itself as shown in Fig. 52, it will be found that the sequence will now satisfy all the requirements.

```
Q S O B C G K . X U T N . D H M V Z E I A Y F J P W
I A Y F J P W Q S O B C G K . X U T N . D H M V Z E
```

FIGURE 52

The sequence is, of course, a decimation of the QUESTIONABLY... sequence, at an interval of $+3$.

54. Solution of subsequent messages enciphered by the same primary components.—*a.* In the discussion of the methods of solving repeating-key ciphers using secondary alphabets derived from the sliding of a mixed component against the normal component (Chapter V), it was shown how subsequent messages enciphered by the same pair of primary components but with different keys could be solved by application of principles involving the completion of the plain-component sequence (pars. 33, 34). The present paragraph deals with the application of these same principles to the case where the primary components are identical mixed sequences.

b. Suppose that the following primary component has been reconstructed from the analysis of a lengthy cryptogram:

Q U E S T I O N A B L Y C D F G H J K M P R V W X Z

A new message exchanged between the same correspondents is intercepted and is suspected of having been enciphered by the same primary components but with a different key. The message is as follows:

```
N F W W P    N O M K I    W P I D S    C A A E T    Q V Z S E    Y O J S C
A A A F G    R V N H D    W D S C A    E G N F P    F A N B N    K R V S A
C W D S L    O U F A Z    N C V X B    I U W A G    S J C F G
```

c. Factoring discloses that the period is 7 letters. The text is transcribed accordingly, and is as follows:

```
N F W W P N O
M K I W P I D
S C A A E T Q
V Z S E Y O J
S C A A A F G
R V N H D W D
S C A E G N F
P F A N B N K
R V S A C W D
S L O U F A Z
N C V X B I U
W A G S J C F
G
```

FIGURE 53

131

d. The letters belonging to the same alphabet are then employed as the initial letters of completion sequences, in the manner shown in Fig. 21 on page 64, using the already reconstructed primary component. The completion diagrams for the first 10 letters of the first three alphabets, together with the 2-category scores, are as follows:

Gen.		Alphabet 1		Alphabet 2		Alphabet 3
1	7	NMSVSRSPRS		~~FKCZCVCFVL~~	9	WIASANAASO
2	6	APTWTVTRVT	∅	GMDQDWDGWY	5	XOBTBABBTN
3	5	BRIXIWIVWI		~~HPFUFXFHXC~~	4	ZNLILBLLIA
4		~~LVOZOXOWXO~~		~~JRGEGZGJZD~~	3	QAYOYLYYOB
5		~~YWNQNZNXZN~~		~~KVHSHQHKQF~~	2	UBCNCYCCNL
6		~~CXAUAQAZQA~~		~~MWJTJUJMUG~~	3	ELDADCDDAY
7		~~DZBEBUBQUB~~		~~PXKIKEKPEH~~	1	SYFBFDFFBC
8	3	FQLSLELUEL		~~RZMOMSMRSJ~~	1	TCGLGFGGLD
9	4	GUYTYSYESY		~~VQPNPTPVTK~~	1	IDHYHGHHYF
10	5	HECICTCSTC	6	WURARIRWIM		~~OFJCJHJJCG~~
11	5	JSDODIDTID		~~XEVBVOVXOP~~		~~NGKDKJKKDH~~
12	5	KTFNFOFIOF		~~ZSWLWNWZNR~~		~~AHMFMKMMFJ~~
13	5	MIGAGNGONG		~~QTXYXAXQAV~~		~~BJPGPMPPGK~~
14	4	POHBHAHNAH		~~UIZCZBZUBW~~	4	LKRHRPRRHM
15		~~RNJLJBJABJ~~		~~EOQDQLQELX~~		~~YMVJVRVVJP~~
16		~~VAKYKLKBLK~~	3	SNUFUYUSYZ		~~CPWKWVWWKR~~
17	∅	WBMCMYMLYM	6	TAEGECETCQ		~~DRXMXWXXMV~~
18	∅	XLPDPCPYCP	5	IBSHSDSIDU		~~FVZPZXZZPW~~
19	4	ZYRFRDRCDR	6	OLTJTFTOFE		~~GWQRQZQQRX~~
20	∅	QCVGVFVDFV	6	NYIKIGINGS		~~HXUVUQUUVZ~~
21	∅	UDWHWGWFGW	6	ACOMOHOAHT		~~JZEWEUEEWQ~~
22		~~EFXJXIXGHX~~		~~BDNPNJNBJI~~		~~KQSXSESSXU~~
23		~~SGZKZJZHJZ~~		~~LFARAKALKO~~		~~MUTZTSTTZE~~
24		~~THQMQKQJKQ~~	1	YGBVBMBYMN		~~PEIQITIIQS~~
25		~~IJUPUMUKMU~~	1	CHLWLPLCPA	8	RSOUOIOOUT
26	6	OKEREPEMPE		~~DJYXYRYDRB~~	9	VTNENONNEI

FIGURE 54

e. The determination of the correct generatrices in Fig. 54 is now an easy matter; however, since in this case the 2-category scores do not at once point to the correct generatrices, a slight experimentation is necessary to arrive at the solution. Logarithmic weights may here be used to by-pass further experimentation; the few generatrices having the best 2-category scores in Fig. 54 are set forth below, with their logarithmic scores:

Gen.		Alphabet 1	Gen.		Alphabet 2	Gen.		Alphabet 3
1	7	NMSVSRSPRS	10	6	WURARIRWIM	1	9	WIASANAASO
		8685888688 = 73			5688888586 = 70			5888888888 = 77
2	6	APTWTVTRVT	17	6	TAEGECETCQ	26	9	VTNENONNEI
		8695959859 = 73			9895979972 = 74			5989888898 = 80
26	6	OKEREPEMPE	19	6	OLTJTFTOFE	25	8	RSOUOIOOUT
		8298969669 = 72			8791969869 = 72			8886888869 = 77
3	5	BRIXIWIVWI	20	6	NYIKIGINGS			
		4883858558 = 62			8682858858 = 66			
10	5	HECICTCSTC	21	6	ACOMOHOAHT			
		7978797897 = 78			8786878879 = 76			
11	5	JSDODIDTID	18	5	IBSHSDSIDU			
		1878787987 = 70			8487878876 = 71			
12	5	KTFNFOFIOF						
		2968686886 = 67						
13	5	MIGAGNGONG						
		6858585885 = 66						

The correct generatrices, as shown by the highest logarithmic scores, are now assembled in columnar fashion and yield the following plain text:

```
1 2 3 4 5 6 7
H A V
E C T
C O N
I M E
C O N
T H O
C O N
S A N
T H E
C T I
```

FIGURE 55

f. The corresponding key letters are sought, using enciphering equations $\theta_{k/c}=\theta_{1/p}$; $\theta_{p/p}=\theta_{c/c}$, and are found to be JOU, which suggests the key word JOURNEY, among others. Testing the key letters RNEY for Alphabets 4, 5, 6, and 7, the following results are obtained:

```
1 2 3 4 5 6 7
J O U R N E Y
N F W W P N O
H A V E D I R
M K I W P I D
E C T E D S E
```

FIGURE 56

The message may now be completed with ease.   It is as follows:

<pre>
          J O U R N E Y   J O U R N E Y
          N F W W P N O   P F A N B N K
          H A V E D I R   S A N C E I N

          M K I W P I D   R V S A C W D
          E C T E D S E   T H E D I R E

          S C A A E T Q   S L O U F A Z
          C O N D R E G   C T I O N O F

          V Z S E Y O J   N C V X B I U
          I M E N T T O   H O R S E S H

          S C A A A F G   W A G S J C F
          C O N D U C T   O E F A L L S

          R V N H D W D   G
          T H O R O R E   X

          S C A E G N F
          C O N N A I S
</pre>

FIGURE 57

g. Another method for the solution of cryptograms when the primary components have been recovered might be mentioned at this point.   This method, based on the analysis of the uniliteral frequency distributions of the individual monoalphabets, is applicable when there are a sufficient number of tallies (say, at least 25 or so) in each distribution; in such situations this method is often easier and quicker than the generatrix method treated in the preceding subparagraphs.

(1) Let us assume that the enemy has been using keyword-mixed sequences based on QUESTIONABLY for the primary components, and that the following message (factoring to five alphabets) with its accompanying frequency distributions are at hand:

<pre>
P F O F R   V V Z D V   Q G Q Y I   E F Q J M   H J I C Y   V A B L Y
Q F Z B V   F B U K V   A U S B Y   M U S K P   M C E A R   F N W I L
D D W Y K   Q J L I R   P A A W R   L B Q F K   C D X A X   J H S A R
D D X B W   F C H A O   B F X A K   E D X O E   Y C H N P   D Q X O E
D D A X O   G B W L T   U H S Y X   H H W Y V   T K U W L   J A Z O S
</pre>

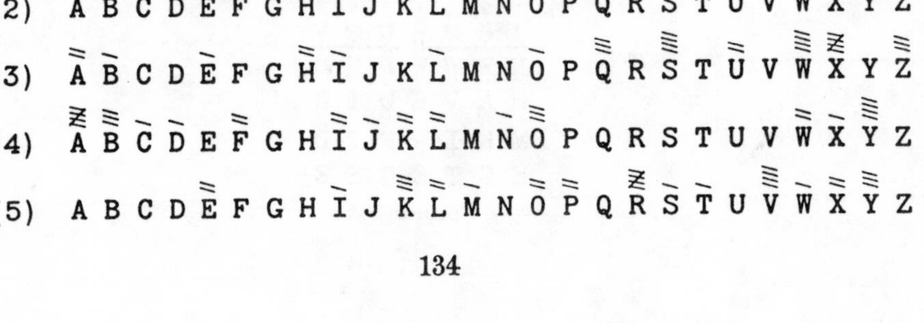

<pre>
(1)   A B C D E F G H I J K L M N O P Q R S T U V W X Y Z

(2)   A B C D E F G H I J K L M N O P Q R S T U V W X Y Z

(3)   A B C D E F G H I J K L M N O P Q R S T U V W X Y Z

(4)   A B C D E F G H I J K L M N O P Q R S T U V W X Y Z

(5)   A B C D E F G H I J K L M N O P Q R S T U V W X Y Z
</pre>

134

In spite of the flatness of the distribution for Alphabet 1 (I.C.=1.08), there is no doubt that the period is 5.

(2) Consider the frequency distribution for the second alphabet, which has several pronounced peaks. The cipher letters D, F, A, B, C, and H are high, with D_c being the highest. *In general*, these letters should represent most of the high-frequency plaintext letters such as E, T, N, R, O, A, I, S, etc. Now prepare two strips bearing keyword-mixed sequences based on QUESTIONABLY; the plain-component strip should be 26 letters long, the cipher-component strip doubled length of 52 letters. Place the D_c on the cipher (long) strip under the E_p on the plain (short) strip, and note what plaintext values of F_c, A_c, B_c, C_c, and H_c are concomitant with $D_c=E_p$. Then place D_c on the cipher strip under T_p, N_p, R_p, etc. in turn, noting what plaintext values of the other cipher letters correspond to each setting. When the correct juxtaposition is made, the values of *all* the cipher letters in Alphabet 2 become known, and the frequencies of the plaintext letters will approximate fairly closely their normal frequencies.

(3) After the correct placement of Alphabet 2 is found, the values for the cipher letters are entered in their proper places in the message. Then the same procedure is applied to each alphabet in turn, and the plaintext values are entered in the message when the correct juxtaposition for the strip is determined. It will be found that the easiest process is to treat the distributions with the most striking peaks (such as those of Alphabets 2 and 3) first, leaving the flattest distributions (such as that of Alphabet 1) until last. Furthermore, after several alphabets have been correctly determined, the clusters of plaintext fragments in the message might suggest complete words, or recovery of part of the key might suggest the entire repeating key, thus rendering unnecessary the placement of the remaining alphabets by the analytic process just described. The solution of this problem is left to the student as an exercise.

55. Solution of repeating-key ciphers in which the identical mixed components proceed in opposite directions.—The secondary alphabets in this case (Case IIc1(b) of par. 8) are reciprocal. The steps in solution are essentially the same as in the preceding case (par. 41); the principles of indirect symmetry of position can also be applied with the necessary modifications introduced by virtue of the reciprocity existing within the respective secondary alphabets (subpar. 44n).

56. Solution of repeating-key ciphers in which the primary components are different mixed sequences.—This is Case IIc2 of par. 8. The steps in solution are essentially the same as in pars. 41 and 44, except that in applying the principles of indirect symmetry of position it is necessary to take cognizance of the fact that the primary components are different mixed sequences (subpar. 44o).

57. Solution of subsequent messages after the primary components have been recovered.—
a. In the case in which the primary components are identical mixed sequences proceeding in opposite directions, as well as in the case in which the primary components are different mixed sequences, the solution of subsequent messages [1] is a relatively easy matter. In both cases, however, the student must remember that before the method illustrated in subpars. 54a–f can be applied it is necessary to convert the cipher letters into their plain-component equivalents *before* completing the plain-component sequence. From there on, the process of selecting and assembling the proper generatrices is the same as usual.

---

[1] That is, messages enciphered with the same primary components (which have now been reconstructed) but enciphered with repeating keys different from those used in the messages upon which the reconstruction of the primary components was accomplished.

b. Perhaps an example may be advisable. Suppose the enemy has been found to be using primary components based upon the key word QUESTIONABLY, the plain component running from left to right, the cipher component in the reverse direction. The following new message has arrived from the intercept station:

```
M V X O X    B Z I Y Z    N L W Z H    O X I E O    O O E P Z    F X S R X

E J B S H    B O N A U    R A P Z I    N R A M V    X O X A I    J Y X W F

K N D O W    J E R C U    R A L V B    Z A Q U W    J W X Y I    D G R K D

Q B D R M    Q E C Y V    Q W
```

c. Factoring discloses that the period is 6 and the message is accordingly transcribed into 6 columns as in Fig. 58. The first 10 letters of these columns are then converted into their plain-component equivalents by juxtaposing the two primary components at any point of coincidence, for example, $Q_p = Z_c$. The converted letters are shown in Fig. 59. The letters of the individual

```
1 2 3 4 5 6
M V X O X B
Z I Y Z N L
W Z H O X I
E O O O E P
Z F X S R X
E J B S H B
O N A U R A
P Z I N R A
M V X O X A
I J Y X W F
K N D O W J
E R C U R A
L V B Z A Q
U W J W X Y
I D G R K D
Q B D R M Q
E C Y V Q W
```

FIGURE 58

```
1 2 3 4 5 6
O S U M U H
Q P F Q K G
E Q B M U P
W M M M W I
Q Y U V T U
W A H V B H
M K J X T J
I Q P K T J
O S U M U J
P A F U E Y
```

FIGURE 59

136

columns are then used as the initial letters of completion sequences, using the QUESTIONABLY primary sequence. The final step is the selection and assembling of the selected generatrices. The results for the first ten letters (using two-category weights) of the first three columns are shown below:

Gen.	Alphabet 1	Alphabet 2	Alphabet 3
1	~~OQEWQWMIOP~~	~~SPQMYAKQSA~~	0 ~~UFBMUHJPUF~~
2	~~NUSXUXPONR~~	3 TRUPCBMUTB	~~EGLPEJKREG~~
3	~~AETZEZRNAV~~	5 IVERDLPEIL	4 SHYRSKMVSH
4	~~BSIQSQVABW~~	5 OWSVFYRSOY	3 TJCVTMPWTJ
5	3 LTOUTUWBLX	4 NXTWGCVTNC	~~IKDWIPRXIK~~
6	~~YINEIEXLYZ~~	~~AZIXHDWIAD~~	~~OMFXORVZOM~~
7	~~COASOSZYCQ~~	~~BQOZJFXOBF~~	~~NPGZNVWQNP~~
8	4 DNBTNTQCDU	~~LUNQKGZNLG~~	~~ARHQAWXUAR~~
9	5 FALIAIUDFE	3 YEAUMHQAYH	~~BVJUBXZEBV~~
10	4 GBYOBOEFGS	~~CSBEPJUBCJ~~	~~LWKELZQSLW~~
11	4 HLCNLNSGHT	~~DTLSRKELDK~~	~~YXMSYQUTYX~~
12	~~JYDAYATHJI~~	3 FIYTVMSYFM	~~GZPTCUEICZ~~
13	~~KCFBCBIJKO~~	3 GOCIWPTCGP	~~DQRIDESODQ~~
14	2 MDGLDLOKMN	5 HNDOXRIDHR	4 FUVOFSTNFU
15	2 PFHYFYNMPA	~~JAFNZVOFJV~~	6 GEWNGTIAGE
16	3 RGJCGCAPRB	~~KBGAQWNGKW~~	5 HSXAHIOBHS
17	1 VHKDHDBRVL	~~MLHBUXAHMX~~	~~JTZBJONLJT~~
18	~~WJMFJFLVWY~~	~~PYJLEZBJPZ~~	~~KIQLKNAYKI~~
19	~~XKPGKGYWXG~~	~~RCKYSQLKRQ~~	3 MOUYMABCMO
20	~~ZMRHMHCXZD~~	1 VDMCTUYMVU	3 PNECPBLDPN
21	~~QPVJPJDZQF~~	3 WFPDIECPWE	6 RASDRLYFRA
22	~~URWKRKFQUG~~	~~XGRFOSDRXS~~	1 VBTFVYCGVB
23	2 EVXMVMGUEH	~~ZHVGNTFVZT~~	1 WLIGWCDHWL
24	~~SWZPWPHESJ~~	~~QJWHAIGWOI~~	~~XYOHXDFJXY~~
25	~~TXQRSRJSTK~~	~~UKXJBOHXUO~~	~~ZONJZFGKZO~~
26	~~IZUVZVKTIM~~	~~EMZKLNJZEN~~	~~QDAKQGHNQD~~

FIGURE 60

Columnar assembling of selected generatrices gives what is shown in Fig. 61.

```
  1  2  3  4  5  6
  F  I  R  .  .  .
  A  V  A  .  .  .
  L  E  S  .  .  .
  I  R  D  .  .  .
  A  D  R  .  .  .
  I  L  L  .  .  .
  U  P  Y  .  .  .
  D  E  F  .  .  .
  F  I  R  .  .  .
  E  L  A  .  .  .
```

FIGURE 61

137

d. The key letters are sought, and found to be NUM, which suggests NUMBER. The entire message may now be read with ease. It is as follows:

```
N U M B E R    N U M B E R    N U M B E R    N U M B E R    N U M B E R
M V X O X B    Z I Y Z N L    W Z H O X I    E O O O E P    Z F X S R X
F I R S T C    A V A L R Y    L E S S T H    I R D S Q U    A D R O N W

E J B S H B    O N A U R A    P Z I N R A    M V X O X A    I J Y X W F
I L L O C C    U P Y A N D    D E F E N D    F I R S T D    E L A Y I N

K N D O W J    E R C U R A    L V B Z A Q    U W J W X Y    I D G R K D
G P O S I T    I O N A N D    W I L L P R    O T E C T L    E F T F L A

Q B D R M Q    E C Y V Q W
N K O F B R    I G A D E X
```

FIGURE 62

e. If the primary components are *different* mixed sequences, the procedure is identical with that just indicated. The important point to note is that *one must not fail to convert the cipher letters into their plain-component equivalents* before the completion-sequence method is applied.

CHAPTER VIII

SPECIAL SOLUTIONS FOR PERIODIC CIPHERS

58. General remarks.—The preceding two chapters have been devoted to an elucidation of the general principles and procedure in the solution of typical cases of repeating-key ciphers. This chapter will be devoted to a consideration of the variations in cryptanalytic procedure arising from special circumstances. It may be well to add that by the designation "special circumstances" it is not meant to imply that the latter are necessarily *unusual* circumstances. *The student should always be on the alert to seize upon any opportunities that may appear in which he may apply the methods to be described.* In practical work such opportunities are by no means rare and are seldom overlooked by competent and experienced cryptanalysts.

59. Deriving the secondary alphabets, the primary components, and the repeating key, given a cryptogram with its plain text.—*a.* It may happen that a cryptogram and its equivalent plain text are at hand, as the result of capture, pilferage, compromise, etc. This, as a general rule, affords a very easy attack upon the whole system.

b. Taking first the case where the plain component is the normal sequence, the cipher component a mixed sequence, the first thing to do is to write out the cipher text with its letter-for-letter decipherment. From this, by a slight modification of the principles of factoring, one discovers the length of the key. It is obvious that when a word of three or four letters is enciphered by the same cipher text, the interval between the two occurrences is almost certainly a multiple of the length of the key.[1] By noting a few recurrences of plaintext and cipher letters, one can quickly determine the length of the key (assuming of course that the message is long enough to afford sufficient data). Having determined the length of the key, we rewrite the message according to its periods, with the plain text likewise in periods under the cipher letters. From this arrangement one can now reconstruct complete or partial secondary alphabets. If the secondary alphabets are complete, they will show direct symmetry of position; if they are but fragmentary in several alphabets, then the primary component can be reconstructed by the application of the principles of direct symmetry of position.

c. If the plain component is a mixed sequence, and the cipher component the normal (direct or reversed sequence), the secondary alphabets will show no direct symmetry unless

---

[1] Again, as a note of caution, see the remark made in footnote 8 on p. 26.

they are arranged in the form of an inverse matrix (such as that illustrated in subpar. 36m(2) on p. 76). The student should be on the lookout for such cases.

d. (1) If the plain and cipher primary components are identical mixed sequences proceeding in the same direction, the secondary alphabets will show indirect symmetry of position, and they can be used for the speedy reconstruction of the primary components (subpars. 44*a* to *m*).

(2) If the plain and the cipher primary components are identical mixed sequences proceeding in opposite directions, the secondary alphabets will be completely reciprocal secondary alphabets and the primary component may be reconstructed by applying the principles outlined in subpar. 44*n*.

(3) If the plain and cipher primary components are different mixed sequences, the secondary alphabets will show indirect symmetry of position and the primary components may be reconstructed by applying the principles outlined in subpar. 44*o*.

e. In all the foregoing cases, after the primary components have been reconstructed, the keys can be readily recovered.

60. Solution of isologs involving the same pair of unknown primary components but with key words of identical length.—*a.* The simplest case of this kind is that involving two monoalphabetic substitution ciphers with mixed alphabets derived from the same pair of sliding components. An understanding of this case is necessary to that of the case involving repeating-key ciphers.

(1) A message is transmitted from Station "A" to Station "B". "B" then sends "A" some operating signals which indicate that "B" cannot decipher the message, and soon thereafter "A" sends a second message, identical in length with the first. This leads to the suspicion that the plain text of both messages is the same. The intercepted messages are superimposed. Thus:

1. NXGRV MPUOF ZQVCP VWERX QDZVX WXZQE TBDSP VVXJK RFZWH ZUWLU IYVZQ FXOAR
2. EMLHJ FGVUB PRJNG JKWHM RAPJM KMPRW ZTAXG JJMCD HBPKY PVKIV QOJPR BMUSH

(2) Initiating a chain of ciphertext equivalents from Message 1 to Message 2, the following complete sequence is obtained:

```
 1  2  3  4  5  6  7  8  9  10 11 12 13 14 15 16 17 18 19 20 21 22 23 24 25 26
 N  E  W  K  D  A  S  X  M  F  B  T  Z  P  G  L  I  Q  R  H  Y  O  U  V  J  C
```

(3) Experimentation along already indicated lines soon discloses the fact that the foregoing component is an equivalent primary component of the original primary cipher component based upon the key word QUESTIONABLY, decimated on the 21st interval. Let the student decipher the cryptogram.

(4) The foregoing example is somewhat artificial in that the plain text was consciously selected with a view to making it contain every letter of the alphabet. The purpose in doing this was to permit the construction of a complete chain of equivalents from only two short messages, in order to give a simple illustration of the principles involved. If the plain text of the message does not contain every letter of the alphabet, then only partial chains of equivalents can be constructed. These may be united, if circumstances will permit, by recourse to the various principles elucidated in par. 44.

(5) The student should carefully study the foregoing example in order to obtain a thorough comprehension of the *reason* why it was possible to reconstruct the primary component from the two cipher messages without having any plain text to begin with at all. Since the plain

text of both messages is the same, the relative displacement of the same primary components in the case of Message 1 differs from the relative displacement of the same primary components in the case of Message 2 by a *fixed* interval. Therefore, the distance between N and E (the first letters of the two messages), on the primary component, regardless of what plaintext letter these two cipher letters represent, is the same as the distance between E and W (the 18th letters), W and K (the 17th letters), and so on. Thus, this fixed interval permits of establishing a complete chain of letters separated by constant intervals and this chain becomes an equivalent primary component.

b. With the foregoing basic principles in mind the student is ready to note the procedure in the case of two repeating-key ciphers having identical plain texts. First, the case in which both messages have key words of identical length but different compositions will be studied.

c. (1) Given the following two cryptograms suspected to contain the same plain text:

Message 1

```
Y H Y E X    U B U K A    P V L L T    A B U V V    D Y S A B    P C Q T U
N G K F A    Z E F I Z    B D J E Z    A L V I D    T R O Q S    U H A F K
```

Message 2

```
C G S L Z    Q U B M N    C T Y B V    H L Q F T    F L R H L    M T A I Q
Z W M D Q    N S D W N    L C B L Q    N E T O C    V S N Z R    B J N O Q
```

(2) The first step is to try to determine the length of the period. The usual method of factoring cannot be employed because there are no long repetitions and not enough repetitions even of digraphs to give any convincing indications. However, a subterfuge will be employed based upon the theory of factoring.

d. (1) Let the two messages be superimposed:

```
      1  2  3  4  5  6  7  8  9 10 11 12 13 14 15 16 17 18 19 20 21 22 23 24 25 26 27 28 29 30
  1.  Y  H  Y  E  X  U  B  U  K  A  P  V  L  L  T  A  B  U  V  V  D  Y  S  A  B  P  C  Q  T  U
  2.  C  G  S  L  Z  Q  U  B  M  N  C  T  Y  B  V  H  L  Q  F  T  F  L  R  H  L  M  T  A  I  Q

     31 32 33 34 35 36 37 38 39 40 41 42 43 44 45 46 47 48 49 50 51 52 53 54 55 56 57 58 59 60
  1.  N  G  K  F  A  Z  E  F  I  Z  B  D  J  E  Z  A  L  V  I  D  T  R  O  Q  S  U  H  A  F  K
  2.  Z  W  M  D  Q  N  S  D  W  N  L  C  B  L  Q  N  E  T  O  C  V  S  N  Z  R  B  J  N  O  Q
```

(2) Now let a search be made of cases of identical superimposition. For example,

$\overset{4}{\underset{}{\text{E}}}\overset{}{\underset{}{\text{L}}}$ and $\overset{44}{\underset{}{\text{E}}}\overset{}{\underset{}{\text{L}}}$ are separated by 40 letters, $\overset{6}{\underset{}{\text{U}}}\overset{18}{\underset{}{\text{U}}}$ and $\overset{30}{\underset{}{\text{U}}}\overset{}{\underset{}{\text{Q}}}$ are separated by 12 letters. Let these intervals

between identical superimpositions be factored, just as though they were ordinary repetitions. That factor which is the most frequent should correspond with the length of the period for the following reason. If the period is the same and the plain text is the same in both messages, then the condition of identity of superimposition can only be the result of identity of encipherments by identical cipher alphabets. This is only another way of saying that the same relative position in the keying cycle has been reached in both cases of identity. Therefore, the distance between identical superimpositions must be either equal to or else a multiple of the length of the period.   Hence, factoring the intervals must yield the length of the period.   The complete list of intervals and factors applicable to cases of identical superimposed pairs is as follows:

Repetition	Interval	Factors
1st EL to 2d EL	40	2, 4, 5, 8, 10, 20.
1st UQ to 2d UQ	12	2, 3, 4, 6.
2d UQ to 3d UQ	12	2, 3, 4, 6.
1st UB to 2d UB	48	2, 3, 4, 6, 8, 12, 24.
1st KM to 2d KM	24	2, 3, 4, 6, 8, 12.
1st AN to 2d AN	36	2, 3, 4, 6, 9, 12, 18.
2d AN to 3d AN	12	2, 3, 4, 6.
1st VT to 2d VT	8	2, 4.
2d VT to 3d VT	28	2, 4, 7, 14.
1st TV to 2d TV	36	2, 3, 4, 6, 9, 12, 18.
1st AH to 2d AH	8	2, 4.
1st BL to 2d BL	8	2, 4.
2d BL to 3d BL	16	2, 4, 8.
1st SR to 2d SR	32	2, 4, 8, 16.
1st FD to 2d FD	4	2.
1st ZN to 2d ZN	4	2.
1st DC to 2d DC	8	2, 4.

(3) The factors 4 and 2 are the only ones common to every one of these intervals, and, since a period of 2 is not very probable, it may be taken that the length of the period is 4.

e. Let the messages now be superimposed according to their periods:

```
1.  Y H Y E    X U B U    K A P V    L L T A    B U V V    D Y S A    B P C Q
2.  C G S L    Z Q U B    M N C T    Y B V H    L Q F T    F L R H    L M T A

1.  T U N G    K F A Z    E F I Z    B D J E    Z A L V    I D T R    O Q S U
2.  I Q Z W    M D Q N    S D W N    L C B L    Q N E T    O C V S    N Z R B

1.  H A F K
2.  J N O Q
```

f. (1) Now distribute the superimposed letters into a reconstruction matrix, thus:

Ø	A	B	C	D	E	F	G	H	I	J	K	L	M	N	O	P	Q	R	S	T	U	V	W	X	Y	Z
1		L		F	S			J	O		M	Y			N					I				Z	C	Q
2	N		C		D	G						B		M	Z			Q				F		L		
3	Q	U	T			O		W	B	E		Z		C			R	V		F				S		
4	H			L	W			Q						A	S		B	T					N			

(2) By the usual methods, construct the primary or an equivalent primary component. Taking lines Ø and 1, we note the following sequences:

BL, DF, ES, HJ, IO, KM, LY, ON, TI, XZ, YC, ZQ.

These, when united by means of common letters and study of other sequences, yield the complete original primary component based upon the key word QUESTIONABLY:

QUESTIONABLYCDFGHJKMPRVWXZ

(3) The fact that the pair of lines with which the process was commenced yields the original primary sequence is purely accidental; it might have just as well yielded an equivalent primary sequence.

g. (1) Having the primary cipher component, the solution of the messages is now a relatively simple matter. An application of the method elucidated in par. 54 is made, involving the completion of the plain-component sequence and the selection of those generatrices which contain the best assortment of high frequency letters.[2] Thus, using Message 1:

Gen.	Alphabet 1	Alphabet 2	Alphabet 3	Alphabet 4
1	~~YXKLBDDBTKE~~	1 HUALUYPUFF	5 YBPTVSCNAI	~~EUVAVAQGZZ~~
2	2 CZMYLFLIMS	4 JEBYECREGG	5 CLRIWTDABO	~~SEWBWBUHQQ~~
3	2 DQPCYGYOPT	3 KSLCSDVSHH	3 DYVOXIFBLN	~~TSXLXLEJUU~~
4	4 FURDCHCNRI	~~MTYDTFWTJJ~~	3 FCWNZOGLYA	~~ITZYZYSKEE~~
5	3 GEVFDJDAVO	~~PICFIGXIKK~~	~~GDXAQNIYCB~~	~~OIQLQCTMSS~~
6	2 HSWGFKFBWN	4 RODGOHZOMM	~~HFZBUAJCDL~~	5 NOUDUDIPTT
7	~~JTXHGMGLXA~~	~~VNFHNJQNPP~~	~~JGQLEBKDFY~~	8 ANEFEFORII
8	~~KIZJHPHYZB~~	~~WAGJAKUARR~~	1 KHUYSLMFGC	6 BASGSGNVOO
9	~~MOQKJRJCQL~~	~~XBHKBMEBVV~~	2 MJECTYPGHD	5 LBTHTHAWNN
10	~~PNUMKVKDUY~~	~~ZLJMLPSLWW~~	~~PKSDICRHJF~~	~~YLIJIJBXAA~~
11	4 RAEPMWMFEC	~~QYKPYRTYXX~~	~~RMTFODVJKG~~	~~CYOKOKLZBB~~
12	3 VBSRPXPGSD	~~UCMRCVICZZ~~	2 VPIGNFWKMH	2 DCNMNMYQLL
13	4 WLTVRZRHTF	~~EDPVDWODQQ~~	~~WROHAGXMPJ~~	2 FDAPAPCUYY
14	~~XYIWVQVJIG~~	3 SFRWFXNFUU	~~XVNJBHZPRK~~	3 GFBRBRDECC
15	~~ZGOXWUWKOH~~	~~TGVXGZAGEE~~	~~ZWAKLJQRVM~~	1 HGLVLVFSDD
16	~~QDNZXEXMNJ~~	~~IHWZHQBHSS~~	~~QXBMYKUVWP~~	1 JHYWYWGTFF
17	~~UFAQZSZPAK~~	~~OJXQJULJTT~~	~~UZLPCMEWXR~~	~~KJCXCXHIGG~~
18	~~EGBUQTQRBM~~	~~NKZUKEYKII~~	~~EQYRDPSXZV~~	~~MKDZDZJOHH~~
19	3 SHLEUIUVLP	5 AMQEMSCMOO	~~SUCVFRTZQW~~	~~PMFQFQKNJJ~~
20	6 TJYSEOEWYR	4 BPUSPTDPNN	~~TEDWGVIQUX~~	~~RPGUGUMAKK~~
21	~~IKCTSNSXCV~~	8 LRETRIFRAA	~~ISFXHWOUEZ~~	3 VRHEHEPBMM
22	5 OMDITATZDW	3 YVSIVOGVBB	~~OTGZJXNESQ~~	~~WVJSJSRLPP~~
23	~~NPFOIBIQFX~~	3 CWTOWNHWLL	~~NIHQKZASTU~~	~~XWKTKTVYRR~~
24	5 ARGNOLOUGZ	~~DXINXAJXYY~~	~~AOJUMQBTIE~~	~~ZXMIMIWCVV~~
25	4 BVHANYNEHQ	~~FZOAZBKZCC~~	5 BNKEPULIOS	~~QZPAPOXDWW~~
26	~~LWJBACASJU~~	~~GQNBQLMQDD~~	7 LAMSREYONT	~~UQRNRNZFXX~~

(2) In this particular case, it is easy to pick out the correct generatrices for Alphabets 2, 3, and 4, since the correct ones have the highest two-category scores. These generatrices are

---

[2] We are assuming in this case that the plain component is identical with the cipher component. If this is not the case, subpars. 61*f* and *g* outline the procedure to be followed in such situations.

143

assembled in columnar fashion in Fig. 63a, below; from this step it is easy to see that the correct generatrix for Alphabet 1 is Generatrix No. 24, as is shown in Fig. 63b:

```
  1 2 3 4        1 2 3 4
  . L L A        A L L A
  . R A N        R R A N
  . E M E        G E M E
  . T S F        N T S F
  . R R E        O R R E
  . I E F        L I E F
  . F Y O        O F Y O
  . R O R        U R O R
  . A N I        G A N I
  . A T I        Z A T I
```

FIGURE 63a   FIGURE 63b

(3) The key letters are sought and give the key word SOUP. The plain text for the second message is now known, and by reference to the cipher text and the primary components, the key word for this message is found to be TIME. The complete texts are as follows:

```
S O U P    S O U P    S O U P    S O U P    S O U P    S O U P
Y H Y E    X U B U    K A P V    L L T A    B U V V    D Y S A
A L L A    R R A N    G E M E    N T S F    O R R E    L I E F

B P C Q    T U N G    K F A Z    E F I Z    B D J E    Z A L V
O F Y O    U R O R    G A N I    Z A T I    O N H A    V E B E

I D T R    O Q S U    H A F K
E N S U    S P E N    D E D X


T I M E    T I M E    T I M E    T I M E    T I M E    T I M E
C G S L    Z Q U B    M N C T    Y B V H    L Q F T    F L R H
A L L A    R R A N    G E M E    N T S F    O R R E    L I E F

L M T A    I Q Z W    M D Q N    S D W N    L C B L    Q N E T
O F Y O    U R O R    G A N I    Z A T I    O N H A    V E B E

O C V S    N Z R B    J N O Q
E N S U    S P E N    D E D X
```

FIGURE 64

61. Solution of isologs involving the same pair of unknown primary components but with key words of different lengths.—a. In the foregoing case the key words for the two messages, although different, were identical in length. When this is not true and the key words are of different lengths, the procedure need be only slightly modified.

b. Given the following two cryptograms suspected of containing the same plain text enciphered by the same primary components but with different key words of different lengths, solve the messages.

Message No. 1

```
V M Y Z G    E A U N T    P K F A Y    J I Z M B    U M Y K B    V F I V V
S E O A F    S K X K R    Y W C A C    Z O R D O    Z R D E F    B L K F E
S M K S F    A F E K V    Q U R C M    Y Z V O X    V A B T A    Y Y U O A
Y T D K F    E N W N T    D B Q K U    L A J L Z    I O U M A    B O A F S
K X Q P U    Y M J P W    Q T D B T    O S I Y S    M I Y K U    R O G M W
C T M Z Z    V M V A J
```

Message No. 2

```
Z G A N W    I O M O A    C O D H A    C L R L P    M O Q O J    E M O Q U
D H X B Y    U Q M G A    U V G L Q    D B S P U    O A B I R    P W X Y M
O G G F T    M R H V F    G W K N I    V A U P F    A B R V I    L A Q E M
Z D J X Y    M E D D Y    B O S V M    P N L G X    X D Y D O    P X B Y U
Q M N K Y    F L U Y Y    G V P V R    D N C Z E    K J Q O R    W J X R V
G D K D S    X C E E C
```

c. The messages are long enough to show a few short repetitions which permit factoring. The latter discloses that Message 1 has a period of 4 and Message 2, a period of 6 letters. The messages are superimposed, with numbers marking the position of each letter in the corresponding period, as shown below:

Message No. 1

```
        1 2 3 4 1 2 3 4 1 2 3 4 1 2 3 4 1 2 3 4 1 2 3 4
No. 1.  V M Y Z G E A U N T P K F A Y J I Z M B U M Y K
No. 2.  Z G A N W I O M O A C O D H A C L R L P M O Q O
        1 2 3 4 5 6 1 2 3 4 5 6 1 2 3 4 5 6 1 2 3 4 5 6

        1 2 3 4 1 2 3 4 1 2 3 4 1 2 3 4 1 2 3 4 1 2 3 4
No. 1.  B V F I V V S E O A F S K X K R Y W C A C Z O R
No. 2.  J E M O Q U D H X B Y U Q M G A U V G L Q D B S
        1 2 3 4 5 6 1 2 3 4 5 6 1 2 3 4 5 6 1 2 3 4 5 6

        1 2 3 4 1 2 3 4 1 2 3 4 1 2 3 4 1 2 3 4 1 2 3 4
No. 1.  D O Z R D E F B L K F E S M K S F A F E K V Q U
No. 2.  P U O A B I R P W X Y M O G G F T M R H V F G W
        1 2 3 4 5 6 1 2 3 4 5 6 1 2 3 4 5 6 1 2 3 4 5 6

        1 2 3 4 1 2 3 4 1 2 3 4 1 2 3 4 1 2 3 4 1 2 3 4
No. 1.  R C M Y Z V O X V A B T A Y Y U O A Y T D K F E
No. 2.  K N I V A U P F A B R V I L A Q E M Z D J X Y M
        1 2 3 4 5 6 1 2 3 4 5 6 1 2 3 4 5 6 1 2 3 4 5 6

        1 2 3 4 1 2 3 4 1 2 3 4 1 2 3 4 1 2 3 4 1 2 3 4
No. 1.  N W N T D B Q K U L A J L Z I O U M A B O A F S
No. 2.  E D D Y B O S V M P N L G X X D Y D O P X B Y U
        1 2 3 4 5 6 1 2 3 4 5 6 1 2 3 4 5 6 1 2 3 4 5 6

        1 2 3 4 1 2 3 4 1 2 3 4 1 2 3 4 1 2 3 4 1 2 3 4
No. 1.  K X Q P U Y M J P W Q T D B T O S I Y S M I Y K
No. 2.  Q M N K Y F L U Y Y G V P V R D N C Z E K J Q O
        1 2 3 4 5 6 1 2 3 4 5 6 1 2 3 4 5 6 1 2 3 4 5 6

        1 2 3 4 1 2 3 4 1 2 3 4 1 2 3 4
No. 1.  U R O G M W C T M Z Z V M V A J
No. 2.  R W J X R V G D K D S X C E E C
        1 2 3 4 5 6 1 2 3 4 5 6 1 2 3 4
```

d. A reconstruction matrix of "secondary alphabets" is now made (cf. Fig. 65) by distributing the letters in respective lines corresponding to the 12 different superimposed pairs of numbers. For example, all pairs corresponding to the superimposition of position 1 of Message 1 with position 1 of Message 2 are distributed in lines Ø and 1 of the matrix. Thus, the very first superimposed pair is $\begin{bmatrix} 1 \\ V \\ Z \\ 1 \end{bmatrix}$; the letter Z is inserted in line 1 under the letter V. The next $\begin{Bmatrix} 1 \\ 1 \end{Bmatrix}$ pair is the 13th superimposition, with $\begin{Bmatrix} F \\ D \end{Bmatrix}$; the letter D is inserted in line 1 under the letter F, and so on. The matrix is then as follows:

	Ø	A	B	C	D	E	F	G	H	I	J	K	L	M	N	O	P	Q	R	S	T	U	V	W	X	Y	Z
1–1		I	J		P		D						Q	G	C	E			K	O		R	Z				
2–2		H	V	N										G		U			W			E	D	M	L	X	
3–3		E					M			X		G		I	D	J		N				R				A	O
4–4					X		O	C						D	K		A	F	Y	Q				V	N		
1–5			B			T	W		L				R		E				N		Y	Q		U	A		
2–6		M	O			I				C				D								U	V			F	R
3–1		O		G			R					L		P		S		D					Z				
4–2		L	P			H				U	V					E	D	M				F					
1–3			Q	J						V	W	K	O	X	Y				M	A							
2–4		B					J		X	P	O						A		F	Y						D	
3–5		N	R			Y							B	C	G								Q	S			
4–6					M			L	O					S	U	V	W	X									

Superimposed pairs

FIGURE 65

e. There are more than sufficient data here to permit the reconstruction of a complete equivalent primary component, for example, the following:

1	2	3	4	5	6	7	8	9	10	11	12	13	14	15	16	17	18	19	20	21	22	23	24	25	26
I	T	K	N	P	Z	H	M	W	B	Q	E	U	L	F	C	S	J	A	X	R	G	D	V	O	Y

f. The subsequent steps in the actual decipherment of the text of either of the two messages are of considerable interest. Thus far the cryptanalyst has only the cipher component of the primary sliding components. The plain component may be identical with the cipher component and may progress in the same direction, or in the reverse direction; or, the two components may be different. If different, the plain component may be the normal sequence, direct or reversed; or it may be a different mixed sequence. Tests must be made to ascertain which of these various possibilities is true.

g. (1) It will first be assumed that the primary plain component is the normal direct sequence. Applying the procedure outlined in par. 33 to the message with the shorter key (Message No. 1, to give the most data per secondary alphabet), an attempt is made to solve the message. It is unnecessary here to go further into detail in this procedure; suffice it to indicate that the attempt is unsuccessful and it follows that the plain component is not the normal direct sequence. A normal reversed sequence is then assumed for the plain component and the proper procedure applied. Again the attempt is found useless. Next, it is assumed that the plain component is identical with the cipher component, and the procedure outlined in par. 54 is tried. This also is unsuccessful. Another attempt, assuming the plain component runs in the reverse direction, is likewise unsuccessful. There remains one last hypothesis, *viz.*, that the two primary components are different mixed sequences.

(2) Below is given Message No. 1 transcribed in periods of four letters. Uniliteral frequency distributions for the four secondary alphabets are shown below in Fig. 66*a*, labeled 1*a*, 2*a*, 3*a*, and 4*a*. These distributions are based upon the normal sequence A to Z. But since the reconstructed cipher component is at hand, these distributions can be rearranged according to the sequence of the cipher component, as shown in distributions labeled 1*b*, 2*b*, 3*b*, and 4*b* in Fig. 66*a*. *The latter distributions may be combined by shifting distributions 2b, 3b, and 4b to proper superimpositions with respect to 1b so as to yield a single monoalphabetic distribution for the entire message. In other words, the polyalphabetic message can be converted into monoalphabetic terms, thus very considerably simplifying the solution.*

Message No. 1

```
VMYZ  GEAU  NTPK  FAYJ  IZMB  UMYK  BVFI
VVSE  OAFS  KXKR  YWCA  CZOR  DOZR  DEFB
LKFE  SMKS  FAFE  KVQU  RCMY  ZVOX  VABT
AYYU  OAYT  DKFE  NWNT  DBQK  ULAJ  LZIO
UMAB  OAFS  KXQP  UYMJ  PWQT  DBTO  SIYS
MIYK  UROG  MWCT  MZZV  MVAJ
```

	A	B	C	D	E	F	G	H	I	J	K	L	M	N	O	P	Q	R	S	T	U	V	W	X	Y	Z
1a.	1	1	1	5	0	2	1	0	1	0	3	2	4	2	3	1	0	1	2	0	5	3	0	0	1	1
2a.	6	2	1	0	2	0	0	0	2	0	2	1	4	0	1	0	0	1	0	1	0	5	4	2	2	4
3a.	4	1	2	0	0	7	0	0	1	0	2	0	3	1	3	1	4	0	1	1	0	0	0	0	7	2
4a.	1	3	0	0	4	0	1	0	1	4	4	0	0	0	2	1	0	3	4	5	3	1	0	1	1	1

	I	T	K	N	P	Z	H	M	W	B	Q	E	U	L	F	C	S	J	A	X	R	G	D	V	O	Y
1b.	1	0	3	2	1	1	0	4	0	1	0	0	5	2	2	1	2	0	1	0	1	1	5	3	3	1
2b.	2	1	2	0	0	4	0	4	4	2	0	2	0	1	0	1	0	0	6	2	1	0	0	5	1	2
3b.	1	1	2	1	1	2	0	3	0	1	4	0	0	0	7	2	1	0	4	0	0	0	0	0	3	7
4b.	1	5	4	0	1	1	0	0	0	3	0	4	3	0	0	0	4	4	1	1	3	1	0	1	2	1

FIGURE 66*a*

(3) Note in Fig. 66*b* how the four distributions are shifted for superimposition and how the combined distribution presents the characteristics of a typical monoalphabetic distribution.

1b. I T K N P Z H M W B Q E U L F C S J A X R G D V O Y

2b. E U L F C S J A X R G D V O Y I T K N P Z H M W B Q

3b. K N P Z H M W B Q E U L F C S J A X R G D V O Y I T

4b. P Z H M W B Q E U L F C S J A X R G D V O Y I T K N

1b.–4b.
combined I T K N P Z H M W B Q E U L F C S J A X R G D V O Y

FIGURE 66b

(4) The letters belonging to Alphabets 2, 3, and 4 of the message may now be converted into terms of Alphabet 1. That is, the two E's of Alphabet 2 become I's; the L of Alphabet 2 becomes a K; the C becomes a P, and so on. Likewise, the two K's of Alphabet 3 become I's, the N becomes a T, and so on. The entire message is then a monoalphabet and can readily be solved. It is as follows:

```
V D V T G    I S W N S    K O F M V    L I R Z Z    U D V O B    U U D V U
E N E M Y    H A S C A    P T U R E    D H I L L    O N E T W    O O N E O

F M O M U    U K W I S    Y V L F C    R D S D L    N S D I U    Z L J U M
U R T R O    O P S H A    V E D U G    I N A N D    C A N H O    L D F O R

S D I U F    M U M K U    W W R P Z    G Z U D C    V M M V A    F V W O M
A N H O U    R O R P O    S S I B L    Y L O N G    E R R E Q    U E S T R

V V D J U    M N V T V    D O W O U    K S L L R    O R U D S    Z O M U U
E I N F O    R C E M E    N T S T O    P A D D I    T I O N A    L T R O O

K W W I U    F Z L P V    W V D O Y    R S C V U    M C V O U    B D J M V
P S S H O    U L D B E    S E N T V    I A G E O    R G E T O    W N F R E

L V M R N    X M U S L
D E R I C    K R O A D
```

(5) Having the plain text, the derivation of the plain component (an equivalent) is an easy matter. It is merely necessary to base the reconstruction upon any of the secondary alphabets, since the plaintext-ciphertext relationship is now known directly, and the primary cipher component is at hand. The primary plain component is found to be as follows:

```
 1  2  3  4  5  6  7  8  9 10 11 12 13 14 15 16 17 18 19 20 21 22 23 24 25 26
 H  M  P  C  B  L  .  R  S  W  .  .  O  D  U  G  A  F  Q  K  I  Y  N  E  T  V
```

(6) The key words for both messages can now be found, if desirable, by finding the equivalent of A_p in each of the secondary alphabets of the original polyalphabetic messages. The key word for No. 1 is STAR; that for No. 2 is OCEANS.

148

(7) The student may, if he wishes, try to find out whether the primary components reconstructed above are the original components or are equivalent components, by examining all the possible decimations of the two components for evidence of derivation from key words.

h. As already treated in par. 37, the χ test may be brought to bear in the process of matching distributions to ascertain proper superimpositions for monoalphabeticity. In the case just considered there were sufficient data in the distributions to permit the process to be applied successfully by eye, without necessitating statistical tests. Where, however, the distributions contain relatively few tallies, the use of statistical methods is imperative.

i. This case is an excellent illustration of the application of the process of *converting a polyalphabetic cipher into monoalphabetic terms.* Because it is a very valuable and important cryptanalytic trick, the student should study it most carefully in order to gain a good understanding of the principle upon which it is based and its significance in cryptanalytics. The conversion in the case under discussion was possible because the sequence of letters forming the cipher component had been reconstructed and was known, and therefore the uniliteral distributions for the respective secondary cipher alphabets could theoretically be shifted to correct superimpositions for monoalphabeticity. It also happened that there were sufficient data in the distributions to give proper indications for their relative displacements. Therefore the theoretical possibility in this case became an actuality. Without these two necessary conditions the superimposition and conversion cannot be accomplished. The student should always be on the lookout for situations in which this is possible.

62. Solution of isologs involving different pairs of unknown primary components.—*a.* If each message of a pair of isologs has been enciphered with a *different* set of primary components, the repeating keys being of different lengths, there are two procedures available for attacking such a situation. The first procedure involves a modification of the principles demonstrated in par. 61; the second procedure involves an entirely different technique, one which effects a direct conversion of the text into monoalphabetic terms. These two procedures will now be treated in the subparagraphs below.

b. Given the following two cryptograms suspected of containing the same plain text enciphered by different sets of primary components and with key words of different lengths, solve the messages.

Message No. 1

```
B W X P S    O B Y I I    U Y H L F    K F S O P    V G E Y W    P B V X O

U G J P B    W D X U G    H S W D H    K H K H C    U A Y K P    N F S P D

O B B Y B    I N K F L    W A B O X    P J X U V    W Q F X R    W X Y W S

S D Y Z Q    Z H E T A    J X X Z W    X J R O S    P D E E W    O J O N K

G I R X R    W U Y D K    N T J W R    E V B U R    D L I S J    B L C K K

F O D E V    D Y Z Q Z    S H C T W    D I E X Z
```

149

Message No. 2

```
J H L E J     M W U A H     J H U I V     Y N C H C     H L P K D     E W Z J J

J N A H B     H Z B I M     T U B Q E     F J A K M     J V B E F     X N C T L

F A A K G     K I A B G     C V F N Y     F W B I Q     G E R S A     T Z U S D

S X B U D     S H A W A     Y X L J D     C Q L E D     H X G Z L     Z W H N B

V T J S A     T S U U C     M I A K K     J E M I Y     D S K G B     V T J Y C

X Y L Z E     C X L S U     M V M N D     O N F J Y
```

c. Factoring discloses that Message No. 1 has a period of 4, and Message No. 2 a period of 5. The messages are superimposed on a width of the least common multiple (20), and a reconstruction matrix is made, following the method outlined in subpar. 61d. This matrix is shown below:

Values, Message No. 1

	A	B	C	D	E	F	G	H	I	J	K	L	M	N	O	P	Q	R	S	T	U	V	W	X	Y	Z
1–1	J			D			V	T		Y						F			M				H	G		
2–2	A						L	V	T			S				E		U					H	X		
3–3	A	M		P	R				K						J								B	L		
4–4			Q											E		G	N						S	K	J	
1–5	G				E		B							A	J				D							
2–1	V		O				K		F			M	E							T	C					
3–2	W				J	N	Q		T		I							S					Z			
4–3		J		F				A								L				Z				U		
1–4			U	B		K	A		Y			E							S	J						
2–5		M			H		C	G			J				D									Y		
3–1			X								M	H			S		J		C							
4–2	V		X		N							Y				I						H				
1–3	F	L	G			U	A												B							
2–4		Z				E	I		N	H									K				U			
3–5	B		V						F	D	K						E	L	Y							
4–1	C	J				Y		X	Z	F								H						S		
1–2	Z	N	H	W														E				X				
2–3	M		A					H					C						B				L			
3–4				N	H	T	S				W	I														
4–5	A		L		M			B				C	Y			Q								U		

FIGURE 67

d. Since the pairs of components for the two messages are different, indirect symmetry will in this case not extend to the Ø line, so all chaining must be done *within* the matrix. Apparent conflicts in the matrix are noted, such as the A's in lines 2–2 and 3–3, the rest of the letters in these lines not being identical as might at first be expected. However, if we restrict our treatment only to the homogeneous lines 1–1, 1–2, 1–3, 1–4, and 1–5 (see the matrix in Fig. 68, below), we will have data which may be interrelated and which will produce an equivalent primary component, either from these data alone or with the help of another family of

150

	A	B	C	D	E	F	G	H	I	J	K	L	M	N	O	P	Q	R	S	T	U	V	W	X	Y	Z
1–1	J		D			V	T		Y				F				M				H	G				
1–2				Z		N		H		W												E			X	
1–3		F		L		G			U		A															B
1–4			U		B			K	A		Y				E							S	J			
1–5		G						E		B								A	J				D			

FIGURE 68

related rows of the matrix, such as 2–1, 2–2, . . . 2–5. The equivalent primary component recovered will be that for Message No. 2, since it is the values for this message which are entered *within* the matrix and which are manipulated. By inverting the matrix so that the values for Message No. 1 are written within the matrix, a similar procedure will yield an equivalent primary component for the first message.

e. An entirely different technique for treating these isologs will now be described. We have factored the two messages as periods of 4 and 5; and now we write out the messages on the width of the least common multiple, retaining indications of the alphabets to which the cipher letters belong, thus:

```
        1 2 3 4 1 2 3 4 1 2 3 4 1 2 3 4 1 2 3 4
No. 1   B W X P S O B Y I I U Y H L F K F S O P
No. 2   J H L E J M W U A H J H U I V Y N C H C
        1 2 3 4 5 1 2 3 4 5 1 2 3 4 5 1 2 3 4 5

        1 2 3 4 1 2 3 4 1 2 3 4 1 2 3 4 1 2 3 4
No. 1   V G E Y W P B V X O U G J P B W D X U G
No. 2   H L P K D E W Z J J J N A H B H Z B I M
        1 2 3 4 5 1 2 3 4 5 1 2 3 4 5 1 2 3 4 5

        1 2 3 4 1 2 3 4 1 2 3 4 1 2 3 4 1 2 3 4
No. 1   H S W D H K H K H C U A Y K P N F S P D
No. 2   T U B Q E F J A K M J V B E F X N C T L
        1 2 3 4 5 1 2 3 4 5 1 2 3 4 5 1 2 3 4 5

        1 2 3 4 1 2 3 4 1 2 3 4 1 2 3 4 1 2 3 4
NO. 1   O B B Y B I N K F L W A B O X P J X U V
No. 2   F A A K G K I A B G C V F N Y F W B I Q
        1 2 3 4 5 1 2 3 4 5 1 2 3 4 5 1 2 3 4 5

        1 2 3 4 1 2 3 4 1 2 3 4 1 2 3 4 1 2 3 4
No. 1   W Q F X R W X Y W S S D Y Z Q Z H E T A
No. 2   G E R S A T Z U S D S X B U D S H A W A
        1 2 3 4 5 1 2 3 4 5 1 2 3 4 5 1 2 3 4 5

        1 2 3 4 1 2 3 4 1 2 3 4 1 2 3 4 1 2 3 4
No. 1   J X X Z W X J R O S P D E E W O J O N K
No. 2   Y X L J D C Q L E D H X G Z L Z W H N B
        1 2 3 4 5 1 2 3 4 5 1 2 3 4 5 1 2 3 4 5

        1 2 3 4 1 2 3 4 1 2 3 4 1 2 3 4 1 2 3 4
No. 1   G I R X R W U Y D K N T J W R E V B U R
No. 2   V T J S A T S U U C M I A K K J E M I Y
        1 2 3 4 5 1 2 3 4 5 1 2 3 4 5 1 2 3 4 5

        1 2 3 4 1 2 3 4 1 2 3 4 1 2 3 4 1 2 3 4
No. 1   D L I S J B L C K K F O D E V D Y Z Q Z
No. 2   D S K G B V T J Y C X Y L Z E C X L S U
        1 2 3 4 5 1 2 3 4 5 1 2 3 4 5 1 2 3 4 5

        1 2 3 4 5 1 2 3 4
No. 1   S H C T W D I E X Z
No. 2   M V M N D O N F J Y
        1 2 3 4 5 1 2 3 4 5
```

151

f. Let us arbitrarily assign the value of A_p as the first letter of the plain text. Since, in Message No. 1, $B_c = A_p$ in Alphabet 1, then every B_c in Alphabet 1 must equal A_p; these values are entered on the work sheet. Now since the 65th and 73d cipher letters of Message No. 1 are A_p, this establishes that the 65th and 73d letters of Message No. 2 (G_c and F_c) are also A_p; therefore, these latter values are entered throughout the work sheet where they occur. Similarly, since every J_c of Alphabet 1 in Message No. 2 equals A_p, this value is entered on the work sheet under those letters. By continuing this process, we shall recover all the A_p's of the pseudo-plain text and the work sheet will now look as shown in Fig. 69, below:

```
      1 2 3 4 1 2 3 4 1 2 3 4 1 2 3 4 1 2 3 4
No. 1 B W X P S O B Y I I U Y H L F K F S O P
No. 2 J H L E J M W U A H J H U I V Y N C H C
      1 2 3 4 5 1 2 3 4 5 1 2 3 4 5 1 2 3 4 5
      A               A   A

      1 2 3 4 1 2 3 4 1 2 3 4 1 2 3 4 1 2 3 4
No. 1 V G E Y W P B V X O U G J P B W D X U G
No. 2 H L P K D E W Z J J J N A H B H Z B I M
      1 2 3 4 5 1 2 3 4 5 1 2 3 4 5 1 2 3 4 5
                      A               A

      1 2 3 4 1 2 3 4 1 2 3 4 1 2 3 4 1 2 3 4
No. 1 H S W D H K H K H C U A Y K P N F S P D
No. 2 T U B Q E F J A K M J V B E F X N C T L
      1 2 3 4 5 1 2 3 4 5 1 2 3 4 5 1 2 3 4 5
                          A

      1 2 3 4 1 2 3 4 1 2 3 4 1 2 3 4 1 2 3 4
No. 1 O B B Y B I N K F L W A B O X P J X U V
No. 2 F A A K G K I A B G C V F N Y F W B I Q
      1 2 3 4 5 1 2 3 4 5 1 2 3 4 5 1 2 3 4 5
              A               A   A       A

      1 2 3 4 1 2 3 4 1 2 3 4 1 2 3 4 1 2 3 4
No. 1 W Q F X R W X Y W S S D Y Z Q Z H E T A
No. 2 G E R S A T Z U S D S X B U D S H A W A
      1 2 3 4 5 1 2 3 4 5 1 2 3 4 5 1 2 3 4 5

      1 2 3 4 1 2 3 4 1 2 3 4 1 2 3 4 1 2 3 4
No. 1 J X X Z W X J R O S P D E E W O J O N K
No. 2 Y X L J D C Q L E D H X G Z L Z W H N B
      1 2 3 4 5 1 2 3 4 5 1 2 3 4 5 1 2 3 4 5

      1 2 3 4 1 2 3 4 1 2 3 4 1 2 3 4 1 2 3 4
No. 1 G I R X R W U Y D K N T J W R E V B U R
No. 2 V T J S A T S U U C M I A K K J E M I Y
      1 2 3 4 5 1 2 3 4 5 1 2 3 4 5 1 2 3 4 5
                      A               A

      1 2 3 4 1 2 3 4 1 2 3 4 1 2 3 4 1 2 3 4
No. 1 D L I S J B L C K K F O D E V D Y Z Q Z
No. 2 D S K G B V T J Y C X Y L Z E C X L S U
      1 2 3 4 5 1 2 3 4 5 1 2 3 4 5 1 2 3 4 5
      A

      1 2 3 4 1 2 3 4 1 2
No. 1 S H C T W D I E X Z
No. 2 M V M N D O N F J Y
      1 2 3 4 5 1 2 3 4 5
                A
```

FIGURE 69

152

g. We will now arbitrarily assign the value B_p to the V_c at the 21st position of Message No. 1; the other V_c of Message No. 1 establishes the E_c of Message No. 2 also as B_p. This procedure is continued, until all the B_p's in the pseudo-plain text are recovered. Continuing in this vein, assigning arbitrary plaintext values to all the cipher letters of Alphabet 1 of Message No. 1, we are able to reduce almost the entire text[3] to monoalphabetic terms. The work sheet will now look as follows:

```
          1 2 3 4  1 2 3 4  1 2 3 4  1 2 3 4  1 2 3 4
No. 1     B W X P  S O B Y  I I U Y  H L F K  F S O P
No. 2     J H L E  J M W U  A H J H  U I V Y  N C H C
          1 2 3 4  5 1 2 3  4 5 1 2  3 4 5 1  2 3 4 5
          A C H D  I I F C  K    A   C C A    F M E  D
          1 2 3 4  1 2 3 4  1 2 3 4  1 2 3 4  1 2 3 4
No. 1     V G E Y  W P B V  X O U G  J P B W  D X U G
No. 2     H L P K  D E W Z  J J J N  A H B H  Z B I M
          1 2 3    4 5 1 2  3 4 5 1  2 3 4 5  1 2 3 4  5
          B        C E   F    L I A  M F   F  B H O A  M
          1 2 3 4  1 2 3 4  1 2 3 4  1 2 3 4  1 2 3 4
No. 1     H S W D  H K H K  H C U A  Y K P N  F S P D
No. 2     T U B Q  E F J A  K M J V  B E F X  N C T L
          1 2 3 4  5 1 2 3  4 5 1 2  3 4 5 1  2 3 4 5
          C E O O  C D   F  C M A J  O D B    M E B O
          1 2 3 4  1 2 3 4  1 2 3 4  1 2 3 4  1 2 3 4
No. 1     O B B Y  B I N K  F L W A  B O X P  J X U V
No. 2     F A A K  G K I A  B G C V  F N Y F  W B I Q
          1 2 3 4  5 1 2 3  4 5 1 2  3 4 5 1  2 3 4 5
          D G F C  A   I F  M A O J  A I H D  F O A
          1 2 3 4  1 2 3 4  1 2 3 4  1 2 3 4  1 2 3 4
No. 1     W Q F X  R W X Y  W S S D  Y Z Q Z  H E T A
No. 2     G E R S  A T Z U  S D S X  B U D S  H A W A
          1 2 3 4  5 1 2 3  4 5 1 2  3 4 5 1  2 3 4 5
          E B      E J C H  C E E L  O O H E  L C F    J
          1 2 3 4  1 2 3 4  1 2 3 4  1 2 3 4  1 2 3 4
No. 1     J X X Z  W X J R  O S P D  E E W O  J O N K
No. 2     Y X L J  D C Q L  E D H X  G Z L Z  W H N B
          1 2 3 4  5 1 2 3  4 5 1 2  3 4 5 1  2 3 4 5
          F O H L  E O     H D E B   O P F O  F I I  F
          1 2 3 4  1 2 3 4  1 2 3 4  1 2 3 4  1 2 3 4
No. 1     G I R X  R W U Y  D K N T  J W R E  V B U R
No. 2     V T J S  A T S U  U C M I  A K K J  E M I Y
          1 2 3 4  5 1 2 3  4 5 1 2  3 4 5 1  2 3 4 5
          G        E J C A  C H D I  I F C    A B G A  H
          1 2 3 4  1 2 3 4  1 2 3 4  1 2 3 4  1 2 3 4
No. 1     D L I S  J B L C  K K F O  D E V D  Y Z Q Z
No. 2     D S K G  B V T J  Y C X Y  L Z E C  X L S U
          1 2 3 4  5 1 2 3  4 5 1 2  3 4 5 1  2 3 4 5
          H A M    F G      N D      H F C O  O H E L
          1 2 3 4  1 2 3 4  1 2
No. 1     S H C T  W D I E  X Z
No. 2     M V M N  D O N F  J Y
          1 2 3 4  5 1 2 3  4 5
          I J G I  E   M A  L H
```

Note the idiomorphic repetition (representing the word ARTILLERY), previously latent, which now becomes patent in the reduction process.

---

[3] Actually in this particular case the reduction is about 85% complete.

153

h. At this point, sequence reconstruction matrices may be made of the two messages, the Ø line representing the pseudo-plain text and the values inside the matrix being the cipher text. These matrices are illustrated in Figs. 70*a* and *b*, below:

```
Ø A B C D E F G H I J K L M N O P Q R S T U V W X Y Z
1 B V H O W J G D S R I X F K Y E
2 L Q W K S E B Z O H     C   X
3 U P V   Q B C X N     S I   W
4 E W Y P X K   R T A   Z G   D
```

FIGURE 70*a*

```
Ø A B C D E F G H I J K L M N O P Q R S T U V W X Y Z
1 J H T F G Y V D M     S     C
2 S E H   U W A Z I V     N     X
3 F   U   C A M L H       K   B G
4 I T K E S Z   U N   A J B Y Q
5 G F E C D B   Y J A   U M   L
```

FIGURE 70*b*

From these matrices, it is a simple matter to chain out the equivalent primary cipher components used for each message. Having reconstructed the cipher component for a message, the alphabets may be aligned and now the entire text converted to monoalphabetic terms. After solution of the messages, it is found that Message No. 1 is a case of direct symmetry with the cipher component being based on the key word HYDRAULIC, and Message No. 2 is a case of indirect symmetry with both components being keyword-mixed sequences based on QUESTIONABLY.

i. The method described in subpars. 62*e* to *h*, above, involves techniques which have a broad application in cryptanalytics, in other fields besides the solution of periodic polyalphabetic cryptograms. But even in this latter field, it might be the only approach to solution where the cryptosystem involves nonrelated, random-mixed secondary alphabets among which *no* symmetry of any sort exists.

j. The two messages used in the example had periods prime to each other. If this had not been the case, only a slight modification of either of the two methods would have been necessary. For the student who cares to investigate this matter further, there is given in Fig. 71, below, a new Message No. 2 to be paired with Message No. 1 in subpar. 62*b*; he can then solve this pair of isologs by either of the two methods demonstrated in this paragraph.

Message No 2

```
T Q L G C   F X Q J M   L Z J D R   C F L G L   D Z H Z E   X A S V F

T J A S T   Y Q A F V   W L Z A U   G X O J J   F Y I B S   P K H B N

U K A I L   D O N K K   I I T G L   G T N T X   C J J L W   Q L I A L

H A B F A   X J N O Y   T N Q Z C   D N A U Y   D D Y O Z   R A P C O

B F J H S   Z T Q L G   C F X Q J   K B J T B   L K F V X   K G R H B

Y R L C W   N Z B C T   C I B G C   N F C H B
```

FIGURE 71

154

63. Solution of a pair of periodic cryptograms involving a "stagger."—*a*. It happens occasionally that the cryptanalyst has two messages with identical beginnings, but after a few letters the cipher texts diverge; and the group counts of the two messages are either identical or nearly identical. This situation could arise in a pair of isologs, when the first message has a letter omitted (or added) at the point of divergence, and the second message (with the identical beginning) has this error corrected. In other words, we have a pair of true isologs except for the deletion (or addition) of a single letter. Such a situation is called a "stagger."[4] By treating the isologous portions of the two messages, we may recover the primary cipher component by the process of indirect symmetry. This is best illustrated by an example.

b. Let us suppose the following two messages are at hand:

Message "A"

```
Z F W A Y   I T B V X   X W Z Q V   P E B G S   G G F I Z   T U A M F→

←R F E Q X   P E P P O   P C N B P   Q P O T X   V N A I H   H V R X C

N H V G M   F R F S I   E S Q M V
```

Message "B"

```
Z F W A Y   I T B V X   X W Z Q V   P D R K F   U S V A G   X L J K C→

←N D V P R   O W B R H   Y F J M S   H R F V S   B A H W G   Z F A J O

J M F A V   C N D V D   O R Z P H   A
```

We note the identical 16-letter beginnings; we also note that Message "B" is one letter longer than Message "A", and that the repeated tetragraphs in Message "B" are spaced identically as in Message "A", except for the fact that the position of the tetragraphs is one letter more than their counterparts in Message "A". Both messages factor to 6 alphabets.

c. These phenomena clearly point to a case of a stagger, with Message "B" containing one more letter than Message "A". If this is the case, and the plain texts are otherwise identical, then the D_c in the 17th position of Message "B" seems to be the extra letter, coming as it does after the identical beginning. The two texts are now superimposed, and the equivalencies are inserted into a sequence reconstruction matrix, as is shown below:

```
        5 6 1 2 3 4 5 6 1 2 3 4 5 6 1 2 3 4 5 6 1 2 3 4 5 6 1 2 3 4 5 6 1 2 3 4 5 6 1 2 3 4 5 6 1 2 3
"A"     E B G S G G F I Z T U A M F R F E Q X P E P P O P C N B P Q P O T X V N A I H H V R X C N H V G M F R F S I E S Q M V
"B"     R K F U S V A G X L J K C N D V P R O W B R H Y F J M S H R F V S B A H W G Z F A J O J M F A V C N D V D O R Z P H A
        6 1 2 3 4 5 6 1 2 3 4 5 6 1 2 3 4 5 6 1 2 3 4 5 6 1 2 3 4 5 6 1 2 3 4 5 6 1 2 3 4 5 6 1 2 3 4
```

	A	B	C	D	E	F	G	H	I	J	K	L	M	N	O	P	Q	R	S	T	U	V	W	X	Y	Z
1–2				B		F	Z							M		P	D		S					X		
2–3	S				V	F					H			R		U	L				B					
3–4					P	S								H			D	J	A							
4–5	K				V		O				H	Y		R	J											
5–6	W				R	A						C		F								O				
6–1	K	J		N			G							V	W			Z								

---

[4] Such errors are more prone to happen in machine cipher systems, when the addition or deletion of a word separator in a pair of otherwise identical cryptograms (enciphered with identical initial settings or keys) causes a stagger. Sometimes the stagger may be progressive, i.e., the interval of the displacement becoming greater and greater as additional word separators are omitted.

The solution, which proceeds in the usual manner, is left as an exercise for the interested student.[5]

64. Solution of a periodic cryptogram containing a long latent repetition.—*a.* It sometimes happens that a periodic cryptogram contains a long passage repeated in its plain text, the second occurrence of which is enciphered at a point in the keying cycle different from that of the first occurrence. The recognition and delineation of the latent repetition may be made possible by the spatial relationships of ciphertext repetitions present within the message.[6] If such a latent repetition is found, and it is long enough, the equivalencies from the two corresponding sequences may be chained together to yield an equivalent primary cipher component, and thus by-pass a more laborious process of solution by the usual method of frequency analysis or making assumptions in the plain text of a polyalphabetic cipher.

b. As an example, let us suppose the following message has been intercepted:

```
A S E X Z    L R C W C    H X R U G    L X A X W    I N Y E H    P J R D X
R D X W M    L A I E K    K T A G Z    F Z N C E    L L T F W    C R B J T
Z L C V H    M A A J R    D X R T F    M T V J H    P G V P I    M W Y R L
R R B J T    Z L C V H    D K J T A    I B L F P    A W N Y E    H P E M G
F I R V A    R X V J F    J A H D F    I V V T N    A E Z A Z    J X V L Y
P J T N Q    A B K X D    J X H A X    Y W P I M    I C G A N    I W E F G
W M I Z J    H V I X V    L Y P G A    Y X Z M E    K L I S B    O T F O M
V W E F G    W M I Z J    D Z A C G    J V M P V    N D K G K    V M A I B
L F P A W    N Y E H P
```

An examination of the cipher text, which factors to a period of 7, reveals the following striking sets of repetitions with identical spatial relationships of the repetitions (beginning at positions 27 and 147 in the cipher text) in the two sets:

Set "A": JRDXR...(25)...RBJTZLCVH...(3)...JRDXR...(18)...RBJTZLCVH
Set "B": XVLYP...(25)...WEFGWMIZJ...(3)...XVLYP...(18)...WEFGWMIZJ

This phenomenon could arise from a repetition of a long section of plain text within the message. The presence of the repetitions at the beginning and end of these sets of sequences delineates the limits,[7] insofar discernible, of the repeated plaintext passage. Since these two sets are

---

[5] Note, in matrices of this kind, how easy it is to align properly the cipher components after the primary cipher component (or an equivalent) has been recovered, thereby expediting the reduction of the cipher text to monoalphabetic terms. From the data in the sequence reconstruction matrix, it is observed that the B_c of Alphabet 2 is under the E_c of Alphabet 1; the V_c of Alphabet 3 is under the F_c of Alphabet 2; the P_c of Alphabet 4 is under the E_c of Alphabet 3, etc.; thus all the cipher components may be quickly put together at their proper relative displacements, revealing the repeating key in the process in one of the columns.

[6] It is also possible that, because of highly stereotyped and redundant plain text of a particular message, there might be two sets of long polygraphic repetitions of the same length in the cipher text. If these sets actually represent the same plain text, they may be chained together as described below to derive a partial or even complete equivalent primary cipher component.

[7] In cases wherein only one polygraphic repetition is present to delineate a portion of the identical plaintext sections, the limits of the identity may be established to the left and right of this portion by the limits of the isomorphism manifested.

equivalent to each other, it is possible to superimpose these sections and distribute the equivalencies into a sequence reconstruction matrix from which an equivalent primary component may be chained, following a procedure similar to that outlined in subpar. 63c. The completion of the solution of this problem, too, is left as an exercise for the student.

65. Solution by superimposition.—*a.* In solving an ordinary repeating-key cipher the first step, that of ascertaining the length of the period, is of no significance in itself. It merely paves the way for and makes possible the second step, which consists in allocating the letters of the cryptogram into individual monoalphabetic distributions. The third step then consists in solving these distributions. Usually, the text of the message is transcribed into its periods and is written out in successive lines corresponding in length with that of the period. The diagram then consists of a series of columns of letters, and the letters in each column belong to the same monoalphabet. Another way of looking at the matter is to conceive of the text as having thus been transcribed into *superimposed periods;* in such a case the letters in each column have undergone the same kind of treatment by the same elements (plain and cipher components of the cipher alphabet).[8]

b. Suppose, however, that the repeating key is very long and that the message is short, so that there are only a very few, if any, complete cycles in the text. Then the solution of the message becomes difficult, if not impossible (unless the alphabets are known), because there is not a sufficient number of superimposable periods to yield monoalphabetic distributions which can be solved by frequency principles. But suppose also that there are many short cryptograms all enciphered by the same key, each message beginning at identical starting points in the key. Then it is clear that if these messages are superimposed "head on" or "in flush depth," (1) the letters in the respective columns will all belong to individual alphabets, and (2) if there is a sufficient number of such superimposable messages (say 25–30, for English), then the frequency distributions applicable to the successive *columns* of text can be solved—*without knowing the length of the key.*[9] In other words, any difficulties that may have arisen on account of failure or inability to ascertain the length of the period have been circumvented. The second step in normal solution is thus by-passed.

c. Furthermore, and this is a very important point, even if an extremely long key is employed and a series of messages beginning at different initial points are enciphered by such a key, this method of solution by superimposition can be employed, provided that the messages can be superimposed correctly, that is, so that the letters which fall in one column really belong to one cipher alphabet.[10] Just how this can be done will be treated in par. 98.

---

[8] The superimposed messages are said to be "in depth."

[9] The assumption of probable initial words of messages and stereotypic beginnings is a powerful method of attack in such situations. Since the superimposed texts in these cases comprise only the beginnings of messages, assumptions of probable words are more easily made than when words are sought in the interiors of messages. Such common introductory words as REQUEST, REFER, ENEMY, WHAT, WHEN, and SEND are good ones to assume. Furthermore, the high frequencies of certain initial digraphs of common words will, of course, manifest themselves in the first two columns of the superimposition diagram; note, in English, the high frequency of the initial digraph RE_p in many good beginning words such as REQUEST, REQUIRE, REFERENCE, REFERRING, REQUISITIONS, REPEAT, RECOMMEND, REPORT, RECONNAISSANCE, REINFORCEMENTS, and REGIMENT. See also in this connection Appendix 4 of *Military Cryptanalytics, Part I.*

[10] The χ test may be used to advantage in finding and combining columns of the superimposition diagram which were enciphered by identical keys, thus assisting in the analysis of frequencies of larger samples than were available before the amalgamation.

66. Additional remarks.—*a.* We have seen in pars. 60–64 that the chaining process between cipher texts applies to the latent characteristics of the *cipher* components, regardless of the identity of the plain components and regardless whether direct or indirect symmetry is involved in the cryptosystems.

b. The observant student will have noted that a large part of the text thus far is devoted to the elucidation and application of a very few basic principles. These principles are, however, extremely important and their proper usage in the hands of a skilled cryptanalyst makes them practically indispensable tools of his art. The student should therefore drill himself in the application of these tools by practicing upon problem after problem, until he acquires facility in their use and feels competent to apply them in practice whenever the least opportunity presents itself. This will save him much time and effort in the solution of bona fide messages.

CHAPTER IX

PROGRESSIVE ALPHABET SYSTEMS

67. Preliminary remarks.—*a.* In progressive alphabet systems the basic principle is quite simple. Two primary components are arranged or provided for according to a key which may be varied from time to time; the interaction of the primary components results in making available for cryptographic purposes a set of cipher alphabets; all the latter are employed in a fixed sequence or progression; hence the designation progressive alphabet system. Since the number of alphabets available for such use is rather small (usually 26), if the text to be enciphered is much longer than the sequence of alphabets, then the system reduces to a periodic method. But if the number of alphabets is large as compared with the text to be enciphered,[1] so that the sequence of alphabets is not repeated, then, of course, the cryptographic text will exhibit no periodic phenomena.

b. The series of cipher alphabets in such a system constitutes a keying sequence. Once set up, often the only remaining element in the key for a specific message is the starting point in the sequence, that is, the initial cipher alphabet employed in enciphering a given message. If this keying sequence must be employed by a large group of correspondents, and if all messages employ the same starting point in the keying sequence, obviously the cryptograms may simply be superimposed without any preliminary testing to ascertain proper points for superimposition. It has already been indicated (cf. par. 65) how cases of this sort may be solved. However, if messages are enciphered with varying starting points, the matter of superimposing them properly takes on a different aspect. This matter will be treated in par. 72.

68. Solution of a progressive alphabet cipher when the cipher alphabets are known.—*a.* The simplest case of a progressive alphabet system involves two interacting primary components which slide against each other to produce a set of 26 secondary alphabets, which are employed one after the other consecutively in the simplest type of progression. Beginning at an initial juxtaposition, producing say, Alphabet 1, the subsequent secondary alphabets are in the sequence 2, 3, . . . 26, 1, 2, 3, . . ., and so on. If a different initial juxtaposition is used, say Alphabet 10 is the first one, the sequence is exactly the same as before, only beginning at a different point.

---

[1] For instance, if the cipher component of a disk cipher device were composed of a random arrangement of 100 different dinomes, and no message were longer than 100 letters, no periodicity would be manifested.

b. Suppose that the two primary components are based upon the key word HYDRAULIC. A message is to be enciphered, beginning with Alphabet 1. Thus:

Plain component: H Y D R A U L I C B E F G J K M N O P Q S T V W X Z
Cipher component: H Y D R A U L I C B E F G J K M N O P Q S T V W X Z H Y D . . .

Letter No:	1	2	3	4	5	6	7	8	9	10	11	12	13	14	15	16	17	18	19	20	21	22	23	24	25	26
Alphabet No:	1	2	3	4	5	6	7	8	9	10	11	12	13	14	15	16	17	18	19	20	21	22	23	24	25	26
Plain text:	E	N	E	M	Y	H	A	S	P	L	A	C	E	D	H	E	A	V	Y	I	N	T	E	R	D	I
Cipher text:	E	O	G	P	U	U	E	Y	H	M	K	Q	V	M	K	Z	S	J	Q	H	E	N	L	H	H	L

Letter No:	27	28	29	30	31	32	33	34	35	36	37	38	39	40	41	42	43	44	45	46	47	48	49	50	51	52	53
Alphabet No:	1	2	3	4	5	6	7	8	9	10	11	12	13	14	15	16	17	18	19	20	21	22	23	24	25	26	1
Plain text:	C	T	I	O	N	F	I	R	E	U	P	O	N	Z	A	N	E	S	V	I	L	L	E	R	O	A	D
Cipher text:	C	V	B	S	S	N	J	E	P	K	D	D	D	G	P	U	H	F	K	H	H	Y	L	H	M	R	D

c. This method reduces to a periodic system involving 26 secondary cipher alphabets and the latter are used in simple progression. It is obvious therefore that the 1st, 27th, 53d, . . . letters are in the 1st alphabet; the 2d, 28th, 54th, . . . letters are in the 2d alphabet, and so on.

d. To solve such a cryptogram, knowing the two primary components, is hardly a problem at all. The only element lacking is a knowledge of the starting point. But this is not necessary, for merely by completing the plain-component sequence and examining the *diagonals* of the diagram, the plain text becomes evident. For example, let us consider that the first two groups of an intercepted message are HIDCT EHUXI..., and let us assume that the components are keyword-mixed sequences based upon HYDRAULIC. If we complete the plain-component sequences initiated by the successive cipher letters, the plain text ENEMY MACHI . . . is seen to come out in successive steps upward in Fig. 72. Had the cipher component been shifted in the opposite direction in encipherment, the steps would have been downward instead of upward. If sliding strips had been set up according to the sequence of cipher letters but on a diagonal, then, of course, the plaintext letters would have reappeared on one generatrix.

e. If the components were two different known mixed sequences, it would of course first be necessary to convert the cipher letters into their plain-component equivalents before completing the plain-component sequences. In any case, faced with an unknown type of progressive alpha-

```
H I D C T E H U X L
Y C R B V F Y L Z I
D B A E W G D I H C
R E U F X J R C Y B
A F L G Z K A B D E
U G I J H M U E R F
L J C K Y N L F A G
I K B M D O I G U J
C M E N R P C J L K
B N F O A Q B K I M
E O G P U S E M C N
F P J Q L T F N B O
G Q K S I V G O E P
```

FIGURE 72

160

bet cipher, completing the plain-component sequences on the hypotheses of direct or reversed standard alphabets is the logical thing to do, and will quickly prove or disprove these hypotheses. If the primary components are not known sequences, the methods given in this paragraph obviously cannot apply; fortunately, however, there exist several methods which can be used in such situations, as will be treated in the succeeding paragraphs.

69. Solution by a method involving the χ test.—*a*. An interesting general solution of a statistical nature of a progressive alphabet system will now be discussed. The problem involves secondary alphabets derived from the interaction of two identical mixed primary components. It will be assumed that the enemy has been using a system of this kind and that the primary components are changed daily.

b. Before attacking an actual problem of this type, suppose a few minutes be devoted to a general analysis of its elements. It is here assumed that the primary components are based upon the HYDRAULIC....Z sequence and that the cipher component is shifted toward the right one step at a time. Consider a cipher square such as that shown in Fig. 73, which is applicable

Alphabet

	1	2	3	4	5	6	7	8	9	10	11	12	13	14	15	16	17	18	19	20	21	22	23	24	25	26
A	A	U	L	I	C	B	E	F	G	J	K	M	N	O	P	Q	S	T	V	W	X	Z	H	Y	D	R
B	B	E	F	G	J	K	M	N	O	P	Q	S	T	V	W	X	Z	H	Y	D	R	A	U	L	I	C
C	C	B	E	F	G	J	K	M	N	O	P	Q	S	T	V	W	X	Z	H	Y	D	R	A	U	L	I
D	D	R	A	U	L	I	C	B	E	F	G	J	K	M	N	O	P	Q	S	T	V	W	X	Z	H	Y
E	E	F	G	J	K	M	N	O	P	Q	S	T	V	W	X	Z	H	Y	D	R	A	U	L	I	C	B
F	F	G	J	K	M	N	O	P	Q	S	T	V	W	X	Z	H	Y	D	R	A	U	L	I	C	B	E
G	G	J	K	M	N	O	P	Q	S	T	V	W	X	Z	H	Y	D	R	A	U	L	I	C	B	E	F
H	H	Y	D	R	A	U	L	I	C	B	E	F	G	J	K	M	N	O	P	Q	S	T	V	W	X	Z
I	I	C	B	E	F	G	J	K	M	N	O	P	Q	S	T	V	W	X	Z	H	Y	D	R	A	U	L
J	J	K	M	N	O	P	Q	S	T	V	W	X	Z	H	Y	D	R	A	U	L	I	C	B	E	F	G
K	K	M	N	O	P	Q	S	T	V	W	X	Z	H	Y	D	R	A	U	L	I	C	B	E	F	G	J
L	L	I	C	B	E	F	G	J	K	M	N	O	P	Q	S	T	V	W	X	Z	H	Y	D	R	A	U
M	M	N	O	P	Q	S	T	V	W	X	Z	H	Y	D	R	A	U	L	I	C	B	E	F	G	J	K
N	N	O	P	Q	S	T	V	W	X	Z	H	Y	D	R	A	U	L	I	C	B	E	F	G	J	K	M
O	O	P	Q	S	T	V	W	X	Z	H	Y	D	R	A	U	L	I	C	B	E	F	G	J	K	M	N
P	P	Q	S	T	V	W	X	Z	H	Y	D	R	A	U	L	I	C	B	E	F	G	J	K	M	N	O
Q	Q	S	T	V	W	X	Z	H	Y	D	R	A	U	L	I	C	B	E	F	G	J	K	M	N	O	P
R	R	A	U	L	I	C	B	E	F	G	J	K	M	N	O	P	Q	S	T	V	W	X	Z	H	Y	D
S	S	T	V	W	X	Z	H	Y	D	R	A	U	L	I	C	B	E	F	G	J	K	M	N	O	P	Q
T	T	V	W	X	Z	H	Y	D	R	A	U	L	I	C	B	E	F	G	J	K	M	N	O	P	Q	S
U	U	L	I	C	B	E	F	G	J	K	M	N	O	P	Q	S	T	V	W	X	Z	H	Y	D	R	A
V	V	W	X	Z	H	Y	D	R	A	U	L	I	C	B	E	F	G	J	K	M	N	O	P	Q	S	T
W	W	X	Z	H	Y	D	R	A	U	L	I	C	B	E	F	G	J	K	M	N	O	P	Q	S	T	V
X	X	Z	H	Y	D	R	A	U	L	I	C	B	E	F	G	J	K	M	N	O	P	Q	S	T	V	W
Y	Y	D	R	A	U	L	I	C	B	E	F	G	J	K	M	N	O	P	Q	S	T	V	W	X	Z	H
Z	Z	H	Y	D	R	A	U	L	I	C	B	E	F	G	J	K	M	N	O	P	Q	S	T	V	W	X

Cipher Letters (label along left side)

(Plaintext letters are within the square proper)

FIGURE 73

161

to the type of problem under study. It has been arranged in the form of a deciphering square. In this square, *the horizontal sequences are all identical but merely shifted relatively; the letters inside the square are plaintext letters.*

c. If, for mere purposes of demonstration, instead of letters within the cells of the square there are placed tallies corresponding in number with the theoretical frequencies per 100 of the letters occupying the respective cells, the cipher square becomes as follows (showing only the first three rows of the square):

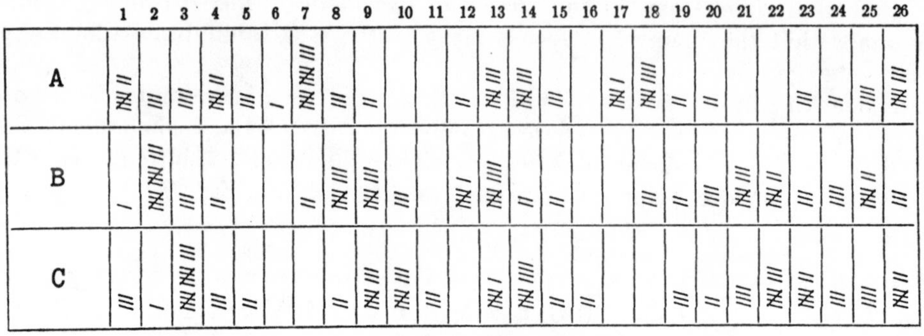

FIGURE 74a

d. It is obvious that here is a case wherein if two distributions pertaining to the square are isolated from the square, the χ test can be applied to ascertain how the distributions should be shifted relative to each other so that they can be superimposed and made to yield a monoalphabetic composite. There is clearly only one correct superimposition out of 25 possibilities. In this case, the "B" row of tallies must be displaced 5 intervals to the right in order to match it and amalgamate it with the "A" row of tallies. Thus:

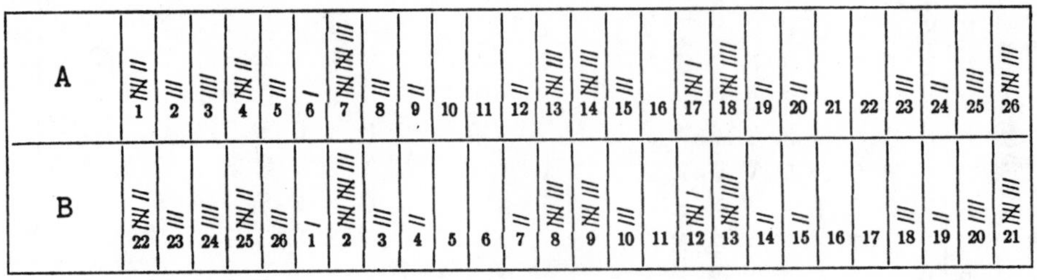

FIGURE 74b

e. Note that the amount of displacement, that is, the number of intervals the "B" sequence must be shifted to make it match the "A" sequence in Fig. 74b, corresponds exactly to the distance between the letters A and B in the primary cipher component, which is 5 intervals. Thus:

```
    0 1 2 3 4 5
... A U L I C B ....
```
The fact that the primary plain component is in this case identical with the primary cipher component has nothing to do with the matter. *The displacement interval is being measured on the cipher component.* It is important that the student see this point very clearly. He can, if he likes, prove the point by experimenting with two different primary components.

f. Assuming that a message in such a system is to be solved, the text is transcribed in rows of 26 letters. A uniliteral frequency distribution is made for each column of the transcribed text,

162

the 26 separate distributions being compiled within a single square such as that shown in Fig. 75. Such a square may be termed a *frequency distribution square*.

g. Now the vertical columns of tallies within such a distribution square constitute frequency distributions of the usual type: they show the distribution of the various cipher letters in each cipher alphabet. If there were many lines of text, all arranged in periods of 26 letters, then each column of the frequency square could be solved in the usual manner, by the application of the simple principles of monoalphabetic frequency. But what do the horizontal rows of tallies within the square represent? Is it not clear that the first such row, the "A" row, merely shows the distribution of A_c throughout the successive cipher alphabets? *And does not this graphic picture of the distribution of* A_c *correspond to the sequence of letters composing the primary plain component?* Furthermore, is it not clear that what has been said of the "A" row of tallies applies equally to the B, C, D, ... Z rows? Finally, is it not clear that the graphic pictures of all the distributions correspond to the *same* sequence of letters, except that the sequence begins with a different letter in each row? In other words, all the horizontal rows of tallies within the distribution square apply to the *same* sequence of plaintext letters, the sequences in one row merely beginning with a different letter from that with which another row begins. The sequences of letters to which the tallies apply in the various rows are merely displaced relative to one another. Now if there are sufficient data for statistical purposes in the various horizontal sequences of tallies within the distribution square, these sequences, being approximately similar, can be studied by means of the χ test *to find their relative displacements*. And in finding the latter, we provide a method whereby the primary cipher component may be reconstructed, since the correct assembling of the displacement data will yield the sequence of letters constituting the primary cipher component. If the plain component is identical with the cipher component, the solution is immediately at hand; if the components are different, the solution is but one step removed. Thus, there has been elaborated a method of solving this type of cipher system *without making any assumptions of values for cipher letters*.

h. We will now take up a typical problem employing the procedures just discussed. The following cryptogram has been enciphered according to the method indicated, by progressive, simple, uninterrupted shifting of a primary cipher component against an identical primary plain component.

163

Cryptogram

```
WGJJM   MMJXE   DGCOC   FTRPB   MIIIK   ZRYNN
BUFRW   WWWYO   IHFJK   OKHTT   AZCLJ   EPPFR
WCKOO   FFFGE   PQRYY   IWXMX   UDIPF   EXMLL
WFKGY   PBBXC   HBFYI   ETXHF   BIVDI   PNXIV
RPWTM   GIMPT   ECJBO   KVBUQ   GVGFF   FKLYY
CKBIW   XMXUD   IPFFU   YNVSS   IHRMH   YZHAU
QWGKT   IUXYJ   JAOWZ   OCFTR   PPOQU   SGYCX
VCXUC   JLMLL   YEKFF   ZVQJQ   SIYSP   DSBBJ
UAHYN   WLOCX   SDQVC   YVSIL   IWNJO   OMAQS
LWYJG   TVPQK   PKTLH   SROON   ICFEV   MNVWN
BNEHA   MRCRO   VSTXE   NHPVB   TWKUQ   IOCAV
WBRQN   FJVNR   VDOPU   QRLKQ   NFFFZ   PHURV
WLXGS   HQWHP   JBCNN   JQSOQ   ORCBM   RRAON
RKWUH   YYCIW   DGSJC   TGPGR   MIQMP   SGCTN
MFGJX   EDGCO   PTGPW   QQVQI   WXTTT   COJVA
AABWM   XIHOW   HDEQU   AINFK   FWHPJ   AHZIT
WZKFE   XSRUY   QIOVR   ERDJV   DKHIR   QWEDG
EBYBM   LABJV   TGFFG   XYIVG   RJYEK   FBEPB
JOUAH   CUGZL   XIAJK   WDVTY   BFRUC   CCUZZ
INNDF   RJFMB   HQLXH   MHQYY   YMWQV   CLIPT
WTJYQ   BYRLI   TUOUS   RCDCV   WDGIG   GUBHJ
VVPWA   BUJKN   FPFYW   VQZQF   LHTWJ   PDRXZ
OWUSS   GAMHN   CWHSW   WLRYQ   QUSZV   DNXAB
VNKHF   UCVVS   SSPLQ   UPCVV   VWDGS   JOGTC
HDEVQ   SIJPH   QJAWF   RIZDW   XXHCX   YCTMG
USESN   DSBBK   RLVWR   VZEEP   PPATO   IANEE
EEJNR   CZBTB   LXPJJ   KAPPM   JEGIK   RTGFF
HPVVV   YKJEF   HQSXJ   QDYVZ   GRRHZ   QLYXK
XAZOW   RRXYK   YGMGZ   BYNVH   QBRVF   EFQLL
WZEYL   JEROQ   SOQKO   MWIOG   MBKFF   LXDXT
LWILP   QSEDY   IOEMO   IBJML   NNSYK   XJZJM
LCZBM   SDJWQ   XTJVL   FIRNR   XHYBD   BJUFI
RJICT   UUUSK   KWDVM   FWTTJ   KCKCG   CVSAG
QBCJM   EBYNV   SSJKS   DCBDY   FPPVF   DWZMT
BPVTT   CGBVT   ZKHQD   DRMEZ   OO
```

i. The message is transcribed in lines of 26 letters, since that is the total number of secondary alphabets in the system.   The transcribed text is shown below:

	1	2	3	4	5	6	7	8	9	10	11	12	13	14	15	16	17	18	19	20	21	22	23	24	25	26
1	W	G	J	J	M	M	M	J	X	E	D	G	C	O	C	F	T	R	P	B	M	I	I	I	K	Z
2	R	Y	N	N	B	U	F	R	W	W	W	W	Y	O	I	H	F	J	K	O	K	H	T	T	A	Z
3	C	L	J	E	P	P	F	R	W	C	K	O	O	F	F	F	G	E	P	Q	R	Y	Y	I	W	X
4	M	X	U	D	I	P	F	E	X	M	L	L	W	F	K	G	Y	P	B	B	X	C	H	B	F	Y
5	I	E	T	X	H	F	B	I	V	D	I	P	N	X	I	V	R	P	W	T	M	G	I	M	P	T
6	E	C	J	B	O	K	V	B	U	Q	G	V	G	F	F	F	K	L	Y	Y	C	K	B	I	W	X
7	M	X	U	D	I	P	F	F	U	Y	N	V	S	S	I	H	R	M	H	Y	Z	H	A	U	Q	W
8	G	K	T	I	U	X	Y	J	J	A	O	W	Z	O	C	F	T	R	P	P	O	Q	U	S	G	Y
9	C	X	V	C	X	U	C	J	L	M	L	L	Y	E	K	F	F	Z	V	Q	J	Q	S	I	Y	S
10	P	D	S	B	B	J	U	A	H	Y	N	W	L	O	C	X	S	D	Q	V	C	Y	V	S	I	L
11	I	W	N	J	O	O	M	A	Q	S	L	W	Y	J	G	T	V	P	Q	K	P	K	T	L	H	S
12	R	O	O	N	I	C	F	E	V	M	N	V	W	N	B	N	E	H	A	M	R	C	R	O	V	S
13	T	X	E	N	H	P	V	B	T	W	K	U	Q	I	O	C	A	V	W	B	R	Q	N	F	J	V
14	N	R	V	D	O	P	U	Q	R	L	K	Q	N	F	F	F	Z	P	H	U	R	V	W	L	X	G
15	S	H	Q	W	H	P	J	B	C	N	N	J	Q	S	O	Q	O	R	C	B	M	R	R	A	O	N
16	R	K	W	U	H	Y	Y	C	I	W	D	G	S	J	C	T	G	P	G	R	M	I	Q	M	P	S
17	G	C	T	N	M	F	G	J	X	E	D	G	C	O	P	T	G	P	W	Q	Q	V	Q	I	W	X
18	T	T	T	C	O	J	V	A	A	A	B	W	M	X	I	H	O	W	H	D	E	Q	U	A	I	N
19	F	K	F	W	H	P	J	A	H	Z	I	T	W	Z	K	F	E	X	S	R	U	Y	Q	I	O	V
20	R	E	R	D	J	V	D	K	H	I	R	Q	W	E	D	G	E	B	Y	B	M	L	A	B	J	V
21	T	G	F	F	G	X	Y	I	V	G	R	J	Y	E	K	F	B	E	P	B	J	O	U	A	H	C
22	U	G	Z	L	X	I	A	J	K	W	D	V	T	Y	B	F	R	U	C	C	C	U	Z	Z	I	N
23	N	D	F	R	J	F	M	B	H	Q	L	X	H	M	H	Q	Y	Y	Y	M	W	Q	V	C	L	I
24	P	T	W	T	J	Y	Q	B	Y	R	L	I	T	U	O	U	S	R	C	D	C	V	W	D	G	I
25	G	G	U	B	H	J	V	V	P	W	A	B	U	J	K	N	F	P	F	Y	W	V	Q	Z	Q	F
26	L	H	T	W	J	P	D	R	X	Z	O	W	U	S	S	G	A	M	H	N	C	W	H	S	W	W
27	L	R	Y	Q	Q	U	S	Z	V	D	N	X	A	N	V	N	K	H	F	U	C	V	V	S	S	S
28	P	L	Q	U	P	C	V	V	W	D	G	S	J	O	G	T	C	H	D	E	V	Q	S	I	J
29	P	H	Q	J	A	W	F	R	I	Z	D	W	X	X	H	C	X	Y	C	T	M	G	U	S	E	S
30	N	D	S	B	B	K	R	L	V	W	R	V	Z	E	E	P	P	P	A	T	O	I	A	N	E	E
31	E	E	J	N	R	C	Z	B	T	B	L	X	P	J	J	K	A	P	P	M	J	E	G	I	K	R
32	T	G	F	F	H	P	V	V	V	Y	K	J	E	F	H	Q	S	X	J	Q	D	Y	V	Z	G	R
33	R	H	Z	Q	L	Y	X	K	X	A	Z	O	W	R	R	X	Y	K	Y	G	M	G	Z	B	Y	N
34	V	H	Q	B	R	V	F	E	F	Q	L	L	W	Z	E	Y	L	J	E	R	O	Q	S	O	Q	K
35	O	M	W	I	O	G	M	B	K	F	F	L	X	D	X	T	L	W	I	L	P	Q	S	E	D	Y
36	I	O	E	M	O	I	B	J	M	L	N	N	S	Y	K	X	J	Z	J	M	L	C	Z	B	M	S
37	D	J	W	Q	X	T	J	V	L	F	I	R	N	R	X	H	Y	B	D	B	J	U	F	I	R	J
38	I	C	T	U	U	U	S	K	K	W	D	V	M	F	W	T	T	J	K	C	K	C	G	C	V	S
39	A	G	Q	B	C	J	M	E	B	Y	N	V	S	S	J	K	S	D	C	B	D	Y	F	P	P	V
40	F	D	W	Z	M	T	B	P	V	T	T	C	G	B	V	T	Z	K	H	Q	D	D	R	M	E	Z
41	O	O																								

j. A frequency distribution square is then compiled, each column of the text forming a separate distribution in columnar form in the square.   The latter is shown in Fig. 75.

165

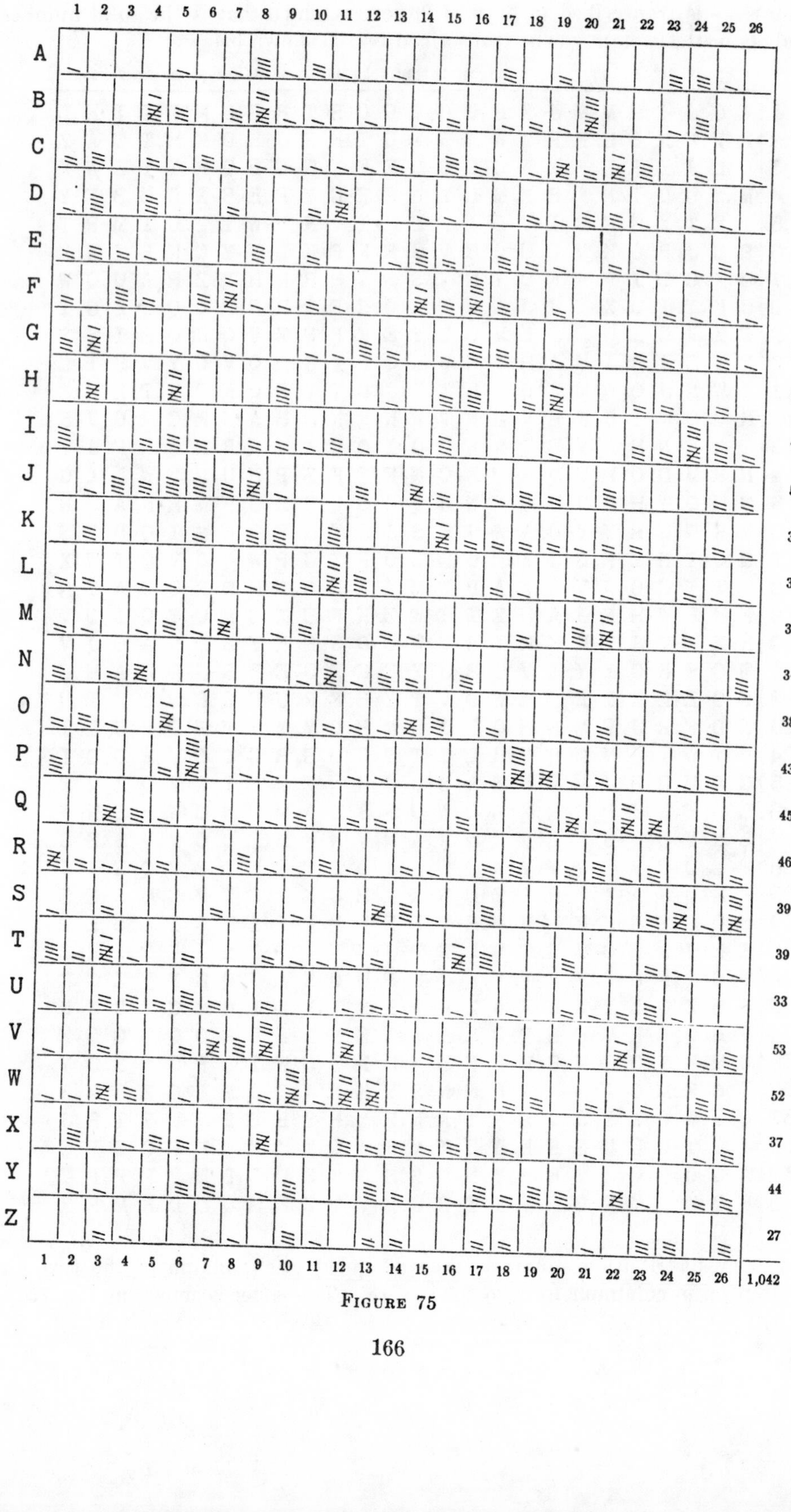

FIGURE 75

166

k. The χ test will now be applied to the horizontal rows of tallies in the distribution square, in accordance with the theory set forth in subpar. 69*g*. Since this test is purely statistical in character and becomes increasingly reliable as the size of the distributions increases, it is best to start by working with the two distributions having the greatest total numbers of tallies. These are the V and W distributions, with 53 and 52 occurrences, respectively. The results of three of the 25 possible relative displacements of these two distributions are shown below, labeled "First test," "Second test," and "Third test." For convenience in estimating the matching propensities, the χ value is expressed in terms of the ξ I. C.[2]

First test

f_V	1	0	2	0	0	2	6	4	8	0	0	7	0	0	2	1	1	1	1	1	0	6	4	0	2	4	$N_V=53$
	1	2	3	4	5	6	7	8	9	10	11	12	13	14	15	16	17	18	19	20	21	22	23	24	25	26	
f_W	24	25	26	1	2	3	4	5	6	7	8	9	10	11	12	13	14	15	16	17	18	19	20	21	22	23	
	0	4	2	1	1	5	3	0	1	0	0	2	8	1	7	6	0	1	0	0	2	3	0	2	1	2	$N_W=52$
$f_V f_W$	0	0	4	0	0	10	18	0	8	0	0	14	0	0	14	6	0	1	0	0	0	18	0	0	2	8	$\Sigma f_V f_W=103$

$$\chi_o=103 \qquad \chi_r=\frac{53\cdot52}{26}=106 \qquad \xi\ I.C.=\frac{103}{106}=0.97$$

Second test

f_V	1	0	2	0	0	2	6	5	8	0	0	7	0	0	2	1	1	1	1	1	0	6	4	0	2	4	$N_V=53$
	1	2	3	4	5	6	7	8	9	10	11	12	13	14	15	16	17	18	19	20	21	22	23	24	25	26	
f_W	18	19	20	21	22	23	24	25	26	1	2	3	4	5	6	7	8	9	10	11	12	13	14	15	16	17	
	2	3	0	2	1	2	0	4	2	1	1	5	3	0	1	0	0	2	8	1	7	6	0	1	0	0	$N_V=52$
$f_V f_W$	2	0	0	0	0	4	0	16	16	0	0	35	0	0	2	0	0	2	8	1	0	36	0	0	0	0	$\Sigma f_V f_W=122$

$$\chi_o=122 \qquad \chi_r=\frac{53\cdot52}{26}=106 \qquad \xi\ I.C.=\frac{122}{106}=1.15$$

Third test

f_V	1	0	2	0	0	2	6	4	8	0	0	7	0	0	2	1	1	1	1	1	0	6	4	0	2	4	$N_V=53$
	1	2	3	4	5	6	7	8	9	10	11	12	13	14	15	16	17	18	19	20	21	22	23	24	25	26	
f_W	4	5	6	7	8	9	10	11	12	13	14	15	16	17	18	19	20	21	22	23	24	25	26	1	2	3	
	3	0	1	0	0	2	8	1	7	6	0	1	0	0	2	3	0	2	1	2	0	4	2	1	1	5	$N_W=52$
$f_V f_W$	3	0	2	0	0	4	48	4	56	0	0	7	0	0	4	3	0	2	1	2	0	24	8	0	2	20	$\Sigma f_V f_W=190$

$$\chi_o=190 \qquad \chi_r=\frac{53\cdot52}{26}=106 \qquad \xi\ I.C.=\frac{190}{106}=1.79$$

l. Since the last of the three foregoing tests gives a value somewhat better than the expected ξ I.C. of 1.73, it looks as though the correct position of the W distribution with reference to the V distribution has been found. In practice, several more tests would be made to insure that other close approximations to 1.73 are not found, but these will here be omitted. The test indicates that the primary cipher component has the letters V and W in these positions:

1 2 3 4
V . . W, since the correct superimposition requires that the 4th cell of the W distribution must be placed under the 1st cell of the V distribution (see the last superimposition above).

m. The next best distribution with which to proceed is the F distribution, with 51 occurrences. Therefore, the F sequence is matched against the W and V sequences separately, and

---

[2] See subpar. 37*e* on p. 80.

167

then against both W and V sequences at their correct superimposition; this procedure serves as a check on the correct matching of the W and V sequences. The following shows the correct relative positions of the three distributions:

f_V
1	0	2	0	0	2	6	4	8	0	0	7	0	0	2	1	1	1	1	1	0	6	4	0	2	4	$N_V=53$
1	2	3	4	5	6	7	8	9	10	11	12	13	14	15	16	17	18	19	20	21	22	23	24	25	26	

f_F
8	9	10	11	12	13	14	15	16	17	18	19	20	21	22	23	24	25	26	1	2	3	4	5	6	7	
1	1	2	1	0	0	6	3	9	3	0	2	0	0	0	2	1	1	1	2	0	4	2	0	3	7	$N_F=51$

f_Vf_F | 1 | 0 | 4 | 0 | 0 | 0 | 36 | 12 | 72 | 0 | 0 | 14 | 0 | 0 | 0 | 2 | 1 | 1 | 1 | 2 | 0 | 24 | 8 | 0 | 6 | 28 | $\Sigma f_Vf_F=212$

$$\chi_o=212 \qquad \chi_r=\frac{53\cdot51}{26}=104 \qquad \xi\ \text{I.C.}=\frac{212}{104}=2.04$$

f_W
1	1	5	3	0	1	0	0	2	8	1	7	6	0	1	0	0	2	3	0	2	1	2	0	4	2	$N_W=52$
1	2	3	4	5	6	7	8	9	10	11	12	13	14	15	16	17	18	19	20	21	22	23	24	25	26	

f_F
5	6	7	8	9	10	11	12	13	14	15	16	17	18	19	20	21	22	23	24	25	26	1	2	3	4	
0	3	7	1	1	2	1	0	0	6	3	9	3	0	2	0	0	0	2	1	1	1	2	0	4	2	$N_F=51$

f_Wf_F | 0 | 3 | 35 | 3 | 0 | 2 | 0 | 0 | 0 | 48 | 3 | 63 | 18 | 0 | 2 | 0 | 0 | 0 | 6 | 0 | 2 | 1 | 4 | 0 | 16 | 4 | $\Sigma f_Wf_F=210$

$$\chi_o=210 \qquad \chi_r=\frac{52\cdot51}{26}=102 \qquad \xi\ \text{I.C.}=\frac{210}{102}=2.06$$

$f_{(V+W)}$
4	0	3	0	0	4	14	5	15	6	0	8	0	0	4	4	1	3	2	3	0	10	6	1	3	9	$N_{V+W}=105$
1	2	3	4	5	6	7	8	9	10	11	12	13	14	15	16	17	18	19	20	21	22	23	24	25	26	

f_F
8	9	10	11	12	13	14	15	16	17	18	19	20	21	22	23	24	25	26	1	2	3	4	5	6	7	
1	1	2	1	0	0	6	3	9	3	0	2	0	0	0	2	1	1	1	2	0	4	2	0	3	7	$N_F=51$

$f_{(V+W)}f_F$ 4 | 0 | 6 | 0 | 0 | 0 | 84 | 15 | 135 | 18 | 0 | 16 | 0 | 0 | 0 | 8 | 1 | 3 | 2 | 6 | 0 | 40 | 12 | 0 | 9 | 63 $\Sigma f_{(V+W)}f_F=422$

$$\chi_o=422 \qquad \chi_r=\frac{105\cdot51}{26}=206 \qquad \xi\ \text{I.C.}=\frac{422}{206}=2.05$$

The test yields the sequence

1	2	3	4	5	6	7	8
V	.	.	W	.	.	.	F

n. The process is continued in the foregoing manner until the entire primary cipher component has been reconstructed. It is obvious that as the work progresses the cryptanalyst is forced to employ smaller and smaller distributions, so that statistically the results are apt to become less and less certain. But to counterbalance this, there is the fact that the number of possible superimpositions becomes progressively smaller as the work progresses. For example, at the commencement of operations the number of possible points for superimposing a second sequence against the first is 25; after the relative positions of 5 distributions have been ascertained and a 6th distribution is to be placed in the primary sequence being reconstructed, there are 20 possible positions; after the relative positions of 20 distributions have been ascertained, there are only 5 possible positions for the 21st distribution, and so on.

o. In the foregoing case the completely reconstructed primary cipher component is as follows:

1	2	3	4	5	6	7	8	9	10	11	12	13	14	15	16	17	18	19	20	21	22	23	24	25	26
V	A	L	W	N	O	X	F	B	P	Y	R	C	Q	Z	I	G	S	E	H	T	D	J	U	M	K

Since it was stated that the problem involves identical primary components, both components are now at hand.[3]

p. Of course, it is probable that in practical work the process of matching distributions would be interrupted soon after the positions of only a few letters in the primary component had been ascertained. For by trying partially reconstructed sequences on the cipher text, the skeletons of some words would begin to show. By filling in these skeletons with the words suggested by them, the process of reconstructing the components is much facilitated and hastened.

q. The components having been reconstructed, only a moment or two is necessary to ascertain their initial position in enciphering the message. It is only necessary to juxtapose the two components so as to give good values for any one of the vertical distributions of Fig. 75. This then gives the juxtaposition of the components for that column, and the rest follows very easily, for the plain text may now be obtained by direct use of the components. The decipherment of the beginning of the cipher text is as follows:

```
        1  2  3  4  5  6  7  8  9 10 11 12 13 14 15 16 17 18 19 20 21 22 23 24 25 26
   1 | W  G  J  J  M  M  M  J  X  E  D  G  C  O  C  F  T  R  P  B  M  I  I  I  K  Z
     | W  I  T  H  T  H  E  I  M  P  R  O  V  E  M  E  N  T  S  I  N  T  H  E  A  I

   2 | R  Y  N  N  B  U  F  R  W  W  W  W  Y  O  I  H  F  J  K  O  K  H  T  T  A  Z
     | R  P  L  A  N  E  A  N  D  T  H  E  M  E  A  N  S  O  F  C  O  M  M  U  N  I

   3 | C  L  J  E  P  P . . .
     | C  A  T  I  O  N . . .
```

r. The student should clearly understand the real nature of the matching process employed to such good advantage in this problem. In practically all the previous cases frequency distributions were made of *cipher letters* occurring in a cryptogram, and the tallies in those distributions represented the actual occurrences of cipher letters. Furthermore, when these distributions were compared or matched, what were being compared were actually cipher alphabets. That is, the text was arranged in a certain way, so that letters belonging to the same cipher alphabet actually fall within the same column and the frequency distribution for a specific cipher alphabet was made by tabulating the letters in that column. Then if any distributions were to be compared, usually the entire distribution applicable to one cipher alphabet was compared with the entire distribution applying to another cipher alphabet. But in the problem just completed, what were compared in reality were not frequency distributions applying to the *columns* of the cipher text as transcribed in subpar. 69*i*, but graphic representations of the variations in the frequencies of *plaintext letters falling in identical sequences, the identities of these plaintext letters being unknown for the moment.* Only after the reconstruction has been completed do their identities become known, when the plain text of the cryptogram is established.

70. Solution by the probable-word method.—*a.* The foregoing method of solution is, of course, almost entirely statistical in nature. There is, however, another method of attack

---

[3] If we did not know in advance that identical primary components were involved, this fact could have been deduced from a study of the frequency distributions in Fig. 75. Note that the distribution for col. 1 may be fitted to the normal; this shows that we have identical components running in the same direction, and that the setting for col. 1 is $A_p = A_c$. Furthermore, after amalgamation of several distributions into a composite distribution more truly representative of the original primary component, it can be deduced that the primary component is not an ordinary keyword-mixed sequence; otherwise an analysis of the composite distribution along the lines indicated in footnote 7 of subpar. 36*g* (on p. 74) would have borne fruit.

which should be brought to notice because in some cases the statistical method, involving the study of relatively large distributions, may not be feasible for lack of sufficient text. Yet in these cases there may be sufficient data in the respective alphabets to permit of some assumptions of values of cipher letters, or there may be good grounds for applying the probable-word method. The present paragraph will therefore deal with a method of solving progressive alphabet cipher systems which is based upon the application of the principles of symmetry of position to certain phenomena arising from the mechanics of the progressive alphabet encipherment method itself.

b. Take the two sequences below and encipher the phrase FIRST BATTALION by the progressive alphabet method, sliding the cipher component to the left one interval after each encipherment.

Components

```
Plain:  H Y D R A U L I C B E F G J K M N O P Q S T V W X Z
Cipher: F B P Y R C Q Z I G S E H T D J U M K V A L W N O X
```

Message

```
        1  2  3  4  5  6  7  8  9  10 11 12 13 14
Plain:  F  I  R  S  T  B  A  T  T  A  L  I  O  N
Cipher: E  I  C  N  X  D  S  P  Y  T  U  K  Y  Y
```

c. Certain letters are repeated in both plain text and cipher text. Consider the former. There are two I's, three T's, and two A's. Their encipherments are isolated below, for convenience in study.

```
        F  I  R  S  T  B  A  T  T  A  L  I  O  N
        1  2  3  4  5  6  7  8  9  10 11 12 13 14
Plain:  .  I  .  .  .  .  .  .  .  .  .  I  .  .   (1)
Cipher: .  I  .  .  .  .  .  .  .  .  .  K  .  .   (2)

Plain:  .  .  .  .  T  .  .  T  T  .  .  .  .  .   (3)
Cipher: .  .  .  .  X  .  .  P  Y  .  .  .  .  .   (4)

Plain:  .  .  .  .  .  .  A  .  .  A  .  .  .  .   (5)
Cipher: .  .  .  .  .  .  S  .  .  T  .  .  .  .   (6)
```

The two I's in line (1) are 10 letters apart; reference to the cipher component will show that the interval between the cipher equivalent of the first I_p (which happens to be I_e) and the second I_p (which is K_e) is 10. Consideration of the mechanics of the enciphering system soon shows why this is so: since the cipher component is displaced one step with each encipherment, two identical letters *n* intervals apart in the plain text must yield cipher equivalents which are *n* intervals apart in the cipher component. Examination of the data in lines (3) and (4), (5) and (6) will confirm this finding. Consequently, it would appear that in such a system the successful application of the probable-word method of attack, coupled with symmetry of position, can quickly lead to the reconstruction of the cipher component.

d. Now consider the repeated cipher letters in the example under subpar. *b.*   There happens to be only two cases of repetition, both involving Y's.   Thus:

```
   1   2   3   4   5   6   7   8   9   10  11  12  13  14
   .   .   .   .   .   .   .   .   T   .   .   .   O   N
   .   .   .   .   .   .   .   .   Y   .   .   .   Y   Y
```

Reference to the plain component will show that the plaintext letters represented by the three Y's appear in the order N O . . . T, that is, reversed with respect to their order in the plain text.   But the intervals between these letters are correct.   Again a consideration of the mechanics of the enciphering system shows why this is so: since the cipher component is displaced one step with each encipherment, two identical letters *n* intervals apart in the cipher text must represent plaintext letters which are *n* intervals apart in the plain component.   In the present case the direction in which these letters run in the plain component is opposite to that in which the cipher component is displaced.   That is, if the cipher component is displaced toward the left, the values obtained from a study of repeated plaintext letters give letters which coincide in sequence (interval and direction) with the same letters in the cipher component; the values obtained from a study of repeated ciphertext letters give letters the order of which must be reversed in order to make these letters coincide in sequence (interval and direction) with the same letters in the plain component.   If the cipher component is displaced toward the right, this relationship is merely reversed: the values obtained from a study of the repeated plaintext letters must be reversed in their order when placing them in the cipher component; those yielded by a study of the repeated ciphertext letters are inserted in the plain component in their original order.

e. Of course, if the primary components are identical sequences the data from the two sources referred to in subpars. *c* and *d* need not be kept separate but can be combined and made to yield the primary component very quickly.

f. With the foregoing principles as background, and given the first few groups of an intercepted message, which is assumed to begin with COMMANDING GENERAL FIRST ARMY (probable-word method of attack), the data yielded by this assumed plain text are shown in Fig. 76.

```
I K M K I   L I D O L   W L P N M   V W P X W   D U F F T   F N I I G
X G A M X   C A D U V   A Z V I S   Y N U N L . . .
```

	1	2	3	4	5	6	7	8	9	10	11	12	13	14	15	16	17	18	19	20	21	22	23	24	25	26
Assumed plain text:	C	O	M	M	A	N	D	I	N	G	G	E	N	E	R	A	L	F	I	R	S	T	A	R	M	Y
Cipher:		I	K	M	K	I	L	I	D	O	L	W	L	P	N	M	V	W	P	X	W	D	U	F	F	T	F

```
     A B C D E F G H I J K L M N O P Q R S T U V W X Y Z
 1   . . I . . . . . . . . . . . . . . . . . . . . . . .
 2   . . . . . . . . . . . . . K . . . . . . . . . . . .
 3   . . . . . . . . . . . . M . . . . . . . . . . . . .
 4   . . . . . . . . . . . K . . . . . . . . . . . . . .
 5   I . . . . . . . . . . . . . . . . . . . . . . . . .
 6   . . . . . . . . . . . . . L . . . . . . . . . . . .
 7   . . . I . . . . . . . . . . . . . . . . . . . . . .
 8   . . . . . . . D . . . . . . . . . . . . . . . . . .
 9   . . . . . . . . . . . . . . O . . . . . . . . . . .
10   . . . . . L . . . . . . . . . . . . . . . . . . . .
11   . . . . . W . . . . . . . . . . . . . . . . . . . .
12   . . . . L . . . . . . . . . . . . . . . . . . . . .
13   . . . . . . . . . . . . . P . . . . . . . . . . . .
14   . . . . N . . . . . . . . . . . . . . . . . . . . .
15   . . . . . . . . . . . . . . . . . M . . . . . . . .
16   V . . . . . . . . . . . . . . . . . . . . . . . . .
17   . . . . . . . . . . . W . . . . . . . . . . . . . .
18   . . . . . P . . . . . . . . . . . . . . . . . . . .
19   . . . . . . . X . . . . . . . . . . . . . . . . . .
20   . . . . . . . . . . . . . . . . . W . . . . . . . .
21   . . . . . . . . . . . . . . . . . . R D . . . . . .
22   . . . . . . . . . . . . . . . . . . . U . . . . . .
23   F . . . . . . . . . . . . . . . . . . . . . . . . .
24   . . . . . . . . . . . . . . . . . . F . . . . . . .
25   . . . . . . . . . . T . . . . . . . . . . . . . . .
26   . . . . . . . . . . . . . . . . . . . . . . . F . .
```

FIGURE 76

Analysis of the data afforded by Fig. 76, in conjunction with the principles of direct symmetry (latent in the *columns* of the figure above), yields the following partial components:

	1	2	3	4	5	6	7	8	9	10	11	12	13	14	15	16	17	18	19	20	21	22	23	24	25	26
Plain:	A	.	L	I	C	.	E	F	G	.	.	M	N	O	.	.	S	.	.	.	.	.	.	Y	D	R
Cipher: {	.	.	M	K	V	.	L	W	N	O	.	F	.	P	.	.	.	.	.	I	.	.	.	T	.
{	D	.	.	.	.	.	.	.	.	.	.	X													

Setting the two partial components into juxtaposition so that $C_p = I_c$ (first encipherment) the 8th value, $I_p = D_c$, gives the position of D in the cipher component and permits the addition of X to it, these being two letters, which until now could not be placed into position in the cipher component. With these two partial sequences it becomes possible now to decipher many other

172

letters in the message, gaps being filled in from the context. For example, the first few letters after ARMY decipher as follows:

```
        1  2  3  4  5  6  7  8  9  10 11 12
Cipher: N  I  I  G  X  G  A  M  X  C  A  D
Plain:  .  I  L  .  .  .  .  E  O  .  .  R
```

The word after ARMY is probably WILL. This leads to the insertion of the letter W in the plain component and G in the cipher component. In a short time both components can be completely established.

g. In passing, it may be well to note that in the illustrative message in subpar. 69*h* the very frequent occurrence of tripled letters (MMM, WWW, FFF, etc.) indicates the presence of a frequently used short word, a frequently used ending, or the like, the letters of which are sequent in the plain component. An astute cryptanalyst who has noted the frequency of occurrence of such triplets could assume the value THE for them, go through the entire text replacing all triplets by THE, and then, by applying the principles of symmetry of position, build up the plain component in a short time. With that much as a start, solution of the entire message would be considerably simplified.

71. Solution by means of isomorphs.—*a.* One of the most powerful attacks in cryptanalytics involves the exploitation of isomorphs, i.e., ciphertext sequences which exhibit an idiomorphism identical with that of another ciphertext sequence; this method finds applicability in many varieties of manual cipher systems, and it also takes on a very important aspect in the solution of many machine cipher systems. In progressive alphabet ciphers, the presence of isomorphs, if they are of fair length and proper composition, might enable the cryptanalyst to derive the complete primary cipher component directly and thus reach a quick and easy solution of a problem; in any case, isomorphs will enable the partial reconstruction of the cipher component, facilitating further analysis and solution.

b. Isomorphic sequences in the cipher text of progressive alphabet systems may be brought about by identical plaintext beginnings [4] of a pair of messages, by identical endings,[5] by a stagger situation, or by a latent repetition occurring within a message or between a pair of messages. Isomorphism may be discovered by examining all pronounced idiomorphic patterns in the cipher text and comparing patterns so disclosed for exact correspondences of repeated letters, i.e., isomorphs. For instance, the two isomorphic ciphertext sequences below may be isolated by searching for all the AA patterns [6] in the cipher texts under examination, and inspecting the

```
(1)  ... C V C N A U H Y H H I T N L C ...
(2)  ... E X E P L I D R D D B W P C E ...
```

letters which precede and follow these AA patterns for further evidences of apparent isomorphism. Obviously, not all sequences surrounding AA patterns will be *causal* isomorphs; this is especially true in the case of short isomorphic sequences, just as short repetitions in cipher text may occur by chance and not be due to causal factors. But if an isomorph can be extended sufficiently (i.e., if further isomorphic patterns about the basic AA patterns are noticed), then the isomorphs

---

[4] These beginnings need not necessarily be stereotyped beginnings. The composition of the plain text is unimportant; the only requisite factor is that the beginnings consist of identical plain text.

[5] This situation is, of course, often brought about by identical signatures at the ends of messages.

[6] In searching for isomorphs, it might be also necessary to examine all A–A patterns, and then A––A patterns, if the AA patterns do not bear fruit.

may be considered valid, and the delineation of the isomorphs to the left and right, insofar as discernible, may be established.[7]

   c. As an example of a solution by means of isomorphs, let us consider the following beginnings of three messages:

Message "A"

```
V N N P H   S M X W I   P U C W R   S T G U C   R M L J J   T U Q R E
H S F V O   J R R T D...
```

Message "B"

```
R W W Z I   Y V U A K   Z G M A E   Y D Q G M   E V J S S   D G W G Z
S T T D B   G T O C N...
```

Message "C"

```
U Z Z Y B   R X I L N   Y K O L G   R A T K O   H Z B T A   G F P M F
B R A X C   V Y E E P...
```

It is noted that Messages "A" and "B" are isomorphic from their beginnings to their 27th letters, and that Message "C" is isomorphic with the other two from its beginning to the 20th letter.[8] The isomorphic portions are now superimposed, as is shown in the diagram below:

```
"A":  VNNPHSMXWIPUCWRSTGUCRMLJJTU
"B":  RWWZIYVUAKZGMAEYDQGMEVJSSDG
"C":  UZZYBRXILNYKOLGRATKO
```

Chains from the foregoing diagram are derived, as follows:

"A"–"B"	"A"–"C"	"B"–"C"
CMVRE	VUK	WZYRUIB
NWA	MXINZ	VX
PZ	PY	DAL
HIK	SRGTA	EGKN
LJSY	WL	MO
XUGQ	CO	QT
TD		

---

[7] The following method facilitating the finding of isomorphs is useful both in analytical machine processing and in manual techniques.   Each ciphertext letter is compared with the 5 or 6 letters or so following, and if there is a reoccurrence of that letter within that span, a numerical indication is placed under the reoccurrence of the letter equal to the interval of the monographic repetition.   For example, in the first cipher sequence given in the text above, the notation would be as follows:

```
... C V C N A U H Y H H I T N L C ...
    2       2 1
```

When all of the cipher text is marked in such a manner, the numerical patterns can be quickly scanned for pattern repetitions; in this case, the identical pattern would be noted at the ciphertext sequence EXEPLIDRDD, and upon
```
                                              2   21
```
further examination it would be observed that the isomorphism could extend for five more letters.

[8] The isomorphism manifested actually begins with the second letters of the messages; it cannot be proved at this point that it includes the first letters, but the absence of contradictory evidence in isomorphs of this length, plus the fact that the isomorphs are at the beginning of the messages, makes this a safe assumption.

Using the principles of indirect symmetry, we recover an equivalent primary cipher component as follows: CMVREOXUGQHIKTDBNWAFPZLJSY. Decimation of this sequence at an interval of —11 brings out the original keyword-mixed sequence, based on HYDRAULIC.

d. With the cipher component now at hand, the text of any one of the messages may now be reduced to monoalphabetic terms, *if we can assume the correct motion of the cipher component;*[9] in other words, a *known motion* makes conversion to monoalphabetic terms possible. Taking the fragment of Message "A" as an example, and assuming that the cipher component is slid to the *right* after each encipherment, we have the following conversion (in terms of an arbitrary A–Z sequence for the plain component) and its accompanying uniliteral frequency distribution:

```
 C: V N N P H S M X W I P U C W R S T G U C R M L J J T
"P": W R S V E Z V F F Q C Q U K R J L D X B X K C K L U

 C: U Q R E H S F V O J R R T D . . .
"P": F U F N E Z R D Z W N O H P
```

                                                                    I.C.=0.90

A B C D E F G H I J K L M N O P Q R S T U V W X Y Z

This is certainly not satisfactory. Assuming that the cipher component is slid to the *left*, we have the following:

```
 C: V N N P H S M X W I P U C W R S T G U C R M L J J T
"P": W P O P W P J R P Y I U W K P F F V N P J U K Q P W

 C: U Q R E H S F V O J R R T D . . .
"P": F S B H W P F P J E T S J P
```

                                                                    I.C.=2.33

A B C D E F G H I J K L M N O P Q R S T U V W X Y Z

Obviously this is the correct case. After solution of the monoalphabet, which is facilitated in this case by the idiomorphic patterns now revealed, it is found that the recovered plain component is the same as the cipher component, except that it runs in the reverse direction.

e. It should be clear why isologous sequences in progressive alphabet systems, unlike isologous sequences in other types of periodic ciphers, produce isomorphs which may be chained without regard to the particular alphabets involved, and also why the conversion process is not affected by the identity of the particular alphabets. In the usual type of repeating-key cipher, the selection of the alphabets used is determined by a key word which is used for this purpose; the letters of the key bear no constant displacement-relationship to each other. However, in the case of a progressive alphabet cipher the successive elements of the key, 26 in number, are a *constant* interval apart from each other as measured on the cipher component; this accounts for the fact that, if one encipherment of a plaintext passage produces an idiomorphic ciphertext sequence, the remaining 25 other possible encipherments will also produce idiomorphic cipher texts which will all be isomorphic to one another.

f. It is important to note that if the cipher component of a progressive alphabet system is recovered from isomorphs, it will probably be an *equivalent primary component* rather than

---

[9] This very important consideration forms the basis of solution of cryptograms produced by many types of cipher devices and cipher machines.

the *original* primary component. If the component recovered is a *decimation* of the original component, the conversion of the cipher text into monoalphabetic terms will be successful only when the cipher component is slid at a constant interval of N places in the appropriate direction, where N is the decimation interval of the original primary component.

72. Solution by superimposition.—*a.* The discussion in this chapter thus far has, except for special solutions, been limited to cases wherein there is available a long message in a progressive alphabet system. Suppose that in the traffic there are no long messages, what then? If a number of short messages are available, then there should be a way to superimpose the messages properly, that is, put them in depth, even if no two messages begin with the same initial key letter, i.e., start at the same point in the key sequence.

b. There are three principal means for superimposing messages in progressive alphabet systems.[10] These are: (1) superimposition by means of known indicators;[11] (2) superimposition by polygraphic ciphertext repetitions; and (3) superimposition by a comparison of columnar frequency distributions. The first of these methods is rather obvious: it goes without saying that if the enemy were still using a compromised or recovered indicator system, then of course all messages could be put in depth without any analysis whatsoever. The second method, that of superimposition by repetition, is also quite obvious: since long repetitions (i.e., long for a given sample size) have a high probability of being causal, then the alignment of messages to make the polygraphic repetitions fall into identical columns of the width of the period will result in the correct superimposition of the messages. The third method, that of comparison of the columnar frequency distributions, will be discussed in detail below.

c. Let us consider a long message in a progressive alphabet cipher, such as that given in subpar. 69*i*, and let us also consider its columnar frequency distributions given in Fig. 75. If we had at hand another long message, which however began at a point in the keying sequence 5 places to the right of the first message, it is clear that col. 1 of the second message would not resemble col. 1 of the first message. Nevertheless, col. 1 of the second message would bear a close resemblance to col. 6 of the first, and col. 2 of the second message would be very similar to col. 7 of the first, and so on. If our two messages had about 40 tallies per distribution (as in the example), there would be little trouble in finding the correct matching of the columns, since this could be done easily by eye. If however we had at hand a pair of *short* messages (say between 100 and 200 letters each), then mere ocular inspection would be of no avail, and recourse must be had to statistical methods to find the proper superimposition.

d. Let us assume that we have for study a set of short messages intercepted on a particular day on a naval circuit known to be passing traffic in progressive alphabet systems. It is further known that the primary components are changed daily; therefore the traffic of one day is expected to be homogeneous with respect to the primary components involved. Two of the longest messages are given below, of lengths 190 and 170 letters, respectively:

Message "A"

```
HFDCS  WTQOO  YCPXF  NWLGP  ULRIU  RHFDQ  HCXPS  SNIPG  NXUVL  CUDAV
WAYNK  ZHKXS  BIPDM  BNKKI  FBLWT  RDAAH  YQSSJ  VSODY  EFFBI  UGXLB
IAYRH  RNMHM  VSUAS  CMFKM  LAFBL  OICZK  KEZVH  JSAGT  ZNEBX  VERGF
ZIAUJ  ZSJFT  WSOQF  GQOKZ  WBREC  EIYCD  VUYXD  MKZKT
```

[10] These means to be described are also applicable for the superimposition of messages in other types of repeating-key systems.

[11] Indicators play an important role in cryptography. An indicator is a symbol (consisting of a letter, a group of letters, a figure, or a group of figures) which indicates the specific key used under the general cryptosystem, or it may indicate which one of a number of general systems has been used, or it may indicate both.

```
KVCRV   FUBOX   SYFGV   ZWTQO   OEAQP   ZKBJW   ZPLEN   WDKJW   WNHLT   PEOYD
PLGRC   UAYVR   RSLAH   OPWYL   WWTRS   QIFFA   DBQSA   IURYA   DZEZS   BXXAE
OPNFF   UKIEL   IVSUA   YGEDI   HSVMP   SQMLI   GEGID   BZEMA   YPNZR   CZTGG
NDAKP   NMKGB   SBLPH   AYAHX
```

e. Since the period of the messages is 26, the messages are written out on this width. What we will now do is align the messages in flush depth and perform a χ test of the corresponding columns, arriving at a value of χ (or a ξ I.C.) for that particular alignment.[12] After this test is completed, we will slide Message "B" over one position with respect to Message "A", and perform the test again; and so on for the 26 possible alignments. In order to facilitate the comparison of the texts, we will write out Message "B" in doubled length, as is shown in Fig. 77 below (for the first comparison); the χ_o values are derived for each column and are indicated under the respective columns.

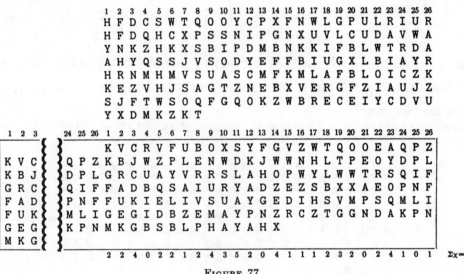

FIGURE 77

f. In the foregoing comparison, we note that the sum of the observed values of χ for all the columns is 51. We will now compute the expected values of χ_m and χ_r with which to compare the χ_o. Since in Fig. 77 we have 8 columns of 8 x 7 letters, 6 columns of 7 x 7 letters, and 12 columns of 7 x 6 letters, the total number of comparisons is $8(8\cdot7)+6(7\cdot7)+12(7\cdot6)=1246$. Thus $\chi_m=.0667(1246)=83.11$, and $\chi_r=\dfrac{1246}{26}=47.92$. The ξ I.C.$=\dfrac{51}{47.92}=1.06$, so instead of arching his eyebrows the cryptanalyst will merely shrug his shoulders and go on to the next test.

g. For the second test, we will move Message "B" one column to the right so that the first letter of Message "B" is under the second letter of Message "A", as shown below, and the χ values are determined as before.

---

[12] This procedure is somewhat akin to that demonstrated in subpar. 18*e*, in connection with the use of the ϕ test to determine the number of alphabets of a relatively short cryptogram of a lengthy period. See also footnote 13 on p. 31.

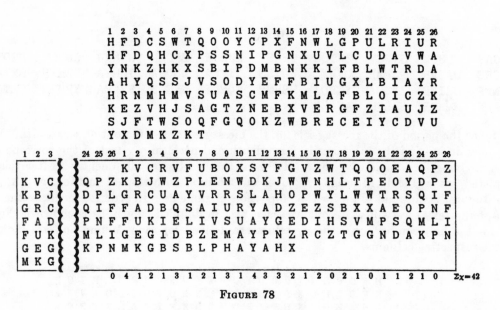

FIGURE 78

For this case, the number of comparisons is $7(8\cdot7)+1(8\cdot6)+7(7\cdot7)+11(7\cdot6)=1245$, thus $\chi_m=$ $.0667(1245)=83.04$, and $\chi_r=\dfrac{1245}{26}=47.88$. Since $\chi_o=42$, the ξ I.C. in this case is $\dfrac{42}{47.88}=0.88$, which means another shrug.

h. Subsequent tests still give ξ I.C.'s in the close vicinity of 1.00, until the 15th test is made, as follows:

FIGURE 79

At this alignment, the number of comparisons is $2(8 \cdot 7)+6(8 \cdot 6)+12(7 \cdot 7)+6(7 \cdot 6)=1240$, thus $\chi_m=.0667(1240)=82.71$, and $\chi_r=\dfrac{1240}{26}=47.69$. The observed χ is 100, so the ξ I.C. here is $\dfrac{100}{47.69}=2.10$, which should gladden the heart of the cryptanalyst. This is it.

i. Just when the cryptanalyst is about to relax and enjoy life, being on the verge of cryptanalytic fructification, he observes with consternation that, at the very next alignment of the messages, a pentagraphic repetition would come in phase, a repetition which somehow he had previously overlooked: at the 16th test, the pentagraph WTQOO would be lined up between the two messages.[13] So with a dejected feeling he superimposes the messages anew, notes that $\chi_m=.0667(1241)=82.77$, $\chi_r=\dfrac{1241}{26}=47.73$, and $\chi_o=65$. This makes the ξ I.C.$=\dfrac{65}{47.73}=1.36$, which in turn makes the cryptanalyst quite unhappy.

j. Grasping at straws, the cryptanalyst tries to save the situation with the ϕ test.[14] For the 15th superimposition, he obtains the following:

$$\phi_o=352$$

$$\phi_r=\frac{2(15 \cdot 14)+18(14 \cdot 13)+6(13 \cdot 12)}{26}=\frac{4632}{26}=178$$

$$\phi_p=.0667(4632)=309$$

$$\delta \text{ I.C.}=\frac{352}{178}=1.98$$

Fine. Now for the 16th superimposition:

$$\phi_o=298$$

$$\phi_r=\frac{3(15 \cdot 14)+16(14 \cdot 13)+7(13 \cdot 12)}{26}=\frac{4634}{26}=178$$

$$\phi_p=.0667(4634)=309$$

$$\delta \text{ I.C.}=\frac{298}{178}=1.67$$

This situation, instead of arching the eyebrows, shrugging the shoulders, or gladdening the heart, now gives a sinking feeling in the pit of the stomach.

k. Impaled on the horns of a dilemma,[15] the cryptanalyst is forced to try both hypotheses; at least there are only *two*—it could have been worse. The 15th superimposition is actually the correct alignment of the messages, so if he trusts the high ξ I.C., the cryptanalyst will be right the first time. The author hastens to assure the reader that, in spite of dark suspicions to the contrary, the accidental pentagraphic repetition was *not* manipulated or forced, but really *did*

---

[13] The mathematical expectation of this phenomenon is calculated as follows: Message "A" is 190 letters long, and thus contains 186 pentagraphs; Message "B", of 170 letters, contains 166 pentagraphs. The number of pentagraphic comparisons is therefore 186x166, or 30,876. Since there are 26^5 different pentagraphs, the probability of a pentagraphic coincidence between these two messages is $\dfrac{30,876}{26^5}$ or .0026; in other words, less than 3 chances in 1,000.

[14] The procedure here is that demonstrated in subpar. 18*e*.

[15] Of, however, a small order of magnitude.

happen accidentally.   What this experience teaches us is that the ξ I.C. is more to be trusted than the δ I.C. in matching distributions,[16] and that, evidently, in samples of this size the probability of a very high ξ I.C. being reached in an *incorrect* case is less than the probability of an accidental pentagraphic repetition.   In passing, it might be well to keep in mind the following excerpt from Kullback: [17]

"It is not very often that statistical analysis alone will enable the cryptanalyst to arrive at the solution of a cryptogram. *Statistical analysis will, however, enable the cryptanalyst to evaluate the desirability of pursuing certain procedures and will indicate the most likely order in which to try various possible steps in solution.*"

While we're at it, it might not hurt to keep in mind also the following quotation from an unidentified author:

"There are three kinds of lies: lies, damned lies, and statistics."

l. It was stated in subpar. *d* that the two messages under discussion were from a set of short messages; the foregoing procedures would be continued, adding more messages to the already established depth, until a sufficient number of messages were put in depth to permit of solution by means of the χ test as treated in par. 69.   These first two messages might by themselves probably be unsolvable; for the student who is interested in solving them, it will be added that the signature TOMLINSON is present in Message "B".

73. Additional remarks.—*a.* As has already been indicated in subpar. 67*a*, the number of different alphabets in progressive alphabet systems is not necessarily confined to 26.   It is possible to have N=25, 27, 30, 32, 36, . . . 100; obviously, where N is greater than 26, the cipher characters cannot be restricted merely to the 26 letters of the alphabet, but must either include additional symbols, or else the cipher text must be represented by digit groups such as dinomes. If a Baudot system incorporated a progressive alphabet principle, then of course the components would involve the 32 characters of the Baudot alphabet.

b. The principles elucidated in this chapter may, of course, also be applied to cases of progressive alphabet systems in which the progression is by regular intervals greater than 1, and, with necessary modifications, to cases in which the progression is not regular but follows a specific pattern, such as the successive displacements 1–2–3–4–5, 1–2–3–4–5, . . . , or 2–5–1–3–1–4–2–3, 2–5–1–3–1–4–2–3, and so on.[18]   The latter types of progression are encountered in certain mechanical cipher devices, the study of which will be reserved for the next text.

---

[16] In *Statistical Methods in Cryptanalysis*, par. 22, Kullback demonstrates the fact that the χ test is preferable to the ϕ test insofar as matching distributions is concerned.   He also shows (p. 49) that if two monoalphabetic distributions have been merged, the expected value of ϕ is given by the formula $\phi=.0667(N-1)-.0564N_1N_2$, where $N=N_1+N_2$.   If the two distributions *are of equal size* (i.e., if $N_1=N_2$), the expected ξ I.C. of two merged nonrelated monoalphabetic distributions will usually be in the vicinity of $\frac{1.73-1.00}{2}=1.37$.   Thus, when Message "A" and Message "B" are incorrectly superimposed in flush depth as in subpar. *e*, the average ξ I.C. of the merged distributions is found to be 1.42, which is just about what is expected.

[17] *Ibid.*, p. 1.

[18] Cases may be encountered in which the selection of alphabets is controlled by a 26-element key comprised by a keyword-mixed sequence as a mnemonic device.

CHAPTER X

REPEATING-KEY SYSTEMS WITH UNRELATED ALPHABETS

74. General remarks.—*a.* In the first nine chapters of this text we have treated only those periodic polyalphabetic systems which involve a relationship among the secondary alphabets. This relationship is brought about by the Vigenère properties of the basic cipher square, or the identical properties possessed by the interaction of sliding primary components. In the case of Porta systems, Vigenère-type properties also exist, but in a modified form. Since the Vigenère square incorporates cyclic permutations of a basic cipher component, the symmetry among the secondary alphabets when related to the original primary plain component is visible or direct; if some other component is considered as the plain component, the relationships among the secondary alphabets will be latent or indirect.

b. If instead of a cipher square of interrelated alphabets there was used a matrix of N different *unrelated* alphabets, of course no symmetry of any kind would be manifested. Therefore the initial solution of a cryptogram in such a system would progress along the usual lines of first principles (i.e., factoring, assumptions of letters based on frequencies or vowel-consonant analysis, attack by the probable-word method, etc.) until the entire cryptogram is solved by the progressive synthesis of the plaintext message. The powerful tool of the reconstruction of the secondary alphabets by principles of direct or indirect symmetry is here inapplicable; therefore the plain text must be coaxed out the hard way in its entirety, and any unrecovered values must remain unrecovered until further traffic establishes these latter values.

c. If the N cipher alphabets of a system involving unrelated alphabets are systematically mixed sequences (e.g., if these sequences are keyword-mixed sequences or transposition-mixed sequences based on different key words), then a partial recovery of the secondary alphabets might reveal what the situation is, and thus make possible the reconstruction of the complete secondary alphabets. If, however, the cipher alphabets are composed of random-mixed sequences, no complete reconstruction would be possible until enough cipher text has been accumulated to permit establishing all the values in all the alphabets.

d. Once the N basic sequences of a cryptosystem with unrelated alphabets are reconstructed, the solution of subsequent messages using the same sequences is a simple matter, even if the sequences are used in a different order, as will presently be demonstrated.

75. Solution of a typical system involving unrelated alphabets.—*a.* The cryptography of a typical cryptosystem involving unrelated alphabets is quite simple. There are available N different alphabets, which may be used in one of the following ways: (1) all of the alphabets are used in the same sequence, starting at the same point in the sequence; (2) all the alphabets are used in the same sequence, but with different starting points; (3) all the alphabets are used, but in a different order, or (4) only a selection of a certain number of alphabets is made, the number and order of which are determined or controlled by a specific key. In Fig. 80, below, we have a total of 25 different cipher sequences [1] of 26 letters each in the form of 26-letter strips; these strips fit horizontally into a frame with space for up to 25 strips, and at the top of the frame there is affixed a normal sequence in which the plaintext letters are to be found.

Plain text

	A B C D E F G H I J K L M N O P Q R S T U V W X Y Z
1	T Q K Z O L R X S P W N A B C E I G D J F V U Y M H
2	S B A C D E H F I J K T L M O U V Y G Z N P Q X R W
3	Y Q R T V W L A D K O M J U B G E P H S C Z I N X F
4	Z S A E D C B I F G J H L K M R U O Q V P T N W Y X
5	S L W E M Z V X G A F N Q U K D O P I T J B R H C Y
6	G P O C I X L U R N D Y Z H W B J S Q F K V M E T A
7	W A H X J E Z B N I K P V R O G S Y D U L C F M Q T
8	G T D X A I H P J O B W K C V F Z L Q E R Y N S U M
9	A J D S K Q O I V T Z E F H G Y U N L P M B X W C R
10	J G H O N M T P R Q S V Z U X Y W I C A K E L B D F
11	V Q P N O H U W D I Z Y C G K R F B E J A L T M S X
12	E W O A M N F L H Q G C U J T B Y P Z K X I S R D V
13	D H B M K G X U Z T S W Q Y V O R P F E A N C J I L
14	D W P K J V I U Q H Z C T X B L E G N Y R S M F A O
15	S G U E N T C X O W F Q D R L J Z M A P B V H I Y K
16	X C S H D E O K F P Y A Q J N U B T G I M W Z R V L
17	N V A R M Y O F T H E U S Z J X D P C W G Q I B K L
18	O Z P L G V J R K Y T F U I W X H A S D M C N E Q B
19	T O J Y L F X N G W H V C M I R B S E K U P D Z Q A
20	Z X Q L Y I O V B P E S N H J W M D G F C K A U T R
21	E Y B F S J M U D Q C L Z W T I P A V N K H R G O X
22	X P U C O T Y A W V S F D L I E B H K N R J Q Z G M
23	E V D T U F O Y H M L S I Q N J C P G B Z A X K W R
24	M V K B Q W U G L O S T E C H N Z F R I D A Y J P X
25	W J L V G R C Q M P S O E X T K I A Z D N B U H Y F

Strip nos.

FIGURE 80

If it were standard practice to select a certain fixed number of strips for the cipher components, these cipher strips would be placed into the device in a predetermined order under the plaintext strip and the process of encryption and decryption would proceed as in any repeating-key cipher using a matrix.[2]

[1] The sequences used in this illustration are actually the sequences used in the obsolete U.S. Army Cipher Device, Type M-94. See in this connection subpar. 6c of Appendix 6, "Cryptographic Supplement."

[2] If 10 different sequences were used for the cipher components, then the number of different permutations of 25 things taken 10 at a time is given by the formula $P_{10}^{25} = \dfrac{25!}{(25-10)!} = \dfrac{25!}{15!} = 11,861,676,288,000$, or, expressed in standard form, approximately 1.19×10^{13}. If only 5 different sequences were used for the cipher components, the number of different permutations is 6.38×10^6; if 15 sequences were used, the number would be 4.27×10^{18}; if 20 were used, the number is 1.29×10^{23}; and if all 25 sequences were used, the number of permutations is 25! or 1.55×10^{25}. However, the fearless cryptanalyst goes ahead and solves his problem anyway, in spite of the fearful magnitude of these awe-inspiring numbers.

b. In Fig. 81 there is illustrated the inverse matrix derived from the previous figure, showing the plaintext equivalents for the 26 cipher letters.

Cipher text

```
     A B C D E F G H I J K L M N O P Q R S T U V W X Y Z
 1   M N O S P U R Z Q T C F Y L E J B G I A W V K H X D
 2   C B D E F H S G I J K M N U O V W Y A L P Q Z X R T
 3   H O U I Q Z P S W M J G L X K R B C T D N E F Y A V
 4   C G F E D I J L H K N M O W R U S P B V Q T X Z Y A
 5   J V Y P D K I X S U O B E L Q R M W A T N G C H Z F
 6   Z P D K X T A N E Q U G W J C B S I R Y H V O F L M
 7   B H V S F W P C J E K U X I O L Y N Q Z T M A D R G
 8   E K N C T P A G F I M R Z W J H S U X B Y O L D V Q
 9   A V Y C L M O N H B E S U R G T F Z D J Q I X W P K
10   T X S Y V Z B C R A U W F E D H J I K G N L Q O P M
11   U R M I S Q N F J T O V X D E C B P Y W G A H Z L K
12   D P L Y A G K I V N T H E F C R J X W O M Z B U Q S
13   U C W A T S F B Y X E Z D V P R M Q K J H O L G N I
14   Y O L A Q X R J G E D P W S Z C I U V M H F B N T K
15   S U G M D K B W X P Z O R E I T L N A F C V J H Y Q
16   L Q B E F I S D T N H Z U O G J M X C R P Y V A K W
17   C X S Q K H U J W O Y Z E A G R V D M I L B T P F N
18   R Z V T X L E Q N G I D U W A C Y H S K M F O P J B
19   Z Q M W S F I K O C T E N H B V Y P R A U L J G D X
20   W I U R K T S N F O V D Q M G J C Z L Y X H P B E A
21   R C K I A D X V P F U L G T Y Q J W E O H S N Z B M
22   H Q D M P L Y R O V S N Z T E B W U K F C J I A G X
23   V T Q C A F S I M P X K J O G R N Z L D E B Y W H U
24   V D N U M R H O T X C I A P J Y E S K L G B F Z W Q
25   R V G T M Z E X Q B P C I U L J H F K O W D A N Y S
```

Strip nos.

FIGURE 81

From the two foregoing matrices, there may be derived diagrams of limitations of the basic matrix. In Fig. 82*a* we have a diagram of the *impossible* ciphertext equivalents of plaintext letters, and in Fig. 82*b* we have a diagram of the impossible plaintext equivalents of ciphertext letters. These two diagrams will be very useful in the analysis of cryptograms enciphered by means of these alphabets, once the basic sequences have been recovered from previous analysis or by compromise.

Plain

```
            A B C D E F G H I J K L M N O P Q R S T U V W X Y Z
            ─────────────────────────────────────────────────
            B D C D B A A C A B A B B A A A A C B C E D B A B C
Impossible  C E E G C B D D C C I D G D D C G E J G H F E C E D
 ciphers    F F F I E D E E E D M G H E E H K J M H I G G D F E
            H I G J F K G H P E N I M F F M L K O L O M J L H G
            I K I P H O K J U F P J O N P P N Q P M Q O K O J I
            K M M Q P P N M X L Q K P O Q Q Q R T O S R O P L J
            L N N U R S P O Y R R R R P R S T U U Q T U P Q N N
            P R T W T U Q S   S U X W S S T X V W R V X V T Z P
            Q U V   W   S T   U V Z X T U V   W X X W   W V     Q
            R   X X   W Z   X X   Y V Y Z   X Y   Y           S
            U   Y Z     Z           Z     Z   Z               U
                Z                                             Z
```

FIGURE 82a

Cipher

```
            A B C D E F G H I J K L M N O P Q R S T U V W X Y Z
            ─────────────────────────────────────────────────
            F A A B B A C A A D A A B B F A A A F C A C D C C C
Impossible  G E C D C B D E B H B J C C H D D B G E B K E E I E
  plains    I F E F E C G H C L F Q H G M E G E H H D N G I M H
            K J H G G E L M D R G T K K N F K J J N F P M J O J
            N L I H H J M P K S L X M N S G O K N P I R R K S L
            O M J J I N Q T L W Q Y P Q T I P L O Q J U S L U O
            P S P L J O T U U Y R   S Y U K Q M P S K W U M   P
            Q W R N N V V Y Z Z W   T Z V M R O U U O X W Q   R
            X Y T O O Y W           V   W N T R Z X R         Y
                X V R   Z           X   O U T       S       S Z
                Z X U               P   X V         V       T
                  Z W               S   Z           Z       V
                    Y               W
                    Z               X
                                    Z
```

FIGURE 82b

c. If strip No. 1 were used in a periodic polyalphabetic cryptogram involving n of the N available sequences, the distribution of the theoretical expectations of the ciphertext frequencies of the No. 1 strip of Fig. 81 would look something like this:

```
    ≡ ≡   ≡           ≡       ≡ ≡
  _ ≡ ≡ ≡ ≡ ≡ _ ≡   ≡ ≡ ≡ _ ≡ ≡ ≡ _ _ ≡ ≡ ≡ ≡ _ ≡   ≡   ≡
  A B C D E F G H I J K L M N O P Q R S T U V W X Y Z
```

Thus, once a periodic cipher in this system is reduced to the proper number of alph ͏ ͏
clear that if strip No. 1 were involved in any of the alphabets of the cryptogram, this facᴛ cͻ ᴌ
be recognized by the goodness of fit of one of the distributions with the distribution of the theoretical ciphertext frequencies for strip No. 1.   In this fashion, the entire array of the seᴄquences

of Fig. 81 could be represented by the theoretical ciphertext frequencies, as shown in Fig. 83, below (where the sum of the frequencies in each row totals to 100):

Theoretical ciphertext frequencies

Strip nos.	A	B	C	D	E	F	G	H	I	J	K	L	M	N	O	P	Q	R	S	T	U	V	W	X	Y	Z
1	2	8	8	6	3	3	8	0	0	9	3	3	2	4	13	0	1	2	7	7	2	2	0	3	0	4
2	3	1	4	13	3	3	6	2	7	0	0	2	8	3	8	2	2	2	7	4	3	0	0	0	8	9
3	3	8	3	7	0	0	3	6	2	2	0	2	4	0	0	8	1	3	9	4	8	13	3	2	7	2
4	3	2	3	13	4	7	0	4	3	0	8	2	8	2	8	3	6	3	1	2	0	9	0	0	2	7
5	0	2	2	3	4	0	7	0	6	3	8	1	13	4	0	8	2	2	7	9	8	2	3	3	0	3
6	0	3	4	0	0	9	7	8	13	0	3	2	2	0	3	1	6	7	8	2	3	2	8	3	4	2
7	1	3	2	6	3	2	3	3	0	13	0	3	0	7	8	4	2	8	0	0	9	2	7	4	8	2
8	13	0	8	3	9	3	7	2	3	7	2	8	0	2	0	3	6	3	0	1	2	8	4	4	2	0
9	7	2	2	3	4	2	8	8	3	1	13	6	3	8	2	9	3	0	4	0	0	7	0	2	3	0
10	9	0	6	2	2	0	1	3	8	7	3	2	3	13	4	3	0	7	0	2	8	4	0	8	3	2
11	3	8	2	7	6	0	8	3	0	9	8	2	0	4	13	3	1	3	2	2	2	7	3	0	4	0
12	4	3	4	2	7	2	0	7	2	8	9	3	13	3	3	8	0	0	2	8	2	0	1	3	0	6
13	3	3	2	7	9	6	3	1	2	0	13	0	4	2	3	8	2	0	0	0	3	8	4	2	8	7
14	2	8	4	7	0	0	8	0	2	13	4	3	2	6	0	3	7	3	2	2	3	1	8	9	0	
15	6	3	2	2	4	0	1	2	0	3	0	8	8	13	7	9	4	8	7	3	3	2	0	3	2	0
16	4	0	1	13	3	7	6	4	9	8	3	0	3	8	2	0	2	0	3	8	3	2	2	7	0	2
17	3	0	6	0	0	3	3	0	2	8	2	0	13	7	2	8	2	4	2	7	4	1	9	3	3	8
18	8	0	2	9	0	4	13	0	8	2	7	4	3	2	7	3	2	3	6	0	2	3	8	3	0	1
19	0	0	2	2	6	3	7	0	8	3	9	13	8	3	1	2	2	3	8	7	3	4	0	2	4	0
20	2	7	3	8	0	9	6	8	3	8	2	4	0	2	2	0	3	0	4	2	0	3	3	1	13	7
21	8	3	0	7	7	4	0	2	3	3	3	4	2	9	2	0	0	2	13	8	3	6	8	0	1	2
22	3	0	4	2	3	4	2	8	8	2	6	8	0	9	13	1	2	3	0	3	3	0	7	7	2	0
23	2	9	0	3	7	3	6	7	2	3	0	0	0	8	2	8	8	0	4	4	13	1	2	2	3	3
24	2	4	8	3	2	8	3	8	9	0	3	7	7	3	0	2	13	6	0	4	2	1	3	0	2	0
25	8	2	2	9	2	0	13	0	0	1	3	3	7	3	4	0	3	3	0	8	2	4	7	8	2	6

FIGURE 83

d. Let us use as an example the following message intercepted on an air force link:

```
G S G P O    Q M H L M    R D N N K    Q D N O N    W G Y C B    Y T K X T
I B J S S    B K Q X C    F G A N K    L Z N D H    S O K G K    B V L U H
H K J Z J    D Z P W C    L S X N E    G D F P T    T T G M V    H M N N G
I T N W G    I B N O Q    H V Q U Y    Y Q P I N    I B J S S    I F O A I
I G N A G    H V V L D    I S X W O    D E V U I    R C X J H    Z O K X H
V O G O B    Y D H H L    V O G C J    J R Q R T    Y G J X G    D V J O L
H R V J B    A Z N C Q    C Q A A G    C O V O F
```

185

Since the cryptogram factors to 10 alphabets, distributions are made accordingly:

I:

II:

A B C D E F G H I J K L M N O P Q R S T U V W X Y Z

III:

IV:

A B C D E F G H I J K L M N O P Q R S T U V W X Y Z

V:

VI:

A B C D E F G H I J K L M N O P Q R S T U V W X Y Z

VII:

VIII:

A B C D E F G H I J K L M N O P Q R S T U V W X Y Z

IX:

X:

A B C D E F G H I J K L M N O P Q R S T U V W X Y Z

e. Matching the distribution for the 1st alphabet against the successive rows of Fig. 83, we obtain the following:

	A	B	C	D	E	F	G	H	I	J	K	L	M	N	O	P	Q	R	S	T	U	V	W	X	Y	Z		
I :			1			1	1	3	5			1						2	1	1		2	1		1			
$\chi(I,1)$:	8			3		8			3									4	7	7		4					=	44
$\chi(I,2)$:	4			3		6	6	35	2									4	7	4					8		=	79
$\chi(I,3)$:	3					3	18	10	2									6	9	4		26	3		7		=	91
$\chi(I,4)$:	3			7			12	15	2									6	1	2		18			2		=	68
$\chi(I,5)$:	2					7		30	1									4	7	9		4	3				=	67
$\chi(I,6)$:	4			9		7	24	65	2									14	8	2		4	8		4		=	151

* * * * *

On the 6th trial, the χ value of 151 is excellent when compared with $\chi_m = .0667(100\text{x}20) = 133.4$ and $\chi_r = .0385(100\text{x}20) = 76.9$; the ξ I.C. is here $\frac{151}{76.9} = 1.96$. Having identified the strip (No. 6) associated with Alphabet I of the cryptogram, the letters of Alphabet I may be deciphered. Alphabet II of the cryptogram when matched with strip No. 1 gives a χ value of 144, which is the highest of the 25 possible matchings; this is equivalent to a ξ I.C. of 1.87, which likewise is very satisfactory; and Alphabet III when matched with strip No. 14 gives a χ of 153, which is a ξ I.C. of 1.99, very good indeed. At this point the cipher letters of the first three alphabets of the cryptogram are deciphered:

```
G S G P O Q M H L M      R D N N K Q D N O N      W G Y C B Y T K X T
A I R                    I S S                    O R T

I B J S S B K Q X C      F G A N K L Z N D H      S O K G K B V L U H
E N E                    T R Y                    R E D

H K J Z J D Z P W C      L S X N E G D F P T      T T G M V H M N N G
N C E                    G I N                    Y A R

I T N W G I B N O Q      H V Q U Y Y Q P I N      I B J S S I F O A I
E A S                    N V I                    E N E

I G N A G H V V L D      I S X W O D E V U I      R C X J H Z O K X H
E R S                    E I N                    I O N

V O G O B Y D H H L      V O G C J J R Q R T      Y G J X G D V J O L
V E R                    V E R                    L R E

H R V J B A Z N C Q      C Q A A G C O V O F
N G F                    D B Y
```

These decipherments certainly look like good plain text.

f. We now continue the matching one more step. In testing the distribution for Alphabet IV, we get a χ of 112 (= ξ I.C. of 1.46) against strip No. 10, a χ of 106 (= ξ I.C. of 1.38) against strip No. 15, and a χ of 100 (= ξ I.C. of 1.30) against strip No. 17. Decipherments of the letters of Alphabet IV on the hypothesis of either strip No. 10 or No. 15 do not produce good plaintext tetragraphs, but when strip No. 17 is tried, good plaintext continuations of the trigraphs are manifest. Note the pentagraphic repetition IBJSS; with the decipherment of the first three letters as ENE$_p$, the word ENEMY may be assumed and thus one may by-pass further χ-test matching. All that is required, after the first three alphabets have been deciphered, is to find what strip will yield an M$_p$ for an S$_c$, and, if there is more than one such strip, to find the one where S$_c$=M$_p$ and also where J$_c$ represents a vowel or an R or L (in the sequence HRVJ$_c$ at position 181 of the message); that is, we test for a strip that yields "good" decipherments for Alphabet IV. In other words, after 3 or 4 distributions have been matched, the plaintext fragments decrypted form a basis for word assumptions, with trials based on the plain-cipher limitations of Figs. 82*a* and *b*. The complete solution now follows easily, and the order of the strips is found to be 6–1–14–17–11–20–4–9–22–24; the message begins with the words **AIR RECONNAIS-SANCE**.

g. If a cryptogram is not long enough to be solved by the procedure just described, it may still succumb to attack by the probable-word method. For example, let us assume the following short cryptogram is at hand:

```
O C X Y D   D L A N L   W B B Y H   S F O A I   B N D Z E   C K S O F
O C X C D   L D N X I   R C X B M
```

187

The message has been intercepted on circuits known to be passing administrative traffic, so a number of probable beginning words will be tried, among which are the following:

ACKNOWLEDGE	CONFIRM	FROM	RECEIPT	REQUIRE
ADVISE	DEPARTURE	INFORM	RECEIVE	REQUISITION
ARRIVAL	DISCONTINUE	IN REPLY	RECOMMEND	RERAD
ATTENTION	EFFECTIVE	ORDERS	REFERENCE	REURAD
CANCEL	EQUIPMENT	OUR	REFERRING	SEND
CITE	EXPEDITE	PARAPHRASE	REPEAT	STATUS
COMMANDING	FOLLOWING	PREPARE	REPORT	SUPPLY
COMMUNICATION	FOR	PROCEED	REQUEST	VERIFY

h. Referring to the diagram of Fig. 82*b*, we note that the first letter of the cryptogram, O_c, cannot represent S_p or V_p; this rules out the beginning words SEND, STATUS, SUPPLY and VERIFY. The second letter of the cryptogram, C_o, cannot represent A, C, E, I, R, T, or X, so that 25 more from the list of 40 words are eliminated. The third cipher letter, X_c, cannot represent L, M, R, or V; therefore 7 more words are eliminated, leaving only CONFIRM, EFFECTIVE, EQUIPMENT, and INFORM remaining under consideration. Since the fourth cipher letter, Y , cannot represent either I_p or O_p, this reduces the possibilities to either CONFIRM or EFFECTIVE; neither one of these words can be eliminated by a continuation of the foregoing process.

i. The possibilities of strip numbers for these two probable words are as follows:

Plain:	C	O	N	F	I	R	M
Cipher:	O	C	X	Y	D	D	L
Strips:	6	1	14	17	3	20	2
	12		25		11		4
					21		

Plain:	E	F	F	E	C	T	I	V	E
Cipher:	O	C	X	Y	D	D	L	A	N
Strips:	1	4	6	20	8	18	24	23	10
	11				9	25		24	15
	22				23				

Since the cryptogram factors to 10 alphabets we will write out the cipher text on this width, and test the assumptions of strip numbers on other rows of the cipher text. Testing the word CONFIRM, with 6–1–14–17 as the first four strip numbers we get the following:

```
6  1  14  17
O C X Y D D L A N L
C O N F

W B B Y H S F O A I
O N O F

B N D Z E D K S O F
P L A N

O C X C D L D N X I
C O N S

R C X B M
I O N X
```

This certainly looks promising. If B_c at the next-to-last position is a null X_p, then M_c might be another X_p null; $M_c = X_p$ on strips 7 and 11, but only on strip 11 does D_c (the fifth letter of the cryptogram) equal I_p, so the correct strip for the fifth position is No. 11. In short order we recover the entire sequence of strips, which is the same as that given in subpar. *f*, above.

j. If a probable word is to be tested somewhere in the message, the position being unknown, then the diagram in Fig. 82*a* is useful.   For instance, if the crib FLIGHT PLAN is to be tested in the cryptogram given in subpar. *g*, it will be found that the only place where this crib will fit without a contradiction (i.e., an impossible plain-cipher equivalency) is at the 15th position, beginning with the letters HSF. . . .   Where the period is known, the possible strip arrangements may be tested against other cycles of the cryptogram to reduce the key to a unique set of strips, as in the example in subpar. *i*.   When the period of a short cryptogram cannot be determined,

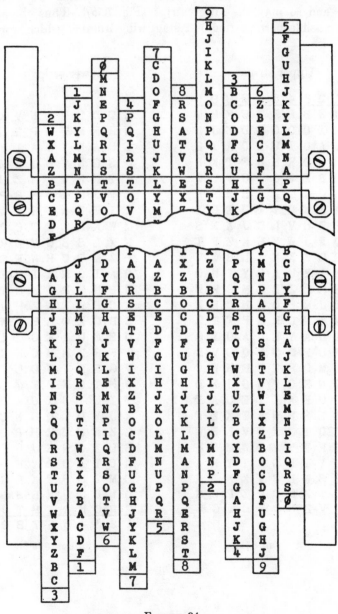

FIGURE 84

189

the placement of a crib will still yield a key, which, even if not unique, can be tested against the rest of the cipher text in the manner described in subpar. 22f(2).

76. **Solution of a second case.**—a. The cryptosystem which will now be treated involves a cipher device marketed in France in the 1930's under the misnomer of "transpositeur à permutations secrètes"; Baudouin [3] describes this device and shows one method of attack, albeit a weak one. This device, illustrated in Fig. 84, comprises a frame in which 10 compound strips, joined in the middle, are slid vertically. The upper halves of the strips (Fig. 85a) may be permuted among themselves, and so may the lower strips (Fig. 85b). Thus there are (10!) x (10!) or 13,168,189,440,000 possible permutations—a staggering number which apparently contributed

Upper strips	Lower strips

```
    Upper strips                    Lower strips

  1 2 3 4 5 6 7 8 9 0
  J W B P F Z C R H M           G Q D L S X N V K T
  K X C Q G B D S J N           H R F M T Z P W L V
  Y A O I U E O A I E           E U A E Y U A I Y O
  L Z D R H C F T K P           J S G N V B Q X M W
  M B F S J D G V L Q           K T H P W C R Z N X
  N C G T K F H W M R           L V J Q X D S B P Z
  A E U O Y I U E O I           I Y E I A Y E O A U
  P D H V L G J X N S           M W K R Z F T C Q B
  Q F J W M H K Z P T           N X L S B G V D R C
  R G K X N J L B Q V           P Z M T C H W F S D
  E I Y U A O Y I U O           O A I O E A I U E Y
  S H L Z P K M C R W           Q B N V D J X G T F
  T J M B Q L N D S X           R C P W F K Z H V G
  V K N C R M P F T Z           S D Q X G L B J W H
  I O A Y E U A O Y U           U E O U I E O Y I A
  W L P D S N Q G V B           T F R Z H M C K X J
  X M Q F T P R H W C           V G S B J N D L Z K
  Z N R G V Q S J X D           W H T C K P F M B L
  O U E A I Y E U A Y           Y I U Y O I U A O E
  B P S H W R T K Z F           X J V D L Q G N C M
  C Q T J X S V L B G           Z K W F M R H P D N
  D R V K Z T W M C H           B L X G N S J Q F P
  U Y I E O A I Y E A           A O Y A U O Y E U I
  F S W L B V X N D J           C M Z H P T K R G Q
  G T X M C W Z P F K           D N B J Q V L S H R
  H V Z N D X B Q G L           F P C K R W M T J S
                                1 2 3 4 5 6 7 8 9 0
```

FIGURE 85a   FIGURE 85b

[3] Captain Roger Baudouin, *Eléments de Cryptographie*, pp. 188–196. Paris, 1939.

no little to the inventor's Gallic exuberance. The secrecy imparted to messages is, we learn, "guaranteed absolute both mathematically and in practice"; as for the device, "if lost it will not enable the finders to decipher messages that might be intercepted." Still glowing with pride, the inventor goes on to say that since there are 13 trillion possibilities which must be tried in order to read an intercepted message, a trial-and-error procedure is rendered *absolument impossible*, thus "baffling all approaches in cryptanalytics used up to the present time." Stifling a slight yawn, we return to the device.

b. There are two fixed reading positions on the device; the upper one is used for the plain text, while the lower one (26 letters below the first one) is used for the cipher. In encryption, the 20 strips are first arranged according to a specific key; then the first 10 letters of the plain are aligned in the upper reading position, and their cipher equivalents are found in the lower reading position. The same treatment is then applied to the second set of 10 letters of the message, and so on. In decryption, after first arranging the strips according to the key for the message, the inverse procedure is followed, setting up the cipher text on the lower reading position and finding the plain text in the upper.

c. Now for some cryptanalytic observations.

(1) First of all, this system yields a periodic polyalphabetic encipherment of only 10 alphabets; any message enciphered by means of this device will always have a period of 10.

(2) In order to take advantage of certain reduced telegraph rates, this system has been constructed so that vowels are enciphered by vowels, and consonants by consonants, so that the resulting cipher text is pronounceable. This is penny wise and cipher foolish—what a wonderful asset in crib-placing! And—further to compound the cryptographic felony—no consonant will ever be enciphered by itself. This system seems to have been designed for cryptanalysis!

(3) It is true that all 20 of the strips are different from each other, so that we have what at first glance might seem to be "unrelated" alphabets. But on closer examination, it will be seen that all of them are but slight modifications of direct standard sequences. Taking upper strip No. 1 as an example,

$$\text{J K Y L M N A P Q R E S T V I W X Z O B C D U F G H,}$$

this may be decomposed as follows:

```
J K   L M N   P Q R   S T V   W X Z   B C D   F G H
    y       a       e       i       o       u
```

All of the remaining 19 strips are, to our delight, constructed along similar lines. Thus, if we compare upper strip No. 1 and lower strip No. 1,

```
J K y L M N a P Q R e S T V i W X Z o B C D u F G H
G H e J K L i M N P o Q R S u T V W y X Z B a C D F
```

we note that we actually have *direct* symmetry among the consonants (arranged *in their normal alphabetical order*) and likewise among the vowels. This property is one more cryptanalytic boon bestowed upon us by the inventor.

d. As an example of solution of a cryptogram produced by the *transpositeur*, let us assume that the following message is at hand:

```
Z K O K C    I B W D T    I P U A F    X O C N E    J R Y M W    G B E D J
X Y O C K    W O G Y D    B F D Y O    X Q C Y A    Z R A N J    O Z I Y J
B I Y Q K    X B A T A    O L S A C    P W A X A    T U Z Y Q    O B E D K
O M G G Y    Q X D E D
```

Since the consonants on the strips are arranged in their normal alphabetical order, we should be able to use the method of completing the plain-component sequence for the 20 possible *consonant* generatrices.[4] This we do forthwith. The completion diagrams for the first five out of the 10 alphabets are as follows:

Gen.	Alphabet 1	Alphabet 2	Alphabet 3	Alphabet 4	Alphabet 5
1	~~ZJXBZBT~~	2 KPRFRLM	1 DSZG	~~KMGNQG~~	~~GFWKJKCQ~~
2	~~BKZCBCV~~	3 LQSGSMN	2 FTBH	2 LNDPRH	~~DGXLKLDR~~
3	Ø CLBDCDW	4 MRTHTNP	Ø GVCJ	~~MPFQSJ~~	1 FHZMLMFS
4	Ø DMCFDFX	~~NSVJVPQ~~	Ø HWDK	~~NQGRTK~~	3 GJBNMNGT
5	1 FNDGFGZ	~~PTWKWQR~~	~~JXFL~~	2 PRHSVL	1 HKCPNPHV
6	Ø GPFHGHB	~~QVXLXRS~~	~~KZGM~~	~~QSJTWM~~	~~JLDQPQJW~~
7	~~HQGJIHJC~~	~~RWZMZST~~	1 LBHN	~~RTKVXN~~	~~KMFRQRKX~~
8	~~JRHKJKD~~	3 SXBNBTV	Ø MCJP	1 SVLWZP	4 LNGSRSLZ
9	~~KSJLKLF~~	1 TZCPCVW	~~NDKQ~~	~~TWMXBQ~~	3 MPHTSTMB
10	1 LTKMLMG	~~VBDQDWX~~	1 PFLR	~~VXNZCR~~	~~NQJVTVNC~~
11	2 MVLNMNH	~~WGFRFXZ~~	1 QGMS	1 WZPBDS	1 PRKVVWPD
12	2 NWMPNPJ	~~XDGSGZB~~	3 RHNT	~~XBQCFT~~	~~QSLXWXQF~~
13	~~PXNQPQK~~	1 ZFHTHBC	1 SJPV	1 ZCRDGV	~~RTMZXZRG~~
14	~~QZPRQRL~~	~~BGJVJCD~~	~~TKQW~~	1 BDSFHW	3 SVNBZBSH
15	4 RBQSRSM	~~CHKWKDF~~	1 VLRX	~~CFTGJX~~	2 TWPCBCTJ
16	6 SCRTSTN	~~DJLXLFG~~	1 WMSZ	~~DGVHKZ~~	~~VXQDCDVK~~
17	3 TDSVTVP	~~FKMZMGH~~	2 XNTB	Ø FHWJLB	1 WZRFDFWL
18	1 VFTWVWQ	2 GLNBNHJ	Ø ZPVC	~~GJXKMC~~	~~XBSGFGXM~~
19	~~WGVXWXR~~	~~HMPCPJK~~	Ø BQWD	1 HKZLND	~~ZGTHGHZN~~
20	~~XHWZXZS~~	~~JNQDQKL~~	1 CRXF	Ø JLBMPF	~~BDVJHJBP~~

The scores to the left of the columns are the sums of the two-category weights described in subpar. 21*g*; even though we are treating only the consonants, this scoring method suffices and there is no need to devise specially any new weights. (For greater sensitivity, we could of course use the $\log_{133}$ weights treated in par. 34.)

---

[4] This easy general solution was overlooked by Baudouin, who employed a much less generally applicable method in his example which depended on a message beginning with a digraph composed of two consonants.

e. The generatrices with the highest scores are assumed to be the correct ones,[5] and the following decipherments result:

```
      1 2 3 4 5 6 7 8 9 10
      Z K O K C I B W D T
      S M   L L
      I P U A F X O C N E
        R   N
      J R Y M W G B E D J
      C T   N G
      X Y O C K W O G Y D
      R   D S
      B F D Y O X Q C Y A
      T H R
      Z R A N J O Z I Y J
      S T   P R
      B I Y Q K X B A T A
      T   R S
      O L S A C P W A X A
        N H   L
      T U Z Y Q O B E D K
      N N   Z
      O M G G Y Q X D E D
      P T H
```

For the vowels, the plain-component completion method is possible but too precarious; it is usually too difficult to distinguish the right answers from the wrong.[6] The simplest thing, having established the consonants for some of the alphabets, is to insert vowels in the word structures on the basis of contextual likelihood; one vowel correctly identified in a particular column will of course identify all the vowels in that column. Thus, in the diagram above, SMθLL$_p$=SMALL and CTθNG$_p$=CTING, etc. Aided as we are both by the plaintext fragments

---

[5] In Alphabet 4 there are two generatrices with equally high scores; however, Generatrix No. 2 produces good consonant digraphs with Alphabet 5, whereas the digraphs produced by Generatrix No. 5 are not nearly as good. This is shown by the centiban scores of logs$_{224}$ (cf. Table 15, Appendix 2, *Military Cryptanalytics, Part I*) of

LL NG DS PR RS
73+73+ 59+ 66+ 75=346,

whereas

PL RG HS SR VS
59+48+ 38+ 42+ 0 =187, thus confirming the choice of Generatrix

No. 2 of Alphabet 4 as the correct one.

[6] It is interesting to point out that in Alphabet 3 where there are 6 vowels, completion of the vowel-sequences together with the deciban scores based on log$_{133}$ weights yields the following, in which the highest generatrix is the correct one:

```
Gen.
  1    O U Y O A Y   42
  2    U Y A U E A   43
  3    Y A E Y I E   46
  4    A E I A O I   49
  5    E I O E U O   48
  6    I O U I Y U   42
```

thus far decrypted, and by the consonant-vowel configuration of the rest of the text, the entire cryptogram may now easily be solved, as follows:

```
1 2 3 4 5 6 7 8 9 10
Z K O K C I B W D T
S M A L L A R M S F

I P U A F X O C N E
I R E I N T E R D I

J R Y M W G B E D J
C T I N G C R O S S

X Y O C K W O G Y D
R O A D S S E V E N

B F D Y O X Q C Y A
T H R E E T H R E E

Z R A N J O Z I Y J
S T O P R E Q U E S

B I Y Q K X B A T A
T A I R S T R I K E

O L S A C P W A X A
O N H I L L N I N E

T U Z Y Q O B E D K
N I N E Z E R O S T

O M G G Y Q X D E D
O P T H O M P S O N
```

f. All that remains now is the matter of the key, i.e., the specific arrangement of the upper and lower strips; given the plain text to the cipher, this is a very easy matter. We note, in Figs. 85a and b, that if S_p is found in upper strip No. 1, the only possible cipher equivalents (found in Fig. 85b on the same line with S_p in Fig. 85a) are as follows:

(lower strip nos.)

$$\begin{array}{cccccccccc} 1 & 2 & 3 & 4 & 5 & 6 & 7 & 8 & 9 & 0 \\ S_p = Q & B & N & V & D & J & X & G & T & F \end{array}$$

Patently, $S_p = Z_c$ is impossible with any combination involving upper strip No. 1. In fact, it is compatible only with the following 7 out of the 100 possible combinations of the strips for the first alphabet:

(upper strip nos.): 2   4   5   6   8   9   0
(lower strip nos.): $\overline{3}$, $\overline{8}$, $\overline{4}$, $\overline{1}$, $\overline{6}$, $\overline{7}$, $\overline{5}$

But, in Alphabet 1, $I_p = I_c$ which should serve to cut down the 7 possibilities above; $I_p = I_c$ in only three of the 7 combinations given above, *viz.*, $\frac{2}{3}$, $\frac{4}{8}$, and $\frac{6}{1}$. Thus, we may limit the possible strip arrangements for the ten alphabets to the following:

Alphabet 1 $(S_p = Z_c,\ I_p = I_c)$: $\frac{2}{3}$, $\frac{4}{8}$, $\frac{6}{1}$

Alphabet 2 $(M_p = K_c,\ O_p = Y_c)$: $\frac{1}{1}$

Alphabet 3 $(R_p = D_c,\ A_p = O_c)$: $\frac{7}{7}$, $\frac{9}{5}$, $\frac{0}{6}$

Alphabet 4 $(L_p = K_c,\ I_p = A_c)$: $\frac{4}{7}$, $\frac{8}{2}$

Alphabet 5 $(L_p = C_c,\ E_p = O_c)$: $\frac{7}{5}$, $\frac{9}{6}$

Alphabet 6 $(T_p = X_c,\ A_p = I_c)$: $\frac{8}{8}$

Alphabet 7 $(R_p = B_c,\ E_p = O_c)$: $\frac{3}{9}$, $\frac{4}{6}$, $\frac{5}{7}$, $\frac{9}{2}$

Alphabet 8 $(M_p = W_c,\ O_p = E_c)$: $\frac{3}{4}$, $\frac{6}{9}$

Alphabet 9 $(S_p = D_c,\ E_p = Y_c)$: $\frac{3}{4}$, $\frac{6}{9}$

Alphabet 10 $(F_p = T_c,\ I_p = E_c)$: $\frac{1}{6}$, $\frac{5}{0}$

g. Since there is only one possibility of a strip pair in Alphabets 2 and 6, the positions of upper strips Nos. 1 and 8 and lower strips Nos. 1 and 8 are now fixed. This means that in Alphabet 4 only the pair $\frac{4}{7}$ will remain, as the upper strip No. 8 in the pair $\frac{8}{2}$ has already been used in Alphabet 6; similarly, in Alphabet 10, only the pair $\frac{5}{0}$ will remain. In Alphabet 1, only $\frac{2}{3}$ will remain; and since for Alphabets 8 and 9 we must have either $\frac{3}{4}$ and $\frac{6}{9}$, or vice versa, the only strip pair that remains for Alphabet 7 is $\frac{9}{2}$. This means that for Alphabet 3 the only strip pair must be $\frac{0}{6}$, and that the only strip pair for Alphabet 5 is $\frac{7}{5}$. The strips that have been fixed are as follows:

Alphabet

	1	2	3	4	5	6	7	8	9	10
upper strips:	2	1	0	4	7	8	9	.	.	5
lower strips:	3	1	6	7	5	8	2			0

195

The identity of the strip pairs for Alphabets 8 and 9 cannot be determined uniquely in this particular example; Alphabet 8 is either $\frac{3}{4}$ or $\frac{6}{9}$, and Alphabet 9 is either $\frac{6}{9}$ or $\frac{3}{4}$; either combination will decipher all cryptograms sent in the same key as the one just solved.

h. The foregoing solution is predicated on a knowledge of the device and its strips. If we had not known anything about the device, a single cryptogram of fair length would have sufficed for solution without much difficulty, and the completely filled-out reconstruction matrix (for the device as set up in Fig. 84, for example) might look like this:

```
P:      A B C D E F G H I J K L M N O P Q R S T U V W X Y Z
     1 │A H J K E L M N I P Q R S T O V W X Z B U C D F Y G│
     2 │I X Z B O C D F U G H J K L Y M N P Q R A S T V E W│
     3 │O M N P U Q R S Y T V W X Z A B C D F G E H J K I L│
     4 │U Z B C Y D F G A H J K L M E N P Q R S I T V W O X│
C:   5 │I R S T O V W X U Z B C D F Y G H J K L A M N P E Q│
     6 │I F G H O J K L U M N P Q R Y S T V W X A Z B C E D│
     7 │I K L M O N P Q U R S T V W Y X Z B C D A F G H E J│
     8 │U L M N Y P Q R A S T V W X E Z B C D F I G H J O K│
     9 │U L M N Y P Q R A S T V W X E Z B C D F I G H J O K│
    10 │Y Q R S A T V W E X Z B C D I F G H J K O L M N U P│
```

FIGURE 86*a*

Indirect symmetry extending to the plaintext line would have been manifest, and the following chains (from lines 4 and 10, as an example) would have been recovered:

(A E I O U Y)   (B R J Z Q H X P G W N F V M D T L C S K)

The consonant chain, if decimated at an interval of −3, would yield the consonants in normal alphabetical order. The matrix might thereupon be rearranged as follows:

```
P:      A E I O U Y B C D F G H J K L M N P Q R S T V W X Z
     1 │A E I O U Y│H J K L M N P Q R S T V W X Z B C D F G│
     2 │I O U Y A E│X Z B C D F G H J K L M N P Q R S T V W│
     3 │O U Y A E I│M N P Q R S T V W X Z B C D F G H J K L│
     4 │U Y A E I O│Z B C D F G H J K L M N P Q R S T V W X│
C:   5 │I O U Y A E│R S T V W X Z B C D F G H J K L M N P Q│
     6 │I O U Y A E│F G H J K L M N P Q R S T V W X Z B C D│
     7 │I O U Y A E│K L M N P Q R S T V W X Z B C D F G H J│
     8 │U Y A E I O│L M N P Q R S T V W X Z B C D F G H J K│
     9 │U Y A E I O│L M N P Q R S T V W X Z B C D F G H J K│
    10 │Y A E I O U│Q R S T V W X Z B C D F G H J K L M N P│
```

FIGURE 86*b*

The cryptanalyst would make mental note of the direct symmetry manifested in Fig. 86*b*; he would see that he could solve further cryptograms by a modification of the plain-component sequence method as demonstrated in subpar. *d*; and he might perhaps be forever blissfully unaware of the existence of the 10 permutable upper strips and the 10 permutable lower strips.

In other words, even though he might never know the exact mechanical details of the system, he could still cryptanalyze the traffic with ease. Situations of this sort are not at all uncommon in operational cryptanalytic practice.

77. Solution of a further example.—*a.* The system to be treated here is one of the machine ciphers used by AGGRESSOR, the maneuver enemy in U.S. joint maneuvers and training exercises. This system is included here because in its cryptanalysis certain interesting and pedagogically valuable techniques come into play, and furthermore some interesting applications of symmetry present themselves, even though the alphabets of the machine are random, nonrelated alphabets.

b. This electromechanical cipher machine is called the ZEN–40; its cryptographic principle embodies a polyalphabetic substitution matrix of 25 reciprocal nonrelated alphabets which are wired electrically in a bank of uniselector switches [7] in the machine's interior. These alphabets are of the Porta type, in which there are two distinct "families" of 13 letters each; a letter in one family has as its equivalents only the 13 letters in the other family. The exact composition of the letters composing the two families is determined by the plugging of a small plugboard located on the front panel of the ZEN–40. The plugboard serves a threefold purpose: (1) it determines the composition of the two families; (2) it changes the identity of the letters in the internally wired matrix into isomorphic equivalents of the rows of the matrix; and (3) it permutes the order of the rows of the basic matrix. These three aspects will be explained in detail subsequently.

c. There are several procedures in using the ZEN–40, giving rise to a number of different types of cryptosystems. The particular cryptosystem with which we will be concerned in this discussion produces cryptograms enciphered by polyalphabetic substitution of a period of 25, with 25 reciprocal, nonrelated, Porta-type alphabets. The two variables in this cryptosystem are (1) the plugging which remains in force for a particular cryptoperiod (usually one day), and (2) the *starting point* (determined by a specific key) of the succession of the 25 alphabets. The specific key may be varied at will by the cipher clerk for each message; these keys are designated by indicators consisting of a consonant-vowel digraph repeated, followed by a fixed letter (usually X), such as in the indicator groups BABAX, VEVEX, etc.

d. In the solution of this cryptosystem, the initial cryptanalysis would be accomplished with a small volume of traffic as a polyalphabetic substitution cipher with 25 nonrelated alphabets, and during the course of solution the phenomena of reciprocity and the Porta-like families would have been observed and used to advantage. The sequence reconstruction matrix might look as in Fig. 87, below, using any one of the alphabets arbitrarily as the starting point for "Alphabet 1" of the matrix; in this case, the sequence of alphabets of a message with the indicator "BABAX" has been used as a base. (All reciprocal values of recoveries have been filled in.) It is noted that the 12 different equivalents for A_p in the order in which they occur in the matrix are as follows: P L I R Y T U M F X W D; the equivalents for B_p are X I P Y M W L Q U. These equivalents for B_p are among the equivalents for A_p, with the addition of Q, which is the last letter comprising one family of 13 letters. It will also be noted that each row of the matrix contains letters exclusively from the one or the other of the two families of 13;[8] thus with but only a few entries in the reconstruction matrix, it is possible to segregate the two families with ease. In this case it is therefore easy to identify the families as (A B C E G H J K N O S V Z)

---

[7] These switches are of the type actuated by dialing in automatic dialing telephone systems.

[8] Each row of the matrix will contain from 9 to 13 different letters belonging to one family, because of the manner in which the internally wired matrix is constructed.

```
        1  2  3  4  5  6  7  8  9 10 11 12 13 14 15 16 17 18 19 20 21 22 23 24 25
   A    P     P  P  L  I  R  I     Y  T  L  U  M  F  Y  X  Y     W  Y     M  D  Y
   B    X        I  P     Y  M  I  W              X  P  I  L     Q           U  P
   C    F  W  I  Q  Y     U     T  I     Y     I  D  L           P  F     U
   D    H  E     S                 Z     S  S  N     C        S  Z  N  J  G  A  J
   E    Q  D  X     X  R  T  X     F  I     L  W  U  F  U  Q  Q  I  P  U  X  I  L
   F    C     G  O  G  G        E     H     K  A  E  N  V  V  J  C              K
   G    M  M  F  R  F  F  W     M  X                 M  R     W     D           U
   H    D  Q        R  L  L     U  U  R  F  I  X  L  I  L        M  I  Y
   I       C  B  K  A  V  A  B  C  E  N  H  C  J  H  B  K     E  K  H  V  E
   J    U  L  L        M              R  P  T        I  U        T  F     D  T  T  D
   K             I                 R  F  T        W  I  U  R  I              F
   L       J  J     A  H  H  S     S  O  A  E  S  H  C  H  B  N        S  Z  O  E
   M    G  G  N        J  N  B  G  N  Z     V  A  Z  O  Z  G  S  N  H        A  S  O
   N    Y  T  M  T  U     M  U  Q  M  Q  I  D  T  R  X  F     L  M  D  X  R  Q  W
   O       X     F     Q     R  W  Q  L  X  W  P  P  M  P  R  Y  U  U  Q     L  M
   P    A     A  A  B     Z        Z  J           O  O  B  O     Z  C  E     S  V  B
   Q    E  H     C     O  S     N  O  N              E  E  B     O        N
   R    S  S     G  H  E  A  O  S  J  H  V  K  V  N  S     O  G  K  Z  V  N
   S    R  R     D  W  Y  Q  L  R  L  D  D  T  L     R  T  D  M        L  P  M
   T       N     N     Z  E  Z  C     A  J  S  N  K     S     J           J  J  Z
   U    J  Z  V     N     C  N  H  H           A     E  J  E     K  O  O  E  C  B  G
   V       Y  U        I     X        R  M  R              F  F        R  I  P
   W       C        S     G     O  B        O  E        K        A  G        Z  N
   X    B  O  E  Z  E        E  V  G     O     H  B  N  A              N  E
   Y    N  V        C  S  B        A     C                 A     A  O     A     H     A
   Z       U     X        T  P  T  D  P  M           M     M     P  D  R     L  W  T
```

FIGURE 87

and (D F I L M P Q R T U W X Y). This matrix may be visualized as a Porta-like matrix of 25 nonrelated alphabets, as illustrated in the fragmentary matrix below:

```
        A  B  C  E  G  H  J  K  N  O  S  V  Z
    1   P  X  F  Q  M  D  U     Y     R
    2         W  D  M  Q  L     T  X  R  Y  U
    3   P     I  X  F     L     M           U
   ~~~~~~~~~~~~~~~~~~~~~~~~~~~~~~~~~~~~~~~~~~~~~
   24   D  U     I           T  F  Q  L  M  P  W
   25   Y  P     L  U     D     W  M           T
```

e. The rows of matrices for subsequent periods will be related to those of Fig. 87, in that there will be a simple substitution of the letters in a row (i.e., preserving the idiomorphic pattern and thus *isomorphic* to the original row), and a transposition or permutation of the rows of the basic matrix.   For example, row "G" of Fig. 87, which begins with the letters M M F R F F... might be shifted to the "X" row of a new matrix, with the identity of the letters changed to L L D C D D... .   The partially recovered plugging, i.e., the simple substitution alphabet

198

(which applies to *both* the isomorphic substitution and to the permutation of the rows of the matrix) is then for this case as follows:

```
"α": A B C D E F G H I J K L M N O P Q R S T U V W X Y Z
"β":       D X           L         C
```

The M M F R F F of "α" will go to L L D C D D of "β" at the same position (i.e., starting in the same alphabet), *if* the two matrices actually start with the same alphabet; if the indicator system has not changed, a pair of messages with identical indicators in two cryptoperiods means that the relative starting points for the sequence of alphabets are identical. If the relative starting points of two reconstruction matrices are *not* the same, then the M M F R F F of row "G" of "α" will still go to L L D C D D of row "X" of "β", but at a displacement equivalent to the relative displacement between the starting points of the two matrices.

   f. In order to illustrate the mechanics of this system, let us assume that we have solved some traffic in a cryptoperiod subsequent to that identified by the matrix in Fig. 87. A portion of the reconstruction matrix for this "β" period (denoting the matrix in Fig. 87 as belonging to the "α" period) is shown below; the beginning point of the sequence of alphabets here too is that for a "BABAX" message.

```
        1 2 3  4 5 6 7 8 9  10 11 12 13 14 15 16 17 18 19 20 21 22 23 24 25
     A |Q Q R      E R X Q         G J O      O Q N      P    J    M  |
(β)  B |W H    U F   X   C I F      I     T            V W          |
     C | R L R    O D O B   J      N R L    N B E          E E     |
```

It is apparent from the foregoing that the "A" and "C" rows are in the same family, and that the two families for the "β" period are (A C F H I K S T U V W Y Z) and (B D E G J L M N O P Q R X). Now we note the idiomorphic sequence of row "A", beginning with Q Q R – – – R; this is identified as the isomorphic equivalent of row "M" of "α", as follows:

```
           1 2 3  4 5 6 7 8 9  10 11 12 13 14 15 16 17 18 19 20 21 22 23 24 25
(β) A:  Q Q R      E R X Q          G J O      O Q N      P    J    M
(α) M:  G G N      J N B G N Z      V A Z O Z G S N H      A S O
```

From this we recover the following plugging (substitution alphabet):

```
"β": A B C D E F G H I J K L M N O P Q R S T U V W X Y Z
"α":       J V   A       O S Z H G N             B
```

And since the "A" row of "β" goes to the "M" row of "α", we may add this equivalent pair to the recovered plugging.

   g. Now we may take row "C", for example, of the "β" matrix and transform it into its exact equivalents in terms of matrix "α", as follows:

```
           1 2 3  4 5 6 7 8 9  10 11 12 13 14 15 16 17 18 19 20 21 22 23 24 25
(β) C:    R L R    O D O B   J E N R L    N B E          E E
(α) ?:    N   N    Z   Z     A   S N      S   J          J J
```

Row "C" of "β" may be identified as row "T" of Matrix "α", which results in the following additional values in both rows:

```
           1 2 3  4 5 6 7 8 9  10 11 12 13 14 15 16 17 18 19 20 21 22 23 24 25
(β) C:    R L R    O D O B   J E N R L    N B E          E E O
(α) T:    N K N    Z E Z C   A J S N K    S C J          J J Z
```

Transferring the equivalent pairs from the foregoing to our recovered plugging, including the pairs $A(\beta)=M(\alpha)$ and $C(\beta)=T(\alpha)$ derived from the permutation of the rows, we now have the following plugging reconstruction:

```
"β": A B C D E F G H I J K L M N O P Q R S T U V W X Y Z
"α": M C T E J   V     A   K O S Z H G N           B
```

h. Enough of the basic theory has been demonstrated how the foregoing procedures could be continued with other rows of a partially recovered new matrix, permitting the easy reconstruction of the relative plugging between key periods. However, a partially recovered matrix of a new cryptoperiod is not a prerequisite for the reconstruction of the new plugging; a simple technique based upon a crib attack will now be demonstrated. This technique, involving an interesting application of symmetry in cross-equating between values of two different key periods, will be treated in the subparagraphs below.[9]

i. Let us assume we have available, in a new key period, the following message suspected of beginning with the opening stereotype "REFERENCE YOUR MESSAGE":

```
B A B A X    P C N J J    Z S Q I Z    I J V D M    H H Z J I    J D Y F K
H N B B F    A S M L T    J M Z A D    N B B P I    U V J I Q
```

The indicator, BABAX, shows that the beginning of the sequence of alphabets starts at the same point in the cycle as the BABAX matrix in Fig. 87 for the earlier cryptoperiod. The recoverable letter-families are observed to be (A D E G O Q R U Y) and (C I J M P V Z), and also (F S) and (H N) which are as yet indeterminate as to which of the larger chains they belong. From this it is obvious that the next word of the crib is *not* "NUMBER," since the 22d letter, D_c, cannot represent U_p because D and U are in the same family.

j. The matched plain-cipher of the crib is set down:

```
  1  2  3  4  5  6  7  8  9 10 11 12 13 14 15 16 17 18 19 20
  R  E  F  E  R  E  N  C  E  Y  O  U  R  M  E  S  S  A  G  E
  P  C  N  J  J  Z  S  Q  I  Z  I  J  V  D  M  H  H  Z  J  I
```

In the 16th and 17th positions, $S_p=H_c$. A search is made in the matrix of Fig. 87 for a repeated letter in these positions in one of the rows, but none is found. (The matrix has been only partially reconstructed, so this correspondence is still hidden.) Since there is also the vertical pair E_p/I_c in positions 9 and 20 of the crib, a search is made in Fig. 87 for corresponding repetitions in the 9th and 20th positions in one of the rows; such a correspondence is found in the "D" and "Z" rows. This means that, in the plugging for the new matrix (β), what is now E_p in β used to be D_p (or Z_p) in α, and what is now I_c in β used to be Z_c (or D_c) in α. Since the plugging effects a simultaneous transformation of both the plain and cipher elements of the basic matrix, whatever correspondence exists in the plain between two matrices will also exist in the cipher of the two matrices. Thus we may make the following diagram, assuming one of the possibilities [10] above that $Z_p(\alpha)=E_p(\beta)$ and $D_c(\alpha)=I_c(\beta)$:

```
              1  2  3  4  5  6  7  8  9 10 11 12 13 14 15 16 17 18 19 20
Plain (α):    Z  Z  Z     Z                       Z                 Z
Plain (β):    R  E  F  E  R  E  N  C  E  Y  O  U  R  M  E  S  S  A  G  E
Cipher (α):                     D  D                                D
Cipher (β):   P  C  N  J  J  Z  S  Q  I  Z  I  J  V  D  M  H  H  Z  J  I
```

FIGURE 88*a*

---

[9] This method was first pointed out to me by Mr. William E. May.

[10] The selection of the possibility to be tried is arbitrary at this stage; if a wrong equivalence is chosen, conflicts will develop during the course of the analysis. (See subpar. 77*n*.)

Note that we have placed a Z over every E (either plain or cipher) and likewise a D over every I (either plain or cipher) of the diagram.

k. Now in position 2, Z_p (of the α period) is found to equal U_c in α, by referring to the matrix of Fig. 87; likewise, Z_p (α) in positions 4, 6, and 15 in Fig. 88*a* may be found, by referring to the corresponding columns in Fig. 87, to equal X_c, T_c, and M_c in α. These equivalencies are set down in Fig. 88*b*, below:

```
                1  2  3  4  5  6  7  8  9  10 11 12 13 14 15 16 17 18 19 20
Plain (α):      Z  Z     Z     Z                    Z              Z
Plain (β):      R  E  F  E  R  E  N  C  E  Y  O  U  R  M  E  S  S  A  G  E
Cipher (α):     U  X     T        D        D                 M              D
Cipher (β):     P  C  N  J  J  Z  S  Q  I  Z  I  J  V  D  M  H  H  Z  J  I
```
FIGURE 88*b*

By transferring values just derived (e.g., a U above C in the cipher may be transferred to other occurrences of U in *either* the cipher or the plain), we obtain the following diagram:

```
                1  2  3  4  5  6  7  8  9  10 11 12 13 14 15 16 17 18 19 20
Plain (α):      Z  Z     Z  U  Z              M  Z                       Z
Plain (β):      R  E  F  E  R  E  N  C  E  Y  O  U  R  M  E  S  S  A  G  E
Cipher (α):     U  X     X  T        D  T  D              M           T  X  D
Cipher (β):     P  C  N  J  J  Z  S  Q  I  Z  I  J  V  D  M  H  H  Z  J  I
```
FIGURE 88*c*

We now look up the equivalents in Fig. 87 for X (in position 5), U (pos. 8), T(10), D(11), M(14), T(18), and X(19), and we record these new values in the diagram, yielding the following:

```
                1  2  3  4  5  6  7  8  9  10 11 12 13 14 15 16 17 18 19 20
Plain (α):      Z     Z  E  Z     U  Z     S  O     M  Z                 Z
Plain (β):      R  E  F  E  R  E  N  C  E  Y  O  U  R  M  E  S  S  A  G  E
Cipher (α):     U     X  X  T        N  D  T  D  X        A  M           T  X  D
Cipher (β):     P  C  N  J  J  Z  S  Q  I  Z  I  J  V  D  M  H  H  Z  J  I
```
FIGURE 88*d*

Since we have $E_p(\alpha) = R_p(\beta)$ in position 5, an E may be inscribed over the R in columns 1 and 13, yielding new cipher values of Q and L in the corresponding positions in the "cipher α" row. The diagram is now as complete as we can make it for the moment with the crib alone; the following is the result obtained:

```
                1  2  3  4  5  6  7  8  9  10 11 12 13 14 15 16 17 18 19 20
Plain (α):      E  Z     Z  E  Z     U  Z     S  O  E  M  Z                 Z
Plain (β):      R  E  F  E  R  E  N  C  E  Y  O  U  R  M  E  S  S  A  G  E
Cipher (α):     Q  U     X  X  T        N  D  T  D  X  L  A  M           T  X  D
Cipher (β):     P  C  N  J  J  Z  S  Q  I  Z  I  J  V  D  M  H  H  Z  J  I
```
FIGURE 88*e*

l. From the foregoing, it is evident that the plugging for the β period (taking α as the base) thus far recovered is the following substitution:

```
α: A B C D E F G H I J K L M N O P Q R S T U V W X Y Z
β: D     I R              V M Q U   P   O Z C     J   E
```

201

Three more values could have been picked up (in columns 10, 18, and 19) if the matrix in Fig. 87 had been complete; any further values must now come from the exploitation of the rest of the message.

m. The entire cipher text is written out on a width of 25, in the manner of the diagrams of Figs. 88*a–e*, and substituted values from the recovered plugging and from the basic matrix are made throughout the message where possible. Thus:

	1	2	3	4	5	6	7	8	9	10	11	12	13	14	15	16	17	18	19	20	21	22	23	24	25
Plain (α):	E	Z		Z	E	Z		U	Z			S	O	E	M	Z				Z					
Plain (β):	R	E	F	E	R	E	N	C	E	Y	O	U	R	M	E	S	S	A	G	E					
Cipher (α):	Q	U		X	X	T		N	D	T	D	X	L	A	M				T	X	D	X	A		
Cipher (β):	P	C	N	J	J	Z	S	Q	I	Z	I	J	V	D	M	H	H	Z	J	I	J	D	Y	F	K

	1	2	3	4	5	6	7	8	9	10	11	12	13	14	15	16	17	18	19	20	21	22	23	24	25
Plain (α):								B					S		F				E	Z	U	S	E	A	W
Plain (β):													O						R	E	C	O	R	D	
Cipher (α):								M				X	M	T		A			Q	D	O	L	X	D	N
Cipher (β):	H	N	B	B	F	A	S	M	L	T	J	M	Z	A	D	N	B	B	P	I	U	V	J	I	Q

Figure 88f

If now an S_p is assumed as the last letter of the message plain text, the diagram above may be expanded to the following, which will result in the recovery of four more equivalent pairs (F–F, G–N, K–H, W–S) in the plugging:

	1	2	3	4	5	6	7	8	9	10	11	12	13	14	15	16	17	18	19	20	21	22	23	24	25
Plain (α):	E	Z	F	Z	E	Z	G	U	Z			S	O	E	M	Z	W	W		Z				K	
Plain (β):	R	E	F	E	R	E	N	C	E	Y	O	U	R	M	E	S	S	A	G	E				H	
Cipher (α):	Q	U	G	X	X	T	W	N	D	T	D	X	L	A	M	K	K	T	X	D	X	A		F	
Cipher (β):	P	C	N	J	J	Z	S	Q	I	Z	I	J	V	D	M	H	H	Z	J	I	J	D	Y	F	K

	1	2	3	4	5	6	7	8	9	10	11	12	13	14	15	16	17	18	19	20	21	22	23	24	25
Plain (α):	M		G					B					S		F				E	Z	U	S	E	A	W
Plain (β):	M		N										O						R	E	C	O	R	D	S
Cipher (α):	K	G		F		W	M					X	M	T		A	G		Q	D	O	L	X	D	N
Cipher (β):	H	N	B	B	F	A	S	M	L	T	J	M	Z	A	D	N	B	B	P	I	U	V	J	I	Q

Figure 88g

The solution would continue in this manner, with the exploitation of further plaintext assumptions or additional cipher text. Any further plaintext assumptions of letters or probable words in the context would of course be based on the 13 possible plaintext equivalents for any given cipher letter in this key period.

n. In subpar. *j*, we started the diagram of Fig. 88*a* with the assumption that $Z_p(\alpha) = E_p(\beta)$ and $D_c(\alpha) = I_c(\beta)$; this subsequently proved to be correct, there being no conflicts in the equivalent pairs developed. If, however, we had started with the other possibility, $D_p(\alpha) = E_p(\beta)$ and $Z_c(\alpha) = I_c(\beta)$, inconsistencies would have developed. For example, in the early stages of analysis of this possibility, the following diagram would have been obtained:

	1	2	3	4	5	6	7	8	9	10	11	12	13	14	15	16	17	18	19	20
Plain (α):	W	D		D	W	D		E	D			D	W	C	D				M	D
Plain (β):	R	E	F	E	R	E	N	C	E	Y	O	U	R	M	E	S	S	A	G	E
Cipher (α):		E		S	S		X	Z		Z	S	O	I	C					S	Z
Cipher (β):	P	C	N	J	J	Z	S	Q	I	Z	I	J	V	D	M	H	H	Z	J	I

202

Note that the tentative plugging D–U in column 12 is inconsistent with the plugging D–E in other columns of the diagram.

o. The examples of theoretical solution thus far demonstrated have involved matrices with identical starting points in the cycle of 25 alphabets. If in the β period we had no message with the indicator BABAX (i.e., starting at the same relative point in the new matrix as the start of the matrix in Fig. 87), and we had a crib in a message having an unknown starting point, we would have to search for isomorphism across all the columns consecutively, instead of searching the rows of specific columns as we did in subpar. *j.* Consider the following:

$$\text{R E F E R E N C E Y O U R M E S S A G E}$$
$$\text{J J N Z Z Z M L M W Z X C U M E A X P X}$$

We note the isomorphism in positions 4 and 6, and also 9 and 15, and we search in the matrix in Fig. 87 for a row with identical letters spaced at a distance of 2, and also 6, as in the matched plain-cipher, above. The only one we find [11] which fits both intervals is in the Z row, in positions 6 and 8, and 11 and 17. Our diagram thus begins as follows:

```
              3  4  5  6  7  8  9  10 11 12 13 14 15 16 17 18 19 20 21 22
Plain (α):             Z     Z        Z              Z
Plain (β):    R  E  F  E  R  E  N  C  E  Y  O  U  R  M  E  S  S  A  G  E
Cipher (α):            T     T        M              M
Cipher (β):   J  J  N  Z  Z  Z  M  L  M  W  Z  X  C  U  M  E  A  X  P  X
```

From here on the solution would proceed as previously demonstrated. Note that the two pairs of identical letters enable us to arrive at once at the correct initial assumption, instead of having two or more possibilities from which to make an arbitrary choice as was the case in subpar. *j.*

78. Solution involving isologs.—*a.* The possibilities for a successful attack on complex cryptosystems by the exploitation of isologs is predicated upon the mechanics of the cryptosystems, and, usually, also upon the presence of special circumstances connected with the isologs. Each case is usually a very special case, dependent upon the amount of cryptanalytic technical information that can be derived from a particular isolog situation.

b. It has been indicated in subpar. 62*i* how the procedures of an attack on isologs may be adapted to a case of isologs involving two different sets of unrelated, random alphabets. For example, even if the two messages in subpar. 62*b* were enciphered with 4 and 5 distinct unrelated alphabets respectively, the procedures given in subpars. 62*e* to *g* could be used for solution. Thus a partial recovery of some of the alphabets of a system such as that described in subpar. 75*a* would be made possible by this special solution.

c. In the case of the strip system described in par. 76, isologs are generally not of much help in solution; but since the general solution described in subpars. 76*d* and *e* is adequate for solving a single message, an isolog attack is only of academic importance. Nevertheless, a pair of very short isologs might still be solvable in this system, if either the plain or the cipher strips are in a fixed order, and this order is known.

d. Isologs in a system such as the ZEN–40 described in par. 77 are again of not much assistance in arriving at a solution, unless further special circumstances also exist. For instance, if we had in this system a pair of cross-period isologs (i.e., in two different pluggings) in which there were two sets of families, and if these families were known, an adaptation of the generatrix

---

[11] It is quite possible that if the matrix in Fig. 87 were completely reconstructed, we might have found one or two other rows (in other columns) with the properties we are seeking; in any case, the selections would be greatly restricted if we had two pairs of identical letters as in the case at hand.

method is possible.[12]   Let us suppose that in the following pair of isologs, the families of Message "A" are known to be (A B D E G H L U V W X Y Z) and (C F I J K M N O P Q R S T), and the families of Message "B" are known to be (A C E G H I J K L M N O P) and

Message "A"

```
M O M O X     O B K X S     D C G W A     M G V G H     U K O H L     L P F Z D
H C Y Y S     G W W C B     Z Z X G X     U U N C C     G H Z A M     X T K W T
G K C C L     Z Z Z H X     K G G B W
```

Message "B"

```
R E R E X     S F S B O     D Y A E T     Z H T F Z     C X B J F     U X B T J
Y G X J O     Y D P R U     E T C F U     C L U B T     O H V J W     J Y S S I
Y S U R E     E T Y R U     T F G Q U
```

(B D F Q R S T U V W X Y Z).   Then by superimposing Message "A" and "B" and writing the *common* letters which can represent decipherments of the vertical pairs, we have the following diagram for the first 30 letters of the messages:

```
 1  2  3  4  5  6  7  8  9 10 11 12 13 14 15 16 17 18 19 20 21 22 23 24 25 26 27 28 29 30
 O  B  K  X  S  D  C  G  W  A  M  G  V  G  H  U  K  O  H  L  L  P  F  Z  D  H  C  Y  Y  S
 S  F  S  B  O  D  Y  A  E  T  Z  H  T  F  Z  C  X  B  J  F  U  X  B  T  J  Y  G  X  J  O
 A  C  A  C  B  C  A  F  F  C  A  F  C  C  C  F  A  A  F  C  C  A  A  C  F  C  B  C  F  B
 E  I  E  I  D  I  E  Q  Q  I  E  Q  I  I  I  Q  E  E  Q  I  I  E  E  I  Q  I  D  I  Q  D
 G  J  G  J  U  J  G  R  R  J  G  R  J  J  J  R  G  G  R  J  J  G  G  J  R  J  U  J  R  U
 H  K  H  K  V  K  H  S  S  K  H  S  K  K  K  S  H  H  S  K  K  H  H  K  S  K  V  K  S  V
 L  M  L  M  W  M  L  T  T  M  L  T  M  M  M  T  L  L  T  M  M  L  L  M  T  M  W  M  T  W
 N     N  X  N           M        N           N  N  N        N  N        N        N  X  N              X
 O     O  Y  O           O        O           O  O  O        O  O        O        O  Y  O              Y
 P     P  Z  P           P        P           P  P  P        P  P        P        P  Z  P              Z
```

FIGURE 89

It is easily seen that, by reading various levels of the generatrices, the cryptanalyst can decipher the first two words of the message as ENEMY PATROLS.   The rest of the plain text can be obtained by following this procedure; the completion of the solution is left to the student as an exercise.   Having the matched plain and cipher, recovery of the plugging follows along the lines indicated in subpars. 77*i* to *o*.

79. Additional remarks.—*a*. The attack on a system such as that illustrated in Fig. 80 is fairly simple because the plain component in this case is the normal sequence; if the plain component had been any other fixed sequence that were *known*, the tables of plain-cipher limitations in Figs. 82*a* and *b* and the table of theoretical ciphertext frequencies in Fig. 83 would have to be modified accordingly.   Instead of the normal sequence, any one of the 25 numbered strips in Fig. 80 could have been used as the plain component; this would complicate the solution to the extent that the table of theoretical ciphertext frequencies would have to be compiled for 25x24 or 600 different distributions, against which the uniliteral frequency distributions for a new cryptogram in this system must be tested.   If the plain component were an entirely unknown sequence, different from any of the 25 numbered strips, solution would be greatly complicated

[12] This situation may of course also arise in modified Porta systems.

and would have to follow along the general lines indicated in subpar. 74*b*, since neither tables of plain-cipher limitations nor a table of theoretical ciphertext frequencies could be constructed. This demonstrates that, even in a cryptosystem employing random cipher alphabets, maximum security is attained when the plain component is also a random sequence.

b. If in a system such as that of Fig. 80, each of the cipher strips were *slidable* against the plain component so as to make possible the juxtaposition of any letter of the cipher component against A_p, then purely manual methods of attack would be too laborious for a practical solution; machine techniques could here be used to good advantage. However, there is still the possibility of getting too many acceptable "good answers," from which the cryptanalyst would have to determine the correct answer.

c. We have seen how easily the strip device treated in par. 76 succumbs to cryptanalytic attack because of the major weaknesses of this system. The same firm that marketed the *transpositeur* later produced a modified *transpositeur* called the "Sphinx"; this latter device also had 10 compound strips, but the 20 half-strips were not limited to an upper or lower position as was the case of the *transpositeur*, so that the number of possible arrangements is 20! or 2.4×10^{18} instead of the 1.3×10^{13} in the case of the *transpositeur*. In the Sphinx device there is no consonant-to-consonant and vowel-to-vowel limitation as there is in the *transpositeur*, so it looks as if the Sphinx is a decided improvement over its predecessor; however, in order to make the system easy to use by a cipher clerk, some of the strips are direct standard, the others are reversed standard sequences. Therefore for each of the 10 columns we will have Vigenère encipherment with either direct or reversed standard alphabets, depending upon the identity of the strips used in the particular positions—what an improvement!

d. The security of the *transpositeur* could have been enhanced considerably by the incorporation of 20 *random* half-strips, not limited to upper or lower position, and by not having fixed plaintext and ciphertext reading positions. This variable-generatrix idea is incorporated in the now obsolete U.S. Army Cipher Device M–94,[13] and in strip systems related to this device.

e. In the solution of the *transpositeur*, as well as in the ZEN–40, we have seen further instances of the general applicability of the generatrix method. It is quite surprising how many times solutions to cryptanalytic problems depend upon or are aided by the generatrix method, with or without minor modifications; the student would do well to keep this always in mind, and try to adapt this method wherever the opportunity presents itself.

f. The reason for emphasizing the large numbers in pars. 75 and 76 is to demonstrate forcibly that numbers of combinations, permutations, or keys *by themselves* often have no bearing upon the cryptanalytic complexity of solution of a system. If some would-be inventors of cryptographic systems would only stop and consider that the number of possible 26-letter *simple substitution alphabets* is 26! or 4.03×10^{26}, and that nevertheless simple substitution ciphers are solved quite readily, they should be more circumspect in bandying about their astronomical numbers too glibly.

g. In passing, it is worth mentioning that, no matter how complex a system is as regards the generation or use of a large number of alphabets, if we have a sufficient number of messages in depth (say 25–30, for English), we will be able to solve the plain texts of the messages, even if the cryptographic features of the system remain an enigma.

---

[13] See subpar. 6*c*, Appendix 6.

POLYALPHABETIC BIPARTITE SYSTEMS

80. General.—*a.* All the systems thus far treated have been characterized by polyalphabetic encipherment of single plaintext letters. Instead of single plaintext letters, the "plain text" to be subjected to polyalphabetic encipherment might be multiliteral elements of a first substitution, such as the left- and right-hand components of a bipartite substitution. This "plain text" may be considered either as a secondary or intermediate plain text, or as a primary encipherment; hereinafter we will use the expression "intermediate plain text" to describe this situation.

b. Periodic bipartite systems may take one of the following four principal forms:

(1) In the simplest form, a succession of n unrelated bipartite matrices is used cyclically to encipher the successive letters of a plaintext message.

(2) A single bipartite matrix with a fixed internal composition is used, the coordinates of which are slid in a manner giving rise to polyalphabetic substitution. For instance, if the row coordinates of a 5 x 5 matrix consisted of the digits 1–5 and the column coordinates consisted of the digits 6–0, the successive letters of the plain text might be enciphered with a cyclical shift of either the row or the column coordinates, or both.

(3) A single bipartite matrix with fixed internal composition and fixed coordinates is used, with a dinomic polyalphabetic substitution applied to the intermediate plain text. The dinomic substitution may involve encipherments interrelated in some manner, or entirely unrelated encipherments.

(4) A single bipartite matrix with fixed internal composition and fixed coordinates is used, with an *additive* superimposed on the primary encipherment to yield a polyalphabetic substitution. The addition of the key might involve either carrying addition, or noncarrying (i.e., mod 10) addition.

c. The following remarks are generalizations of the cryptanalytic attack on the foregoing systems:

(1) In the case under subpar. *b*(1), it is obvious that solution must be predicated on the recovery of the n different matrices involved. If there is no latent relationship among the various matrices, exploitation of such a system cannot be aided by any method of equating or correlating cipher values belonging to different matrices.

(2) In the case under subpar. *b*(2), an entering wedge might be forced into the system under the supposition that the matrices were unrelated; but if the frequency distributions for the row and column coordinates are closely examined, the phenomena associated with the use of sliding coordinates would soon manifest themselves and give an indication as to the true nature of the system under study, and thus could simplify the problem greatly.

(3) The case under subpar. $b(3)$ would have to be attacked as the general case under $b(1)$, above; any relationship among the coordinates uncovered between the different matrices could be exploited to reduce the problem to simplest cryptographic terms.

(4) The fourth case, that under subpar. $b(4)$, is the more general case of polyalphabetic bipartite systems. The techniques of solution are sufficiently detailed and specialized to warrant thorough treatment; this will be done in the paragraphs that follow.

81. Analysis of a simple case: the "Nihilist" cipher.—*a.* The first system we shall treat is that known in cryptologic literature as the "Nihilist" cipher,[1] so named because it was first used by anti-Tsarist factions in Russia in the latter part of the 19th century; the basic idea is so simple that it has been "invented" many times since. This system embraces a dinome substitution followed by a cyclic numerical key as an additive. The dinome substitution is accomplished by means of a 5 x 5 bipartite square in which a normal alphabet ($I=J$) is inscribed, the coordinates of which are the digits 1 to 5 in normal order; the plain text undergoes a primary encipherment, and to this encipherment is added (by *carrying* addition) a cyclic numerical key obtained by the encipherment of a key word with the basic matrix. Thus we have a polyalphabetic dinome encipherment with a period equal to the length of the key word.

b. An example of encipherment is given to illustrate this system. The basic matrix is that shown in Fig. 90; let the key word be WHITE, from which is derived the numerical key 52 23 24 44 15, and let the message be as follows: RESISTANCE ENCOUNTERED NORTH OF VILLAGE.

```
    1 2 3 4 5
  1 A B C D E
  2 F G H I K
  3 L M N O P
  4 Q R S T U
  5 V W X Y Z
```

FIGURE 90

The plain text is written on a width of five (i.e., equal to the length of the key word), and the primary bipartite encipherment accomplished as shown in Fig. 91a. The dinomes of the key are added to the dinomes of the primary encipherment, as shown in Fig. 91b. Note the four values in the fifth column in Fig. 91b in which the carrying addition gives a different result from that of the customary cryptographic noncarrying (or mod 10) addition.

---

[1] This is one of the several types of cipher systems known by the same name; this appellation has also been given to a kind of false double transposition, as well as to simple bipartite encipherment with the matrix in Fig. 90, without further complexities. This last system is still encountered occasionally in prisons for "grapevine" communications of the inmates.

```
Key word:   W   H   I   T   E                      W   H   I   T   E
                                     Additive:  52  23  24  44  15
         _____
P :  R   E   S   I   S                         R   E   S   I   S
C₁:  42  15  43  24  43                         42  15  43  24  43
                                     C₂:  94  38  67  68  58

     T   A   N   C   E                           T   A   N   C   E
     44  11  33  13  15                          44  11  33  13  15
                                                 96  34  57  57  30

     E   N   C   O   U                           E   N   C   O   U
     15  33  13  34  45                          15  33  13  34  45
                                                 67  56  37  78  60

     N   T   E   R   E                           N   T   E   R   E
     33  44  15  42  15                          33  44  15  42  15
                                                 85  67  39  86  30

     D   N   O   R   T                           D   N   O   R   T
     14  33  34  42  44                          14  33  34  42  44
                                                 66  56  58  86  59

     H   O   F   V   I                           H   O   F   V   I
     23  34  21  51  24                          23  34  21  51  24
                                                 75  57  45  95  39

     L   L   A   G   E                           L   L   A   G   E
     31  31  11  22  15                          31  31  11  22  15
                                                 83  54  35  66  30

        FIGURE 91a                                 FIGURE 91b
```

The final cipher text, if transmitted in dinome groupings, would be as follows:

94 38 67 68 58 96 34 57 57 30 67 56 37 78 60 85 67 39 86 30
66 56 58 86 59 75 57 45 95 39 83 54 35 66 30

Since the enciphering equation is $P+K=C$, the deciphering equation is $P=C-K$; thus in decipherment the key dinome must be subtracted (with *borrowing* subtraction) from the cipher text to yield the plaintext dinome.

c. It will be observed that the lowest possible cipher value is 22 (arising from A_p+A_k), and that the highest cipher value is 110 (arising from Z_p+Z_k). But in Nihilist encipherment the trinomes from 100 to 110 (excluding the impossible 101) are customarily treated as dinomes by dropping the first digit; no ambiguity is present because the lowest *bona fide* dinome is 22, thus an initial "0" or "1" at once indicates the special situation involved. The student should note that in the Nihilist system there are certain cipher dinomes which arise from a unique combination of plain+key; these are:

(1) $22 = A_p + A_k (= 11 + 11)$ only,

(2) $30 = E_p + E_k (= 15 + 15)$ only,

(3) $02 = V_p + V_k (= 51 + 51)$ only, and

(4) $10 = Z_p + Z_k (= 55 + 55)$ only.

The first two dinomes, 22 and 30, can occur quite frequently, but the other two have a much smaller probability of occurrence.[2] A further observation in the Nihilist system is that if the units digit of a cipher dinome is $\emptyset$, it could have arisen only from a plaintext 5 enciphered by a key of 5; and if either the units or the tens digit of a cipher dinome is 2, it could have arisen only from a plaintext 1 enciphered by a key of 1. These points are very helpful in analysis, as will subsequently be seen.

d. The classic Nihilist system may be recognized by the virtual absence of the digit "1"; this digit cannot occur at all in the units position of dinomes, and in the tens position it can occur only in the very rare case where Z_p is enciphered by Z_k, resulting in the dinome 10. The usual principles of factoring apply of course to a Nihilist cipher; the period will be a factor of the interval between two occurrences of a long repetition, and the ϕ test may be used to confirm a tentative period. But in the Nihilist cipher, advantage may be taken of its cryptographic idiosyncrasies to permit factoring a cryptogram much more quickly than would be possible with the usual procedures, and to enable factoring a much shorter message than would otherwise be possible with the usual procedures for the determination of the period. The specific location in a cryptogram of cipher dinomes 22, 30, 02, and 10 may furnish clues not only as to possible periods, but also as to *impossible* periods. For instance, if a pair of 22's is found 24 dinomes apart, the period may be taken to be one of the factors of 24 (unless of course there is more than one A in the key word); conversely, if a 22 is found at a distance of 45 dinomes from a 30, the period cannot possibly be 5 or 9, since a 22 is predicated upon a key of 11 and a 30 is contingent upon a key of 15, and thus there would be a clash of key values if the cipher were written out on a width of either 5 or 9.

e. Once a Nihilist cipher is recognized as such, the easiest line of attack is by capitalizing on the cryptographic weaknesses of the system. These points are enumerated below:

(1) The distance between two *identical* dinomes of the (22, 30, 02, 10) class will be a multiple of the period, unless there are repeated letters in the key word.

(2) The interval between two *different* dinomes of the (22, 30, 02, 10) class *cannot* be a multiple of the period, since the keys involved must be different.

(3) The maximum difference between the units digits of dinomes enciphered by the same key is 4. Since the maximum *plaintext* difference is 4 (i.e., 5–1), the addition of a key digit from 1 to 5 will not alter this characteristic in the cipher text. For instance, in the key of C(13), $E_p(15)$ becomes 28, and $F_p(21)$ becomes 34; the difference between the cipher dinomes (treating the units and the tens positions separately) is 14, which is the same as the difference between plaintext 15 and 21.

(4) The maximum difference between the tens digits of dinomes enciphered by the same key is also 4, if allowance is made for situations wherein the units digit is a $\emptyset$, in which case, for example, a cipher dinome 40 must be treated as (3, 10) for the tens and units positions, respectively. For instance, in the key of E(15), $E_p(15)$ becomes 30, and $F_p(21)$ becomes 36; cipher 30 must however be treated as (2, 10) in the tens and units positions, so that the difference between (2, 10) and 36 is 14, which is the same as the difference between plaintext 15 and 21.

(5) From items (3) and (4), it therefore follows that if the difference between two cipher dinomes is 5 or more in either the units or the tens position, the dinomes cannot possibly belong

---

[2] Since the key in the Nihilist system is derived from plain text, the probability of a 30 occurring is the square of the probability of E_p in English, i.e., $(.1300)^2$ or .0169; the probability of a 22 is .0054; the probability of an 02 is .0002; and the probability of a 10 is only .000001.

to the same cipher alphabet. It also follows that if a difference of 5 or more is found in either the units or the tens position, this rules out a Nihilist cipher with a single dinome as key, i.e., a monoalphabetically enciphered dinome system.

(6) In Fig. 92, below, is given a table of possible key digits derivable from the range of low-high cipher digits in the Nihilist system. As an illustration of its use, let us say that in a particular column of a factored Nihilist message the lowest tens (or units) digit is a 5, the highest a 9; from the table, it is seen that the only key digit possible is 4. If on the other hand the lowest tens (or units) digit were a 4, the highest a 7, it is seen that the key is not unique, but must be either a 2 or a 3.

Highest cipher digit

Lowest cipher digit	2	3	4	5	6	7	8	9	Ø
2	1	1	1	1	1				
3		1,2	1,2	1,2	1,2	2			
4			1,2,3	1,2,3	1,2,3	2,3	3		
5				1,2 3,4	1,2 3,4	2,3,4	3,4	4	
6					1,2,3 4,5	2,3 4,5	3,4,5	4,5	5
7						2,3 4,5	3,4,5	4,5	5
8							3,4,5	4,5	5
9								4,5	5
Ø									5

FIGURE 92.

(7) Once several key digits have been established, either uniquely or with variants, it is possible to recover the entire literal key by anagramming among the choices of key possibilities. Even if the numerical key is not derived from a Nihilist encipherment of a plaintext word, the unique key values established can be used to decipher the particular columns pertaining to this key, and a selection from among the other multiple keys can be made on the basis of weights of trial plaintext decipherments; the weights used may be either monographic or digraphic weights.

211

f. It is time to try out theory in practice. Let us assume the enemy has been using the Nihilist system with periods up to 20, and that we have at hand the following cryptogram:

```
57  59  55  49  66  66  84  26  74  48  98  59  25  48  26  30  48  77  55  45
76  57  99  30  56  30  27  48  67  86  86  34  65  45  78  39  45  46  28  39
55  67  86  32  55  75  70  59  66  49  27  26  76  67  54  22  56  39  97
```

The cipher text is scanned, and it is noted that a 30 is found as the 16th, 24th, and 26th dinomes, and that there is a 22 in the 56th dinome. From the first 30 to the 22 is an interval of 40; from the second 30 to the 22 is an interval of 32; and from the third 30 to the 22 is an interval of 30. From this we determine that the period of the cryptogram cannot be any of the factors of 40, 32, or 30, so this rules out 2, 3, 4, 5, 8, 10, 15, 16, and 20 as possible periods. The intervals between the three 30's are 2, 8, and 10—but since these possible periods have been eliminated no encouragement is obtained from these intervals, fraught as they are with naught.

(1) Rather than write out the cipher text in various widths, we will try to reject trial periods on the basis of differences of 5 or more in the tens or units digits, using a short-cut procedure. Assuming first a period of 6, we examine the first and seventh dinomes, the 2d and 8th dinomes, etc., until we come to the 7th and 13th positions where the dinomes 84 and 25 have a difference of 6 in the tens digits, causing us to reject the hypothesis of a period of 6. A period of 7 is assumed, and this too is quickly rejected from the 2d and 9th positions where the dinomes 59 and 74 have a difference of 5 in the units digits. 9 is rejected as a period from the 7th and 16th positions, where the dinomes 84 and 30 have a difference of 5 in the tens digits, and a period of 11 is rejected from the 13th and 24th positions, where the dinome 25 could not have been homogeneous with 30, since we know 30 *must* come from a key of 15 (see subpar. *c*, above). When we try a period of 12, no inconsistencies develop, so we assume that this is the correct period.

(2) The cryptogram is written out on a width of 12, and the four columns containing the unique dinomes 30 and 22 are deciphered at once, as is shown in Fig. 93, below:

```
Key:      15        15              11              15
       57  59  55  49  66  66  84  26  74  48  98  59
           44        34              15              44
           T         O               E               T
       25  48  26  30  48  77  55  45  76  57  99  30
           33        15              34              15
           N         E               O               E
       56  30  27  48  67  86  86  34  65  45  78  39
           15        33              23              24
           E         N               H               I
       45  46  28  39  55  67  86  32  55  75  70  59
           31        24              21              44
           L         I               F               T
       66  49  27  26  76  67  54  22  56  39  97
           34        11              11
           O         A               A
```

FIGURE 93

The key for the tenth column can be determined uniquely, since the range of the low-high digits (3–7) in the tens position indicates a key of 2, and the range (5–9) in the units position indicates

212

a key of **4**. Furthermore, the presence of the digit 2 in the tens positions of the first and third columns fixes the key as 1 in these positions, and the presence of the digit Ø in the units position of the 11th column fixes the key in this position as 5. The keys for the rest of the positions are not unique; by referring to the table of Fig. 92, the keys (with multiple values included) are found to be as follows:

```
                          2
      2              33  1      21
      3      3      23 44 32    32      4
     14  15  14  15 34 55 43 11 43 24 55 15
```

(3) Since there are only three key possibilities (12, 13, or 14) for the first column, we will make trial decipherments and score these decipherments with the deciban weights with which the student is now familiar (cf. subpars. 34*c* and *f*). This information is shown in the diagram below:

Trial key of 12		Trial key of 13		Trial key of 14	
	Wgt.		Wgt.		Wgt.
45		44		43	
U	6	T	9	S	8
13		12		11	
C	7	B	4	A	8
44		43		42	
T	9	S	8	R	8
33		32		31	
N	8	M	6	L	7
54		53		52	
Y	6	X	3	W	5
Scores:	36		30		36

With such scanty data of only five letters available per column, the deciban scores are not immediately conclusive; apparently the keys of 12 and 14 are equally good, with the key of 13 a third choice. However, since the second column of Fig. 93 has been deciphered, a much more sensitive discrimination among the three key possibilities for the first column may be obtained by the use of *digraphic* weights. The three sets of digraphs formed by the three possible decipherments of column 1 taken with the decipherment of column 2 are shown in the diagram below, together with the centiban weights of the digraphs (cf. Table 15 on p. 285 of *Military Cryptanalytics, Part I*).

Case I		Case II		Case III	
UT	58	TT	67	ST	88
CN	13	BN	00	AN	89
TE	91	SE	84	RE	96
NL	42	ML	00	LL	73
YO	55	XO	13	WO	67
Scores:	259		164		413

It is clear from the high score of 413 that Case III has the best statistical probability [3] of being the correct case; thus the key for the first column should be 14. This process could be continued with other columns where necessary, until sufficiently long plaintext polygraphs are deciphered to permit finishing the solution by contextual analysis. The message is found to begin with the words STRONG RESISTANCE and the key is now derived uniquely.

(4) When the key has been derived from the bipartite encipherment with the Nihilist square of a plaintext word, another approach is via the anagramming of the key word from the multiple possiblities; this is especially easy when the data are sufficient to reduce the number of multiple values. In the case just studied the key recovered in subpar. 81*f*(2) is given below, together with the multiple keyletter values involved:

				2						
				33	1		21			
2										
3	3		23	44	32		32		4	
14	15	14	15	34	55	43	11	43	24	55	15

B	E	C	E	H	M	L	A	F	I	U	E
C		D		I	N	M		G		Z	
D				N	O	N		H			
				O	P	Q		L			
				R	R			M			
				S	S			N			
				T				Q			
				U				R			
				W				S			
				X							
				Y							
				Z							

A few moments' inspection of the beginning and ending portions establishes that the key word is DECENTRALIZE.

g. We have seen how simple it is to solve a Nihilist cipher if the square is known. If the square had the row and column coordinates in an unknown permutation of the digits 1–5, or if the internal composition of the square consisted of an unknown mixed sequence, solution is hardly more difficult, as will now be demonstrated.

(1) Let us consider the following Nihilist cryptogram enciphered with a modified square:

```
87 53 74 67 49 48 66 55 66 87 42 65 57 58 76 45 66 75 75 74
67 75 58 48 44 62 86 75 35 65 64 36 46 56 56 66 87 36 96 68
58 48 46 85 59 97 55 85 68 78 87 36 62 87 97 54 96 84 47 48
44 56 66 87 52 06 65 38 49 66 55 67 98 55 96 68 66 55 46 84
67 07 45 96 85 68 67 44 84 65 86 54 07 86 56 87 24 62 67 99
53 95 87 50 77 56 74 59 68 73 96 68
```

There are no occurrences of the unique dinomes 22, 30, 02, or 10, nor are there any readily discernible long polygraphic repetitions; nevertheless factoring is very easy by the process of inspec-

---

[3] Case III is better than Case I by a factor of $224^{1.54} = 4163$; that is, the difference between 413 and 259, treated as an exponent of the base (224) of the logarithmic weights.

tion outlined in subpar. $f(1)$, above. All periods between 1 and 20 are eliminated, except 9 and 18, so it is assumed that 9 is the correct period and the cryptogram is written out as is shown below:

1	2	3	4	5	6	7	8	9
87	53	74	67	49	48	66	55	66
87	42	65	57	58	76	45	66	75
75	74	67	75	58	48	44	62	86
75	35	65	64	36	46	56	56	66
87	36	96	68	58	48	46	85	59
97	55	85	68	78	87	36	62	87
97	54	96	84	47	48	44	56	66
87	52	06	65	38	49	66	55	67
98	55	96	68	66	55	46	84	67
07	45	96	85	68	67	44	84	65
86	54	07	86	56	87	24	62	67
99	53	95	87	50	77	56	74	59
68	73	96	68					

(2) Referring to the table of Fig. 92, it may be seen that the keys for the columns must be as follows:

Cols.:	1	2	3	4	5	6	7	8	9
Keys:	54	21	52	33	25	34	11	31	34
			53	43			12	41	44
							13		

Since the keys for cols. 1, 2, 5, and 6 are unique, these keys are subtracted from the corresponding cipher dinomes to yield a *reduction to monoalphabetic terms*. This reduction is shown below:

Cols.:	1	2	3	4	5	6	7	8	9
Keys:	54	21			25	34			
	33	32			24	14			
	33	21			33	42			
	21	53			33	14			
	21	14			11	12			
	33	15			33	14			
	43	34			53	53			
	43	33			22	14			
	33	31			13	15			
	44	34			41	21			
	53	24			43	33			
	32	33			31	53			
	45	32			25	43			
	14	52							

The distributions for these columns are given below:

Col. 1:

Col. 2:

11 12 13 14 15 21 22 23 24 25 31 32 33 34 35 41 42 43 44 45 51 52 53 54 55

Col. 5:

Col. 6:

11 12 13 14 15 21 22 23 24 25 31 32 33 34 35 41 42 43 44 45 51 52 53 54 55

The ϕ counts for col. 1 (16) and col. 6 (14) are excellent, but those for col. 2 (6) and col. 5 (6) are very poor. Nevertheless, the χ test performed between the distributions for cols. 1 and 2, and between cols. 1 and 5, give excellent results, thereby indicating that they belong together. The combined distribution of cols. 1, 2, 5, and 6 is as follows:

11 12 13 14 15 21 22 23 24 25 31 32 33 34 35 41 42 43 44 45 51 52 53 54 55   N = 50

The I.C. of this distribution [4] is $\dfrac{25\Sigma f(f-1)}{50\times49}=1.82$, which is excellent.

(3) The key for col. 3 is either 52 or 53; what we will do now is make trial decipherments of col. 3 with both of these keys, and we will compare these decipherments with the combined distribution of cols. 1, 2, 5, and 6 to find the best match. This is shown below:

Col. 3:
(k=52)

11 12 13 14 15 21 22 23 24 25 31 32 33 34 35 41 42 43 44 45 51 52 53 54 55

Col. 3:
(k=53)

11 12 13 14 15 21 22 23 24 25 31 32 33 34 35 41 42 43 44 45 51 52 53 54 55

The key of 52 gives a χ value of 24, and the key of 53 gives a χ value of 41; this shows that the key for col. 3 should be 53.

(4) The entire tabulation of trial keys for the five nonunique columns are given below, together with the χ values as compared with the combined distribution of cols. 1, 2, 5, and 6.

─────────

[4] In this case, we must remember that a *25*-element alphabet is involved and modify the formula for the I.C. accordingly.

Col. Key		11	12	13	14	15	21	22	23	24	25	31	32	33	34	35	41	42	43	44	45	51	5	53	54	55	x
		1	1	1	6	2	4	1		2	1	2	3	10	2		1	1	4	1	1		1	5			
3	52		2		1		1							1				1·	5						1	1	24
	53		2		1		1						1					1	5						1	1	41
4	33									1	1		1	5			1		1	1	1		1				13
	43				1	1				1	5		1				1	1	1	1							27
7	11		1							1			3	1	2				2							2	36
	12	1								1			3	1	2				2						2		28
	13	1							1				3	1	2				2					2			48
8	31									2	2	3		1				1							2	1	26
	41				2	2	3						1					1		2	1						48
9	34									2	1	3	3		1					1	1						49
	44							2	1	3	3			1				1	1								18

From the foregoing, it is evident that the keys for the nine columns are as follows:

1	2	3	4	5	6	7	8	9
54	21	53	43	25	34	13	41	34

(5) All nine columns of the cryptogram may now be reduced to monoalphabetic terms, as follows:

```
33 32 21 24 24 14 53 14 32
33 21 12 14 33 42 32 25 41
21 53 14 32 33 14 31 21 52
21 14 12 21 11 12 43 15 32
33 15 43 25 33 14 33 44 25
43 34 32 25 53 53 23 21 53
43 33 43 41 22 14 31 15 32
33 31 53 25 13 15 53 14 33
44 34 43 25 41 21 33 43 33
53 24 43 42 43 33 31 43 31
32 33 54 43 31 53 11 21 33
45 32 42 44 25 43 43 33 25
14 52 43 25
```

The simple dinome substitution is readily solvable, and the plain text is found to begin with the words NO ADDITIONAL. The square as recovered is shown in Fig. 94a; upon observing the phenomena characteristic of a keyword-mixed sequence inside the square, we permute the

	1	2	3	4	5
1	B	L	U	I	C
2	A	Y	H	D	R
3	S	O	N	P	
4	M	F	E	G	K
5		V	T	W	

FIGURE 94a

	3	2	4	5	1
2	H	Y	D	R	A
1	U	L	I	C	B
4	E	F	G	K	M
3	N	O	P	Q	S
5	T	V	W	X	Z

FIGURE 94b

rows and columns of the reconstruction square to yield the original enciphering square as shown in Fig. 94b. The additive key, when deciphered through the reconstructed square, is found to be based on WATER PUMP.

82. Analysis of a more complicated example.—*a.* In the next case to be considered, it will be assumed that the enemy is known to be using various types of dinome matrices in conjunction with an additive superencipherment, the arithmetic being performed mod 10. The following message has been intercepted:

```
91 67 92 80 74 71 05 60 80 36 99 87 80 10 49 64 39 92 73 64
53 88 26 46 61 67 17 52 37 91 57 17 88 50 95 15 75 21 02 61
76 35 39 58 58 72 96 86 58 47 21 77 00 99 79 50 65 21 72 16
56 47 20 61 16 26 60 59 29 00 90 57 08 43 60 24 42 00 72 76
73 37 79 78 44 31 17 91 04 07 06 70 17 13 19 31 65 38 33 31
63 88 90 10 94 63 82 29 72 62 03 66 38 40 00 56 75 87 83 76
95 02 52 48 87 03 05 03 60 16 28 79 68 04 07 92 72 86 30 00
98 35 58 13 67 26 05 52 78 67 63 70 48 77 16 23 17 88 50 95
15 72 22 34 31 99 44 37 80 48 51 77 91 03 30 64 40 69 41 25
35 85 83 73 02 64 15 86 30 41
```

The polygraphic repetition present at an interval of 125 dinomes suggests that the basic period is five dinomes (i.e., a 10-digit additive sequence). Since the message above is already written on a width of 20 dinomes, it will be convenient to make a distribution of the 10 columns, as follows:

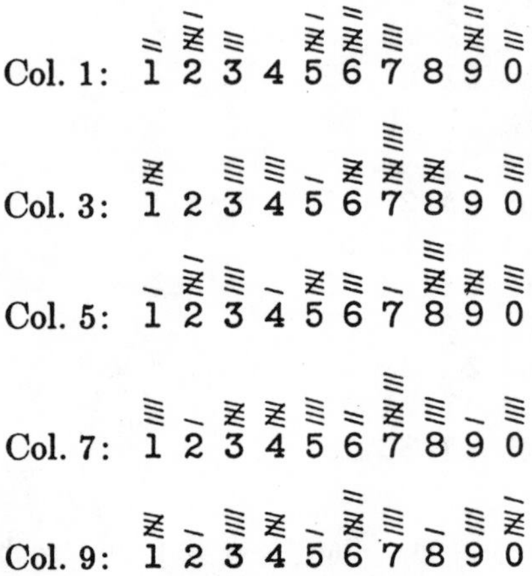

Col. 1: 1 2 3 4 5 6 7 8 9 0   Col. 2: 1 2 3 4 5 6 7 8 9 0

Col. 3: 1 2 3 4 5 6 7 8 9 0   Col. 4: 1 2 3 4 5 6 7 8 9 0

Col. 5: 1 2 3 4 5 6 7 8 9 0   Col. 6: 1 2 3 4 5 6 7 8 9 0

Col. 7: 1 2 3 4 5 6 7 8 9 0   Col. 8: 1 2 3 4 5 6 7 8 9 0

Col. 9: 1 2 3 4 5 6 7 8 9 0   Col. 10: 1 2 3 4 5 6 7 8 9 0

FIGURE 95a   FIGURE 95b

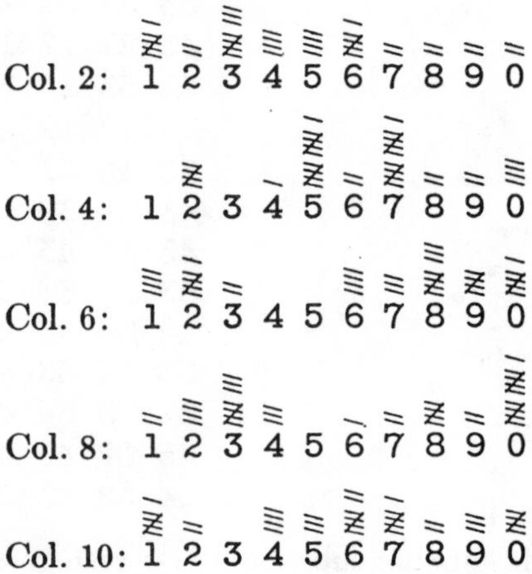

b. It will be observed that the foregoing distributions may be classed into two families, one comprising the odd columns and the other comprising the even columns;[5] the reason for this is that the frequencies of the row coordinates of the underlying matrix have a distinct pattern

---

[5] Note that this is further proof that the underlying text is in dinomes. If the intermediate plaintext had consisted of trinomes, or monomes and dinomes, the columnar distributions would not have fallen into two families; instead there would have been only one family discernible, and solution would progress by matching all the distributions together, without regard to their parity. See in this connection subpar. 86g.

218

of peaks and troughs, and likewise the frequencies of the column coordinates have a distinct pattern, different from that of the row coordinates. The addition, mod 10, of a key digit merely displaces the entire pattern of peaks and troughs, just as in a standard alphabet cipher a change of key letter displaces the distribution by the value of the key letter (mod 26).[6] Therefore the distributions within each of the families may be slid to find the best match, and we have the following:

Col. 1: 1 2 3 4 5 6 7 8 9 0   Col. 2: 1 2 3 4 5 6 7 8 9 0

Col. 3: 2 3 4 5 6 7 8 9 0 1   Col. 4: 5 6 7 8 9 0 1 2 3 4

Col. 5: 4 5 6 7 8 9 0 1 2 3   Col. 6: 6 7 8 9 0 1 2 3 4 5

Col. 7: 9 0 1 2 3 4 5 6 7 8   Col. 8: 8 9 0 1 2 3 4 5 6 7

Col. 9: 5 6 7 8 9 0 1 2 3 4   Col. 10: 4 5 6 7 8 9 0 1 2 3

FIGURE 96a   FIGURE 96b

c. The relative displacements of the odd columns, in terms of col. 1, are 0, 1, 3, 8, and 4; the relative displacements of the even columns, in terms of col. 2, are 0, 4, 5, 7, and 3. Therefore if we arbitrarily treat the additive for the first dinome as 00, the second dinome has a relative key of 14, the third dinome a relative key of 35, the fourth a key of 87, and the fifth

---

[6] Mod 10 addition is really a digital version of a Vigenère table with standard alphabets, as will be seen from the following diagram:

Plaintext digit

	0	1	2	3	4	5	6	7	8	9
0	0	1	2	3	4	5	6	7	8	9
1	1	2	3	4	5	6	7	8	9	0
2	2	3	4	5	6	7	8	9	0	1
3	3	4	5	6	7	8	9	0	1	2
4	4	5	6	7	8	9	0	1	2	3
5	5	6	7	8	9	0	1	2	3	4
6	6	7	8	9	0	1	2	3	4	5
7	7	8	9	0	1	2	3	4	5	6
8	8	9	0	1	2	3	4	5	6	7
9	9	0	1	2	3	4	5	6	7	8

Key digit / Cipher

a key of **43**.[7] The key digits are subtracted from the cipher, to yield a reduction in terms of the first of the five dinome columns.   This is illustrated in the work sheet below:

Additive: <u>00 14 35 87 43</u> <u>00 14 35 87 43</u> <u>00 14 35 87 43</u> <u>00 14 35 87 43</u>

Cipher text: 91 67 92 80 74 71 05 60 80 36 99 87 80 10 49 64 39 92 73 64

Plain text: 91 53 67 03 31 71 91 35 03 93 99 73 55 33 06 64 25 67 96 21

```
          53 88 26 46 61   67 17 52 37 91   57 17 88 50 95   15 75 21 02 61
          53 74 91 69 28   67 03 27 50 58   57 03 53 73 52   15 61 96 25 28

          76 35 39 58 58   72 96 86 58 47   21 77 00 99 79   50 65 21 72 16
          76 21 14 71 15   72 82 51 71 04   21 63 75 12 36   50 51 96 95 73

          56 47 20 61 16   26 60 59 29 00   90 57 08 43 60   24 42 00 72 76
          56 33 95 84 73   26 56 24 42 67   90 43 73 66 27   24 38 75 95 33

          73 37 79 78 44   31 17 91 04 07   06 70 17 13 19   31 65 38 33 31
          73 23 40 91 01   31 03 66 27 64   06 66 82 36 76   31 51 03 56 98

          63 88 90 10 94   63 82 29 72 62   03 66 38 40 00   56 75 87 83 76
          63 74 65 33 51   63 78 94 95 29   03 52 03 63 67   56 61 52 06 33

          95 02 52 48 87   03 05 03 60 16   28 79 68 04 07   92 72 86 30 00
          95 98 27 61 44   03 91 78 83 73   28 65 33 27 64   92 68 51 53 67

          98 35 58 13 67   26 05 52 78 67   63 70 48 77 16   23 17 88 50 95
          98 21 23 36 24   26 91 27 91 24   63 66 13 90 73   23 03 53 73 52

          15 72 22 34 31   99 44 37 80 48   51 77 91 03 30   64 40 69 41 25
          15 68 97 57 98   99 30 02 03 05   51 63 66 26 97   64 36 34 64 82

          35 85 83 73 02   64 15 86 30 41
          35 71 58 96 69   64 01 51 53 08
```

FIGURE 97

d. A dinome distribution is now taken on the pseudo-plain text; this is as follows:

	1	2	3	4	5	6	7	8	9	0	
1		1	1	2	3						7
2	4		3	4	2	3	6	3	1		26
3	3		6	1	2	4		1		1	18
4		1	1	1						1	4
5	7	4	6		1	4	2	2		2	28
6	3		6	6	2	5	6	2	2		32
7	4	1	9	2	2	2		2			22
8		3	1	1							5
9	7	1	1	1	5	4	2	4	2	2	29
0	2	1	11		1	3		1			19
	30	12	45	18	18	25	16	15	5	6	

FIGURE 98

[7] This relative additive differs from the true additive by a dinome constant.

Matching propensities are detected among the rows of the matrix, but not among the columns; this points to the possibility of a variant matrix of 10 columns and perhaps three rows. This assumption is strengthened by the local variation among the distributions for the even columns in Fig. 95b (these variations being a direct function of the plain text being enciphered), and by the pronounced similarity of the distributions for the odd digits in Fig. 95a (the similarity of these distributions being caused by a "check-off" procedure in the variant usage).

e. We note in Fig. 98 that rows 1, 4, and 8 are homogeneous and that therefore they belong to one family. Row 6, with 32 tallies, is the row with the heaviest distribution; therefore we shall begin by taking the cross-products sum of row 6 with the remaining six rows that come into consideration (excluding the 1–4–8 family).[8] This is shown in the diagram below:

	1	2	3	4	5	6	7	8	9	Ø	
$\chi(6,2)$:	12	–	18	24	4	15	36	6	2	–	= 117
$\chi(6,3)$:	9	–	36	6	4	20	–	2	–	–	= 77
$\chi(6,5)$:	21	–	36	–	2	20	12	4	–	–	= 95
$\chi(6,7)$:	12	–	54	12	4	10	–	4	–	–	= 96
$\chi(6,9)$:	21	–	6	6	10	20	12	8	4	–	= 87
$\chi(6,0)$:	6	–	66	–	2	15	–	2	–	–	= 91

It is clear that there is an outstandingly good match between row 6 and row 2, so these rows belong to the same family. The other χ values are less clear, except for the outstandingly low value of the match 6–3, which indicates that 3 is in a *different* family.

f. We now compare row 3 with the remaining four rows, and we get the following:

	1	2	3	4	5	6	7	8	9	Ø	
$\chi(3,5)$:	21	–	36	–	2	16	–	2	–	2	= 79
$\chi(3,7)$:	12	–	54	2	4	8	–	2	–	–	= 82
$\chi(3,9)$:	21	–	6	1	10	16	–	4	–	2	= 60
$\chi(3,0)$:	6	–	66	–	2	12	–	1	–	–	= 87

From this we see that row 3 and row Ø undoubtedly belong together, and that in all probability row 9 (the lowest χ value) does not belong with 3 and Ø; this would imply that row 9 belongs with rows 2 and 6, since the family of 1–4–8 is distinctive enough to permit no other additions. However, we shall leave this decision to one more test.

g. The only rows left to place are the 5, 7, and 9 rows. In order to facilitate the matching of these rows with the rows of the 2–6 and the 3–0 families, we will first amalgamate the members of the families as we have them so far so that we may have more typical distributions for these families; this amalgamation is as follows:

	1	2	3	4	5	6	7	8	9	Ø
α = (1+4+8):	–	5	3	4	3	–	–	–	–	1
β = (2+6):	7	–	9	10	4	8	12	5	3	–
γ = (3+0):	5	1	17	1	3	7	–	2	–	1

---

[8] See also pp. 112–113 of *Military Cryptanalytics, Part I*, in connection with the use of the cross-products sum in the analysis of a variant system.

We will now take the cross-products sum between the β row and rows 5, 7, and 9; and likewise between the γ row and rows 5, 7, and 9.   This yields the following:

	1	2	3	4	5	6	7	8	9	Ø	
$\chi(\beta,5)$:	49	–	54	–	4	32	24	10	–	–	= 173
$\chi(\beta,7)$:	28	–	81	20	8	16	–	10	–	–	= 163
$\chi(\beta,9)$:	49	–	9	10	20	32	24	20	6	–	= 170
$\chi(\gamma,5)$:	35	4	102	–	3	28	–	4	–	2	= 178
$\chi(\gamma,7)$:	20	1	153	2	6	14	–	4	–	–	= 200
$\chi(\gamma,9)$:	35	1	17	1	15	28	–	8	–	2	= 107

It is apparent that row 7 belongs to the γ family, since $\chi(\gamma,7)$ has the high value of 200 whereas the $\chi(\beta,7)$ has the much lower score of 163.   Furthermore, the lowest score of 107 for $\chi(\gamma,9)$ when compared with the value of 170 for $\chi(\beta,9)$ confirms that row 9 belongs with the β family rather than with the γ family.   The family relationship of row 5 is still indeterminate statistically, because the methods we are using do not have sufficient discriminatory power for us to be able to place row 5 with any confidence.   Our consolidated frequency distribution (less the tallies of row 5) now looks as follows:

	1	2	3	4	5	6	7	8	9	Ø
148	–	5	3	4	3	–	–	–	–	1
269	14	1	10	11	9	12	14	9	5	2
370	9	2	26	3	5	9	–	4	–	1

h. We will now convert the intermediate text of Fig. 97 to true monoalphabetic terms using the consolidated frequency matrix just obtained, calling the three rows "1", "2", and "3". The dinomes beginning with the digit 5 we will leave unchanged, since we do not know the relationship of this row. This conversion is shown in Fig. 99, below.

```
91 53 67 03 31 71 91 35 03 93 99 73 55 33 06 64 25 67 96 21
21    27 33 31 31 21 35 33 23 29 33    33 36 24 25 27 26 21

53 74 91 69 28 67 03 27 50 58 57 03 53 73 52 15 61 96 25 28
   34 21 29 28 27 33 27          33    33    15 21 26 25 28

76 21 14 71 15 72 82 51 71 04 21 63 75 12 36 50 51 96 95 73
36 21 14 31 15 32 12    31 34 21 23 35 12 36       26 25 33

56 33 95 84 73 26 56 24 42 67 90 43 73 66 27 24 38 75 95 33
   33 25 14 33 26    24 12 27 20 13 33 26 27 24 38 35 25 33

73 23 40 91 01 31 03 66 27 64 06 66 82 36 76 31 51 03 56 98
33 23 10 21 31 31 33 26 27 24 36 26 12 36 36 31    33    28

63 74 65 33 51 63 78 94 95 29 03 52 03 63 67 56 61 52 06 33
23 34 25 33    23 38 24 25 29 33    33 23 27    21    36 33

95 98 27 61 44 03 91 78 83 73 28 65 33 27 64 92 68 51 53 67
25 28 27 21 14 33 21 38 13 33 28 25 33 27 24 22 28          27

98 21 23 36 24 26 91 27 91 24 63 66 13 90 73 23 03 53 73 52
28 21 23 36 24 26 21 27 21 24 23 26 13 20 33 23 33    33    →

15 68 97 57 98 99 30 02 03 05 51 63 66 26 97 64 36 34 64 82
15 28 27    28 29 30 32 33 35    23 26 26 27 24 36 34 24 12

35 71 58 96 69 64 01 51 53 08
35 31    26 29 24 31       38
```

FIGURE 99

223

The dinome of outstanding frequency, **33**, may be assumed to be E_p; this, coupled with the idiomorphic pattern of the message beginning, establishes that the first word is INTELLIGENCE and places the "5" row in the 2–6–9 family. The text is easily solved, and a reconstruction matrix obtained as shown in Fig. 100*a*, which may be permuted into the matrix shown in Fig. 100*b*.

```
          1 2 3 4 5 6 7 8 9 Ø                    2 4 3 8 5 9 0 1 6 7
     148 | U   W V Y         |             2569 | M O N A R C H I S T |
    2569 | I M N O R S T A C H|              370 | B D E F G J K L P Q |
     370 | L B E D G   P   F K|              148 | U V W X Y Z         |
```

FIGURE 100*a*   FIGURE 100*b*

i. A closer examination of the sequence of digits comprising the column coordinates reveals that, if we subtract 7 (mod 10) from each of these digits, we will have a numerical key based upon the key word MONARCHIST—in other words, we are able to reduce the even digits of the dinome additives to their primary instead of relative equivalents. It will also be discovered that if 5 is subtracted from the digits comprising the row coordinates, we will get an assembly of digits that can be put into a logical numerical order which undoubtedly is the original set of row coordinates; or, if the lateral differences (called in cryptologic language the "deltas") between the dinomes of the relative additive key 00 14 35 87 43 are examined, the delta sequence 14 21 52 66 is the same as the dinome delta sequence of the numerical key based on MONARCHIST. This now proves the original primary enciphering matrix, as well as the original primary additive key. The true additive key is 57 61 82 34 90, and the original matrix is that shown in Fig. 100*c*, below.

```
          5 7 6 1 8 2 3 4 9 0
    0741 | M O N A R C H I S T |
     852 | B D E F G J K L P Q |
     963 | U V W X Y Z         |
```

FIGURE 100*c*

j. We have shown (in subpars. *b* and *c*) with this problem only one method of equating columns of additive-enciphered dinome text. In the next paragraph there will be shown several other methods applicable for reducing polyalphabetically enciphered dinome text to simple (i.e., monoalphabetic) terms, without regard to the mechanics used to produce the dinome intermediate text.

83. Analysis of syllabary square systems with superencipherment.—*a*. A logical extension of the idea of bipartite systems with encipherment is a system wherein the original plaintext is first enciphered with a syllabary square or a code chart, followed by a superimposed additive upon the primary encipherment. In the problem next to be considered, we will assume that the enemy is using the syllabary square illustrated in Fig. 101, below, in conjunction with a cyclic additive. For this first situation we will assume that the coordinates are known sequences, and that they are the digits 1–Ø in normal order.

	1	2	3	4	5	6	7	8	9	Ø
1	A	1	AL	AN	AND	AR	ARE	AS	AT	ATE
2	ATI	B	2	BE	C	3	CA	CE	CO	COM
3	D	4	DA	DE	E	5	EA	ED	EN	ENT
4	ER	ERE	ERS	ES	EST	F	6	G	7	H
5	8	HAS	HE	I	9	IN	ING	ION	IS	IT
6	IVE	J	Ø	K	L	LA	LE	M	ME	N
7	ND	NE	NT	O	OF	ON	OR	OU	P	Q
8	R	RA	RE	RED	RES	RI	RO	S	SE	SH
9	ST	STO	T	TE	TED	TER	TH	THE	THI	THR
Ø	TI	TO	U	V	VE	W	WE	X	Y	Z

FIGURE 101

b. The following cryptogram is available for study:

```
72 99 32 93 76 12 12 81 66 34 32 28 49 43 32 00 43 22 28 99
80 01 59 97 31 57 97 26 47 39 25 14 62 63 49 53 76 12 12 81
66 20 37 96 71 24 16 00 61 61 95 13 68 12 41 51 97 28 23 89
85 43 04 90 74 61 41 60 47 33 31 33 24 78 72 47 40 76 41 78
39 41 86 11 74 05 41 60 47 33 31 78 62 57 37 38 02 22 04 99
67 43 09 31 41 65 95 80 70 39 25 03 85 43 77 15 04 99 22 98
22 09 26 21 62 48 46 72 41 52 14 60 76 03 62 76 58 31 47 47
95 55 64 76 58 39 82 60 49 70 12 19 46 85 62 21 09 75 23 89
74 73 80 38 75 12 93 24 31 09 56 03 99 28 55 33 47 55 80 96
51 96 74 53 52 47 50 91 62 26 93 44 04 38 09 60 67 18 14 24
28 10 04 57 18 67 77 62 67 70 08 90 74 43 23 25 71 67 64 96
72 32 12 41 58 40 37 74 28 99 08 38 58 28 93 31 33 48 64 62
61 55 37 87 96 52 58 57 28 66 37 33 51 32 61 82 43 22 51 04
49 52 64 76 58 39 74 08 98 82 46 47 46 05 61 87 21 83 06 05
22 78 12 87 50 36 61 82 18 75 34 53 96 55 14 94 91 67 51 29
66 73 04 90 74 14 36 03 71 66 37 68 96 39 23 56 86 85 12 87
71 49 76 00 04 77 23 15 62 26 93 97 67 43 09 31 41 81 87 27
76 05 14 96 62 15 77 70 60 08 49 82 96 32 82 03 72 09 28 55
88 40 93 01 98 34 47 91 86 09 26 46 74 66 37 00 47 12 30 53
15 77 49 82 71 28 92 00 12 39 14 68
```

The longer polygraphic repetitions present have a common factor of 8; but there are several shorter repetitions which factor to 4, so it will be assumed that the additive is 4 dinomes. (If we wished to play it safe, we could have made distributions on the basis of 8 dinome columns; this would have disclosed good matching between the distributions for the 1st and 5th columns, etc., revealing that the period is actually four dinomes.)

c. Dinome distributions are made for the four dinome columns, as follows:

I

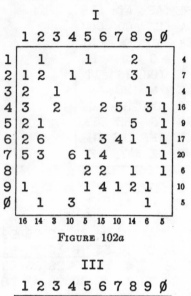

FIGURE 102*a*

II

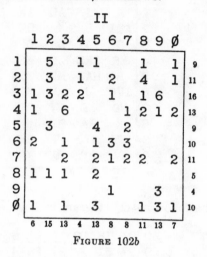

FIGURE 102*b*

III

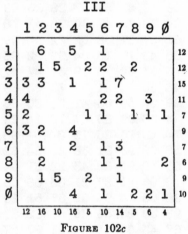

FIGURE 102*c*

IV

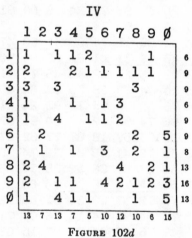

FIGURE 102*d*

We will now attempt to equate the first digits (1 and 3) of the dinome columns I and II, and also the second digits (2 and 4) of cols. I and II.   This is shown in Figs. 103a and b, below:

$\chi(1,3)$

4	7	4	16	9	17	20	6	10	5	
9	11	16	13	9	10	11	5	4	10	= 976
11	16	13	9	10	11	5	4	10	9	= 898
16	13	9	10	11	5	4	10	9	11	= 820
13	9	10	11	5	4	10	9	11	16	= 888
9	10	11	5	4	10	9	11	16	13	= 907
10	11	5	4	10	9	11	16	13	9	= 935
11	5	4	10	9	11	16	13	9	10	=1061
5	4	10	9	11	16	13	9	10	11	=1072
4	10	9	11	16	13	9	10	11	5	=1038
10	9	11	16	13	9	10	11	5	4	=1009

FIGURE 103a

$\chi(2,4)$

16	14	3	10	5	15	10	14	6	5	
6	15	13	4	13	8	8	11	13	7	= 917
15	13	4	13	8	8	11	13	7	6	=1088
13	4	13	8	8	11	13	7	6	15	= 927
4	13	8	8	11	13	7	6	15	13	= 909
13	8	8	11	13	7	6	15	13	4	= 992
8	8	11	13	7	6	15	13	4	13	= 949
8	11	13	7	6	15	13	4	13	8	= 950
11	13	7	6	15	13	4	13	8	8	=1019
13	7	6	15	13	4	13	8	8	11	= 944
7	6	15	13	4	13	8	8	11	13	= 909

FIGURE 103b

In Fig. 103a, the matching of the row digits gives three outstanding χ values, but these values are too close together to permit an easy choice among them.   On the other hand, the matching of the column digits produces one outstanding very high χ value, 1088, which indicates that the column digits of II have a relative displacement of $+1$ in relation to the column digits of I. In order to be able to discriminate among the three likely choices for the matching of the row coordinates of I and II, we will perform the χ test on *dinome* distributions; this test with dinomes is much more powerful than matching on the basis of single-digit distributions, not only because the latent primary encipherment has strong dinome characteristics, but also because of the *cohesion* of plain language, i.e., given a particular plaintext letter, the occurrence of the next letter is not based upon a random choice from a [biased] population of plaintext frequencies but is governed by the cohesion or affinity of letters forming plaintext *digraphs*.

d. Since the relationship of the column coordinates of II in reference to I has been determined, and since the three highest χ values for the row coordinates of II indicate slides of 7, 6, and 8 with respect to I, we will rewrite the dinome distribution for II in three ways to permit an easier (and less subject to error) matching of the dinome distributions of I and II.   The three transformations of the distribution for II are shown below:

	2	3	4	5	6	7	8	9	∅	1
8	1	1		2						1
9				1			3			
∅		1		3			1	3	1	1
1	5		1	1				1		1
2	3		1		2		4			1
3	3	2	2		1		1	6		1
4		6				1	2	1	2	1
5	3			4		2				
6		1		1	3	3				2
7		2		2	1	2	2			2

FIGURE 104a

	2	3	4	5	6	7	8	9	∅	1
7		2		2	1	2	2			2
8	1	1		2						1
9				1			3			
∅		1		3			1	3	1	1
1	5		1	1				1		1
2	3		1		2		4			1
3	3	2	2		1		1	6		1
4		6				1	2	1	2	1
5	3			4		2				
6		1		1	3	3				2

FIGURE 104b

	2	3	4	5	6	7	8	9	∅	1
9				1			3			
∅		1		3			1	3	1	1
1	5		1	1				1		1
2	3		1		2		4			1
3	3	2	2		1		1	6		1
4		6				1	2	1	2	1
5	3			4		2				
6		1		1	3	3				2
7		2		2	1	2	2			2
8	1	1		2						1

FIGURE 104c

The cross-products sum of the dinome distributions is taken by multiplying the entries in each cell of I with the *corresponding* cell of II, and then adding up all the cross-products thus derived. (For example, cell 1–1 of I is compared with cell 8–2 of II; cell 1–2 of I is compared with cell 8–3 of II; etc.) The χ test of the dinome distribution of I against the dinome distributions of Figs. 104a, b, and c yields χ values of 123, 91, and 236, respectively; thus it is indicated that row 9 of II is equated to row 1 of I, or a slide of +8. This now means that if col. I is arbitrarily considered to have the additive 00, this fixes the relative additive for col. II as 81. The merged distribution for dinome columns I and II properly equated is now as follows:

	1	2	3	4	5	6	7	8	9	Ø	
1		1			2			5			8
2	1	3		4			1	6	1	1	17
3	7		2	1			1		2		13
4	6		3		2	2	9		4	1	27
5	5	3	2		1		1	11		2	25
6	2	12				4	6	2	2	2	30
7	8	3		10	1	6				1	29
8		1		1	5	5		1		3	16
9	1	2		2	2	6	3	2	3		21
Ø	1	2		5					1	1	10
	31	27	7	23	13	23	21	27	13	11	

FIGURE 105

e. The process of equating dinome columns III and IV with the merged distribution for I and II continues as before, relying on the single-digit distributions for obtaining the best two or three choices or so, and then determining the correct choice by the χ-test analysis of the dinome distributions as was performed in subpar. d, above. By this process the relative additive for the four dinome columns is derived as 00 81 75 39. These key digits are now subtracted from the cipher text of the cryptogram given in subpar. b; this reduces the complex text to monoalphabetic terms. The first line of the conversion is therefore as follows:

Additive:	00 81 75 39	00 81 75 39	00 81 75 39	00 81 75 39	00 81 75 39
Cipher text:	72 99 32 93	76 12 12 81	66 34 32 28	49 43 32 00	43 22 28 99
Plain text:	72 18 67 64	76 31 47 52	66 53 67 99	49 62 67 71	43 41 53 60

The conversion of the entire text to monoalphabetic terms is given in Fig. 106, below:

```
72 18 67 64    76 31 47 52    66 53 67 99    49 62 67 71    43 41 53 60
80 20 84 68    31 76 22 97    47 58 50 85    62 82 74 24    76 31 47 52
66 49 62 67    71 43 41 71    61 80 20 84    68 31 76 22    97 57 58 50
85 62 39 61    74 80 76 31    47 52 66 04    24 97 07 18    40 95 76 49
39 60 11 82    74 24 76 31    47 52 66 49    62 76 62 09    02 41 39 60
67 62 34 02    41 84 20 51    70 58 50 74    85 62 02 86    04 18 57 69
22 28 51 92    62 67 71 43    41 71 49 31    76 22 97 47    58 50 72 18
95 74 99 47    58 58 17 31    49 99 47 80    46 04 97 92    09 94 58 50
74 92 15 09    75 31 28 95    31 28 81 74    99 47 80 04    47 74 15 67
51 15 09 24    52 66 85 62    62 45 28 15    04 57 34 31    67 37 49 95
28 39 39 28    18 86 02 33    67 99 33 61    74 62 58 96    71 86 99 67
72 51 47 12    58 69 62 45    28 18 33 09    58 47 28 02    33 67 99 33
61 74 62 58    96 71 83 28    28 85 62 04    51 51 96 53    43 41 86 75
49 71 99 47    58 58 09 79    98 01 71 18    46 24 96 58    21 02 31 76
22 97 47 58    50 55 96 53    18 94 69 24    96 74 49 65    91 86 86 90
66 92 39 61    74 33 61 74    71 85 62 39    96 58 58 27    86 04 47 58
71 68 01 71    04 96 58 86    62 45 28 68    67 62 34 02    41 00 12 98
76 24 49 67    62 34 02 41    60 27 74 53    96 51 17 74    72 28 53 26
88 69 28 72    98 53 72 62    86 28 51 17    74 85 62 71    47 31 65 24
15 96 74 53    71 47 27 71    12 58 49 39
```

FIGURE 106

All we need now is a *single* dinome as a corrective to convert the entire cipher text from our arbitrary base to the true base which would enable the reading of the message directly with the syllabary square shown in Fig. 101. As an easy solution, if the cryptogram in Fig. 106 ends with a signature, it is possible that the last element is an F_p (from INF); or the sequence 58 58 in the 4-dinome repetition of the 8th line of Fig. 106 may be tried as a doubled S_p, P_p, or L_p. The corrective for the additive is thus found to be 93, making the true additive sequence 93 74 68 22 which will decipher the beginning of the message as SECOND REGIMENT.... .

f. Note that there are three sets of 5-dinome repetitions present in the cryptogram given in subpar. b. It is quite possible that two of these sets might represent identical plain text; if this is so, it will make possible a very easy method of equating the columns without recourse to analysis of distributions. For instance, let us suppose that the repeated sequences (76 12 12 81 66) and (41 60 47 33 31) actually are identical in their underlying plain text, and that the cryptogram has been factored to a period of 4. The sequences are aligned under their respective dinome columns thus:

```
     I    II   III  IV
    (76   12   12   81
     66)      (41   60
     47   33   31)
```

Then if the additive for col. I is taken as 00, it is clear that, if 41. (III) is to represent 76, the additive for col. III must be 75; this shows the method how a relative additive can quickly be recovered by exploiting isologous ciphertext sequences. (The validity of the additive is confirmed if latent repetitions are now uncovered in other parts of the cipher text.) The student should keep this method in mind for possible use in the analysis of other types of systems which might lend themselves to this attack.

g. It should be clear to the student that the column-equating methods treated in the foregoing subparagraphs do not depend upon any known factors concerning the composition of the matrix or of the coordinates. One more generally applicable method of equating will now be demonstrated; and, in order to illustrate a different case, we will assume that the matrix is still that of Fig. 101, except that the coordinates are unknown mixed sequences. The following message, factoring [9] to a period of 6, will be studied:

```
 41 30 07 04 63 53   61 21 53 79 39 04   74 34 51 93 60 29   60 25 89 68 74 34
 83 51 94 19 17 84   66 04 04 53 24 20   42 92 20 23 92 55   11 26 36 92 13 69
 13 05 99 56 98 09   42 10 40 99 48 82   95 20 72 75 24 12   42 92 20 23 92 90
 04 66 60 80 16 71   42 48 72 78 03 17   44 13 35 45 17 87   12 48 04 04 91 95
 71 42 72 78 97 37   84 80 26 56 86 89   44 26 51 28 24 11   11 80 85 36 08 83
 19 10 91 25 31 37   17 52 23 95 23 55   83 51 94 19 17 84   66 50 11 17 24 11
 11 34 45 06 40 69   37 16 36 83 48 55   89
```

FIGURE 107

This message is too short to permit analysis of the frequency distributions with confidence; and there are no sets of equal-length repetitions to allow us to equate columns by the method indicated in subpar. *f*, above. Nevertheless, the dinome columns may be equated if we can discover some *latent* repetitions in the cipher text which could then be exploited in a manner similar to that shown in subpar. *f*. These latent repetitions may be made patent by means of a differencing technique now to be described.

h. Let us examine the following isologous encipherments produced with the square of Fig. 101 and the additive 74 31 89 60 25 12:

74	31	89	60	25	12
D	I	V	IS	ION	HE
31	54	04	59	58	53
05	85	83	19	73	65
A	D	Q	U	AR	TER
11	31	70	03	16	96
85	62	59	63	31	08
S					
88					
52					

FIGURE 108a

74	31	89	60	25	12
		D	I	V	IS
		31	54	04	59
		10	14	29	61
ION	HE	A	D	Q	U
58	53	11	31	70	03
22	84	90	91	95	15
AR	TER	S			
16	96	88			
80	27	67			

FIGURE 108b

Referring to Fig. 108a, if we subtract (mod 10) each cipher dinome from the cipher dinome just below it (i.e., in the corresponding position of the next cycle of the period), we will derive the "delta" or difference stream 80 87 76 54 68 43 77; if we difference the *plaintext* dinomes the same way, we will get the identical delta stream. The reason for this is that the difference between two plaintext elements, $\alpha - \beta$, is unchanged if the same constant "k" is added to each of the elements; or, expressed algebraically, $(\alpha + k) - (\beta + k) = (\alpha - \beta)$. In other words, the differ-

---

[9] See in this connection subpar. 84*d*.

230

ence between the cipher elements at an interval corresponding to the period represents the *difference between the underlying plaintext elements*, thus removing the effect of the additive. Once therefore having established the period in a numerical system with additive superencipherment, if we derive a delta stream at an interval corresponding to the period, any long latent polygraphic repetitions will be uncovered in this process. The delta streams obtained from Figs. 108a and b are shown below:

I	II	III	IV	V	VI
80	87	76	54	68	43
77					

FIGURE 108c

I	II	III	IV	V	VI
		80	87	76	54
68	43	77			

FIGURE 108d

The repetitions in the delta stream are of such length that they must be interpreted as having arisen *causally*, just as long ciphertext repetitions in a relatively small sample of text have to be attributed to the effect of identical keys applied to identical plain text, producing identical cipher text. The method of exploitation of the delta repetitions from this point on will be discussed in subpar. *j* below.

i. The isologous passages in Figs. 108a and b were enciphered by two full cycles of the period. Note the examples below, in which the isologous plain text is less than two cycles in length:

74	31	89	60	25	12
O	B	SE	R	V	AT
74	22	89	81	04	19
48	53	68	41	29	21

ION	P	O	ST		
58	79	74	91		
22	00	53	51		

FIGURE 109a

74	31	89	60	25	12
	O	B	SE	R	V
	74	22	89	81	04
	05	01	49	06	16

AT	ION	P	O	ST	
19	58	79	74	91	
83	89	58	34	16	

FIGURE 109b

	I	II	III	IV	V	VI
Delta:	84	57	95	10		

FIGURE 109c

	I	II	III	IV	V	VI
Delta:	84	57	95	10		

FIGURE 109d

The delta repetition is four dinomes in length, which is one cycle less than the length of the isologous plain text; i.e., $10-6=4$. Note, however, the following examples:

74	31	89	60	25	12
P	O	IN	T	F	IVE
79	74	56	93	46	61
43	05	35	53	61	73

SE	VE	N	F	OU	R
89	05	60	46	78	81
53	36	49	06	93	93

FIGURE 110a

74	31	89	60	25	12
			P	O	IN →
			79	74	56
			39	99	68

T	ON	E	SE	VE	N →
← 93	76	35	89	05	60
67	07	14	49	20	72

F	I	VE			
← 46	54	05			
10	85	84			

FIGURE 110b

	I	II	III	IV	V	VI
Delta:	10	31	14	53	32	20

FIGURE 110c

	I	II	III	IV	V	VI
Delta:				10	31	14 →
	53	88	70 ←			

FIGURE 110d

Here the delta repetition is four dinomes also; this repetition, however, arises not from a long plaintext repetition, but from identical sets of a 4-dinome repetition in the plain text over another 4-dinome repetition in the plain text. This means that, if a delta repetition does not extend to a full cycle or more of the period, we must not jump to conclusions that a short delta repetition is the result of a single long plaintext repetition; in Figs. 110c and d, the 4-dinome repetition, as may be seen, is *not* the result of a 10-dinome plaintext repetition.

j. Now to get back to the cryptogram of Fig. 107. Since the cipher text factors to 6 dinomes, we will subtract each dinome from the one six places to the right of it to obtain the delta stream; this is shown in Fig. 111, below:

```
41 30 07 04 63 53   61 21 53 79 39 04   74 34 51 93 60 29   60 25 89 68 74 34
                    20 91 56 75 76 51   13 13 08 24 31 25   96 91 38 75 14 15

83 51 94 19 17 84   66 04 04 53 24 20   42 92 20 23 92 55   11 26 36 92 13 69
23 36 15 51 43 50   83 53 10 44 17 46   86 98 26 70 78 35   79 34 16 79 21 14

13 05 99 56 98 09   42 10 40 99 48 82   95 20 72 75 24 12   42 92 20 23 92 90
02 89 63 64 85 40   39 15 51 43 50 83   53 10 32 86 86 30   57 72 58 58 78 88

04 66 60 80 16 71   42 48 72 78 03 17   44 13 35 45 17 87   12 48 04 04 91 95
62 74 40 67 24 81   48 82 12 98 97 46   02 75 63 77 14 70   78 35 79 69 84 18

71 42 72 78 97 37   84 80 26 56 86 89   44 26 51 28 24 11   11 80 85 36 08 83
69 04 78 74 06 42   13 48 54 88 99 52   60 46 35 72 48 32   77 64 34 18 84 72

19 10 91 25 31 37   17 52 23 95 23 55   83 51 94 19 17 84   66 50 11 17 24 11
08 30 16 99 33 54   08 42 32 70 92 28   76 09 71 24 94 39   83 09 27 08 17 37

11 34 45 06 40 69   37 16 36 83 48 55   89
55 84 34 99 26 58   26 82 91 87 08 96   52
```

FIGURE 111

Two sets of repetitions are revealed in the delta stream, one of 7 dinomes and one of 4 dinomes. The longer one must perforce represent a repeated plaintext passage beginning 6 dinomes to the left of the delta repetition, but there is no assurance that the 4-dinome delta repetition represents a longer plaintext repetition; in any case, we shall use only the information derived from the lengths of the delta repetitions as disclosed.

(1) Let us record the original ciphertext sequences which stand above the 7-dinome delta repetitions of Fig. 111; allocated into their proper positions in the key cycle, these are as follows:[10]

I	II	III	IV	V	VI
		(94	19	17	84
66	04	04)			
		(10	40	99	48	82
95	20)				

FIGURE 112

We will now arbitrarily assume that the initial 10_c in the second sequence represents 10_p; this of course gives us an additive of 00 for col. II. The 94_c in the initial position of the first sequence must also represent 10_p, so therefore the additive for col. III has to be 84. This additive, when applied to the second dinome of the second sequence, 40_c, deciphers it as 66_p. This zigzagging process is continued, quickly deriving the relative additive as follows:

```
      91   00   84   53   71   17
C:              (94   19   17   84
P:               10   66   46   77

C:   66   04   04)
P:   75   04   20

C:         (10   40   99   48   82
P:          10   66   46   77   75

C:   95   20)
P:   04   20
```

FIGURE 113

[10] If these delta repetitions had not extended for at least a full cycle of the period, we would have had to take into consideration the entire sets of ciphertext equivalents of the latent plaintext repetition, beginning in positions 21 and 50.

(2) With a relative additive at hand, we now reduce the text of the cryptogram to mono-alphabetic terms, as follows:

```
91 00 84 53 71 17    91 00 84 53 71 17    91 00 84 53 71 17    91 00 84 53 71 17
41 30 07 04 63 53    61 21 53 79 39 04    74 34 51 93 60 29    60 25 89 68 74 34
50 30 23 51 92 46    70 21 79 26 68 97    83 34 77 40 99 12    79 25 05 15 03 27 →

83 51 94 19 17 84    66 04 04 53 24 20    42 92 20 23 92 55    11 26 36 92 13 69
92 51 10 66 46 77    75 04 20 00 53 13    51 92 46 70 21 48    20 26 52 49 42 52
←

13 05 99 56 98 09    42 10 40 99 48 82    95 20 72 75 24 12    42 92 20 23 92 90
22 05 15 03 27 92    51 10 66 46 77 75    04 20 98 22 53 05    51 92 46 70 21 83

04 66 60 80 16 71    42 48 72 78 03 17    44 13 35 45 17 87    12 48 04 04 91 95
13 66 86 37 45 64    51 48 98 25 32 00    53 13 51 92 46 70    21 48 20 51 20 88

71 42 72 78 97 37    84 80 26 56 86 89    44 26 51 28 24 11    11 80 85 36 08 83
80 42 98 25 26 20    93 80 42 03 15 72    53 26 77 75 53 04    20 80 01 83 37 76

19 10 91 25 31 37    17 52 23 95 23 55    83 51 94 19 17 84    66 50 11 17 24 11
28 10 17 72 60 20    26 52 49 42 52 48    92 51 10 66 46 77    75 50 37 64 53 04 →

11 34 45 06 40 69    37 16 36 83 48 55    89
20 34 61 53 79 52    46 16 52 30 77 48    98
←
```

FIGURE 114

All of the polygraphic repetitions originally present in the plain text are now disclosed. Since the matrix involved is the same as that in Fig. 101 except that the coordinates have been scrambled, we must make some plaintext assumptions. The best assumption for the repetition 20 26 52 49 42 52 is P O S IT ION S, based not only on the idiomorph present, but also on the fact that the first two dinomes begin with the same digit (P and O are in the same row of the matrix); moreover, by the time we have recorded the coordinates for the values P, O, S, and IT, the dinome 42 automatically gives the value ION, thus furnishing confirmation of the validity of the plaintext assumption. The derived coordinates are placed in the proper positions outside the basic matrix, so it now looks like this:

				6				2	Ø	9
	A	1	AL	AN	AND	AR	ARE	AS	AT	ATE
	ATI	B	2	BE	C	3	CA	CE	CO	COM
	D	4	DA	DE	E	5	EA	ED	EN	ENT
	ER	ERE	ERS	ES	EST	F	6	G	7	H
4	8	HAS	HE	I	9	IN	ING	ION	IS	IT
	IVE	J	Ø	K	L	LA	LE	M	ME	N
2	ND	NE	NT	O	OF	ON	OR	OU	P	Q
5	R	RA	RE	RED	RES	RI	RO	S	SE	SH
	ST	STO	T	TE	TED	TER	TH	THE	THI	THR
	TI	TO	U	V	VE	W	WE	X	Y	Z

234

From here on the rest of the solution follows easily, the deciphered values furnishing clues around which to make a few further assumptions until all ten row and column coordinates are recovered. For example, the repetition 51 92 46 70 21 (the middle dinome of which deciphers to I_p) must begin with one of the R or S groups of row 5; if 51 represents RE, then 21 automatically deciphers as NT, suggesting that the repetition represents RE G I ME NT, especially since the column coordinates for G and ME have already been placed by the first assumption.

(3) Since the additive recovered is on a relative base, so are the reconstructed coordinates on a relative base. The actual additive was 14 23 07 76 94 30, which can be derived from our recovered relative additive by adding a corrective of 23 to all the dinomes of the key; the matrix coordinates would then be changed by adding 8 to all the row coordinates, and 7 to all the column coordinates. But there is no way of deriving or of proving the correct base; besides, this point is only of academic importance.

k. The initial entry in the example in Fig. 114 was made by means of a repetition which was identified as representing POSITIONS; this pat solution may appear to the student as a very fortunate piece of hindsight indeed, in view of the fact that the author made up the problem. For the skeptical reader with a jaundiced eye, there will now be presented a mathematical method of arriving at several row and column coordinates (thereby identifying a number of plaintext values in the cipher), without recourse to any plaintext assumptions whatsoever.

(1) If the matrix in Fig. 101 were a known matrix, recovered from previous solution, a tabulation could be made of the frequencies of occurrence of the various plaintext elements within the matrix. Such a tabulation is shown in Fig. 115, below, wherein are listed the fre-

	1	2	3	4	5	6	7	8	9	Ø	
1	30	6	3	2	3	13	3	1	14	3	78
2	1	10	3	8	20	1	3	8	6	3	63
3	26	1	5	5	30	5	4	5	9	1	91
4	10	1	1	2	1	18	1	22	1	15	72
5	1	3	4	36	1	19	8	14	7	8	101
6	1	2	7	7	28	3	9	23	8	28	116
7	1	6	10	28	11	17	13	12	50	4	152
8	31	8	22	1	1	4	13	54	10	1	145
9	13	15	22	3	2	2	10	6	2	3	78
Ø	6	13	26	10	9	15	6	3	15	1	104
	120	65	103	102	106	97	70	148	122	67	1000

FIGURE 115

quencies of over 1400 plaintext values from representative messages, reduced to a base of 1000. Note that the highest-frequency element, 88 (representing S_p), has a relative frequency of 54 in 1000 (i.e., 5.4%); the next highest, 79 (representing P_p), a relative frequency of 50; etc. Note also that the sums of the entries in the rows have greatly varying frequencies, and likewise the columnar sums.

(2) Referring back to Fig. 114, we will now take a dinome distribution of the monoalphabetically converted text; this is shown below:

	1	2	3	4	5	6	7	8	9	Ø	
1		1	3		3	1	1			4	13
2	4	2	1			3	5	2	1	9	27
3		1		2			3			2	8
4		4			1	8		5	2	1	21
5	9	6	7							2	24
6	1			2		4		1		1	9
7		2			4	1	6		3	4	20
8			3			1		1		3	8
9		7	1				1	4	1		14
Ø	1		3	4	3					2	13
	15	23	18	8	14	20	13	12	6	28	

FIGURE 116

Row 2 of this distribution, with 27 tallies, and row 5, with 24 tallies, should correspond either to true row 7 (weight of 152) and true row 8 (weight of 145) of Fig. 115, or vice versa; let us assume that true row 7 (with the higher score) is the correct equivalent for row 2. Col. Ø, with 28 tallies, should be one of the three highest columns of Fig. 115: true col. 8 (weight of 148), true col. 9 (weight of 122), or true col. 1 (weight of 120). But cell 2–Ø (with a high count of 9 tallies) should correspond to one of the following true row-column combinations: 7–8 (weight of 12), 7–9 (weight of 50), or 7–1 (weight of 1). The correct choice for cell 2–Ø is obviously true 7–9. This means then that row 5 (with 27 tallies) should be true row 8 (weight of 145).

(3) Since col. Ø (which has been identified as true col. 9) is not true col. 8 (which has a high weight of 148), true col. 8 should be col. 2 (with 23 tallies, the second ranking column); this is substantiated by cell 5–2 (with a frequency of 6), which shows a correspondence with true 8–8 (weight of 54). Now cells 5–1 (9 tallies) and 5–3 (7 tallies) should represent true 8–1 (weight of 31) or true 8–3 (weight of 22); in light of the higher number of tallies (18) of col. 3, this column should correspond to true col. 1 (weight of 120), making col. 1 (15 tallies) equal to true col. 3 (weight of 103). Cell 9–2 (7 tallies) should correspond to true 6–8 (weight of 23) or to true 4–8 (weight of 22); but comparing row 9 (14 tallies) with true row 6 (weight of 116) and with true row 4 (weight of 72), the agreement of row 9 is best with true row 4.

(4) Placing the recovered coordinates for three of the rows and four of the columns in position on the matrix, we have the following:

```
      3        1              2    Ø
   | A    1   AL   AN  AND  AR  ARE  AS   AT   ATE |
   | ATI  B   2    BE  C    3   CA   CE   CO   COM |
   | D    4   DA   DE  E    5   EA   ED   EN   ENT |
 9 | ER  ERE  ERS  ES  EST  F   6    G    7    H   |
   | 8   HAS  HE   I   9    IN  ING  ION  IS   IT  |
   | IVE  J   Ø    K   L    LA  LE   M    ME   N   |
 2 | ND  NE   NT   O   OF   ON  OR   OU   P    Q   |
 5 | R   RA   RE   RED RES  RI  RO   S    SE   SH  |
   | ST  STO  T    TE  TED  TER TH   THE  THI  THR |
   | TI  TO   U    V   VE   W   WE   X    Y    Z   |
```

236

The plaintext values for the dinomes whose coordinates have been recovered are now placed in the cryptogram, yielding the following:

```
 50 30 23  51 92 46  70 21  79 26 68 97  83 34 77 40 99 12  79 25  05 15 03 27 →
 89  9 71  83 48      9 73   7     4      1        9  4  8    7            1  7
 SE ND RE  G           NT

 92 51 10 66 46 77  75 04 20  00 53 13  51 92 46 70 21 48  20 26 52 49 42 52
 48 83  9            79  9 81   1 83 48       9 73       79  7 88       8 88
 G  RE              P      R   RE G         NT          P    S          S

 22 05 15 03 27 92  51 10 66 46 77 75  04 20 98 22 53 05  51 92 46 70 21 83
 78       1  7 48   83  9                79  4 78 81       83 48       9 73  1
 OU           G     RE                   P    OU R         RE G          NT

 13 66 86 37 45 64  51 48 98 25 32 00  53 13 51 92 46 70  21 48 20 51 20 88
  1                 83     4  7     8  9 81  1 83 48        9  73 79 83 79
                    RE                 R    RE G           NT    P  RE P

 80 42 98 25 26 20  93 80 42 03 15 72  53 26 77 75 53 04  20 80 01 83 37 76
  9  8  4  7  7 79  41  9  8  1      8  81  7       81     79  9  3  1
                    P  ER              R           R      P

 28 10 17 72 60 20  26 52 49 42 52 48  92 51 10 66 46 77  75 50 37 64 53 04 →
  7  9     8  9 79   7 88       8 88    48 83  9          89       81
                    P     S        S   G  RE             SE        R

 20 34 61 53 79 52  46 16 52 30 77 48  98
 79     3 81    88         88  9
 P      R  S                S
```

Not only do the skeletal plaintext values constitute a nucleus for further assumptions, but derived *single* coordinates for the rows or columns (such as in the second dinome where 30= –9) serve as a guide for the choice of additional values. The solution from here on is very straightforward.

(5) If the sample of text were large enough, it might be possible to recover most or even all of the row and column coordinates mathematically. But if we are to use statistical tools intelligently, and not merely for their own sake,[11] we should use just what is needed for the quickest solution possible.

l. In the foregoing subparagraphs there have been treated enciphered syllabary square systems wherein the composition of the matrix is known. If nothing were known about the basic matrix, solution would proceed by factoring and determining the period, and then reducing the cipher text to monoalphabetic terms by one of the methods already outlined. The last step, that of breaking into the reduced cipher text, is accomplished by attacks based on probable words, repetitions and similar sequences, idiomorphs, isologs, and other phenomena or special situations which can and will occur, sooner or later when the system is used for regular traffic; the analysis of syllabary squares and code charts has been given adequate treatment in par. 80 of Chapter XI in *Military Cryptanalytics, Part I,* and in the associated problems (Appendix 9 of that text, pp. 423–427).

---

[11] See in this connection some remarks made by C. H. O'D. Alexander quoted on p. 223 of *Military Cryptanalytics, Part I.*

84. Additional remarks.—*a.* The discussion of additive systems in this chapter has been limited to superenciphered *numerical* bipartite systems, i.e., where the matrix coordinates consist of digits. If the coordinates consisted of letters, and if these letters were enciphered with, say, direct standard alphabets, the techniques presented in this chapter can be adapted to this situation because the arithmetic is being performed on a *known* modulus (in this case, mod 26; e.g., B+E=G, X+C=A, etc.). If the superencipherment involves unknown mixed cipher alphabets, the ordinary modular relationships do not obtain; therefore solutions must be based on a volume of traffic, plus whatever fortunate special situations may be present in the system as used by the enemy. However, the majority of cases of superenciphered bipartite systems encountered have involved matrices with numerical coordinates and mod 10 addition.

b. The cryptographic arithmetic treated in this chapter is the *additive method*, where P+K= C, and C−K=P. There are two other arithmetical methods of encipherment: the *subtractive method*, where P−K=C, and C+K=P; and the *minuend method*, where K−P=C, and K−C=P. Additive, subtractive, and minuend methods are complementary: an additive system may be solved as a subtractive system or a minuend system; any one of these may be solved as either of the other two. If an additive system is assumed and the cipher is actually a subtractive system, all that will happen is that a complementary key will be derived (e.g., in subpar. 82*i* the recovered key would have been 53 49 28 76 10 instead of the 57 61 82 34 90 as derived). If a minuend system is solved as an additive or subtractive system, the intermediate plaintext digits will be the complements of the true intermediate plain (with or without the addition of a constant). In any case, the derived key can always be converted into the true key either (a) by the addition of a constant, or (b) by the addition of a constant to the *complements* of the derived key. Situations where it makes any difference if the correct method has not been assumed usually involve certain aspects of key analysis, or situations wherein the true intermediate plaintext values are known. This matter will be dealt with at greater length in the next volume.

c. It should be clear to the student that if there are any limitations in either the left- or right-hand components of the dinome intermediate text, such limitations will simplify the problem of reduction to monoalphabetic terms.

d. The cryptogram in Fig. 107 was factorable by means of the polygraphic repetitions patent in the cipher text. The student should note that if these repetitions had not been in evidence, we still could have factored the cryptogram by generating delta streams at various intervals and examining these streams for evidences of long polygraphic repetitions; when the interval of 6 dinomes was considered, we would have the diagram as illustrated in Fig. 111, revealing from the latent repetitions now disclosed that the length of the period is 12 digits.

e. One further tool for factoring might occur to the student: the use of an I.C. to determine when the correct write-out has been reached, in the manner of that described in subpar. 18*e*. This very valuable method, especially rewarding in difficult cases, warrants detailed treatment; the application of this procedure will be taken up in the next chapter in subpars. 86*b*–*d*.

f. Attacks based on cribs, isologs, and other special situations may be devised to fit the specific situation at hand; the alert cryptanalyst should always be on the lookout for the possibility of exploitation by means of these methods in a particular case under study.

CHAPTER XII

MONOME-DINOME SYSTEMS WITH CYCLIC ADDITIVES

85. General remarks.—*a.* In the preceding chapter we have seen demonstrated the various methods of attack on dinome systems superenciphered by cyclic additives. The determination of the length of the additive was made by the general method of factoring the interval between long (i.e., *causal*) repetitions; in the case of the Nihilist system the determination of the period was made by taking advantage of the cryptographic idiosyncracies of that system (as regards the "unique dinomes" 02, 10, 22, and 30).

b. The matrices in the foregoing chapter were dinome matrices, their particular dimensions being irrelevant. The reduction of the columns of the additive-enciphered text was accomplished (1) by equating the monomic distributions (cf. subpars. 82*b* and *c*), or (2) by equating the dinomic columns (as in subpar. 83*d*), or (3) by comparing sets of identical-length ciphertext repetitions assumed to contain identical underlying plain text (subpar. 83*f*), or (4) by analysis of the delta stream at an interval corresponding to the period (subpar. 83*j*).

c. If a cyclic additive encipherment is applied to intermediate plain text produced by a *monome-dinome* system, the problem gets more complicated, especially as regards column equating. The determination of the period may be made by the usual process of factoring; but if no long repetitions are in evidence, we must rely on deriving a columnar I.C. statistic for each width that comes into consideration,[1] hoping that the correct width will have a predominant I.C. and that there will be no other "good" answers for the incorrect widths. We might even apply the delta-stream method and with luck uncover possible latent sets of long plaintext repetitions which would then indicate that the interval of the delta stream tried is equivalent to the true period or a multiple of the period; but this method is hardly to be recommended except in cases where it is known that the additive is very short in comparison with the length of the message.

d. In additive-enciphered monome-dinome systems, once the period has been determined, the equating of columns is accomplished by sliding the monomic distributions to a correct match when there are a sufficient number of tallies per column. What constitutes "a sufficient number of tallies per column" is dependent on the over-all I.C. of the cipher text produced by the underlying monome-dinome matrix; if the matrix had the highest frequency letters in the monome row, much larger distributions would be necessary for column equating than if some medium or low frequency letters were represented by monomes. The problem of column equating is all the more complicated because each columnar distribution contains a mixture of monome elements and only one of the elements of a dinome—thus there is a "watering down" of the information that might have been available if the distributions pertained only to left-hand or right-hand members of dinomes as in the systems illustrated in the preceding chapter.

---

[1] Cf. the method shown in subpar. 18*e*.

e. If there are several messages in the same system which have been enciphered at various points along the keying cycle, their correct superimpositions may be determined by locating long repetitions between messages and aligning them so that the repetitions are exactly superimposed. Otherwise, once the period has been determined, even without the presence of long repetitions we may still align the messages correctly by a variation of the χ-test method demonstrated in par. 72.

86. Analysis of a general case of an additive-enciphered monome-dinome system.—*a.* In this first case we will treat the cryptanalysis of a system involving an unknown monome-dinome matrix with an additive of unknown length; for purposes of illustration, it will be assumed that the enemy is known to be using additives from 20 to 40 digits in length. The following two messages are available for study:

Message "A"

90723	78168	94849	15771	16844	17454	66220	88312	87103	45436
51844	80725	95351	25207	71062	43897	67340	60921	05986	85348
28147	15733	58293	45515	05206	88337	34666	19895	67818	09150
66954	13321	61791	75797	51414	31979	86210	85627	71095	58825
20894	16966	09087	59634	80149	82880	81862	77470	01320	13674
11794	57837	24849	06800	00520	19613	90147	16045	20150	35129
06260	72364	91991	17821	62194	36516	06329	85610	90458	05395
55013	35800	92354	04365	92886	96225	20858	05926	00264	38137
81653	45991	26864	97686	06029	44327	74662	65027		

Message "B"

60542	47550	69060	75362	54662	15457	59157	87473	49316	85347
71001	54092	60653	01924	46954	28733	91803	65347	43818	08626
06354	13674	11794	57837	25513	51562	06723	19962	51163	49777
57217	35540	01953	28138	90813	05530	07142	06526	06554	84334
34903	31904	26742	97424	04573	22367	17863	25890	59816	42517
30323	83618	80859	15433	25890	58254	60200	14378	99263	49028
67137	40325	53354	15374	24063	75498				

There are many short repetitions present, but since the causal cases cannot be distinguished from the random, there is no information in the repetitions to indicate the length of the period. Furthermore, we really do not know whether or not the two messages are even in the same system; and if they are, whether the messages are in flush depth or at an offset in the key cycle.

b. Since the additive sequences used by the enemy in the past have been from 20 to 40 digits long, we will transcribe Message "A", the longer of the two, into the various widths successively, deriving the sum of the I.C.'s of the columns for each particular width.[2] The

---

[2] The process of transcribing text into a multitude of widths and making all the necessary computations is a laborious task when performed by hand; where machine methods are available, this presents no problem.

columnar frequencies for Message "A" when written out on a width of 20 are shown in the diagram below:

```
      1 2 3 4 5 6 7 8 9 10 11 12 13 14 15 16 17 18 19 20
 ∅    4 6 1 2 4 5 1 1 2 3  5  3  4     3        1  1  1  3   ∅
 1    1 3 5 2 2 5     2 1  2  1  7  1  2  1  5  1  2  4  3   1
 2    4 2 3 3     1 2 1 4     2  1  3  3  3        1  7  1   2
 3        4     3 1 1 5 3  1  1        1     2  4  2  3  3  1  3
 4        1 1 6 4.3 2 2 1 3     3  1  2  6  2        1  1  1   4
 5        2     5       8 1  2  3  4  2  1  2  1  3  7  1     5   5
 6    4 4 1 1 1 1 4 2 4 4  2  4  2  6  3  1  1  4        1   6
 7        3 2     2 3 1 2 1  5  3        1     1  1  4  2  3  4   7
 8    4 1 5     3.3 2 2 1 1  1  1  5  3     4  3  6  1  1   8
 9    5        3 3     1 4 3     3  1  3  4  2  2  3  1  2  2   9

 φ=  68 58 60 66 46 58 74 42 40 52 48 68 46 60 52 54 68 52 68 46      Σφ=1126
```

The sum of all the columnar φ values is 1126. Since in writing out the message (440 digits) on a width of 20, we get 20 columns of 22 tallies each, the ϕ_r is $\frac{20(22 \cdot 21)}{10} = 924$; thus the I.C. for this width is $\frac{1126}{924} = 1.22$, which seems surprisingly good for a random case, if it *is* random. Since the cryptanalyst should have learned by now that it is well to regard with suspicion *any* very good result on the very *first* trial, he proceeds to test other widths. The data for the first 10 tests are tabulated below:

Width	I.C.	Width	I.C.
20	1.22	25	0.97
21	0.93	26	0.92
22	0.91	27	0.91
23	1.01	28	1.06
24	1.11	29	1.11

c. The next width to be considered is 30, so the message is written out accordingly, as follows:

```
  1 2 3 4 5 6 7 8 9 10 11 12 13 14 15 16 17 18 19 20 21 22 23 24 25 26 27 28 29 30
  9 0 7 2 3 7 8 1 6 8  9  4  8  4  9  1  5  7  7  1  1  6  8  4  4  1  7  4  5  4
  6 6 2 2 0 8 8 3 1 2  8  7  1  0  3  4  5  4  3  6  5  1  8  4  4  8  0  7  2  5
  9 5 3 5 1 2 5 2 0 7  7  1  0  6  2  4  3  8  9  7  6  7  3  4  0  6  0  9  2  1
  0 5 9 8 6 8 5 3 4 8  2  8  1  4  7  1  5  7  3  3  5  8  2  9  3  4  5  5  1  5
  0 5 2 0 6 8 8 3 3 7  3  4  6  6  6  1  9  8  9  5  6  7  8  1  8  0  9  1  5  0
  6 6 9 5 4 1 3 3 2 1  6  1  7  9  1  7  5  7  9  7  5  1  4  1  4  3  1  9  7  9
  8 6 2 1 0 8 5 6 2 7  7  1  0  9  5  5  8  8  2  5  2  0  8  9  4  1  6  9  6  6
  0 9 0 8 7 5 9 6 3 4  8  0  1  4  9  8  2  8  8  0  8  1  8  6  2  7  7  4  7  0
  0 1 3 2 0 1 3 6 7 4  1  1  7  9  4  5  7  8  3  7  2  4  8  4  9  0  6  8  0  0
  0 0 5 2 0 1 9 6 1 3  9  0  1  4  7  1  6  0  4  5  2  0  1  5  0  3  5  1  2  9
  0 6 2 6 0 7.2 3 6 4  9  1  9  9  1  1  7  8  2  1  6  2  1  9  4  3  6  5  1  6
  0 6 3 2 9 8 5 6 1 0  9  0  4  5  8  0  5  3  9  5  5  5  0  1  3  3  5  8  0  0
  9 2 3 5 4 0 4 3 6 5  9  2  8  8  6  9  6  2  2  5  2  0  8  5  8  0  5  9  2  6
  0 0 2 6 4 3 8 1 3 7  8  1  6  5  3  4  5  9  9  1  2  6  8  6  4  9  7  6  8  6
  0 6 0 2 9 4 4 3 2 7  7  4  6  6  2  6  5  0  2  7
```

241

The diagram for the columnar frequencies at this width is given below:

	1	2	3	4	5	6	7	8	9	10	11	12	13	14	15	16	17	18	19	20	21	22	23	24	25	26	27	28	29	30	
Ø	9	3	2	1	5	1			1	1		3	2	1		1		2		1		3	1		2	3	2		2	4	Ø
1		1		1	1	3		2	3	1	1	6	4		2	5					3	1	3	2	3		2	1	2	2	1
2		1	5	6				1	1	1	3	1	1	2			2		1	1	4		5	1	1		1			4	2
3			4		1	1	2	7	3	1	1				2		1	1	3	1			1		2	4					3
4				3	1	2		1	3		2	1	4	1	3			1	1		1	1	4	6	1		2		1		4
5		3	1	3		1	4		1				2	1	2	7				5	4	1		2		4	2	2	2		5
6	2	6		2	2			5	3		1		3	3	2	1	2			1	3	2		2		1	3	1	1	4	6
7		1		1	2			1	5	3	1	2		2	1	2	1	1	4		2				1	3	1	2			7
8	1		2		5	4			2	3	1	2	1	1	1	6	1			1	1	8		2	1			2	1		8
9	3	1	2		2		2			5		1	4	2	1	1	3	5				3	1	1	1	4			2		9
φ=	80	42	36	40	30	28	30	64	24	28	32	40	24	32	12	28	46	38	38	38	38	16	58	28	36	20	26	20	20	28	Σφ=1020

The sum of all the columnar φ values here is 1020. Since we have 20 columns of 15 tallies and 10 columns of 14 tallies, $\phi_r = \dfrac{20(15 \cdot 14) + 10(14 \cdot 13)}{10} = 602$, and the I.C. is therefore $\dfrac{1020}{602} = 1.69$. With such a high I.C., there is hardly any question that the correct period is 30.

d. We now transcribe Message "B" on a width of 30 as shown below, together with its accompanying frequency diagram:

1	2	3	4	5	6	7	8	9	10	11	12	13	14	15	16	17	18	19	20	21	22	23	24	25	26	27	28	29	30
6	0	5	4	2	4	7	5	5	0	6	9	0	6	0	7	5	3	6	2	5	4	6	6	2	1	5	4	5	7
5	9	1	5	7	8	7	4	7	3	4	9	3	1	6	8	5	3	4	7	7	1	0	0	1	5	4	0	9	2
6	0	6	5	3	0	1	9	2	4	4	6	9	5	4	2	8	7	3	3	9	1	8	0	3	6	5	3	4	7
4	3	8	1	8	0	8	6	2	6	0	6	3	5	4	1	3	6	7	4	1	1	7	9	4	5	7	8	3	7
2	5	5	1	3	5	1	5	6	2	0	6	7	2	3	1	9	9	6	2	5	1	1	6	3	4	9	7	7	7
5	7	2	1	7	3	5	5	4	0	0	1	9	5	3	2	8	1	3	8	9	0	8	1	3	0	5	5	3	0
0	7	1	4	2	0	6	5	2	6	0	6	5	5	4	8	4	3	3	4	3	4	9	0	3	3	1	9	0	4
2	6	7	4	2	9	7	4	2	4	0	4	5	7	3	2	2	3	6	7	1	7	8	6	3	2	5	8	9	0
5	9	8	1	6	4	2	5	1	7	3	0	3	2	3	8	3	6	1	8	8	0	8	5	9	1	5	4	3	3
2	5	8	9	0	5	8	2	5	4	6	0	2	0	0	1	4	3	7	8	9	9	2	6	3	4	9	0	2	8
6	7	1	3	7	4	0	3	2	5	5	3	3	5	4	1	5	3	7	4	2	4	0	6	3	7	5	4	9	8

	1	2	3	4	5	6	7	8	9	10	11	12	13	14	15	16	17	18	19	20	21	22	23	24	25	26	27	28	29	30	
Ø	1	2			1	3	1			2	5	2	1	1	2					2	2	3		1		2	1	2			Ø
1			3	4		2		1			1		1		4		1	1		2	4	1	1	1	2	1					1
2	3		1		3		1	1	5	1			1	2		3	1			2	1		1		1	1			1	1	2
3		1		1	2	1		1		1	1	1	4		4		2	6	3	1	1				7	1		1	3	1	3
4	1			3		3		2	1	3	2	1		4		2		1	3		3			1	2	1	3	1	1		4
5	3	2	2		2	1	5	2	1	1		2	5		3				2			1		2	6	1	1				5
6	3	1	1		1		1	1	2	2	4		1	1		2	3			1	5		1								6
7		3	1		3		3		1	1		1	1		1	3	2	1	1	1			1	1	1	4					7
8		3		1	1	2				3	2		3	1		4				2		2									8
9		2		1	1	1		2	2			1	1		3	1	1	1	1		2	1	3								9
φ=	18	12	14	20	14	14	10	22	22	10	24	16	16	22	26	24	12	32	18	16	10	20	14	26	42	6	32	10	12	16	Σφ=550

The ϕ_o is 550; the $\phi_r = \dfrac{30(11 \cdot 10)}{10} = 330$. The I.C. is $\dfrac{550}{330} = 1.67$, which substantiates the assumption that 30 is the correct period for this message also.

242

e. Now comes the problem of determining the relative juxtaposition of the two messages (if they are indeed homogeneous). Following the general procedure illustrated in par. 72 in connection with progressive alphabet systems, we will match the columnar frequency diagram of Message "B" at all possible offsets with the columnar frequency diagram of Message "A", deriving the columnar χ values for the columns at each juxtaposition.[3] The first test is shown below:

	1	2	3	4	5	6	7	8	9	10	11	12	13	14	15	16	17	18	19	20	21	22	23	24	25	26	27	28	29	30	
φ	9	3	2	1	5	1			1	1		3	2	1		1		2		1		3	1		2	3	2		2	4	φ
1	1		1	1	3		2	3	1	1	6	4		2	5				3	1	3	2	3		2	1	2	2	1		1
2		1	5	6		1	1	1	3	1	1	2			2		1	1	4		5	1	1		1			4			2
3		4		1	1	2	7	3	1	1				2		1	1	3	1		1		2	4							3
4			3	1	2			1	3			2	1	4	1	3		1	1			1	1	4	6	1		2		1	4
5		3	1	3		1	4		1		2	1	2	7		5	4	1		2			4	2	2	2					5
6	2	6		2	2			5	3		1		3	3	2	1	2		1	3	2		2		1	3	1	1	4		6
7		1		1	2			1	5	3	1	2		2	1	2	1	1	4		2			1	3	1	2				7
8	1		2		5	4		2	3	1	2	1	1	1	6	1		1	1	8		2	1		2	1					8
9	3	1	2		2		2		5		1	4	2	1	1	3	5			3	1	1	1	4			2				9

	1	2			29	30	1	2	3	4	5	6	7	8	9	10	11	12	13	14	15	16	17	18	19	20	21	22	23	24	25	26	27	28	29	30	
φ	1	2			1	2	1	2			1	3	1		2	5	2	1	1	2							2	2	3		1		2	1	2		φ
1								3	4			2		1		1	1		4		1	1		2	4	1	1	1	2	1							1
2	3				1	1	3		1		3		1	1	5	1		1	2		3	1		2	1		1	1			1	1			2
3		1			3	1		1		1	2	1		1		1	1	1	4		4		2	6	3	1	1			7	1		1	3	1		3
4	1				1	1	1			3		3		2	1	3	2	1		4		2		1	3		3			1	2	1	3	1	1		4
5	3	2			1		3	2	2	2		2	1	5	2	1	1		2	5		3			2		1			2	6	1	1				5
6	3	1					3	1	1		1		1	1	1	2	2	4		1	1		2	3			1	5		1							6
7		3			1	4		3	1		3		3		1	1		1	1		1		1	3	2	1	1	1			1	1	1	1	4		7
8					2			3		1	1	2						3	2			3	1		4					2		2					8
9		2			3			2		1	1		1				2	2			1	1			3	1	1	1			2	1	3					9

$\chi=$ 15 20 8 10 12 14 13 13 23 19 3 14 6 14 14 24 27 10 13 9 16 23 37 18 22 15 30 17 10 9

The sum of the columnar χ values at this juxtaposition is 478. The expected sum of the cross products in a random case, χ_r, is

$$\frac{20(15 \cdot 11) + 10(14 \cdot 11)}{10} = 484,$$

so the ξ I.C. at this particular alignment of the two messages is $\frac{478}{484} = 0.99$.

f. We now slide the frequency diagram for Message "B" one position to the right with respect to the diagram for Message "A", and we derive the ξ I.C. for this setting. This ξ I.C.,

---

[3] A cutout mask, exposing corresponding cells in the two frequency diagrams, will be found useful in avoiding errors in deriving the cross products.

1.04, is likewise void of cryptanalytic pith.   After 20 unsuccessful trials,[4] on the 21st we finally reach the setting illustrated below:

```
    1  2  3  4  5  6  7  8  9 10 11 12 13 14 15 16 17 18 19 20 21 22 23 24 25 26 27 28 29 30
ø   9  3  2  1  5  1        1  1        3  2  1        1        2        1        3  1     2  3  2        2  4  ø
1      1        1  1  3        2  3  1  1  6  4        2  5              3  1  3  2  3        2  1  2  2  1  1
2      1  5  6        1  1  1  3  1  1  2        2        1  1  4        5  1  1        1                 4     2
3         4        1  1  2  7  3  1  1        2        1  1  3  1        1        2  4                          3
4            3  1  2        1  3        2  1  4  1  3        1  1              1  1  4  6  1        2        1  4
5      3  1  3        1  4        1              2  1  2  7        5  4  1        2              4  2  2  2  5
6   2  6        2  2        5  3        1        3  3  2  1  2              1  3  2        2        1  3  1  1  4  6
7      1        1  2        1  5  3  1  2        2  1  2  1  1  4        2              1  3  1  2        7
8   1        2        5  4        2  3  1  2  1  1  1  1  6  1        1  1  8        2  1        2  1        8
9   3  1  2        2        2        5        1  4  2  1  1  3  5              3  1  1  1  4              2  9
```

```
    1  2       11 12 13 14 15 16 17 18 19 20 21 22 23 24 25 26 27 28 29 30  1  2  3  4  5  6  7  8  9 10     29 30
ø   1  2       5  2  1  1  2                    2  2  3     1     2  1  2  1  2              1  3  1        2     1  2  ø
1               1     1     4     1  1     2  4  1  1  1  2  1              3  4        2  1                          1
2      3                 1  2     3  1        2  1     1     1  1           1  1  3     1     3     1  1  5  1     1  1  2
3         1    1  1  4     4     2  6  3  1  1           7  1     1  3  1     1     1  2  1     1     1        3  1  3
4      1       2  1        4     2     1  3     3              1  2  1  3  1  1  1        3     3     2  1  3     1  1  4
5   3  2       1     2  5        3              2        1     2  6  1  1     3  2  2  2     2  1  5  2  1     1     5
6   3  1       2  4     1  1        2  3           1· 5     1           · 3  1  1     1     1  1  1  2              6
7      3             1  1     1     1  3  2  1  1  1        1  1  1  1  4     3  1     3     3     1  1        1  4  7
8                       3  2        3  1     4              2     2        3     1  1  2              2     8
9      2             2  2        1  1        3  1  1  1  1     2  1  3     2     1  1     1  1              3     9
 x=   49 33 30 31 28 32 31 54 25 28 25 37 22 24 21 23 46 24 30 19 36 16 31 31 11 18 20 19 29 21
```

Here the sum of the columnar cross products is 844, so the ξ I.C. is $\frac{844}{484}=1.74$, evidencing that the two messages *are* homogeneous after all, and that they may be correctly juxtaposed as indicated.

g. We may now consolidate the corresponding columnar distributions of Message "A" and Message "B", in order to obtain more data and thus facilitate the equating of the monomic distributions by sliding them to the best fit. In Fig. 117a, below, we show the consolidated data for the first 6 columns of the combined distributions; and in Fig. 117b we have equated these distributions in terms of col. 1. This process is continued with the remaining columns; and, since we happen to have plenty of data to work with, the entire additive is obtained quite easily, yielding the following 30-digit sequence:

0 6 9 2 0 8 5 3 3 4 9 1 8 6 3 1 5 4 9 7 2 7 8 1 4 0 7 5 2 6

---

[4] The student might wish to see the results of the first 20 trials. These are tabulated in the diagram below, wherein the entries under "slide" indicate the displacement of the frequency diagram for Message "B" to the right with respect to the frequency diagram for Message "A".

Slide	ξ I.C.	Slide	ξ I.C.	Slide	ξ I.C.	Slide	ξ I.C.
ø	0.99	5	0.83	10	0.93	15	0.92
1	1.04	6	1.06	11	0.82	16	0.99
2	0.90	7	1.01	12	0.94	17	0.86
3	1.16	8	1.14	13	1.13	18	1.01
4	0.86	9	0.89	14	0.94	19	1.04

This is probably a *relative* additive; there is no way of proving at this point which one of the ten equivalent additive sequences is the original.

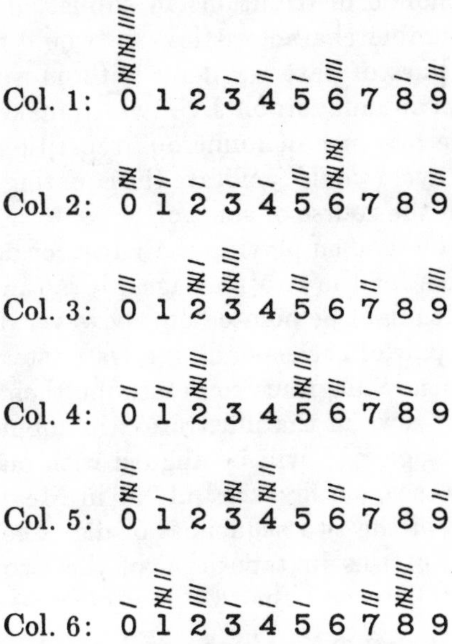

Col. 1: 0 1 2 3 4 5 6 7 8 9   Col. 1: 0 1 2 3 4 5 6 7 8 9

Col. 2: 0 1 2 3 4 5 6 7 8 9   Col. 2: 6 7 8 9 0 1 2 3 4 5

Col. 3: 0 1 2 3 4 5 6 7 8 9   Col. 3: 9 0 1 2 3 4 5 6 7 8

Col. 4: 0 1 2 3 4 5 6 7 8 9   Col. 4: 2 3 4 5 6 7 8 9 0 1

Col. 5: 0 1 2 3 4 5 6 7 8 9   Col. 5: 0 1 2 3 4 5 6 7 8 9

Col. 6: 0 1 2 3 4 5 6 7 8 9   Col. 6: 8 9 0 1 2 3 4 5 6 7

FIGURE 117a   FIGURE 117b

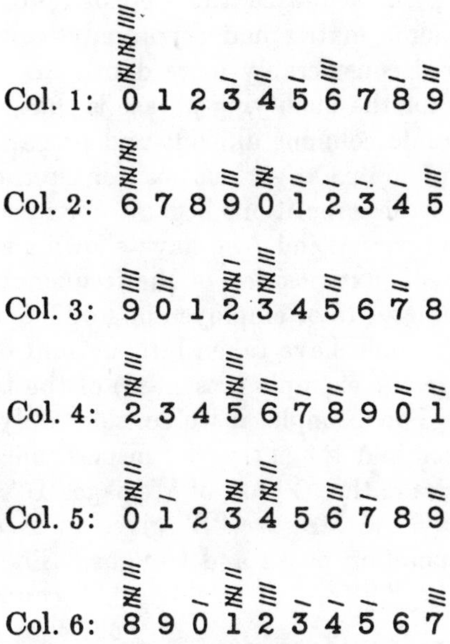

h. Having recovered the additive, we proceed to apply it to Message "A" to reduce the cipher to monoalphabetic terms. The first 60 digits of the message and their conversion are shown in the illustration below:

```
   0 6 9 2 0 8 5 3 3 4 9 1 8 6 3 1 5 4 9 7 2 7 8 1 4 0 7 5 2 6
C: 9 0 7 2 3 7 8 1 6 8 9 4 8 4 9 1 5 7 7 1 1 6 8 4 4 1 7 4 5 4
P: 9 4 8 0 3 9 3 8 3 4 0 3 0 8 6 0 0 3 8 4 9 9 0 3 0 1 0 9 3 8

C: 6 6 2 2 0 8 8 3 1 2 8 7 1 0 3 4 5 4 3 6 5 1 8 4 4 8 0 7 2 5...
P: 6 0 3 0 0 0 3 0 8 8 9 6 3 4 0 3 0 0 4 9 3 4 0 3 0 8 3 2 0 9
```

Once the entire cryptogram has been reduced to monoalphabetic terms, the solution is quite straightforward, following the lines already discussed at length in the previous text.[5] The digits Ø and 3 are identified as row coordinates, and when the converted text is divided accordingly the plain text is recovered, with Message "A" beginning with the words "REPORTS OF INTERROGATION. . ." The monome-dinome matrix is reconstructed as follows:

```
    9 4 8 1 2 7 6 5 0 3
  - R E P U B L I C ░ ░
  Ø A D F G H J K M N O
  3 Q S T V W X Y Z .
```

Since the additive sequence has probably been recovered on a relative base, the matrix coordinates are also relative.

---

[5] Cf. Chapter X, *Military Cryptanalytics, Part I*.

i. In order to illustrate the general theory and techniques of solution of an additive-enciphered monome-dinome system, we have used in the foregoing example a matrix with a very favorable I.C. This facilitated the step of matching monomic distributions in subpar. *g*. If the monome-dinome matrix had cryptanalytically unfavorable characteristics, we would probably have required considerably more depth than the 26 lines of text we dealt with in subpar. *g*. The reason for the qualifying phrase is that, even with an unfavorable I.C. (which makes equating of monomic columns difficult and precarious), the presence of numerous repetitions in the underlying plain text at various positions in the keying cycle would facilitate the equating process, once some of these reptitions began to be uncovered in the course of solution.

j. In subpars. *e* and *f* we have shown a sensitive method employing the χ test for determining the correct juxtaposition of the frequency diagrams for the two messages; it is the method which would have to be employed in a difficult case. It might be pointed out, however, that as a short cut we could have taken into account only one pair of corresponding rows (instead of the 10 pairs as in the example presented) of the two frequency diagrams to determine their relative placement. For example, if we consider only the "$\emptyset$" rows in the illustration in subpar. *e*, we should expect that the entry "9" in position 1 of Message "A" will be aligned with one of the highest entries in the "$\emptyset$" row of Message "B". In this case, our first trial of "9" in Message "A" against the "5" in Message "B" gives an excellent fit of the two sequences of digits as regards their corresponding peaks and troughs. The χ value at this juxtaposition of the two rows is 111; since the "$\emptyset$" row of message "A" contains 50 tallies, and the "$\emptyset$" row of Message "B" contains 34 tallies, the value of χ_r is $\frac{50 \cdot 34}{30} = 56.6$, and the ξ I.C. is $\frac{111}{56.6} = 1.96$. If we have to choose between two or more high scores obtained by this method, this preliminary test could be checked by performing the χ test on several entire columns of the diagram.

87. Analysis of a second case.—*a*. If an additive-enciphered monome-dinome system were used operationally, it is quite possible that the basic rectangle and coordinates might remain in force for a considerable period of time, so that cryptographic clerks might more easily memorize the equivalents for most or all of the letters and thus speed up operations. In such a case, then, the only major variable element in the cryptosystem would be the length and composition of the additive sequence used to encipher the intermediate text.[6] If the basic matrix becomes known through previous solution, we may have recourse to a statistical method for reading traffic enciphered with the same matrix but with an unknown additive.

b. Let us assume that the enemy is still using the same monome-dinome matrix which was recovered in the previous paragraph, *viz.*:

```
        9 4 8 1 2 7 6 5 0 3
      ┌─────────────────────┐
    - │ R E P U B L I C ███  │
    ∅ │ A D F G H J K M N O  │
    3 │ Q S T V W X Y Z      │
      └─────────────────────┘
```

Since the ten cipher digits have greatly varying probabilities, we can calculate a set of weights which will be most useful in solving further systems incorporating the same matrix. First we

---

[6] Another variable might be the specific starting point in the additive cycle.

shall replace the plaintext entries of the matrix with their theoretical frequencies in 1000 letters,[7] thus:

	9	4	8	1	2	7	6	5	Ø	3
−	76	130	27	26	10	36	74	31		
Ø	74	42	28	16	34	2	3	25	79	75
3	3	61	92	15	16	5	19	1		

The theoretical frequency of the digit Ø will be the sum of all the entries in the "Ø" row, plus the entries in the "Ø" column; this is found to be 457. The theoretical frequency of the digit 3 will likewise be the sum of all the entries in the "3" row plus the entries in the "3" column; this is 287. The expected frequencies of the remaining digits will be the sum of the entries in each of the columns corresponding to the particular digit. Thus the theoretical distribution of the 10 digits obtained in the encipherment of 1000 letters of English plain text will be as follows:

Ø	1	2	3	4	5	6	7	8	9
457	57	60	287	233	57	96	43	147	153

These frequencies will be used in the derivation of logarithmic weights, following the general procedure outlined in subpars. 34d and e on pp. 66–67.

  c. In the table below, column (a) represents the frequencies of the ten digits comprising a plaintext "alphabet" of 10 categories; col. (b) represents the logarithms (to the base 10) of

	(a)	(b)	(c)	(d)	(e)
Ø	457	2.6599	1.0264	.99	9
1	57	1.7559	0.1224	.12	1
2	60	1.7782	0.1447	.14	1
3	287	2.4579	0.8244	.80	8
4	233	2.3674	0.7339	.71	7
5	57	1.7559	0.1224	.12	1
6	96	1.9823	0.3488	.34	3
7	43	1.6335	0.0000	.00	0
8	147	2.1673	0.5338	.51	5
9	153	2.1847	0.5512	.53	5

these frequencies; col. (c) contains adjusted logarithms, obtained by subtracting the logarithm of the lowest frequency (43) from all the entries in col. (b), which is equivalent to dividing all the entries in col. (a) by 43;[8] col. (d) contains two-digit logarithms to a new base (10.88); and col. (e) represents deciban weights of col. (d), obtained by multiplying the entries in col. (d) by 10 and dropping the fractional part. The new base, C, is derived as follows:

$$\text{Let } \frac{457}{43} = C^{0.99}$$

$$\text{Then } (\text{Log}_{10}457 - \text{Log}_{10}43) = \text{Log}_{10}C^{0.99}$$

$$= (0.99)(\text{Log}_{10}C)$$

$$C = \text{Antilog } \frac{(\text{Log}_{10}457 - \text{Log}_{10}43)}{0.99} = \text{Antilog } \frac{1.0264}{0.99} = \text{Antilog } 1.0368$$

$$C = 10.88$$

---

[7] Cf. p. 28, *Military Cryptanalytics, Part I.*

[8] The purpose of this step is to reduce the lowest frequency, 43, to 1 on an arithmetical scale. The computations which follow are similar to those in subpar. 34e, where the rationale of the procedure was developed.

Logarithms to a new base may be computed by the formula

$$Log_C Y = \frac{Log_{10} Y}{Log_{10} C}$$

Therefore if the entries in col. (c) are divided by 1.0368, we obtain the figures in col. (d) which are logarithms to the base 10.88.

d. For a demonstration problem, we will use Message "B" given in subpar. 86a; we will assume that the additive is unknown, but that the monome-dinome rectangle has been recovered from other messages. Since the message factors to a period of 30, it is written out on this width:

1	2	3	4	5	6	7	8	9	10	11	12	13	14	15	16	17	18	19	20	21	22	23	24	25	26	27	28	29	30
6	0	5	4	2	4	7	5	5	0	6	9	0	6	0	7	5	3	6	2	5	4	6	6	2	1	5	4	5	7
5	9	1	5	7	8	7	4	7	3	4	9	3	1	6	8	5	3	4	7	7	1	0	0	1	5	4	0	9	2
6	0	6	5	3	0	1	9	2	4	4	6	9	5	4	2	8	7	3	3	9	1	8	0	3	6	5	3	4	7
4	3	8	1	8	0	8	6	2	6	0	6	3	5	4	1	3	6	7	4	1	1	7	9	4	5	7	8	3	7
2	5	5	1	3	5	1	5	6	2	0	6	7	2	3	1	9	9	6	2	5	1	1	6	3	4	9	7	7	7
5	7	2	1	7	3	5	5	4	0	0	1	9	5	3	2	8	1	3	8	9	0	8	1	3	0	5	5	3	0
0	7	1	4	2	0	6	5	2	6	0	6	5	5	4	8	4	3	3	4	3	4	9	0	3	3	1	9	0	4
2	6	7	4	2	9	7	4	2	4	0	4	5	7	3	2	2	3	6	7	1	7	8	6	3	2	5	8	9	0
5	9	8	1	6	4	2	5	1	7	3	0	3	2	3	8	3	6	1	8	8	0	8	5	9	1	5	4	3	3
2	5	8	9	0	5	8	2	5	4	6	0	2	0	0	1	4	3	7	8	9	9	2	6	3	4	9	0	2	8
6	7	1	3	7	4	0	3	2	5	5	3	3	5	4	1	5	3	7	4	2	4	0	6	3	7	5	4	9	8

e. Consider the digits comprising col. 1: one of the ten possible additive digits, when applied to the cipher digits of col. 1, will yield a set of plaintext digits belonging to the theoretical distribution (given at the end of subpar. *b*) of our known matrix. This gives us our clue for a *modus operandi*, and we once again bring to bear the versatile and valuable tool of the generatrix method. The top row of Fig. 118a, below, consists of the digits of col. 1. In the succeeding nine rows we have completed the normal numerical sequence; this is equivalent to trying all ten digits as additives for the column. In Fig. 118b, we have replaced the digits of Fig. 118a by their deciban equivalents derived in subpar. *c*.[9] The sums of the log weights given at the right of Fig. 118b provide a means for evaluating the relative merits of each decipherment

	Generatrices		Decibans	Σ
	<u>6 5 6 4 2 5 0 2 5 2 6</u>		3 1 3 7 1 1 9 1 1 1 3	31
	7 6 7 5 3 6 1 3 6 3 7		0 3 0 1 8 3 1 8 3 8 0	35
	8 7 8 6 4 7 2 4 7 4 8		5 0 5 3 7 0 1 7 0 7 5	40
	9 8 9 7 5 8 3 5 8 5 9		5 5 5 0 1 5 8 1 5 1 5	41
	0 9 0 8 6 9 4 6 9 6 0		9 5 9 5 3 5 7 3 5 3 9	63
1.	1 0 1 9 7 0 5 7 0 7 1		1 9 1 5 0 9 1 0 9 0 1	36
	2 1 2 0 8 1 6 8 1 8 2		1 1 1 9 5 1 3 5 1 5 1	33
	3 2 3 1 9 2 7 9 2 9 3		8 1 8 1 5 1 0 5 1 5 8	43
	4 3 4 2 0 3 8 0 3 0 4		7 8 7 1 9 8 5 9 8 9 7	78
	5 4 5 3 1 4 9 1 4 1 5		1 7 1 8 1 7 5 1 7 1 1	40

FIGURE 118a   FIGURE 118b

---

[9] The easiest procedure here is to complete the log sequences *vertically*, starting at the proper initial point determined by the appropriate digit in the top row of Fig. 118a. If desired, strips may be prepared as an aid in this process.

(i.e., each row) in Fig. 118a on the same row as the corresponding log weights in Fig. 118b. The predominantly high score of 78 indicates that the first cipher digit, 6_c, should be a 4_p; therefore the correct additive for col. 1 is 2.

    f. The completion diagrams and the log weighting for the next nine columns of the cryptogram in subpar. d are shown below:

		0 9 0 3 5 7 7 6 9 5 7	9 5 9 8 1 0 0 3 5 1 0	41
		1	1 9 1 7 3 5 5 0 9 3 5	48
		2	1 1 1 1 0 5 5 5 1 0 5	25
		3	8 1 8 3 5 9 9 5 1 5 9	63
		4	7 8 7 0 5 1 1 9 8 5 1	52
2.	5		1 7 1 5 9 1 1 1 7 9 1	43
	6		3 1 3 5 1 8 8 1 1 1 8	40
	7		0 3 0 9 1 7 7 8 3 1 7	46
	8		5 0 5 1 8 1 1 7 0 8 1	37
	9		5 5 5 1 7 3 3 1 5 7 3	45

		5 1 6 8 5 2 1 7 8 8 1	1 1 3 5 1 1 1 0 5 5 1	24
	6		3 1 0 5 3 8 1 5 5 5 1	37
	7		0 8 5 9 0 7 8 5 9 9 8	68
	8		5 7 5 1 5 1 7 9 1 1 7	49
	9		5 1 9 1 5 3 1 1 1 1 1	29
3.	0		9 3 1 8 9 0 3 1 8 8 3	53
	1		1 0 1 7 1 5 0 8 7 7 0	37
	2		1 5 8 1 1 5 5 7 1 1 5	40
	3		8 5 7 3 8 9 5 1 3 3 5	57
	4		7 9 1 0 7 1 9 3 0 0 9	46

		4 5 5 1 1 1 4 4 1 9 3	7 1 1 1 1 1 7 7 1 5 8	40
	5		1 3 3 1 1 1 1 1 1 9 7	29
	6		3 0 0 8 8 8 3 3 8 1 1	43
	7		0 5 5 7 7 7 0 0 7 1 3	42
	8		5 5 5 1 1 1 5 5 1 8 0	37
4.	9		5 9 9 3 3 3 5 5 3 7 5	57
	0		9 1 1 0 0 0 9 9 0 1 5	35
	1		1 1 1 5 5 5 1 1 5 3 9	37
	2		1 8 8 5 5 5 1 1 5 0 1	40
	3		8 7 7 9 9 9 8 8 9 5 1	80

		2 7 3 8 3 7 2 2 6 0 7	1 0 8 5 8 0 1 1 3 9 0	36
	3		8 5 7 5 7 5 8 8 0 1 5	59
	4		7 5 1 9 1 5 7 7 5 1 5	53
	5		1 9 3 1 3 9 1 1 5 8 9	50
	6		3 1 0 1 0 1 3 3 9 7 1	29
5.	7		0 1 5 8 5 1 0 0 1 1 1	23
	8		5 8 5 7 5 8 5 5 1 3 8	60
	9		5 7 9 1 9 7 5 5 8 0 7	63
	0		9 1 1 3 1 1 9 9 7 5 1	47
	1		1 3 1 0 1 3 1 1 1 5 3	20

249

<u>4 8 0 0 5 3 0 9 4 5 4</u>

5	7 5 9 9 1 8 9 5 7 1 7	68
6	1 5 1 1 3 7 1 9 1 3 1	33
7	3 9 1 1 0 1 1 1 3 0 3	23
8	0 1 8 8 5 3 8 1 0 5 0	39
9	5 1 7 7 5 0 7 8 5 5 5	55
0	5 8 1 1 9 5 1 7 5 9 5	56
1	9 7 3 3 1 5 3 1 9 1 9	51
2	1 1 0 0 1 9 0 3 1 1 1	18
3	1 3 5 5 8 1 5 0 1 8 1	38
	9 0 5 5 7 1 5 5 8 7 8	59

6. (label beside 9)

<u>7 7 1 8 1 5 6 7 2 8 0</u>

8	0 0 1 5 1 1 3 0 1 5 9	26
9	5 5 1 5 1 3 0 5 8 5 1	39
0	5 5 8 9 8 0 5 5 7 9 1	62
1	9 9 7 1 7 5 5 9 1 1 8	62
2	1 1 1 1 1 5 9 1 3 1 7	31
3	1 1 3 8 3 9 1 1 0 8 1	36
4	8 8 0 7 0 1 1 8 5 7 3	48
5	7 7 5 1 5 1 8 7 5 1 0	47
6	1 1 5 3 5 8 7 1 9 3 5	48
	3 3 9 0 9 7 1 3 1 0 5	41

7. (label beside 2)

<u>5 4 9 6 5 5 5 4 5 2 3</u>

6	1 7 5 3 1 1 1 7 1 1 8	36
7	3 1 9 0 3 3 3 1 3 8 7	41
8	0 3 1 5 0 0 0 3 0 7 1	20
9	5 0 1 5 5 5 5 0 5 1 3	35
0	5 5 8 9 5 5 5 5 5 3 0	55
1	9 5 7 1 9 9 9 5 9 0 5	68
2	1 9 1 1 1 1 1 9 1 5 5	35
3	1 1 3 8 1 1 1 1 1 5 9	32
4	8 1 0 7 8 8 8 1 8 9 1	59
	7 8 5 1 7 7 7 8 7 1 1	59

8. (label beside 0)

<u>5 7 2 2 6 4 2 2 1 5 2</u>

6	1 0 1 1 3 7 1 1 1 1 1	18
7	3 5 8 8 0 1 8 8 1 3 8	53
8	0 5 7 7 5 3 7 7 8 0 7	56
9	5 9 1 1 5 0 1 1 7 5 1	36
0	5 1 3 3 9 5 3 3 1 5 3	41
1	9 1 0 0 1 5 0 0 3 9 0	28
2	1 8 5 5 1 9 5 5 0 1 5	45
3	1 7 5 5 8 1 5 5 5 1 5	48
4	8 1 9 9 7 1 9 9 5 8 9	75
	7 3 1 1 1 8 1 1 9 7 1	40

9. (label beside 0)

```
     0 3 4 6 2 0 6 4 7 4 5        9 8 7 3 1 9 3 7 0 7 1   55
     1                            1 7 1 0 8 1 0 1 5 1 3   28
     2                            1 1 3 5 7 1 5 3 5 3 0   34
     3                            8 3 0 5 1 8 5 0 9 0 5   44
     4                            7 0 5 9 3 7 9 5 1 5 5   56
10.  5                            1 5 5 1 0 1 1 5 1 5 9   34
     6                            3 5 9 1 5 3 1 9 8 9 1   54
     7                            0 9 1 8 5 0 8 1 7 1 1   41
     8                            5 1 1 7 9 5 7 1 1 1 8   46
     9                            5 1 8 1 1 5 1 8 3 8 7   48
```

g. Some of the columns show a single generatrix with an outstandingly high score. This leaves but little doubt as to the validity of the selection of the proper generatrix (e.g., 78 for col. 1, 80 for col. 4, and 75 for col. 9).[10] In other columns, such as col. 5 (with three close scores of 63, 60, and 59) and col. 10 (with the close scores of 56, 55, and 54), there are two or more possible choices for the correct generatrix. What we will do is to set down the possible plaintext digits for the first 10 digits of the cryptogram, and try to get started with a good plaintext fragment. From the foregoing generatrix diagrams, the following are the possible plaintext digits for the first 10 ciphers:

```
        1  2  3  4  5  6  7  8  9  10
   C:   6  0  5  4  2  4  7  5  5  0
   P:   4  3  7  3  9  4  9  0  3  4
               8        0        0
               3        6
```

We proceed to take the various possibilities into consideration, and we make trial decipherments as follows:

```
1.   4/3 7/3 9/4/9/0 3/4/
     E   X   Q  ER  O  E

2.   4/3 7/3 8/4/9/0 3/4/
     E   X   T  ER  O  E

3.   4/3 7/3 3/4/9/0 3/4/
     E   X   ?  ER  O  E

4.   4/3 7/3 9/4/0 0/3 4/
     E   X   Q   E  N   S

5.   4/3 7/3 8/4/0 0/3 4/
     E   X   T   E  N   S
```

---

[10] In order to appreciate the significance of the scores, we should know the expected score for a correct generatrix, as well as the expected score for an incorrect one. For a correct case, the expected score is calculated by multiplying the probability of each digit by its log weight, summing the products thus obtained; this sum is then multiplied by the number of digits in the generatrix. In a random case, the expected score is the sum of the log weights in the scale (40) divided by 10, multiplied by the number of digits in the generatrix. Thus, the expected score in a correct case is 6.3N, and the random score is 4N, where N is the number of digits in the generatrix. (See also footnote 2 on p. 67.)

On the fifth trial, the beginning of the word EXTENSIVE manifests itself, and we are off to a flying start. We derive the additive, and decipher down the columns, yielding the following decipherments:

```
2 7 8 1 4 0 7 5 2 6
6 0 5 4 2 4 7 5 5 0 ...
4/3 7/3 8/4/0 0/3 4/
 E    X    T  E  N    S

5 9 1 5 7 8 7 4 7 3
3 2/3 4/3 8/0 9/5/7/
   S    T    A  C  L

6 0 6 5 3 0 1 9 2 4
4/3 8/4/9/0 4/4/0 8/
   T  E  R    D  E  F

4 3 8 1 8 0 8 6 2 6
2/6/0 0/4/0 1/1/0 0/
 I  N  E    G  U  N

2 5 5 1 3 5 1 5 6 2
0 8/7/0 9/5/4/0 4/6/
   L  A    C  E  D  I

5 7 2 1 7 3 5 5 4 0
3 0 4/0 3/3 8/0 2/4/
       O    T  H  E

0 7 1 4 2 0 6 5 2 6
8/0 3/3 8/0 9/0 0/0
   O    T  A  N

2 6 7 4 2 9 7 4 2 4
0 9/9/3 8/9/0 9/0 8/
   R  T  R    A  F

5 9 8 1 6 4 2 5 1 7
3 2/0 0/2/4/5/0 9/1/
   N  BE C  A  U

2 5 8 9 0 5 8 2 5 4
0 8/0 8/6/5/1/7/3 8/
   F  IC U  L  T

6 7 1 3 7 4 0 3 2 5
4/0 3/2/3 4/3 8/0 9/
   O  B  S    T  A
```

The rest of the solution follows easily by extending the plain text already recovered.

h. The foregoing figure has given us a clue as to the method to be followed when we have a *placed* crib, either at the very beginning or the very end of the message. If we had had the probable word EXTENSIVE as a stereotyped beginning, we would have obtained the same results.

If, however, a crib must be dragged throughout a message, the procedure is quite laborious. In the absence of words, we could drag short plaintext fragments through the cipher, and examine the decipherments at cyclic recurrences of the key.[11] For example, suppose we were to drag TION, represented by the digits 3860300, through the message under examination. If we start TION at the fourth cipher digit (as being the earliest position TION could reasonably be expected to occur), we would get the decipherments shown in Fig. 119a. We then slide the crib over one position, and we get the decipherments shown in Fig. 119b.

```
        1 4 8 7 2 5 0                       9 6 1 5 2 0 6
6 0 5 4 2 4 7 5 5 0 6 9...         6 0 5 4 2 4 7 5 5 0 6 9...
      /3 8/6/0 3/0 0/                     /3 8/6/0 3/0 0/
        T  I  O  N                         T  I  O  N
5 9 1 5 7 8 7 4 7 3 4 9           5 9 1 5 7 8 7 4 7 3 4 9
      4/3 0/0 2/2/3                       8/2/6/9/5/3 8/
        H     B                           B  I  R  C  T
6 0 6 5 3 0 1 9 2 4 4 6           6 0 6 5 3 0 1 9 2 4 4 6
      4/9/2/4/7/7/4/                       4/4/0 4/0 4/8/
        R  B  E  L  L  E                   E     D     D  P
4 3 8 1 8 0 8 6 2 6 0 6           4 3 8 1 8 0 8 6 2 6 0 6
      0 4/2/1/4/7/6/                       9/4/7/1/0 6/4/
        B  U  E  L  I                       E  L  U  K  E
2 5 5 1 3 5 1 5 6 2 0 6           2 5 5 1 3 5 1 5 6 2 0 6
      0 9/7/4/3 1/2/                       4/9/0 0/4/2/4/
        L  E  V  B                         R  N  E  B  E
5 7 2 1 7 3 5 5 4 0 0 1           5 7 2 1 7 3 5 5 4 0 0 1
      0 3 5/8/3 9/0                         8/7/4/0 2/0 4/
        P     Q                            L  E  H  D
0 7 1 4 2 0 6 5 2 6 0 6           0 7 1 4 2 0 6 5 2 6 0 6
      3 8/2/9/3 7/6/                       3 4/5/0 0/6/4/
        B  R  X  I                         C  N  I  E
2 6 7 4 2 9 7 4 2 4 0 4           2 6 7 4 2 9 7 4 2 4 0 4
      3 8/1/0 2/7/4/                       3 3 6/9/0 4/4/
        U  H  L  E                             R  D  E
5 9 8 1 6 4 2 5 1 7 3 0           5 9 8 1 6 4 2 5 1 7 3 0
      0 2/6/5/3 6/7/                       7/8/1/0 9/7/7/
        I  C  Y  L                         P  U  A  R R
2 5 8 9 0 5 8 2 5 4 6 0           2 5 8 9 0 5 8 2 5 4 6 0
      8/6/7/1/0 0/4/                       1/9/7/7/3 4/0
        I  L  U  N  E                       R  L  L  S
6 7 1 3 7 4 0 3 2 5 5 3           6 7 1 3 7 4 0 3 2 5 5 3
      2/3 6/3 1/7/5/                       8/8/9/8/0 5/9/
        Y  V  L  C                         P  R P  M  R
```

FIGURE 119a   FIGURE 119b

---

[11] The procedure here would be to derive a trial additive and write this additive on a slip of paper, then slide the additive down the column, noting what decipherments result. These decipherments are then partitioned into monomes and dinomes as far as possible, and the equivalent plaintext letters are judged as to their relative merits.

The patient cryptanalyst will, on the 136th trial, reap his just reward when he finally uncovers the following stretches of good English plain text:

```
                                        3 4 9 1 8 6 3
    6 0 5 4 2 4 7 5 5 0 6 9 0 6 0 7 5 3 6 2 5 4 6 6 2 1 5 4 5 7
                                        3 8/6/3 8/0 9/
                                          I T   A
    5 9 1 5 7 8 7 4 7 3 4 9 3 1 6 8 5 3 4 7 7 1 0 0 1 5 4 0 9 2
                                        1/3 8/0 2/4/8/
                                          T   H E P
    6 0 6 5 3 0 1 9 2 4 4 6 9 5 4 2 8 7 3 3 9 1 8 0 3 6 5 3 4 7
                                        0 9/0 0/0 4/0
                                            N   D
    4 3 8 1 8 0 8 6 2 6 0 6 3 5 4 1 3 6 7 4 1 1 7 9 4 5 7 8 3 7
                                        4/0 2/0 9/3 1/
                                          H   A V
    2 5 5 1 3 5 1 5 6 2 0 6 7 2 3 1 9 9 6 2 5 1 1 6 3 4 9 7 7 7
                                       /3 8/6/0 3/0 0/
                                          T I O   N
    5 7 2 1 7 3 5 5 4 0 0 1 9 5 3 2 8 1 3 8 9 0 8 1 3 0 5 5 3 0
                                        0 4/0 9/0 5/0
                                          A   M
    0 7 1 4 2 0 6 5 2 6 0 6 5 5 4 8 4 3 3 4 3 4 9 0 3 3 1 9 0 4
                                        0 0 4/3 1/4/0
                                          V   E
    2 6 7 4 2 9 7 4 2 4 0 4 5 7 3 2 2 3 6 7 1 7 8 6 3 2 5 8 9 0
                                        3 3 2/6/0 0/0
                                          I   N
    5 9 8 1 6 4 2 5 1 7 3 0 3 2 3 8 3 6 1 8 8 0 8 5 9 1 5 4 3 3
                                        8/4/9/9/0 9/6/
                                          E R R A   I
    2 5 8 9 0 5 8 2 5 4 6 0 2 0 0 1 4 3 7 8 9 9 2 6 3 4 9 0 2 8
                                        4/4/0 8/4/0 0/
                                          E F E N
    6 7 1 3 7 4 0 3 2 5 5 3 3 5 4 1 5 3 7 4 2 4 0 6 3 7 5 4 9 8
                                        4/0 3/3 2/0 0/
                                          O   W N
```

FIGURE 119c

If we were unlucky with TION, we would try other polygraphic cribs. As a last resort, we might even have to be content with dragging the digit equivalents of plaintext digraphs such as TH, IN, ON, etc. (Digraphs such as RE and ER would be unsatisfactory, because the component letters are represented in the rectangle by monomes, so our decipherments would be next to useless—in fact, useless.)

i. As an illustration of the effectiveness of testing even a short crib through a cipher text, let us consider dragging the digraph TH (which has the tetranome equivalent 3802) through the message we have been using as an example. In Fig. 120a, below, we assume that TH begins the

254

3 2 5 2
6 0 5 4 2 4 7 5 5 0...
3 8/0 2/
　T H
5 9 1 5 7 8 7 4 7 3
2/7/6/3
　L I　　　　　7,8
6 0 6 5 3 0 1 9 2 4
3 8/1/3
　　U　　　　　6
4 3 8 1 8 0 8 6 2 6
1/1/3 9/
　U Q　　　　　6,2
2 5 5 1 3 5 1 5 6 2
9/3 0/9/
　　R　　　　　8
5 7 2 1 7 3 5 5 4 0
2/5/7/9/
　C L R　　　　7,7,8
0 7 1 4 2 0 6 5 2 6
7/5/6/2/
　C I B　　　　7,8,4
2 6 7 4 2 9 7/4 2 4
9/4/2/2/
　E B B　　　　9,4,4
5 9 8 1 6 4 2 5 1 7
2/7/3 9/
　L Q　　　　　7,2
2 5 8 9 0 5 8 2 5 4
9/3 3/7/
　　? L　　　　Ø,7
6 7 1 3 7 4 0 3 2 5
3 5/6/1/
　　I U　　　　7,6
　　　　　　　　　125

FIGURE 120a

　　　　4 9 1 8
...7 5 3 6 2 5 4 6 6 2...
　　　　8/6/3 8/
　　　　　I T　　　　8,9
8 5 3 4 7 7 1 0 0 1
3 8/0 2/
　　　　　T H
2 8 7 3 3 9 1 8 0 3
9/0 0/0
　　　　　N　　　　8
1 3 6 7 4 1 1 7 9 4
0 2/0 9/
　　　　　A　　　　8
1 9 9 6 2 5 1 1 6 3
8/6/0 3/
　　　　　I O　　　8,8
2 8 1 3 8 9 0 8 1 3
4/0 9/0
　　　　　A　　　　8
8 4 3 3 4 3 4 9 0 3
0 4/3 1/
　　　　　V　　　　5
2 2 3 6 7 1 7 8 6 3
3 2/6/0
　　　　　I　　　　8
8 3 6 1 8 8 0 8 5 9
4/9/9/0
　　　　　R R　　　8,8
1 4 3 7 8 9 9 2 6 3
4/0 8/4/
　　　　　F E　　　6,9
1 5 3 7 4 2 4 0 6 3
0 3/3 2/
　　　　　W　　　　5
　　　　　　　　　　　106

FIGURE 120b

message; we derive the additive and decipher down the columns, and we partition the intermediate plain text as far as we can with assurance—then we decrypt the partitioned plain as
shown. In Fig. 120b, where the TH happens to be placed *correctly* (starting at the 50th digit),
we get the decipherments shown in that figure. With so much depth, it is no problem to pick
out the correct case by eye from among a set of trials. If, however, the cryptanalyst were
testing a much shallower depth (i.e., fewer repetitions of the keying cycle), a statistical weighting
of the decipherments would be necessary to enable recognition of the best case or cases from
among the many trials. The scoring of the decipherments in Figs. 120a and b is accomplished

by assigning to the deciphered plaintext letters (less the original TH) the deciban weights given in subpar. 34c (excluding the period for which no weight has been calculated), summing these weights, and dividing by the number of monomes and dinomes exposed in the partitioning process—this yields an average for the column. Thus, in Fig. 120a, the sum of the weights of the decrypted plaintext letters (including a weight of ∅ for the nonexistent dinome 33, is 124; the number of intermediate plaintext groupings (excluding the dinome 30 representing a period) is 21; therefore the average score is $\frac{124}{21}=5.9$. In the case of Fig. 120b, the sum of the weights of the decrypted letters is 106, which when divided by 14 (the number of intermediate plaintext groupings in this case) gives an average of 7.6. Since the expected average score for an incorrect case is 5.8, and the expected average score for a correct case is 7.6,[12] it is clear that Fig. 120a is no better than random, while Fig. 120b is in all probability valid and can be used to extend further plain text.

88. Analysis involving isologs.—*a*. In enciphered monome-dinome systems, attacks based on the exploitation of isologs are particularly valuable, especially in those cases wherein the monome-dinome matrix has a low I.C., or where coordinates or additive keys are changed so frequently that not enough homogeneous traffic is available for study. Several typical examples of isolog attacks will be presented in the succeeding subparagraphs.

b. Let the following two messages be examined:

Message "A"

80404	31105	22961	61428	00434	28663	47839	25767	04100	20012
07149	90313	87161	34078	16767	04100	20681	06449	73411	56005
13305	20885	09483	46222	99725	01138	00999	03729	43177	53265
12159	65970	19302	33919	12775	00560	33436	82551		

Message "B"

04378	88147	20798	22772	39352	81140	51367	49631	51142	28849
68493	29231	40648	48506	30631	51142	28418	67793	02339	19582
27833	44759	56425	44059	50079	30056	63476	17257	67041	00207
10986	26224	48220	96496	26203	24434	80478	80388		

Both messages are of the same length, and both messages have a long internal repetition beginning with the 38th and 73d digits; furthermore, there is a long repetition between the two messages, beginning with the 162d digit of Message "A" and the 89th digit of Message "B". These phenomena, among other considerations (in particular, the δ and ξ I.C.'s), confirm the period as 35, show that the messages are isologs, and indicate that Message "B" is +3 on the keying cycle with respect to Message "A".

---

[12] Derivation of these constants has been shown in footnote 2 on p. 67.

c. The messages are now written out as follows:

```
 1  2  3  4  5  6  7  8  9 10 11 12 13 14 15 16 17 18 19 20 21 22 23 24 25 26 27 28 29 30 31 32 33 34 35
 8  0  4  0  4  3  1  1  0  5  2  2  9  6  1  6  1  4  2  8  0  0  4  3  4  2  8  6  6  3  4  7  8  3  9
 2  5  7  6  7  0  4  1  0  0  2  0  0  1  2  0  7  1  4  9  9  0  3  1  3  8  7  1  6  1  3  4  0  7  8
 1  6  7  6  7  0  4  1  0  0  2  0  6  8  1  0  6  4  4  9  7  3  4  1  1  5  6  0  0  5  1  3  3  0  5
 2  0  8  8  5  0  9  4  8  3  4  6  2  2  2  9  9  7  2  5  0  1  1  3  8  0  0  9  9  9  0  3  7  2  9
 4  3  1  7  7  5  3  2  6  5  1  2  1  5  9  6  5  9  7  0  1  9  3  0  2  3  3  9  1  9  1  2  7  7  5
 0  0  5  6  0  3  3  4  3  6  8  2  5  5  1
```

```
 1  2  3  4  5  6  7  8  9 10 11 12 13 14 15 16 17 18 19 20 21 22 23 24 25 26 27 28 29 30 31 32 33 34 35
          0  4  3  7  8  8  8  1  4  7  2  0  7  9  8  2  2  7  7  2  3  9  3  5  2  8  1  1  4  0  5  1
 3  6  7  4  9  6  3  1  5  1  1  4  2  2  8  8  4  9  6  8  4  9  3  2  9  2  3  1  4  0  6  4  8  4  8
 5  0  6  3  0  6  3  1  5  1  1  4  2  2  8  4  1  8  6  7  7  9  3  0  2  3  3  9  1  9  5  8  2  2  7
 8  3  3  4  4  7  5  9  5  6  4  2  5  4  4  0  5  9  5  0  0  7  9  3  0  0  5  6  6  3  4  7  6  1  7
 2  5  7  6  7  0  4  1  0  0  2  0  7  1  0  9  8  6  2  6  2  2  4  4  8  2  2  0  9  6  4  9  6  2  6
 2  0  3  2  4  4  3  4  8  0  4  7  8  8  0  3  8  8
```

We will assume arbitrarily that the additive for col. 1 is $\emptyset$; this makes the first digit of Message "A" an 8_p. The first digit of Message "B" must also be an 8_p, so the additive for col. 4 is 2, which makes the 4th digit of Message "A" a $\emptyset$. This crisscross process is continued, until the complete additive is recovered. The recovery of the entire additive is possible here because the displacement interval of the two messages, 3, is not a factor of nor has it a factor in common with the period, 35. If the displacement interval had been, say, 14, the common factor (7) would have resulted in a closed chain of additives for cols. 1, 8, 15, 22, and 29; thus there would be 7 distinct chains in all.

d. After the additive has been recovered in the foregoing problem, Message "A" is reduced to monoalphabetic terms; this is shown below, together with the recovered additive:

```
 1  2  3  4  5  6  7  8  9 10 11 12 13 14 15 16 17 18 19 20 21 22 23 24 25 26 27 28 29 30 31 32 33 34 35
 0  3  4  2  7  3  9  1  8  6  1  2  8  1  0  6  4  7  2  5  0  7  9  3  6  8  5  4  4  8  9  2  5  0  6
 8  7  0  8  7  0  2  0  2  9  1  0  1  5  1  0  7  7  0  3  0  3  5  0  8  4  3  2  2  5  5  5  3  3  3
 2  2  3  4  0  7  5  0  2  4  1  8  2  0  2  4  3  4  2  4  9  3  4  8  7  0  2  7  2  3  4  2  5  7  2
 1  3  3  4  0  7  5  0  2  4  1  8  8  7  1  4  2  7  2  4  7  6  5  8  5  7  1  6  6  7  2  1  8  0  9
 2  7  4  6  8  7  0  3  0  7  3  4  4  1  2  3  5  0  0  0  0  4  2  0  2  2  5  5  5  1  1  1  2  2  3
 4  0  7  5  0  2  4  1  8  9  0  0  3  4  9  0  1  2  5  5  1  2  4  7  6  5  8  5  7  1  2  0  2  7  9
 0  7  1  4  3  0  4  3  5  0  7  0  7  4  1
```

The presence of the dinome 22 before and after the tripled digits [13] in two portions of the message makes the assumption of 2 as a row coordinate reasonable, and the four consecutive occurences of the digit $\emptyset$ makes this also a likely row coordinate. When the intermediate plain text is partitioned according to this hypothesis, the message plain text can be recovered easily, beginning with the words TO COMMANDING OFFICER... The matrix is reconstructed as follows:

```
      4 8 1 3 7 9 5 6 Ø 2
    - E T N R O A I S ■
    Ø B C D F G H J K L M
    2 P Q U V W X Y Z . #
```

---

[13] See footnote 3 on p. 191 of *Military Cryptanalytics, Part I.*

e. The period of the isologs in subpar. *b*, above, was determined from the occurrence of a long internal polygraphic repetition within each message. If this repetition had not been present, we still could have factored the isologs by superimposing them and subtracting the cipher of Message "A" from that of Message "B". Since the plain text of the two messages is identical, these differences will represent the difference between the *key digits* at an interval corresponding to the relative displacement of the isologs; therefore these differences will repeat *at an interval corresponding to the length of the period.* The beginnings of the messages and their differences are shown in the following diagram:

```
"B": 04378 88147 20798 22772 39352   81140 51367 49631 51142 28849...
"A": 80404 31105 22961 61428 00434   28663 47839 25767 04100 20012...
     24974 57042 08837 61354 39928   63587 14538 24974 57042 08837
```

The differences repeat at an interval of 35 digits, revealing the length of the period. Note that the sequence of these differences is identical to the delta (or *lateral* differences) of the additive at an interval of 3 (i.e., the displacement interval of the two messages). If we take the delta at an interval of 3 of the key shown in subpar. *d*, we will obtain the stream 24974..., which is the same as the differences just derived above. If we had subtracted Message "B" from Message "A", we would of course have obtained the *complements* of these differences.

f. Isologs involving identical matrices and coordinates, but having additive keys of different lengths and composition, are readily susceptible to attack providing the additive lengths are relatively prime. As a demonstration of this, let us suppose that we have a pair of isologs, factoring to 15 and 16, respectively. The first 80 digits of the messages are shown in Figs. 121*a* and *b*, below:

Message "A"

```
 1  2  3  4  5  6  7  8  9 10 11 12 13 14 15
 8  1  7  3  8  6  3  3  5  1  0  5  0  3  8
 0  1  4  5  4  6  4  8  3  0  3  8  1  0  2
 5  9  0  8  4  8  3  6  7  2  6  0  9  0  1
 1  2  9  5  3  0  4  7  5  6  8  8  3  6  4
 0  6  4  7  4  0  3  8  0  4  0  8  2  2  7
 7  9  7  7  5...
```

FIGURE 121*a*

Message "B"

```
 1  2  3  4  5  6  7  8  9 10 11 12 13 14 15 16
 1  2  8  4  2  4  9  8  3  1  1  9  3  6  1  7
 0  2  8  9  5  7  2  8  9  6  3  1  4  6  5  2
 6  8  1  8  7  7  1  8  8  7  0  1  6  2  8  9
 3  7  2  9  9  6  1  7  4  6  8  6  2  3  7  9
 6  9  0  1  2  6  8  1  4  6  0  6  7  1  2  1...
```

FIGURE 121*b*

If we assume an arbitrary additive of ∅ for the first column of Message "A", we get the decipherments shown in Fig. 122*a*. These decipherments are now cribbed into Message "B", as shown in Fig. 122*b* together with the derived additive; this latter is used to decipher more digits in Message "B", and these decipherments in turn are cribbed into Message "A", and so on until all the intermediate plaintext has been recovered.[14]

g. The foregoing situation is easily exploitable no matter what the lengths of the periods are, so long as they are prime to each other. If the lengths of the periods are not relatively prime, the general approach in the previous subparagraph may still be used, if not to reduce the entire text to monoalphabetic terms, at least to reduce the text to several sets of families which might then be amalgamated by other means. In passing, it might be pointed out that a difference of 1 in the lengths of additives of a pair of isologs might arise from an error in copying out the additive, resulting in an added or a dropped digit.

[14] The plain text and basic matrix in this example are the same as those given in the preceding subparagraph.

Message "A"

```
 1  2  3  4  5  6  7  8  9 10 11 12 13 14 15
∅
 8  1  7  3  8  6  3  3  5  1  0  5  0  3  8
 8
 0  1  4  5  4  6  4  8  3  0  3  8  1  0  2
 0
 5  9  0  8  4  8  3  6  7  2  6  0  9  0  1
 5
 1  2  9  5  3  0  4  7  5  6  8  8  3  6  4
 1
 0  6  4  7  4  0  3  8  0  4  0  8  2  2  7
 0
 7  9  7  7  5 ...
 7
```

FIGURE 122a

Message "B"

```
 1  2  3  4  5  6  7  8  9 10 11 12 13 14 15 16
 3                                  9  2  1  0  7
 1  2  8  4  2  4  9  8  3  1  1  9  3  6  1  7
 8                                              0
 0  2  8  9  5  7  2  8  9  6  3  1  4  6  5  2
 5
 6  8  1  8  7  7  1  8  8  7  0  1  6  2  8  9
 1
 3  7  2  9  9  6  1  7  4  6  8  6  2  3  7  9
 0
 6  9  0  1  2  6  8  1  4  6  0  6  7  1  2  1...
 7
```

FIGURE 122b

h. In the next situation, we will assume that we have a pair of messages factoring to 15, having identical beginnings 20 digits long. The first 80 digits of these messages are given below:

Message "A"

```
 1  2  3  4  5  6  7  8  9 10 11 12 13 14 15
 8  1  7  3  8  6  3  3  5  1  0  5  0  3  8
 0  1  4  5  4  1  1  1  7  5  1  7  4  3  2
 3  7  0  7  3  9  5  3  0  7  9  7  3  9  5
 2  4  9  9  4  0  3  7  2  5  3  3  6  8  9
 7  6  0  9  3  1  8  5  4  5  2  9  9  5  2
 0  6  1  6  9 ...
```

FIGURE 123a

Message "B"

```
 1  2  3  4  5  6  7  8  9 10 11 12 13 14 15
 8  1  7  3  8  6  3  3  5  1  0  5  0  3  8
 0  1  4  5  4  6  4  8  3  0  3  8  1  0  2
 5  9  0  8  4  8  3  6  7  2  6  0  9  0  1
 1  2  9  5  3  0  4  7  5  6  8  8  3  6  4
 0  6  4  7  4  0  3  8  0  4  0  8  2  2  7
 7  9  7  7  5 ...
```

FIGURE 123b

Let us take the difference stream (designated as "Δ") for the two messages at an interval corresponding to the period. If each row is subtracted from the row immediately beneath, we have the following:

Δ, Message "A"

```
 1  2  3  4  5  6  7  8  9 10 11 12 13 14 15
 2  0  7  2  6  5  8  8  2  4  1  2  4  0  4
 3  6  6  2  9  8  4  2  3  2  8  0  9  6  3
 9  7  9  2  1  1  8  4  2  8  4  6  3  9  4
 5  2  1  0  9  1  5  8  2  0  9  6  3  7  3
 3  0  1  7  6 ...
```

FIGURE 124a

Δ, Message "B"

```
 1  2  3  4  5  6  7  8  9 10 11 12 13 14 15
 2  0  7  2  6  0  1  5  8  9  3  3  1  7  4
 5  8  6  3  0  2  9  8  4  2  3  2  8  0  9
 6  3  9  7  9  2  1  1  8  4  2  8  4  6  3
 9  4  5  2  1  0  9  1  5  8  2  0  9  6  3
 7  3  3  0  1 ...
```

FIGURE 124b

The difference streams for the two messages, beginning with the 19th digit of the Δ for Message "A" and the 21st digit of the Δ for Message "B", are identical. This is clear proof that the two messages are isologs;[15] the messages start out with the same plain text enciphered with identical keys, and then evidently a 2-digit stagger takes place. If we assume an arbitrary additive of Ø for column 1, we derive plaintext values which can be cribbed from one message to the other, and both messages can be reduced to monoalphabetic terms, as in subpar. *f*, above. The cause of the error, after the intermediate plain text is solved, is discovered to be that, in Message "A", an F_p (=Ø3) was left out of the word OFFICER, thus producing a stagger situation at an offset of 2 digits.

i. In the foregoing situation, the possibility that the two messages are isologs might have been indicated by their near-correspondence in length, Message "A" being two digits shorter than Message "B". But even if the texts of the two messages diverged completely after the 80 digits shown in Figs. 123*a* and *b*, the length of the exact correspondence of plain text would be revealed by the delta streams as shown in Figs. 124*a* and *b*, and solution would still go on as before. This is one more demonstration of the value of stagger situations, once they are recognized and exploited.

j. For the last example of an isolog situation, we will treat the case where a cipher clerk incorrectly enciphered a message using the equation P−K=C (i.e., corresponding to the *deciphering* equation) instead of the correct P+K=C, and subsequently he sent the corrected version. This is called an *encipher-decipher bust*.

(1) Let us examine the following pair of messages. (For the sake of illustration, we will assume the matrix to be known, and that it is the REPUBLIC matrix of subpar. 86*h*.)

Message "A"

| 77421 | 29282 | 51449 | 98657 | 94622 | 91878 | 57896 | 14694 | 85074 | 34064 |
| 24606 | 42952 | 61890 | 94115 | 05362 | 50380 | 91241 | 69655 | 52623 | 97711 |

Message "B"

| 11685 | 81828 | 31247 | 92253 | 14086 | 75038 | 99034 | 98098 | 23472 | 96842 |
| 48022 | 88116 | 29870 | 74575 | 67308 | 98706 | 95465 | 47095 | 96463 | 73999 |

All the differences of the corresponding digits between the two messages are even, pointing to the type of error involved. The length of the key is not known, nor can it be determined from the two messages at hand; nevertheless, solution of the plain text will proceed *without* knowing this length, and the additive will be recovered as the very last step in the process.

(2) The first thing we will do is *add* the two cipher texts, as shown below; this has the effect of giving us 2P, or twice the value of the plaintext digit for each position, vitiating the effect of the key. Next, this value of 2P is decomposed into the two possible plaintext digits it can represent (for instance, a 2P of 8 could arise from a 4+4, or a 9+9). Then, knowing the matrix, it is a simple matter to recover the original plain text from the double stream of intermediate plaintext digits. The message text is recovered, beginning with the words RECONNAISSANCE

---

[15] If these messages had been very short, both their periods and the fact that they are isologs could have been discovered by taking their individual difference streams at various intervals corresponding to trial periods; when a period of 15 was tried, we would have gotten the results as shown above.

260

```
C₁:   77421  29282  51449  98657  94622    91878  57896  14694  85074  34064
C₂:   11685  81828  31247  92253  14086    75038  99034  98098  23472  96842
2P:   88006  00000  82686  80000  08608    66806  46820  02682  08446  20806
   ⎧  44003  00000  41343  40000  04304    33403  23410  01341  04223  10403
P: ⎨
   ⎩  99558  55555  96898  95555  59859    88958  78565  56896  59778  65958

C₁:   24606  42952  61890  94115  05362    50380  91241  69655  52623  97711
C₂:   48022  88116  29870  74575  67308    98706  95465  47095  96463  73999
2P:   62628  20068  80660  68680  62660    48086  86606  06640  48086  60600
   ⎧  31314  10034  40330  34340  31330    24043  43303  03320  24043  30300
P: ⎨
   ⎩  86869  65589  95885  89895  86885    79598  98858  58875  79598  85855
```

PATROLS. Finally, the actual intermediate plain text is set against the cipher text of Message "B", and it is found that the additive is a 51-digit repeating sequence.[16]

(3) If the matrix were *not* known, it still might be possible to analyze the double plaintext stream if a favorable crib began the message. In the previous example, the probable word RECONNAISSANCE will permit the identification of the two row coordinates (in variant form, of course) and the equivalents for the 8 letters; but unless there are enough *different* letters in the crib, it will be very difficult to recover the remainder of the plain text from the several variant decipherments for the rest of the cipher text.[17] In any case, the row- and column coordinates cannot be determined uniquely, but may be recovered on a relative base because of the variant aspects inherent in the solution.

89. **Additional remarks.**—*a.* In the examples in the preceding paragraphs, only one type of monome-dinome matrix has been used; viz., matrices with two row coordinates. Of course, any type of monome-dinome matrix (such as one of those given in par. 75, *Military Cryptanalytics, Part I*) might have been used for producing the intermediate text, but this is immaterial insofar as the general methods for reducing to monoalphabetic terms are concerned. What *does* matter, as has already been remarked in subpar. 85d, is the theoretical I.C. of the intermediate text produced by a specific matrix. Several cases will be cited in the subparagraphs following.

b. The I.C. of the REPUBLIC matrix illustrated in pars. 86 and 87 may be calculated from the expected frequencies of the digits given in subpar. 87b. However, instead of the δ I.C. formula of $\frac{c\Sigma f(f-1)}{N(N-1)}$, we shall use a statistic known as the *gamma* (γ) *I.C.*,[18] calculated by the formula

---

[16] This sequence is the value of *e*, the base of natural or Napierian logarithms, 2.71828 . . ., taken to 50 decimals. There have been cases in cryptographic practice when key digits have been obtained from mathematical tables (such as tables of logarithms, trigonometric functions, etc.), or have been derived from a fraction yielding a long repeating decimal, or have been generated by some mathematical formula. In other cases, key has been derived from literal text by enciphering the latter with the monome-dinome rectangle, as in the Nihilist method treated in the preceding chapter.

[17] This is similar to the process of solution of the Edgar Allen Poe cipher with variant *plaintext* values (cf. footnote 2, subpar. 2d), except that in this case the process is considerably more complicated in its application to monome-dinome ciphers.

[18] If we assume that the data in subpar. 87b (i.e., the reduction to 1000 letters of the results of counting a sample of 50,000 letters of English plain text) afford an accurate approximation to the true probabilities of occurrence of English letters, then the γ I.C. is the correct statistic to express the ratio of the expected number of coincidences between a sample of text in a language (in this case, digital text resulting from the encryption of plain text with the REPUBLIC matrix) and a sample of the same size drawn from a flat population. However, the δ I.C. (which approaches the γ I.C. as N grows large) suffices for most purposes, and is in fact preferable in treating small samples, since it gives an unbiased estimate of the roughness, independent of sample size.

$\frac{c\Sigma f^2}{N^2}$, where c is the number of categories (in this case, 10). Thus in this example, since the sum (N) of the frequencies given in subpar. 87b is 1590, and the sum of the squares (Σf^2) of the frequencies ($457^2 + 57^2 + \ldots + 147^2 + 153^2$) is 411,688, the γ I.C.$= \frac{10(411,688)}{1590^2} = 1.63$.

c. The I.C. of a particular matrix depends not only on what letters constitute the monome row, but also on the composition and arrangement of the letters in the dinome rows with respect to the letters in the monome row. Thus, in the following two matrices, Fig. 125a has an I.C.

```
   0 1 2 3 4 5 6 7 8 9          0 1 2 3 4 5 6 7 8 9
 -|E T N R O A I S    █|       -|█    E T N R O A I S|
 8|B C D F G H J K L M|       Ø|B C D F G H J K L M|
 9|P Q U V W X Y Z    |       1|P Q U V W X Y Z    |
```

FIGURE 125a FIGURE 125b

of 1.14, while Fig. 125b has an I.C. of 1.16. The theoretical lower and upper limits of I.C.'s for matrices with two row coordinates are 1.03 and 2.11; these are the I.C.'s of the matrices in Figs. 125c and d respectively, given below:

```
   0 1 2 3 4 5 6 7 8 9          0 1 2 3 4 5 6 7 8 9
 -|E T N R O A I S    █|       -|B X Q K J Z      █|
 8|Q B V G U P H L Z J|       8|E T N R O A I S D L|
 9|K X W Y M F C D    |       9|H C F P U M Y G W V|
```

FIGURE 125c FIGURE 125d

Where the monome row consists of a key word, it has been found that the I.C.'s of such matrices are usually in the vicinity of 1.30 to 1.50, for what this generalization of the range might be worth.

d. Matrices with more than two row coordinates should be expected to have higher I.C.'s than matrices with only two row coordinates; however, in the matrix below, which has been manipulated to yield the lowest possible theoretical I.C., we get an I.C. of 1.002.

```
   0 1 2 3 4 5 6
 -|E T N R O A I|
 7|  B Q G U H L|
 8|  D J W M F P|
 9|V Z S C Y X K|
```

FIGURE 125e

e. In subpar. 86b we noted that the I.C. of the 440 digits of the cipher text, when written out on a width of 20, yielded an I.C. of 1.22, remarking that this I.C. "seems surprisingly good for a random case, if it *is* random." We subsequently found out that the correct width for this cryptogram was 30, so the reason for the "surprisingly good" I.C.[19] is now clear: on a width of 20 each column is actually composed not of an assortment of digits belonging to all possible families (and therefore possessing random characteristics), but of digits belonging to only three of these families.[20] If we had written out the cipher on a width of 15, we would have obtained an I.C. of 1.27, understandable since each column is now composed of digits from only two families instead of digits from the total population of equiprobable families.[21]

f. Dinome and "split dinome" (i.e., A–A) counts might theoretically be useful in equating columns in enciphered monome-dinome systems; however, in actual practice if there is enough material to use these methods with confidence, there is also usually enough material to equate columns by means of monomic distributions. Nevertheless, in difficult cases the cryptanalyst might have no choice but to use these methods.

g. The higher the I.C. of the underlying monome-dinome matrix, the less material is generally necessary for the successful equating of columns. Thus, in subpar. 86*c*, it is possible to equate the columns of Message "A" without Message "B", but not without considerable trouble.

h. In systems employing matrices of very low I.C.'s (such as an I.C. of 1.03 for the matrix in Fig. 125*c*), the monomic roughness is not significantly above random to permit the use of the monomic δ I.C. in establishing the period or in equating columns. Nevertheless, the pronounced *dinomic* roughness inherent in *all* monome-dinome systems is enough to enable the factoring and subsequent equating of columns, given sufficient material.

i. It might not be amiss to observe that additive-enciphered *dinome* systems employing a single-digit word separator will give rise to manifestations of an additive-enciphered *monome-dinome* system. The processes of factoring and equating of columns here will be pursued as in monome-dinome systems, until the evidence of such a word-separator usage is uncovered and exploited.

j. Note that, in the two messages given in subpar. 86*a et seq.*, Message "B" begins at the very next position in the keying cycle where Message "A" stopped. This phenomenon, known as *tailing*, can be used to "set" messages along the keying cycle without resort to exhaustive trials to prove the correct superimposition, if it has been observed that traffic emanating from a particular originator exhibits a high incidence of this situation.

k. This chapter has concerned itself entirely with additive-enciphered *monome-dinome* systems as illustrations of the methods of attack on periodic encipherments of mixed-length intermediate plaintext elements. It is clear, however, that the general approaches treated apply

---

[19] The reader with a background in statistics will realize that the phrase "surprisingly good" is certainly an understatement, to say the least. It can be shown that the sigmage of this I.C. is $\dfrac{440(1.22-1.00)}{\sqrt{2(20 \cdot 9)}} = 5.1\ \sigma$, which may be translated as odds of 1 chance in 200,000. (We use here the χ^2 distribution for an evaluation of the sigmage, not the normal [Gaussian] distribution, since it has been established that the χ^2 estimate is closer to the true value than is the normal estimate.) This certainly shows that *causal* factors are responsible for this I.C.; but in view of the explanation given, it also shows the student that he must use cryptomathematics intelligently—not blindly jump to conclusions when he gets a high score in a particular test. The I.C. of 1.22 is doubtlessly causal, but it is not the *right* answer.

[20] Since our distributions consist of the merger of three separate families or distributions, the expected I.C. (when the families are equiprobable) is 1.00 plus one-third of the "bulge" between the I.C. of random and the I.C. of the matrix. In this case, the REPUBLIC matrix has a theoretical I.C. of 1.63, therefore on a width of 20 the expected I.C. is $1.00 + \dfrac{.63}{3} = 1.21$.

[21] The expected I.C. in this case is $1.00 + \dfrac{.63}{2} = 1.32$, as explained in footnote 20, above.

equally well in those cases where the intermediate plain text is composed of dinomes and trinomes, or other similar variations of mixed-length systems.

l. The observations made in subpar. 84*b* with respect to additive, subtractive, and minuend encipherments in the systems of the preceding chapter of course also apply to monome-dinome systems.

m. As a final remark, it might be noted that situations wherein the composition of the matrix is known, but the coordinates are unknown, is not of much help in attacking a cryptogram in the initial stages, unless a crib is also available.[22] As an example, let us consider the following cryptogram, factoring to 35:

```
 1  2  3  4  5  6  7  8  9 10 11 12 13 14 15 16 17 18 19 20 21 22 23 24 25 26 27 28 29 30 31 32 33 34 35
 8  0  4  0  4  3  1  1  0  5  2  2  9  6  1  6  1  4  2  8  0  0  4  3  4  2  8  6  6  3  4  7  8  3  9
 2  5  7  6  7  0  4  1  0  0  2  0  0  1  2  0  7  1  4  9  9  0  3  1  3  8  7  1  6  1  3  4  0  7  8
 1  6  7  6  7  0  4  1  0  0  2  0  6  8  1  0  6  4  4  9  7  3  4  1  1  5  6  0  0  5  1  3  3  0  5
 2  0  8  8  5  0  9  4  8  3  4  6  2  2  2  9  9  7  2  5  0  1  1  3  8  0  0  9  9  9  0  3  7  2  9
 4  3  1  7  7  5  3  2  6  5  1  2  1  5  9  6  5  9  7  0  1  9  3  0  2  3  3  9  1  9  1  2  7  7  5
 0  0  5  6  0  3  3  4  3  6  8  2  5  5  1
```

It will be assumed that the enemy has been using a matrix with internal composition as shown

FIGURE 126

in Fig. 126, above, but that we are faced with unknown coordinates. It is further believed that the cryptogram begins with the opening stereotype "TO COMMANDING OFFICER."

(1) It will be noted that the plaintext letters of the crib C, M, D, G, and F, must all come from the same row of the matrix; therefore the first digits of all these dinome equivalents must be identical. If we arbitrarily assume this digit to be plaintext Ø, we derive the relative additive for the appropriate columns which we use to decipher down the columns. Thus:

```
 1  2  3  4  5  6  7  8  9 10 11 12 13 14 15 16 17 18 19 20 21 22 23 24 25 26 27 28 29 30 31 32 33 34 35
       4        3     1        2           6        2  0     3
 8  0  4  0  4  3  1  1  0  5  2  2  9  6  1  6  1  4  2  8  0  0  4  3  4  2  8  6  6  3  4  7  8  3  9
       /  /0 /     /0 /0 /  /  /0 /  /  /0 /  /0 /0 /  /0 /  /  /
 T     O     C     O  M     M  A     N  D     I  N     G     O  F     F     I     C     E  R
 2  5  7  6  7  0  4  1  0  0  2  0  0  1  2  0  7  1  4  9  9  0  3  1  3  8  7  1  6  1  3  4  0  7  8
       3        7     0        8           4        2  9     8
 1  6  7  6  7  0  4  1  0  0  2  0  6  8  1  0  6  4  4  9  7  3  4  1  1  5  6  0  0  5  1  3  3  0  5
       3        7     0        8           4        2  7     8
 2  0  8  8  5  0  9  4  8  3  4  6  2  2  2  9  9  7  2  5  0  1  1  3  8  0  0  9  9  9  0  3  7  2  9
       4        7     3        4           3        0  0     0
 4  3  1  7  7  5  3  2  6  5  1  2  1  5  9  6  5  9  7  0  1  9  3  0  2  3  3  9  1  9  1  2  7  7  5
       7        2     1        0           0        5  1     7
 0  0  5  6  0  3  3  4  3  6  8  2  5  5  1
       1        0     3        0
```

---

[22] Even in simple monoalphabetic substitution, a known *plain* component is of no assistance in the early stages, and in later stages is helpful only if the cipher component has been derived in some systematic fashion.

We will call this family of columns the "α" family, for convenience. The distribution for the decipherments of the α family, excluding the digits from the original crib, is as follows:

$$\emptyset \quad 1 \quad 2 \quad 3 \quad 4 \quad 5 \quad 6 \quad 7 \quad 8 \quad 9$$

(2) Since T_p and C_p come from the same column of the matrix, it is obvious that cols. 1, 4, and 25 belong to one family; likewise, since O_p and G_p come from the same column of the matrix, it is clear that cols. 2, 5, 17, and 18 belong to one family, different from the two other families just established. By examining the plaintext letters composing the original crib, we will arrive at the following designation of families:

T	O	C	M	M	A	N	D	I	N	G	O	F	F	I	C	E	R
β	γ	$\alpha\beta$	γ	$\alpha\delta$	$\alpha\delta$	ϵ	ζ	$\alpha\zeta$	η	ζ	$\alpha\gamma$	γ	$\alpha\theta$	$\alpha\theta$	η	$\alpha\beta$	ι	θ

A total of 12 families is possible, which may be collapsed eventually into 10 families representing the equivalents for the 10 digits.

(3) Since the γ family is the heaviest family, next to α, we will take a distribution of the γ family equated in terms of an arbitrary *additive* $\emptyset$ for col. 2, again excluding the elements derived from the assumed crib. This is as follows:

$$\emptyset \quad 1 \quad 2 \quad 3 \quad 4 \quad 5 \quad 6 \quad 7 \quad 8 \quad 9$$

We will now perform a cross-products sum test between the distribution for α and all possible slides for γ; this is shown below:

```
       9 3 3 5 4 1 - 6 4 1
1:     1 - 5 1 3 3 1 1 - 3   53
2:     - 5 1 3 3 1 1 - 3 1   59
3:     5 1 3 3 1 1 - 3 1 -   99
4:     1 3 3 1 1 - 3 1 - 5   47
5:     3 3 1 1 - 3 1 - 5 1   68
6:     3 1 1 - 3 1 - 5 1 3   83
7:     1 1 - 3 1 - 5 1 3 3   52
8:     1 - 3 1 - 5 1 3 3 1   59
9:     - 3 1 - 5 1 3 3 1 1   56
```

It is apparent that γ is at a slide of 3 with respect to α; the combined distribution for $(\alpha+\gamma)$ is therefore as follows:

$$\emptyset \quad 1 \quad 2 \quad 3 \quad 4 \quad 5 \quad 6 \quad 7 \quad 8 \quad 9$$

(4) The work sheet for the cryptogram will now look like this:

```
 1  2  3  4  5  6  7  8  9 10 11 12 13 14 15 16 17 18 19 20 21 22 23 24 25 26 27 28 29 30 31 32 33 34 35
 β  γ  α  β  γ  α  δ  α  δ  ε  ζ  α  ζ  η  ζ  α  γ  γ  α  θ  α  θ  η  α  β  ι  θ
    3  4     7  3        1                 2                 6  4  7  2        0        3
_____
 8  0  4  0  4  3  1  1  0  5  2  2  9  6  1  6  1  4  2  8  0  0  4  3  4  2  8  6  6  3  4  7  8  3  9
 /7/0    /7/0    /0    /  /  /0    /  /  /0  7/7/0    /0    /  //0  /  /  /
 T  O     C  O  M     M  A  N     D  I  N     G  O  F     F  I  C     E  R
 2  5  7  6  7  0  4  1  0  0  2  0  0  1  2  0  7  1  4  9  9  0  3  1  3  8  7  1  6  1  3  4  0  7  8
    2  3     0  7     0              8              4  3  4  2        9              8

 1  6  7  6  7  0  4  1  0  0  2  0  6  8  1  0  6  4  4  9  7  3  4  1  1  5  6  0  0  5  1  3  3  0  5
    3  3     0  7     0              8              4  2  7  2        7              8

 2  0  8  8  5  0  9  4  8  3  4  6  2  2  2  9  9  7  2  5  0  1  1  3  8  0  0  9  9  9  0  3  7  2  9
    7  4     8  7     3              4              3  5  0  0        0              0

 4  3  1  7  7  5  3  2  6  5  1  2  1  5  9  6  5  9  7  0  1  9  3  0  2  3  3  9  1  9  1  2  7  7  5
    0  7     0  2     1              0              0  1  2  5        1              7

 0  0  5  6  0  3  3  4  3  6  8  2  5  5  1
    7  1     3  0     3              0
```

At this point the 10-digit repetition in the second and third lines is examined. If the 07 is a proper dinome, it represents G_p; and the repetition is just the right length for the assumption of REGIMENT. (Furthermore there is a hit with the cipher dinome 10 which is an M_p from COMMANDING.) This gives us $R_p=3$, and $T_p=8$; therefore $C_p=08$ (cols. 4 and 25), which yields, in col. 4, $E_p=4$. Substituting $E_p=4$ in cols. 10 and 26, $T_p=8$ in col. 1, and $R_p=3$ in col. 27 we now get the following:

```
 1  2  3  4  5  6  7  8  9 10 11 12 13 14 15 16 17 18 19 20 21 22 23 24 25 26 27 28 29 30 31 32 33 34 35
 β  γ  α  β  γ  α  δ  α  δ  ε  ζ  α  ζ  η  ζ  α  γ  γ  α  θ  α  θ  η  α  β  ι  θ
 0  3  4  2  7  3        1     6     2                 6  4  7  2        0        3  6  8  5
_____
 8  0  4  0  4  3  1  1  0  5  2  2  9  6  1  6  1  4  2  8  0  0  4  3  4  2  8  6  6  3  4  7  8  3  9
 8/7/0 8/7/0    /0    /9/ /0    /  /  /0  7/7/0    /0    /  /  /0  8/4/3/
 T  O     C  O  M     M  A  N     D  I  N     G  O  F     F  I  C     E  R
 2  5  7  6  7  0  4  1  0  0  2  0  0  1  2  0  7  1  4  9  9  0  3  1  3  8  7  1  6  1  3  4  0  7  8
 2  2/3/4/0 7/    /0    /4/   /8/          4  3  4  2        9           8  7  0  2
       R     E  G     I  M  ENT
 1  6  7  6  7  0  4  1  0  0  2  0  6  8  1  0  6  4  4  9  7  3  4  1  1  5  6  0  0  5  1  3  3  0  5
 1  3/3/4/0 7/    /0    /4/   /8/          4  2  7  2        7           8  5  7  1
       R     E  G     I  M  ENT
 2  0  8  8  5  0  9  4  8  3  4  6  2  2  2  9  9  7  2  5  0  1  1  3  8  0  0  9  9  9  0  3  7  2  9
 2  7  4  6  8  7     3     7     4                 3  5  0  0        0           0  2  2  5

 4  3  1  7  7  5  3  2  6  5  1  2  1  5  9  6  5  9  7  0  1  9  3  0  2  3  3  9  1  9  1  2  7  7  5
 4  0  7  5  0  2     1     9     0                 0  1  2  5        1           7  6  5  8

 0  0  5  6  0  3  3  4  3  6  8  2  5  5  1
 0  7  1  4  3  0     3              0  0
```

266

(5) The coordinates thus far reconstructed are the following:

```
 4 8   3 7 9     0
 ┌─────────────────┐
-│E T N R O A I S ██│
0│B C D F G H J K L M│
 │P Q U V W X Y Z . #│
 └─────────────────┘
```

We note that in col. 7, the additive must be such as to derive values where 1_c and 4_c do not yield any of the plain digits already recovered, *viz.*, 0, 3, 4, 7, 8, or 9; the only possible additive for the column that meets this requirement is 9, which makes $1_c=2_p$ and $4_c=5_p$. The last two coordinate digits, 1 and 6, are now quickly determined from the context of the decipherments obtained thus far, so that the completed matrix is as follows:

```
 4 8 1 3 7 9 5 6 0 2
 ┌───────────────────┐
-│E T N R O A I S ██│
0│B C D F G H J K L M│
2│P Q U V W X Y Z . #│
 └───────────────────┘
```

The last 8 digits of the additive sequence and the remainder of the message plain text are easily recovered by extending the already derived plain text.

CHAPTER XIII

PERIODIC DIGRAPHIC SYSTEMS

90. General.—In the usual literal periodic polyalphabetic systems, the plaintext units treated are single letters. It might occur to a cryptographer that, since ordinary [monoalphabetic] digraphic substitution is in principle considerably more difficult [1] of solution than monoalphabetic monographic substitution, it follows that a polyalphabetic system where the unit of substitution is a *digraph* will give considerably more security than a polyalphabetic monographic substitution. This premise can be easily demonstrated in practice; a much larger volume of text and a larger number of favorable circumstances usually are prerequisites to the successful cryptanalysis of polyalphabetic digraphic ciphers. Fortunately, such systems are rarely encountered; the cryptography of systems suitable for practical use has inherent weaknesses which cannot be avoided except at the expense of inordinate complications in the work of the cipher clerks performing the encryption. In the next paragraph we will treat the cryptography of typical polyalphabetic digraphic systems where the "alphabets" [2] are used cyclically.

91. Cryptography of typical periodic digraphic systems.—*a.* The most elementary idea of a periodic digraphic system is perhaps a scheme incorporating *n* unrelated digraphic systems used in a cyclical fashion. For instance, four independent 26x26 digraphic tables might be drawn up; Table I would be used to encipher the 1st, 5th, 9th . . . plaintext digraphs, Table II would be used for the 2d, 6th, 10th . . . plaintext digraphs, etc. Since, however, such a scheme is rather clumsy in operation, it might occur to a cryptographer to use only *one* basic table and modify it so as to yield a polyalphabetic digraphic substitution. This might be accomplished through the use of a table such as the one illustrated in Fig. 127, below. This table, yielding pseudo-digraphic [3] encipherments, produces periodic encipherments of a period of 4 digraphs. The first letters of plaintext digraphs are enciphered monographically by means of the four alphabets at the side of the table; the second letters of digraphs are *digraphically* enciphered by the equivalents within the table proper, the particular encipherment being governed by the identity of the first letter of the plaintext digraph. This scheme could be extended to include more alphabets for the encipherments of the first letters of digraphs; these alphabets might be slides of a basic sequence (as in the example above), or they might be *n* different, unrelated alphabets.

---

[1] See subpar. 64*e*, *Military Cryptanalytics, Part I.*

[2] Each "alphabet" contains 26² elements bearing a one-to-one correspondence between plaintext and ciphertext units. Hence we can appreciate the notions of "monoalphabeticity" and "polyalphabeticity" as applied to digraphic systems.

[3] Cf. subpar. 68*a*, *Military Cryptanalytics, Part I.*

θ_c^1 $\qquad\qquad\qquad\qquad\qquad\qquad\qquad$ θ_p^2

	1	2	3	4	A	B	C	D	E	F	G	H	I	J	K	L	M	N	O	P	Q	R	S	T	U	V	W	X	Y	Z
A	W	I	R	E	G	E	N	R	A	L	C	T	I	O	M	P	Y	B	D	F	H	J	K	Q	S	U	V	W	X	Z
B	E	N	B	S	E	N	R	A	L	C	T	I	O	M	P	Y	B	D	F	H	J	K	Q	S	U	V	W	X	Z	G
C	S	G	K	T	N	R	A	L	C	T	I	O	M	P	Y	B	D	F	H	J	K	Q	S	U	V	W	X	Z	G	E
D	T	H	C	I	R	A	L	C	T	I	O	M	P	Y	B	D	F	H	J	K	Q	S	U	V	W	X	Z	G	E	N
E	I	O	D	N	A	L	C	T	I	O	M	P	Y	B	D	F	H	J	K	Q	S	U	V	W	X	Z	G	E	N	R
F	N	U	F	G	L	C	T	I	O	M	P	Y	B	D	F	H	J	K	Q	S	U	V	W	X	Z	G	E	N	R	A
G	G	A	J	H	C	T	I	O	M	P	Y	B	D	F	H	J	K	Q	S	U	V	W	X	Z	G	E	N	R	A	L
H	H	R	L	O	T	I	O	M	P	Y	B	D	F	H	J	K	Q	S	U	V	W	X	Z	G	E	N	R	A	L	C
I	O	B	M	U	I	O	M	P	Y	B	D	F	H	J	K	Q	S	U	V	W	X	Z	G	E	N	R	A	L	C	T
J	U	K	P	A	O	M	P	Y	B	D	F	H	J	K	Q	S	U	V	W	X	Z	G	E	N	R	A	L	C	T	I
K	A	C	Q	R	M	P	Y	B	D	F	H	J	K	Q	S	U	V	W	X	Z	G	E	N	R	A	L	C	T	I	O
L	R	D	V	B	P	Y	B	D	F	H	J	K	Q	S	U	V	W	X	Z	G	E	N	R	A	L	C	T	I	O	M
M	B	F	X	K	Y	B	D	F	H	J	K	Q	S	U	V	W	X	Z	G	E	N	R	A	L	C	T	I	O	M	P
N	K	J	Y	C	B	D	F	H	J	K	Q	S	U	V	W	X	Z	G	E	N	R	A	L	C	T	I	O	M	P	Y
O	C	L	Z	D	D	F	H	J	K	Q	S	U	V	W	X	Z	G	E	N	R	A	L	C	T	I	O	M	P	Y	B
P	D	M	W	F	F	H	J	K	Q	S	U	V	W	X	Z	G	E	N	R	A	L	C	T	I	O	M	P	Y	B	D
Q	F	P	E	J	H	J	K	Q	S	U	V	W	X	Z	G	E	N	R	A	L	C	T	I	O	M	P	Y	B	D	F
R	J	Q	S	L	J	K	Q	S	U	V	W	X	Z	G	E	N	R	A	L	C	T	I	O	M	P	Y	B	D	F	H
S	L	V	T	M	K	Q	S	U	V	W	X	Z	G	E	N	R	A	L	C	T	I	O	M	P	Y	B	D	F	H	J
T	M	X	I	P	Q	S	U	V	W	X	Z	G	E	N	R	A	L	C	T	I	O	M	P	Y	B	D	F	H	J	K
U	P	Y	N	Q	S	U	V	W	X	Z	G	E	N	R	A	L	C	T	I	O	M	P	Y	B	D	F	H	J	K	Q
V	Q	Z	G	V	U	V	W	X	Z	G	E	N	R	A	L	C	T	I	O	M	P	Y	B	D	F	H	J	K	Q	S
W	V	W	H	X	V	W	X	Z	G	E	N	R	A	L	C	T	I	O	M	P	Y	B	D	F	H	J	K	Q	S	U
X	X	E	O	Y	W	X	Z	G	E	N	R	A	L	C	T	I	O	M	P	Y	B	D	F	H	J	K	Q	S	U	V
Y	Y	S	U	Z	X	Z	G	E	N	R	A	L	C	T	I	O	M	P	Y	B	D	F	H	J	K	Q	S	U	V	W
Z	Z	T	A	W	Z	G	E	N	R	A	L	C	T	I	O	M	P	Y	B	D	F	H	J	K	Q	S	U	V	W	X

θ_p^1 at left, θ_c^2 at right.

FIGURE 127

b. Another system for polyalphabetic digraphic encipherment might incorporate a 26x26 table such as that shown in Fig. 128; the coordinates in this case are written on strips which may be slid to any point of juxtaposition against a predetermined reference point (for example, the cell in the upper left-hand corner). The same key word or two different key words might be employed to set the two coordinate strips for a periodic digraphic system with a limited period; or the two strips might be moved one position at a time, to yield what for all intents and purposes is a progressive alphabet *digraphic* system with a period of 26 digraphs.

c. Instead of 26x26 tables, small matrices such as four-squares, two-squares, or Playfairs might be used as a basis for cryptographic treatment in periodic digraphic systems. Since these matrices do not involve coordinates (as do the large tables), periodicity of encipherment would have to be obtained either (1) by the use of *n* different, unrelated small matrices for the succession of *n* digraphs in the period, or (2) by some scheme for permuting or deriving additional matrices from a basic matrix. In the two following subparagraphs there will be illustrated some typical means for deriving a multiplicity of matrices from a basic matrix, using a 5x5 Playfair square for the examples.

d. Let us assume that our basic Playfair matrix is that shown in Fig. 129*a*, below. We take the first four letters of the top row, HYDR, and we inscribe them on a diagonal to the right of the

270

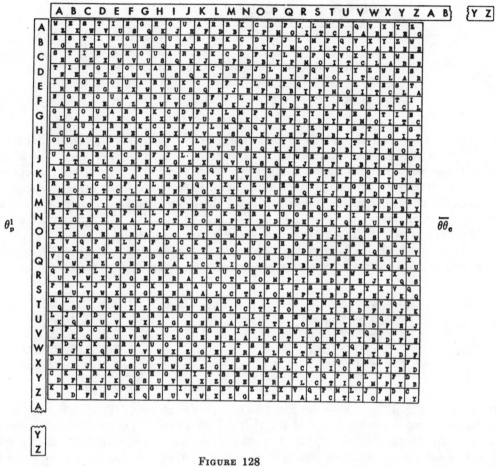

FIGURE 128

Playfair square, as shown in Fig. 129b. In Fig. 129c, we complete these four skeletal columns by permuting vertically the first four columns of the Playfair square, using the diagonally inscribed letters as reference points; this now yields a total of 5 Playfair squares, starting in each of the first 5 columns as shown in the figure. The next four letters in the top row of our new

```
H Y D R A
U L I C B
E F G K M
N O P Q S
T V W X Z
```

FIGURE 129a

```
 1
H Y D R A
U L I C B H
E F G K M     Y
N O P Q S         D
T V W X Z             R
```

FIGURE 129b

```
1 2 3 4 5
H Y D R A T O G C
U L I C B H V P K
E F G K M U Y W Q
N O P Q S E L D X
T V W X Z N F I R
```

FIGURE 129c

diagram are ATOG; we inscribe these letters diagonally to the right of the diagram, and permute the columns as before. After performing this process five times, we have the diagram shown in Fig. 129d, below, which would then start to repeat itself. The reference numbers 1–20 are

271

```
U V W X Y Z
A B C D E F G H I J K L M N O P Q R S T
1 2 3 4 5 6 7 8 9 10 11 12 13 14 15 16 17 18 19 20
H Y D R A T O G C Z E Y P R M T L G Q Z H Y D R
U L I C B H V P K A N L W C S H F P X A U L I C
E F G K M U Y W Q B T F D K Z U O W R B E F G K
N O P Q S E L D X M H O I Q A E V D C M N O P Q
T V W X Z N F I R S U V G X B N Y I K S T V W X
```

FIGURE 129d

inscribed over the diagram, as well as the key letters A–Z (which could be used for indicator purposes). This Playfair system actually consists, then, of a "band" composed of 20 interrelated Playfair squares, which are denoted either by the number or a letter over the upper left-hand corner of each square. In using the Playfair band, a 5x5 cutout mask (provided with an aperture to expose the particular square indicator) is slid along the band according to a prearranged periodic key; or each square could be used successively to encipher the digraphs of the plain text, yielding a progressive alphabet digraphic system of a period of 20.

e. In the next scheme for deriving a plurality of Playfair squares, we will generate a band of 25 squares by a method of permuting two columns at a time. We start with our basic Play-

```
   1   2
 H Y D R A  H F
 U L I C B  Y N
 E F G K M  U O
 N O P Q S  L T
 T V W X Z  E V
```

FIGURE 130a

```
  1   2   3
 H Y  D R A H F  D K
 U L  I C B Y N  R P
 E F  G K M U O  I Q
 N O  P Q S L T  C W
 T V  W X Z E V  G X
```

FIGURE 130b

fair square in Fig. 130a, taking the first two letters of each row (HY, UL, EF, NO, and TV) of the square, inscribing them vertically to the right of the square; this produces the second Playfair square. We now take the square just derived and, as shown in Fig. 130b, we go through the same process as before, the first two letters of each row in the second square being recorded in two columns to the right of the second square, yielding the third square. This procedure is continued for a total of 25 squares, as shown in Fig. 130c, after which point the band will repeat itself.

```
 1   2   3   4   5   6   7   8   9   10  11  12  13
 H Y D R A H F D K A U F I K B U N I P B S N T P W S Z T V
 U L I C B Y N R P H S D T A W F Z K V U X I E B G N M P O
 E F G K M U O I Q B L N C P Y S R T H W D Z A V F X K E U
 N O P Q S L T C W Y Z R V H X D E A G F M K O U Q I L B C
 T V W X Z E V G X M E O G Q M L O C Q Y L R C H Y D R A H
                                                    (check)
 13  14  15  16  17  18  19  20  21  22  23  24  25
 W S Z T V W X Z E V G X M E O G Q M L O C Q Y L R C   H Y D   R A
 G N M P O S Q T L W C Z Y V R X H E D G A M F O K Q   U L I   C B
 F X K E U G I M B O N Q P L S C T Y W R Z H V D X A   E F G   K M
 Q I L B C N Y P R S H T D W A Z F V K X U E I G B M   N O P   Q S
 Y D R A H F D K A U F I K B U N I P B S N T P W S Z   T V W   X Z
```

FIGURE 130c

272

(In Fig. 130c we have split the band into two sections for convenience, repeating the 13th square at the beginning of the second section to avoid errors.)

f. Many other methods for permuting a series of squares from a basic square are of course possible; the particular system of generation will determine just how many derived squares will be produced, and how many *different* encipherments of a given plaintext digraph will be available.[4]

g. In the foregoing system of 25 squares, there are numerous possibilities that lend themselves to keying procedures. In one system, the 25 squares might be used in cyclic order, beginning with any desired square;[5] this amounts to a progressive alphabet digraphic system of a period of 25. In another system, there might be used a 25-element numerical key derived from a literal key, such as the numerical sequence given below,

```
          5           10          15          20          25
H Y D R A U L I C A N A L O G I E S H Y D R A U L,
10 24 6 19 1 22 14 12 5 2 17 3 15 18 9 13 8 21 11 25 7 20 4 23 16
```

as a means of disarranging the normal 1, 2, 3, . . . progression of the Playfair squares in order to remove the cryptographic weakness of three columns in common between the squares used to encrypt adjacent plaintext digraphs. For instance, if the first plaintext digraph were enciphered in square number 6 as a starting point, the succeeding digraphs would be enciphered in square numbers 19 1 22 14 12 . . . . . 23 16 10 24 6, at which point the cycle repeats. Many other variations in the keying of this and other systems are possible. For example, in the system described in subpar. *e*, a selection of a small number of the squares might be made on the basis of a repeating key, such as the "G", "R", "A", "N", and "D" squares to yield a period of 5; or a 25-letter mixed sequence might be used.

92. Analysis of a first case.—*a.* We will now consider a problem from the diagnostic stage to its ultimate solution. The following message is to be examined:

```
DVLTZ  ZLJDV  BMSUT  HKGII  TMEBS    CLQDJ  NHYLO  FCKDC  OEBVY  LCEJM
RPRKP  TNPQU  DJVRR  VOUDZ  NARRO    EIWCL  OROCZ  EMPJP  GUMVC  OCLCK
YNLLG  WOVTM  PTDIR  FTSDE  LPQPK    UUVKO  LLQYD  GBYXW  YCEQO  ROFUC
ITKCB  BMYIR  LMLGD  VDLMT  UPNNI    TTFBG  TGBFR  PYTKO  UUGXB  EDVTH
BXIVR  KSLGG  JBBFQ  BMGQU  DGNIA    NICZC  UUSCX  GDFUU  IVNLK  NKHLP
IEMQU  TITBU  IGEQL  VGUZL  EBTVR    PTGPB  WQBVY  CLJKL  UQSRN  TOUXT
RVEJC  QMRTG  PECEV  PZRXG  VADVK    HCCOU  YXSUT  HKGII  TMEBS  CUHMD
OGLCZ  ZSUCJ  BMMRT  GPECE  VKYHZ    YPPRP  RRJMW  JXWSO  XARVN  LQDFI
OUUQS  RNTWK  XTRPB  DIZOF  ZRKHK    CVKTP  OPYXQ  ZTVMP  CRGHX  EBFMW
QUWRL  MELBU  JXQUB  SXYDT  MPCRN    KMDOG
```

[4] In the system described in subpar. *d*, a particular plaintext digraph will have either 1, 6, or 8 different cipher equivalents, owing to the weak nature of the permutation used for deriving additional squares. However, in the system illustrated in subpar. *e*, there will be from 12 to 18 different equivalents for a digraph, with a mode of 13 occurring in slightly more than one-third of the cases. In other words, this latter system is a periodic digraphic system of a period of 25, involving an equivalent of 12 to 18 different Playfair squares.

[5] The indicator procedure might consist of the numerical designation of the selected square used to start the encipherment; or, since it will be noticed that each of the 25 letters occupies the upper left-hand corner of one particular square and one square only, a square may be designated by the letter occupying this position. Thus, square number 6 may also be designated as the "U" square. In an indicator such as AABUU, the first three letters might designate a particular numerical key (such as the one derived from HYDRAULIC ANALOGIES in this subparagraph) from among a set of keys, the last two letters showing the starting point in the sequence.

The presence of several long repetitions at intervals factorable by 8 leads us to believe that we have here a periodic system of 8 alphabets.   The message is transcribed accordingly and uni-literal distributions are taken on the columns, as shown below:

```
D V L T Z S L J      D V B M S U T H      K G I I T M E B      S C L Q D J N H
Y L O F C K D C      O E B V Y L C E      J M R P R K P T      N P Q U D J V R
R V O U D Z N A      R R O E I W C L      O R O C Z E M P      J P G U M V C O
C L C K Y N L L      G W O V T M P T      D I R F T S D E      L P Q P K U U V
K O L L Q Y D G      B Y X W Y C E Q      O R O F U C I T      K C B B M Y I R
L M L G D V D L      M T U P N N I T      T F B G T G B F      R P Y T K O U U
A N I C Z C U U      B X I V R K S L      G G J B B F Q B      M G Q U D G N I
I T B U I G E Q      S C X G D F U U      I V N L K N K H      L P I E M Q U T
K L U Q S R N T      L V G U Z L E B      T V R P T G P B      W Q B V Y C L J
V A D V K H C C      O U X T R V E J      C Q M R T G P E      C E V P Z R X G
L C Z Z S U C J      O U Y X S U T H      K G I I T M E B      S C U H M D O G
W J X W S O X A      B M M R T G P E      C E V K Y H Z Y      P P R P R R J M
I Z O F Z R K H      R V N L Q D F I      O U U Q S R N T      W K X T R P B D
M W Q U W R L M      K C V K T P O P      Y X Q Z T V M P      C R G H X E B F
                     E L B U J X Q U      B S X Y D T M P      C R N K M D O G
```

1. A B C D E F G H I J K L M N O P Q R S T U V W X Y Z

2. A B C D E F G H I J K L M N O P Q R S T U V W X Y Z

3. A B C D E F G H I J K L M N O P Q R S T U V W X Y Z

4. A B C D E F G H I J K L M N O P Q R S T U V W X Y Z

5. A B C D E F G H I J K L M N O P Q R S T U V W X Y Z

6. A B C D E F G H I J K L M N O P Q R S T U V W X Y Z

7. A B C D E F G H I J K L M N O P Q R S T U V W X Y Z

8. A B C D E F G H I J K L M N O P Q R S T U V W X Y Z

274

b. The I.C.'s of the distributions (comprising 60 tallies each) and the observed number of blanks (Λ) for each are tabulated in the diagram below:

Alph.	Λ	I.C.		Alph.	Λ	I.C.
1	6	1.29		5	9	2.07
2	3	1.29		6	3	1.07
3	9	1.66		7	6	1.25
4	6	1.32		8	6	1.31

Except for alphabets 3 and 5, the I.C.'s are far from satisfactory; the period is unquestionably 8, but it does not appear that we have 8 monoalphabetic distributions. The average of the I.C.'s is $\frac{11.26}{8} = 1.41$, a figure considerably above random but nevertheless not nearly close enough to the expected I.C. of plain text for a sample of text this size. We note, however, that the average I.C. of the odd columns is $\frac{6.27}{4} = 1.57$, while the average I.C. of the even columns is $\frac{4.99}{4} = 1.25$; this strikes us as being especially significant.[6] Furthermore, the average Λ for the odd columns is $\frac{30}{4} = 7.5$, while that of the even columns is $\frac{18}{4} = 4.5$; these figures are compared with the expected Λ_p of 8 and the Λ_r of 2.5 for distributions of this size.[7] Perhaps the odd columns *do* represent monoalphabetic encipherment of plain text after all, while the even columns have undergone different cryptographic treatment. We will pursue this matter further.

c. One of the possibilities that comes to mind to explain the foregoing phenomena is a pseudo-digraphic encipherment in which the initial letters of plaintext pairs are monographically enciphered. If this were the case the *digraphic* I.C.'s of columns 1-2, 3-4, 5-6, and 7-8 should be close to the expected 4.66 for English plain text;[8] these digraphic I.C.'s are 5.38, 7.31, 7.31, and

---

[6] It can be shown that the I.C. of the odd columns, 1.57, represents a sigmage of $\frac{240(1.57-1.08)}{\sqrt{2(25\cdot 4)}} = \frac{117.6}{14.14} =$ 8.3 σ, whereas the I.C. of the even columns, 1.25, represents a deviation of $\frac{240(1.25-1.08)}{\sqrt{2(25\cdot 4)}} = \frac{40.8}{14.14} = 2.9\ \sigma$ above random. (We used 1.08 in the formula instead of 1.00, because the former figure is the I.C. of the overall cipher text.)

[7] Cf. Chart 6 on p. 39 of *Military Cryptanalytics, Part I.*

[8] Cf. subpar. 67c, *Military Cryptanalytics, Part I.*

8.09, respectively, giving statistical credence to the hypothesis that the four pairs of adjacent columns represent digraphically enciphered plaintext.[9]

d. The 14-letter repetition in the message is now examined. The uniliteral frequencies of the first letters of the cipher digraphs lend support to the assumption that this repetition represents the encipherment of RECONNAISSANCE, giving us the equivalents of C_p and N_p in column 1, A_p in col. 3, R_p and S_p in col. 5, and A_p and C_p in col. 7, in addition to the 7 values within the large square of the reconstruction matrix. The third letter of the repetition MR TG PE CE thus turns out to be S_p; frequency considerations of the first letters of these cipher digraphs make it quite likely that this repetition represents POSITION which gives us additional values in our reconstruction matrix. Finally, the six digraphs at the beginning of the message just before RECONNAISSANCE are studied, and, from the standpoint of the length of the ciphertext passage, plus the AB —— —— —— AB idiomorph exhibited, plus a consideration of the uniliteral frequencies of the initial letters of the digraphs, the opening word is assumed to be PHOTOGRAPHIC. The values from these three plaintext assumptions are set forth in the reconstruction matrix in Fig. 131a, below:

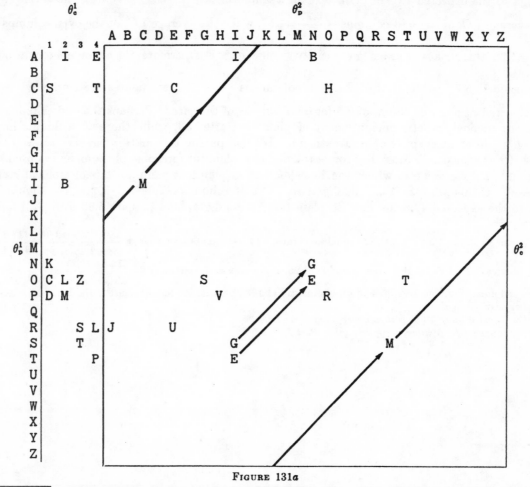

FIGURE 131a

---

[9] See also subpar. 95a for further lines of attack on this problem if the digraphic I.C.'s of the pairs of adjacent columns had not been satisfactory.

e. Evidence of vertical direct symmetry, as well as of diagonals of repeated letters characteristic of Vigenère-type squares, are manifested within the matrix, as shown by the lines in the foregoing figure; from these characteristics it appears that both the θ_p^1 and θ_p^2 sequences of this digraphic matrix consist of the normal A–Z sequence. If this is so, then direct symmetry should also be manifested among the four cipher sequences used to encipher the first letters of digraphs. Taking advantage of the principles of direct symmetry of position, the matrix in Fig. 131a is amplified into that shown in Fig. 131b, below:

```
                    θ¹c                                    θ²p

                                A B C D E F G H I J K L M N O P Q R S T U V W X Y Z
                 1 2 3 4
      A |       I       E |   G E   R     C T I   M       B     H J     S U V
      B |     E   B S   |   E   R     C T I   M       B     H J     S U V       G E
      C |     S   K T   |     R     C T I   M       B     H J     S U V       G E
      D |     T   C I   | R     C T I   M       B     H J     S U V       G E
      E |     I   D     |   C T I   M       B     H J     S U V       G E R
      F |               |   C T I   M       B     H J     S U V       G E R
      G |               |   C T I   M       B     H J     S U V       G E R
      H |         L     | T I   M       B     H J     S U V       G E R       C
      I |       B M     | I   M       B     H J     S U V       G E R       C T
      J |       K P     |   M       B     H J     S U V       G E R       C T I
      K |       C       | M       B     H J     S U V       G E R       C T I
 θ¹p  L |       D     B |   B     H J     S U V       G E R       C T I   M          θ²c
      M |     B   K     |   B     H J     S U V       G E R       C T I   M
      N |     K       C | B     H J     S U V       G E R       C T I   M       B
      O |     C L Z D   | B     H J     S U V       G E R       C T I   M       B
      P |     D M       |   H J     S U V       G E R       C T I   M       B
      Q |       P   E   | H J     S U V       G E R       C T I   M       B     H
      R |         S L   | J     S U V       G E R       C T I   M       B     H J
      S |     L   T M   |   S U V       G E R       C T I   M       B     H J
      T |     M   I P   |   S U V       G E R       C T I   M       B     H J
      U |     P         | S U V       G E R       C T I   M       B     H J
      V |       Z       | U V       G E R       C T I   M       B     H J       S
      W |               | V       G E R       C T I   M       B     H J       S U
      X |       E       |   G E R       C T I   M       B     H J       S U V
      Y |       S     Z |   G E R       C T I   M       B     H J       S U V
      Z |     Z T       | G E R       C T I   M       B     H J       S U V
```

FIGURE 131b

The frequencies of the additional values placed by direct symmetry in the four monographic columns are checked, and they are found to correspond generally with the expected frequencies of their plaintext equivalents; this, then, is confirmation of the type of matrix assumed.

f. From the partially reconstructed matrix in Fig. 131*b*, above, the derived values may be entered on the work sheet, as follows:

```
DV  LT  ZS  LJ    DV  BM    SU  TH    KG  II  TM  EB    SC  LQ  DJ  NH
PH  OT  OG  RA    PH  IC    RE  CO    NN  AI  SS  AN    CE  O       EN

YL  OF  CK  DC    OE  BV    YL  CE    JM  RP  RK  PT    NP  QU  DJ  VR
        D   OS        IO        NO                TO                EN

RV  OU  DZ  NA    RR  OE    IW  CL    OR  OC  ZE  MP    JP  GU  MV  CO
        E              T   N             ON  S              IO  N

CL  CK  YN  LL    GW  OV    TM  PT    DI  RF  TS  DE    LP  QP  KU  UV
O   K       R              SS  TO    PT      SC  O              CT

KO  LL  QY  DG    BY  XW    YC  EQ    OR  OF  UC  IT    KC  BB  MY  IR
N   O       OM    M             A                 DE    NT  IF  I   DA

LM  LG  DV  DL    MT  UP    NN  IT    TF  BG  TG  BF    RP  YT  KO  UU
SS  OM  ES  O     TO            DE    D   IS  SI  L             C

GX  BE  DV  TH    BX  IV    RK  SL    GG  JB  BF  QB    MG  QU  DG  NI
    IT  ES  CO    M   AW                     B                 EW

AN  IC  ZC  UU    SC  XG    DF  UU    IV  NL  KN  KH    LP  IE  MQ  UT
    AG  OS                  E         ES      C   ME    S   AB  I

IT  BU  IG  EQ    LV  GU    ZL  EB    TV  RP  TG  PB    WQ  BV  YC  LJ
ED  IN  TH  A     SE        O   AN    DT      SI  TU        IO      RA

KL  UQ  SR  NT    OU  XT    RV  EJ    CQ  MR  TG  PE    CE  VP  ZR  XG
N       RM                      AR    O   PO  SI  TI    ON      OP

VA  DV  KH  CC    OU  YX    SU  TH    KG  II  TM  EB    SC  UH  MD  OG
    LL  CO  NT              RE  CO    NN  AI  SS  AN    CE      I

LC  ZZ  SU  CJ    BM  MR  TG  PE    CE  VK  YH  ZY    PP  RP  RR  JM
SO      RE  NE    MY  PO  SI  TI    ON          Y     U

WJ  XW  SO  XA    RV  NL  QD  FI    OU  UQ  SR  NT    WK  XT  RP  BD
        R                           RM                       L

IZ  OF  ZR  KH    KC  VK  TP  OP    YX  QZ  TV  MP    CR  GH  XE  BF
E       OP  ME    NT      S         SE  S   OP                L

MW  QU  WR  LM    EL  BU  JX  QU    BS  XY  DT  MP    CR  NK  MD  OG
T           RT    B   IN            MI      ED  S     OP          I
```

278

From here on the addition of further values will snowball, and in very short order the plain text is solved in its entirety, and the enciphering matrix completed; the latter is found to be identical with the matrix illustrated in Fig. 127.

g. The steps in the solution of the foregoing problem were simple. The diagnosis of the system was straightforward, and the reconstruction of the plain text and of the matrix was begun by three word assumptions. In actual practice, the solution of a single message may not be so fortunate, but, as usual, we have shown the theoretical steps involving a single message which has been manipulated to make possible a solution on this limited traffic; in operational practice, several messages would probably have been required in order to find the two or three cribs necessary for solution. If the θ_p^1 and θ_p^2 sequences had been unknown mixed components, then the phenomena of indirect symmetry would have prevailed, and additional plaintext assumptions in the message would probably have been necessary in order to exploit the symmetrical phenomena in such a case.

h. A few remarks on the I.C.'s given in subpar. *b* might be added at this time. Alphabets 1 and 7 were a trifle low, and the average I.C. of 1.57 for the odd columns was also lower than we would have liked to have seen for monoalphabetic text. The vagaries of the plain text as it was allocated into the columns were responsible for this, since the over-all I.C. of the plaintext message may be found to be 1.74. On the other hand, the average I.C. of the even columns should have been lower than the observed 1.25,[10] but again this is "one of those things." The prudent cryptanalyst is prudent in his reverence for probabilities, small or large.

93. Analysis of a second case.—*a.* For our next example we will assume that the enemy is known to be using a system involving a multiplicity of Playfair squares to accomplish a poly-

---

[10] The expected I.C. for the second letters of digraphs of English text enciphered in a pseudo-digraphic system is $26(.0667)^2 = 1.16$, as compared with the usual I.C. of $26(.0667) = 1.73$. This I.C. of 1.16 is characteristic of *plaintext autokey* systems (cf. subpar. 99*e*)

alphabetic digraphic substitution. The following are the beginnings of 40 messages available for study:

	1	2	3	4	5	6	7	8	9	10
1.	IG	WN	CM	TO	SM	WT	LK	ET	RA	LN...
2.	HK	HV	YG	RT	MZ	EF	YO	DR	IM	OV...
3.	HK	CI	NT	IG	OE	OL	FC	NX	PI	FP...
4.	BS	UO	RO	CO	FR	DF	EN	ZO	AB	UV...
5.	LQ	IB	VY	CN	IH	FG	ZN	ZD	ZO	FL...
6.	OV	KH	LF	RC	GT	TU	NZ	RG	MT	YV...
7.	HZ	SF	WD	CQ	QE	YU	VO	PI	CA	AI...
8.	HK	HV	PG	IC	CO	DG	RM	NS	EA	XD...
9.	HA	PN	WE	ZU	VZ	NG	IR	OZ	HT	OE...
10.	NM	IF	HK	RC	CT	FR	FQ	EO	PI	MG...
11.	HK	LK	ZL	YF	VD	UC	OD	TS	AB	CI...
12.	NT	ZU	NB	FY	OF	ZL	RG	IR	PI	XV...
13.	UN	FZ	BH	NC	UC	ZU	CS	IX	DZ	CZ...
14.	QP	PB	CO	TO	DE	UO	ZO	BX	TE	NE...
15.	IG	WN	CM	TO	NG	BM	QW	UE	NQ	NP...
16.	HK	LK	CI	MU	VD	UC	OD	TS	BX	SV...
17.	HU	CD	AR	FY	HI	CU	NZ	UT	EL	UE...
18.	OV	KH	LF	SG	IT	EO	IZ	KB	SD	SL...
19.	UN	FZ	BU	DY	TA	LO	LI	UZ	NT	AT...
20.	HR	ZF	RT	VZ	FR	MS	RQ	TU	AK	KT...

	1	2	3	4	5	6	7	8	9	10
21.	HR	IG	CO	TO	UB	ZO	KI	ZL	TO	XO...
22.	TD	VY	MC	RC	GT	TU	NZ	QC	LD	OD...
23.	LQ	OY	LV	HD	PG	AW	PI	EO	BV	SX...
24.	HK	NK	PV	HF	UT	DW	IR	GN	CA	CK...
25.	FS	WV	NU	DS	ZO	IT	OX	IR	RC	TI...
26.	QD	BP	TO	GS	TL	PH	FI	EO	TS	SR...
27.	LV	KH	YG	DC	EO	CD	TB	MD	CM	HX...
28.	FS	WV	UZ	OV	FD	OL	XO	SB	IP	PN...
29.	UP	NT	BI	FY	FG	RO	HZ	QT	PI	OP...
30.	HZ	SF	WD	NQ	DP	NQ	ZO	LF	IR	XR...
31.	HU	HX	XY	BU	LO	WZ	PD	CR	RL	ZB...
32.	HK	PG	UZ	OV	UB	ZQ	FH	LP	ET	EA...
33.	NT	ZU	BH	NC	UC	ZU	CS	KU	EO	TC...
34.	AH	IG	IT	BV	EA	VF	PT	AK	NZ	ZU...
35.	NM	WV	OV	SP	OX	BG	OZ	YK	SC	RC...
36.	BR	IB	HE	AM	BU	DA	OX	YD	IM	OV...
37.	HK	TG	NC	VS	OE	XB	GE	XO	OZ	PN...
38.	GL	WV	YG	DC	EO	CD	RL	ZD	ZO	FL...
39.	GL	AQ	SN	FY	HI	CU	NZ	LC	KP	PK...
40.	LQ	KZ	UO	RO	BI	CT	NZ	KB	HW	TX...

From the repetitive phenomena observed, it is concluded that the messages are in flush depth; i.e., each column represents a digraphic "monoalphabet."

b. Abridged digraphic distributions are now made for the first few digraphic columns; these are shown on the next page.

280

```
1. A B C D E F G H I J K L M N O P Q R S T U V W X Y Z
   H S           S L K G       Q   M V   P       D N
   R             S L K G       Q   T V   D         N
                       Z           V   T         P
                       K           Q   M
                       A
                       K
                       K
                       U
                       R
                       R
                       K
                       Z
                       U
                       K
                       K

2. A B C D E F G H I J K L M N O P Q R S T U V W X Y Z
   Q P I         Z   V B   H K   K Y N     F G O Y N       U
       D         Z   V F   H K   T   B     F           N   F
                 X   G H           G       V               U
                     G Z                   V
                     B                     V
                                           V

3. A B C D E F G H I J K L M N O P Q R S T U V W X Y Z
   R H M           K T     F C T V G   O N O Z Y D Y G L
   U   O           E     F   B   V   T   Z   E   G
   I   M           V     U           O   D   G
   H   I           C
   O

4. A B C D E F G H I J K L M N O P Q R S T U V W X Y Z
   M U O Y     Y S D G         U C V     T G O   Z     F U
   V N S       Y F C           Q V       C P O   S
   Q C C       Y               C         C   O
     C C       Y                         C   O
                                         O

5. A B C D E F G H I J K L M N O P Q R S T U V W X Y Z
   U O E O R T I H     O Z G E G E   M A C Z         O
   I T P A R T I T         F         L B D
     O D                 X           T D
       G                 E           B
                                     C
```

Note is taken of the high frequency digraphs in the columns, and also of the reversible digraphs. What follows now is a brief synopsis of the initial entries into the problem. In col. 1, HK_c, with 8 occurrences, is in all probability RE_p. Next, we study the tetragraphic repetition CO TO in Msg #14 and 21, and the repetition IG WN CM TO in #1 and 15; it is assumed that these represent TI ON and DI VI SI ON, respectively. Msg #32 is now assumed to begin with the word

281

RE GI ME NT, which would make MO VE ME NT in #28. In #38, we have GL WV=FI VE;
in #27 we have LV KH=YO UR and in #6 we have OV KH LF=FO UR TH. The 8-letter repetition between #6 and #22 is assumed to be DI VI SI ON; Msg #2 now appears to begin with the
word RE FE RE NC E, which makes #8 RE FE RX RI NG TO. The initial word in #22 is
assumed to be WH EN, and in #3, RE IN FO RC EM EN TS.

c. At this point the work sheet with the assumptions entered will now look as follows:

```
    1   2   3   4   5   6   7   8   9   10              1   2   3   4   5   6   7   8   9   10
 1. IG  WN  CM  TO  SM  WT  LK  ET  RA  LN...     21. HR  IG  CO  TO  UB  ZO  KI  ZL  TO  XO...
    DI  VI  SI  ON                                        TI  ON
 2. HK  HV  YG  RT  MZ  EF  YO  DR  IM  OV...     22. TD  VY  MC  RC  GT  TU  NZ  QC  LD  OD...
    RE  FE  RE  NC  E                                     WH  EN  IS  DI  VI  SI  ON
 3. HK  CI  NT  IG  OE  OL  FC  NX  PI  FP...     23. LQ  OY  LV  HD  PG  AW  PI  EO  BV  SX...
    RE  IN  FO  RC  EM  EN  TS
 4. BS  UO  RO  CO  FR  DF  EN  ZO  AB  UV...     24. HK  NK  PV  HF  UT  DW  IR  GN  CA  CK...
                                                         RE
 5. LQ  IB  VY  CN  IH  FG  ZN  ZD  ZO  FL...     25. FS  WV  NU  DS  ZO  IT  OX  IR  RC  TI...
                            NO                            MO  VE
 6. OV  KH  LF  RC  GT  TU  NZ  RG  MT  YV...     26. QD  BP  TO  GS  TL  PH  FI  EO  TS  SR...
    FO  UR  TH  DI  VI  SI  ON                                                ER
 7. HZ  SF  WD  CQ  QE  YU  VO  PI  CA  AI...     27. LV  KH  YG  DC  EO  CD  TB  MD  CM  HX...
                                                         YO  UR  RE  GI  ME  NT
 8. HK  HV  PG  IC  CO  DG  RM  NS  EA  XD...     28. FS  WV  UZ  OV  FD  OL  XO  SB  IP  PN...
    RE  FE  RX  RI  NG  TO                                MO  VE  ME  NT      EN
 9. HA  PN  WE  ZU  VZ  NG  IR  OZ  HT  OE...     29. UP  NT  BI  FY  FG  RO  HZ  QT  PI  OP...

10. NM  IF  HK  RC  CT  FR  FQ  EO  PI  MG...     30. HZ  SF  WD  NQ  DP  NQ  ZO  LF  IR  XR...
                DI
11. HK  LK  ZL  YF  VD  UC  OD  TS  AB  CI...     31. HU  HX  XY  BU  LO  WZ  PD  CR  RL  ZB...
    RE
12. NT  ZU  NB  FY  OF  ZL  RG  IR  PI  XV...     32. HK  PG  UZ  OV  UB  ZQ  FH  LP  ET  EA...
                                                         RE  GI  ME  NT
13. UN  FZ  BH  NC  UC  ZU  CS  IX  DZ  CZ...     33. NT  ZU  BH  NC  UC  ZU  CS  KU  EO  TC...

14. QP  PB  CO  TO  DE  UO  ZO  BX  TE  NE...     34. AH  IG  IT  BV  EA  VF  PT  AK  NZ  ZU...
            TI  ON
15. IG  WN  CM  TO  NG  BM  QW  UE  NQ  NP...     35. NM  WV  OV  SP  OX  BG  OZ  YK  SC  RC...
    DI  VI  SI  ON                                        VE
16. HK  LK  CI  MU  VD  UC  OD  TS  BX  SV...     36. BR  IB  HE  AM  BU  DA  OX  YD  IM  OV...
    RE
17. HU  CD  AR  FY  HI  CU  NZ  UT  EL  UE...     37. HK  TG  NC  VS  OE  XB  GE  XO  OZ  PN...
                        ON                                RE          EM
18. OV  KH  LF  SG  IT  EO  IZ  KB  SD  SL...     38. GL  WV  YG  DC  EO  CD  RL  ZD  ZO  FL...
    FO  UR  TH  RE  GI  ME  NT                            FI  VE  RE  GI  ME  NT  S
19. UN  FZ  BU  DY  TA  LO  LI  UZ  NT  AT...     39. GL  AQ  SN  FY  HI  CU  NZ  LC  KP  PK...
                            NE                            FI                  ON
20. HR  ZF  RT  VZ  FR  MS  RQ  TU  AK  KT...     40. LQ  KZ  UO  RO  BI  CT  NZ  KB  HW  TX...
                                                                             ON
```

282

In the course of experimenting with the partial reconstruction of the Playfair squares for each column, we are able to determine that, in col. 4, $CO_c=TI_p$, $CN_c=TR_p$, $NC_c=RT_p$, $DS_c=-R_p$, $VS_c=EN_p$, and $RO_c=NI_p$. These recoveries facilitate further assumptions, and in reasonably short order we would have our work sheet looking like this:

```
      1   2   3   4   5   6   7   8   9   10              1   2   3   4   5   6   7   8   9   10
 1.  IG  WN  CM  TO  SM  WT  LK  ET  RA  LN...      21.  HR  IG  CO  TO  UB  ZO  KI  ZL  TO  XO...
     DI  VI  SI  ON                                     AD  DI  TI  ON  AL
 2.  HK  HV  YG  RT  MZ  EF  YO  DR  IM  OV...      22.  TD  VY  MC  RC  GT  TU  NZ  QC  LD  OD...
     RE  FE  RE  NC  E                                  WH  EN  IS  DI  VI  SI  ON
 3.  HK  CI  NT  IG  OE  OL  FC  NX  PI  FP...      23.  LQ  OY  LV  HD  PG  AW  PI  EO  BV  SX...
     RE  IN  FO  RC  EM  EN  TS
 4.  BS  UO  RO  CO  FR  DF  EN  ZO  AB  UV...      24.  HK  NK  PV  HF  UT  DW  IR  GN  CA  CK...
             TI                                         RE  CO  NX  NA  IS  SA  NC  E
 5.  LQ  IB  VY  CN  IH  FG  ZN  ZD  ZO  FL...      25.  FS  WV  NU  DS  ZO  IT  OX  IR  RC  TI...
             TR          NO                             MO  VE  YO  UR
 6.  OV  KH  LF  RC  GT  TU  NZ  RG  MT  YV...      26.  QD  BP  TO  GS  TL  PH  FI  EO  TS  SR...
     FO  UR  TH  DI  VI  SI  ON                         PR  IS  ON  ER
 7.  HZ  SF  WD  CQ  QE  YU  VO  PI  CA  AI...      27.  LV  KH  YG  DC  EO  CD  TB  MD  CM  HX...
                                                        YO  UR  RE  GI  ME  NT
 8.  HK  HV  PG  IC  CO  DG  RM  NS  EA  XD...      28.  FS  WV  UZ  OV  FD  OL  XO  SB  IP  PN...
     RE  FE  RX  RI  NG  TO                             MO  VE  ME  NT  OF  EN  EM  Y
 9.  HA  PN  WE  ZU  VZ  NG  IR  OZ  HT  OE...      29.  UP  NT  BI  FY  FG  RO  HZ  QT  PI  OP...
                                                        IN  FO  RM  AT  IO  N
10.  NM  IF  HK  RC  CT  FR  FQ  EO  PI  MG...      30.  HZ  SF  WD  NQ  DP  NQ  ZO  LF  IR  XR...
     SE  ND  AD  DI  TI  ON  AL
11.  HK  LK  ZL  YF  VD  UC  OD  TS  AB  CI...      31.  HU  HX  XY  BU  LO  WZ  PD  CR  RL  ZB...
     RE  QU  ES  TA  RT  IL  LE  RY
12.  NT  ZU  NB  FY  OF  ZL  RG  IR  PI  XV...      32.  HK  PG  UZ  OV  UB  ZQ  FH  LP  ET  EA...
     EN  EM  YP  AT  RO  L                              RE  GI  ME  NT  AL
13.  UN  FZ  BH  NC  UC  ZU  CS  IX  DZ  CZ...      33.  NT  ZU  BH  NC  UC  ZU  CS  KU  EO  TC...
     HE  AV  YA  RT  IL  LE  RY                         EN  EM  YA  RT  IL  LE  RY
14.  QP  PB  CO  TO  DE  UO  ZO  BX  TE  NE...      34.  AH  IG  IT  BV  EA  VF  PT  AK  NZ  ZU...
     PO  SI  TI  ON                                     RA  DI  O
15.  IG  WN  CM  TO  NG  BM  QW  UE  NQ  NP...      35.  NM  WV  OV  SP  OX  BG  OZ  YK  SC  RC...
     DI  VI  SI  ON                                     SE  VE  N
16.  HK  LK  CI  MU  VD  UC  OD  TS  BX  SV...      36.  BR  IB  HE  AM  BU  DA  OX  YD  IM  OV...
     RE  QU  IR  EA  RT  IL  LE  RY
17.  HU  CD  AR  FY  HI  CU  NZ  UT  EL  UE...      37.  HK  TG  NC  VS  OE  XB  GE  XO  OZ  PN...
     TH  IR  DB  AT  TA  LI  ON                         RE  PO  RT  EN  EM  Y
18.  OV  KH  LF  SG  IT  EO  IZ  KB  SD  SL...      38.  GL  WV  YG  DC  EO  CD  RL  ZD  ZO  FL...
     FO  UR  TH  RE  GI  ME  NT                         FI  VE  RE  GI  ME  NT  S
19.  UN  FZ  BU  DY  TA  LO  LI  UZ  NT  AT...      39.  GL  AQ  SN  FY  HI  CU  NZ  LC  KP  PK...
     HE  AV  Y           NE                             FI  RS  TB  AT  TA  LI  ON
20.  HR  ZF  RT  VZ  FR  MS  RQ  TU  AK  KT...      40.  LQ  KZ  UO  RO  BI  CT  NZ  KB  HW  TX...
     AD  VA  NC  E                                          NI          ON
```

283

d. With so many plain-cipher equivalencies per column, reconstruction of the squares will be a very easy matter. The squares as recovered for the first three columns are the following:

```
F G K M E        Z E V W X        D K A H F
O P Q S N        A H F D R        R P B Y N
V W     T        B Y N I C        I   M U O
Y D R A H        M U O G K        C   S L T
L I     U        S L T P Q          X Z E V
```
Square No. 1   Square No. 2   Square No. 3

Square No. 1 is recognized as containing a keyword-mixed sequence, so this square is rewritten in its original form, with the missing letters filled in. It is noticed that three of the columns of square No. 1 are common to square No. 2, and that three of the columns of this latter square are common to square No. 3; these three squares are therefore rewritten as follows:

```
H Y D R A        D R A H F        A H F D K
U L I C B        I C B Y N        B Y N R P
E F G K M        G K M U O        M U O I
N O P Q S        P Q S L T        S L T C
T V W X Z        W X Z E V        Z E V   X
```
Square No. 1   Square No. 2   Square No. 3

A few moments' inspection will now reveal the relationships among the three squares; each succeeding square is derived from its predecessor by permuting two columns at a time, as demonstrated in subpar. 91*e*. Since we now know the method of square generation, we may read any message in its entirety without further ado after we have generated the pertinent band of Playfair squares.

e. The foregoing system was fairly easy to solve because of its progressive 1, 2, 3 . . . selection of the Playfair squares from the band. If the order of square selection had been different, say in a scrambled order of 25 squares as treated in subpar. 91*g*, it would probably have been necessary to make entries in quite a few columns in order to reconstruct enough partial squares before we would have been able to see any relationships among the squares.

f. Once the Playfair band has been recovered, a message starting at any arbitrary point in the band may of course be read, since one of the 25 possible trials will yield plain text. If the same band continues to be used, but there is employed an unknown mixed sequence to govern the progression of enciphering squares, then a modification of the generatrix method is here applicable. For example, let us consider the following cryptogram, known to have been enciphered with the Playfair band just recovered, but with an unknown 25-element progression:

```
RQ  CP  CI  IT  TP  CL  ZL  GP  TD  GH  SC  XW  RQ  XV  EI
EW  ZC  RW  ZN  HS  PY  BT  WM  KY  QD  TF  NI  UX  XY  FG
DI  PV  MT  VG  VY
```

The procedure here is to complete the "plain component (digraphic) sequence" from the cipher digraphs by deciphering each digraph successively through all 25 squares. For example,

284

the first digraph RQ_c represents XK_p in squares No. 1 and 2, PI_p in squares No. 3 and 4, WN_p in square No. 5, etc. The complete generatrix diagram for the first ten digraphs is the following:

	RQ	CP	CI	IT	TP	CL	ZL	GP	TD	GH...
1.	XK	IQ	IL	UW	WN	IU	VB	IG	WH	ED
2.	XK	IQ	IN	NP	LT	YQ	ES	IG	PF	UD
3.	PI	WR	IR	OC	WN	TS	ES	XR	CF	ED
4.	PI	WR	IR	OC	WN	ZI	LS	XR	CF	MR
5.	WN	QT	TG	GI	DT	NB	LS	XT	DS	MT
6.	HO	NC	TG	GI	AC	NY	LS	QC	DS	QV
7.	PO	RC	TG	GI	AC	SG	FO	QC	FV	QV
8.	HO	QI	AC	CK	HI	OM	FO	HQ	SA	HV
9.	HO	QI	AC	CK	HI	OY	XO	HQ	RW	HV
10.	LC	QT	RE	EN	NT	RY	DR	HQ	SA	HV
11.	YK	HT	RE	EN	NT	RY	DR	BW	SA	BY
12.	YL	HT	DO	OS	ZT	RO	RK	BW	SC	BY
13.	YL	BO	BQ	BS	AT	BI	RK	OM	SA	OY
14.	DM	BO	YU	EX	AT	BY	RK	ES	XA	UF
15.	YL	RY	YU	MQ	ZM	RO	ET	MN	QK	UF
16.	YL	TH	QN	MQ	ZM	WT	ET	ZH	QK	FN
17.	TB	YN	ZF	TQ	DQ	WY	CY	MN	HT	FN
18.	ZS	YN	ZF	TQ	DQ	VN	VQ	MN	HT	FN
19.	HO	ST	TN	FH	CT	SP	WC	MC	PF	QX
20.	HO	YN	TN	FH	YI	WG	KG	MN	WH	QX
21.	TO	MN	QN	FH	YI	OM	WC	ES	WH	DA
22.	HO	YN	YU	EP	NT	OY	WC	FS	BM	MR
23.	LC	YN	YU	EP	NT	RY	DC	IW	WH	ED
24.	CK	YZ	YM	NP	ZT	RY	WC	IW	WE	NL
25.	CK	DM	DQ	UW	WN	YQ	VQ	IG	WH	ED

By reading various levels of the generatrix diagram, it may be seen that the message begins "HOSTILE PATROL SIGHTED..."

g. It will be noted that the equivalency $CP_c = ST_p$ is unique to square No. 19, and that $CI_c = IL_p$ is unique to square No. 1; therefore these squares may be ruled out as key squares for any other positions along the cycle of 25. The multiple keys for the first 10 digraphs are as follows:

C:	RQ	CP	CI	IT	TP	CL	ZL	GP	TD	GH...
P:	HO	ST	IL	EP	AT	RO	LS	IG	HT	ED
	6	19	1	22	13	12	4	2	17	3
	8			23	14	15	5	25	18	23
	9						6			25
	20									
	22									

The first 10 keys might be made unique by considering the decipherments of the cipher digraphs in the next cycle. Since we have limited the possible keys in the foregoing diagram, only *those* keys come into question in the corresponding positions of the next cycle. The decipherments, therefore, of the digraphs in the next cycle are as follows:

	TF	NI	UX	XY	FG	DI	PV	MT	VG	VY
1.	....	....	CT							
2.	....	....	....	....	....	....	....	OS		
3.	....	....	....	....	....	....	....	....	....	EN
4.	....	....	....	....	....	....	NX			
5.	....	....	....	....	....	....	TW			
6.	DI	....	....	....	....	....	CH			
7.										
8.	SK									
9.	WA									
10.										
11.										
12.	....	....	....	....	IX					
13.	....	....	....	GW						
14.	....	....	....	NS						
15.	....	....	....	....	YQ					
16.										
17.	....	....	....	....	....	....	....	....	....	EV
18.	....	....	....	....	....	....	....	....	....	EC
19.	....	UN								
20.	FI									
21.										
22.	PM	....	IO							
23.	....	....	....	VR	....	....	....	....	FP	
24.										
25.	....	....	....	....	....	....	....	NZ	....	OV

The plain text revealed, "...DJ UN CT IO NS IX TW OS EV EN," is in this case found in unique squares, so the unambiguous key for the first 10 positions is found to be 6 19 1 22 14 12 5 2 17 3. When the rest of the plain text is solved, it will be found that of the remaining 15 columns, all but 4 will yield unique keys; if we had available another message or two, the ambiguity could probably be removed from the 4 ambiguous columns.

94. Analysis of other types of periodic digraphic systems.—a. Since there is a plethora of possible basic digraphic systems which may be used in conjunction with a polyalphabetic scheme, each case will present different aspects in its solution, depending on what may be known initially about the system, and what phenomena are uncovered *and recognized* during the process of solution. A sufficient volume of traffic, plus the inevitable cryptanalytic breaks which may be expected to occur in the course of the use *and misuse* of the system, are the deciding factors for successful solution.

b. In a system such as that illustrated in Fig. 128, once the period has been determined by factoring (with perhaps the digraphic ϕ test being used to prove the period), plaintext assumptions in the messages would be recorded intially in several skeleton 26x26 matrices, one for each column of the period, until enough data have accumulated to permit the revelation of the relationships latent among the matrices and among the sets of coordinates. If the composition of the interior of the matrix were known, even a single crib of moderate length might suffice to establish enough values in the sliding coordinates which would result in further automatic decryptions and rapid completion of the solution.

c. In those digraphic systems which yield trinomes for the ciphertext equivalents for plaintext digraphs, the primary cipher text might be subjected to encipherment by a cyclic additive as means of increasing the security of the system. For example, the basic system might incorporate a matrix such as that illustrated in Fig. 132, below: [11]

$$\theta_p^2$$

	J	U	P	I	T	E	R	A	B	C	D	F	G	H	K	L	M	N	O	Q	S	V	W	X	Y	Z
V	001	002	003	004	005	006	007	008	009	010	011	012	013	014	015	016	017	018	019	020	021	022	023	024	025	026
E	027	028	029	030	031	032	033	034	035	036	037	038	039	040	041	042	043	044	045	046	047	048	049	050	051	052
N	053	054	055	056	057	058	059	060	061	062	063	064	065	066	067	068	069	070	071	072	073	074	075	076	077	078
U	079	080	081	082	083	084	085	086	087	088	089	090	091	092	093	094	095	096	097	098	099	100	101	102	103	104
S	105	106	107	108	109	110	111	112	113	114	115	116	117	118	119	120	121	122	123	124	125	126	127	128	129	130
A	131	132	133	134	135	136	137	138	139	140	141	142	143	144	145	146	147	148	149	150	151	152	153	154	155	156
B	157	158	159	160	161	162	163	164	165	166	167	168	169	170	171	172	173	174	175	176	177	178	179	180	181	182
C	183	184	185	186	187	188	189	190	191	192	193	194	195	196	197	198	199	200	201	202	203	204	205	206	207	208
D	209	210	211	212	213	214	215	216	217	218	219	220	221	222	223	224	225	226	227	228	229	230	231	232	233	234
F	235	236	237	238	239	240	241	242	243	244	245	246	247	248	249	250	251	252	253	254	255	256	257	258	259	260
G	261	262	263	264	265	266	267	268	269	270	271	272	273	274	275	276	277	278	279	280	281	282	283	284	285	286
H	287	288	289	290	291	292	293	294	295	296	297	298	299	300	301	302	303	304	305	306	307	308	309	310	311	312
I	313	314	315	316	317	318	319	320	321	322	323	324	325	326	327	328	329	330	331	332	333	334	335	336	337	338
J	339	340	341	342	343	344	345	346	347	348	349	350	351	352	353	354	355	356	357	358	359	360	361	362	363	364
K	365	366	367	368	369	370	371	372	373	374	375	376	377	378	379	380	381	382	383	384	385	386	387	388	389	390
L	391	392	393	394	395	396	397	398	399	400	401	402	403	404	405	406	407	408	409	410	411	412	413	414	415	416
M	417	418	419	420	421	422	423	424	425	426	427	428	429	430	431	432	433	434	435	436	437	438	439	440	441	442
O	443	444	445	446	447	448	449	450	451	452	453	454	455	456	457	458	459	460	461	462	463	464	465	466	467	468
P	469	470	471	472	473	474	475	476	477	478	479	480	481	482	483	484	485	486	487	488	489	490	491	492	493	494
Q	495	496	497	498	499	500	501	502	503	504	505	506	507	508	509	510	511	512	513	514	515	516	517	518	519	520
R	521	522	523	524	525	526	527	528	529	530	531	532	533	534	535	536	537	538	539	540	541	542	543	544	545	546
T	547	548	549	550	551	552	553	554	555	556	557	558	559	560	561	562	563	564	565	566	567	568	569	570	571	572
W	573	574	575	576	577	578	579	580	581	582	583	584	585	586	587	588	589	590	591	592	593	594	595	596	597	598
X	599	600	601	602	603	604	605	606	607	608	609	610	611	612	613	614	615	616	617	618	619	620	621	622	623	624
Y	625	626	627	628	629	630	631	632	633	634	635	636	637	638	639	640	641	642	643	644	645	646	647	648	649	650
Z	651	652	653	654	655	656	657	658	659	660	661	662	663	664	665	666	667	668	669	670	671	672	673	674	675	676

θ_p^1 (left coordinate) $\overline{\theta\theta}_s$ (right coordinate)

FIGURE 132

Such an additive-enciphered digraphic system could pose considerable obstacles in the way of cryptanalysis; nevertheless, given enough traffic, and given enough special circumstances which, as the student has come to appreciate, are inevitable when any system is used among a group of correspondents over a period of time, solution of such a system by a staff of expert and trained cryptanalysts is only a matter of time and labor. If the matrix and its coordinates become

[11] For another type of trinome-digraphic system, see subpar. 66*f*, in *Military Cryptanalytics, Part I.*

known, either through compromise or by analytical reconstruction, then a crib attack is an easy entry into what would otherwise be a very difficult system.

95. Additional remarks.—*a.* The question of diagnosis and recognition of periodic digraphic systems has been touched on rather lightly in our discussion thus far. It will be helpful to illustrate some general concepts which might facilitate the identification of this family of systems.

(1) Let us suppose a hypothetical system, in which four 4-square matrices are used in succession in a message. That is, the 1st, 5th, 9th... digraphs are enciphered with Matrix No. 1; the 2d, 6th, 10th... digraphs are enciphered with Matrix No. 2; etc. This may be diagrammed as follows, where the ligatures designate the letters enciphered digraphically:

$$\widehat{\theta\theta}\ \widehat{\theta\theta}\ \widehat{\theta\theta}\ \widehat{\theta\theta}$$

The characteristics of such a system would be: (a) the absence of one letter, usually J, in the traffic; (b) the presence of cyclical phenomena in the polygraphic repetitions present that would indicate a period of 8; (c) the general inadequacy of the monographic ϕ tests for the 8 distributions, *including* an insufficiency for the most part in the expected number of blanks; (d) the prevalence of repetitions of an *even* number of letters, which repetitions would begin for the most part in alphabets 1, 3, 5, and 7, and would have the tendency to end in alphabets 2, 4, 6, and 8; (e) good results in digraphic distributions, when the digraphic ϕ test is applied to the pairs 1–2, 3–4, 5–6, and 7–8, and poor results when the test is applied to the pairs 2–3, 4–5, 6–7, and 8–1; and (f) negative results when the digraphic χ test is applied, showing that the four digraphic encipherments are cryptographically nonhomogeneous.

(2) Now let us consider what would happen if instead of the digraphic encipherment of successive pairs of letters, some other type of pairing is used, such as one of the following examples:

Case a: $\theta\ \theta\ \theta\ \theta\ \theta\ \theta\ \theta$

Case b: $\theta\ \theta\ \theta\ \theta\ \theta\ \theta\ \theta$

Case c: $\theta\ \theta\ \theta\ \theta\ \theta\ \theta\ \theta$

When counts are made on the digraphs composed of enciphered *adjacent* letters of plain text, as in the example in the preceding subparagraph, the digraphic κ_p is .0069; it is this constant which will be used in the digraphic ϕ and χ tests as a measure of the relative "digraphicity" of the cipher text.[12] If, however, the plaintext elements which are digraphically enciphered are *not* adjacent letters in running plain text but are *widely* separated, then the digraphs thus formed do not follow the frequency of English plaintext digraphs, but instead depend upon the *product of the individual probabilities* of English plaintext letters, so that our κ_p in this instance will be the square of the monographic κ_p, $(.0667)^2 = .0044$. This same constant, .0044, would be true in any digraphic encipherment of a more-or-less random assortment of letters taken from a population having the probabilities of English plaintext letters; thus it applies to a digraphic

---

[12] The κ_r constant is the reciprocal of the number of elements possible in the distribution; thus the usual value for the digraphic κ_r is $\dfrac{1}{676} = .00148$. In the case of systems employing 4-square or 2-square matrices, the κ_r is $\dfrac{1}{625} = .00160$; if the system employed Playfair squares, the digraphic κ_r is $\dfrac{1}{600} = .00167$, since doubled letters are usually excluded in this cipher.

encipherment of a transposition cipher, or the encipherment of the vertical pairs in a periodic "seriation" such as in the following example:[13]

```
R E F E R      O U R M E      N U M B E
( ( ( (        ( ( ( (        (
E N C E Y      S S A G E      R . . .
```

The highest frequency digraph of the units thus formed would be EE_p; next would be the digraphs ET_p and TE_p; and so on, in descending order of the products of the probabilities of the individual letters composing the digraphs.

(3) In case a, above, the digraphic κ_p would be less than .0069, but higher than .0044, since the frequencies of repeated trigraphs in English plain text govern an affinity of combination for certain letters with others; e.g., the frequent trigraphs ENT_p, ION_p, AND_p, ING_p, . . . will influence the higher probability of the separated digraphs ET_p, IN_p, AD_p, IG_p, etc. In case b, however, the digraphic κ_p would be .0044; and in case c, whereas the κ_p of the digraphs 1–8 and 2–7 would be .0044, the κ_p of the digraph 3–6 would theoretically be a shade above .0044 (a refinement indistinguishable in actual practice), while the digraph 4–5 would of course have a κ_p of .0069.

(4) It follows, then, that given enough material, the digraphic ϕ test may be used to diagnose a periodic digraphic cipher, to include the manner of pairing the plaintext letters to produce the cipher digraphs. Furthermore, the digraphic χ test may be employed to discover whether all the digraphic encipherments are cryptographically unique, or whether the same digraphic treatment has been applied to more than one pairing in the periodic digraphic system. A résumé of the formulas used in digraphic analysis is given below. When the digraphs are composed of enciphered adjacent letters,

$$_2\phi_p = .0069N(N-1) \qquad _2\chi_m = .0069N_1N_2$$
$$_2\phi_r = .0015N(N-1) \qquad _2\chi_r = .0015N_1N_2$$

For digraphs composed of enciphered separated letters,

$$_2\phi_p \geq .0044N(N-1) \qquad _2\chi_m \geq .0044N_1N_2$$
$$_2\phi_r = .0015N(N-1) \qquad _2\chi_r = .0015N_1N_2$$

(5) A rather important consideration that may be overlooked or forgotten by the student of cryptanalytics, is that the ϕ tests on the initial and final letters of a digraphic substitution employing 4-square, 2-square, or Playfair matrices are far from being random distributions. Since these matrices produce only a *partially digraphic* encipherment, then the encipherments of EN_p, ER_p, ES_p, ET_p . . . may result in a series of cipher digraphs in which the E_p has been enciphered more-or-less monoalphabetically. However, the use of a *well-constructed* 26x26 table will yield a digraphic encipherment wherein the uniliteral frequency distributions of the initial letters and final letters have random characteristics.

(6) Some pertinent observations may be made here regarding repetitive phenomena in cases such as a, b, and c of subpar. (2), above. In case a, repetitions will begin *predominantly* in alphabets 1 and 5, and end in alphabets 4 and 8; in case b, repetitions will usually begin in alphabet 1 and end likewise in alphabet 8; and in case c, the delineations of the repetitions will either be from alphabet 1 to alphabet 8, or alphabet 2 to alphabet 7, or alphabet 3 to alphabet 6.

---

[13] In this example, having a seriation interval of 5, if the last block of 10 letters were incomplete, it would be padded by enough nulls to permit the encipherment of the five vertical digraphs.

Thus, causal tetragraphic repetitions are possible in case *a* in the first four or last four letters, and tetragraphic repetitions are also possible in case *c* in the *middle* four letters; but in case *b*, causal tetragraphic repetitions have been effectively suppressed.

b. It might be of interest to point out that periodic cryptosystems have been constructed which contain intermixtures of monographic and digraphic treatment, usually for the purpose of achieving a "complexity" in the cryptographic system and thereby defeating enemy cryptanalysis. Such poor subterfuges are—as we have just said—poor; nevertheless, similar ideas are sometimes encountered in examples of poor cryptography. The monographic encipherments in these systems might be uniliteral in form, or biliteral; and in the latter case, the two cipher elements concerned might be adjacent elements in the cipher text, or separated in the cycle of a period-length—as another cryptographic trick to deter cryptanalysis.

c. The superimposition of messages enciphered in periodic digraphic systems is accomplished generally in the same manner as is the case with monographic ciphers, i.e., aligning the messages by means of known indicators, or juxtaposing messages so that long polygraphic repetitions present are exactly superimposed. In addition, long messages might be correctly superimposed by means of a modification of the kappa test; this test will be treated in the next chapter.

CONCLUDING REMARKS

96. Miscellaneous periodic polyalphabetic systems.—*a.* In all the systems treated thus far in this text, each alphabet was used successively to encipher successive single plaintext elements, monographic or digraphic. There is no reason, however, why each alphabet might not be used to encipher 2, 3, or more successive letters at a time; this has the apparent effect of doubling, tripling, or n-tupling the length of the fundamental period, but at the expense of a corresponding reduction in the cryptographic security of the system.

b. As an example of such a system, we may cite that used by the Russians during World War I and known in cryptologic literature as the "Sprungchiffre"; this is illustrated in Fig. 133, below: [1]

	А	Б	В	Г	Д	Е	Ж	З	И	К	Л	М	Н	О	П	Р	С	Т	У	Ф	Х	Ц	Ч	Ш	Щ	Ъ	Ю	Я	Ь	Ъ	Ы	Й	I
3	31	61	81	79	57	35	12	56	46	74	37	41	89	43	45	47	97	65	32	59	24	39	38	86	13	84	23	85	62	17	54	58	14
1	31	21	81	79	42	56	72	26	83	27	37	61	89	43	28	23	97	13	29	59	36	32	38	73	63	24	64	85	41	17	25	51	46
4	15	37	21	64	31	17	67	25	49	69	18	23	35	93	59	86	52	13	46	89	74	98	28	47	72	42	45	24	48	87	34	65	39
5	86	92	52	23	18	97	36	13	46	67	54	71	19	14	65	27	93	85	16	79	12	58	76	48	83	34	26	74	62	38	37	29	81
6	25	31	17	42	38	13	41	61	23	45	89	15	84	75	48	54	34	73	14	53	37	24	64	18	28	12	95	57	93	78	82	76	27
7	41	64	84	43	92	53	85	34	67	71	27	26	46	49	24	58	31	75	18	23	98	29	62	39	42	51	96	65	17	96	13	91	94
8	12	56	82	74	13	38	96	54	61	37	83	26	49	68	39	65	57	16	23	95	48	31	78	17	59	73	14	72	98	52	41	53	69
2	73	86	31	93	42	56	21	62	19	47	75	61	32	59	28	84	14	71	35	91	87	69	16	13	25	76	89	38	64	94	95	83	29

FIGURE 133

(1) This basically is a dinome-for-letter substitution with 8 random, unrelated alphabets,[2] used in conjunction with a special indicator procedure. The enciphering clerk begins his message with a 5-digit "stutter" group chosen at random, such as **44444**, which indicates how many consecutive plaintext letters are to be enciphered by each alphabet. He then enciphers the first four letters (if **44444** is the indicator) with the alphabet labeled "1", after which he enciphers the next four letters with alphabet "2", and so on, repeating the cycle after alphabet "8" is used. At any point during the encipherment after a block of letters (in this case, 4) has been encrypted, the clerk might introduce a new stutter group, such as **66666**, which would indicate that each alphabet from now on (without disturbing the sequence of alphabets) will be used to encipher *six* consecutive plaintext letters. The final cipher text was transmitted in 5-digit groups. For decipherment, a separate deciphering table was necessary.

[1] The matrix illustrated and a description of the cryptography of the system were taken from Andreas Figl, *Systeme des Chiffrierens*, Graz, 1926, pp. 84–85 and Appendix 19.

[2] The dinomes in the cipher components did not include the digit 0, nor were there any doublets such as 11, 22, etc.

(2) Changes of keys in this system were effected merely by changing the designations of the 8 alphabets, the basic matrix remaining fixed for a considerable period; in fact, according to official German historical records, the random cipher components of the matrix seem to have been changed only twice during the life of this cryptosystem.[3]

(3) The cryptanalysis of this system is obvious. If the matrix and details of the system were unknown, the study of even a small amount of traffic in the same key would establish the meaning of the stutter indicator group, disclosing the basic periodicity as 8 alphabets. The general method of attack is then along the lines indicated in subpar. 74b. In this latter connection, we would be aided by the idiomorphisms which will manifest themselves when a single alphabet is used to encipher several consecutive plaintext letters; the word КОМИССИЯ, for instance, will quite likely yield an ABBA pattern in the cipher if the indicator is 44444 or higher. Once the matrix becomes known, new alphabet keys may be recovered by a modification of the usual generatrix method.[4]

c. The 4-level dinome variant system illustrated in subpar. 58c of *Military Cryptanalytics, Part I*, lends itself to polyalphabetic treatment. The basic system, as the student will recall, involves a matrix with a 25-letter (I=J) plain component, and four cipher sequences consisting of 25 dinomes each (in normal numerical order, 01–25, 26–50, 51–75, and 76–00). These sequences, aligned according to a specific key, constitute a matrix providing four cipher equivalents for each plaintext letter.

(1) In Fig. 134, below, there is illustrated a polyalphabetic modification of this system:

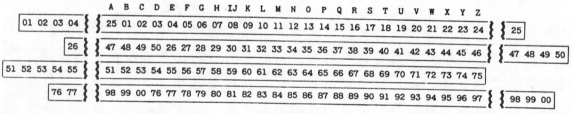

FIGURE 134

The four sequences are printed on sliding strips which are free to slide individually in a frame against a normal plain component. The initial dinomes (01, 26, 51, 76) of the strips are here shown aligned to the letters B, E, A, D, respectively, constituting the first specific key. These strips are now locked into place with respect to each other, and the entire compound strip is moved to provide a feature of polyalphabeticity, controlled by a second specific key. For instance, if the dinome 01 in the now-fixed compound strip were set successively against the letters B, A, S, K, E, T during the encipherment of successive plaintext letters, we will have a periodic polyalphabetic substitution system with variants.

---

[3] This system, introduced toward the end of 1914, was so clumsy to use and caused so many requests for retransmissions—because the Russians were often unable to read their own traffic—that it was withdrawn even before the year was up. The Russians, unaccustomed to such complications, reverted to the simple substitution ciphers (!) they had previously been using.

[4] We could even identify a particular alphabet from occurrences of certain dinomes which are unique in the matrix (such as, in Fig. 133, the dinome 63 in alphabet labelled "1" and 68 in alphabet labelled "8"), or from the ten different dinomes which occur in only two of the alphabets (such as 15, occurring in alphabets labelled "4" and "6").

(2) The cryptanalysis of this system, too, is quite apparent. What we have fundamentally is a repeating-key system with *standard alphabets*. This gives us at once the obvious cue: factor the message, convert the cipher letters of each alphabet into their plain-component equivalents, and complete the plain-component sequence. The particular steps for such a system have been treated in subpars. 60*n–p* of *Military Cryptanalytics, Part I*.

(3) If the alphabets had not been standard alphabets, the story would be quite different. Fortunately, in such a case the system would become operationally preposterous, with the probable result that the enemy's cryptocommunications would break down if such a system were introduced. But even if such a system with mixed alphabets *were* used, the application of the principles expounded in this text, and the availability of a reasonable amount of traffic, would lead to solution, albeit laborious.

d. Polyalphabetic systems have been encountered in which vowels have been enciphered by vowels, and consonants by consonants.[5] This feature usually has been prompted for reasons of economy existing in once prevailing telegraph company rates. The following *sectional matrix*[6] is an example of a system possessing the vowel-to-vowel feature:

```
A E I O U Y B C D F G H J K L M N P Q R S T V W X Z
┌─────────┬───────────────────────────────────────┐
│ U E I O A Y │ Q S T N B L C D F G H J K M P R V W X Z │
│ E I O A Y U │ N B L C D F G H J K M P R V W X Z Q S T │
│ I O A Y U E │ C D F G H J K M P R V W X Z Q S T N B L │
│ O A Y U E I │ G H J K M P R V W X Z Q S T N B L C D F │
│ A Y U E I O │ K M P R V W X Z Q S T N B L C D F G H J │
│ Y U E I O A │ R V W X Z Q S T N B L C D F G H J K M P │
└─────────┴───────────────────────────────────────┘
```

FIGURE 135

Other sectional matrices might be constructed in which the cipher equivalents for plaintext vowels are chosen from a group of six cipher letters. In such a system, the plaintext letters AEIOUY, comprising 40% of the text, will be replaced by the six new vowel-equivalents in question. The vowel-equivalents can be picked out of the uniliteral distributions on the basis of their outstanding frequencies; and supporting evidence may be found in the "vowel-like" *positional* spacing of these letters in the cipher text of a cryptogram. While we're on the subject of sectional matrices, it might be mentioned that matrices with multiple sections are also possible, as exemplified in Fig. 136, below:

```
A B C D E F G H I J K L M N O P Q R S T U V W X Y Z
┌───────────┬─────────────┬───────────┬─────────┐
│ Q U E S T │ I O N A B │ L Y C D F │ G H K M P │ R V W X Z │
│ U E S T Q │ O N A B I │ Y C D F L │ H K M P G │ V W X Z R │
│ E S T Q U │ N A B I O │ C D F L Y │ K M P G H │ W X Z R V │
│ S T Q U E │ A B I O N │ D F L Y C │ M P G H K │ X Z R V W │
│ T Q U E S │ B I O N A │ F L Y C D │ P G H K M │ Z R V W X │
└───────────┴─────────────┴───────────┴─────────┘
```

FIGURE 136

e. Periodic cryptosystems have been encountered in which the alphabets used consisted of both direct standard and reversed standard alphabets. The rule governing the choice of one

---

[5] We have already seen an example of this in the system described in par. 76.

[6] A sectional matrix is, as the term implies, a polyalphabetic substitution matrix with two or more distinct sections. The Porta table is an example of a sectional matrix, as is demonstrated by the equivalent matrix illustrated in subpar. 23*a*, on p. 45.

293

type or the other, might be based (1) on the *position* of the key letter in the repeating key (e.g., the odd letters of the key to be enciphered with direct standard alphabets, the even letters with reversed standard), or (2) on the *parity* of the key letter in the normal alphabetical sequence (e.g., key letters in the ACEGI... family to be enciphered with direct standard, and key letters in the BDFHJ... family to be enciphered with reversed standard alphabets). Examples such as these should pose no difficulties; the principles of their cryptanalysis have been covered in Chapter IV.

f. The student has seen that, when the cipher component in a periodic cipher is the normal sequence (or any other *known* sequence), matching of the individual uniliteral frequency distributions for each alphabet is possible, reducing the polyalphabetic cryptogram to a monoalphabetic cipher.[7] Now let us assume we have at hand a particular periodic polyalphabetic cipher of several hundred letters, factoring to six alphabets. We observe that we are able to slide the uniliteral distributions for alphabets 1 and 2 to an excellent match, confirmed by the χ test; alphabets 3 and 4 are also slid to an excellent fit with respect to each other; and likewise alphabets 5 and 6 are also slid to a correct match. Yet we find it impossible to obtain a good match for the three combined distributions, in spite of the paradoxical fact that the cipher component *must* have been the normal sequence to enable us to match *any* distributions at all! The obvious explanation (which incidentally was far from obvious when this situation was first encountered) is that the cipher components for the first two alphabets consisted of the normal sequence, the cipher components for alphabets 3 and 4 consisted of a *decimation* of the normal sequence, and the cipher components for alphabets 5 and 6 consisted of a different decimation of the normal sequence; the plain component was a mixed sequence.[8] This demonstrates to the student once again that he must always keep an open mind in explaining phenomena, however "incongruous" or "inexplicable" they may be. It is the "improbable" system which may resist the efforts of the cryptanalyst, until he casts aside preconceived *idées fixes* and rationalizes the causes of the manifestations present to reach an ultimate solution.[9]

97. Periodic Baudot systems.—*a.* In the previous text we became familiar with the international Baudot code used in teleprinter communication.[10] This code is reproduced for convenience in Fig. 137, below:

UPPER CASE	WEATHER SYMBOLS	↕	⊕	○	∕	3	→	↘	↑	8	↗	←	↖	•	⊛	9	∅	1	4	⌂	5	7	⊙	2	∕	6	+	−	⟨	⫴					
	COMMUNICATIONS	−	?	:	$	3	↑	ə	£	8	'	(	)	•	¬	9	∅	1	4	⌂	5	7	;	2	∕	6	"	⁇	⟨						
LOWER	CASE	A	B	C	D	E	F	G	H	I	J	K	L	M	N	O	P	Q	R	S	T	U	V	W	X	Y	Z	BLANK	C.R.	L.F.	SPACE	LTR. SHIFT	FIG. SHIFT

FIGURE 137

There are many methods for accomplishing the encryption of teleprinter signals, ranging from primitive switching devices yielding nothing more than a simple substitution, to systems involving complicated apparatus producing encrypted signals of great security.

---

[7] Cf. par. 36.

[8] This situation could also have arisen if all the cipher components consisted of the normal sequence, and the plain components involved three different mixed sequences.

[9] In this connection, the student would do well to spend 60 seconds in meditation on the quotation from Aristotle on the back of the title page of this text (from the *Politics*, i. 2. 9. 1253 a).

[10] At this point it is recommended that the student review the material covered in par. 56 of *Military Cryptanalytics, Part I.*

294

b. The first encrypted teleprinter system was invented during World War I by an American engineer, Gilbert S. Vernam, who called it the "Cipher Printing Telegraph System." Basically, the Vernam system incorporated a specially prepared tape of random teleprinter characters used to key another tape containing the plain text to be encrypted. The two tapes were fed into a "tape reader," and the impulses from these two tapes were combined by what is known as "encipherment according to the Vernam rule," or, more simply, "Baudot addition." That is, like impulses or bauds combine to form a "mark" (symbolized by +), whereas unlike impulses result in a "space" (symbolized by -). For example, if the character on the keying tape is -+++- (=C) and the character on the plaintext message tape is ++--- (=A), then the result by Baudot addition is -+--+ (=L). Of course, by a simple modification of the electrical circuit, the rule of addition could be changed to one where like bauds produce a space and unlike bauds a mark; but the general nature of Baudot addition remains the same.

c. The Vernam system was designed originally to use a long keying tape of approximately 100,000 characters. If a [statistically] reasonably flat tape were actually generated at random and if it were used only once (i.e., if *no* portion of the tape were ever used for more than one message), then the system would impart absolute security to the traffic. However, the practicability of production and distribution of these tapes becomes quite a problem, especially if the traffic transmitted is large in volume, and if there are a large number of correspondents who must intercommunicate in the system. Therefore Vernam proposed that *two* key tapes in the form of continuous loops be used together, the lengths of which should be prime to each other; the interaction of these tapes would generate a very long keying sequence. For instance, if the two key loops consisted of 1,000 and 999 characters, respectively, then the resultant key would be the product of the lengths of the tapes, or 999,000 characters. This key would not be, strictly speaking, a purely random key, since it is derived from the interaction of two primary components; nor would the security offered, under actual operating conditions, be as great as might be imagined. For certain types of traffic, Vernam even proposed as a convenience the use of a single tape loop constituting a short repeating key; the security of *this* scheme is either negligible, or only two or three times that amount.

d. Let us now consider the mechanics of Baudot encipherment. Since the international Baudot code is a *known* alphabet, it follows that we should be able to read two or more messages enciphered with identical keys. Suppose we have the following beginnings of two messages which possessed identical indicators, and are therefore assumed to be in flush depth:

Msg "A": -+--+ +++++ ++--- ++-++ --+-+ ---+- --+-- -+++- ...

Msg "B": +--++ -+--+ +-+-+ ----- ----- +--+- -+--- +--+- ...

If we assume that the first message begins with RE$_p$ (= -+-+- +----), we will derive as key [11] the fragment +++-- +---- (=UE$_k$). This key, when applied to the beginning of Message "B", yields +---- --++- (=EN$_p$). This certainly looks promising, and if we extend the RE$_p$ into REQUEST, we will get ENEMY PA... in Message "B". And so on.

e. In practice, teleprinter signals are not analyzed baud by baud as in the foregoing example; instead, each group of five bauds is transcribed as a single Baudot character, and treatment is

---

[11] We are assuming here the keying convention that like impulses produce a "+", unlike a "−". This assumption, however, is immaterial; the opposite rule might actually have been employed in the encryption, without our either knowing it or being able to prove it.

applied to the 32 Baudot characters resulting from this transcription.[12]   In cryptanalysis, we make use of *Baudot combination tables* which contain all possible combinations of the 32 characters and their Baudot sum.   Such a table is illustrated in Fig. 138a, containing Baudot sums combined according to the rule that like bauds produce a "+", unlike a "—".[13]   In Fig.

$$\theta^2$$

	A	B	C	D	E	F	G	H	I	J	K	L	M	N	O	P	Q	R	S	T	U	V	W	X	Y	Z	3	4	5	7	8	9
A	8	S	L	Y	X	Z	I	3	G	Q	W	C	7	T	9	R	J	P	B	N	5	4	K	E	D	F	H	V	U	M	A	O
B	S	8	3	K	U	J	M	L	7	F	D	H	G	R	V	T	Z	N	A	P	E	O	Y	5	W	Q	C	9	X	I	B	4
C	L	3	8	0	T	M	J	S	Q	G	V	A	F	X	D	U	I	5	H	E	P	K	4	N	9	7	B	W	R	Z	C	Y
D	Y	K	0	8	Q	5	N	4	T	X	B	9	R	G	C	7	E	M	W	I	Z	3	S	J	A	U	V	H	F	P	D	L
E	X	U	T	Q	8	W	9	R	O	Y	Z	N	4	L	I	3	D	H	5	C	B	7	F	A	J	K	P	M	S	V	E	G
F	Z	J	M	5	W	8	3	I	H	B	X	7	C	V	R	9	S	O	Q	4	Y	N	E	K	U	A	G	T	D	L	F	P
G	I	M	J	N	9	3	8	Z	A	C	R	Q	B	D	X	W	L	K	7	Y	4	5	P	O	T	H	F	U	V	S	G	E
H	3	L	S	4	R	I	Z	8	F	7	9	B	Q	U	W	X	M	E	C	5	N	Y	O	P	V	G	A	D	T	J	H	K
I	G	7	Q	T	0	H	A	F	8	L	P	J	S	Y	E	K	C	W	M	D	V	U	R	9	N	3	Z	5	4	B	I	X
J	Q	F	G	X	Y	B	C	7	L	8	5	I	3	O	N	4	A	V	Z	9	W	R	U	D	E	S	M	P	K	H	J	T
K	W	D	V	B	Z	X	R	9	P	5	8	4	N	M	3	I	U	G	Y	7	Q	C	A	F	S	E	O	L	J	T	K	H
L	C	H	A	9	N	7	Q	B	J	I	4	8	Z	E	Y	5	G	U	3	X	R	W	V	T	O	M	S	K	P	F	L	D
M	7	G	F	R	4	C	B	Q	S	3	N	Z	8	K	5	Y	H	D	I	W	9	X	T	V	P	L	J	E	O	A	M	U
N	T	R	X	G	L	V	D	U	Y	O	M	E	K	8	J	S	9	B	P	A	H	F	7	C	I	4	5	Z	3	W	N	Q
O	9	V	D	C	I	R	X	W	E	N	3	Y	5	J	8	Z	T	F	4	Q	7	B	H	G	L	P	K	S	M	U	O	A
P	R	T	U	7	3	9	W	X	K	4	I	5	Y	S	Z	8	V	A	N	B	C	Q	G	H	M	O	E	J	L	D	P	F
Q	J	Z	I	E	D	S	L	M	C	A	U	G	H	9	T	V	8	4	F	O	K	P	5	Y	X	B	7	R	W	3	Q	N
R	P	N	5	M	H	O	K	E	W	V	G	U	D	B	F	A	4	8	T	S	L	J	I	3	7	9	X	Q	C	Y	R	Z
S	B	A	H	W	5	Q	7	C	M	Z	Y	3	I	P	4	N	F	T	8	R	X	9	D	U	K	J	L	O	E	G	S	V
T	N	P	E	I	C	4	Y	5	D	9	7	X	W	A	Q	B	O	S	R	8	3	Z	M	L	G	V	U	F	H	K	T	J
U	5	E	P	Z	B	Y	4	N	V	W	Q	R	9	H	7	C	K	L	X	3	8	I	J	S	F	D	T	G	A	O	U	M
V	4	0	K	3	7	N	5	Y	U	R	C	W	X	F	B	Q	P	J	9	Z	I	8	L	M	H	T	D	A	G	E	V	S
W	K	Y	4	S	F	E	P	O	R	U	A	V	T	7	H	G	5	I	D	M	J	L	8	Z	B	X	9	C	Q	N	W	3
X	E	5	N	J	A	K	O	P	9	D	F	T	V	C	G	H	Y	3	U	L	S	M	Z	8	Q	W	R	7	B	4	X	I
Y	D	W	9	A	J	U	T	V	N	E	S	O	P	I	L	M	X	7	K	G	F	H	B	Q	8	5	4	3	Z	R	Y	C
Z	F	Q	7	U	K	A	H	G	3	S	E	M	L	4	P	O	B	9	J	V	D	T	X	W	5	8	I	N	Y	C	Z	R
3	H	C	B	V	P	G	F	A	Z	M	O	S	J	5	K	E	7	X	L	U	T	D	9	R	4	I	8	Y	N	Q	3	W
4	V	9	W	H	M	T	U	D	5	P	L	K	E	Z	S	J	R	Q	O	F	G	A	C	7	3	N	Y	8	I	X	4	B
5	U	X	R	F	S	D	V	T	4	K	J	P	O	3	M	L	W	C	E	H	A	G	Q	B	Z	Y	N	I	8	9	5	7
7	M	I	Z	P	V	L	S	J	B	H	T	F	A	W	U	D	3	Y	G	K	O	E	N	4	R	C	Q	X	9	8	7	5
8	A	B	C	D	E	F	G	H	I	J	K	L	M	N	O	P	Q	R	S	T	U	V	W	X	Y	Z	3	4	5	7	8	9
9	0	4	Y	L	G	P	E	K	X	T	H	D	U	Q	A	F	N	Z	V	J	M	S	3	I	C	R	W	B	7	5	9	8

θ^1 (left margin) $(\theta^1 + \theta^2)$ (right margin)

FIGURE 138a

---

[12] As mentioned in the previous text, it is customary in cryptanalytic work to symbolize the character representing the carriage return by the digit "3", the line feed by "4", the figure shift by "5", the blank by "7", the letter shift by "8", and the space by "9".   The beginner should be careful not to confuse these *symbols* with plain-text digits.

[13] The student will note that in Baudot addition, because of the binary basis of the arithmetic, P+K=C, P+C=K, and C+K=P.   Thus, in Fig. 138a, it will be seen that, for example, any combination of two of the characters A, B, and S will yield the third character given.

θ^2

	A	B	C	D	E	F	G	H	I	J	K	L	M	N	O	P	Q	R	S	T	U	V	W	X	Y	Z	3	4	5	7	8	9
A	7	G	F	R	4	C	B	Q	S	3	N	Z	8	K	5	Y	H	D	I	W	9	X	T	V	P	L	J	E	O	A	M	U
B	G	7	Q	T	0	H	A	F	8	L	P	J	S	Y	E	K	C	W	M	D	V	U	R	9	N	3	Z	5	4	B	I	X
C	F	Q	7	U	K	A	H	G	3	S	E	M	L	4	P	O	B	9	J	V	D	T	X	W	5	8	I	N	Y	C	Z	R
D	R	T	U	7	3	9	W	X	K	4	I	5	Y	S	Z	8	V	A	N	B	C	Q	G	H	M	0	E	J	L	D	P	F
E	4	0	K	3	7	N	5	Y	U	R	C	W	X	F	B	Q	P	J	9	Z	I	8	L	M	H	T	D	A	G	E	V	S
F	C	H	A	9	N	7	Q	B	J	I	4	8	Z	E	Y	5	G	U	3	X	R	W	V	T	O	M	S	K	P	F	L	D
G	B	A	H	W	5	Q	7	C	M	Z	Y	3	I	P	4	N	F	T	8	R	X	9	D	U	K	J	L	O	E	G	S	V
H	Q	F	G	X	Y	B	C	7	L	8	5	I	3	0	N	4	A	V	Z	9	W	R	U	D	E	S	M	P	K	H	J	T
I	S	8	3	K	U	J	M	L	7	F	D	H	G	R	V	T	Z	N	A	P	E	O	Y	5	W	Q	C	9	X	I	B	4
J	3	L	S	4	R	I	Z	8	F	7	9	B	Q	U	W	X	M	E	C	5	N	Y	O	P	V	G	A	D	T	J	H	K
K	N	P	E	I	C	4	Y	5	D	9	7	X	W	A	Q	B	O	S	R	8	3	Z	M	L	G	V	U	F	H	K	T	J
L	Z	J	M	5	W	8	3	I	H	B	X	7	C	V	R	9	S	O	Q	4	Y	N	E	K	U	A	G	T	D	L	F	P
M	8	S	L	Y	X	Z	I	3	G	Q	W	C	7	T	9	R	J	P	B	N	5	4	K	E	D	F	H	V	U	M	A	0
N	K	Y	4	S	F	E	P	O	R	U	A	V	T	7	H	G	5	I	D	M	J	L	8	Z	B	X	9	C	N	W	3	
O	5	E	P	Z	B	Y	4	N	V	W	Q	R	9	H	7	C	K	L	X	3	8	I	J	S	F	D	T	G	A	O	U	M
P	Y	K	O	8	Q	5	N	4	T	X	B	9	R	G	C	7	E	M	W	I	Z	3	S	J	A	U	V	H	F	P	D	L
Q	H	C	B	V	P	G	F	A	Z	M	O	S	J	5	K	E	7	X	L	U	T	D	9	R	4	I	8	Y	N	Q	3	W
R	D	W	9	A	J	U	T	V	N	E	S	O	P	I	L	M	X	7	K	G	F	H	B	Q	8	5	4	3	Z	R	Y	C
S	I	M	J	N	9	3	8	Z	A	C	R	Q	B	D	X	W	L	K	7	Y	4	5	P	O	T	H	F	U	V	S	G	E
T	W	D	V	B	Z	X	R	9	P	5	8	4	N	M	3	I	U	G	Y	7	Q	C	A	F	S	E	O	L	J	T	K	H
U	9	V	D	C	I	R	X	W	E	N	3	Y	5	J	8	Z	T	F	4	Q	7	B	H	G	L	P	K	S	M	U	O	A
V	X	U	T	Q	8	W	9	R	O	Y	Z	N	4	L	I	3	D	H	5	C	B	7	F	A	J	K	P	M	S	V	E	G
W	T	R	X	G	L	V	D	U	Y	O	M	E	K	8	J	S	9	B	P	A	H	F	7	C	I	4	5	Z	3	W	N	Q
X	V	9	W	H	M	T	U	D	5	P	L	K	E	Z	S	J	R	Q	O	F	G	A	C	7	3	N	Y	8	I	X	4	B
Y	P	N	5	M	H	O	K	E	W	U	G	U	D	B	F	A	4	8	T	S	L	J	I	3	7	9	X	Q	C	Y	R	Z
Z	L	3	8	0	T	M	J	S	Q	G	V	A	F	X	D	U	I	5	H	E	P	K	4	N	9	7	B	W	R	Z	C	Y
3	J	Z	I	E	D	S	L	M	C	A	U	G	H	9	T	V	8	4	F	O	K	P	5	Y	X	B	7	R	W	3	Q	N
4	E	5	N	J	A	K	O	P	9	D	F	T	V	C	G	H	Y	3	U	L	S	M	Z	8	Q	W	R	7	B	4	X	I
5	0	4	Y	L	G	P	E	K	X	T	H	D	U	Q	A	F	N	Z	V	J	M	S	3	I	C	R	W	B	7	5	9	8
7	A	B	C	D	E	F	G	H	I	J	K	L	M	N	O	P	Q	R	S	T	U	V	W	X	Y	Z	3	4	5	7	8	9
8	M	I	Z	P	V	L	S	J	B	H	T	F	A	W	U	D	3	Y	G	K	O	E	N	4	R	C	Q	X	9	8	7	5
9	U	X	R	F	S	D	V	T	4	K	J	P	O	3	M	L	W	C	E	H	A	G	Q	B	Z	Y	N	I	8	9	5	7

θ^1 (left margin) $(\theta^1+\theta^2)$ (right margin)

FIGURE 138b

138b we have the complementary table of Baudot sums combined according to the rule that *unlike* bauds produce a "+", like bauds a "−". As has already been mentioned, it is immaterial which rule of addition is assumed; but once a convention is established, it must be continued in the particular problem under study. For the sake of uniformity, in this and the following texts we will always assume the convention that, unless otherwise specified, like bauds produce a "+", unlike a "−".[14]

---

[14] The reason for the inclusion here of the complementary Baudot table illustrated in Fig. 138b, is for purposes of reference in following other technical treatments in which the inverse convention might be used. The table in Fig. 138b can be derived from that in Fig. 138a by adding +++++ (=8) to all the values in that table.

f. The complete texts of the two messages in flush depth given in subpar. *d*, above, are as follows:

Message "A"

```
L8A5H   39CTB   KNMIH   KEAFR   UGGPZ   U3P8Y   EE5ZX   JBD3K   WWV8D   9ZEFE
NOIS7   FPZVG   NAXJR   NQGVH
```

Message "B"

```
BLY77   D4DAG   VOD9J   KSHCR   80D77   3LSSZ   45YAU   KCCE5   FELG8   TPLWV
CKYRH
```

Let us suppose that, in order to illustrate the method of sliding a probable word, we had not already made an entry into the texts, and let us assume that the word ARTILLERY is in one of the messages. The first thing we will do is to superimpose the two cipher texts and *add* these texts together, using the Baudot combination table for this purpose. Since the messages are in depth, this is equivalent to removing the effect of the key.[15] The combined cipher stream is shown below:

```
L8A5H   39CTB   KNMIH   KEAFR   UGGPZ   U3P8Y   EE5ZX   JBD3K   WWV8D   9ZEFE
BLY77   D4DAG   VPD9J   KSHCR   80D77   3LSSZ   45YAU   KCCE5   FELG8   TPLWV
HLD9J   VBONM   CJRX7   853M8   UXNDC   TSNS5   MSZFS   530PJ   EFWGD   JONE7

NOIS7   FPZVG   NAXJR   NQGVH
CKYRH
─────────────────────────────
X3NTJ
```

Our next step is to use a diagram similar to that in Fig. 15 (in par. 22) to facilitate sliding the probable word. In the diagram below, the first row under the combined cipher stream represents the plaintext equivalents in one of the messages if the other contains the A_p of the probable word; the second row represents the equivalents on the trial that the message in question contains the R_p of the probable word; and so forth for all of the letters of the probable word being tried. If our assumption is correct, the word ARTILLERY, when correctly placed, will yield plain text

---

[15] This may be demonstrated mathematically by the following:

$$(1) \quad P_1 + C_1 = K = P_2 + C_2$$
$$(2) \quad P_1 + C_1 = P_2 + C_2$$
$$(3) \quad P_1 - P_2 = C_2 - C_1$$
$$(4) \quad P_1 + P_2 = C_1 + C_2$$

(The fourth equation follows from the third because of the fact that in Baudot systems, addition is identical with subtraction.) The sum of the ciphers is proved to equal the sum of their plaintext equivalents; the effect of the key is thereby eliminated. The use of the combined cipher stream makes unnecessary the two-step process of $P_1 + C_1 = K$, followed by $K + C_2 = P_2$.

along a diagonal, representing the plain text of the other message.[16]   The beginning of this diagram is illustrated in Fig. 139, below:

```
           5        10        15        20        25        30        35
   H L D 9 J V B O N M C J R X 7 8 5 3 M 8 U X N D C T S N S 5 M S Z F S
 A 3 C Y O Q 4 S 9 T 7 L Q P E M A U H 7 A 5 E T Y L N B T B U 7 B F Z B
 R   U M Z V J N F B D 5 V 8 3 Y R C X D R L 3 B M 5 S T B T C D T 9 0 T
 T     I J 9 Z P Q A W E 9 S L K T H U W T 3 L A I E 8 R A R H W R V 4 R
 I       X L U 7 E Y S Q L W 9 B I 4 Z S I V 9 Y T Q D M Y M 4 S M 3 H M
 L         I W H Y E Z A I U T F L P S Z L R T E 9 A X 3 E 3 P Z 3 M 7 3
 L           W H Y E Z A I U T F L P S Z L R T E 9 A X 3 E 3 P Z 3 M 7 3
 E             U I L 4 T Y H A V E S P 4 E B A L Q T C 5 L 5 S 4 5 K W 5
 R               F B D 5 V 8 3 Y R C X D R L 3 B M 5 S T B T C D T 9 0 T
 Y                 I P 9 E 7 Q R Y Z 4 P Y F Q I A 9 G K I K Z P K 5 U K
```

FIGURE 139

From the plaintext fragment ALLY9ACTI revealed along the diagonal, starting at the 20th position, it is clear that both the presence and placement of the probable word ARTILLERY are confirmed.   The two plain texts are now inserted in the messages, arbitrarily assuming that ARTILLERY is in Message "A", and they are extended in both directions, yielding the following decryption.[17]

```
         5        10        15        20        25        30        35
Key:U E J A R L J Y N K B Y W 8 W M X C P P L Y A 5 M B X M 9 K B 3 L P 3
C₁: L 8 A 5 H 3 9 C T B K N M I H K E A F R U G G P Z U 3 P 8 Y E E 5 Z X
P₁: R E Q U E S T 9 A D D I T I O N A L 9 A R T I L L E R Y 9 S U P P O R

C₂: B L Y 7 7 D 4 D A G V O D 9 J K S H C R 8 0 D 7 7 3 L S S Z 4 5 Y A U
P₂: E N E M Y 9 P A T R O L S 9 U N U S U A L L Y 9 A C T I V E 9 N O R T
```

```
         40        45        50        55        60        65        70
Key:9 4 T 5 H P I 7 E G S 3 N 7 8 Q 4 0 H K R A
C₁: J B D 3 K W W V 8 D 9 Z E F E N O I S 7 F P Z V G N A X J R N Q G V H
P₁: T 9 I N 9 G R E E N V I L L E 9 S E C T O R

C₂: K C C E 5 F E L G 8 T P L W V C K Y R H
P₂: H W E S T 9 0 F 9 G R E E N V I L L E 9
```

g. In the preceding subparagraph it was stated that, even after the presence of the probable word ARTILLERY was confirmed, we *arbitrarily* assumed the crib to be in Message "A".   It is important to note that there is an element of ambiguity in reading a Baudot depth of two; if two messages are of the same length, it is possible to recover the entire texts of the messages, but the plain texts corresponding to the particular messages might be inverted, i.e., the plain text recovered for Message "A" *really* belongs to Message "B", and vice versa.   This phenom-

---

[16] At this stage we are not sure which message contains the word ARTILLERY; this point will be resolved in the next subparagraph.

[17] The last 13 characters of Message "A" cannot be decrypted at this time, since in these positions we do not have a second message upon which to test key obtained from plaintext assumptions.   If there is a systematic method for the generation of key, and if this method is successfully analyzed, then it will be possible to read the "depth of one" at the end of Message "A".

enon, characteristic of Baudot depths only, is brought about by the binary addition inherent in the cryptographic process. An assurance that we have the right plain text with the right cipher is obtained only if (a) one message is longer than the other (in which case the logical continuation of the longer message will indicate which of the two plain texts belongs to the message), or (b) a third message is available on which to test the derived key. For example, if the plain texts to our two messages in the preceding subparagraph had been inverted, we would have obtained the following result, shown only in part:

```
              5            10        50          55        60          65          70
Key:  N N X O V W F L 8 N     7 Y Y J 5 5
 C₁:  L 8 A 5 H 3 9 C T B.....E N O I S 7 F P Z V G N A X J R N Q G V H
 P₁:  E N E M Y 9 P A T R     V I L L E 9

 C₂:  B L Y 7 7 D 4 D A G.....V C K Y R H
 P₂:  R E Q U E S T 9 A D     E 9 S E C T
```

The last word in the second message, SECT(OR?), seems to have been throttled; unless a group is missing, this is indicative that the plain texts of the messages have been inverted. Further confirmation could be obtained if we had a third message against which to try our derived key. For example, let the third message, starting at the same point [18] in the key as the other two, begin with the cipher text VLTPH 5I8Q7... In Fig. 140a, the key derived above yields gibberish,

```
"Key":  N N X O V W F L 8 N        Key:  U E J A R L J Y N K
  C₃:  V L T P H 5 I 8 Q 7          C₃:  V L T P H 5 I 8 Q 7
  P₃:  F E L Z Y Q H L Q W          P₃:  I N 9 R E P L Y 9 T
```

FIGURE 140a   FIGURE 140b

whereas in Fig. 140b the key recovered in the preceding subparagraph produces valid plain text for the third message.

h. In subpar. *f* we recovered 57 elements of key, and the key did not repeat within this stretch. If the key is periodic, we would need additional traffic to establish the length of the period, unless the period is too long to make feasible this determination. But even if the key has a long period, if this key has been produced by the interaction of two short key loops, we will be able to partition the key into its two components and reconstruct two equivalent loops with which we could generate the entire key; thus we would be able to read all messages encrypted with these tapes.[19]

i. Let us assume that the key recovered in subpar. *f* has been produced by two short loops of unknown lengths between 11 and 50 characters, so that the total key might be from 132 (=11x12) to 2450 (=49x50) characters long. The first thing to be determined is the length of the two tapes concerned. What we will do is write out the key successively on various widths,

---

[18] If this third message were not in flush depth with the other two, we could use a modification of the diagram in Fig. 139 to test the first few letters of the third message against the recovered key (or its complement), and then, if necessary, the last few letters of the third message against the key (or its complement).

[19] Once we have possession of the entire key, a new message could be read by sliding, say, the first 10 cipher characters of the message against the key stream, in a manner identical to that illustrated in Fig. 139. If the indicator system were known, or if there were a long polygraphic repetition in common with an already solved message, a new message could be read without further ado. See also par. 98 (and, in particular, subpar. 98j) in connection with the kappa test for message placement.

starting at a width of 11.   Consider the following transcriptions of the key on widths of 11, 12, and 13:

```
 1  2  3  4  5  6  7  8  9 10 11
 U  E  J  A  R  L  J  Y  N  K  B
 Y  W  8  W  M  X  C  P  P  L  Y
 A  5  M  B  X  M  9  K  B  3  L
 P  3  9  4  T  5  H  P  I  7  E
 G  S  3  N  7  8  Q  4  0  H  K
 R  A
```
FIGURE 141a

```
 1  2  3  4  5  6  7  8  9 10 11 12
 U  E  J  A  R  L  J  Y  N  K  B  Y
 W  8  W  M  X  C  P  P  L  Y  A  5
 M  B  X  M  9  K  B  3  L  P  3  9
 4  T  5  H  P  I  7  E  G  S  3  N
 7  8  Q  4  0  H  K  R  A
```
FIGURE 141b

```
 1  2  3  4  5  6  7  8  9 10 11 12 13
 U  E  J  A  R  L  J  Y  N  K  B  Y  W
 8  W  M  X  C  P  P  L  Y  A  5  M  B
 X  M  9  K  B  3  L  P  3  9  4  T  5
 H  P  I  7  E  G  S  3  N  7  8  Q  4
 O  H  K  R  A
```
FIGURE 141c

Now if we take each one of the foregoing transcriptions and add the first row of key to the second row, the second row to the third, and so on, we will be negating the effect of the key, producing what amounts to a delta or difference stream.[20]   *At the correct assumption of the length of one of the tapes, the delta stream will repeat itself at an interval corresponding to the length of the other tape.*[21]   The deltas at the foregoing three widths are shown below:

```
 1  2  3  4  5  6  7  8  9 10 11
 F  F  J  K  D  T  G  M  S  4  W
 D  Q  M  Y  V  V  Y  I  T  S  O
 R  N  U  9  L  O  K  I  7  Q  N
 W  L  W  Z  K  5  M  J  E  J  Z
 K  B
```
FIGURE 142a

```
 1  2  3  4  5  6  7  8  9 10 11 12
 J  E  U  7  3  A  4  M  E  S  S  Z
 T  B  Z  8  I  V  T  E  8  M  H  7
 E  P  B  Q  F  P  I  P  Q  N  8  Q
 X  T  W  D  Z  F  T  H  I
```
FIGURE 142b

```
 1  2  3  4  5  6  7  8  9 10 11 12 13
 U  F  3  E  5  5  4  0  I  W  X  P  Y
 X  T  U  F  3  E  5  5  4  0  I  W  X
 P  Y  X  T  U  F  3  E  5  5  4  0  I
 W  X  P  Y  X
```
FIGURE 142c

It is clear from the repeated delta stream manifested in Fig. 142c that the lengths of the two tapes are 13 and 15 characters.

j. Now that we know the lengths of the tapes, we can reconstruct equivalent tapes which will be cryptographically identical with the original tapes.[22]   The 57 elements of recovered key are written on a width of 13 (the length of the shorter tape), allowing space between successive rows; and on this diagram every 15 characters (the length of the longer tape) are blocked off beneath the key.   We will now arbitrarily assume that the first character on tape II (the longer

```
              1  2  3  4  5  6  7  8  9 10 11 12 13
Tape I:  8
   Key:  U  E  J  A  R  L  J  Y  N  K  B  Y  W
Tape II: U
         8  W  M  X  C  P  P  L  Y  A  5  M  B
                                             ⌐U
         X  M  9  K  B  3  L  P  3  9  4  T  5
                                             ⌐U
         H  P  I  7  E  G  S  3  N  7  8  Q  4
                                             ⌐U
         O  H  K  R  A
```
FIGURE 143a

```
              1  2  3  4  5  6  7  8  9 10 11 12 13
Tape I:  8  5  9  U  E  L  X  L  A  9  H  Q  H
   Key:  U  E  J  A  R  L  J  Y  N  K  B  Y  W
Tape II: U  S  T  5  H  8  D  O  T  H  L  X  O
         8  W  M  X  C  P  P  L  Y  A  5  M  B
         8  Q  U  S  T  5  H  8  D  O  T  H  L
         X  M  9  K  B  3  L  P  3  9  4  T  5
         X  O  8  Q  U
         H  P  I  7  E  G  S  3  N  7  8  Q  4
                                             ⌐U
         O  H  K  R  A
```
FIGURE 143b

---

[20] As has already been noted, in Baudot arithmetic subtraction is identical with addition.

[21] See also subpar. 88h for an analogous situation involving additive-enciphered monome-dinome systems.

[22] These tapes will differ from the original tapes by a constant Baudot character added to all the elements of each key tape.

tape) is a "U"; since the first *key* character is also a "U", this would make the first element of tape I (the shorter tape) an "8" in order to satisfy the equation $U_1 + 8_2 = U_k$. The "U's" are written under the key at every cyclic repetition of tape II, and, adding these U's to their corresponding key letters, we obtain elements belonging to tape I; this is shown in Fig. 143*a*, above. By continuing this process, we are able to reconstruct both tapes in their entirety, as is shown in Fig. 143*b*. With these tapes at hand, we can generate the entire key of 195 characters, the first 90 of which are shown below:

```
            5          10         15         20       25          30
Tape I:  8 5 9 U E L X L A 9 H Q H 8 5 9 U E L X L A 9 H Q H 8 5 9 U
Tape II: U S T 5 H 8 D O T H L X O 8 Q U S T 5 H 8 D O T H L X O 8 Q
   Key:  U E J A R L J Y N K B Y W 8 W M X C P P L Y A 5 M B X M 9 K

                  35         40         45         50         55         60
         E L X L A 9 H Q H 8 5 9 U E L X L A 9 H Q H 8 5 9 U E L X L
         U S T 5 H 8 D O T H L X O 8 Q U S T 5 H 8 D O T H L X O 8 Q
         B 3 L P 3 9 4 T 5 H P I 7 E G S 3 N 7 8 Q 4 0 H K R A Y X G

              65         70         75         80         85         90
         A 9 H Q H 8 5 9 U E L X L A 9 H Q H 8 5 9 U E L X L A 9 H Q
         U S T 5 H 8 D O T H L X O 8 Q U S T 5 H 8 D O T H L X O 8 Q
         5 V 5 W 8 8 F A 3 R 8 8 Y A N N F 5 5 T 9 Z I X P 8 E A H 8
```

With the key extended to the 70th position, we are now able to read the end of Message "A" which was previously denied to us because the depth of two did not extend that far. The decryption of the last four groups of Message "A" is now revealed as follows:[23]

```
             55         60         65         70
   Key:   Q 4 0 H K R A Y X G 5 V 5 W 8 8 F A 3 R
Cipher:   N O I S 7 F P Z V G N A X J R N Q G V H
 Plain:   9 S E C T O R 5 M 8 3 4 B U R N S I D E
```

98. The κ (kappa) test for the superimposition of messages.—*a*. In subpar. 65*c*, in connection with a discussion on placing polyalphabetically enciphered messages in depth, it was stated that "even if an extremely long key is employed and a series of messages beginning at different initial points are enciphered by such a key, this method of solution by superimposition can be employed, provided that the messages can be superimposed correctly, that is, so that the letters which fall in one column really belong to one cipher alphabet." In subpar. 72*b*, in connection with a discussion on the solution of progressive alphabet systems, it was stated that there are three principal means of superimposing messages, as follows: (1) superimposition by means of known indicators; (2) superimposition by ciphertext repetitions; and (3) superimposition by a comparison of columnar frequency distributions. It was furthermore indicated, in an accompanying footnote to subpar. 72*b*, that the foregoing three means are also applicable for the superimposition of messages in other types of repeating-key systems. If the repeating key is very long (or, for that matter, if the period is undeterminable), then we can bring to bear a statistical method for placing messages in depth, even if the indicator system is unknown and there are no long polygraphic repetitions in common among the messages. This statistical method will be described in the subparagraphs below.

---

[23] Note the appearance in the plain text of the punctuation and of the carriage-return and line-feed functions.

b. One of the most important techniques in cryptanalytics is that known as the "kappa test." This test is useful for several cryptanalytic purposes and one of the most important of them is to ascertain when two or more sequences of letters are correctly superimposed. By the word "correctly" in this case is merely meant that the sequences are so arranged relative to one another as to facilitate or make possible a solution. The test has for its theoretical basis the following circumstances:

(1) If any two rather lengthy sequences of letters are superimposed, it will be found, on examining both members of the successive pairs of letters brought into vertical juxtaposition, that *in a certain number of cases the two superimposed letters will coincide.* If both sequences of letters constitute random text taken from a 26-letter alphabet, there will be about 38 or 39 such cases of coincidence per thousand pairs examined. This, of course, is because the "kappa" or repeat rate for single letters (i.e., the probability of monographic coincidence) of random text is the reciprocal of the number of elements in the alphabet; so for a 26-character alphabet the κ_r (kappa random) is $\frac{1}{26} = .0385$. If both sequences of letters constitute English plain text, there will be about 66 or 67 such cases of coincidence per thousand pairs examined. This is because the κ_p or repeat rate for single letters of English plain text is .0667. (The student will note that these two constants, κ_r and κ_p, are the ones he has been using in the monographic ϕ and χ tests when 26-letter text has been involved.)

(2) If the superimposed sequences are wholly monoalphabetic encipherments of plain text by the same cipher alphabet, there will still be about 66 or 67 cases of coincidence in each 1,000 cases examined, because in monoalphabetic substitution there is a fixed or unvarying relationship between plaintext and ciphertext letters, so that for statistical purposes mono-alphabetic cipher text behaves just the same as if it were normal plain text.

(3) Even if the two superimposed sequences are not monoalphabetically enciphered text, but are polyalphabetic in character, there will still be about 66 or 67 cases of identity between superimposed letters per thousand cases examined, *provided that the two sequences really belong to the same cryptographic system and are superimposed at the proper point with respect to the keying sequence.* The reasons for this will be set forth in the succeeding subparagraphs.

(4) Consider the two messages below. They have been enciphered polyalphabetically by the same two primary components sliding against each other. The two messages use the same keying sequence, beginning at the same initial point in that sequence; that is, they are in flush depth. Consequently, the two messages are identically enciphered, letter for letter, and the only differences between them are those occasioned by differences in plain text. Note, now,

No. 1 ⎰ Alphabets: 16 21 13 5 6 4 17 19 21 21 2 6 3 6 13 13 1 7 12 6
     ⎱ Plain text: W H E N I N T H E C O U R S E L O N G M...
       Cipher   E Q N B T F Y R C X X L Q J N Z O Y A W...

No. 2 ⎰ Alphabets: 16 21 13 5 6 4 17 19 21 21 2 6 3 6 13 13 1 7 12 6
     ⎱ Plain text: T H E G E N E R A L A B S O L U T E L Y...
       Cipher: P Q N T U F B W D J L Q H Y Z P T M Q I...

that (a) in every case in which two superimposed cipher letters are the same, the plaintext letters are identical, and (b) in every case in which two superimposed cipher letters are different, the plaintext letters are different. In such a system, even though the cipher alphabet changes from letter to letter, the number of cases of identity or coincidence in the two

303

members of a pair of superimposed cipher letters will still be about 66 or 67 per thousand cases examined, *because the two members of each pair of superimposed letters are in the same cipher alphabet and it has been seen in (2) that in monoalphabetic cipher text κ is the same as for plain text,*[24] *viz., .0667.* The two messages may here be said to be superimposed correctly, that is, brought into proper juxtaposition with respect to the keying sequence.

(5) But now suppose the same two messages are superimposed incorrectly, that is, they are no longer in proper juxtaposition with respect to the keying sequence. Thus:

No. 1
Alphabets:	16	21	13	5	6	4	17	19	21	21	2	6	3	6	13	13	1	7	12	6
Plain text:	W	H	E	N	I	N	T	H	E	C	O	U	R	S	E	L	O	N	G	M
Cipher:	E	Q	N	B	T̲	F	Y	R	C	X	X	L̲	Q	J	N	Z̲	O	Y	A	W

No. 2
Alphabets:	16	21	13	5	6	4	17	19	21	21	2	6	3	6	13	13	1	7	12
Plain text:	T	H	E	G	E	N	E	R	A	L	A	B	S	O	L	U	T	E	L
Cipher:	P	Q	N	T̲	U	F	B	W	D	J	L̲	Q	H	Y	Z̲	P	T	M	Q

It is evident that the two members of every pair of superimposed cipher letters are no longer in the same cipher alphabet, and therefore, if two superimposed cipher letters *are* identical this is merely an "accident," for now there is no basic or general cause for the similarity, such as is true in the case of the correct superimposition. The similarity, if present, is, as already stated, due to chance and the number of such cases of similarity should be about the same as though the two cipher letters were drawn at random from random text, in which $κ_r = .0385$. It is no longer true that (a) in every case in which two superimposed cipher letters are the same, the plaintext letters are identical, or (b) in every case in which two superimposed cipher letters are different, the plaintext letters are different. Note, for example, that the superimposed T_c's represent two different plaintext letters and that the S_p of the word COURSE in the first message gives J_c while the S_p of the word ABSOLUTELY in the second message gives H_c. Thus, it becomes clear that in an incorrect superimposition two different plaintext letters enciphered by two different alphabets may by chance produce identical cipher letters, which on superimposition yield a coincidence having no external indications as to dissimilarity in plaintext equivalents. Hence, if there are no other factors which enter into the matter and which might operate to distort the results to be expected from the operation of the basic factor, the expected number of cases of identical cipher letters brought together by an incorrect superimposition will be determined by the value $κ_r = .0385$.

(6) But now note also that in the foregoing incorrect superimposition there are two Z_c's and that they represent the same plaintext letter L. This is occasioned by the fact that the plaintext messages happened to have L's in just those two places and that the cipher alphabet happened to be the same both times. Hence, it becomes clear that the same cipher alphabet brought into play twice may by chance happen to encipher the same plaintext letter both times, thus producing identical cipher letters. In some systems this source of identity in superimposed cipher letters is of little importance; in other systems, it may materially affect the actual number of coincidences. For instance, if a system is such that it produces a long secondary keying cycle composed of repetitions of short primary keying cycles, an incorrect superimposition of two cryptograms may bring into juxtaposition many of these short cycles, with the result that

---

[24] The fact that in this case each monoalphabet contains but two letters does not affect the theoretical value of κ; and whether the actual number of coincidences agrees closely with the expected number based upon κ = .0667 depends upon the *lengths* of the two superimposed sequences.

the actual number of cases of identical superimposed cipher letters is much greater than the expected number based upon $\kappa_r = .0385$. Thus, this source for the production of identical cipher letters in an incorrect superimposition operates to increase the number of cases to be expected from the fundamental constant $\kappa_r = .0385$.

(7) In some systems, where nonrelated cipher alphabets are employed, it may happen that two identical plaintext letters may be enciphered by two different cipher alphabets which, by chance, have the same equivalent for the plaintext letter concerned. This is, however, a function of the particular cryptographic system and can be taken into account when the nature of the system is known.

(8) In general, then, it may be said that in the case of a correct superimposition the probability of identity or coincidence in superimposed cipher letters is .0667; in the case of an incorrect superimposition, the probability is at least .0385 and may be somewhat greater, depending upon special circumstances. The foregoing situation and facts make possible what has sometimes been referred to as the "coincidence test." Since this test uses the constant κ, the specific designation "kappa test" is more appropriate.

c. The way in which the kappa test may be applied will now be explained. The statement that $\kappa_p = .0667$ means that in 1,000 cases where two letters are drawn at random from a large volume of plain text, there will be about 66 or 67 cases in which the two letters coincide, that is, are identical. Nothing is specified as to what the two letters shall be; they may be two Z's or they may be two E's. This means that if many *comparisons* of single letters are made, the letters being drawn *at random* from among those constituting a large volume of *plain* text, 6.67 per cent of these comparisons made will yield coincidences. So, if 2,000 such comparisons are made, the theory indicates that there should be about $.0667 \times 2,000 = 133$ coincidences; if there is sufficient text to permit making 20,000 comparisons, there should be about 1,334 coincidences, and so on.

d. Another way of handling the matter is to find the ratio of the observed number of coincidences to the total number of cases in which the event in question might possibly occur, i.e., the total number of comparisons of superimposed letters. When this ratio is closer to .0667 than it is to .0385, the correct superimposition has been ascertained. This is true because in the case of a correct superimposition both members of each pair of superimposed letters actually belong to the same monoalphabet and therefore the probability of their coinciding is .0667; whereas in the case of an incorrect superimposition the members of each pair of superimposed letters belong, as a general rule, to different monoalphabets,[25] and therefore the probability of their coinciding is nearer to .0385 than to .0667.

e. From the foregoing, it becomes clear that the kappa test involves acertaining the total number of comparisons that can be made in a given case, as well as ascertaining the actual number of coincidences in the case under consideration. When only two messages are superimposed, this is easy: the total number of comparisons that can be made is the same as the number of superimposed pairs of letters. But when more than two messages are superimposed in a *superimposition diagram* it is necessary to make a simple calculation, based upon the fact that

---

[25] The qualifying phrase "as a general rule" is intended to cover any distortion in results occasioned by the presence of an unusual number of those cases of coincidence described under subpars. *b*(6) and (7).

n letters yield $\frac{n(n-1)}{2}$ pairs or comparisons, where n is the number of letters in the column.[26]

For example, in the case of a column of 3 letters, there are $\frac{3\text{x}2}{2}=3$ comparisons; in the case of a column of 4 letters, there are $\frac{4\text{x}3}{2}=6$ comparisons; and so on. If a superimposition diagram contains columns of various lengths, one merely adds together the number of comparisons for the columns of different lengths to obtain a grand total.[27]

f. In ascertaining the number of coincidences in the case of a column containing several letters, it is again necessary to use the formula $\frac{n(n-1)}{2}$, only in this case n is the number of identical letters in the column. The reasoning, of course, is the same as before. The total number of coincidences is the sum of the number of coincidences for each case of identity. For example, in a column consisting of the ten letters CKBKZKCBBK, there are 3 B's, 2 C's, 4 K's, and 1 Z. The 3 B's yield 3 coincidences, the 2 C's yield 1 coincidence, and the 4 K's yield 6 coincidences. The sum $3+1+6$ makes a total of 10 coincidences in the $\frac{10\text{x}9}{2}=45$ comparisons.

g. The steps in applying the foregoing principles to a typical case will now be described. Suppose several messages enciphered by the same keying sequence but each beginning at a different point in that sequence are to be solved. The indicated method of solution is that of superimposition, the problem being to determine just where the respective messages are to be superimposed so that the cipher text within the respective columns formed by the superimposed messages will be monoalphabetic. From what has been indicated above, it will be understood that the various messages may be shifted relative to one another to many different points of superimposition, there being but one correct superimposition for each message with respect to all the others. First, all the messages might be numbered according to their lengths, the longest being assigned the number 1. Commencing with messages 1 and 2, and keeping number 1 in a fixed position, we place message 2 under it so that the intitial letters of the two messages coincide. Then the two letters forming the successive pairs of superimposed letters are examined and the total number of cases in which the superimposed letters are identical is noted, this giving the observed number of coincidences. Next, the total number of superimposed pairs is ascertained, and the latter is multiplied by .0667 to find the expected number of coincidences. If the observed number of coincidences is considerably below the expected number, or if the ratio of the observed number of coincidences to the total number of comparisons is nearer .0385 than to .0667, the superimposition is incorrect and message 2 is shifted to the next superimposition, that is, so that its first letter is under the second of message 1. Again the observed number of coincidences is ascertained and is compared with the expected number. Thus, by shifting message

---

[26] This formula is merely a special case under the general formula for ascertaining the number of combinations that may be made of n different things taken r at a time, which is $_nC_r=\frac{n!}{r!(n-r)!}$. In studying coincidences by the method indicated, since only two letters are compared at a time, r is always 2; hence the expression $\frac{n!}{r!(n-r)!}$, which is the same as $\frac{n(n-1)(n-2)!}{2(n-2)!}$, becomes $\frac{n(n-1)}{2}$ when $(n-2)!$ is cancelled.

[27] We have already seen examples of this in subpars. 18*e* and 86*c*, in connection with the ϕ test. (By definition ϕ is twice the number of coincidences.)

2 one space at a time (to the right or left relative to message 1) the kappa test finally should indicate the proper relative positions of the two messages. When the correct point of superimposition is reached, the cryptanalyst is rarely left in doubt, for the results are sometimes quite startling. After messages 1 and 2 have been properly superimposed, message 3 is tested first against messages 1 and 2 separately, and then against the same two messages combined at their correct superimposition.[28] Thus message 3 is shifted a step each time until its correct position with respect to messages 1 and 2 has been found. Then message 4 is taken and its proper point of superimposition with respect to messages 1, 2, and 3 is ascertained. The process is continued in this manner until the correct points of superimposition for all the messages have been found. It is obvious that, as messages are added to the superimposition diagram, the determination of correct points of superimposition for subsequent messages becomes progressively more certain and therefore easier.

h. In the foregoing procedure it is noted that there is necessity for repeated displacement of one message against another or other messages. Therefore, it is advisable to transcribe the messages on long strips of cross-section paper, joining sections accurately if several such strips are necessary to accommodate a long message. Thus, a message once so transcribed can be shifted to various points of superimposition relative to another such message, without repeatedly rewriting the messages.[29]

i. In subpar. *d,* above, we mentioned that in applying the kappa test we might consider a *ratio* of the observed number of coincidences to an expected number. Since the statistic δ I.C. is defined as the ratio $\frac{\phi_o}{\phi_r}$ and the ξ I.C. is defined as $\frac{\chi_o}{\chi_r}$, we may express the value of kappa as a "κ I.C."; this κ I.C. will be defined as the ratio of the observed number of coincidences to the expected number of coincidences for random.[30] The advantage of expressing coincidences as a κ I.C. is particularly evident when we are testing digital traffic, wherein the value of κ_p for the underlying intermediate plain text might be unknown.

j. The κ_r constant for digital text is of course $\frac{1}{10} = .1$, and the κ_r for Baudot text is $\frac{1}{32} = .0313$; these are the constants to be used in deriving the κ I.C. for digital and teleprinter traffic. If the exact nature of digital intermediate plain text is known (such as has been indicated, for example, in subpars. 89*a–c* with respect to monome-dinome systems), the κ_p for a particular digital system may be calculated. As for the κ_p in Baudot text, an analysis of 300 teleprinter messages (totalling 53,281 characters) revealed that .0566 is the κ_p for English Baudot text.[31]

---

[28] At first thought the student might wonder why it is advisable or necessary to test message 3 against messages 1 and 2 separately before testing it against the combination of messages 1 and 2. The first two tests, it seems to him, might be omitted and time saved thereby. The reason for this is that if messages 1 and 2 are correctly superimposed, it might be possible that at an *incorrect* juxtaposition of message 3 we would still get a high number of coincidences against the *combination* of messages 1 and 2, whereas if we were to try message 3 separately against message 1 and then against message 2, our superimposition error would be disclosed. *Thus, a correct superimposition for one of the three combinations may yield such good results as to mask the bad results for the other two combinations.*

[29] Machinery for automatically comparing letters in applying the kappa test has been devised. Such machines greatly facilitate and speed up the procedure, and make possible a comparison of many messages among themselves which would otherwise require enormous labor if performed by manual methods.

[30] The expression "κ I.C." is introduced here to eliminate the confusion which heretofore existed in designating the I.C. derived from aligning two sequences. In the past, designations such as "I.C." or (incorrectly) "ξ I.C." have given rise to ambiguity; likewise, the term "kappa test" is preferable to the former designations "counting coincidences" or "applying the coincidence test," which are broad expressions covering a multitude of syncrasies.

[31] The δ I.C. of English Baudot text is therefore $32(.0566) = 1.81$.

k. The student is again cautioned that the kappa test is especially reliable only when the messages to be superimposed are rather long (say, 500 letters or more), so that there are a sufficient number of comparisons to permit unequivocal manifestations of the laws of probability. If the messages are too short, an incorrect superimposition may yield an inordinate number of coincidences; or, worse yet, the correct superimposition may not produce a high enough score.

99. Fundamental principles of aperiodic systems.—*a.* Virtually all systems based upon the principle of a repeating key can be solved because of cyclic or periodic phenomena which are produced externally or internally in the cryptograms through the use of a repeating key. There are methods for preventing the external manifestation in the cryptograms of these phenomena, or methods for their suppression and disguise if present internally. In some, the principle is to make the elements of a fixed or invariable-length key apply to variable or irregular-length groupings of the plain text so that no cyclic phenomena are exhibited by the cryptograms. In others, the principle is to apply irregular-lengths of the key, or a variable-length key to regular and fixed groupings of the plain text, with the same object in view. In still other methods, both principles are combined, or the key itself is of such a nature that it does not repeat itself. This may be brought about by constructing or establishing a nonrepeating key, or by employing the key in a special manner. Systems in which the successive letters of the cipher text (or successive letters of the plain text) after the initial letter serve as successive key letters are also used with the object of avoiding or eliminating periodicity. The subparagraphs following will be devoted to a description and discussion of the methods of suppressing periodicity in cryptosystems. These methods as a class are designated as *aperiodic* systems, as contrasted with the more simple periodic or repeating-key systems we have been studying in this text.

b. One of the simplest methods of avoiding periodicity is to use as the key for the encipherment of one or more messages a series of letters or characters that does not repeat itself. The running text of a book, identical copies of which are in possession of the correspondents, may serve as the key for this purpose. It is only necessary for the correspondents to agree as to the starting point of the key, or to arrange a system of indicating this starting point by means of an indicator letter or group in a fixed position of a cryptogram, usually at the very beginning. Various types of cipher alphabets may be employed in this system: direct or reversed standard alphabets, mixed alphabets drawn up at random, or secondary alphabets resulting from the interaction of two primary sliding components. Such a system is called a *running-key system;* other names applied to it are *nonrepeating-, continuous-,* or *indefinite-key* systems. Telephone directories, the Bible, novels, long poems, standard reference works, numerical tables such as logarithmic and trigonometric tables, etc., have often been used as source books for such keys.

c. In the preceding subparagraph it was shown how suppression of periodicity could be accomplished by means of a continuous key. However, periodicity may also be avoided by special manipulation of an otherwise finite, repeating key. A key word, though limited in length, may nevertheless be applied to variable or invariable-length sections of the plain text. When, for example, each letter of the key serves to encipher a single letter of the plain text, the encipherment is said to be *invariable* or *fixed* in this respect. The same is true even if a single letter of the key serves to encipher regular sets of letters of the plain text; for example, each letter of the key may serve to encipher 2, 3, 4 . . ., letters of the text. In these cases periodicity would be manifested externally by the cryptograms, provided that there is a sufficient amount of text to be examined. But if each letter of the key serves to encipher *irregular*

308

or variable-length groupings of the plain text, then periodicity cannot appear except under rather remote contingencies. Suppose, for example, that so simple a scheme is used as letting each letter of the key serve to encipher a complete word of the text; since words are of irregular lengths and there is no regularity whatever in the sequence of words with respect only to their lengths, periodicity cannot appear. Or, instead of enciphering according to natural word lengths, the irregular groupings of the text might be regulated by other agreements; for example, it might be agreed that every key letter will be used to encipher a number of letters corresponding to the numerical value of the key letter in the normal alphabet. If the key word in the foregoing two systems is short and the message is long, periodicity may creep in despite the irregular groupings in the encipherment. Sufficient evidence may even be obtained to lead to a disclosure of the length of the key. But if the key consists of a long word, or of a complete phrase or sentence, the text would have to be very long in order that sufficient evidences of periodicity be found to make possible the determination of the length of the key.

d. In the preceding subparagraph, periodicity was suppressed by enciphering variable-length groupings of the *plain text*. It will now be shown how periodicity may be avoided by enciphering by variable-length groupings of the *key*. The method consists in *interrupting* the key; given a key word, it can become a variable-length key by interrupting it according to some prearranged plan, so that it becomes equivalent to a series of keys of different lengths. Thus, the single key word QUESTIONABLY, for example, might be expanded into a sequence of irregular lengths, such as QUESTIONA/QUESTIONAB/QUE/QUESTI/, etc.[32]

(1) Various schemes for indicating or determining the interruptions may be adopted. For example, suppose it may be agreed that the interruption will take place immediately after and every time that the letter R occurs in the plain text; this is the *plaintext interruptor* method. If the key word were QUESTIONABLY it would then be interrupted as shown in the following example:

```
K:   QUEQU QUEST IONAB QUEST QUESQ UE
P:   OURFR ONTLI NESAR ENOWR EPORT ED...
```

Since this scheme is cryptographically objectionable because of a preponderance in the key of the first few letters of the key word, it might be advantageous to use the key interruption (in this case, the presence of an R_p in the text being enciphered) either to cause the key to "stutter," or to skip an element in the key; these effects are shown in the following examples:

```
K:   QUEES STION ABLYQ QUEST TIONN AB
P:   OURFR ONTLI NESAR ENOWR EPORT ED...
```

```
K:   QUETI NABLY QUEST ONABL QUESI ON
P:   OURFR ONTLI NESAR ENOWR EPORT ED...
```

(2) An alternative to the foregoing method is that employing the idea of a *ciphertext interruptor* letter. In this case, the interruption of the key takes place every time a designated letter shows up in the cipher text.

---

[32] Note that here the key word is being interrupted according to its derived numerical key, i.e., first after

$$\begin{array}{cccccccccccc} 8 & 11 & 3 & 9 & 10 & 4 & 7 & 6 & 1 & 2 & 5 & 12 \\ Q & U & E & S & T & I & O & N & A & B & L & Y \end{array}$$

the digit 1, then after the digit 2, etc. The example in this subparagraph shows how a long key sequence may be derived from a short basic key.

(3) It is possible to apply an interrupted key to variable-length groupings of the plain text. In illustrating this method, an indicator (for instance, the letter X) will be inserted in the plain text to show when the interruption takes place. For example, if the plain text is poly-alphabetically enciphered by word lengths and one letter of the key word QUESTIONABLY is skipped when the interruptor letter is used, we would have the following:

```
K:   QUE STIONA LYQUE STI ONAB YQUESTIO
P:   OUR FRONTX LINES ARE NOWX REPORTED...
```

Many other variations of the interruptor method are of course possible; *Military Cryptanalytics, Part III*, will contain more on the cryptography of these systems, as well as include detailed treatment of their cryptanalysis.

e. The last major class of aperiodic systems is that of *autokey systems* in which the key is automatically derived either from the cipher text (in the case of *ciphertext autokey* systems) or from the plain text (in *plaintext autokey* systems).

(1) Suppose, for example, that two correspondents agree to use the word TRUE as an *initial key* in a ciphertext autokey system, in conjunction with reversed standard alphabets, and the message to be enciphered begins HEAVY INTERDICTION FIRE FALLING AT... The first four letters are enciphered as follows:

```
K:   TRUE
P:   HEAVY INTER DICTI ONFIR EFALL INGAT...
C:   MNUJ
```

The cipher letters MNUJ now form the key letters for enciphering the next four plaintext letters, $YINT_p$, yielding $OFHQ_c$. The latter then form the key letters for enciphering the next four letters, and so on, resulting in the following:

```
K:   TRUEM NUJOF HQKOE IIVWU VQODR LOSGD
P:   HEAVY INTER DICTI ONFIR EFALL INGAT...
C:   MNUJO FHQKO EIIVW UVQOD RLOSG DBMGK
```

(2) Instead of using the cipher letters in sets, as shown above, the last cipher letter given by the use of the key word may become the key letter for enciphering the next plaintext letter; this new cipher resultant then becomes the key letter for enciphering the following letter, and so on to the end of the message. Thus:

```
K:   TRUEJ LDQXT CZRPW OANIA JFAAP EWJDA
P:   HEAVY INTER DICTI ONFIR EFALL INGAT...
C:   MNUJL DQXTC ZRPWO ANIAJ FAAPE WJDAH
```

It is obvious that an initial key word is not necessary; a single prearranged letter will do.

(3) In plaintext autokey systems, the plain text itself serves as the key, after an initial group or an initial letter. This is shown in the following example, wherein the text of the message itself, after the prearranged initial key word TRUE, forms the key text (the enciphering alphabets, as before, are reversed standard alphabets):

```
K:   TRUEH EAVYI NTERD ICTIO NFIRE FALLI
P:   HEAVY INTER DICTI ONFIR EFALL INGAT...
C:   MNUJJ WNCUR KLCYV UPOAX JAIGT XNFLP
```

310

(4) One serious objection to plaintext autokey systems is that the results of errors are cumulative; one error affects all the succeeding letters, and if several errors are made, the messages are difficult to decrypt. (This disadvantage can be minimized by the use of automatic cipher devices suitably constructed to accomplish the encipherment with speed and accuracy.) The serious weakness of ciphertext autokey systems, on the other hand, is that the key of an intercepted message is already *in the possession of the enemy cryptanalyst*, since the cipher text itself is the key. How these systems are solved merits detailed treatment; their cryptanalysis will be discussed in the next volume.

f. There are many elementary cryptomechanisms and cipher devices which have as their principle the suppression of periodicity. A description of some of the more important of these is contained in Appendix 6, "Cryptographic Supplement."

100. Final remarks.—*a.* In subpars. 13*f–h* we stated that there are twelve different equations possible for establishing the manner in which two sliding primary components may be used. It was furthermore stated that twelve square tables, equivalent to the twelve different equations, can readily be constructed. Using the two components given in the example,

(1) A B C D E F G H I J K L M N O P Q R S T U V W X Y Z
(2) F B P Y R C Q Z I G S E H T D J U M K V A L W N O X

and the twelve enciphering equations

$$(1)\ \theta_{k/2}=\theta_{1/1};\ \theta_{p/1}=\theta_{c/2} \qquad (7)\ \theta_{k/2}=\theta_{p/1};\ \theta_{1/2}=\theta_{c/1}$$
$$(2)\ \theta_{k/2}=\theta_{1/1};\ \theta_{p/2}=\theta_{c/1} \qquad (8)\ \theta_{k/2}=\theta_{c/1};\ \theta_{1/2}=\theta_{p/1}$$
$$(3)\ \theta_{k/1}=\theta_{1/2};\ \theta_{p/1}=\theta_{c/2} \qquad (9)\ \theta_{k/1}=\theta_{p/2};\ \theta_{1/1}=\theta_{c/2}$$
$$(4)\ \theta_{k/1}=\theta_{1/2};\ \theta_{p/2}=\theta_{c/1} \qquad (10)\ \theta_{k/1}=\theta_{c/2};\ \theta_{1/1}=\theta_{p/2}$$
$$(5)\ \theta_{k/2}=\theta_{p/1};\ \theta_{1/1}=\theta_{c/2} \qquad (11)\ \theta_{k/1}=\theta_{p/2};\ \theta_{1/2}=\theta_{c/1}$$
$$(6)\ \theta_{k/2}=\theta_{c/1};\ \theta_{1/1}=\theta_{p/2} \qquad (12)\ \theta_{k/1}=\theta_{c/2};\ \theta_{1/2}=\theta_{p/1}$$

we can produce the corresponding twelve square tables, the first four rows of which are shown below: [33]

		A	B	C	D	E	F	G	H	I	J	K	L	M	N	O	P	Q	R	S	T	U	V	W	X	Y	Z
	A	A	L	W	N	O	X	F	B	P	Y	R	C	Q	Z	I	G	S	E	H	T	D	J	U	M	K	V
Table	B	B	P	Y	R	C	Q	Z	I	G	S	E	H	T	D	J	U	M	K	V	A	L	W	N	O	X	F
No. 1[34]	C	C	Q	Z	I	G	S	E	H	T	D	J	U	M	K	V	A	L	W	N	O	X	F	B	P	Y	R
	D	D	J	U	M	K	V	A	L	W	N	O	X	F	B	P	Y	R	C	Q	Z	I	G	S	E	H	T

		A	B	C	D	E	F	G	H	I	J	K	L	M	N	O	P	Q	R	S	T	U	V	W	X	Y	Z
	A	A	H	L	U	R	G	P	S	O	V	Y	B	X	D	E	I	M	K	Q	T	W	Z	C	F	J	N
Table	B	T	A	E	N	K	Z	I	L	H	O	R	U	Q	W	X	B	F	D	J	M	P	S	V	Y	C	G
No. 2	C	P	W	A	J	G	V	E	H	D	K	N	Q	M	S	T	X	B	Z	F	I	L	O	R	U	Y	C
	D	G	N	R	A	X	M	V	Y	U	B	E	H	D	J	K	O	S	Q	W	Z	C	F	I	L	P	T

[33] It is understood that the plaintext letters are to be found in the normal sequence above the square proper, the key letters in the sequence to the left of the square, and the resultant cipher letters within the square.

[34] This table is cryptographically identical with that given in Fig. 9 on p. 17, even though for comparison purposes the horizontal rows of the latter have been interchanged so as to begin successive alphabets with the successive letters of the normal sequence.

```
        A B C D E F G H I J K L M N O P Q R S T U V W X Y Z
      A|F B P Y R C Q Z I G S E H T D J U M K V A L W N O X
Table B|X F B P Y R C Q Z I G S E H T D J U M K V A L W N O
No. 3 C|O X F B P Y R C Q Z I G S E H T D J U M K V A L W N
      D|N O X F B P Y R C Q Z I G S E H T D J U M K V A L W

        A B C D E F G H I J K L M N O P Q R S T U V W X Y Z
      A|U B F O L A J M I P S V R X Y C G E K N Q T W Z D H
Table B|V C G P M B K N J Q T W S Y Z D H F L O R U X A E I
No. 4 C|W D H Q N C L O K R U X T Z A E I G M P S V Y B F J
      D|X E I R O D M P L S V Y U A B F J H N Q T W Z C G K

        A B C D E F G H I J K L M N O P Q R S T U V W X Y Z
      A|A V K M U J D T H E S G I Z Q C R Y P B F X O N W L
Table B|B F X O N W L A V K M U J D T H E S G I Z Q C R Y P
No. 5 C|C R Y P B F X O N W L A V K M U J D T H E S G I Z Q
      D|D T H E S G I Z Q C R Y P B F X O N W L A V K M U J

        A B C D E F G H I J K L M N O P Q R S T U V W X Y Z
      A|A T P G J U L I M F C Z D X W S O Q K H E B Y V R N
Table B|H A W N Q B S P T M J G K E D Z V X R O L I F C Y U
No. 6 C|L E A R U F W T X Q N K O I H D Z B V S P M J G C Y
      D|U N J A D O F C G Z W T X R Q M I K E B Y V S P L H

        A B C D E F G H I J K L M N O P Q R S T U V W X Y Z
      A|G H I J K L M N O P Q R S T U V W X Y Z A B C D E F
Table B|Z A B C D E F G H I J K L M N O P Q R S T U V W X Y
No. 7 C|V W X Y Z A B C D E F G H I J K L M N O P Q R S T U
      D|M N O P Q R S T U V W X Y Z A B C D E F G H I J K L

        A B C D E F G H I J K L M N O P Q R S T U V W X Y Z
      A|U V W X Y Z A B C D E F G H I J K L M N O P Q R S T
Table B|B C D E F G H I J K L M N O P Q R S T U V W X Y Z A
No. 8 C|F G H I J K L M N O P Q R S T U V W X Y Z A B C D E
      D|O P Q R S T U V W X Y Z A B C D E F G H I J K L M N

        A B C D E F G H I J K L M N O P Q R S T U V W X Y Z
      A|A B C D E F G H I J K L M N O P Q R S T U V W X Y Z
Table B|V F R T S X I E Z D M A U W N B C Y G H J K L O P Q
No. 9 C|K X Y H G O Z S Q T U V J L W F R P I E D M A N B C
      D|M O P E I N Q G C H J K D A L X Y B Z S T U V W F R
```

[35] An interesting fact about this case is that if the plain component is made identical with the cipher component (both being the sequence FBPY...), and if the enciphering equations are the same as for Table No. 1, then the resultant cipher square is identical with Table No. 9, except that the key letters at the left are in the order of the reversed mixed component, FXON... In other words, the secondary cipher alphabets produced by the interaction of two identical mixed components are the same as those given by the interaction of a mixed component and the normal component.

```
              A B C D E F G H I J K L M N O P Q R S T U V W X Y Z
            A A B C D E F G H I J K L M N O P Q R S T U V W X Y Z
 Table    B L P Q J H B S T G U V W K O X Y Z C E D M A N F R I
 No. 10³⁶ C W Y Z U T P E D S M A N V X F R I Q H J K L O B C G
            D N R I M D Y H J E K L O A F B C G Z T U V W X P Q S

              A B C D E F G H I J K L M N O P Q R S T U V W X Y Z
            A G Z V M P A R O S L I F J D C Y U W Q N K H E B X T
 Table    B H A W N Q B S P T M J G K E D Z V X R O L I F C Y U
 No. 11   C I B X O R C T Q U N K H L F E A W Y S P M J G D Z V
            D J C Y P S D U R V O L I M G F B X Z T Q N K H E A W

              A B C D E F G H I J K L M N O P Q R S T U V W X Y Z
            A F X O N W L A V K M U J D T H E S G I Z Q C R Y P B
 Table    B B F X O N W L A V K M U J D T H E S G I Z Q C R Y P
 No. 12   C P B F X O N W L A V K M U J D T H E S G I Z Q C R Y
            D Y P B F X O N W L A V K M U J D T H E S G I Z Q C R
```

b. When these tables are examined carefully, certain interesting points are noted. In the first place, the tables may be paired so that one of a pair may serve for enciphering and the other of the pair may serve for deciphering, or vice versa. For example, Tables 1 and 2 bear this reciprocal relationship to each other; similarly, Tables 3 and 4, 5 and 6, 7 and 8, 9 and 10, and 11 and 12 also show this relationship. In the second place, although the tables are derived from the same pair of components, the internal dispositions of the letters are quite diverse. For example, in Table 1 the horizontal sequences are identical with those of the square in Fig. 9 (on p. 17), but are merely displaced to the right and to the left at different intervals according to the successive key letters. Hence Table 1 shows a horizontally displaced, direct symmetry of the cipher component. Vertically, no symmetry is in evidence; [37] but when Table 1 is more carefully examined, a latent symmetry may be discerned where at first glance it is not apparent. If one takes any two *columns* of the table, it is found that the interval between the members of any pair of letters in one column is the same as the interval between the member of the homologous pair of letters in the other column, *if the distance is measured on the cipher component.* For example, consider the 2d and 15th columns (headed by L and I, respectively); take the letters P and G in the 2d column, and J and W in the 15th column. The distance between P and G on the cipher component is 7; the distance between J and W on the same component is *also* 7. This, of course, is a manifestation of indirect symmetry inherent in the cipher square. It follows, then, that every table which sets forth in systematic fashion the various secondary alphabets, derivable by sliding two primary sequences through all points of coincidence to find cipher equivalents, must show some kind of symmetry both horizontally and vertically. The symmetry is termed visible or direct, if the sequences of letters in the rows (or columns) are the same throughout and are identical with that of one of the primary components; it is termed hidden or indirect if the

---

[36] The foregoing footnote also applies to this table, except that the key letters at the left will follow the order of the direct mixed component.

[37] It is true that the first column within the table shows the plain-component sequence, but this is merely because the method of finding the equivalents in this case is such that this sequence is bound to appear in that column, since the successive key letters are A, B, C, ... Z, and this sequence happens to be identical with the plain component in this case. The same is true of Table Nos. 5 and 11; it is also applicable to the first row of Table Nos. 9 and 10.

sequences of letters in the rows or columns are different, apparently not related to either of the components, but which are in reality decimations of one of the primary components.

c. When the twelve tables are examined in the light of the foregoing remarks, the type of symmetry found in each may be summarized in the following manner:

Table No.	Horizontal				Vertical			
	Direct symmetry		Indirect symmetry		Direct symmetry		Indirect symmetry	
	Follows plain component	Follows cipher component	Follows plain component	Follows cipher component	Follows plain component	Follows cipher component	Follows plain component	Follows cipher component
1	------	x	------	------	------	------	------	x
2	------	------	x	------	------	------	x	------
3	------	x	------	------	------	x	------	------
4	------	------	x	------	x	------	------	------
5	------	x	------	------	------	------	------	x
6	------	------	x	------	------	------	x	------
7	x	------	------	------	------	------	x	------
8	x	------	------	------	------	------	x	------
9	------	------	------	x	------	------	------	x
10	------	------	------	x	------	------	------	x
11	------	------	x	------	x	------	------	------
12	------	x	------	------	------	x	------	------

Of these twelve types of cipher squares, corresponding to the twelve different ways of using a pair of sliding primary components to derive secondary alphabets, the ones best known and most often encountered in cryptologic studies are Tables 1 and 2, referred to as being of the Vigenère type; Tables 5 and 6, referred to as being of the Beaufort type; and Tables 9 and 10, referred to as being of the Delastelle type.[38] The foregoing exposition might serve to clarify the relationships present among the twelve different cryptographic equations and their associated derived tables.

d. Not much has been said in this text concerning the use of word separators in polyalphabetic systems. This usage is not often encountered in periodic systems; nevertheless, a few words on the subject may not be amiss. Word separators may be incorporated in the cryptosystem in both enciphered and unenciphered form, as follows:

(1) A rare letter, such as X_p, might be used as a word separator in the plain text of a message; this separator would then be enciphered by the alphabets used in the polyalphabetic system. In such a case, the cipher equivalents of X_p, when the periodic cipher text is allocated into its constituent monoalphabetic distributions, will have a predominant frequency.[39]

(2) A 25-letter cipher alphabet might be used, with, say, the letter X_c missing in the cipher component; this X_c could then be used as a word separator during the course of the periodic

---

[38] It will be noted that the tables of the Delastelle type show no direct or visible symmetry, either horizontally or vertically, and because of this fact some authors have declared that they yield more security than do any of the other types of tables; this supposed increase in security is, as the student has come to learn, more illusory than real.

[39] See footnote 8 on p. 96, *Military Cryptanalytics, Part I*, for the frequency characteristics of English plain text which includes a word separator.

encipherment, without disturbing the period (i.e., as if X_o was the ciphertext equivalent of a word separator in all the alphabets). In such a case, the overwhelming frequency of X_o in the *over-all* cipher text, together with its characteristic positional appearance spaced throughout the cipher text, would at once proclaim what is going on.

(3) If the X_o in subpar. (2), above, were inserted in the cipher text *after* periodic encipherment, it would disturb the cyclic phenomena that otherwise might be present in the cryptogram, giving the impression (on hasty analysis) of an aperiodic system. Nevertheless, as in the preceding case, the startling frequency of X_o in the over-all cipher text, coupled with its positional appearance, would enable the cryptanalyst to interpret its significance. Once the X_o's have been eliminated, the cryptogram would be back in periodic form—with the added help of the now known word divisions!

(4) Unenciphered word separators need not be as unsophisticated as in cases (2) and (3), above. For example, in a 25-letter alphabet with a missing X_o, this X_o is first used to replace the second letters of all ciphertext doublets; then the last cipher letter of every word is doubled, to indicate word divisions. (If a word ends in a doubled cipher letter, the second letter of the doublet has been replaced by an X_o, followed in this case by another X_o to indicate the end of a word.) In other words, there will be 26 different letters used for word separators, in what appears to be a random selection. Such a case, when first encountered, might be hard to diagnose because of possible mental blocks on the part of the cryptanalyst; nevertheless, the manifestations of the extraordinarily high doublet rate in the cipher text (16% instead of the expected 3.8% for random), the absence of any tripled letters in the cipher text, and the positional appearance of the doublets scattered throughout the text, should be enough clues to enable the correct interpretation of these phenomena.

(5) In polyalphabetic systems yielding digits for the cipher text, a particular digit, not otherwise used in the cryptographic scheme, might be reserved as a word separator, which is then enciphered along with the rest of the text, similar to case (1), above. Or, in the case of additive-enciphered systems, using a monome-dinome system as an example, the digit "9" might be missing in the row and column coordinates; the addition of the key would be performed *mod 9* (producing cipher text containing only the digits 0 through 8). The digit 9 is then inserted in the cipher text, to show word divisions, disturbing the cyclic repetitions of the key in the process, similar to case (3), above. Such a scheme might be troublesome, especially since, with a 10-element alphabet, the frequency of the digit 9 might be very close to the random expectation of 10%; but the absence of doubled 9's, and the positional appearance of the 9's in the cipher text, should once again lead to a correct interpretation of the phenomena.

e. The student has seen in subpar. 97*f* how we are able to read a depth of two in a Baudot system where the key is longer than either of the two messages. The reason this is possible with such a shallow depth is, of course, that the alphabet is a *known* alphabet. If our depth of two were in a literal system with known alphabets (say, reversed standard alphabets), solution would still be possible, regardless of the length of the total key or its composition; likewise, in a digital system, such as an additive-enciphered monome-dinome system, wherein the matrix and coordinates are *known*, solution of a depth of two is also possible. In certain situations, it is even possible to read a *single* message enciphered with an unknown long, nonrepeating key, *if the key is a plaintext key or is derived from plain text;*[40] in effect what we really have is a depth

---

[40] As an example of key derived from plain text, consider an additive-enciphered monome-dinome system in which the key consists of plain text taken from a book in the possession of the correspondents; this key text is then converted into digital form by enciphering it through the same matrix used for encrypting the message.

of *two* in these situations, since a correct plaintext assumption in the message will yield plain text in the key, and vice versa.[41]

f. Now that the formal part of this second volume in a comprehensive series of six basic texts on cryptanalytics is drawing to a close, there are still several topics which must be included if, as indicated at the end of *Military Cryptanalytics, Part I,* the first two volumes are to contain most of the necessary fundamentals of the science; this information is included in some of the appendices which follow.

(1) Although considerable treatment has been devoted to the solution of monoalphabetic and polyalphabetic substitution ciphers, we have not yet, except for a few remarks of a very general nature, touched upon that other large and important class of ciphers, *viz., transposition.* The fourth volume in this series will deal extensively with these latter systems; in the meanwhile, the student can learn the general methods of solution of some of the more elementary types of transposition systems by studying Appendix 5, "Introduction to the solution of transposition ciphers."

(2) In order to round out the student's background in the cryptography of codes,[42] and of certain aperiodic systems and representative machine ciphers, this information is contained in Appendix 6, "Cryptographic supplement."

---

[41] Perhaps this is as good a place as any to make some observations which are of general interest in connection with the running-key principle. Suppose a basic, unintelligible, random sequence of keying characters which is not derived from the interaction of two or more shorter keys and which *never repeats* is employed *but once* as a key for encipherment. Can a cryptogram enciphered in such a system be solved? The answer to this question must unqualifiedly be this: even if the cipher alphabets are known sequences, cryptanalytic science is certainly powerless to attack such a cryptogram. Furthermore, so far as can now be discerned, no method of attack is likely ever to be devised. Short of methods based upon the alleged phenomena of telepathy—the objective existence of which is denied by most sane investigators today—it is impossible to conceive of any way of attacking such a cryptogram.

This is a case (and perhaps the only case) in which the impossibility of cryptanalysis is mathematically demonstrable. Two things are involved in a complete solution in mathematics: not only must an answer to the problem be offered, but also it must be demonstrated that the answer offered is *unique*, that is, the only possible one. (The mistake is often made that the latter phase of what constitutes a valid solution is overlooked—and this is the basic error which numerous alleged Bacon-Shakespeare "cryptographers" commit.) To attempt to solve a cryptogram enciphered in the manner indicated is analogous to an attempt to find a unique solution for a single equation containing two unknowns, with absolutely no data available for solution other than those given by that equation itself. It is obvious that no unique solution is possible in such a case, since *any one quantity whatsoever* may be chosen for one of the unknowns and the other will follow as a consequence. Therefore an infinite number of different answers, all equally valid, is possible. In the case of a cryptogram enciphered in the manner indicated, there is the equivalent of an equation with two unknowns; the key is one of the unknowns, the plain text is the other. One may conjure up an infinite number of different plain texts and offer any one of them as a "solution." One may even perform the perfectly meaningless labor of reconstructing the "key" for this selected "solution"; but since there is no way of proving from the cryptogram itself, or from the reconstructed key (which is unintelligible) whether the "solution" so selected is *the* actual plain text, all of the infinite number of "solutions" are equally valid. Now since it is inherent in the very idea of cryptography as a practical art that there must and can be only *one* actual solution (or plain text), and since none of this infinite number of different solutions can be proved to be *the one and only* correct solution, therefore, our common sense rejects them one and all, and it may be said that a cryptogram enciphered in the manner indicated is impossible to solve.

The foregoing statement is no longer true when the running key constitutes intelligible text, or if it is used to encipher more than one message, or if it is the secondary resultant of the interaction of two or more short primary keys which go through cycles themselves. For in these cases there is additional information available for the limitation of one of the unknowns, and hence a unique solution becomes possible.

[42] Elementary principles of code solution have in effect been touched upon in the discussion on cryptosystems employing syllabary squares and code charts, in par. 80 of *Military Cryptanalytics, Part I.*

(3) In this and the preceding volume there have been numerous references on the importance of the assistance rendered by machine aids in cryptanalysis.[43] In modern communication intelligence operations, these aids play a paramount role, just as they do in other scientific and technological fields. At this point in our studies, it is desirable to have an appreciation of the potentialities of some of the more elementary aids, *viz.*, punched card business machines; Appendix 4, "Applications of electrical tabulating equipment in cryptanalysis," provides this background.

(4) Appendix 7, "Introduction to traffic analysis," will give the student a basic understanding of this important branch of cryptology, and will help him realize the close bond between cryptanalysis and traffic analysis. Appendix 8, "The ZENDIAN Problem: an exercise in communication intelligence operations," presents a simulated operational situation involving traffic analysis and cryptanalysis on a volume of traffic intercepted during a hypothetical amphibious operation.

g. As was the case with the previous text, mere reading of the methods of solution of the various types of cryptosystems covered in this volume is not enough to insure complete understanding of the principles and techniques presented. It is therefore strongly recommended that the student solve the problems contained in Appendix 9, "Problems—Military Cryptanalytics, Part II," as a means of acquiring facility and adroitness in the solution of periodic polyalphabetic ciphers. For further study, the messages of the Zendian Problem will provide valuable experience in attacking unknown cryptosystems of all classes, especially as regards cryptanalytic diagnosis.

h. The formal portion of this text will be closed with a synoptic chart of cryptography (continuing the series of charts established in the first volume), found on the next page, showing the relationships among the various cryptosystems treated in *Military Cryptanalytics, Part II*. This chart is a continuation of the chart on p. 227 of *Military Cryptanalytics, Part I*, if we consider the present chart as an amplification of the box labelled "Polyalphabetic" in the previous chart.

YYJIU KDPRJ ZCZUO OVHTR BEFLA E

---

[43] Cf. the first reference on machine aids in subpar. 2*f*(6), *Military Cryptanalytics, Part I*.

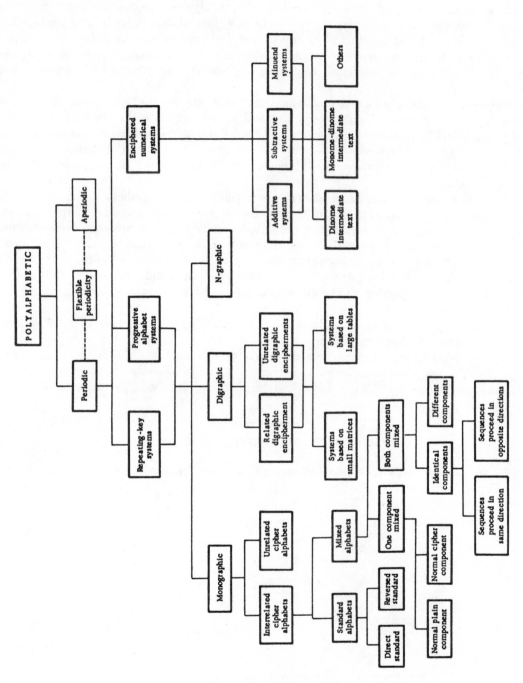

Synoptic chart of cryptography for *Military Cryptanalytics, Part II.*